A Child Goes Forth
A Curriculum Guide for Preschool Children

Tenth Edition

Barbara J. Taylor
Brigham Young University, Emerita

PEARSON

Merrill
Prentice Hall

Upper Saddle River, New Jersey
Columbus, Ohio

Library of Congress Cataloging in Publication Data

Taylor, Barbara J.
    A child goes forth: a curriculum guide for preschool children / Barbara J. Taylor.—10th ed.
        p. cm.
    Includes bibliographical references and index.
    ISBN 0-13-048116-5
    1. Education, Preschool—Curricula.   I. Title.

LB1140.4.T388 2005
372.19—dc21

2003053993

Vice President and Executive Publisher: Jeffery W. Johnston
Publisher: Kevin M. Davis
Editorial Assistant: Autumn Crisp
Production Editor: Sheryl Glicker Langner
Production Coordination: Jan Braeunig, Carlisle Publishers Services
Design Coordinator: Diane C. Lorenzo
Photo Coordinator: Valerie Schultz
Cover Designer: Ali Mohrman
Cover Photo: Dee R. Taylor
Production Manager: Laura Messerly
Director of Marketing: Ann Castel Davis
Marketing Manager: Amy June
Marketing Coordinator: Tyra Poole

This book was set in New Century Schoolbook by Carlisle Communications, Ltd. It was printed and bound by Banta Book Group. The cover was printed by Phoenix Color Corp.

Photo Credits: Wallace G. Barrus: pp. 5, 7, 9, 10, 18, 20, 25, 30, 36, 40, 48, 54, 60, 76, 77, 82, 95, 104, 119, 125, 134, 137, 139, 141, 152, 159, 163, 180, 183, 206, 223, 260, 276, 278, 283, 284, 297, 300, 323, 339, 342, 347, 349, 353, 379, 381, 384, 414, 416, 432, 433; Scott Cunningham/Merrill: pp. 2, 242, 334, 359, 389, 406, 428; Lloyd Lemmerman/Merrill: p. 44; Anthony Magnacca/Merrill: pp. 116, 123, 167, 302, 426; Karen Mancinelli/Pearson Learning: p. 63; Mike Provost/Silver Burdett Ginn: p. 320; Silver Burdett Ginn: 252; Dee R. Taylor: pp. 15, 35, 72, 94, 97, 101, 102, 105, 130, 142, 158, 182, 202, 216, 225, 228, 235, 265, 282, 292, 295, 315, 325, 337, 354, 370, 372, 377, 392, 394, 422, 440; Anne Vega/Merrill: pp. 66, 176, 188, 236, 258, 270, 310, 312, 366, 374

Pearson Prentice Hall™ is a trademark of Pearson Education, Inc.
Pearson® is a registered trademark of Pearson plc
Prentice Hall® is a registered trademark of Pearson Education, Inc.
Merrill® is a registered trademark of Pearson Education, Inc.

Pearson Education Ltd.
Pearson Education Singapore Pte. Ltd.
Pearson Education Canada, Ltd.
Pearson Education—Japan
Pearson Education Australia Pty. Limited
Pearson Education North Asia Ltd.
Pearson Educación de Mexico, S.A. de C.V.
Pearson Education Malaysia Pte. Ltd.

10 9 8 7 6 5 4 3 2
ISBN: 0-13-048116-5

To young children everywhere

Preface

As I finish the tenth edition of *A Child Goes Forth,* I look back over my years of schooling and my years of teaching. I had completed two years of my university education when I was married. We moved to Inglewood, California, we had one son, and my husband completed his architecture degree at University of Southern California. We moved back to Utah, where my husband was employed by a local architect. I had begun working as a secretary for one of the university presidents when we decided that it was possible for me to go back to school and finish my degree. I enrolled in child development classes, which was a wonderful choice. Not only was my line of study useful in my life, but I enjoyed the classes very much. I finished my bachelor's degree and was offered a graduate assistantship. The years flew by as I taught undergraduate students and was a head teacher in the preschool. Then the pressure began—either get a doctorate or move on. I found much joy and satisfaction in working with young children and university students. What to do!!!

By now my husband had his own architectural firm, we had a second child, and further education seemed out of the question—BUT in a family council, we decided that I could go on with my schooling (which the university insisted be out-of-state and at a notable university). Again, a family council! Our oldest son was in the third grade, our youngest son was a preschooler, and my husband's firm was growing. We looked at several universities that were "tops" in early childhood education and child development. We decided upon Florida State in Tallahassee. I was already acquainted with many faculty members, and I held their program in high regard. We packed up and off we went! My husband flew to Tallahassee as often as his business permitted, our oldest son was in the third grade, and our youngest son was cared for by loving and qualified people.

I finished my necessary course work at Florida State, and we moved back to Utah. I returned to teaching and finishing courses such as statistics, languages, and more. Time marches on—I was ready to complete my dissertation, take my exams, teach classes, and finish my degree. Everything fell into place and it was time for graduation!! What a welcome day!

But how does *A Child Goes Forth* fit into this? One semester I was teaching my usual child development courses and gave the students a reading list. One brave student raised her hand and said, "Can't you give us some articles to read so that we don't have to spend all that time at the library looking them up and reading them there?" It was a worthy idea—and my reply was, "I can't for this semester, but I will for the students next semester." I am not sure how well that satisfied my present students, but it was a great help to the later ones. I did put together a reading packet—**and that was the beginning of my writing career!**

The first edition of *A Child Goes Forth* was a spiral book of readings with a cover designed by my husband. That edition in 1964 was published by the Brigham Young University Press, and it was followed by subsequent editions in 1966, 1972, and 1975, also by the BYU Press. By some means (unknown to me) the BYU Press sold the rights to Burgess Publishing Company, who published the fifth edition in 1980. Then it was sold to Macmillan College Publishing Company, who printed editions in 1985, 1991, 1995, and 1999.

Here it is 2003, and this is the **tenth** edition! It takes a lot of time to revise a text. I have tried to bring attention to early educators and theories, to changes over time, and to current thinking. There are many new ideas yet to come. Let's hope they are in the best interest of young children!

Overview of the Tenth Edition

In many places, including our own country, children are still undervalued, underfed, exploited, or inappropriately cared for. We still have a long time to go. But are we headed in the right direction, and are children and families any better off? Progress is often slow and rocky, and sometimes unfair. Again (as in the ninth edition) I ask, "How can early childhood educators make the road a little safer, a little easier, and more rewarding for children, parents, and educators?" This is a daunting task; however, this edition of *A Child Goes Forth* is yet another attempt to provide some guidance and reassurance along the way. This text is written with a sincere desire to offer logical information, based on knowledge and experience, and encouragement to adults who love, learn with, and live with young children. One begins at the beginning—the environments that produce happier, healthier, and more productive citizens—without the assurance that it will be the "best" way for each child.

Chapter 1 describes developmentally appropriate practices (DAP) and names some important educators who promoted this concept many years ago, as well as currently. DAP was popularized by the National Association for the Education of Young Children (NAEYC). Theories of early educators are mentioned, reinforced by current theories and practices. Knowing the names and philosophies of influential educators is important in the field of early childhood education. Some theories remain unchanged; others are modified by current research.

"Reflections" appear in each chapter; they are intended to help you focus on words and ideas that can make a difference in daily lives and to encourage you to ponder possible solutions and then reflect on how and why you would respond.

"Notable Quotes" reflect various educators' thinking. Read them carefully and see how they help you further understand past and present research.

Figures and tables are placed throughout the text in order to clarify, condense, and inform you of important facts. Study them carefully as you read the chapters.

Curriculum chapters have been updated in an effort to show how each topic not only stands alone, but affects each child's total growth and development. Original and subsequent information is very important in understanding thoughts and ideas over time, through research, and the direction ahead. It has tremendous influence upon the total growth and development of each young child and for each teacher! Teachers may have curriculum preferences—as children do—but the total experience helps both teachers and children have a better understanding of the world in which we live.

Guidance Techniques, the subject of Chapter 2, are necessary in all walks of life and provide ways for children and teachers to act and interact in more positive, productive, and acceptable ways.

In researching Chapter 3, "The Value of Play," I became more convinced that we need to accept and understand the ways of children if we are to be advocates for them and if we are to be instruments in promoting better kinds of behavior.

Curriculum development, the subject of Chapter 4, must change constantly to meet the needs of children and teachers. Webbing, flexibility, multicultural education, and other aspects make for an interesting learning experience.

"Language Arts," Chapter 5, takes on greater meaning as more and more cultures are mixing together. Early experiences with books are invaluable in teaching about ourselves and cultures of others.

"Creative Arts," Chapter 6, does more than teach us about being "artists." We learn about cultures, uses of materials, activities, appreciation, and many other personal and group values.

Where more and more cultures are mixing together, we can increase our knowledge and appreciation for one another through music and movement (Chapter 7).

Again, I was pleased and excited to see how the science and math scores of American children have improved in recent years. I believe that through the encouragement of teachers and parents, young children can become more interested and proficient in these topics. Exploration, experimentation, and science in general are worthwhile and vital (Chapter 8).

Over the past few years, American children have been gaining better understanding of math. There are many ways we can continue this trend (Chapter 9).

I have made a deliberate attempt to focus upon the individual and how he feels about himself and others. There is much diversity in living environments today. Personal and multicultural experiences and attitudes are important aspects of learning. Improving our social relationships with people of other cultures, ages, and various differences will improve our understanding (Chapter 10).

If we are to be a healthy society, we must pay more attention to nutrition and health, immunizations, personal hygiene, and exercise (Chapter 11).

Chapter 12 contains a variety of activities that help children make transitions between activities. Some ideas will become favorites of the children and give them new meaning in moving from one activity, or place, to another.

Appendix A lists some curriculum topics appropriate for young children and different ways of "changing from one place to another" or "changing from one activity to another."

Appendix B suggests some miniplans related to Chapters 5 through 11.

My personal hope is that you will enjoy planning for and being with young children as much as I do!

In Walt Whitman's poem "Autumn Rivulets," a child becomes part of all he sees and does. Children of all ages are curious, imitative, and growing, and the title *A Child Goes Forth* reflects this involvement of children with the world around them. Part of what makes *A Child Goes Forth* a successful text for early childhood education courses is the book's emphasis on the individuality of each child, and in each edition there is greater emphasis on and clarity in providing programs and activities that are *developmentally appropriate* for children. In order to provide such programs, parents and teachers should understand and insist upon the components necessary for good environments for young children—inside and outside the home. Adults should not be intimidated by commercial materials, academic pressures, or outspoken but uninformed adults. All facets of a child's personality—social, intellectual, spiritual, physical, and emotional—are interrelated; a relaxed, unstructured, yet carefully planned atmosphere is most conducive to effective learning.

Acknowledgments

I extend a special thank you to the reviewers of this text at all stages of its development: Janice K. Ewing, Colby-Sawyer College; John R. Hranitz, Bloomsburg University of Pennsylvania; Steven Reuter, Minnesota University, Mankato; Edythe J. Schwartz, California State University, Sacramento; and Lorraine A. Shanoski, Bloomsburg University of Pennsylvania.

Discover the Companion Website Accompanying This Book

The Prentice Hall Companion Website: A Virtual Learning Environment

Technology is a constantly growing and changing aspect of our field that is creating a need for content and resources. To address this emerging need, Prentice Hall has developed an online learning environment for students and professors alike—Companion Websites—to support our textbooks.

In creating a Companion Website, our goal is to build on and enhance what the textbook already offers. For this reason, the content for each user-friendly website is organized by topic and provides the professor and student with a variety of meaningful resources. Common features of a Companion Website include:

For the Professor—

Every Companion Website integrates **Syllabus Manager**™, an online syllabus creation and management utility.

- ➤ **Syllabus Manager**™ provides you, the instructor, with an easy, step-by-step process to create and revise syllabi, with direct links into Companion Website and other on-line content without having to learn HTML.
- ➤ Students may log on to your syllabus during any study session. All they need to know is the web address for the Companion Website and the password you've assigned to your syllabus.
- ➤ After you have created a syllabus using **Syllabus Manager**™, students may enter the syllabus for their course section from any point in the Companion Website.
- ➤ Clicking on a date, the student is shown the list of activities for the assignment. The activities for each assignment are linked directly to actual content, saving time for students.
- ➤ Adding assignments consists of clicking on the desired due date, then filling in the details of the assignment—name of the assignment, instructions, and whether or not it is a one-time or repeating assignment.

➤ In addition, links to other activities can be created easily. If the activity is online, a URL can be entered in the space provided, and it will be linked automatically in the final syllabus.

➤ Your completed syllabus is hosted on our servers, allowing convenient updates from any computer on the Internet. Changes you make to your syllabus are immediately available to your students at their next logon.

For the Student—

➤ **Introduction**—General information about the topic and how it will be covered in the website.

➤ **Web Links**—A variety of websites related to topic areas.

➤ **Timely Articles**—Links to online articles that enable you to become more aware of important issues in early childhood.

➤ **Learn by Doing**—Put concepts into action, participate in activities, examine strategies, and more.

➤ **Visit a School**—Visit a school's website to see concepts, theories, and strategies in action.

➤ **For Teachers/Practitioners**—Access information you will need to know as an educator, including information on materials, activities, and lessons.

➤ **Current Policies and Standards**—Find out the latest early childhood policies from the government and various organizations, and view state, federal, and curriculum standards.

➤ **Resources and Organizations**—Discover tools to help you plan your classroom or center and organizations to provide current information and standards for each topic.

➤ **Electronic Bluebook**—Paperless method of completing homework or essays assigned by a professor. Finished work can be sent to the professor via email.

➤ **Message Board**—Virtual bulletin board to post and respond to questions and comments from a national audience.

To take advantage of these and other resources, please visit the *A Child Goes Forth: A Curriculum Guide for Preschool Children,* Tenth Edition, Companion Website at

www.prenhall.com/taylor

Educator Learning Center: An Invaluable Online Resource

Merrill Education and the Association for Supervision and Curriculum Development (ASCD) invite you to take advantage of a new online resource, one that provides access to the top research and proven strategies associated with ASCD and Merrill—the Educator Learning Center. At www.EducatorLearningCenter.com you will find resources that will enhance your students' understanding of course topics and of current educational issues, in addition to being invaluable for further research.

How the Educator Learning Center Will Help Your Students Become Better Teachers

With the combined resources of Merrill Education and ASCD, you and your students will find a wealth of tools and materials to better prepare them for the classroom.

Research

- More than 600 articles from the ASCD journal *Educational Leadership* discuss everyday issues faced by practicing teachers.
- A direct link on the site to Research Navigator™ gives students access to many of the leading education journals, as well as extensive content detailing the research process.
- Excerpts from Merrill Education texts give your students insights on important topics of instructional methods, diverse populations, assessment, classroom management, technology, and refining classroom practice.

Classroom Practice

- Hundreds of lesson plans and teaching strategies are categorized by content area and age range.
- Case studies and classroom video footage provide virtual field experience for student reflection.
- Computer simulations and other electronic tools keep your students abreast of today's classrooms and current technologies.

Look Into the Value of Educator Learning Center Yourself

Preview the value of this educational environment by visiting www.EducatorLearningCenter.com and clicking on "Demo." For a free 4-month subscription to the Educator Learning Center in conjunction with this text, simply contact your Merrill/Prentice Hall sales representative.

Introduction

A Note About the Child on the Cover

Bre is 4 years old. She was born in Western Samoa and now resides in the United States with her parents, an older sister (age 6), an older brother (age 18), and two frisky dogs. She has had many experiences in her young life that encourage her to be curious, outgoing, friendly, secure, and teachable.

While the primary focus of this text is on children between the ages of 2 and 6, the preparation that occurs before and the experiences that occur before and after these ages are vital in the total learning and development of children of all ages. A brief overview of the chapters in this text can also relate to younger children or children who do not attend preschools or child-care centers before entering public school. Children of all ages need to have experiences in each of the following 11 areas, which correspond to the chapters of this book:

1. Participate in *environments* that include happy and healthy homes and neighborhoods; love and respect for themselves and others; and conditions where simple, inexpensive, and wholesome experiences are prevalent. Bre attends a nearby private preschool three mornings a week.

   Example: Bre has freedom of movement, but unsafe conditions are noted and corrected or guarded against; she feels loved and valued; and many of her daily activities revolve around simple activities available in the home and her preschool.

2. Know that her parents and others will provide appropriate *guidance* to the young children who are inexperienced and in developing stages of growth. She lives near one set of grandparents, enjoys visiting them, and feels free to ask Grandpa for special favors.

   Example: Bre is redirected from areas and activities that may cause her harm: open staircases, unsafe places to climb, toys that are inappropriate, and so forth. As a result she has learned to go up and down stairs safely and to play in secure places.

3. Explore and play.

   Example: Bre likes to explore new areas, play with familiar and new things, and repeat prior activities. She knows how to play alone, but prefers playmates. She has learned to follow rules regarding play equipment.

4. Utilize available materials and learn personal responsibility.

   Example: Bre knows how to care for her toys and put them where they belong when they are not in use (blocks are stacked, books are shelved, pieces are grouped), but may need a reminder. Her use of toys increases as she develops new skills.

5. Hear and use language.

   Example: Bre has had many experiences with language—through stories, music, movement, and other involvement. She uses complex sentences and can explain her needs and desires. Since her birth, parents and others have read to her, shown her pictures and objects, played with her, and made her a very active part of the family. She sits quietly and looks at books or feels free to ask an adult to read to her. She eagerly climbs up beside the adult and listens carefully to the story, a skill that will aid in the development of later reading ability. She recognizes letters by name. Being born in Western Samoa, she has frequent exposure to that language and culture.

6. Be creative and self-expressive.

   Example: Bre is learning to do things in a variety of ways and to express her needs and desires in acceptable ways. She asks someone to sit by her and read a book; she invites someone to play with her. She wants someone to talk with her about her activities and to value her ideas and abilities. Her attempts are acknowledged and appreciated.

7. Hear and enjoy music and movement activities.

   Example: Bre sings and dances often—especially when she recognizes the tunes. A scarf or different rhythms encourage locomotion, and the activity itself encourages her body usage, self-confidence, motor and social skills, and memory improvement.

8. Experience science concepts.

   Example: Bre is fascinated by motion: air, water, weather, toys, and her own body. She experiences things such as bubbles, magnets, changes in weather (falling snow or rain, gentle breezes), and sensory objects. Opportunities for exploration are always available and inexpensive (concepts of time, sequencing of events, labels for objects or activities, experimenting with colors, etc.).

9. Learn math skills.

   Example: Bre loves to count—numbers, objects, just about anything. She knows about one-to-one correspondence and about sequencing events: First put on your pajamas, go to the bathroom, and then we'll read a bedtime story.

10. Build social relationships.

    Example: Bre is a very social person who likes to be included in whatever is going on or to know the reason she is excluded. She uses many of the social graces (please, thank you) and knows that they are important to those around her. She plays cooperatively and accepts taking turns. She especially likes to visit Grandma and Grandpa. She has great ideas about what Grandpa should prepare for dinner when she comes to visit!

11. Develop and maintain a strong and healthy body.

    Example: Bre's personal and health needs are important to her. Her immunizations are on schedule, her illnesses are promptly cared for, and she loves to eat whatever others are eating and to be a part of a family setting.

    Bre can ride a small two-wheel bicycle and is now learning to ice skate. She thinks both of these activities reflect her body skills!

In preparing this text, it has been a joy to have Bre as a guide and model for me. She has emphasized the importance of very young children—they are not just waiting to grow up and "be" something, they are already *something very special!*

In summary, activities for all ages (sometimes divided by category and sometimes combined with other topics) should be **enjoyable** rather than restrictive, **growth promoting** rather than growth stunting (stereotyping), **positive** rather than negative, and often **child initiated** rather than adult imposed. Adults need to be aware of the following at all times:

➤ Very young children are active learners and will respond positively or negatively depending on how the environment is planned and utilized.
➤ It is very easy to stimulate and encourage young children to value themselves and their environment.
➤ "A child goes forth" from a very young age, and individuals in their environment can be positive, negative, or noninfluential.
➤ *Every* child deserves the right to a happy, productive, and enriched life!

Brief Contents

Contents

Chapter 3: The Value of Play   73

Chapter 4: Curriculum Development   117

Chapter 7: Music/Movement   253

Chapter 8: Science and Technology   293

Chapter 9: Mathematics 335

Chapter 10: Social Studies, Anti-Bias Curriculum, and Field Trips 367

NOTE: Every effort has been made to provide accurate and current Internet information in this book. However, the Internet and information posted on it are constantly changing, and it is inevitable that some of the Internet addresses listed in this textbook will change.

CHAPTER

1

Good Environments for Young Children, Teachers, and Families

Main Principles

In order for good teaching/learning environments to occur, the teacher must consider the following – individually and collectively:

1. *The teachers* (adults) must be committed to building positive relationships with all children, families, colleagues, and others involved in the teaching process. *Teachers must:*

   ➤ receive proper training through approved training and experience (pp. 5–8);

   ➤ know and support a code of ethics (pp. 7–8);

   ➤ become certified (pp. 8–10);

   ➤ know the philosophy and rationale of recognized leaders in the field of early childhood education (pp. 10–12);

   ➤ reflect on how philosophy and application support good practices ("reflections," pp. 10–13 and throughout each chapter);

   ➤ be knowledgeable about advanced and delayed needs of children (pp. 13–14);

   ➤ recognize, support, and provide for different age (and ability) preschool children (pp. 14–18);

   ➤ recognize and promote developmentally appropriate practices (pp. 19–22). It is also assumed that teachers will keep physically fit and mentally alert as they learn how to focus on and use developmentally appropriate ideas and programs that meet the individual and group needs of all persons in the classroom.

2. *The children* must receive individual attention and appreciation and have their needs met through developmentally appropriate programs.

   To this end *teachers must:* (pp. 22–25)

   ➤ learn about each child individually;

   ➤ maintain awareness of individual environments;

➤ promote healthy peer interaction;

➤ be aware of community resources for children and families who need additional or specialized services.

3. *The families* must be willing to understand, cooperate with, and participate in good settings for their children.

To this end *teachers must:* (pp. 22–25)

➤ become acquainted with the families in order to understand their needs;

➤ know how to interact with families to receive and give necessary information;

➤ know of and share information about child care and education available to the families

4. *The philosophy of the program* must be of high quality and ideally accredited by an organization with a strong foundation in early childhood education. (p. 25)

Although accreditation is strictly voluntary, many early childhood professionals believe that accreditation is the pinnacle of high quality in early childhood programs and should be achieved by any center that is truly trying to meet the needs of children, families, and center staff. Programs of high quality include the National Academy of Early Childhood Programs (NAECP), the National Association for the Education of Young Children (NAEYC), and National Academy of Teacher Educators (NCATE). Readers are encouraged to read and study various programs.

Introduction

How often have you heard the statement, "Children are our best resources," and then wondered just what was meant? If this statement refers to a child in a family, a community, or anywhere in the world, it could mean that the hopes of the family, the community, or the world reside in the abilities and performance of that child. Take, for example, the role of the *expecter,* who assumes that great rewards, returns, and benefits will occur (internally and externally) for individuals or groups. Then take, for another example, the role of the *expectee.* Will the child receive assistance, guidance, and encouragement along the way, or must the child stumble and progress as well as possible? Sometimes the messages that are sent and those that are received are quite different—depending on the frame of reference, confidence, and desired outcome of the sender and receiver. Expecting too much too soon, and without thinking through the myriad implications and complications, may invite early failure or total disaster.

Adults who work with young children are really involved with the "pot of gold at the end of the rainbow." Young children are tender, malleable, trusting, lovable, curious, and teachable. It is as if the teacher or parent were seated at the potter's wheel, about to take the lump of clay and mold it into a thing of beauty and value. At the same time, the adult does not have the privilege of molding a child into a preconceived idea of "perfection"; rather, the adult must help the child to capitalize on his individual talents and abilities so he can live happily and healthily in his world and feel good about himself and his contribution.

This chapter identifies some of the important considerations in providing good learning and living environments for young children.

Most of the classroom examples in this book involve female teachers. Unfortunately, men have had a certain reluctance to enter an occupation that has been traditionally "female"; men in the field of education are often teaching older children or holding administrative positions. Nevertheless, young children need and want male teachers, and one hopes there will be an increasing trend toward more men teaching young children.

Caring adults help children develop confidence and initiative.

Role of the Teacher (Adults)

The role of the teacher is vital in all aspects of teaching, curriculum planning, and personal interaction with each child and parent, other teachers, staff members, and all who are associated with the facility and particular classroom. The teacher must be current in her teaching methods and aware of which current trends are best for the young children in the *present classroom.*

The teacher plays a personal multifaceted role by activities such as the following:

Oneself: Keeping physically fit and mentally alert.

Learning, evaluating, and implementing developmentally appropriate ideas and programs that meet the individual and group needs of the present children and adults in the classroom.

Keeping current! Being aware of resources for teaching, parent education, current trends and events, organizations, publications, etc.

Focusing on issues and practices that improve one's teaching and personal interactions.

Children: Learning about and furthering the growth and development of each one through personal interest, activities, dedication, and study.

Providing stimulating and growth-promoting activities in all areas of curriculum with all children.

Adults: Getting to know and understand the needs of parents, co-workers, minority groups, and others who influence the children within and outside the classroom.

Building a strong commitment to better lives through education, health, relationships, and other special areas.

At an earlier period there was a separation between the role of the parent and the role of the school—it could have even been called a chasm over which neither ventured. The child was shuttled between two different settings. Now both teachers and parents are more accepting of each other's role in an effort to better educate children. However, teachers and parents are still learning how to deliver and receive messages that are accurate, clear, and helpful.

Building relationships within the classroom: In earlier studies, peer relationships in child care settings were identified:

1. Children who had secure attachment relationships with their teachers were more gregarious, engaged in more complex play, and displayed more behavioral flexibility than did those with less secure teacher attachments.
2. Children who had higher emotional security with their teachers displayed fewer withdrawn behaviors and less hostile aggression toward peers.
3. When teachers mediated positively during peer interactions (for example, offering verbal or physical assistance), children were more likely to be accepted by their peers, whereas negative teacher mediation (interruption, punishment, or separation) was related to children's withdrawn behaviors and hostile aggression toward others.
4. Children's relationships with teachers may have even stronger effects on their peer relationships than do their relationships with parents because the teacher is available and ready to guide children in peer situations (Howes Matheson, & Hamilton, 1994).
5. Finally, we have evidence that secure attachment relations with parents and teachers provide the greatest positive influence on young children's competence with peers. Children who had formed secure attachments with their teachers but not with their parents were more socially competent than those who had not formed secure attachments to *either* parents *or* teachers. Researchers suggest that having a secure attachment with a teacher or caregiver may at least partially compensate for insecure attachment with a parent.
6. Look at each individual child in your classroom and identify each one's strengths, interests, misconceptions, goals, weaknesses, etc. Get to know each child personally.

Training

It is critical that teachers of early childhood education be properly and completely trained for their profession. Most states, and some districts, have carefully outlined courses for such training, which should differ from the training for elementary or secondary teachers.

In the March 2002 issue of *Young Children,* NAEYC announced new standards for preparing tomorrow's teachers. They report that while the central values of the revised standards remain the same as they were in the past, by Spring 2003, new highlights for all higher-education institutions seeking NCATE approval must prepare tomorrow's professionals to:

➤ "work effectively with young children with disabilities in inclusive settings;
➤ promote the learning of children from many cultures and language groups;
➤ build strong relationships with all families and in all communities;
➤ use more in-depth knowledge of early childhood assessment practices and issues\integrate essential content knowledge in literacy, mathematics, and other disciplines with knowledge of child development and learning; and
➤ go beyond textbook knowledge to demonstrate real competence in making a difference for children" (Hyson, 2002, p. 78).

The article continues: tomorrow's teachers should be able to:

1. promote child development and learning through understanding what young children are like and what influences their development;

2. create good environments where all children can thrive;
3. build family and community relationships;
4. observe, document, and assess individuals and programs to build sound discipline and advocate for children, families, and the profession.

The complete document, "NAEYC Standards for Early Childhood Professional Preparation: Baccalaureate or Initial Licensure Level" (revised 2001) with detailed explanations and references, may be downloaded from *www.naeyc.org/profdev*.

In researching how education and experience affect teachers of young children, Kontos and Wilcox-Herzog (2001) report a synthesis from three research studies. Their summary and implications tell us: "(1) teachers' formal education correlates with overall classroom quality; (2) specialized education is correlated with effective teacher behavior, and (3) teachers' experience cannot be consistently linked to overall classroom quality or effective behavior" (p. 89).

Because teacher requirements vary for the age of the children taught, between states, in longevity, and in transferability between states, the reader is encouraged to seek current local, state, and national requirements from appropriate departments of education.

Code of Ethics

As with other occupations and because of the great impact teachers have on the lives of children and families, it is understandable and important to have standards of ethical conduct. The National Association for the Education of Young Children (NAEYC) adopted a *code of ethics* in 1989, revised in 1997. (A copy was received on March 12, 2002, from the Internet.) It summarizes a code of ethics as statements about right or good conduct in the course of implementing one's goals and about courage to act in accordance with professional judgment of what is best for individuals served, even when they may not agree.

Teachers can support children through language and action.

In 1991, Katz and Ward prepared an expanded edition of ethical behavior for the National Association for the Education of Young Children, which includes the NAEYC code of ethical conduct and statement of commitment adopted in July 1989.

Many daily decisions, moral and ethical, are required of those who work with young children and their families, and of those who administer and license programs. In behalf of these children and adults, NAEYC (Katz and Ward, 1996) has set forth a code of ethical conduct, describing paramount responsibilities for:

➤ *children*—"to provide safe, healthy, nurturing, and responsive settings . . . to support children's development, respect individual differences, help children learn to live and work cooperatively, and promote health, self-awareness, competence, self-worth, and resiliency" (p. 58).

➤ *families*—"to bring about collaboration between the home and school in ways that enhance the child's development" (p. 58).

➤ *colleagues*—(co-workers, employers, employees): "to establish and maintain settings and relationships that support productive work and meet professional needs. The same ideals that apply to children are inherent in our responsibilities to adults" (p. 59).

➤ *communities and society*—"to provide programs that meet its needs and to cooperate with agencies and professions that share responsibility for the welfare and protection of children . . . to serve as a voice for children everywhere" (p. 60).

The main features of the NAEYC code of ethics are the group's beliefs about:

➤ what is right rather than expedient,
➤ what is good rather than simply practical, and
➤ what acts members must never engage in or condone, even if those acts would work or if members *could get away with* such acts, acts to which they must never be accomplices, bystanders, or contributors (Katz & Ward, 1996, p. 4).

"In summary, . . . it seems reasonable to suggest that the actual problems encountered by practitioners in the course of daily practice typically reflect combinations of several of these aspects" (Katz & Ward, 1996, p. 8).

Why is a code of ethics important? Katz and Ward (1996) identify and summarize a four-part answer:

1. *High power and low status of practitioners:* greater necessity for internalized restraints against abusing power (p. 4).
2. *Multiplicity of clients:* parents are the primary group, children secondary, the employing agency and the larger community next. "Each group of clients in the hierarchy may be perceived as exerting pressures for practitioners to act in ways that may be against the best interest of another client group" (p. 7).
3. *Ambiguity of the data base:* "to remind practitioners to eschew orthodoxies, strive for settings and relationships that support productive work and meet professional needs. The same ideals that apply to children are inherent in our responsibilities to adults" (p. 59).
4. *Communities and society:* "to provide programs that meet its needs and to cooperate with agencies and professions that share responsibility for the welfare and protection of children . . . to serve as a voice for children everywhere" (p. 60).

Early Childhood Teacher Certification

The Executive Summary of a position statement of the National Association of Early Childhood Specialists in State Departments of Education (NAECS/SDE) and the National Association for Early Childhood Teacher Educators (NAECTE) supports and builds upon the joint position statement of the NAEYC and the Association of Teacher

A friendly suggestion by an adult can *stimulate the play of children without being directive or critical.*

Educators (ATE). These organizations believe there is an urgent need for legislative and policy support of initial early-childhood teacher and administrator preparation in order to:

➤ provide well-trained educators;
➤ meet early-childhood teacher certification established by the NAEYC and the ATE;
➤ create and maintain high-quality early-childhood educator preparation programs in college and universities; and
➤ provide opportunities for related career advancement for Head Start and child-care personnel (information received on the Internet 3-13-02).

NAECTE and NAECS/SDE *support* the following PRINCIPLES:

➤ Early-childhood teachers of children from birth through 8 years of age need a baccalaureate education and specialized professional preparation.
➤ All states in the United States need an early-childhood teacher certificate for new teachers, separate from elementary or secondary teacher certification.
➤ It is essential that the initial professional preparation of building principals and school district administrators include study and experiences to initiate and support early-childhood teacher programs.

NAECTE and NAECS/SDE *recognize* the following FINDINGS:

➤ Young children are more likely to have an effective education when taught by teachers who have had specialized college preparation to work in early-childhood settings.
➤ Gains associated with programs using specially prepared early-childhood teachers who intervene with low-income children show that government received as high as $6 worth of benefits for every $1 spent on early education, because there is less retention, there are fewer special-education placements, and there is less juvenile delinquency.
➤ There are proven United States college and university programs that provide usable models to prepare early-childhood teachers.

➤ Variability exits in states' definitions of early-childhood education and early-childhood teacher preparation. Standards range from minimal to comprehensive and cover varied age ranges and different expectations of expertise (3 references).

➤ Building principals significantly influence school climate and the nature of learning in schools.

In addition to the above findings, there are recommendations of study that will better prepare teachers for working with young children, such as study of individual and group development and assessment, sociocultural and linguistic opportunities, and integrated study of children with special learning needs. Reflective studies would include observation-based approaches; work with multiple small groups; adaptations to meet special learning needs; and related, authentic assessment. A guided practice in full-time student teaching would include placements in both primary and preprimary settings that are exemplary and accredited and field placements that also include family study settings and accredited, exemplary infant/toddler settings. See also Internet: http://ericps.crc.uiuc.edu/naecs/position/ecteacher.html.

Two early promoters of early childhood education were the Swiss Jean Piaget (1896–1980) and his contemporary, Russian Lev Vygotsky (1896–1934). See Figure 1.1 to read about their influence on the field.

"Reflection" Symbol and Exercises

Before we proceed further, a symbol that will appear throughout the text needs to be introduced. To demonstrate a point, to give the reader an opportunity to visualize a

Theories promoted by Piaget and Vygotsky are frequently played out in classroom settings.

"Researchers such as Mestre (1991), citing Resnick (1987), Von Glasersfeld (1989), and others caution that if we as educators do not take students' prior knowledge into consideration, it is likely that the message we think we are sending will not be the message received" (Lind, 1997, p. 79).

Inasmuch as Jean Piaget and Lev Vygotsky are of prime importance to this chapter, more details will be given about them here. Selected other American and foreign educators who also play an important role in the progress of American (and world) early childhood education will be listed in Chapter 3.

Jean Piaget (1896–1980)

Jean Piaget was a Swiss epistomologist, biologist, psychologist, and astute observer of child development. As a highly original thinker, he has fueled decades of discussion and research throughout much of the world. His constructivist view places the major focus on the child as an intellectual explorer, who makes discoveries and constructs independent knowledge.

Piaget formulated a model for the stages of individual development in children as follows (1974):

Stage 1: Sensorimotor (0 to 24 months of age). Learning through the five senses and the emerging ability to control one's body movement are both crucial during this time.

Stage 2: Preoperational (2 to 7 years of age). During this period, children are somewhat self-centered; are still oriented toward learning through the senses and body skills; live in the here-and-now world; and need concrete experiences. They begin to handle abstract concepts, although the ideas of past and future are difficult for them. Most experiences need to be positive to develop their self-confidence.

Stage 3: Concrete operational (7 to 11 years of age).

Stage 4: Formal operational (11 years of age on).

(The third and fourth stages, concrete operational and formal operational, are beyond the scope of this book; however, the reader may find value in investigating these later stages. Many child-development texts or articles in professional journals are good sources of information.)

To achieve movement from one "stage" to the next, children engage in two cognitive processes that complement and coincide with each other:

accommodation: the process of learning something totally new; and
assimilation: the process of assimilating new information into old information.

The two processes explain what happens within the individual and enables the child to achieve equilibration, which provides a place for each new bit of knowledge the child constructs. "This kind of learning is playful, and can even be defined as play" (Krogh, 1997, p. 35).

Piaget's theories include:

1. Activity directed by the child is primary in his development (Van Hoorn et al. 1993, p. 237).
2. Through initiative and effort, the child modifies and builds upon already constructed mental patterns to try to make sense of new experiences (Cowan, 1978).
3. Knowledge is based on what the individual child brings to each situation rather than on what the child accumulates from the environment (Van Hoorn et al. 1993, p. 15).

Piaget's influence began in the 1950s, accelerated in the 1960s, and is very strong at present. An early contemporary of Lev Vygotsky, Piaget, and his work, became more widely known because of the suppression of Vygotsky's writing in Russia at the time. They both place emphasis on play in intellectual development and provide strong arguments for children's use of objects and their interaction with peers as the basis for early childhood curriculum.

Another important fact of Piaget's theory of development is what happens within the individual child. "Piaget assumed that the child's thought becomes more like that of an adult when children become developmentally ready to notice deficiencies in their immature, illogical reasoning and abandon it in favor of a logical approach to the world. Indeed, Piaget regarded the thought of the young child and that of more mature peers and adults not as collaborative and complementary but rather as in conflict" (Tudge & Winterhoff, 1993, p. 74).

Piaget's work is described as a cognitive-development theory: Children "construct" their own knowledge, facilitated by the teacher, through reflection on their experiences, their choices, and playing with peers. Learning and development are separate entities, but learning depends on development (Berk & Winsler, 1995, pp. 100–103).

Piaget was a strong supporter of play and hands-on experiences. He believed that children actually think differently than adults. He encouraged learning centers with materials for art, block play, writing, drawing, dramatic play, and exploration with raw materials (dirt, sand, water, and so on) for both individual and group projects. (DeVries & Kohlberg, 1987; Wasserman, 1992.)

Behaviorism (identified with direct teaching instruction) and maturationism (leading to a more hands-off teaching approach) were both employed during Piaget's lifetime. He rejected neither of these approaches, feeling that each had something to offer, as they interact with elements in children's lives.

Figure 1.1 Two Early Promoters of Early Childhood Education

Related directly to educational interactions with young children is Piaget's theory of *heteronomy* (being dependent upon others) and *autonomy* (personal conviction and some self-assurance). The more experience children have in making personal decisions, the more quickly they develop autonomous behavior.

Lev Vygotsky (1896–1934)

Vygotsky, a contemporary of Piaget, wrote copiously; however, his work was unpublished until after his death. Both Vygotsky and Piaget viewed the child as a biological organism; each credits the other for help in developing his theory.

Vygotsky had two major goals:

1. to create a Marxist psychology that would solve problems in psychology and guide the Russian people in their newly designed country, and
2. to help children solve physical and psychological problems through
   - dialogue with peers and adults; a process referred to as scaffolding (a term not introduced by Vygotsky but used to describe his work) denotes important components of tutoring (Wood, 1989) and connotes and supports a sensitive cooperation promoting children to take over more responsibility for tasks as their skill increases (Berk & Winsler, 1995, p. 32); and
   - zone of proximal development: the body of knowledge, tasks, and skills that a child is ready to reach through guidance and interactions from adults or more mature peers.

His ideas were sufficiently threatening to Soviet Union authorities that his work was suppressed and untranslated until the mid-1950s. Vygotsky today is recognized for his emphasis on socially constructed knowledge. His work has become fairly well known in recent years and complements Piaget's work.

SIMILARITIES between Piaget and Vygotsky:

These two men

were born the same year (1896);
credit each other for help in developing his own theory;
value play as an activity critically important to children's learning and development;
agree upon rules of behavior or symbolic meanings (dramatic play);
agree that dramatic or pretend (representational play) play offers opportunities to develop the concept that one object can symbolize another;
share understandings (Vygotsky's *intersubjectivity* is demonstrated in dramatic play when the necessary social give-and-take results in agreed-upon rules of behavior or symbolic meanings);
have strongly influenced current-day early childhood educational theory and practices;
view children as actively constructing their own knowledge; and
view the child as a biological organism (Krogh, 1997, p. 36).

DIFFERENCES between Piaget and Vygotsky:

Vygotsky believed that play gave children opportunities to act out the rules of society beginning in the toddler years, and he was more impressed than Piaget *by the importance of social interactions* as demonstrated in dramatic play through the necessary social give-and-take.

Vygotsky argued that social interaction was more important to education than Piaget believed (Krogh, 1997, p. 36).

Vygotsky's ideas on child development were sufficiently threatening to authorities that his publications were suppressed and untranslated until the mid-1950s.

Vygotsky's theory is sociocultural, emphasizing socially constructed knowledge.

Vygotsky agreed with those who criticized Piaget for not taking "into account the importance of the social situation and milieu" (opportunity to act out the rules of society) (Krogh, 1997, p. 36).

Piaget's theory of development stresses what happens within the individual. Rules of society would first be learned in elementary-school years when games containing rules would become more prevalent in children's lives than simple dramatic play.

Piaget's research and findings were published as they were completed.

There are many other important past, contemporary, and future educators who are not mentioned here. (See Chapter 3.) Nevertheless, they have made, are making, and will make valuable contributions and raise thought-provoking issues in attempts to improve life, health, and education for young children everywhere!

Figure 1.1 Continued

situation, to bring in practical experience, and to bring past and future learning into focus, *Reflections* will be used. The symbol denoting such examples is

In studying the image, one notes that a child stands amid four arrows, used to signify learning and interaction between the child and her environment. The arrow on the left refers to the child's past experiences that have influenced and will influence present and future learning. The arrow on the right indicates that with experience and maturity, the child's horizontal learning increases—that is, she learns about different topics.

The arrow on the top refers to vertical (or depth) learning: at first the child learns few things about a topic, then—indicated by the arrow beneath the child—she learns more things about the same topic. As she grows and experiences, the child will learn *some* about more topics (breadth) and *more* about the same topics (depth).

Read the "planting" Reflection on page 14. See if you can determine how Shaun's past experiences and the hands-on activity increased his knowledge and feelings about planting. Then ponder how a planting experience could be integrated with other topics to give meaning to both (water, tools, weather, different ways to plant, satisfaction, and so on). Stretch your imagination, if necessary, to reflect on your similar past experiences and what would have helped you develop a more positive attitude toward tasks for children, planting and harvesting crops, independence, commitment, and so on.

As you probably discovered in this exercise, some situations are not black or white. For example, if a child cries when left in a strange situation, does it necessarily mean that the child was raised in a distrusting environment? Respond to each item in the exercise in two ways: (1) what would be the most common or expected reaction, and (2) what modifications would ensure growth for each child?

Values for Children
Children with Special (Advanced or Delayed) Needs

(This topic is mentioned throughout various chapters.)

Much needs to be said about children with special needs (gifted, talented, disabled, neglected, mistreated, poor health, low income, one parent, etc.). Caregivers, parents, and teachers should be aware of all of these conditions in their classrooms, in children's homes, and other areas. They should be willing and able advocates for these children.

As both an opportunity for and a challenge to professionals and parents, the demand for early education and care continues to increase among economically diverse families. Quality programs need to be designed to help children from low-income families, disabled children, families with special needs, and also to be challenging for "gifted" children.

 **Reflection**

A group of preschool children were involved in a planting experience. They had a bucket of dirt, individual containers, spoons, bulbs, seeds, and a small watering can. Unnoticed by the children, the teacher became distracted. The children busied themselves with the task at hand. Shaun filled his container. Then, realizing it might not be a good idea just to lay the bulbs and seeds on top of the dirt, he emptied his container. This time he put the seeds and bulbs in the bottom and filled the jar with soil. Thoughtfully, he looked at the jar. Evidently deciding that this also was not the best idea, he spooned the dirt out until he reached the bulbs and seeds. The bulbs were easily retrieved, but the seeds became a problem. Carefully, he spooned the dirt onto the table. At first he tenderly stirred the dirt with his spoon but finally resorted to using his fingers to pick out the seeds one by one. Then he remembered how they had used cotton balls when they sprouted seeds previously. He got some small, white cotton balls from the shelf, lightly dampened them at the sink, and returned to the activity. He picked up each seed and placed it on a cotton ball. This time, as he filled his jar, he was very precise in placing the dirt, bulbs, and seeds. When the jar was full, he patted the dirt gently and slowly poured water from the can. His masterpiece was finished! By now the teacher had returned and was quietly observing the different skills and methods of the children. Shaun showed her his jar and told her of his different attempts at planting the bulbs and seeds and how he had finally succeeded. One could tell from the look of satisfaction on his face that Shaun was pleased with his planting experience. The teacher's smile and interest confirmed his ability to solve his problem.

Using the Reflection symbol (child with arrows on p. 13) and its definition, described previously, what possible changes occurred for both children through vertical and horizontal learning (for example, past experiences, learning or progress, and so on)? As a teacher, how can you provide experiences so all children in your classroom will show self-confidence, security, and positive ways of expressing themselves? How would you as a teacher respond to Shaun's planting experience?

The reader is encouraged to get assistance from individuals who have experience in working with these special children, who know the literature, and can give guidance in planning curriculum and activities for them. This is beyond my knowledge and expertise!

In the interest of focus, however, one article will be referenced here (Campbell & Taylor, 1996):

To provide a definitive investigation of the effects of preschool interventions for children from low-income families, a Consortium for Longitudinal Studies was formed in which eleven investigators followed up their participants to learn how long early benefits persisted. The consortium found important, lasting benefits in terms of: (a) fewer retentions in grade and fewer placements into special education for treated children; (b) positive changes in parental educational and employment levels; (c) modest but long-lasting IQ gains; (d) higher academic test scores and better progress through school; (e) "No one model emerges as clearly superior to another: positive benefits were found for limited interventions as well as for the most massive"; (f) greater cognitive gains when intervention begins in very early childhood; (g) care must be of the highest quality with particular attention being paid to socioemotional factors; (h) more research is needed on how best to foster healthy emotional growth in young children; (i) early childhood programs ultimately save taxpayer dollars in terms of reductions in the costs of education, welfare, and crime (p. 79).

What Young Children Are Like

What a child is and does as a 2-year-old certainly is reflected in what she is and does as an older child. Likewise, how a child reacts as she moves into schoolwork will also depend on how she has spent her earlier years.

Children with delayed development learn from other children and adults.

At the outset, the reader must be cautioned about individual differences of children in age, skills, interest, family backgrounds, and opportunity. The following paragraphs note some expected behavior of children ages 2 through 5. Just knowing whether behavior is typical of an age can help the adult in planning for and understanding children, but it does not take into account deviations from the "norms."

2-Year-Olds

Adam and Beth have recently passed their second birthday. Adam, seated on the floor near Beth, plays quietly with a few assorted toys. Beth is handling a book, which is upside down. As she attempts to turn the pages, she accidentally drops the book, which starts a wheel toy in motion. Both Beth and Adam reach for the toy and begin to scuffle over it. They begin jabbering at each other and pulling on the toy. A teacher steps in and offers a similar toy to each child. The children hear music and hurry to join in songs, stories conversation, and other activities. They are semi-involved in a movement experience, but their jumping, running, and imitating are immature, uncoordinated, and slower than that of the other children; however, they are great imitators, curious, and full of energy. They soon tire and then individually drift off to another activity.

Characteristics: Play is usually solitary; children have a short attention span and are easily distracted. They use limited and often unclear language, often need adult assistance, and exhibit uncoordinated physical development.

3-Year-Olds

Cristi is attempting a puzzle and Devin, playing nearby, is using blocks to make a garage for his car. Cristi becomes distracted as Devin's blocks fall on his car. Cristi moves near Devin and asks, "What's happening?" Devin shrugs his shoulders and starts restacking the blocks. Cristi watches, gets an idea, sits down by Devin, and hands him a block. He takes it and makes a roof for his garage; the "roof" slides off and lands on his car. Cristi shows him how to move the blocks closer so the roof is supported by two blocks. Devin looks at her, accepts the solution, hands her another car, and asks her to help with building a barn. They play side by side with limited conversation until Cristi returns to her puzzle, picks up a piece, and talks to it as if it were "real." The teacher announces lunch; Devin and Cristi hurry to wash their hands and find chairs next to each other at the table.

Characteristics: Children play near others (parallel) and begin cooperative play—a move from watching to "doing"; an increased attention span leads to more independence, more interaction, more cooperation, and increasing skills; verbalization consists of longer sentences, more ideas, and more use of language, but children may still participate in collective monologue. Large muscles are increasing in strength and coordination; however, agility is lacking. Use of small muscles is still limited, even though it is increasing all the time. Lack of eye-hand coordination and of precision in small muscles makes it tiring for a 3-year-old to stay with small-muscle activities (puzzles, pegboards, or scissors).

The child's ability to distinguish reality from fantasy is limited—everything is possible, and the 3-year-old attempts to demonstrate rather than verbalize ideas.

Growth tapers off, causing dawdling over food and poor appetite.

4-Year-Olds

Ethan and Frankie are heading for the playground. They find the shed latched, but not locked. Ethan gets a box to stand on while Frankie steadies the box. Grace approaches and offers suggestions, which are ignored by the boys. Finally getting a stick to knock the latch out of the clasp, the boys race inside, get matching trikes, and speed off, apparently continuing play of a prior time. Their conversation, ranging from moderate to loud, directs and reflects accurate portrayal of their play, and sometimes addresses the activities of other children.

Characteristics: Children make definite strides for independence and for the most part, are assertive and boastful. They express caring behavior toward others and usually prefer a friend of the same sex. Their interests are much broader and continued play is common. They want realistic props and roles for each participant. Attention is gained by showing off, expressing displeasure, and being aggressive or loud. Gross and fine muscles are becoming better coordinated, but large-muscle activities are still preferred over small-muscle tasks.

Language is used increasingly in accurate reflection of the child's play, in interaction with others, to gain desired things, to gain information, and in self-expression. Serious answers are wanted with verbiage.

Four-year-olds make some distinction between reality and fantasy, but there is still some confusion. When such actions as displays of superhuman strength or impossible feats are viewed on television or in movies, 4-year-olds insist they can be performed.

5-Year-Olds

Hettie, Ivan, Jacquie, Kenna, and Lamont are busily engaged in reenacting their roles of the previous day. Sequences have been briefly reviewed and minor adjustments have been made. Periodically they stop to make additional minor adjustments in order to modify the direction of their play. As their interest begins to dwindle, they leave their dramatic play to participate in other attractive activities. Hettie and Kenna move to where a teacher and a few children are making applesauce for lunch, Ivan and Lamont head for the woodworking table, and Jacquie joins a group of children who are dancing with scarves and lively music.

Characteristics: Children at 5 years of age are more independent, dependable, self-assured, and conforming than younger children, but they like approval from others. They are protective toward younger siblings. They prefer to play with children of the same sex and age, and their play is cooperative, sustained, and more complex than formerly. Eye-hand coordination, gross and fine muscle movements, and ideas work cooperatively. Body control is good; they can throw and catch a ball, jump rope, skip and use their skills to interact with other people. They use scissors with more precision than younger children and enjoy making things. They love stories and school and can remember sequences of numbers or letters. Although 5-year-olds tend to be obedient, cooperative, and empathetic, they also brag about accomplishments, exaggerate, and enter into short quarrels. They understand and use language freely in expressing their feelings and in complying with requests. They differentiate better between truth and make-believe and can verbally explain some differences. They still enjoy dramatic play but are interested in the "real" world.

Summary

Specific differences can be noted among children between ages 2 and 5; however, the match between a child and his age characteristics is another thing. Some fit so well that the movement from one age to the next is evident; others pass casually through the stages. Along with individual differences are periods when development is more continuous and smooth than others. When children are in a period of rapid development, behavior is less stable than when development is slower. For instance, the behavior of 2- and 4-year-olds, who are in periods of rapid development, reflects more negativism or egocentrism than that of 3- and 5-year-olds.

Young children from financially, educationally, nutritionally, or experientially restricted backgrounds may have the same tendencies toward these characteristics, but may not have the opportunity to explore or experience, or be motivated or encouraged.

Let us make a quick note about *attention* and *interest,* mentioned earlier. *Webster's New World Dictionary* makes the following distinctions: "Attention: the ability to give heed or observe carefully." "Interest: a share or participation in something." It may be said that young children have short attention spans. That is very logical if they are expected to observe carefully. Participating or sharing in an experience is very different. Young children are not observers—they are participants. If their attention or longer involvement is desired, active involvement rather than "showing" is required. Here is an example of how the interest span of a group of 2-year-olds was lengthened.

 **Reflection**

Balls of play dough were placed in front of each child. Without delay, it was tasted, pinched, and smelled. This wasn't too exciting or interesting. As two children started to leave the table, the teacher brought out some flour sifters and flour. The children turned back to the activity. Sifting flour was fun for a few minutes; rolling the flour into the dough also took some concentration. Again a couple of the children were ready to leave. The teacher placed a small rolling pin in front of each child. Nothing was said, but eager hands reached for the pins. Now the children were tasting, pinching, flouring, and rolling. This continued for several minutes. Then, as lack of interest began to set in, the teacher placed cookie cutters and a pan on the table. Again, the eager fingers and minds were diverted back to the activity. All in all, the children stayed at the activity for a length of time that was notable, especially considering their age and short interest span.

What was it that kept the children interested? New and varied materials, attention from the teacher, peers, or success? Each of these components must have added to the experience.

How do the following children respond?

1. a 2-year-old
2. a 3-year-old
3. a 4-year-old
4. a 5-year-old

Using the Reflection symbol (child with arrows) and its definition, described on page 13, explain what possible changes occurred through vertical and horizontal learning (for example, past experiences, learning or progress, and so on). As a teacher, how can you provide experiences so all children in your classroom will show self-confidence, security, and positive ways of expressing themselves?

How Young Children Learn

In early European history, children were treated like adults, were dressed like adults, worked like adults, and were considered adult in all ways except size. They were expected to carry their full share of responsibility in providing for the family. In some cases, children performed tasks that adults could not: they crawled into small openings while working in mines, spent long hours in the fields, and survived on less food and sleep.

During the past century, observation and research confirmed that children are not miniature adults. They do have feelings similar to those of adults, such as fear, joy, and pain, etc., but their learning patterns are different from those of adults.

Many approaches, theories, and practices have been introduced regarding the growth, behavior, and learning of young children. This text promotes the premise that experiences for young children should be based on abilities, interests, and experiences that are developmentally appropriate for each individual child. Theorists who advocate these ideas include Piaget, Erikson, Dewey, Vygotsky, Malaguzzi (founder of the Reggio Emilia approach). See Figure 1.1, pp. 11–12, and Table 3.1, p. 75.

Each student is highly encouraged to seek further information from original writings of each theorist, and from educators who are well versed in the trends of early childhood education.

Misconceptions About Behavior and Learning Styles

Adults who have been around young children will quickly recognize some points as **myths** and react accordingly. For example:

Children are most like adults in their thinking and least like them in their feelings.
Children learn best while sitting still and listening.
Children can learn and operate according to rules.
Acceleration is preferable to elaboration.
Parents and teachers can raise the IQ of children (Elkind, 1972).

Solitary play can occur at any age and often leads to group activity.

Adults whose experience with young children is limited, however, will have to be observant to avoid the above pitfalls. Young children do share the same emotional feelings with adults, but their cognitive structure is immature. They are doers—their thinking pattern does not allow them to sit and listen or to absorb and follow rules at this young age. They need *time* and *opportunities* to learn about their environment. Additional misconceptions could be added—for example, "All children of the same chronological age have the same interests, attention span, and abilities," "Extrinsic rewards are better than intrinsic rewards," or "Children learn through vicarious experiences."

Since the publication of Elkind's list above, support for his ideas has grown, research has been conducted, programs have been initiated, and national and local organizations have contributed to this philosophy (Bredekamp & Copple, 1997).

In general, when 2-year-olds are mentioned, one's first thoughts are of behavior:

Age + negativism = "terrible twos"

Negative behavior might be expressed more vigorously at 2 years than at most other ages, but this is not the only age when a person is negative. Some individuals never get beyond this stage. But because negativism is so often associated with the young child, this concept is briefly explored here. (See also Chapter 2.)

Some young children are very negative. They may constantly use the word "NO!" even when they want the opposite; they may become rigid or limp all over; they may use aggressive behavior, such as biting, kicking, and scratching; they may run away; or worst of all, they may throw a tantrum. They cannot verbalize feelings or desires, so they revert to behavior—with vigor—even though it may be short-lived! Instead of ignoring or playing down the behavior, adults often force more negativism. The 2-year-old then sees that negative behavior has to increase in intensity or duration in order to get results. This tendency can result from aggressive discipline, intolerance toward normal childish behavior, refusal by the child to carry out a request when and how the adult requires, adult interference, inconsistent training (such as toilet training or reaction to people of different tempos). Negativism begins at about 18 months of age, reaches a peak between 3 and 6 years of age, and then recedes rapidly, partly from social influence, partly because children learn that compliance is to their advantage, and partly because adults learn to show more respect for the children.

Negativism is usually more frequent and more severe in poorly adjusted children, but also appears in well-adjusted children. Between the ages of 4 and 6 children change resistance from physical to verbal forms. They also pretend not to hear or understand, refuse to see the point, insist on reopening issues, and complain or act irresponsibly.

Negativism is a part of the young child's life, but duration, intensity, and frequency depend in large measure on the response of the adult. Through behavior, adults can increase or decrease negativism by planning for and interacting with young children. Adults must see that issues are resolved without causing children to suffer loss of face, without trying to win a power struggle, and through a loving relationship. When thoughtfully handled, not only will the "terrible twos" be changed to the "terrific twos," but other ages and stages will be less stressful for both children and adults. In a broad generality, many adults try to do too much for a child at each age when the child is trying to become more and more independent, that is, a person in his own right with his own needs, abilities, and desires.

Negativism and other aspects of behavior (such as independence, confidence, security conformity, and conflict) recur throughout the child's life cycle, becoming notable again during adolescence and young adulthood.

Developmentally Appropriate Practices

Some important highlights:

1. Developmentally appropriate practice is **NOT** a curriculum or a method, but a way of thinking about and working with children (Wilt, Vander, & Monroe, 1998, p. 17).

Children learn from each other if they have time, materials, and opportunities which encourage cooperation.

2. Teachers in early childhood settings, particularly in prekindergarten programs, have long subscribed to many of the tenets spelled out in *Developmentally Appropriate Practice in Early Childhood Programs . . . from Birth through Age 8* (Bredekamp 1987; Bredekamp & Copple, 1997).

3. It results from the process of professionals making decisions about the well-being and education of children based on at least three important kinds of information or knowledge about: (a) child development and learning, (b) the strengths, interests, and needs of each individual child in the group, and (c) the social and cultural contexts in which children live (Bredekamp & Copple, 1997, p. 8 & 9).

4. NAEYC has modified its former standards from "either/or" to "both/and" thinking: For example: Children (1) construct their own understanding of concepts **and** benefit from instruction by more competent peers and adults; (2) learn through integration of curriculum **and** in-depth study; (3) benefit from making choices **and** from having boundaries; and (4) develop their own self-identity **and** respect for differences of others. Additional examples are given in the NAEYC position statement (Bredekamp & Copple, 1997, p. 23).

5. Good environments for children are also good environments for parents.

6. The terms **DAP** (Developmentally Appropriate Practices) and **DIP** (Developmentally Inappropriate Practices) were coined and popularized by NAEYC and are descriptive terms.

7. The revised NAEYC pamphlet addresses age appropriateness and individual appropriateness in the areas of physical, motor, language, cognitive, social, and emotional development at the different age levels. It also provides guidelines for (a) creating a caring community of learners, (b) teaching to enhance development and learning, (c) constructing appropriate curriculum, (d) assessing children's learning and development, and (e) establishing reciprocal relationships with families.

8. The environment where the child feels secure and happy is where she does best.

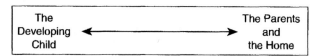

Figure 1.2   The Child Is Part of the Family Unit.

Some Misconceptions About Developmentally Appropriate Practices

There are some myths associated with developmentally appropriate practices:

➤ There are two dichotomous positions: one always right, the other always wrong.
➤ Teachers are required to abandon all their prior knowledge and experience; former learning is unacceptable.
➤ Classrooms are unstructured and chaotic.
➤ Teachers offer no instructions; a traditional, "watered-down" curriculum results in less learning.
➤ The DAP program meets the needs of only certain kinds of children.
➤ DAP is a fad—soon to be replaced by another; perhaps opposite, trend (Kostelnik, 1992, pp. 17–23).

As a matter of fact, teachers are most successful in developmentally appropriate practices when they capitalize on their prior knowledge, long-range objectives, fluid decision making, and input from the children (in the form of their asking questions, suggesting alternatives, expressing interest, developing plans, and looking for new directions in learning).

In planning for young children, one must consider *the children, the curriculum, adult-child interaction, developmental evaluation of the children, and other influences*, such as the growing child's having more and more out-of-home influences. Perhaps the child will attend a preschool or child-care center, which expands experience as illustrated in Figure 1.2 and Figure 1.3

Parents want the best opportunities for each of their children, but suppose that parents want to give their children "all the things I never had." Then the situation moves from a dyad (two components) to a triad (three components), to multi-involvement; for example, parents may enroll their children in athletic programs, in music programs, in

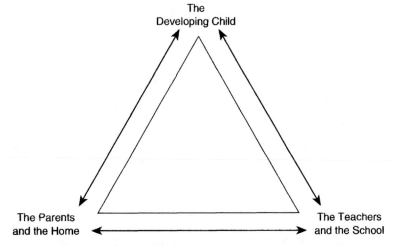

Figure 1.3   The Child Is the Connecting Link Between Home and School.

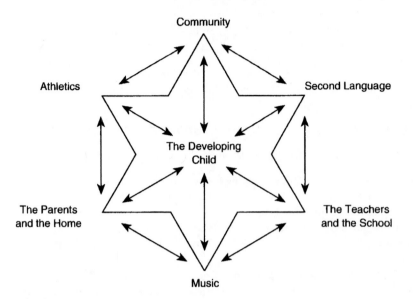

Figure 1.4   Influences Outside the Home Increase the Complexity of the Child's Environment.

learning a second language, in academic acceleration, and so on. The child's world looks more like the one shown in Figure 1.4.

Children also have to deal with various sources of energy, identified by Elkind as *clock energy* (pursuing the tasks of daily living) and *calendar energy* (involved in growth and development (1984).

There should be diversity in programs to create awareness of different cultures, abilities, and needs of individual children, who come from varied backgrounds, genetic make-ups, cultures, and so on. What fits one may not fit another, and vice versa. Sighted and hearing children have different modes of learning than children who have sight or hearing deficiencies, for example. Programs must be carefully planned and administered so that they will be of value to the children who participate in them now—today! Children and parents have goals for "regular" learning—reading, writing, and arithmetic—but how and when children use these experiences and information may be vastly different for each child. Various types of diversity (such as gender, culture, race, physical abilities, and so on) are further addressed in Chapter 10.

The Relationship Between Home and School Environments

Parents play a vital role in the education of their children, for even when they think they are not teaching, they are visual, verbal, and physical models. Parents shouldn't feel that "teaching" is the sole responsibility of "teachers." Regardless of age, setting, or title, we are all TEACHERS and learners.

Readiness for school means that "all children in America will be ready to learn." This is the most significant statement ever made by one of our nation's leaders acknowledging the critical importance of early childhood experiences to later success in school and life (U. S. Department of Education, 1991, p. 38).

Specifics of this report include the following:

1. All "special-needs children" (delayed or advanced) will have access to high-quality and developmentally appropriate preschool programs that help prepare children for school.
2. Every parent in American will be the child's first teacher and devote time each day to helping his or her preschool children learn; parents will have access to the training and support they need.

 *Reflection*

Prior to the summer vacation, the teacher is planning a social with the children who have been in her preschool classroom for the past school year. She sends a vague invitation home with each child—it's unclear who is invited, whether it is a come-and-go or a stay affair, what the purpose is, how long it lasts, and so on.

Intentions of the teacher: The festivities will be simple, fairly short, outdoors, with light refreshments, a chance for the teacher to say good-bye to the child and for parents to pick up any items the child has left at school.

Interpretation of the parents: This will be a graduation for the child (even if he will return after summer), "I won't have to fix dinner," "We'll all need to dress up," "It will be difficult getting all of us ready and there on time," "It will be an opportunity for my child to perform for the other parents and children," "This will give my younger children a chance to play on the playground," "We had better invite all our relatives for this 'educational' achievement," and other parental hopes and anticipations.

The party does not meet the expectations of the teacher, the children, or the parents.

Exercise: With a partner, role play assuming you are the teacher. What message did you want to give to the parents? Why were your intentions misunderstood? Why were the parents so angry and resentful? Did any good things happen?

In a few minutes, switch roles and assume that you are the parent. Did you understand the teacher's intentions or did you feel you had to make them up? Did that disappoint you and/or your children? Do you have a basis for being angry or do you just accept things as they unravel? Will this incident interfere with relationships between the home and school? How could future misunderstandings be avoided between the teacher and the parent?

3. Children will receive the nutrition and health care needed to arrive at school with healthy minds and bodies, and the number of low-birth-weight babies will be significantly reduced through enhanced prenatal health systems.

Head Start, NAEYC, ATE, educators, researchers, and others advocate a strong and reciprocal relationship between the school and the home, and give their full support to the above goals, which encourage schools to get ready to serve all children. These supporters urge that any definition of readiness must address both characteristics of the child and characteristics of the school (U.S. Department of Education, 1991).

NAEYC summarizes its commitment to universal school readiness by:

1. addressing the inequities in early life experiences so that all children have access to the opportunities that promote school success;
2. recognizing and supporting individual differences among children; and
3. establishing reasonable and appropriate expectations of children's capabilities on school entry.

Head Start funds have continually increased as a means of preventing young children from experiencing those things that diminish their self-image, health, learning abilities, and optimism for the future. Organizations and individuals have devised and implemented ways to help parents within the home, but the goal of reaching all children in need has not been rapidly or completely accomplished. Out-of-home experiences have

Notable Notes

University researchers, preschool teachers and staff, elementary school staff, parents, and others have joined to design, implement, and conduct research on an intervention to improve transitions to kindergarten. They confirm the importance of "a shared mission, communication, mutual respect, and value of collaboration for all involved" (Pianta et al., 2001).

"Recent data from the Census Bureau tell us that during a typical week, 14 million young children, or three-fourths of all children under age five, are in some form of regular child care arrangement. On average, young children spent 28 hours per week in child care. When parents work or are in school, the average time children spend in child care increases to 35 hours per week (Smith 2000). These hours and days in care provide us with a new opportunity to encourage early learning and family support" (Lombardi, 2001, p. 74).

"One factor that has interfered with a comprehensive understanding of developmentally appropriate practice is confusion regarding what it is. This has led to different interpretations, with the result that educators may say they are implementing DAP when in fact they are not" (Wilt, Vander, & Monroe, 1998, 17).

". . . education that is DAP requires a sensitivity that is both age and individually appropriate. Teachers must be aware of and account for the typical sequences of growth and change in children. This means that teachers need a much stronger grounding in child development than most of them have. . . . Teachers must *also* be aware of and account for individual children's development, understanding, interests, and cultural background" (Wilt, Vander, & Monroe, 1998, p. 18).

"The 'schedule,' determined by the 'clock,' often interrupts productive play and intrudes upon young children's natural, creative business, which creates unnecessary transitions and stress" (Wien & Kirby-Smith, 1998, p. 9).

Teachers want to develop DAP practices in their centers—not scripts inherited from previous teachers and carried on because no one has time to think consciously about doing things differently (Wien, 1996 p. 50).

not always been available or desirable for many diverse reasons. To make the most of schooling for young children, parents, families, and teachers, there should be provision for home visits by teachers and for parental visits to classrooms.

In early childhood education there are advantages in making a tie between school and home. Some teachers think they are too busy to make home visits—and some parents feel uncomfortable about teachers visiting the home.

home visits: (give teachers a better understanding between the two environments). Some visits are more successful than others!

> On one of my home visits the child had showed me his room and told me about his family, friends, and dog. We went into the living room to continue our visit. His mother brought in a plate of cookies. She said to the child, "Give your teacher a cookie!" The child picked up a cookie and gently tossed it to me across the room. The child had answered the request. The mother was embarrassed, but I just said, "Thank you," and we went on with our visit!

> Children love the visits! ("You came to MY house!") One of the greatest rewards is an improved relationship between children, parents, and teachers.

home kits: (requests of parents or suggestions by teachers). Some items are more valuable than others!

parental visits to classroom: Some visits are helpful to parents: better understanding of school goals, volunteering, feeling a part of a team, and the like. Some visits are more helpful to children: feeling a tie between two environments. Some are more

Good environments for children include indoor and outdoor play with peers.

helpful to teachers (Bredekamp & Copple, 1997; Gorter-Reu & Anderson, 1998; Powell, 1998; Hurt, 2000).

The environment where the child feels secure and happy is where she does best, where this child fits developmentally. Pushing ahead or holding back may please parents, but may not be best for the child. The child's behavior age, not her birthday age, should determine the time of school entrance and of subsequent promotions.

An important consideration of parents should be the philosophy of the center. Is it based on developmentally appropriate practices supported by research? Is it the best setting for *this particular child and family?* Will expectations cause undue stress on either the family or the center? When there is conflict, it is the child who is usually in the middle—uncomfortable at school and at home. More information is presented in subsequent chapters.

Application of Principles

1. Teachers and researchers are encouraged to learn how to use the Socratic method of teaching or discussion: "in which one asks a series of easily answered questions that inevitably lead the answerer to a logical conclusion foreseen by the questioner. . . ." (Webster's Dictionary, 1959, 1385). Use Socratic questions to elicit prosocial planfulness and recognition of responsibility.

   For example:

   a. A teacher may show pictures of an easily recognized animal and ask open-ended questions, such as: What is the name of the mother animal, the father animal, the baby animal? What color(s) do you see on this animal? What does this animal like to eat? What do we get from this animal (to eat, wear, do)? Where would you go to see a "live" animal like this one?

   b. A teacher may show a replica (or real object) of a toy and ask the children how they would play with it—or what its use is.

    c. A teacher may show various products and ask the children which ones they would need to make: a snack (beverage, breakfast cereal, sandwich, etc.), a creative-arts activity (easel, paint, dough clay, earth clay), dramatic play (clothes, shoes, hats, working items) and the like. Be creative! Help the children learn to plan for their own activities.

    d. Think of the many ways children can use their own creative thinking skills in: dramatic play; creative arts; social thinking; using nice talk ("please", "thank you," greetings, seeking assistance); listening; being helpful, cooperative, generous, patient; sharing; providing alternates to aggression.

    e. Preschool children can be encouraged to use polite words, listen to person who is talking, participate with a peer in an activity, share, take turns, and help another person have fun. How can you help the children in your classroom do the same? "Be sure to help children become aware of how the child being helped feels and how the child who has been helpful or generous will feel about himself or herself" (Wittmer & Honig, 1994, p. 9).

2. Name some characteristics of a good environment for:
    a. Young children.
    b. Teachers of young children.
    c. Interaction between home and school. What advice would you give to parents considering enrolling their child in a child-care/education center?

3. Recall one of the theorists outlined in the chapter:
    a. Give some examples of his/her beliefs.
    b. Specifically, how would you use this information in preparing for or teaching young children?

4. Select a "misconception" listed in the chapter and indicate how you would correct or diffuse it.

5. Give three examples of developmentally appropriate and developmentally *inappropriate* activities; give examples of differences between age-appropriate and individually appropriate activities.

6. Think of a child between ages 3 and 5. What are some of the influences in that child's life? How could you help the child simplify some of the negative influences?

7. Consider two children who are fighting over a toy. How could you help each one become more friendly?

8. As a future teacher of young children, what personal and professional characteristics would you most desire to develop? Suggest ways you could build good relationships with children, colleagues, and parents.

9. What are the differences between child-centered and adult-centered activities?

10. In what ways do adults "hurry" or put stress on young children?

11. Contact a department of education to get the requirements for becoming a certified teacher of child care and/or a teacher of preschool children in your area.

References

Association of Teacher Educators (ATE). (1991). Early childhood teacher certification: A position statement of the Association of Teacher Educators and the National Association for the Education of Young Children (NAEYC). *Young Children, 47* (1), 16–21.

Barnett, W. S. (1995). Long-term effects of early childhood programs on cognitive and school outcomes. *The Future of Children, 5*(3), 25–50.

Bergen, D., Reid, R., & Torelli, L. (2001). *Educating and caring for very young children: The infant/toddler curriculum.* Early Childhood Education Series. January. Williston, VT: Teacher's College Press. (P.O. Box 20, Williston, VT 05495-0020. Tel: 800-575-6566; fax: 802-864-7626; website: http://www.teacherscollegepress.org.)

Berk, L. E. (1994). Vygotsky's theory: The importance of make-believe. *Young Children, 50*(1), 30–39.

Berk, L. E., & Winsler, A. (1995). *Scaffolding children's learning: Vygotsky and early childhood education.* Series #7. National Association for the Education of Young Children (NAEYC) Research into Practice Series. Washington, DC: National Association for the Education of Young Children. (1509 16th Street, N. W., Washington, DC 20036-1426.)

Bodrova, E. & Leong, D. J. (1996). *Tools of the mind: The Vygotskian approach to early childhood education.* Columbus, OH, and Upper Saddle River, NJ: Merrill.

Bowman, B. T., Donovan, M., & Burns, M. S. (Eds.). (2001). Eager to learn: Educating our preschoolers. (Full report and executive summary.) Washington, DC: National Academy Press. (2101 Constitution Ave., N. W., Lockbox 285, Washington DC 20055. 888-624-8373 [toll free]; fax: 202-334-2451; website: http://www.nap.edu.) (Paper or microfiche.)

Bredekamp, S. (Ed.). (1987). *Developmentally appropriate practice in early childhood programs serving children from birth through age 8,* expanded edition. Washington, DC: NAEYC.

Bredekamp, S., & Copple, C. (Eds.). (1997). *Developmentally appropriate practice in early childhood programs* (rev. ed.) Washington, DC: NAEYC.

Byrnes, J. P. (2001). *Minds, brains, and learning: Understanding the psychology and educational relevance of neuroscientific research.* New York: Guilford Press.

Cadwell, L. B. (1997). *Bringing Reggio Emilia home.* Early Childhood Education Series. New York: Teachers College Press, Columbia University.

Caine, G., & Caine, R. L. (1997). *Education on the edge of possibility.* Alexandria, VA: Association for Supervision and Curriculum Development (ASCD).

Campbell, F. A., & Taylor, K. (1996, May). Early childhood programs that work for children from economically disadvantaged families. *Young Children, 51*(4), 74–80.

Cowan, P. A. (1978). *Piaget with feelings.* New York: Holt, Rinehart & Winston.

DeVries, R., & Kohlberg, L. (1987/1990). *Constructivist early education: Overview and comparison with other programs.* Washington, DC: NAEYC.

Edwards, C. (1993). Partner, nurturer, and guide. The roles of the Reggio teacher in action. In C. Edwards, L. Gandini, & G. Forman (Eds.), *The hundred languages of children: The Reggio Emilia approach to early childhood education,* 151–170. Norwood, NJ: Ablex Publishing.

Elkind, D. (1972). Misunderstandings about how children learn. *Today's Education,* 125–126.

Elkind, D. (1981). *The hurried child.* Reading, MA: Addison-Wesley.

Elkind, D. (1984). *All grown up and no place to go: Teenagers in crisis.* Reading, MA: Addison-Wesley.

Elkind, D. (1986). Formal education and early childhood education: An essential difference. *Phi Delta Kappan,* 67, 631–636.

Elkind, D. (1988). Educating the very young: A call for clear thinking. *NEA Today, 6*(6), 22–26.

ERIC DIGEST. Protecting children from inappropriate practices. ERIC 326305 1990-00-00. At http://www.ed.gov/databases/ERIC_digest/ed326305.

Gandini, L. (1993). Fundamentals of the Reggio approach to early childhood education. *Young Children, 48*(1), 4–8.

Gorter-Reu, M. S., & J. M. Anderson. (1998). Home kits, home visits, and more! *Young Children, 53*(3), 71–73.

Hart, C. H., Burts, D. D., and Charlesworth, R. (1997). *Integrated curriculum and developmentally appropriate practice: Birth to age eight.* Albany: State University of New York Press.

Howes, C., & Clements, D. (1994). Adult socialization of children's play in child care. In Goelman, H. (Ed.), *Play and child care.* Albany: State University of New York Press.

Howes, C., Matheson, C. C., & Hamilton, C. E. (1994). Maternal, teacher, and child care history correlates of children's relationships with peers. *Child Development, 65,* 264–273.

Hurt, J. A. (2000). Create a parent place: Make the invitation for family involvement real. *Young Children, 55* (5), 88–92.

Hyson, M. (2002). Professional development: Preparing tomorrow's teachers: NAEYC Announces new standards. *Young Children, 56*(3), 78–79.

Katz, L. G., & Ward, E. H. (1991, 1996). *Ethical behavior in early childhood education,* (expanded ed.). Washington, DC: NAEYC.

Kontos, S., & Wilcox-Herzog, A. (2001). How do education and experience affect teachers of young children? *Young Children, 56*(4), 85–91.

Krechevsky, M., & Gardner, H. (1990). The emergence and nurturance of multiple intelligences: The Project Spectrum approach. In M. J. A. Howe (Ed.), *Encouraging the development of exceptional skills and talents.* Leicester, Eng.: British Psychological Society.

Krechevsky, M., & Gardner, H. (2001). What is Project Spectrum 2061? *Young Children, 56*(4).

Krogh, S. (1997). How children grow and why it matters: The foundation for the developmentally appropriate integrated early childhood curriculum. In C. H. Hart, D. D. Burts, and R. Charlesworth, *Integrated curriculum and developmentally appropriate practice: Birth to age eight* (pp. 29–48). Albany: State University of New York Press.

Lewin, A. (1995). *The fundamentals of the Reggio approach.* Presentation to visiting delegation at the Model Early Learning Center, Washington, DC.

Lind, K. K. (1997). Science in developmentally appropriate integrated curriculum. In C. H. Hart, D. D. Burts, and R. Charlesworth (Eds.), *Integrated curriculum and developmentally appropriate practice: Birth to age eight* (pp. 75–101). Albany: State University of New York Press.

Lombardi, J. (2001). It's time to redesign child care to create 21st century early education. *Young Children, 3,* 74–77.

Lowery, L. (1998). How new science curriculums reflect brain research. *Educational Leadership, 56,* 27–30.

Mestre, J. (1991). Learning and instruction in pre-college physical science. *Physics Today, 44,* 56–62.

National Academy Press. At www.nap.edu.

National Association of Early Childhood Specialists in State Departments of Education (NAECS/SDE) and National Association for Early Childhood Teacher Educators (NAECTE): Executive Summary. Retrieved March 13, 2002, from http://ericps.crc. uiuc.edu/naecs/position/ecteachr.html.

National Association for the Education of Young Children (NAEYC). *Code of ethical conduct.* Adopted 1989. Amended 1997. Retrieved March 12, 2002, from http//:www. NAEYC.org/resources/position_statements/

National Association for the Education of Young Children (NAEYC). (1998). Real-life ethical problems early childhood professionals face. NAEYC's *Code of ethical conduct and statement of commitment.* NAEYC Brochure #503.

National Association for the Education of Young Children (NAEYC) & National Association of Early Childhood Specialists in State Departments of Education (NAECS/ SDE. (1991). Guidelines for appropriate curriculum content and assessment in programs serving children ages 3 through 8. *Young Children, 46*(3), 21–38. Also in Bredekamp, S. K., & Rosegrant, T. (Eds.). (1992). *Reaching potentials: Appropriate curriculum and assessments for young children* (pp 9–27). Washington, DC: NAEYC.

National Academy of Early Childhood Programs (NAECP) (1991) *Accreditation Criteria and Procedures.* Rev. Ed. Washington, DC: NAEYC.

National Institute of Mental Health. At www.nimh.nih.gov/childhp/collabor.html.

Piaget, J. (1974). *The child and reality: Problems of genetic psychology.* Trans. A. Rosin. New York: Viking.

Pianta, R. C., Kraft-Sayre, M., Rimm-Kaufman, S., Gercke, N., & Higgins, T. (2001). Collaboration in building partnerships between families and schools: The National Center for Early Development and Learning's Kindergarten Transition Intervention. *Early Childhood Research Quarterly, 16,* 117–132.

Powell, D. R. (1998). Reweaving parents into the fabric of early childhood programs. *Young Children, 53*(5), 60–67.

Reggio Emilia. Website prepared by Lella Gandini, July 1998, at www.mhhe.com/socscience/education/cybereducator.

Resnick, L. B. (1987). *Education and learning to think.* Washington, DC: National Academy Press.

Shepard, L. A., Kagan, S. L., & Wurtz, E. (1998). Goal 1: Early childhood assessments Resource Group Recommendations. *Young Children, 53*(3), 52–54. (Reprinted from *Principles and recommendations for early childhood assessments,* pp 20–21, by L. A. Shepard, S. L. Kagan, and E. Wurtz, Eds., 1998, Washington, DC: National Educational Goals Panel.

Shonkoff, J. P., & Phillips, D. A. (Eds.). (2000). *From neurons to neighborhoods: The science of early childhood development.* Washington, DC: National Academy Press.

Smith, K. (2000). *Who's minding the kids? Child care arrangements: Fall 1995.* Current population reports. Washington, DC: U.S. Bureau of the Census.

Tudge, J. R. H., & Winterhoff, P. A. (1993). Vygotsky, Piaget, and Bandura: Perspectives on the relations between the social world and cognitive development. *Human Development, 36,* 61–81.

Van der Veer, R., & Valsiner, J. (1991). *Understanding Vygotsky.* Cambridge: Blackwell.

Van Hoorn, J., Nourot, P., Scales, B., & Alward, K. (1993). *Play at the center of the curriculum.* Upper Saddle River, NJ: Merrill/Prentice Hall.

Vinson, B. M. (2001). Fishing and Vygotsky's concept of effective education. *Young Children, 56*(1), 88–89.

Von Glasersfeld, E. (1989). Cognition, construction of knowledge, and teaching. *Syntheses, 80,* 121–40.

Vygotsky, L. S. (1978). *Mind in society: The development of higher psychological processes.* Cambridge, MA: Harvard University Press.

Vygotsky, L. S. (1993, 1987). *Collected works of L. S. Vygotsky,* Vol. 1, Eds. R. Rieber & A. S. Carton. New York: Plenum Press. (Originally 1920–30).

Vygotsky, L. S. (1997). Play and its role in the mental development of the child. In Bruner, J. S., Jolly, A., & Sylva, K., (Eds.). *Play: Its role in development & evolution* (pp. 537–554). New York: Basic Books. (Original work published in 1966.)

Wasserman, S. (1992). Serious play in the classroom. *Childhood Education, 68*(3), 133–30.

Webster's College Edition. Webster's New World Dictionary of the American Language (1959). p. 1385. Cleveland and New York: World Publishing Co.

Wien, C. A. (1996). Time, work, and developmentally appropriate practice. *Early Childhood Research Quarterly, 11,* 377–403.

Wien, C. A., & Kirby-Smith, S. (1998). Untiming the curriculum: A case study of removing clocks from the program. *Young Children, 53*(5), 8–13.

Wilt, J., Vander, L., & Monroe, V. (1998). Successfully moving toward developmentally appropriate practice: It takes time and effort. *Young Children, 53*(4), 17–23.

Wittmer, D. S., & Honig, A. S. (1994). Encouraging positive social development in young children. *Young Children, 49*(4), 4–12.

Wolfe, P. (1998). Revisiting effective teaching. *Educational Leadership, 56,* 61–64.

Wood, D. J. (1989). Social interaction as tutoring. In M. H. Bornstein & J. S. Bruner, (eds.), *Interaction in human development,* 59–80. Hillsdale, NJ: Erlbaum.

2

Guidance Techniques Built on Understanding the Child's Personal Development

"It is not possible that a family desires to delegate to a school such an important task as education of their child . . . so schools and parents must communicate and work together for children."

–Loris Malaguzzi (See McBride, 1999).

Main Principles

1. High-quality settings outside the home are vital for the growth, development, enhanced learning opportunities, and reduced behavior problems of young children (p. 32).

2. Reports confirm strong research evidence that good early education has a positive impact on school success (pp. 32–33).

3. Adults play an important role in the lives of children by helping them develop needed and wanted prosocial attitudes and behaviors (p. 33).

4. Teachable moments enhance learning (p. 33).

5. How children define and deal with conflict has a great deal to do with solutions (p. 32).

6. Preschool class management, based on eight positive steps, helps to enhance learning and to reduce behavior problems (p. 33).

7. Interactive guidance principles may be *direct* or *indirect* (p. 33).

8. Always be alert to teachable moments (p. 36).

9. Developmentally appropriate guidance techniques are important and effective (pp. 35–38).

10. Uses of and cautions about praise (pp. 51–52).

Introduction

Two important recently released reports from the National Research Council confirm the importance of quality child care. The first, *From Neurons to Neighborhoods: The Science of Early Childhood Development,* reminds us that "second only to the immediate family, child care is the context in which early childhood unfolds, starting in infancy" (Shonkoff & Phillips 2000). The second report, *Eager to Learn: Educating Our Preschoolers,* points out that care and education cannot be thought of as separate entities in dealing with young children (Bowman, Donovan, & Burns 2000). Both reports reaffirm the strong research evidence that good early education has a positive impact on school success (Lombardi, 2001, p. 74).

Recent data from the Census Bureau: during a typical week, 14 million young children, or three fourths of all children under age 5, are in some form of regular child-care arrangement (spending 28 hours per week). Working parents and school-attending parents place their children in child care about 35 hours per week (Smith, 2000).

In studying children in kindergarten through third grade, researchers have assessed how conflicts developed over time and what methods the children used to resolve them. They found that how the children defined the conflict had a great deal to do with its solutions. Kindergartners see conflict in the present moment, in physical terms, and egocentrically. Time helps them to see it from another's point of view and in a more broad and abstract manner—such as underlying motives, feelings, and intentions. Learning to negotiate is difficult for young children; however, when their thinking becomes more flexible and interconnected, they can see options for solutions. By helping young children to develop problem-solving skills, adults help them gain skills of empowerment and techniques of getting along with others: "I (we) can solve problems and make each other happy!" Children in the early grades can learn through class meetings, group discussions, and even role playing. These techniques help young children feel that they are problem solvers!

When caregivers and teachers take time to encourage, facilitate, and teach prosocial behaviors, children's prosocial interactions increase while aggression decreases. In one study, children (ages 3 months to kindergarten) who attended an experimental child-care program that focused on intellectual growth were rated by their kindergarten teachers as more aggressive than a control group of children who attended community child-care programs during their preschool years for a shorter amount of time.

Developmental theory predicts that with age, as children's thinking becomes more logical and flexible, they will become better able to think of win/win solutions.

Studies have found that when children are encouraged in child-sensitive high-quality care in classroom behaviors (use cooperation rather than competition; use conflict resolution in games and sports; hear empathy and caring in literature; discuss feelings; practice social interaction with special-needs children; train older children as peer mediators, etc.), they have less bullying or rejection by other children. The more nurturing parents and caregivers are—the more positive affection and responsive, empathetic care they provide—the more positively children will relate in social interactions with teachers, caring adults, and peers in cooperating with classroom learning goals, as well.

Still other authors suggest preschool classroom management based on "loosening up" with eight positive steps:

1. Be a committed preschool teacher.
2. Show respect to each other.
3. Deal in a positive atmosphere.
4. Be guided by consistency, structure, and routine.
5. "Mean what you say and say what you mean."
6. Encourage choice but still maintain control.
7. Be willing to clarify.
8. "If it doesn't work, scrap it!" (McCloskey, 1996).

Role of the Teacher

Three major, very different approaches to child rearing, which usually result in the development of quite different kinds of character, are outlined in Table 2.1, Approaches to Child Rearing and Child Care. However, in cases of harm, danger, or destruction, the teacher steps in immediately and stops the behavior without a second thought about which type of guidance he or she prefers.

Proactive guidance, in which teachers and children anticipate possible problems and consider acceptable solutions, is far superior to *reactive* guidance, in which interaction is generally negative or one-sided.

Example:

A group of 3-year-olds is going on a spring walk. In *proactive* guidance, the children and teachers discuss the route, expected behavior at various points, the purpose of the trip, items they will be taking, when they will return, and so on. The excursion is pleasant and satisfying to all involved. In *reactive* guidance, the children frolic freely, disregard any cautions, refuse to follow rules, and are unruly. Teachers become upset, children are ridiculed, and the excursion turns out to be unpleasant for all involved.

Guidance techniques are built on the child's understanding, personal development, and ability to follow through, and the safety involved (rather than "because I said so!").

Observational strategies (types of guidance) may be recorded through time sampling, anecdotal records, or specific focus, depending on the type and reason for the observation.

There are many approaches a teacher can take to a variety of situations within the classroom to reduce discipline problems. This method, called *indirect guidance,* shows in the organization of curriculum areas, materials, traffic patterns, sequencing of events, use of space and time, and other items that consider the needs of the children individually or as a group. The following are some examples.

- ➤ The classroom is "culturally friendly."
- ➤ Democracy and curiosity are encouraged.
- ➤ Children select the areas and amount of time spent in play.
- ➤ Children have individual spaces for their personal items.
- ➤ Health and safe limits are identified and enforced.

Table 2.1   Approaches to Child Rearing and Child Care

Types of Child-Rearing Patterns	Parent Behavior	Type of Preschool Education Preferred
Authoritarian (autocratic, external control)	Values obedience over independence, conformity and convention over creativity. Punitive; as a result, children most likely react with anger, resentment, or submission.	Academic; authoritarian teachers. Rigid schedules and behavior. Seat work, where children work individually at their own pace. Little child-child interaction. Conformity.
Permissive (laissez-faire)	Extremely indulgent. Lacks limits in setting standards, behavioral and/or intellectual challenges, and development of social skills.	Pleasant setting but little intellectual content or challenge to children's thinking or social development. Laissez-faire teachers spend limited time (a) planning and/or preparing curriculum, (b) enriching play or providing meaningful activities, (c) helping children develop democratic interactional skills, and (d) providing guidance or suitable responses to individual children's needs. The need to play and other physical needs are seriously neglected.
Democratic (an approach advocated by Dewey, who defined it as a cluster of characteristics, interests, and motivations in an individual that are at once self-fulfilling and of benefit to the group. [Greenberg, 1992, March, p. 61] Dewey disagreed that all children of the same age have the same skill development, knowledge, and understanding, a common thought of teachers and parents who dominated children. An easily implemented approach that benefits and addresses rights, abilities, responsibilities, and actions of each person.)	Aware of and concerned with social interaction, thinking, and learning. Expects and recognizes behavior that is developmentally appropriate. Parents discuss necessary rules with children and build a democratic setting. Adults use proactive rather than reactive guidance.	Developmentally appropriate settings and learning experiences. Caring teachers, flexible activities, and a democratic atmosphere blend into a coherent setting of fulfillment for one's self and others.

Adapted from Greenberg, P. (1992, March). Why not academic preschool? Part 2. Autocracy or democracy in the classroom? *Young Children, (47)3*, 54–64.

➤ Incompatible areas and/or materials are separated within the classroom (for example, water is away from books, quiet areas are away from active activities).

➤ Art projects are open-ended.

➤ Tools are appropriate in size, weight, and intended use.

➤ Blocks are used out of traffic areas and on a surface that muffles the sound.

➤ Bathroom fixtures and classroom furniture are child-sized.

➤ Needs of children with disabilities are met.

➤ Teachers are accessible when needed.

➤ Group activities are kept to a minimum.

Some children prefer solitary play.

➤ Tension-reducing activities and methods are appropriate.
➤ Alternative plans and activities are available.
➤ Materials are easily accessed and replaced, are self-help, and encourage repeated and cooperative play.
➤ Activities and materials are flexible depending on the skills, interests, and needs of individual children.
➤ Duplicate materials are available to encourage cooperative play.

Developmentally Appropriate Guidance Techniques

For approaches to classroom and home guidance that support and are consistent with developmentally appropriate practices, consider three areas of research: *early emotional development, motivation,* and *sociomoral understanding and prosocial behavior* (Piaget: influenced by their level of cognitive development) (Hyson & Christensen, 1997, 291–301).

The above three areas of theory and research, together with the NAEYC standards for the guidance of children's socioemotional development (Bredekamp, 1987; Bredekamp & Copple, 1997), suggest four key guidance goals:

1. self-regulation (to reach their goals);
2. self-efficacy and respect (to "tackle difficult learning problems with zest and persistence");
3. emotional understanding (respond to uniting human quality; honor differences); and
4. sociocultural competence ("skilled in living and working within a community").

Note: Teachers who use developmentally appropriate practices meet the developmental needs of children through guidance strategies and curriculum focus. Brazelton and Greenspan (both holding M.D. degrees, and known and respected in medical and child development fields) enumerate seven irreducible needs of children (2000,

Teachers need to be aware of unsafe use of equipment (children sitting on high benches).

p. 8) repeated in an interview (Greenberg, 2001). They include: (1) ongoing nurturing relationships; (2) physical protection, safety, and regulation; (3) individual differences; (4) developmentally appropriate experiences; (5) limits, structure, and expectations; (6) stable, supportive communities and cultural continuity; and (7) protecting the future.

Guidance at School and Home

In order to understand and promote good environments for children, adults need to develop skills in solving problems, asking questions, talking with others, planning and adjusting, and having time to explore and reflect. For each teacher in the classroom, it is important to develop observation skills and an opportunity to discuss with others, experienced and inexperienced, what they have seen and interpreted.

Are there some activities or items that could be implemented to better help children understand and utilize more variety (special needs of children, more understanding of principles and procedures, cultural interpretations, better use of toys and/or materials, development of large and/or small muscles, etc.)?

What types of activities encourage or discourage language and interaction? Which children always seek out (or avoid) certain activities or playmates? What types of activities discourage language and social interaction? Do some children always want to play in a particular setting? Why do some children avoid indoor activities and other children avoid outdoor activities? How could both environments be more inviting and growth-promoting to all children?

Teachable Moments

Always be on the lookout for precious teachable moments. When one arises, use it! If it doesn't arise, MAKE ONE! Teachers can do this by following a child's lead, by listening carefully to what children have to say, by sharing important ideas, information visuals, and the like to increase their knowledge and to show sincere personal interest.

So many things that adults take for granted are very new to children! Special days and activities, such as field trips or guests, provide opportunities to engage children and help them build new interests.

But even everyday activities, such as sharing a story, painting, counting, or finding a way to share materials fairly, are opportunities for children to share their thinking, build confidence, and learn new things. For child-care providers, as for *all* teachers, these experiences can provide wonderful opportunities to listen to children, to learn about their thoughts and feelings, and to share something of ourselves with them.

Encourage and compliment children for offering good ideas or making valid requests.

Observation Skills

Some *observation skills* that need to be cultivated might include: learning what to look for and how to interpret what they have seen; learning how to use specific information; observing each child's fine/gross motor skills; observing relationships between children; interpreting the observations; and making other uses of the information.

If adults do not already have some good observation skills, they should carefully consider what they need to do in order to better understand the needs of the children. They could consider the following:

Objective evaluations: These include making written notes of exactly what is occurring, without bias, prejudice, or interpretation.

Example: #1
Tim and Sarah are digging in the sand. Tim quickly fills his bucket by using a large shovel and quick movements, compacting the sand after each shovelful. He then turns the bucket upside down and taps the bottom of it with his shovel. Carefully, he lifts the bucket up and observes a mound in the shape of his bucket. He says to Sarah, "Look, I've got an empty bucket and a full pile." Sarah looks at him, smiles, and continues putting sand in her bucket.

Subjective evaluations: These include recording not only what is observed, but interpretive feelings, ideas, or impressions of the person making the observation.

Example: #2
Tim and Sarah are digging in the sand. Tim likes playing in the sand, but Sarah is afraid of getting dirty. Tim pretends to be a giant steam shovel as he piles sand in the bucket. When he is satisfied with the amount of sand in his bucket, he turns it upside down. In the meantime, Sarah acts uninterested, thinks about a story they heard yesterday, and wishes she were painting a picture or wearing a hat to keep the sun out of her eyes.

Think carefully about the differences in the examples. Which evaluation would be more meaningful in a child's file? What are the dangers of subjective evaluations? What conclusions could parents make from each of the above examples?

Supervisors or directors can assist novice teachers to develop and sharpen their observation skills by giving simple observation assignments and providing verbal or written feedback. Another option is to have trainees observe as a trainer points out activities or relationships that are occurring within the classroom. These two steps may be inverted (observation and discussion with a more experienced person and then individual observation). Observers must be taught how to record what transpires within the classroom without imposing their own feelings, motives, or prejudices.

Through training and experience, novice teachers can understand the needs and development of the young child. In many settings, academic skills are reinforced and children participate as a group, in circles, and within a time limitation. In DAP programs, play skills are emphasized (see Chapter 3, The Value of Play). As Piaget stated, "To understand is to invent," and children learn most important things by interaction with the physical world, with other children, and by constructing their own knowledge. Adults at school and home should have these same opportunities to construct their knowledge. In this way adults have a better opportunity to connect theory and practice for themselves and the young children they teach.

And what about the teachers who have not developed a feeling of self-esteem—which some children also lack? By helping these adults experience their world firsthand (and through observing the actions of children), they can enhance their feelings about themselves, their willingness to try new things, and their interaction with others.

Parents should be encouraged to visit the classroom to do some inconspicuous observations of *all* children so as to get a clear picture of what children are like and what they do at certain ages. It often makes parents feel more comfortable and confident in how their children behave. If possible, a supervisor or teacher could observe with the parents and point out some important happenings (curriculum areas, child interaction, language development, child reaction to materials/activities, and so on).

Parents can also be invited to participate in observing their child (and other children) at home or in various settings, looking at the same behaviors just outlined, and to share their observations with teachers during conferences or casual conversations. Some parents will be objective, some will be defensive, and some will use the information to learn more about their child and children in general.

Good observational skills and accurate interpretation are great assets when guiding others. The following section lists some techniques that adults in the school and/or home will find fruitful and easy to use. They are not presented in any particular order; they just work. Read through them and pick out one or two that you would like to try. Be persistent. Give each one a fair trial. After you have mastered some, select others. Undoubtedly there will be a change in behavior for both you and the children you teach—at home or at school. The bibliography at the end of the chapter can lead you to further examine the issues.

 *Reflection*

A prospective parent is visiting your classroom. Together you glance around the classroom and notice that some of the children are in the domestic area, some are building with table blocks and others with large unit blocks, some are painting at the easel, some are quietly looking at books and using visual aids on the flannel board, and still others are outside digging and planting a garden, riding trikes, and climbing.

The parent remarks: "I think it is a rather expensive program for children to just play all the time. And how do you keep track of all the children at once?"

What a golden moment and what a captive audience for the teacher to show the parent the philosophy of the classroom as the following items are pointed out:

1. Children manage most of their own activities because of the types of things provided.
2. Children are free to remain or leave according to their interests.
3. Children assist each other.
4. Teachers are aware of all the children, position themselves strategically, and assist if needed.
5. Children gain self-esteem and self-discipline because of the attitude of teachers and security in the environment.
6. Planned and spontaneous learning occurs in all areas of curriculum and through personal interaction.

Guidance Techniques for School and Home

There are many techniques a teacher can use in a variety of classroom situations to eliminate or reduce discipline problems. Consider and carefully evaluate the following techniques to help teachers become aware of some "problems" and "solutions" to inevitable situations. Add some "personal" goals!

Ultimate Goals Help the Child To Develop Self-Esteem and Self-Discipline. Some adults like knowing they can control someone or something. Children feel undervalued or unimportant when they are expected to conform with little or no consideration.

One way adults express their power to children is by saying, "I like the way . . . " for example, that Charles is sitting, or Debbie waited for her turn to talk, and so on. (See discussion on "I Like . . . " later in this chapter.) The situation could be turned more to the child's behavior by saying, "Thanks, Charles, for sitting up at story time," "Debbie, it was thoughtful of you to wait until Susan was through talking before giving us your ideas," "What a good idea you had, Stephen, about wiping your brush on the side of the jar to keep the paint from dripping on the floor," and so on.

Self-esteem, how we value ourselves, reflects how others view us as well. If individuals become more competent, the feedback they receive, both from the accomplishment of tasks and from others' view of the accomplishment, becomes enhanced. The school's role in enhancing self-esteem must (first) help children cope with ambiguities and discontinuities in their lives, and (second) help them deal with the persistent correlation between self-esteem and a number of school-related variables (such as participation, competition, behavior, self-direction, achievement, and others). One might expect children to be active in participation and classroom governance where there is heterogeneous grouping and cooperative learning with emphasis on personal and social meanings.

Lest any gains in self-esteem resulting from classroom activity be washed away by conditions outside the classroom, educators become more active as advocates for children. Children cannot grow with dignity and self-esteem if they must live in a world that mitigates against these qualities, particularly for those who are not white, male, and middle-class.

For children to survive in this complex world, they must be able to take responsibility for their own actions, practice self-control when they are ready and able, and develop trust and confidence in their ability to make and carry out decisions and to accept the consequences. Help them feel worthy of trust through your sincere remarks.

Listen *to* Children and Talk *with* Them.   Adults often give their undivided attention to another adult but fail to hear the words of children—who sometimes have to tug and pull at us before we give them even divided attention. Children do have important things to say and ask. We should listen and respond in an affectionate and interested manner.

Young children often have difficulty expressing themselves because their thoughts move faster than their mouths. When they are rushed or listeners are only partially interested, children do not often return for information or conversation. Listening adults find out information about the child's interests and needs, and thereby are able to help the child gain confidence in himself and with others.

Undivided attention is given to a child by an adult who stoops, kneels, gives eye-contact, touches, concentrates on the message, or by other means shows interest in the child. (If you have ever studied a foreign language, you will be more sympathetic to the child's difficulty in communicating.)

Besides being poor listeners to children, adults may speak differently to them—talking down in tone or ideas. Instead, speak normally, avoid unnecessary lectures, and talk about things of their interest. At times it will be important to reflect children's feelings

Teachers involve children in conversation and activities.

to them—not by putting ideas into their heads or words into their mouths, but by helping them put feelings into words. Efforts to comfort, argue a child out of his feelings, point a moral, criticize his attitude, or make up with him when he is angry are valueless. The best response communicates both understanding of the feelings and acceptance of them.

Plan Experiences That Are Challenging but Successful.   Young children need to have successful experiences at least 80 percent of the time if they are going to develop confidence in themselves. Everyone likes success, but it is especially important to young children. They need encouragement to try new activities and to repeat old ones.

Being in the sensorimotor stage of development, children need appropriate experiences with brief explanations. Children sense the adult's confidence, which is important in attempting something new or difficult. Mastery brings about competence: competence brings about mastery.

Observe each child carefully, then give individual responsibilities and privileges accordingly. Express your honest appreciation and encouragement frequently. Let the child determine when her activity is finished and satisfying.

Send and Receive Clear Messages.   When you make a request of children, be sure they understand what you mean. If they act unsure, then repeat, define, or clarify, but not in a belittling way.

For example, at the center, Rojas would stand near the gate until no one was looking, then run into the parking lot. The teacher showed him how busy the lot was, how fast cars went past the gate, and how difficult it was to see him because of his height. Her words went unheeded, so she warned him that the next time he went out of the gate, she would call his mother to come and take him home. His chance came, and he slipped out of the gate and was gone again. Because of her warning and the presence of real danger, the teacher called his mother, who came and took Rojas home. The next day when he arrived at school, he went to each child and said, "Do you know what happens if you run

Reflection

Provide toys and materials for activities than can be concluded at any time or that can be extended if desired (block building, art materials, outdoor play, and so on). Suppose a child began making a collage out of the many types of materials to cut and paste. He can conclude the activity with few or many objects pasted on his masterpiece—and who is to say that it isn't finished or that the child hasn't had satisfaction in the process?

If children experience only situations they can manage easily, they will tend to repeat those and ignore challenging opportunities. If experiences are always too difficult, children turn away from them. Failure is an unpleasant feeling. Watch the children. See what interests them and how they attack various problems. Help them develop problem-solving abilities by providing toys and materials with endless experimental possibilities to stimulate curiosity. Plan time for their exploration. Introduce them to some new experiences to widen their horizons, but make sure these experiences are based on needs, levels of development, and interests. Avoid pushing when children are not ready, but keep curiosity alive when they are ready.

out of the gate?" and then explained, "Your mother comes and takes you home." He had omitted the reasons, but he was clear on the result.

Requests made of children should be reasonable, clear, and simple. Too many commands or directions that seem unreasonable or complicated cause children to hesitate rather than respond. Think carefully what you are requesting, then be prepared to follow through, as in the case of Rojas. Your hesitancy or inability to follow through adds to the children's confusion.

Speak with confidence, and children respond in the same way. When you end a request with "Okay?" it means you are seeking their agreement to conform, and the children are frequently confused by this action. Another familiar phrase is, "You need to . . ." Griffin (1982) defines this as meaning that the teacher will not change his mind and that he has a good reason for anything he requires. Just use your voice as a teaching tool and expect the children to carry the request through matter-of-factly.

While sending good messages to children, be alert in receiving their messages. Are their words saying what they mean? Are there nonverbal messages? Gestural language often conveys more clues than verbal language. Let children know you understand their feelings by defining them. "I know you are mad because you can't swing. It's Lisa's turn, but when she is through, it will be your turn. Let's find something else to do while you wait." "It really hurts when you fall on the cement. A cool cloth will help your knee feel better."

Be honest in your praise of children and their accomplishments. They will appreciate your sincerity as well as your time to talk and to listen.

Reinforce the Positive Actions So They Will Be Repeated. It seems much easier (or perhaps more common) to comment on negative rather than positive behavior. Communication with a particular child may be only to describe her "bad" behavior. To get any recognition at all, she repeats the negative behavior. Is it better to have negative attention than none at all? Adults who look for and reward acceptable behavior indicate to children the types of actions that are accepted and expected. When children exhibit negative or undesirable behavior, they need to know it is the *behavior* that is unacceptable, not the children themselves.

Suppose a child picks up his toys and you say, "Thanks for picking up your toys. Your room looks so nice when your toys are on the shelf." By commenting, you are increasing the possibility of his repeating the behavior. But if you say nothing, he may think, "Why should I pick up my toys? Mother (or teacher) doesn't care. She'll just pick them up later." But how do you show approval for something that has never occurred (the child has never picked up his toys)? You have to watch for the behavior, or even catch the child doing the task. Even if he picked up only one toy, say, "That truck looks good on the shelf. Now it won't get stepped on," or "You'll be able to find your truck the next time you want it because it is on the shelf." The next time he may pick up two toys. Again, give honest praise. He will probably continue until all the toys are picked up if he gets more recognition for picking them up than for leaving them around. Notice when he is doing good things and acknowledge them.

If you look for good behavior to reinforce, you are likely to find it. If you look for the bad, you are also likely to find it. The more closely a reinforcement (a reward, an approval, a privilege) follows an action, the more likely that action is to be repeated. In fact, if you reinforce a child's action every time she exhibits good behavior, and then begin to taper off to reinforcing less frequently, she will continue to repeat that pattern, looking for the approval. Reinforce her occasionally and she'll continue the behavior, wanting the approval but not knowing when it will come.

In reinforcing actions, identify what was appropriate. Rather than saying, "You did a good job," or "I like what you did," say, "You did a good job in sweeping the floor and putting the broom in the closet," or "Thanks for putting the puzzle together. Now the pieces won't get lost." Kind words *(thank you, please, excuse me)* are important to children *and* adults.

Two schools of thought deal with inappropriate behavior. One is to ignore it; however, the behavior may increase in intensity and frequency as the child tries to regain attention. When the child finds this behavior unrewarded, it will likely be discontinued. The second thought is that if inappropriate behavior is ignored, children may interpret this laissez-faire attitude as permission—if you're angry, hitting somebody feels pretty good. It is important to take assertive action and stop undesirable behavior rather than let it slip past on the grounds that it will go away!

Use a Positive Approach, but Do Not Hesitate to Stop Inappropriate Behaviors. When I tell my university students to use a positive rather than a negative approach, some of them rebel. A familiar comment is, "We've heard nothing but negative comments all our lives. Now we are expected to adopt a different approach—just like that!" It is difficult to see value in and to use an opposing technique at first. But through diligent effort, students see children responding more favorably when positive rather than negative statements are used. The effort pays off. In fact, some of the students say, "The children are using our techniques! Quick, teach us the next step!" My answer is: "If it is a good technique, and it works, why can't children use it?" Why do adults think they always have to be one step ahead of children?

Occasionally, an adult should analyze how his verbalizations appear to others: If the teacher thoughtfully considers the words that he uses in speaking to children, he may realize that many of them communicate disapproval, disappointment, criticism, impatience, and other negative attitudes, even though his general attitude toward children is a positive one.

Always telling children what *cannot* be done creates defiance. Turn that around: when children are told what *can* be done, all sorts of possibilities arise, creating a different attitude and encouraging rather than discouraging participation.

Think how you would respond to the following sets of statements:

"Hammer your nail in that wood," or "Don't hammer the table."
"Hang your jacket in your locker," or "Don't throw your jacket on the floor."
"Pour just what you want to drink," or "Don't waste juice!"

If the first of each pair of statements seems too commanding, read them again. Realize that the child is being redirected, that is, given a possible response, an appropriate action. The second statement in each pair leaves him hanging: "Well, what *do* you expect me to do?" He may continue the behavior because no alternative is available.

Positive statements work well with anyone. When a person knows how she is expected to act, the chance of her acting that way is increased. Most people respond better when addressed in a positive way. They feel respected and appreciated. The world of preschoolers is so full of "*don'ts, quits,* and *stops*" that the children are left with the feeling, "Whatever I do is wrong." Using the positive approach opens new avenues for children and their behavior, as do humor and modeling.

Pay particular attention to ways to appreciate positive behavior, ways to cope with troublesome behavior, qualities of significant adults in the lives of children, and ways to involve parents in their children's schooling.

Now a few *DON'T*s along with the previous *Do*s. *First,* do not be misled about *never* using negative statements. When danger is imminent, do whatever it takes to stop the action before an injury occurs. Then survey the situation and proceed with positive words and actions. *Second,* don't overuse praise! It can become so common that the children see no value in it and can almost mock the teacher's words before she says them: "Oh, that is so *wonderfully wonderful!*" Make sure your praise is appropriate and honest and fits the situation. *Third,* teachers should intervene when children send messages that are never acceptable—such as remarks intended to exclude anyone because of race, skin color, nationality, and the like. See discussion on pp. 63–65.

Provide Guidelines for Behavior.   Good discipline includes creating an atmosphere of firmness, clarity, conscientiousness, and reasoning. In other words, it must be clear what is expected and why it is important. Bad discipline involves unduly harsh and inappropriate punishment and is often associated with verbal ridicule and attacks on the child's integrity.

As an undergraduate student, I remember learning early about the three red flags in discipline: The child is not allowed to hurt himself, hurt someone else, or destroy property. This advice has served me well and has been passed on to my students.

Limits should be considered very carefully and important ones upheld. Unimportant limits should be discarded. Nothing is magical about a set number of limits—have only those that are important for the health and safety of the children and teachers. Help children understand what the limits are and why they are necessary, and give as much freedom as possible. As children grow and develop, alter the guidelines. Children's increasing reasoning power, skills, and experiences cause them to act more independently. Be consistent, but not inflexible, in enforcing the guidelines. Certain conditions call for altering guidelines, not breaking them or removing them.

If possible, let the children help establish rules. "What do you think we ought to do about . . . " "Can you think of something that would make that situation safer?" "Where should you ride the trike?" Allow for discussions. Establish reasons why a certain thing

Reflection

As a little homework, keep track of your interaction with a child (or adult) for a few days. Mark down every time you respond to that person and see whether your positive responses outweigh your negative ones *and* whether you use a variety of appropriate responses.

does or does not occur. Keep stating the reasons (from time to time) until the children understand the rationale. Reasons are important in their learning.

The best time to handle a situation is before it occurs. Watch for trouble spots. Talk about and set up limits before there is an accident. ("When we cross the street on our walk today, we will wait at the corner and all cross together.") With prior admonition, children will know what is to occur and as a consequence will behave acceptably.

It has been said that there are classrooms with "16 million rules and regulations" and those with only the most general rules: "Be kind to other people" or "Take good care of property." A three-step method was suggested three decades ago, and is still valid:

Step One: Build understandings (reasons).
Step Two: Set up only necessary rules (i.e., for health and safety).
Step Three: Be sensitive to the present children (Hymes, 1981).

Most teachers feel that setting limits is probably the most difficult part of teaching.

Children need to feel that limits are for their health and safety. They need to be prevented from doing some things, and they need to be required to do some things. More important than what limits are set or required is recognition of a child's feelings about those limits and requirements. Limits are for safety and health. Inappropriate behavior must be rebuked. In such a circumstance, make sure (1) that the children are aware of the seriousness of the offense, (2) that you reprimand only their action, communicating that you still love and care for them by the tone of your voice, the gentleness of your touch, and closeness to them, and (3) that the punishment fits the crime. Do not be like the old woman in the shoe, who didn't know what to do with all her children, so first she fed them (a common reinforcer and perhaps a mind reliever) and then she punished them all in the same manner. Were they bad for being children or for being too numerous? Did they misbehave? Will their punishment prevent misbehavior

Enthusiasm and puppets make a good learning environment.

(whatever it was) from happening again? What did they learn from the episode? What did the old woman learn?

Whenever a child has been removed from a situation or activity, some legitimate way of returning is extremely important: the child must decide when she is ready, and she must have another chance to participate where she misbehaved. Without these two conditions, how can she build self-control?

Show Respect for Children.   When an adult shows respect for children, the children increase in feelings of competence and value while also improving their relationships with peers. It is important for children to develop good feelings about themselves, about their peers and the other humans around them, about the world of reality in which they live.

Children who are totally immersed in activities that need to be prematurely terminated appreciate a friendly notice. For example, Lee was used to a few minutes' warning before lunch, but he finished his activity early one day. He called, "Mother, aren't you going to tell me it's a few minutes before lunch?" She replied, "Not quite yet." Lee stood silently for several minutes until Mother's warning. Happily, he washed his hands and went to the table.

Another way to show respect for children involves their personal belongings. Encourage them to share as good social etiquette, but never force them. If a child has a personal possession that he doesn't want to share, say to the other child (or children), "This is very special to him. He wants to keep it now, so we'll look for something for you." The child is not made to feel guilty because he does not share; rather, he feels that his rights are respected. Remember that sharing *follows* possessing! At school the problem of sharing may arise infrequently because all the toys belong to everyone; however, one child may be using a particular toy when another wants it. Be fair when handling disagreements between two children. When possible, allow them to settle their own differences. Allow each child to maintain her dignity; avoid forcing guilt feelings on her. Be proactive!

Children should also be respected for the individuals they are, for what they can do, and for just being themselves. Help them build a good self-image by pointing our assets: "You are able to ride the bike so well." "You have the prettiest blue eyes." "My, but you are strong to help move the table." Show in words and actions that you value them. Avoid comparing abilities, characteristics, activities, and behavior with those of other children. Such comparisons breed dislike and unhappiness.

Guide Through Love Instead of Fear or Guilt.   When an offense occurs, place emphasis on the action and not on the child. In a loving and kind way, help the child to see the infraction and how to resolve it in ways other than blind obedience. Then let him know that you reprimand only his action and that you still love and care for him.

When appropriate, ask the children to define the situation. "Do you know why you can't do this?" If they are inaccurate or unclear, explain: "Because it is very dangerous, and you might get hurt [or whatever is the case]. I love you, and I would feel very sad if something happened to you." Or "I care enough about you to stop you when you are doing something that could hurt you or someone else."

Trying to rule through fear or guilt is a growth-stunting procedure; children never learn to make valid decisions or see true issues. Instead, build a loving and trusting relationship so that you both are able to survive the inevitable rough times.

Be a Good Role Model.   When we ask or expect children to act in a certain manner, and then we do the opposite, they receive mixed messages. Consider the teacher who tells the children that it is time for *everybody* to go inside, and then turns back into the playground to put away some equipment. Or the parent who strikes a child, at the same time saying, "How many times have I told you not to hit your little brother?"

The mere fact that we are moving, speaking beings means that we are providing a model for someone. Imitations of good qualities are flattering, but imitations of bad qualities are embarrassing. As parents or teachers we see behavior reflected in the words and actions of children (a comment, a gesture). Sometimes we recognize these behaviors as our own; sometimes, oblivious, we wonder where the children could have seen or heard such a thing!

If we have a happy attitude, the children around us are likely to have the same attitude. If we are harsh and critical, so will the children be. Be sure your words and actions say the same thing. If you tell your child to get ready for supper, you get ready, too. If you continue to sit and read the paper while you are telling her to hurry, she becomes confused. If she sits (as you are doing), do not get angry with her for imitating you. She usually follows your actions more readily than your words. When your actions and words do not support each other, you are sending a mixed message.

Keep calm. Be nurturing. Give valid reasons for what you request from the children. An adult who is authoritarian, permissive, or inconsistent does not help the children to form productive behavior patterns. If you are unappreciative of the way the children are acting at home or in the classroom, try to analyze what the problem may be. The best way to change someone else's behavior is to change your own. Maybe you are expecting too much or not enough; maybe you aren't sure what to expect! Maybe you act defensively, and so do those around you. Try to be more understanding and patient; look for the other person's point of view. Pleasant understanding reduces tension. Evaluate carefully and then make specific plans for improvement.

Be on Guard for Warning Signals. When you anticipate that a dangerous situation is about to occur and immediate action is called for, step in unhesitatingly and stop the behavior. If verbal means deter the action, fine ("Put that shovel down," or "Don't hit him with the shovel!"). If that doesn't stop the action, physical means may be necessary ("I'll have to hold onto your arm so you won't hit him with the shovel."). Then discuss the situation with those involved. "When he stepped on your road, it made you want to hit him; but when you hit him, he doesn't know what you want. Tell him with words." Let the child know that you understand his behavior but that there are other, more positive ways of expressing his feelings. Children will not learn the value of property if they are allowed to destroy it. They will not build good interpersonal relationships if they are allowed to harm another individual. Being inquisitive is one thing, but deliberate destruction or injury must not be tolerated.

Being observant can reduce or prevent misbehavior. Children usually give some signals. You can see the tension building in the block area or other places. Children who cannot see at group time will begin subtle physical or verbal actions. Children who need to use the toilet begin to wiggle. The signs are there—learn how to read and respond to them before a problem arises.

A number of authors list causes of misbehavior. For example, Hymes (1981) says there are four causes of misbehavior: (1) the stage of growth the child is presently in, (2) unmet needs, (3) the present environment, and (4) lack of knowledge that the behavior is inappropriate. Other authors identify the following reasons for misbehavior: to gain attention, to display power, to gain revenge, and to express inadequacy and passivity—that is, to give up. To be sure, children misbehave for different reasons.

Recently there has been much discussion and research about the stress in the lives of young children—both in and out of the home. Teachers who are aware of problems or difficult situations the children face can deal with them in more direct and kindly ways. Angry feelings, associated with feelings of dependency, sadness, or depression, should be distinguished from aggression. Anger is a temporary emotional state caused by frustration, and aggression is often an attempt to hurt a person or to destroy property (the red flags). When either of these feelings arise, they call for action that teaches and protects, not punishes.

 **Reflection**

Tommy, a 3-year-old, was brought to a center by his mother. He was new and uncomfortable. As they approached the door, he began to draw back, cry, and hit his mother. She could not understand why he acted this way, but because she was in a hurry, she pushed him in the door. His feet stood firm, and he leaned back against her with all his strength. She tried reasoning, threatening, and then bribing. Still he refused. Even the teacher's invitation was not accepted. Finally the mother bribed him with gum (and who knows what else), and he reluctantly and stubbornly entered the room. He went from toy to toy, kicking or throwing each one. He pushed the other children and took their toys. The teacher's first inclination was to tell him that if he was unable to act friendly, he would not be able to come to the center. That was just what he wanted! Instead, she tried to involve him in interesting activities, one after another. He momentarily became involved—and then remembered to throw the toys and hit the children. It took the entire morning, under the teacher's watchful eye, to help him settle in. His best involvement was in large-muscle, vigorous activity where he could legitimately "let it out."

In an article about attitudes toward crying in young children, the following factors were reported:

1. Crying is less acceptable in boys than girls; however, crying is an important and beneficial physiological process that helps children cope with stress.
2. Children become enthusiastic and successful learners when a emotional release is recognized and accepted.
3. Sources that bring stress into children's lives and create a need for crying include: *abuse* (physical, sexual, verbal), *pain* (neglect; illnesses, injuries, and hospitalization); *emotional distress* (confusion, anxiety; quarreling, separation, divorce), *parental misbehavior* (substance abuse); violence (war, death, misbehavior); disruption of familiar patterns (moving, new sibling, fatigue, hunger) (Solter, 1992, p. 67).

Children need an environment that permits them to cry without being distracted, ridiculed, or punished. In this manner they can help free themselves from the effects of frustrating, frightening, or confusing experiences (Solter, 1992, p. 67).

Avoid Power Struggles.   Adults may make a demand or a request of children. When the children do not comply, the adults become angry. They ask or tell the children again. If this still is unsuccessful, adults become defensive, especially if they are questioned or ignored. Do children have the right to question adults? When they are told to do something, they should obey! Or should they? Are the requests reasonable? Do the children understand the nature of the requests? What do adult actions mean to children? Are children being deliberately disobedient? If both adults and children analyze the situation, if adults give rationales for requests, if children verbalize noncompliance, the situation is resolvable. If, on the other hand, each decides stubbornly to win, a power struggle results, and neither wins.

Try resolving conflicts through negotiation by (1) identifying what the conflict is, and then (2) listing, evaluating, and ranking possible or alternate solutions. Discuss these issues rationally.

Offer Legitimate Choices and Accept Decisions.   Choice making should be a practice developed from early childhood. Choices should be within the child's ability, legitimate, and character-building.

Some interesting research from the Gesell Institute of Child Development suggests that ease or difficulty of choice making is related to age. The average child of 3, 5, 7, or 10 has an easier time deciding between two alternatives because at these ages he is under less inner stress and strain than at other ages. He is therefore able to accept choices without too much emotional conflict. Children do not make good decisions at any age when they are ill, fatigued, bombarded, or pressured. Are adults any different?

If a child has a legitimate choice, let her practice decision making. Bearing in mind that you must be prepared to accept her decision, be careful to form appropriate choices: "You can wear your blue shirt or your green one." "You can play inside or outside." "You can either hear one more story or play a short game before bedtime." If she has no choice, you make a simple outright statement about what is to occur: "Put on your blue shirt." "You will have to stay inside." "It is time for bed now." To offer a child a choice ("Do you want to drink your milk?") and then refuse to accept his answer ("Well, that's too bad; you have to, anyway") increases the negative aspect of his world. Also remember that when a question is worded in such a way that either yes or no can be the answer, the child is most likely to answer in the negative, even if she really wants it to be positive.

Sometimes adults think they are democratic in offering choices to children, when in reality they are weighting the questions in their favor. "Do you want to watch TV, or do you want to help me so we can go and get a treat?" "Do you want to pick up your toys or go to your room?" If children are going to be able to make good decisions, they need to develop a sound basis on which to make choices. They need legitimate choices for practice. They also need to be willing and able to handle the consequences of their choices.

Young children learn to be independent.

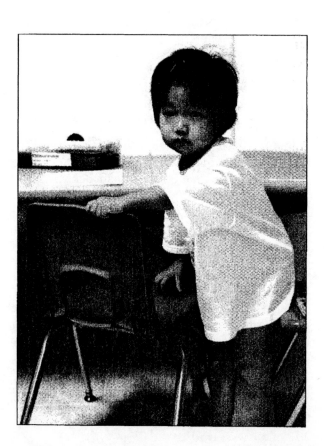

Encourage Independence.   Preschool children like to do things themselves. Often, in the interest of time or energy, the parent or teacher assists the children or actually does the task rather than letting children try their skills or problem-solving abilities. Admittedly, some tasks are too difficult for preschoolers to attempt. In such instances, the adult can offer assistance and encouragement. If the task is one the children can handle, let them. It might take longer, but the results are worth the patience.

Encouragement is essential in building independence. "Try, and if you need help, I'll help you" is often enough incentive to get the children started. Then remain nearby. If assistance is needed, help—through either verbal or physical means. On completion, give some honest praise: "You did that so well," or "I'm glad you tried. I think you will be able to do it by yourself next time."

Seek long-range goals for children—development of good work habits, initiative, self-direction, and the ability to tackle a job.

Provide Acceptable Avenues for Release of Feelings.   Frustration and anger come easily to preschoolers. They need to express these feelings in such a way that they feel better—not worse. If they are hitting, tell them to hit the clay, the stuffed animal, the punching bag, the pillow, or other suitable objects; but they cannot hit the baby, the television set, or people. Large-muscle activities—such as painting with big strokes, moving to music, riding a stick horse, throwing a ball, or finger painting—are often suitable outlets. At any rate, look for activities that help each child to release his feelings.

The younger the child, the more likely she is to use physical rather than verbal releases. With encouragement, experience, and practice, she will learn acceptable verbal ways of releasing and defining feelings.

Help Children Learn Through Participation.   Children can learn through observation or lecture, but the most efficient way is through participation. Instead of always telling them, provide opportunities for them to experience the results firsthand. Allow plenty of time and materials for exploration.

When asked to perform a task, children should be allowed to do it their way, unless it is dangerous or harmful. Offer suggestions only if the children need them. With freedom to try ideas, children may find better ways to do tasks.

Develop Your Own Skills.   Repeatedly, research shows that the single most important factor in children's learning is the effectiveness of the teacher. Similarly, in counseling, regardless of the method employed, the counselor makes the difference in the therapy. As an adult involved with young children, you are both a teacher and a counselor. You have the responsibility of seeing that your attitudes and personal attributes are such that they will be more instrumental in helping children reach their potential than if your life had not crossed theirs.

➤ PRACTICE PATIENCE.
➤ GAIN KNOWLEDGE ABOUT EFFECTS OF DIFFERENT TYPES OF DISCIPLINE ("Time out" for example).
➤ SEEK GROWTH-BUILDING RESULTS FOR YOUNG CHILDREN.

School and Home Working Together

Because teachers and parents share in the care and education of young children, they should develop good communication skills between themselves. Teachers who use educational jargon need to make sure the parents interpret the messages accurately.

Table 2.2   Ongoing Contacts

About the School	About the Child(ren)	With the Home
Philosophy and procedures	Enrollment procedures/forms	Explain and show "Learning Cards"
Parent handbook	Home visits	Explain and show "Learning Packets"
Daily contact with parents	Daily contact with parents	Ways home can supplement school
Newsletters	Telephone messages	Feedback on ideas or material used
Bulletin boards	Conferences	Ideas initiated at home
Parent education	Individual needs	Home visits
Parent meetings	Written communications	Telephone messages
Announcements about school and community events	School participation (artifacts, job)	Written messages
Suggestion box	Materials available for check-out	School visits
Teaching calendar of events and home follow-up	Small study or discussion groups	Receiving child's materials, when appropriate

Some schools or teachers offer individual conferences or home visits to families of children in their classrooms. When handled carefully, these interactions can be helpful to all parties. Both teachers in the schools and families in the home can share information and "fill in gaps" between the two settings.

Schools can choose from a number of methods to inform and encourage parents. The initial contact will undoubtedly be for information. Further contacts deal with more specific details: daily routines, commitments, responsibilities, privileges of home and school, and so on.

Primary contacts will be casual and information-gathering, such as parents-teacher orientation, philosophy, schedule, and the like.

Secondary contacts (individual and/or group) broaden the scope of the home-school relationship and may be more focused and encourage team cooperation.

Ongoing contacts are suggested in Table 2.2. As a part of "ongoing contacts" when I was a preschool teacher, I frequently had comments and requests from parents about what we did at school and how they could enhance these experiences. The children wanted to sing songs, do art projects, read books, or have other activities as an extension of the classroom. **Learning cards** resulted—actually, they began as 3″ × 5″ note cards, and the children wouldn't go home without their "card." See Figure 2.1.

Date: Theme: Color

    Today we talked about the primary colors—red, yellow, and blue. We sang a song about the colors in the children's clothing and noticed different colors in our classroom and playground. At creative art time we mixed the primary colors and then let the children use the colors separately and combined. At snack we talked about the color of the food; we heard a story and used a record game about colors.

    When appropriate, talk with your child about the colors he is wearing or those around him. Be patient in helping him learn the names of colors. Play color games with your child now (for example, What things can you see that are blue?) and at a later date (for example, What things can you think of that are blue?). Make color learning fun and not a dreaded activity.

Figure 2.1   Learning Card Example of a Day on Color

The cards were tedious to prepare each day, so we prepared a weekly sheet for the parents, rewritten in the vein of developmentally appropriate philosophy. We included the date and theme (for future reference for parents and teachers), a brief overview of the related activities, and then casual suggestions that could easily be carried out at any time.

Materials that go into the home should stress the individuality of families and needs of young children (such as approximate ages at which children can handle suggestions). "The wrong things at the wrong time" can only create stress, frustration, and a sense of failure in young children (Elkind, 1997). Parents need to know what to expect of children at different ages and with individual characteristics.

We also tried *learning packets,* which consisted of a manila envelope containing a single item (such as an article on a prescribed topic) or several items (articles, community resources, art activities to do at home, suggestions for children's story books, songs that we had sung at school, or materials informing parents on current issues or things happening in the community, requesting suggestions from parents, and so on). The contents varied weekly.

Learning packets may be helpful in:

➤ establishing lines of communication between school and home;
➤ providing parents with access to information appropriate for their child's stage of development, written by reliable writers and researchers;
➤ providing helpful and convenient resources for busy parents;
➤ being concise and easy to read; and
➤ making parents aware of inexpensive and readily available materials (and activities) that are pleasurable for themselves and their children (for example, how to read to young children, topics children enjoy, values of activities, art and music experiences, simple science, physical activities, and so on).

Other options: *group parent meetings, individual parent conferences, participation at school or on field trips, newsletters* (about the school, the community, suggestions for home participation, health services available), and other means convenient and appropriate for particular parents and families. Successful parent involvement must meet the needs of the parents, the children, the school, and the community.

To Praise or Not to Praise—That Is the Question!

Some teachers use lavish praise, some use moderate praise, and some use *no praise!* Where is the appropriate balance on the scale?

Publicly praising positive behavior (avoiding the use of negative comments) has been advocated by teachers and teacher educators for generations. Is it a good classroom practice?

When a teacher says, "I like the way . . ." (Kohn, 2000a), it can create problems in the classroom, such as:

➤ being used in unequal and biased ways;
➤ regulating children's behavior in unnatural ways;
➤ teaching children to focus on approval rather than on learning;
➤ expecting other children to model the target child's actions;
➤ emphasizing approval of the teacher;
➤ creating unhealthy feelings between conforming and nonconforming children;
➤ becoming a meaningless and monotonous statement; and
➤ causing other specific problems for both children and teachers.

Kohn (2000a), a noted psychologist, asks: "What could be wrong with telling our kids we like what they are doing?"—and then answers his own question with one word: "Plenty." He continues by saying that it:

Reflection

What successful, and meaningful, alternates (excluding "I like the way . . . ," which is likely to have undesirable side effects) could you as a teacher or parent use to gain cooperation from young children?

Did you consider any of the following alternate techniques?

stating what action is expected: what the child *is* to do—"please hang your sweater in your cubby" (rather than dropping it on the floor);

helping children figure out *what* they need to be ready to learn: "find a comfortable place," "think about the experience," "put the toys on the shelf";

giving expectations and reasons: "it's time to put items away so your hands will be ready for the next activity" or "we need everyone's help to . . . ";

allowing personal choice (within reasonable limits);

using techniques you'd like to try but haven't had the courage or opportunity.

Which of the above techniques (or others) foster self-regulation, long-term effect, and self-motivated behaviors? (Some ideas adapted from Kohn, 2000a.)

➤ "can be manipulative" (children crave our approval);
➤ "creates praise junkies" (children rely on other's decisions about what is good and bad);
➤ "usurps a child's pride" (by telling child how to feel while being judged); and
➤ "diminishes their interest–the greater the reward, the less interest one has."

Removing the emphasis on the adult ("**I like** . . . "), Kohn offers four child-growth-promoting alternatives:

➤ "Say nothing." Children can discover intrinsic value for themselves.
➤ "Report what you see." A short reply tells the child you noticed his achievement.
➤ "Emphasize the impact on others." Explain how others, rather than the adult, feel about the incident.
➤ "Ask questions." What does the child like best about what he (she) has done?

Rather than hearing the teacher using that "tone of voice" and monotonous statement, children would prefer a more positive personal response: that their efforts are seen and actually appreciated. Who wants to always be compared to that "model" student? Children who never hear praise often have a poor self-concept and a resentment toward those who frequently hear the meaningless phrase.

Standardized Testing

In addition to Kohn's treatise about "I like & . . ." he offers some clear counsel about testing of young children (2001). He states that testing is harmful when it "seeps down into primary classrooms," because standardized tests are (1) "based on the premise that all children at a particular grade level must become academically proficient at the same things at the same time," (2) "young children are rarely able to communicate the depth of understanding in the formats typically used by standardized assessments," and (3) "stress that tests create in young children is particularly intense" (p. 19). In addition, he outlines 14 steps in taking a stand against testing young children—which suggests a bumper sticker with slogans such as "**Standardized testing is dumbing down our schools.**" He suggests going through his website (www.alfiekohn.org), clicking on Standards and Testing, and following the links, or going to that of the nation's leading organization challenging standard testing, FairTest (www.fairtest.org).

NAEYC also has issued a viewpoint: "Standardized tests do not equal assessment or accountability." It states: "It is important that concerns about the misuse of testing not be extended to argue against assessment or greater accountability." The following *principles* are drawn from the 1990 NAEYC joint position statement with the National Association of Early Childhood Specialists in State Departments of Education (NAECS/SDE) regarding program evaluation and accountability (*Young Children, 56*(2), p. 18).

In testing, it is assumed that:

1. **No principles of appropriate curriculum are violated** in constructing assessment procedures to evaluate programs or determine their accountability.
2. **Children's performance data collected by teacher to aid in planning instruction** are used to evaluate *how well a program is meeting its goal* for children and families.
3. **Programs use multiple indicators of progress** in all developmental domains to evaluate the programs' effect on children's development and learning. Standardized achievement tests are prohibited before third grade, preferably the fourth.
4. **To judge program effectiveness, all components of a program are considered** within the overall context of opportunities for children and families, including staff development/evaluation, parent satisfaction, program administration, physical environment, and health and safety. Outside, independent evaluation such as program accreditation is useful.
5. **Programs employ sampling methods whenever feasible** if they are mandated to use standardized tests of children's progress for program evaluation/accountability. This sampling approach eliminates subjecting all children to testing, which can consume large blocks of time, cause children undue stress, and result in unwarranted decisions about individual children.

Greater accountability is helpful, especially if we consider how well schools and communities are fully supporting *each* child's educational achievement.

Guidelines for Appropriate Curriculum Content and Assessment in Programs Serving Children Ages 3 through 8—NAEYC and *NAECS/SDE* position statement is available online at www.naeyc.org/resources/position_statements/pscag98.pdf.

Time-Out Procedure

Time-out, a procedure frequently used with toddlers, preschoolers, and sometimes older children (or may even be "self-imposed"), is an enforced time alone as a consequence for unwanted, unacceptable, or harmful behavior. Its effectiveness varies. Some children misbehave to get away from frustrating situations or annoying peers and/or adults. Some view

---

If you are observing unusual amounts of negative behavior in your classroom, check: (a) the physical facilities, (b) the number of children, (c) the number of teachers and how effective they work with the children, and (d) other conditions which may apply to your specific circumstances.

Most child development specialists feel strongly that physical punishment is never appropriate. It: increases rather than decreases negative acts, promotes low self-image, does not teach constructive ways to resolve conflicts or problems, exposes children to and makes them victims of violence, and provides children with a context of learning violence. Haim Ginott wrote more than 40 years ago, "Each time I spank, I'm teaching 'When you're angry, hit.' I've never known a child who was spanked into becoming a more loving human being" (WestEd 1993, 128).

Even teachers need help.

the procedure as humane; however, it can "be deceptive because objectionable behavior is immediately controlled and extinguished" (Schreiber, 1999, p. 22). In other words, the child's misbehavior is controlled by others rather than the child's being assisted to control his/her own actions and build an acceptable means of controlling future misbehavior.

Some early childhood experts have suggested the use of time-out as a preferred method for setting limits with preschool children. However, time-out is *not* recommended by many early childhood leaders, especially with toddlers (Schreiber, 1999).

Time-out is usually an *undesirable* practice for several reasons:

Children of different ages react differently to isolation.
Children of varying levels and kinds of skills can handle misbehavior in acceptable ways:
- *verbally*—through discussing, answering questions, posing other responses, giving one's viewpoint, requesting acceptance, using adult-assisted negotiation, and so on.
- *actions*—by helping to restore prior situation, showing one's reasoning, bringing something to the play, having an alternate behavior demonstrated while waiting for a turn, etc.

Impose external means of control; the child feels powerless.
Reduce the child's opportunity to build inner controls.
Does not teach the child alternate strategies.
Has a negative effect on child's developing sense of self-worth and self-confidence.
Is confusing; has an indirect relationship between action and consequence.
Has no direct and immediate assistance in better behavior.
Isolates child from discussing or resolving the problem.
Provides no opportunity to rectify the problem—either physically or verbally.

Knowing the limited and immature characteristics of toddlers, adults can:

➤ Help children model or verbalize what is happening (limited to individual child's abilities).
➤ Show child how to negotiate (even though skills are immature and limited).

 *Reflection*

In evaluating the information in this section, what techniques do you think would be most growth promoting to specific young children and their future interactions with others?

Observing the behavior of toddlers/preschoolers (T/P), respond "T" (true) or "F" (false) to the following situations, then *explain* your answers (Do some of these situations warrant a T *and* F answer?):

1. Toddlers and/or preschool children have fewer conflicts than older children. T or F
2. The best way of solving problems with T/P is a "lecture." T or F
3. You only have to tell T/P once and they have learned the rule. T or F
4. A toy (activity) has no appeal unless there is personal involvement. T or F
5. Grabbing a toy is the best way to get your turn. T or F
6. Teachers should let the children solve their own personal problems. T or F
7. Young children are most cooperative when they are tired and/or hungry. T or F
8. Small groups of young children encourage interest, cooperation, and peace. T of F
9. Teachers should always demonstrate the use of a toy or activity. T or F
10. If a T/P reacts aggressively, he/she should be removed for the activity. T or F
11. Animals give T/P a feeling of belonging. T or F
12. "Offending" children should be restricted to only one chance. T or F
13. The efforts and needs of the adult should be of prime importance. T or F
14. Animals belong in an early-childhood classroom. T or F
15. Because of the lack of social competence in T/P, teachers must mediate all conflicts. T or F

➤ Realize the child's limited independence and interaction.
➤ Keep groups small, under control, and friendly.
➤ Be alert to possible problems or child combinations.
➤ Prepare environment for the needs of the children (time, amount of toys, interest, easy flow, small group interaction).
➤ Encourage compatible toddler-toddler, toddler-adult behavior.
➤ Respect toddler needs (time, amount of toys, space, independence).

In part two of a two-part article on prosocial behavior in classrooms, families, schools, and communities, Honig and Wittmer (1996) encourage child-sensitive high-quality care in classrooms because those attributes promote prosocial behaviors. For example: emphasize cooperation rather than competition; teach cooperative and conflict-resolution games and sports; set up play spaces and materials to facilitate cooperative play; use children's literature that includes empathy and caring; have discussions about feelings that encourage social interaction with special-needs children; train older children as peer mediators; work closely with families; and use other age-appropriate techniques. They conclude:

> The more cherished a child is, the less likely he or she is to bully others *or* to be rejected by other children. The more nurturing parents and caregivers are—the more positive affection and responsible, empathetic care they provide—the more positively children will relate in social interactions with teachers, caring adults, and peers and in cooperating with classroom learning goals, as well (p. 70).

Reflection

1. What do you do with a child who **always** whines, complains, pouts, withdraws, rebels, argues, or blames someone else when things don't go his way?
2. How can you set the stage for interruptions, changes, or new procedures so that a child will not whine, complain, pout, withdraw, rebel, argue, or blame someone else?

Violence in the Lives of Young Children (See also Chapter 3)

Violence is becoming more and more evident in our lives today—not just in the media, but in our personal and global lives as well. Shidler defines violence as "both verbal and nonverbal aggressive behavior toward another person" (2001, p. 67). Would you define it differently?

"... we know that *only* when children feel emotionally and physically safe do they grow, develop, and learn at their best. Consistent, reliable, loving care has a profound effect on their future."

(Anderson, 2001, p. 4)

Statistics about widespread school violence show that the chances of being seriously physically injured at school are minimal.

"Less than one percent of all school-age homicides occur in school groups or en route to and from school" (Kachur, Stinnes, & Powell, 1996).

"A more pressing problem associated with violence in the schools is corporal punishment. In the United States, only 27 of the 50 states have banned use of corporal punishment in the schools" (United States Department of Education, Office for Civil Rights, 1997).

Making violence *unacceptable* is discussed by Remboldt (1998), who reports:

1. It is a program that empowers concerned adults to compassionately combat violence in schools (p. 32).
2. A two-year study of violence in schools was conducted by the Johnson Institute to gain a clear understanding of the problem and to develop an effective solution. The program, *Respect and Protect: Prevention and Intervention,* paves the way for schools and communities to actually establish a safe learning environment for children.
3. The key to preventing violence "lies in shaping children's beliefs, attitudes, and behaviors before violence becomes an automatic manifestation of their anger" (p. 33).

The Institute's *Respect and Protect Violence Prevention and Intervention Program* for schools and communities is based on the following ideas:

➤ respecting and protecting of the rights of others;
➤ adopting a policy of non-tolerance of violence;
➤ stopping the enabling behaviors of staff, students, and parents that sustain attitudes of entitlement;
➤ clearly defining unacceptable behavior;
➤ distinguishing and addressing two types of violence—bully-victim violence and violence that stems from normal conflicts; and
➤ identifying both adult- and student-centered prevention components, such as environmental control, intervention component, contracts, and the like.

The idea that children and adolescents are influenced more by their peers than by adults is questioned by Remboldt (1998), who says, "Not necessarily so." She continues that:

➤ Students do expect adults to be responsible and do something about school violence, but many students feel that support for such change is inadequate or misguided.

Notable Notes

Numerous studies report that violence and violent behavior are learned behaviors. Those who care for young children (teachers, parents, and others) know that *only* when children feel emotionally and physically safe do they grow, develop, and learn at their best. Consistent, reliable, loving care has a profound effect on their future.

NAEYC and the American Psychological Association (APA) have joined efforts to develop a national multimedia campaign and a community-based training program focused on adults who raise, care for, or teach young children ages birth through age eight (Anderson, 2001, p. 60).

Research continues to show that high-quality programs (inside and outside the home) help reduce behavior problems in later childhood and beyond. Adults are encouraged to provide daily experiences that build and promote frequent, positive, emotional, and meaningful relationships with children and adults; support learning; promote positive social and emotional competence; strengthen children's skills to interact meaningfully as positive role models; and foster problem solving with respectful words and actions.

The ACT Against Violence, grounded in behavioral and social science research on early childhood development, brain development, violence, aggression, and violence prevention, emphasizes that violent behavior is, in large part, learned early in life, and habits of aggression and violence can be prevented if addressed when children are young.

Teacher and parent brochures are available online through NAEYC affiliate groups at www.actagainstviolence.org or by calling 1-877-ACT-WISE, toll free.

➤ *Respect and Protect* provides a strategic framework within which one can respond to, rather than control, violence.
➤ When adults firmly state what they mean and reinforce their convictions, there is a new feeling of safety for children and respect for adults.

Adult-Sanctioned Violence

Violence occurs each day within earshot of adults (teachers, parents, program leaders, etc.). It may be in various forms—verbal taunts or pushing, shoving, and other types of physical contact. Do these adults act, react, ignore, move away, or find another way to do nothing? Teacher-sanctioned violence is indicative of destructive conflict management. Students' violent behaviors go unchallenged by teachers and administrators, and may result in significant damage to students' self-esteem and sense of dignity.

In a survey of nearly 600 teachers who were asked to define behaviors as either violent or nonviolent, they identified the following as **nonviolent** (Shidler, 2001):

➤ an adult pulling a child by the arm (65 percent)
➤ a child being struck by another child (11.65 percent)
➤ a child being paddled/spanked by a parent (71.5 percent)
➤ a student being paddled/spanked in school (65 percent)
➤ a child being struck about the body (excluding the buttocks) (8.15 percent)
➤ a child witnessing an adult striking another individual (6.35 percent)
➤ a child witnessing the use of weapons against another individual (3.85 percent)
➤ a child being verbally assaulted by another individual (28 percent)

As children witness these behaviors, they sometimes imitate what they have experienced or observed (Shidler, 2001, p. 168).

Reflection

Over the preschool and kindergarten years, children:

Increase capability of voluntary control of their emotions, their interactions
with others, and their problem-solving abilities.
Have longer attention spans.
Follow more complex directions and comply with rules more reliably.
Increase their ability to interact cooperatively with peers and others.
Internalize the values, behavior, and achievement of those around them.

Teachers must model positive behaviors, minimize exposure to violent or antisocial models, expect and encourage independent and responsible effort, and use
guidance strategies that provide reasons for rules and help children understand
the consequences of their actions (Bronson, 2000, p. 36).
Knowing the above facts, how would you expect teachers to change their personal planning for and reactions to all children in their classrooms?

In an attempt to use peers to mediate conflict resolution in a Head Start class, Gillespie and Chick (2001) used a *Fussbuster Program*. The teachers told the students that if
two children have a conflict not involving immediate health or safety issues, the two children should talk things over at the *Peace Table*. They should ask a friend—a Fussbuster—to accompany them and help them come to an agreement. The rules and
procedures (in the children's own language) were:

1. No physical contact.
2. Talk things over (use a helper—a Fussbuster if desired).
3. One person (talking) at a time.
4. Take a helper—a Fussbuster who takes his/her role seriously.
5. Stay until the problem is solved.
6. Shake hands at the end.
7. You get your spot back (where you were playing).

Teacher intervention was minimal, and often not welcomed by students while at the
Peace Table. By the end of the school year, the children reported positive experiences and
thought the program was a helpful addition to their classroom.

Teasing and Bullying

Teasing and bullying can be problems at any age and can have negative effects on the
physical, emotional, and social development of young children. How we approach it in
preschool and early grades can make a difference in its future application. Research indicates that both boys and girls find themselves the targets of bullies and may themselves initiate teasing and bullying. As educators and parents, we can take action against
such behavior in young boys and girls to "counteract the persistent messages they receive
from the media and society at large" (Froschl & Sprung, 1999, p. 70).

The role of the early childhood teacher:

1. In general teachers do relatively little to put a stop to bullying behavior. It is critical
   for teachers and parents, through understanding and empathy, to address inappropriate behavior before it becomes a way for children to solve their problems.

2. Reasons teachers gave for not intervening include:
   Unawareness;
   Expecting children to solve their own problems;
   Not knowing how to eliminate it;
   Thinking it is a part of childhood;
   Being more involved in curriculum/classroom activities, and/or other personal reasons.
   Wanting to treat all children fairly, regardless of color, religion, language, ethnics, etc.
3. Ways to counteract violence:
   Listen and respond to *every child every day.*
   Strive to develop a positive relationship with each child.
   Look for and acknowledge courteous behavior as it occurs.
   Arrange classroom to encourage respect and cooperation.
   Make a chart of times and children who are responsible for classroom management.
   Take appropriate action when aggressive behaviors begin.
   Help children/adults work together in planned and unplanned activities.
   Be ever alert for "teachable moments."
   Be a role model in helping children develop positive socialization skills.
   Use growth-promoting guidance when infractions occur!
   Learn more about people being violated and those who violate them.
   Work with parents and community (Froschl & Sprung, 1999).

Values for Children
Problem solving

Parents, teachers, caregivers, and others can help young children identify:

➤ Conflicts, personal feelings, and the like: Why is there a problem?
➤ Personal goals: What are they trying to accomplish? Are the goals simple or complex; realistic or unrealistic for the individual?
➤ Procedures: What are some possible resolutions and consequences?
➤ Involvement: Are other individuals involved—if so, what are their feelings? Is cooperation needed? If so, how can others be helpful?
➤ Outcomes: How can outcomes be evaluated? Should an alternate be tried? What are the needs and feelings of all those involved? Would these same outcomes apply to other situations?

> A quick way to determine the cause of misbehavior is to check: the **weather,** the season (holidays), and the **classroom:** temperature, lighting, curriculum areas, number of bodies, individual children, and teachers (preparedness, number, attitude, and capabilities.)

Depending on how it is handled, conflict can be describe as:

| Negative: | dysfunctional | or destructive |
| Positive: | functional | or constructive |

Learning to handle conflict constructively is the goal of conflict resolution. It is a process involving cooperative negotiation to achieve mutually acceptable (win/win) solutions and may need the help of a stable adult. Children can learn positive skills to effectively deal with conflicts while developing independence, competence, and strong self-esteem, a process usually referred to as "social problem solving."

With young children, an adult usually serves as the facilitator, whose focus is on the behaviors, feelings, and desires, not on whether the child is "good" or "bad." Learning positive skills to effectively deal with these conflicts develops independence, competence, and strong self-esteem.

Teachers convey three attitudes about social problem solving:

1. Conflicts occur frequently, but can be reduced in number and intensity in a developmentally appropriate environment (ample supplies, adequate space and time, etc.).

Children may need suggestions on how to solve problems.

2. There can be a win/win situation.
3. Problem solving can be growth-promoting.

Through practicing social problem solving, over and over, young children learn these three skills:

1. to generate alternative solutions,
2. to evaluate consequences, and
3. to predict the consequences of their actions.

From these actions, children learn to accept and express their feelings and needs.

When a child is hurting himself, hurting someone else, or destroying property, the adult needs to step in immediately! The teacher and child can decide the next step of action such as:

The process of problem solving is more important than an optimal outcome.

➤ Gather the facts as each person sees them.
➤ Restate the problem as clearly as possible for all parties.
➤ Determine how the situation became a problem.
➤ Generate alternative solutions.
➤ Make some *safe* solutions that both children can accept.
➤ Follow through with both parties to make sure the solutions have brought "closure."

All solutions do not work all of the time. In order for them to be more successful, they need the following components: (1) trust (in facilitator); (2) time and energy (to redirect, restructure, or offer choices); and (3) basic communication skills (words and ideas the children understand).

Problem solving is a part of our daily life. Practicing it is valuable for later in life. If we can learn good and useful skills at an early age, we can deal more effectively with personal and professional conflicts throughout our lives and in many difficult situations.

1. The **values** you want to encourage.

2. How to plan and **model prosocial behaviors**—setting a good example!

3. Ways to introduce, label, and **acknowledge appropriate behaviors:** "helpful," "good," "nice," or words to the children.

4. Giving children ideas about how to **interact with others in a positive way.**

5. **Role playing.**

6. **Consequences of positive and negative behavior** upon the aggressor and the receiver.

7. Ways to **express interaction** between two parties (happiness, empathy, etc.)

8. **Alternate solutions** to problems.

9. Pictures, books, games, and other materials that **support cooperation, helpfulness, kindness.**

10. **Growth-promoting discipline strategies** when appropriate.

11. **Non-competitive games,** quiet activities, and support of another person.

12. Ways to **foster friendships** (boy-boy, girl-girl, boy-girl, child-teacher).

13. **Developing personal behaviors,** language, relationships, and other aspects to help you be a better, more understanding teacher of young children.

14. **Interaction with other cultures** (visitors, dress, food, customs, play, music, etc.)

15. **Interaction with children and adults who have disabilities.**

Figure 2.2   Effecting Changes in Attitudes and Behaviors

Social Development

The core of the curriculum in nursery schools and kindergartens was "social development" until the late 1960s. During an interim period, a cognitive emphasis was very strong. Social development has recently been getting renewed attention from early childhood education leaders. Skilled teachers of young children implement prosocial goals that emphasize

> showing sympathy and kindness, helping, giving, accepting food or toys, sharing, showing positive verbal and physical contact, comforting another person in distress, donating to others who are less fortunate, showing concern, responding to bereaved peers, taking the perspective of another person, showing affection, and cooperating with others in play or to complete a task (Wittmer & Honig, 1994, p. 4).

Prerequisite for learning about other cultures is first learning about one's own culture, in which children need to take pride. Then they can observe cultural differences and similarities. Concepts should be clear and developmentally appropriate for the age of the child (Salmon, with Akaran, 2001, p. 30). For preschool children, emphasize the child's own culture before introducing local ethnic groups (one at a time), involve firsthand experiences (either in a close location or in the classroom), and give the children opportunities to practice what they have learned with other children and adults. Too advanced planning will result in misunderstandings and disinterest. Repeat information, model, and bring appropriate props (clothing, food, books) about a culture rather than trying to introduce too many different cultures at one time. "If social development is considered a vital component of all activities in which children are engaged, development will be optimized in all areas of children's lives" (DeWolf & Benedict, 1997, 276–77).

In evaluating teaching and the curriculum, teachers could ask themselves: What have the children learned about other cultures? Are they developing cultural prosocial attitudes and behavioral changes? Cite evidence of increased understanding or decreased aggression toward other cultures. See Figure 2.2.

Reflection

Following is a list of negative/positive options:

Put an "N" in front of the guidance techniques that are to be avoided (negative) and a "P" in front of the ones that give better guidance (positive):

_____ Spank _____ Threaten _____ Bribe _____ Reward system (star, food) _____ Restructure the environment _____ Assign time-out _____ Ignore situation _____ Offer legitimate choices _____ Redirect children _____ Substitute toys _____ Listen attentively _____ Withhold privileges _____ Ask child for solutions _____ (Fill in the blank) _____ (Fill in the blank) _____ (Fill in the blank)

Ways Children and Teachers Can Benefit from Interacting with Each Other

Children can:

Learn acceptable ways to express feelings and fulfill desires.

Practice receptive and expressive communication skills.

Develop interest and skills in firsthand, hands-on experiences.

Learn negotiation and analytical thinking skills.

Learn how to solve own problems, generate alternatives solutions, predict and evaluate consequences.

Practice cooperative skills: patience, listening, taking turns.

Solve social problems; interact with others.

Enhance self-esteem, gain independence and cooperation.

Mature in social skills and learn to predict consequences of their behavior.

The reader is invited to add more benefits for children.

Teachers (adults) can:

Prepare the classroom for social activity (room arrangement, ample supplies, adequate time and space, variety of activities, supervision, etc.).

Acknowledge that conflicts will occur (seek for solutions not blame).

Focus on behaviors, feelings, and desires.

Spend more time on positive than on negative behaviors.

Notable Notes

DeWolf and Benedict (1997, p. 277) prepared a table for ways teachers can facilitate children's social development, which include:

- promoting prosocial skills,
- care and respect for all people,
- peer interactions,
- diverse social interactions,
- unstructured, open-ended play materials,
- materials and activities representing and respecting diverse radial, cultural, and class background and abilities,
- positive discipline, and
- reasons children may be isolated socially.

"Track" progress of children (and self).

Oversee the total program.

Give constructive feedback to others: parents, staff, children, self.

Help children (and others) to see and accept solutions to problems.

Initiate ways to discuss and resolve social issues.

Serve as a facilitator.

Learn positive skills to deal effectively with conflicts (they develop independence, competence, and self esteem, etc.).

Mature in optimal ways to redirect/guide young children.

The reader is invited to add more benefits for teachers.

Diversity in the Classroom

Children who are different from others (color, handicaps, language, customs, dress, etc.) may feel harmed in ways that are irreparable if excluded from activity (Elswood, 1999, p. 62).

The concepts about children of COLOR AND OTHER DIFFERENCES must be included throughout our classrooms. Children with differences MUST see evidence of their worth: pictures on the wall, books, songs, toys, actions, dramatic play, verbalization from others (children and adults)—whatever it takes to know they have worth! "They must take an *equal place, not a token place, in the classrooms and the everyday lives of our children* if children of color (or other differences) are to be included and feel that they truly belong" (Elswood, 1999, p. 65). It is never acceptable to exclude anyone because of race, color, ability, or any other reason! Even if a teacher is shocked, embarrassed, or caught off-guard, it is important to step in and take some positive and reassuring action—make sure the action does not complement the infraction! "Be nice to each other" does little to reassure an offended child and "fails to teach the child making the remark that it is wrong to do so" (Elswood, 1999, p. 65).

There are differences other than color that distress children and teachers. Consider differences in languages, customs, dress, food preferences, personal habits, mental and

Sharing ideas is great fun!

Reflection

Two children are trying to figure as many ways as they can to eliminate a "different" child (one of color, one with a handicap, one speaking only a foreign language, or a more appropriate one—YOU DECIDE WHICH). How many **positive** solutions can you generate? What harm can be inflicted on children by exclusion (for any reason) in the social interaction of play?

As a consultant during the early days of Head Start, I was sent to a state and area that was very unfamiliar to me. I was the only white person; however, I did have black curly hair. The children and teachers viewed me from a distance for some time. One child finally came close enough to touch my hair, then another child rubbed my cheek. We initiated a conversation. Other children came. They invited me to join in their activities. How did they feel about me? How did I feel about them (and myself)? If you are the only adult in your classroom who is of a particular color, ethnic group (dress, hair color, language), or other difference, how well do you cope?

Inclusion is much more than simply opening up our classroom doors; we must open up our minds and our hearts!

physical handicaps, holidays, and even differences within each single category. Personal understanding of and appropriate behavior toward each of these differences (and many other unnamed ones) can be growth promoting for adults and children. Parents, professionals, and individuals across many circumstances are willing to help teach young children more tolerance for differences (and likenesses)! Always be alert to ways to inform children about the wonderful world in which we live. In my experiences as an early childhood professional, I have broadened my learning through consulting with different types of groups (Head Start, university, private, Indian, ethnic, handicapped, hospital, language specific, and others). My contacts with educators, teachers, children, and parents throughout this country have broadened my experiences and opened my mind!

Each person needs to feel a personal worthiness. Individual self-concepts are socially constructed and so must be maintained in social interactions (Vygotsky, 1978)

Peer support and interactions are very influential and sometimes difficult for adults to counteract. Teachers may have to send strong and frequent messages to some defiant children and/or adults but **"when racist remarks have been made, the children hurt need to hear that others want to play with them *not* in spite of their color, but because they are who they are. Children value everything they are, including their color"** (Elswood, 1999, p. 64). Our responsibility as teachers and parents is to *help children ACT rather than to react*!!

Here are **some ways** adults can help children feel that they belong:

➤ Help them believe that they are valued.
➤ Convey an attitude of protecting every child.
➤ Provide a developmentally appropriate setting.
➤ Encourage them to make good choices and taking responsibility for solving conflicts without constant adult intervention.
➤ Foster positive social interactions in a child-sensitive environment.
➤ Provide models in books, music, toys, activities, and other materials.

Reflection

Intervention strategies between teacher and **EACH** child should include:

Listening: Become a role model of cross-cultural interactions, and those reflecting other differences (such as disabilities, ethics, etc.).

Teachers should intervene when children make racist or derogatory remarks about others who are different from themselves (color, language, dress, customs, ideas, etc.).

Procedures: Practice and actions infused throughout the classroom and curriculum (visuals, literature, guests, etc.).

Support: From and to each other).

Implementation: A check on progress.

Practice direct intervention (see Chapter 1). It is *never* acceptable to exclude anyone on the basis of race or skin color. Diversity must be valued by adults and children if they are sensitive to the needs and feelings of others.

Now you add some appropriate items that may apply specifically to your group or to specific children!

Practicing Direct Intervention

Teachers should neither be embarrassed by racist remarks or be unsure how to address them. When uncertainty exists, we may unwillingly permit children to be victims of racist remarks. Teacher responses such as "we are all friends here," or "I don't like to hear you say things that make children feel sad," do little to reassure a child who has been excluded from the group because of skin color, and also fails to teach the remark-making child more appropriate responses.

We teach children to defend their bodies by telling their peers that they may not hit or kick them. We can also help children learn to defend themselves verbally against racist and exclusionary remarks and learn not to hurt the feelings of others.

Teachers need to examine their own actions and interactions before implementing curricular or environmental changes. For example, how well do minority and nonminority staff get along well together? How do teachers treat parents of minority children? Do children visit or receive visits from "community helpers" from a variety of backgrounds, including people of color, people with disabilities, older adults, and people whose first language is other than English?

Conclusion

Inclusion is much more than simply opening up our doors; we must open up our hearts. We adapt our physical space to accommodate children with diverse abilities, so must we adapt our curriculum and our interactions—everything we do in our schools—to be truly inclusive of all children.

Watch each child carefully to determine if misbehavior is caused by (1) the present developmental stage, (2) personal temperament difference, (3) the present environment, (4) growing into a more mature stage, (5) unmet needs, or (6) a combination of factors. Realize that a child who continually harms himself or other children should be stopped and that professional assessment may be needed.

Preschoolers enjoy the company of others while carrying out personal ideas.

Application of Principles of Classroom Guidance

Apply the principles in the classroom

1. Point out the appropriate behavior of children. (It was so kind of you to help _____ when he "was feeling sad" or "hurt his knee," etc.)
2. Help children put feelings into words and to understand these feelings. A teacher might make comments such as "You are so happy today. Tell me what makes you so happy," or "It looks like you are feeling angry. How can I help you?"
3. Help young children notice and respond to the feelings of others: Make kindly remarks when someone else is in distress.
4. Encourage children to role play stories they have heard in order to become aware of how the characters feel.
5. Help a child focus on the effects of hurtful and antisocial behaviors, such as hitting or pinching. Results of a study of how children learned altruism at home revealed that parents of the most prosocial toddlers had emphasized the negative consequences of their toddlers' aggressive acts on other children. Patiently point out the consequences of the child's aggressive behavior. Discuss the results of hurtful actions upon another person. Choose statements such as "Look—that hurt him!" "He is sad and crying." "I cannot let you hurt another child, and I do not want anyone to hurt you." "Let's help each other feel happy and safe in this class."
6. Help timid children become more assertive concerning prosocial matters. Practice verbalization and behaviors that will help develop skills and language in dealing with aggressive behaviors of others.
7. Encourage means/ends and alternative-solution thinking in conflict situations. Help children think through, step-by-step, their reasoning about how to respond when they are having a social problem with a peer.
8. Involve young children in creating and implementing "behavior rules" in your classroom for situations such as: working together in pairs or small groups; coping with frustration, anger, and stress; creating new noncompetitive activities; or similar sit-

uations. (Think and use activities that would calm the children: modeling clay, wood-working, water play, physical activity, music, etc.)

9. Show children how to use their voices as "teaching tools" (soft voices can get attention, show consideration, be influential, give satisfaction, and other personal results.)
10. Make a chart listing each child in your group. Observe and record the behavior of each child. Which ones need help in social situations, physical development, or self-confidence? How can you help each child?
11. Make sure you know and understand the "rules" of your group.
12. Practice offering choices. Is there really a choice? How do you follow through when you have offered an inappropriate choice?

Think the principles through:

1. Get a reliable source and find out at what ages young children understand emotions (empathy, anger, sadness, distress). Compare the statistics with children you teach.
2. Describe the advantages and disadvantages of using positive discipline (prosocial behaviors and less aggression), noncompetitive activities, and quieting activities in a classroom of young children.
3. List and prioritize optimum learning conditions for young children in out-of-home settings.
4. Describe a "teachable moment" for young children.
5. Describe what qualities are important to you in learning settings for young children. How would you plan to carry out your ideas?
6. Define different types of guidance (authoritarian, totally permissive, etc.) and place yourself in one of the categories. Do you need to reevaluate your position?
7. Describe when and how to use praise? How effective is praise?
8. Give some examples of positive discipline for a child who is prosocial; aggressive; verbally abusive; negative; defiant.
9. Describe how adults (teachers, parents, friends) can help foster friendships between children (same and/or opposite sex; various ages; cultural differences, etc.).

Make and use a personal file of activities and information to help you become more comfortable in teaching young children:

1. Compile a file of resource materials such as visual aids, books, songs, visitors, and other available means to foster empathy, understanding, appreciation, kind responses, and other positive qualities in young children.
2. Identify and use ways adults (teachers and parents) can help reduce conflicts between young children.
3. List methods of promoting good child behavior instead of saying, "*I* like the way. . ." (see pp. 12, 34 and 39).
4. Identify, contrast, and give examples of the three major types of guidance. Select one you would like to work on. Practice it. After a period, evaluate your progress.
5. To be prepared for a child or parent who needs professional help, identify and make a list of agencies in your community that counsel on mental, social, emotional, and physical problems.
6. Describe how you can change or eliminate the behavior of someone who is inappropriately controlling you.
7. Practice your observations skills. Record children in different types of activities. Ask a colleague or teacher to evaluate how often you record objective information and subjective information.
8. Select a method of contact with the home (learning packet, newsletter, meeting, phone call, "Notes to Home," "Notes from Home," or another method) and propose a way to use it.
9. List what you need to do to make your experience with young children more meaningful to you and to each child and parent.

References

Anderson, M.P. (2001). ACT against violence. *Young Children, 56*(4), 60–61.

Bandura, A. (1973). *Aggression: A social learning analysis.* Englewood Cliffs, NJ: Prentice-Hall.

Bowman, B. T., Donovan, S. M., & Burns, S. M. (Eds.). (2000). *Eager to learn: Educating our preschoolers.* Washington, DC: National Academy Press.

Brazelton, T. B., & Greenspan, S. I. (2000). *The irreducible needs of children: What every child must have to grow, learn, and flourish.* Cambridge, MA: Perseus. (Also in *Young Children, (56)*2, 6–13. Interview conducted by Polly Greenberg.)

Bredekamp, S. (Ed.). (1987). *Developmentally appropriate practice in early childhood programs serving children from birth to age 8.* Washington, DC: NAEYC.

Bredekamp, S., & Copple, C. (Eds.). (1997). *Developmentally appropriate practice in early childhood programs* (Rev. ed.). Washington, DC: NAEYC.

Bronson, M. B. (2000). Recognizing and supporting the development of self-regulation in young children. *Young Children, 55*(2), 32–36.

Carlsson-Paige, N., & Levin, D. E. (2000). *Before push comes to shove: Building conflict resolution skills with children.* St. Paul, MN: Redleaf.

Center on the Social and Emotional Foundations for Early Learning, funded by the Head Start Bureau and the Child Care Bureau in the U.S. Department of Health and Human Services. Four national associations (NAEYC, National Head Start Association, NACCRA, and DEC) working together on the social and emotional development of children. For more information: http://csefel.uiuc.edu.

Chamberlain, J. (2000). Working to create a violence-free future for young children. *Monitor on Psychology, 31*(8), 54–55.

Conflict references: Early childhood conflict resolution program. Search at www.google .com and www.yahoo.com.

Curwin, R., & Mendler, A. (1988). *Discipline with dignity.* Alexandria, VA: Association for Supervision and Curriculum Development.

Da Ros, D. A., & Kovach, B. A. (1998). Assisting toddlers and caregivers during conflict resolutions: Interactions that promote socialization. *Childhood Education, 75*(1), 25–30.

Derman-Sparks, L. (1989). *Anti-bias curriculum: Tools for empowering young children.* NAEYC Order #242/$8. ISBN 0-935989-20-X.

DeVries, R., & Zan, B. (1994). In C. H. Hart, D. C. Burts, & R. Charlesworth (Eds.), *Integrated curriculum and developmentally appropriate practice: Birth to age eight* (p. 299). Albany: State of New York University Press.

Dewey, J. (1900, 1969). *The school and society.* New York: Free Press.

Dewey, J. (1916, 1945). *Democracy and education.* Chicago: University of Chicago Press.

Dewolf, M., & Benedict, J. (1997). Social development and behavior in the integrated curriculum. In Hart, Burts, & Charlesworth 257–284.

Division for Early Childhood (DEC) of the Council for Exceptional Children (endorsed by NAEYC). (2001). *Position Statement on Interventions for Challenging Behavior.* Retrieved from DEC website at http://www.decsped.org/positions/chalbeha.html.

Elkind, D. (1997, May). The death of child nature: Education in the post modern world. *Phi Delta Kappan,* 241–245.

Elswood, R. (1999). Really including diversity in early childhood classrooms. *Young Children, 54*(4), 62–66.

Fleege, P. O., Charlesworth, R., Burts, D. C., & Hart, C. H. (1992). Stress begins in kindergarten: A look at behavior during standardized testing. *Journal of Research in Child Education, 7,* 20–26.

Fleege, P. O. (1997). Assessment in an integrated curriculum. In C. H. Hart, D. C. Burts, & R. Charlesworth (Eds.), *Integrated curriculum and developmentally appropriate practice: Birth to age eight* (pp. 313–334). Albany: State of New York University Press.

Froschl, M., & Sprung, B. (1999). On purpose: Addressing teasing and bullying in early childhood. *Young Children, 54*(2), 70–72.

Gardner, H. *Multiple intelligences: The theory in practice.* New York: Basic.

Gartrell, D. J. (1997). Beyond discipline to guidance. *Young Children, 52*(6), 34–42.

Gartrell, D. J. (1998). *A guidance approach for the encouraging classroom.* Albany, NY: Delmar/Thompson.

Gartrell, D. J. (2001). Replacing time-out: Part 1—Using guidance to build an encouraging classroom. *Young Children, 56*(6), 8–16.

Gartrell, D. J. (2002). Replacing time out: Part 2—Using guidance to maintain an encouraging classroom. *Young Children, 57*(2), 36–43.

Gillespie, C. W., & Chick, A. (2001, Summer). Fussbusters: Using peers to mediate conflict resolution in a Head Start classroom. *Childhood Education,* 192–195.

Gilligan, C., Garbarino, J., Gilligan, J., & Thompson, M. (1999). Boys to men: Questions of violence. Transcript of forum that took place 15 April 1999 at Harvard Graduate School of Education. Available online at http://edletter.org/past/issues/1999-ja forum.shtml.

Goldstein, J. (1986). *Aggression and crimes of violence.* New York: Oxford Press.

Goodrow, M. E. (2000). The teachable moment. *Young Children, 55*(4), 42–43.

Gorter-Reu, M.S., & Anderson, J. M. (1998). Home kits, home visits, and more! *Young Children, 53*(3), 71–73.

Greenberg, P. (1990). Why not academic preschool? Part 1. *Young Children, 45*(2), 70–80.

Greenberg, P. (1992). Way not academic preschool? Part 2—Autocracy or democracy in the classroom? *Young Children, 47*(5), 10–17.

Greenberg, P. (1992). How to institute some simple democratic practices pertaining to respect, rights, roots, and responsibilities in any classroom (without losing your leadership position). *Young Children, 47*(5), 10–17.

Greenberg, P. (2001). The irreducible needs of children: An interview with T. Berry Brazelton, M.D., and S. I. Greenspan, M.D. *Young Children, 56*(2), 6–13.

Harris, T. T., & Fuqua, J. D. (2000). What goes around comes around: Building a community of learners through circle times. *Young Children, 55*(1), 44–47.

Hart, C. H., Burts, D. C., & Charlesworth, R. (Eds.). (1997). *Integrated curriculum and developmentally appropriate practice: Birth to age eight.* Albany: State of New York University Press.

Honig, A. S., & Wittmer, D. S. (1996). Helping children become more prosocial: Ideas for classrooms, families, schools, and communities. *Young Children, 51*(2), 62–70.

Howes, C., Matheson, C. C., & Hamilton, C. E. (1994). Maternal, teacher, and child care history correlates of children's relationships with peers. *Child Development, 65,* 264–273.

Hurt, J. A. (2000). Create a parent place: Make the invitation for family involvement real. *Young Children, 55*(5), 88–92.

Hymes, J. (1981). *Teaching the child under six.* Upper Saddle River, NJ: Merrill/Prentice Hall.

Hyson, M. (2002). Professional development: Yesterday, today, and tomorrow—with your help. Curriculum and assessment in early childhood programs. Summary of NAEYC and NAECS/SDE 1990 position statement—Guidelines for appropriate curriculum and assessment in programs serving children ages 3 through 8. *Young Children, 57*(3), 57.

Hyson, M. C., & Christensen, S. L. (1997). Developmentally appropriate guidance and the integrated curriculum. In C. H. Hart, D. C. Burts, & R. Charlesworth (Eds.), *Integrated curriculum and developmentally appropriate practice: Birth to age eight* (pp. 285–312). Albany: State of New York University Press.

Kachur, S., Stinnes, G., & Powell, K. (1996). School-associated violent deaths in the United States, 1992–1994. *Journal of American Medical Association (JAMA) 275,* 1729–1733.

Katz, L. G. (1997, April). A developmental approach to assessment of young children. *ERIC Digest.* Publication NO. EDO-PS-97-18.

Kohn, A. At www.alfiekohn.org.

Kohn, A. (1993). *Punished by rewards: The trouble with gold stars, incentive plans, A's, praise, and other bribes.* Boston: Houghton Mifflin.

Kohn, A. (1999). *The schools our children deserve: Moving beyond traditional classrooms and "tougher standards."* Boston: Houghton Mifflin.

Kohn, A. (2000a). *The case against standardized testing: Raising the scores, ruining the schools.* Portsmouth, NH: Heinemann.

Kohn, A. (2000, May). Hooked on praise. *Parents' Magazine,* 39–41.

Kohn, A. (2001). Fighting the tests: Turning frustration into action. *Young Children, 56*(2), 19–24.

Lindquist, B., & Molar, A. (1995). Children learn what they live. *Educational Leadership, 52,* 47–51.

Lombardi, J. (2001). It's time to redesign child care to create 21st century early education. *Young Children, 56*(3), 74–77.

Malloy, H. L., & McMurray, P. (1996). Conflict strategies and resolutions: Peer conflict in an integrated early childhood classroom. *Early Childhood Research Quarterly, 11,* 185–206.

Marshall, H. H. (1995). Beyond "I like the way . . . ". *Young Children, 50*(2), 26–28.

McBride, S. L. (1999). Family-centered practices. Research in Review. *Young Children, 54*(3), 62–68.

McClosky, C. M. (1996). Taking positive steps toward classroom management in preschool: Loosening up without letting it all fall apart. *Young Children, 51*(3), 14–16.

McCracken, J. B. *Valuing diversity: The primary years.* NAEYC Order #238/$5. ISBN 0-935989-55-2.

Meisels, S. J. (2000). On the side of the child: Personal reflections on testing, teaching, and early childhood education. *Young Children, 55*(6), 16–19.

National Association for the Education of Young Children (NAEYC) Guidelines for Appropriate Curriculum Content and Assessment in Programs Serving Children Ages 3 through 8. NAEYC and NACS/SDE position statement is available on line at www.naeyc.org/resources/position_statements/pscag98.pdf. (2001. *Young Children (56)* 2, p. 18).

National Association for the Education of Young Children (NAEYC). For reprints on line: www.naeyc.org/resources/journal.

National Association for the Education of Young Children (NAEYC). Call 1-877-ACT-WISE, toll free, or see www.actagainstviolence.org.

National Association for the Education of Young Children (NAEYC). (1998). Real-life ethical problems early childhood professionals face. *NAEYC'S Code of Ethical Conduct and Statement of Commitment.* NAEYC brochure #503.

NAEYC code of ethical conduct: Guidelines for responsible behavior in early childhood education. (1996). *Young Children, 51*(3), 57–60.

Neugebauer, B. (Ed.). *Alike and different: Exploring our humanity with young children* (rev. ed.). NAEYC Order #240/$8. ISBN 0-935989-8.

Peth-Pierce, R. (2000). *A good beginning: Sending America's children to school with the social and emotional competence they need to succeed.* Monograph from the Children's Mental Health Foundations and Agencies Network (FAN). Bethesda, MD: National Institute of Mental Health. Available on line at www.nimh.nih.gov/childhp/fdnconsb.htm.

Piaget, J. (1932, 1960). *The moral judgment of the child.* Glencoe, IL: Free Press.

Pianta, R. C., Kraft-Saure, M., Rimm-Kaufman, S., Gercke, N., & Higgins, T. (2001). Collaboration in building partnerships between families and schools: The National Center for Early Development and Learning's Kindergarten Transition Intervention. *Early Childhood Research Quarterly, 16,* 117–132.

Pines, M. (1979). Good Samaritans at age two? *Psychology Today, 13,* 66–77.

Popham, W. J. (2000). *Testing! Testing! What every parent should know about standardized testing: Raising the scores, ruining the schools.* Portsmouth, NH: Heinemann.

Remboldt, C. (1998, September). Making violence unacceptable. *Association for Supervision and Curriculum Development, 53*(5), 32–38.

Rourke, M. T., Wozniak, R. H., & Cassidy, K. W. (1999). The social sensitivity of preschoolers in peer conflicts. Do children act differently with different peers? *Early Education and Development, 10*(2), 209–227.

Salmon, M., with Akaran, S. E. (2001). Enrich young kindergarten program with a cross-cultural connection. *Young Children, 56*(4), 30–32.

Schreiber, M. E. (1999). Time-outs for toddlers: Is our goal punishment or education? *Young Children, 54*(4), 22–25.

Shepard, L. A., Kagan, S. L., & Wurtz, E. (1998). Goal 1 Early Childhood Assessments Resource Group Recommendations. *Young Children, 53*(3), 52–54. (Reprinted from *Principles and recommendations for early childhood assessments,* pp. 20–21, by L. A. Shepard, S. L. Kagan, & E. Wurtz, Eds., 1998, Washington, DC: National Educational Goals Panel).

Shonkoff, J. P., & Phillips, D. A. (Eds.). (2000). *From neurons to neighborhoods: The science of early childhood development.* Washington, DC, National Academy Press.

Shidler, L. (2001, Spring). Teacher-sanctioned violence. *Childhood Education,* 167–168.

Slaby, R., Rodell, W., Arezzo, D., & Hendrix, K. (1995). *Early violence prevention: Tools for teachers of young children.* Washington, DC: National Association for the Education of Young Children.

Smith, K. (2000). *Who's minding the kids? Child care arrangements: Fall 1995.* Current population reports. Washington, DC: U.S. Bureau of the Census.

Solter, A. (1992). Understanding tears and tantrums. *Young Children, 47*(4), 64–68.

Stipek, D. (1998). *Motivation to learn: From theory to practice.* Englewood Cliffs, NJ: Prentice Hall.

Stone, J. G. (2001). *Building classroom community: The early childhood teacher's role.* Washington, DC: NAEYC.

Swope, K., & Miner, B. (2000). *Failing our kids: Why the testing craze won't fix our schools.* Milwaukee: Rethinking Schools.

United States Department of Education, Office for Civil Rights. (1997). *Elementary and secondary school civil rights compliance report.* Washington, DC: Author.

Using NAEYC's Code of Ethics. "What happens when school/parent relationships aren't good?"

Vygotsky, L. S. (1978). *Mind in society: The development of higher mental processes.* (M. Cole, V. John Steiner, S. Scribner & E. Sauberman, Eds. & Trans.). Cambridge, MA: Harvard University Press.

Wardle, F. (1999). In praise of developmentally appropriate practice. *Young Children, 54*(6), 4–12.

Wesson, K. A. (2001). The "Volvo Effect"—Questioning standardized tests. *Young Children, 56*(2), 16–18.

Wien, C. A., & Kirby-Smith, S. (1998). Untiming the curriculum: A case study of removing clocks from the program. *Young Children, 53*(5), 8–13.

Wilt, J. L. V., & Monroe, V. (1998). Successfully moving toward developmentally appropriate practice: It takes time and effort. *Young Children, 53*(4), 17–23.

Wittmer, D. S., & Honig, A. S. (1994). Encouraging positive social development in young children. *Young Children, 49*(4), 4–12.

Websites

Act Against Violence: www.actagainstviolence.org General information on violence. Also call 1-822-ACT-WISE, TOLL FREE.

Center on the Social and Emotional Foundations for Early Learning: http://csefel.uiun.edu

The Division for Early Childhood (DEC) of the Council for Exceptional Children: www.dec-sped.org/

ERIC Clearinghouse on Elementary and Early Childhood Education: http://ericcec.org/

3

The Value of Play

Main Principles

1. Violence may be a learned behavior that begins early in the lives of young children. Its prevention and/or control needs serious attention.

2. Play is a part of growing up for young children and needs to be encouraged.

3. Through play a child grows and develops in many ways: motor skills, social-emotional skills, cognitive-language skills, combinations of body parts, overall development, and other supporting factors (pp. 75–82).

4. The teacher plays an important role in the child's attitudes, behaviors, and development of play patterns (pp. 82–109).

5. *Dramatic play* is important in the child's development (pp. 83–86).

6. Block play has been an important activity for young children for many years (pp. 86–90).

7. Early and important promoters of children's play are Piaget and Vygotsky (pp. 90–92).

8. There are helpful ways for teachers to encourage children's play (pp. 92–98).

9. Children learn many values from dramatic play (pp. 98–109).

10. Teachers must take precautions in indoor areas and outdoor areas to see that play is growth promoting and safe for young children (pp. 92–98).

11. There are government standards for keeping playgrounds safe for young children (p. 99).

12. Many educators acclaim the benefits of children's play.

13. Of great concern to teachers and parents is the negative role of violence in children's play (pp. 106–109).

14. Application of principles at the end of the chapter can assist students in planning more appropriate play experiences for young children (p. 109).

Introduction

Note to reader: ***Violence*** is discussed in Chapter 2. However, a few helpful reminders are included throughout this chapter. See section at end of chapter. Violence may be a learned behavior that begins at an early age (Bandura, 1973; Goldstein, 1986). Children may witness and become a part of the violence through interactions with others in the family, neighborhood, child-care settings, or other places. *Respect and Protect Program,* a system-based program, empowers concerned adults to compassionately combat violence in schools.

To prevent verbal (taunts) and nonverbal (physical contact, corporal punishment) aggression, we must shape children's beliefs, attitudes, and behaviors before they become an outgrowth of their anger. We do this by respecting and protecting the rights of others, stopping enabling behaviors, clearly defining violence, and teaching children and adults acceptable ways of dealing with their frustrations.

Play can be positive and help develop good social and intellectual behaviors. How one reflects on one's own childhood is a personal matter. Some adults recall playing neighborhood games such as tag, hide and seek, kick-the-can, marbles, hopscotch, follow-the-leader, jump rope, cops and robbers—depending on where and when they grew up. Some adults recall games and activities where play space was limited in size, opportunity, and safety. Others made up their own activities—role playing occupations, pretending to be famous people in sports, movies, science, or other timely topics—with and without props.

At times games were short-lived; at others the play continued for hours, days, or even months. Our games taught us language skills, how to take turns, learning and following rules, different roles, positive human relations, imagination, skills and competence, and change. Perhaps if adults returned to thoughts of their growing-up years, they would have a better appreciation for the play needs of children.

Refer to Chapter 1 for some basic information regarding theories of early childhood education as it relates to the importance of play in the lives of young children.

Why do some people question the value of play for young children? Are they so product- and time-conscious that they want the children to get past playing and get on to "learning"? Do they realize the importance of firsthand experiences? A child may seem to be wasting time at play, but to the child, play is his work, his way of learning about his environment.

Educators in many settings (classroom, spontaneous conversations, departments of education, coffee shops, and so on) are discussing and accepting the importance of developmentally appropriate practice (DAP) (Bredekamp, 1987; Bredekamp & Copple, 1997) but when it comes to actually putting it into practice, there are as many differences in

---

Notable Quotes

"Many animals play, but primates play more, and humans play the most" (Eibl-Eibesfeldt, 1970; Bruner, 1976).

"The child's play interests reveal many of the interests of humankind" (Piaget, 1963; Vygotsky, 1976).

"We are curious about the social and physical world and reach out to explore it . . . to see what will happen and how things and people function. . . . [P]lay reveals children's interests and nourishes the growing edges of their competence . . . [they] try to play with everything in their environments and with each of their own motor and mental capacities" (Bronson, 1995).

"Human play is characteristically imaginative and symbolic" (Piaget, 1962; Werner & Kaplan, 1963).

definition and practice as there are individuals discussing it. One central issue is the inability of teachers/leaders to define the best practice for play of young children in the curriculum. The most common answer is that play is the child's work or one's way of learning. Play is complex and multifaceted. Another answer may be that play is a waste of time and energy.

"To understand is to invent" is a reminder from Piaget. Young children learn most important things through personal involvement—through play—not by being told but by constructing knowledge for themselves in interaction with the physical work and with other children. Teachers can carefully observe the play of children and try to interpret it as the children do—not through the mind and experiences of the teacher, but teachers can use the play theories and application through study and discussions with others in an attempt to better understand it. For values children receive from play, see Table 3.1

Table 3.1   Values of Play for Young Children

Domain	Enhancement
Motor	Health, perceptual-motor abilities, physical fitness; rejuvenation; new or advanced skills; coordination; fine and gross muscle development.
Social-emotional	Freedom to explore rich environments; builds knowledge of self and others; self-esteem and personal power; builds the foundation for success and personal competence; teaches us to value differences; cooperation through curriculum areas; healthy competition; sharing; lengthening interest span.
Cognitive-language	Increased verbal fluency; thinking; problem solving; planning; cooperation; imagination; developing powers of concentration, curiosity, and self-determination.
Combination of domains/body parts	Using arms, legs, and eyes together; using hands, fingers, and eyes together; remembering what is seen; remembering what is heard; communicating with others through expressive language; listening to others; showing interest in words and books; classifying; comparing, and sequencing; understanding numbers; comprehending stories; controlling and expressing emotions.
	Skills required in sociodramatic play are related to the cognitive skills required for academic success and the social skills required for successful school adjustment (Smilansky and Shefatya, 1990).
Overall	Play is more than running off excess energy; relaxing and relieving tension; reliving earlier periods and preparing for later ones; it is somewhat archaic with insufficient explanations (Frost, 1992).
Other factors	A well-organized classroom environment; ability and opportunity to play; brainstorming; spontaneity; ability to solve problems; choice; responsibility and follow-through; a feeling of belonging; culture; novelty; complexity and realism; adult and peer models; role play ideas from life, media, books, and so on.

Development During Years 2 Through 5

Freud and Erikson, psychoanalysts, maintain that play contributes to the development of a healthy personality. Piaget determined that play affects cognitive development as children note cause-and-effect relationships in the process of constructing their own knowledge about their environment. But play is a topic of many disciplines—not just child development and psychology (for example, anthropology, sociology, physical education, education). Frost (1992) concludes the following:

> After having reviewed major theories of play spanning the last 3,000 years, from Plato to Piaget, it is still not possible to arrive at a simple, clear, scientific definition of play. Erikson advises that play has a very personal meaning for each individual. Perhaps the best thing that we as adults can do to discover this meaning is to go out and play; to reflect upon our own childhood play; to once again look at play through the eyes of the child (p. 21).

Motor Development

Physical changes in the young child are more obvious than changes in other areas of development. Through physical increase, the child gains independence, develops body skills and coordination, masters her environment, and learns to cooperate. Her body is used as a vehicle of expression. Through body movements, she learns spatial relationships and bilateral movements. She learns about motion, speed, and force. Many of these activities are symbolic and are satisfying at the time and also in later learning. Numerous studies have shown the important relationship between a child's physical skills and her self-concept. When she feels competent, she is willing to attempt new and different experiences.

For the most part, and mainly because of inadequate space indoors, most large-muscle activities are performed outside. However, some provision should be made for indoor large-muscle play, giving consideration to space needs, type of equipment, appropriate activities, and noise level. Children should play outdoors each day, even during inclement weather, but sustained large-muscle development is difficult when it is wet or cold. On such days children profit from indoor large-muscle activities. A portable jungle gym, ladders, and boxes can be brought in, or sheets thrown over furniture can suffice for props. Set up the limits—the stick horses can be ridden in one room, but not throughout the building—and watch the enjoyment!

Having a teacher nearby can aid in social development.

Outdoor play can be invigorating and pleasurable.

Social Development

Social-skill learning, a complex task, can be fostered through play. Some skills are self-related and some are interpersonally related. Every child wants to participate with other children, and the first few years are the most important for practicing social living.

Unfortunately, there are times in children's lives when they are not free to play, such as in new, strange, or feared situations—for example, war, accidents, or family deaths. But it is important that all children have the opportunity to use play to relieve feelings of disorganization, distrust, fear, and uncertainty. The events at the World Trade Center in New York City, war in various geographical locations, floods, disease, and other uncontrollable events add to the insecurity of children and families.

Children at all ages, but especially those at ages 4 and 5, need constructive play experiences to express creative thought, decision making, and the ability to cope with stressful situations. The American Academy of Pediatricians has expressed concern about the dramatic increase of "stress-related" symptoms being seen in young children.

In their study of play behaviors, Quay, Weaver, and Neel (1986) find that children engage in more social than nonsocial and more positive than negative behavior (also stated by Marcus [1987] and Read, Gardner, & Mahler [1987]). More negative social behavior occurred in woodworking and doll/dollhouse environments. By gender, boys played more in woodworking, manipulative, and language centers; girls played more in paints, housekeeping, games, art, and book centers.

Maturation is a factor to consider in assessing a child's readiness for specific types of play activities. It sets limitations on his skills, experience, and techniques.

Studies over several decades show the relationship between the absence of pleasure and the failure to develop normally. Some years ago, Spitz observed that infants in a founding home developed severe psychological disturbances even though physical care was adequate.

Some play is not without conflict. In her concluding paragraph of a study on kindergarten children, Ditchburn (1988) states:

Conflict management is a requisite social skill at every stage of life and in all social situations. Further, conflict is endemic in our stressful, modern society. That young children demonstrate sophistication in conflict management gives some pause for reflection. Play is readily available, cost efficient, and a safe occasion for the exercise of socially acceptable conflict management.... Learning through play is not merely a trite phrase supporting academically impoverished practice—rather play is a lesson in life. One cautionary note, however, is in order. We need to examine which strategies achieve desired ends and which children typically achieve their conversational goals in situations of conflict. There are important moral and gender-related questions which have not been addressed in the literature on children's conflict. (p. 69)

Play helps young children learn and practice roles of leading and following, essential aspects of effective social participation. Trawick-Smith (1988) found the following:

Never to lead is never to be heard, never to have ideas carefully considered by others, and never to have an impact on the behaviors or thinking of peers. Never to follow, on the other hand, is never to benefit from the ideas of others or be swayed to another's viewpoint. Total absence of the skill or the confidence to lead or follow, when these are genuinely desired or needed, can be a barrier to human interaction that teachers can help young children overcome. Helping young children develop leadership abilities, whether a child chooses to exercise these frequently or only occasionally, is a worthwhile objective of early childhood programs. (p. 58)

During the ages from 2 to 4, the child is less inhibited that she will ever be. Her self-image during this period depends on her play. She is very egocentric and desires power. Healthy personality development is tied to each child's own biological time clock, to personal endowment, and to very early life experiences.

See Figure 3.1 regarding types of children's play.

Emotional Development

Some adults have little patience with and understanding of a child's emotional development. That is one reason why play opportunities are so important for young children. Through play, children learn trust and confidence in themselves, in others, and in their environment. They recognize their self-worth and develop inner satisfaction. Instead of feeling helpless in many situations and showing fear or rage, they reduce these feelings or gain mastery over them and formulate acceptable age-related emotional releases. In play they can exercise rule making and direction following; both are important for interaction with others and for later learning.

Play is a medium through which children can express their positive or negative feelings. For a time they do not have to conform to adult ways and can have relief from high expectations in childlike ways. Whenever a child has a successful experience, her feelings of self-worth and ability increase. Success also releases her from a sense of powerlessness. She actually can control and manipulate her environment.

Within a group of peers, the child can learn about sharing, taking turns, and property rights. She learns that at school there are toys, activities, and people to be shared. At times she uses these things; at times someone else uses them—but sharing is *not* giving up one's rights. A child who has had opportunities to possess (at home or elsewhere) finds that rather than relinquishing all rights, she will again be able to use the item(s). And while she

Simple	One child plays alone (solitary)—looking at books, manipulating toys, entertaining self.
Complex	Usually two to four children (parallel or cooperatively)—with art materials, at water/sand table, in block area.
Super	Usually up to eight children (cooperatively)—in dramatic play, construction, table, or floor games.

Figure 3.1   Suggested Types of Play in Young Children

is sharing, she should be redirected to another activity or toy, rather than just wait! Then, at the appropriate time, the child is offered another opportunity to use the shared item.

At times some children become so upset that they cannot control themselves. On these occasions, so that the child does not lose face or upset the other children, it may be wise to remove the child. Help her to gain control and return to the setting without her feeling the isolation as a form of punishment or rejection.

Current thinking has replaced games of exclusion (musical chairs, for example) with those that foster *inclusion,* that encourage collaboration rather than competition, and that allow play time for all rather than the varsity-bound, the most popular, or the most aggressive. Activities that teach skills such as trust, initiative, and autonomy are welcome. All of these activities build self-esteem and foster peace (in the world, the school, and the neighborhood) through social interaction, as they generate alternatives, promote working together, and imbue respect for both body and soul.

Teachers and parents should actively discourage the use of elimination and competition with young children in games such as dodge ball; "Duck, Duck, Goose"; kickball; relay races; and of course musical chairs. They should advocate games that give every child lots of turns, that permit success at various skill levels, and that allow social acceptance (not ridicule) of differences in ability. Elimination games may cause children to feel sad, worthless, lazy, squashed, lacking in body skills, friendless, and dumb.

Competitive and large-group games do not meet the needs of the young child. Rules are hard to interpret and follow, skills are limited, waiting for a turn is difficult, and playing for an extended time (as many games require) is exhausting. It appears that small-group games can be beneficial if they do not occur too frequently, everybody gets lots of chances, the emphasis is placed on the fun and excitement, and each child feels successful. This would be developmentally appropriate for young children.

Help teachers and parents understand the complexities of play and what the child is learning. Offer suggestions on ways that teachers and parents can extend the child's play experiences at home. Ask open-ended questions while moving the conversation in a specific direction, such as what kinds of toys were used or roles were played. Teachers and parents are facilitators of play experiences as they offer new materials, comment on what they observe, and offer suggestions of new things to try.

Cognitive and Language Development

Many people think intellectual development must be taught through structured academic experience. They think that children must be taught early to perform the three Rs. Some teachers are so anxious to look good and to prepare children for the next grade that they are introducing topics earlier and earlier. Hymes calls this the "dribble down disease" (1981, p. 25). Why are adults not just as concerned about training children in the basics of life? Have they ever stopped to think that children who are helped to live fully as 3-, 4-, 5-, 6-, or whatever-year-olds will be happier and more productive throughout their entire schooling and lives? Young children may read, write, or do arithmetic, but do they know how to play?

The preschool period is not a valueless waiting time. Much is to be gained from play experiences: sustained attention and deep concentration, so necessary for reading; imagination; curiosity to explore, examine, and discover; initiative to try one's own ideas; opportunity to use memory in relating, recalling, and thinking; a chance to play and organize; leadership and group participation; a larger repertoire of responses; language development; creativity; acquisition of knowledge; self-enhancement; flexibility; understanding of one's personal problems; and the ability to exercise divergent thinking.

How can children or adults be expected to make good decisions based on logic, cause and effect, value, or consequences if opportunities are not provided throughout their lives to exercise judgment, originality, and independence? Development and use of the ability to think divergently are essential.

Earlier extensive review of research on the role of play in language and cognitive development showed that it:

➤ stimulates innovation in language;
➤ introduces and clarifies new words and concepts;
➤ motivates language use and practice;
➤ develops mentalinguistic awareness;
➤ encourages verbal thinking (Levy, 1984).

See Table 3.2 for a list of instructional items to provide for the various ages and areas of development.

Table 3.2   Areas of Development

Age	Motor	Social and Emotional	Cognitive and Language
2–3	blocks: unit, hollow, plastic, and cardboard wooden figures rocking boat simple climbing equipment large wooden nesting boxes big cars and trucks wheel toys easels, paints, and brushes manipulative toys	dollhouse dolls stuffed toys simple doll clothes and blankets telephones child-sized furniture domestic-play items dress-up clothes riding toys music	books with action, rhyming records record player puzzles crayons markers paste brushes clay soft balls
4	**add:** walking boards planks, boxes wheelbarrows tricycles swings slide woodworking bench and tools sand toys triangle set coaster wagon jungle gyms stick horses balls hoops	**add:** chest of drawers sand and water table clothesline and pins puppets puppet theater career clothing costumes wheel toys multicultural books and toys	**add:** chalk, peg, and bulletin boards blunt scissors large colored beads and patterns for stringing manipulative toys card games aquarium pets cooking opportunities
5	**add:** giant dominoes construction sets balls roller skates scooter ladders, ropes jump ropes obstacle courses	**add:** small tent traffic signs	**add:** flannel board and counting set counting games magnets magnifying glasses games with rules action books

Stages of Play in Young Children

Parten's traditional stages of play (1932–33; Table 3.3) have been useful in identifying when young children develop certain skills in playing with each other during the early years.

Parten's descriptions of play are now referred to as the *traditional* view and were formulated when most research involved young children whose interactions with peers were limited to occasional play groups of short duration. Current research is not entirely consistent with the traditional view mainly because today children spend more time in the company of peers in child-care centers, family child-care homes, and other programs, which necessitates reassessing the age ranges and kinds of play in which they participate. A second reason is that more research is being conducted on the topic.

Recent research shows that, given the opportunity to be with peers, even infants participate in parallel play, which had previously been considered to be absent from children's repertoires until the age of 2. As early as 12 months of age, infants have been observed spending more time watching the activity of their peers than that of their mothers, and they were more likely to touch, get close to, look at, and imitate a friend than a stranger. Important opportunities to practice social skills in the early years and to learn new ones through frequent and sustained peer contacts encourage 2- and 3-year-olds to engage in associative and cooperative play (Anselmo & Franz, 1995).

Ross and Lollis (1989), observing 20- and 30-month-old children over time in small peer-group play sessions, found that (1) even at that young age, children formed relationships with individual friends that were qualitatively different from their interactions with other people; and (2) these special relationships continued across a number of play sessions with surprising stability. They suggest that it is possible that positive interactions draw children into social relationships and once these relationships are established, conflict naturally emerges as a normal part of social development.

Caplan et al. (1991) studied conflict in the peer relationships of 12- and 24-month-old toddlers, examining the theory that conflict is due to frustration over play equipment and toys. They found that rather than the scarcity of toys being related to conflict, the greatest amount of conflict occurred among 24-month-olds when there were scarce resources and no duplicate toys available. The conflict among the 12-month-olds, however, occurred when the toddlers found a toy attractive when another child had it—even if there was another duplicate toy available in the room and sometimes even when the child was holding the duplicate toy. The ability to cooperate increases over the ages of 12 to 30 months, due to the child's ability to separate himself from others cognitively, known as *self-other differentiation* (Brownell & Carriger, 1990).

> Conclusion: The vast literature on children's play reveals that its contributions to child development can be looked at from diverse vantage points. Psychoanalytic theorists have highlighted the emotionally integrative function of pretense, pointing out that anxiety-provoking events, such as a visit to the doctor's office or discipline by a parent, are likely to be revised in the young child's play, but with roles reversed so that the child is in command and compensates for unpleasant experiences in real life (Erikson, 1950).

Table 3.3 Parten's Traditional Stages of Play

Age	Name of Play	Brief Description
0–24 months	Solitary	Children interact only with an object or familiar person
2–3 years	Parallel	Children play near each other but independently
3–4 years	Associative	Children participate in small groups but have a very limited sharing or interaction with each other
4 years on	Cooperative	Children share ideas and roles and interact in increasingly more complex play

Thinking up and carrying out one's ideas is growth promoting.

Piaget underscored the opportunities that make-believe affords for exercising symbolic schemes. And both Piaget and Vygotsky recognized that pretense allows children to become familiar with social-role possibilities. In cultures around the world, young children act out family scenes and highly visible occupations—police officer, doctor, and nurse in Western nations; rabbit hunter and potter among the Hopi; and hut builder and spear maker among the Baka of West Africa (Garvey, 1990). In this way, play provides children with important insights into the link between self and wider society (Berk & Winsler, 1995, p. 79).

Role of the Teacher

The teacher or parent should accept the challenge of designing and providing appropriate play activities that enhance the child's intellectual development. Most kinds of opportunities, such as dramatic, sensory, or scientific exploration, are *meaningful,* but especially so are creative or artistic endeavors. Deciding *what* to do and *how* to do it sharpens the child's intellect. These activities also provide for exercise of the brain, eye, hand, and other parts of the body.

Intellectual development can be developed through play experiences. For example, attitudes about curiosity, divergent thinking, motivation, and so on, are so essential to learning math and science. These attitudes are formed during play activities.

Play themes are acquired in many ways—from books and stories children see and hear, daily episodes they see, their own imaginations, vicarious experiences, media, curiosity, spontaneous or planned activities, ignorance, or a desire to test and learn about the world. All these ways, and many more, cause the child to develop and stretch his mental capacities.

Maturation is a factor to consider in assessing a child's readiness for specific types of play activities. It sets limitations on one's skills, experience, and techniques. Also, teachers should be aware of the style differences between girls' and boys' play. See Figure 3.2.

Girls	Boys
• More advanced socially	• More rough-and-tumble play
• More advanced in cognitive and language development	• More aggression and fighting
• Prefer table play and sitting activities	• Prefer floor play, push-pull toys, blocks, wheel toys, and sand
• Prefer arts, crafts, puzzles, coloring, dolls	• Prefer outdoors
• Use materials in a more educational way	• Choose superhero play
• Prefer domestic activities	• Boisterous
• Less active and noisy	• More gender-role oriented

Figure 3.2   Some Differences Between Young Girls' and Boys' Style of Play

Dramatic Play

Dramatic play, sometimes referred to as *sociodramatic play,* is defined as "a form of voluntary social play activity in which young children participate" (Smilansky & Shefatya, 1990). Its importance in the preschool curriculum cannot be underestimated because it gives children a chance to touch and live different ways of life (See Table 3.4).

Table 3.4   Ideas to Encourage Dramatic Play

Type of Activity	Suggested Props
Family/home	Dress-up clothes—masculine and feminine, occupational, multicultural. Full-length or hand-held mirrors. Different rooms, different activities, different family members. A visit by child's family. Pictures of children in various kinds of activities posted at eye level. A mother bathing a baby. Books, stories, and pictures.
Clothing	Ethnic, gender, specialty articles of clothing (sports, occupational, etc.). Nonsexist ideas and discussion. Books, stories, and pictures.
Government offices—post office, bank, school, museum, police or fire station, etc.	Appropriate clothing and tools (badges, kits, bags, money, vehicles, etc.). Practicing courtesy and safety. Books, stories, and pictures.
Animals	Different habitats—pet shop, kennel, zoo, natural settings. Items for pet care. Replicas of different kinds of animals: zoo, farm, circus, and dinosaurs. Healthy and friendly animals within the classroom or on a field trip. A bug hunt on the playground. A bird's nest, a beehive, a cocoon. Books, stories, and pictures.
Food	Furniture and equipment for a restaurant, tools for planting, equipment and opportunity for food preparation, plastic replicas, good pictures. A field trip to a bakery, grocery store, pizza shop, produce farm, etc. Books, stories, and pictures.

(continued)

Table 3.4   continued

Type of Activity	Suggested Props
Local industry	Depends on individual community: farm, dairy, water sport or fishing, etc. A safe and interesting place recognized by the children. An involved parent, clothing worn, and good pictures. Books, stories, and pictures.
Health center—doctor's office, clinic, hospital, etc.	Medical clothing and equipment. A unit on health. A visitor to the classroom. Books, stories, and pictures.
Water	Cooking and eating utensils. Boats, funnels, tubes, measuring equipment, water wheel, and water. Mixing paints for use. Investigating porous and nonporous materials. Doll clothes, a washtub, and soap. Books, stories, and pictures.
Environment	Rearrange, rotate, and add something special. Observe and discuss pollution—noise, litter, water, air. Child-sized and easily moved equipment and furniture. Combination of equipment and activities within the classroom. Enough (or duplicate) items for cooperative and sustained play. Manipulative toys for construction and building. Items to encourage singing, dancing, moving (records and recorders, tapes and cassettes, musical instruments, streamers, soft balls, scarves, etc.) A flannel board and objects of different colors, sizes, shapes, animals, people, etc. Books, stories, and pictures.
Sports	Family members to demonstrate their sport activities. Different sports items (hats, shoes, equipment). Books, stories, and pictures.
Nature	A walk during different seasons of the year, noting the surroundings. Items for making a collage. Places animals live and what they eat. Weather conditions at your center and those in other climates. Local and seasonal items of nature—leaves, snow, flowers, etc. Books, stories, and pictures.
Transportation	Uses of different vehicles. Sounds of different vehicles. Vehicles added to blocks, table toys, sand, etc. Books, stories, and pictures.
Interests of individual children	To be filled in by individual teacher.
Things to introduce to the children	To be filled in by individual teacher.

Some centers have a policy of restricting items from home (toys, food, pets, or other unnamed items). In this way toys and opportunities are not lost, broken, misplaced, or unjustly claimed. Some centers find that play is more spontaneous and inclusive when certain items are not available—clothing fads (Superman cape, hero toys), media themes, food advertising, and so on. War play can be disruptive, negative, and exclusive; so can hero play. (See section "Violent Play" in Chapter 2.)

 **Reflection**

It is not unusual for a child to dramatize a familiar theme. Simon and Ann were playing in the domestic area. Ann handed a block (representing his lunch bucket) to Simon and told him to go to work. He did so. Shortly she called to him and told him it was time to come home. Dutifully he returned, only to have her throw her arms around him and say, "Oh darling, I'm so glad you're home." Startled, Simon dropped the block and said, "Let me out of here!" With that, he ran to another area. This may have been a familiar scene to Ann, but it was foreign to Simon.

Dramatic play occurs in any area: domestic, block, sand, art, snack, language arts, or anywhere children are. Teachers of children can be the initiators, but the actual activity should be child centered. A story may trigger an activity, or the teacher can initiate dramatization of a story the children have just heard. A field trip is reinforced by dramatizing it upon return. See Figure 3.3 on how to sustain children's play.

Do	**Don't**
• Plan daily free-play periods of a *minimum* of 30 minutes —with longer periods at least several times during the week.	• Use elimination of play or exclusion from the group as a means of punishment. (Disruptive children need experiences with other children and activities—but recall the three red flags.)
• Plan sustained times rather than brief periods scattered through the day.	• Use outdoor time just to get rid of wiggles, release tension, or reduce energy levels.
• Have sustained play periods when most (or all) of the children are present.	• Overload play periods with academic performance (counting, sorting, and so on).
• Reduce the amount and kinds of interruptions.	• Set unnecessary restrictions on children or uses of materials.
• Reinforce the importance of play with the children (in the physical environment, interest areas, stimulating materials and activities, and so on), in staff training (personal and curriculum development), and interaction with parents (interest areas, workshops, newsletters, meetings, informal conversations, community events, check-out materials, and so on).	• Let adults dominate the play of the children.
• Help the children to be successful in play activities.	• Be unnecessarily restrictive on the noise or activity level in the classroom and playground.
• Plan frequent opportunities to play outdoors.	• Provide props (books, clothing, occupation, and so on) that encourage gender, cultural, economic, or other biases.
• Vary the kinds of play and vary the manner of play (repetitive or prolonged).	• Provide materials that could cause harm or danger to the children.
• Watch for the interest levels of children and provide items that will increase their participation and development.	• Use materials that are especially fragile.
• Frequently add new materials or activities to stimulate their thinking.	• Promote games that exclude children because of skills.
• Observe the children carefully in order to meet their individual and group needs.	• Expect children to be excited over a long period of time with the same toys.
	• Expect the children to have the same interests, skills, and attention span.

Figure 3.3   Hints for Sustaining Children's Play

Notable Quotes

From "What Grownups Understand about Child Development": Source of National Survey commissioned by Zero to Three, Civitas Initiative, and Brio Corporation (June/July 2000).

Many parents and other adults regard play as an important part of a child's development based on research that shows it as a factor in healthy development (reading and/or talking with their child(ren), providing a sense of safety and security, etc. (Lally, Lerner, & Lurie-Hurvitz, 2001, pp. 50–53)

Parents and child development researchers differ on some forms of play for helping a child's intellectual development. For example:

Parents rated as "very effective" for helping 2-year-olds develop intellectually:

educational flashcards (68%); solitary play on the computer (48%); educational TV (62%) (p. 51)

Early childhood research confirms that play is critical for the healthy development of all ages (references).

Parents *incorrectly* believe:

that children get an equal benefit from hearing someone talk on TV as hearing them in the same room (32%);

that play is more important for older (5-year-olds) than younger children (10-month-olds);

that play is very important for a 5-year-old's healthy development (86% of all adults versus 71% of parents and 60% of all adults who believe this is so for a 10-month-old); and

that "children usually have stronger bonds with parents who do not work and stay at home than they do with parents who work full-time outside of the home" (a large majority of adults—53% of moms and 72% of dads) (p. 52).

Blocks

Blocks are important in the education of young children both at home and at school.

The importance of block usage is reflected in the many early proponents of blocks. (see Table 3.5.)

Types and Use

Blocks are of many different kinds: large and hollow with handle openings, solid, unit, dimensionally proportioned, plastic, cardboard, vinyl, or fabric. Some are intended for use on the floor, others for use on tables. They are made in different sizes, shapes, and colors. Children enjoy putting blocks together to make new shapes or color combinations. Dramatic play is often enhanced with the addition of props to blocks. Two areas in the center may be joined together with the use of blocks (blocks and trucks, blocks used to enclose a reading area, and so on).

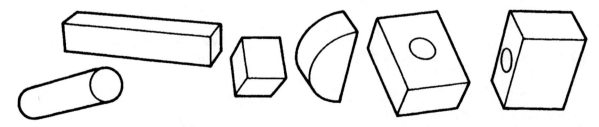

Table 3.5 Early Promoters and Contributions to Block Building

Proponent	Time Frame	Contribution
Plato	429–345 B.C.	Block play is mentioned in his writings.
Comenius	1592–1670	Block play is mentioned in his writings.
John Locke	1693	"Learning anything they should be taught, might be made as much a recreation to their play, as their play is to learning." (*Some Thoughts Concerning Education*)
Johann Pestalozzi	1746–1827	Hands-on learning.
Frederick Froebel	1826–1887	Influenced by Pestalozzi (hands-on). Froebel's blocks were austere and monochromatic, and emphasized the structural relationships between units. His ideas were highly abstract, symbolized by blocks and other three-dimensional materials; the fact that children were given physical objects to play with as the basis for learning revolutionized early childhood education (Hewitt, 2001, p. 9). By the 1890s his materials and methods were under attack by kindergarten reformers, who criticized the formal, sequential use of the gifts, the lack of what they considered self-determined purpose in the child's play, the small size of the items, and the emphasis on sedentary activities (Hewitt, 2001, p. 9).
John Dewey	1859–1952	His philosophy implied radical change in curriculum (physical activity, free play, democracy, cooperation, field trips, etc.) He coined the word *occupation* to describe the "focused doing" of children.
Milton Bradley	1836–1911	An enterprising lithographer who began manufacturing "Gifts and Occupations" for the American school market (Hewitt, 2001, p. 9).
Maria Montessori	1870–1952	"Using her objective and scientific observation skills, she saw how young children learn and what they are naturally drawn to learn at various ages and stages of development. . . All children around the world experience these stages, each child in his or her own time" (Kramer, 1976). Her designed materials were monochromatic (or of natural color) and emphasized the structural relationships between units. At Casa dei Bambini in Italy, Montessori originated a series of blocks called "didactic materials" based on the systematic training of the senses as a way for children to understand the world. She designed the "Pink Tower," a nine-unit tower of solid pink blocks graduated in size and small enough for immature hands to use on a table. In *Spontaneous Activity in Education,* she describes her materials to analyze and represent things of dimension, forms, colors, texture, weight, temperature, flavor, and sound. She explains, "It is the qualities of the object, not the objects themselves, which are important, although these qualities, isolated one for the other, are themselves represented by objects" (1970, p. 203).
Jean Piaget	1896–1980	Piaget was a strong believer in make-believe play and hands-on learning. Blocks fit nicely into his theory.
Patty Smith Hill	1868–1946	As a member of the faculty of Teachers College/Columbia University (1905), Hill questioned the lack of free play, the need for large-motor activity, and the needs of the child as a social being. These concerns led to her modification and design of larger blocks (in a series, square pillars, and metal rods that secured the pieces), first manufactured by the Schoenhut Company in Philadelphia (these were modified in form into the 1950s). Because of their size and weight, the blocks necessitated the involvement and cooperation of several children to construct a building (Hewitt, 2001, p. 9).

(continued)

Table 3.5   continued

Proponent	Time Frame	Contribution
Caroline Pratt	1913	Her materials were austere and monochromatic, emphasizing the structural relationships between the units. Educated in woodworking training in Sweden, Pratt developed unit system blocks for her experimental classroom at Harley House and at the City and Country School she helped found in New York City. She designed "do-withs," wooden figures of family and community workers, to accompany the unit blocks. Her designs and pioneering work on block use focused on the block work of children 14 months to 3 years old at the Nursery School, a project of Bureau of Educational Experiments, organized in New York City in 1917 by Harriet Johnson, Caroline Pratt, and Lucy Sprague Mitchell. "The City and Country School and Bank Street School for Children still carry on this strong block-building tradition." (Hewitt, 2001, p. 10).
J. Crandall, S. L. Hill, & R. Bliss		The alphabet and pictures blocks manufactured by these individuals were "decorated with colorful images, following Locke's idea of mixing pleasure with learning" (Hewitt, 2001, p. 9).

Good planning should go into the purchase of blocks. All blocks should be designed to fit together mathematically, each size twice as long or wide as the preceding size. Not only will they serve better purposes in building, but they will stack compactly when not in use. All types of blocks should be either shellacked or waxed. This finish will be more practical than paint.

Introduction of Blocks into the Curriculum for Young Children

Children have countless ways to use blocks: in building and knocking down; with enclosures and gaps, adjusting and readjusting. They have great interest in and spend endless time with blocks—using versatility and originality.

The perception of children's block play has implications for early-childhood teacher education. Teachers need to be aware of (1) how to facilitate children's social play, (2) how to encourage children's active problem solving while working with the medium, (3) how to evaluate complexity and quality of the children's work, and (4) how and when to in-

---

Notable Quotes

The rich potential of blocks as a learning tool for young children to invent and represent ideas is still a challenge for teachers today (Hewitt, 2001, p. 12).

Children have built, knocked down, enclosed, made gaps, pushed, designed and redesigned, and thoroughly enjoyed the versatility and origination of blocks (Hewitt, 2001, p. 12).

"Children's impulse to construct is inherent and connected to learning is an old idea" (Hewitt, 2001, p. 6).

"Although many theorists study the play behavior of children, only a few go on to design play/learning material and to write passionately about its use" (Hewitt, 2001, p. 9).

tervene in the activity. Findings from studies reveal that high-quality play environments also create more complex block structures (Eberly and Golbeck, 2001).

An excellent way to help young children learn about their community is through expression with blocks, which give them the opportunity to recreate the world they have physically explored (or will explore) and to learn how they can locate themselves in space (Seefeldt, 1997).

Unit blocks are favorites of teachers and children in most preschools, nursery schools, kindergartens, special-needs units, and many homes. They are enjoyed by children of all ages and often involve families and/or older children. They can be used as math manipulatives (early and advanced exercises), floor toys, table toys, and other ways of expressing one's interests. They can support and enhance learning in various areas of curricula.

One note of caution: Block play may be constructive or destructive—a fact that makes some adults shy away from it. It can invite quiet or active play. Children need an environment with open-ended materials and teachers who understand, encourage, build on, and even participate in a basic and complex mode of learning. This includes having enough

➤ space devoted to block play;
➤ time set aside for serious and ongoing play;
➤ focus on block work as evidenced by teachers' interaction with children through observation, documentation, revising structures, and sometimes participating in the play process; and
➤ time for teachers to share observations with colleagues and understand how children's block play connects with the development of other curriculum and personal areas (Hewitt, 2001, p. 12).

A teacher wanted to promote block play with a group of 4-year-old children. The space in the room was limited, so she moved out part of the furniture and the domestic equipment. The first day after the equipment was gone, the children all asked, "Who took our stove?" "Where did the refrigerator go?" They wandered around aimlessly. The second day, they noticed a stack of large blocks in the corner and began using the blocks in their play. By the end of the week, they had experienced many joys from using these blocks— They worked cooperatively and came up with some rather ingenious ideas—including making furniture. The use of blocks was no longer a problem.

Plenty of space and uninterrupted time are necessary for good block play. As in the preceding example, equipment can be moved to another area or room if necessary to provide sufficient floor space. Because of the noise they create, blocks are used on a rug or carpet if at all possible. This protects the blocks from damage when they tumble down, keeps the children's knees from a cold or hard surface, and softens sounds.

Blocks should be out of the traffic pattern. For several days, two children had tried to build a block fence to house some new farm animals. Every time they got ready to play with their creation, either someone knocked it down or they had to pick it up. This day they were determined to have success. Quickly they gathered up the needed blocks and animals. They selected a different spot and started building. Soon one child after another rushed past and down went the blocks. In total disgust, they complained to the next child, who replied, "I didn't mean to—but I just had to get in to the toilet." The children had selected the most vulnerable spot in the room—right in front of the bathroom door!

A unit of time should be allotted to use a completed structure. At one center, day after day the children played that they were going to Africa to catch zoo animals. One child had recently been to a nearby zoo and had shared his ideas. Seeing how sustained the play was, the teacher began the basic structure so the children could finish it and get on with their trip to Africa. Otherwise, they never would have been able to play—they would always be building!

The teacher should be conscious of the time and warn the children in advance to end the activity at the appropriate time. Sometimes good constructive play can be continued and some other activity shortened or eliminated. Simply saying, "It's almost time to pick up the blocks," or "It will soon be time for snack" gives the children an opportunity to prepare to end the activity. If possible, the structure is left up for later play.

The teacher should indicate to the children what the guidelines are for the block area. She should be nearby, but need not actively participate. Her verbal support is often enough to sustain activity in this area.

When structures get too tall or wobbly, a positive suggestion redirects the activity. Statements such as "Build as high as your nose," or "It's time to start another stack," are usually readily accepted by the children. Safety is important. The teacher should show appreciation for a structure but avoid overemphasis, never giving the children the idea that they must make certain structures in order to gain approval.

To interest children in the block area, a teacher may have to provide a pacesetter, that is, an eye-catcher or attention-getter. It should not be elaborate—just attract the children. One day it may be a tall structure, another day a farm or single block road leading to transportation vehicles.

In addition to those early promoters previously listed in Table 3.5, consider the thoughts of Vygotsky and Piaget listed in Figure 3.4.

Vygotsky

Because he died at the age of 38, his work was suppressed by the Russian government, and he was a contemporary of Piaget, Vygotsky's work was not well known during his life.

He had some very specific ideas regarding children and play including the following:

1. Make-believe
   (a) is the ultimate activity for nurturing capacities that are crucial for academics as well as later-life success (Berk & Winsler, 1995, p. 79);
   (b) helps children understand the meaning and function of culture, life plans, and volitional motives (Vygotsky, 1978, p. 2);
   (c) is valuable for stretching children's development (zone of proximal development): Children function above their normal level of ability when challenged by peers in their play.
2. Play has two critical features: "all representational play creates an imaginary situation that permits the child to grapple with unrealized desires, and it contains rules for behavior that children must follow to successfully act out the play scene" (Berk, 1994, p. 32). This theory is described as a sociocultural theory (Berk & Winsler, 1995, p. 100); learning and development combine in a complex interrelated fashion such that *instruction leads*, or *elicits, development*.
3. Language is central; teachers ask real and important questions to determine what children know about the world. There are no single "right answers." The child is active; social environments collaborate to produce development (Berk & Winsler, 1995, p. 101).
4. Vygotsky's main tenet is that "people are products of their social and cultural worlds and that to understand children, we must understand the social, cultural, and societal contexts in which they develop" (Berk & Winsler, 1995, p. 12).
5. Four distinct characteristics of Vygotsky-based curricular reform in his early childhood classrooms are:
   (a) heavy emphasis on teacher-child and child-child relationships;
   (b) use of whole language theory rather than meaningless drills;
   (c) relevant activities related to children's interests and competencies; and
   (d) suggested broadening of the ZPD (Zone of Proximal Development) to expert partners, such as mixed-age grouping (Moll & Whitmore, 1993).
6. *Scaffolding,* a term not introduced by Vygotsky but used to describe his work, denotes important components of tutoring (Wood, 1989) and connotes and supports a sensitive cooperation promoting children to take over more responsibility for tasks as their skill increases (Berk & Winsler, 1995, p. 32).
7. Play is valuable for stretching children's zone of proximal development through challenges of peers and play.

Figure 3.4   Some Thoughts About Play from Vygotsky and Piaget

Piaget

Piaget's influence began in the 1950s, accelerated in the 1960s, and is still prominent today. Piaget was an early contemporary of Lev Vygotsky, but Piaget and his work became more widely known because of Vygotsky's early death and the suppression of Vygotsky's writings.

Piaget's theories included the following:
1. Activity directed by the child is primary in his/her development (Van Hoorn et al., 1993, p. 237).
2. Through her own initiative and effort, the child modifies and builds upon already constructed mental patterns to try to make sense of new experiences (Cowan, 1978).
3. Knowledge is based on what the individual child brings to each situation rather than on what is accumulated from the environment (Van Hoorn et al., 1993, p. 15).
4. Children's thought becomes more like that of adults when they become developmentally ready to notice their own deficiencies in immature, illogical reasoning and abandon it in favor of a logical approach to the world. Indeed, Piaget regarded the thought of the young child and that of more mature peers and adults not as collaborative and complementary but rather as in conflict (Tudge & Winterhoff, 1993, p. 74).
5. His work is described as a cognitive-developmental theory: Children "construct" their own knowledge, facilitated by the teacher, through reflection on their experiences, their choices, and their playing with peers. Learning and development are separate entities, identical, and lead to development (Berk & Winsler, 1995, pp. 100–103).
6. He was a strong supporter of play and hands-on experiences. He believed that children progress through universal and invariant sequences of development (maturation and transaction), with each stage marked by a characteristic way of organizing thoughts and activities; in other words, children actually think differently than adults. (See Chapter 1.) He encouraged learning centers with materials for art, block play, writing, drawing, dramatic play, and exploration with raw materials (dirt, sand, water, and so on) for both individual and group projects (DeVries & Kohlberg, 1987; Wasserman, 1990).

Both Vygotsky and Piaget
1. Both credit each other for help developing their theories—Vygotsky (1934/1987) about Piaget's work on self-directed speech in cognitive development and Piaget (1962/1979) about Vygotsky's interpretation of egocentric speech. They both started with the same basic view of the child as a biological organism. Vygotsky explored how social experience might cause important revisions in the child's thinking to come about (Berk & Winsler, 1995, p. 109). Piaget focused on what it is within the organism that leads to cognitive change. Because both shared basic beliefs about development, the two theories are best viewed as complementary rather than in opposition to one another, as checks and balances (Glassman, 1994, p. 186).
2. Both educators' theories have become influential in the educational theory and practice of the 1970s, 1980s, and 1990s, and into the 2000s.
3. They both place emphasis on play in intellectual development and provide strong arguments for children's use of objects and in interaction with peers as the basis for early childhood curriculum.
4. Both note that play characterizes language, artistic, and literacy activities during the preschool years (Berk & Winsler, 1995, p. 31).
5. Both recognize that pretense allows children to become familiar with social role possibilities. In cultures around the world, young children act out family scenes and highly visible occupations. In this way, play provides children with important insights into the link between self and wider society (Berk & Winsler, 1995, p. 79).
6. "Young children who especially enjoy pretending or who are given encouragement to engage in fantasy play score higher on tests of imagination and creativity" (Dansky, 1980; Pepler & Ross, 1981).
7. "In sum, fantasy play continues to social maturity and the construction of diverse aspects of cognition. When children use play objects in novel ways, the objects seem to stimulate the discovery of new relationships and enhance children's ability to think flexibly and inventively" (Berk & Winsler, 1995, p. 34).

Figure 3.4 continued

Reflection

What is the role of the adult in helping each child feel that he/she can succeed in the following circumstances:

1. Activities that are open-ended (flexible): blocks, dramatic play, art, (add more).
2. Activities that are closed-ended (one right way): puzzles, handling animals, use of some toys, number of persons in one activity or area, for specific purposes—hopefully these are limited.
3. Setting up and cleaning up play areas.
4. Interacting with new toys, different peers, guests, and/or animals.
5. Separating from a parent.
6. Add some of your own favorites.

The Role of the Teacher Is Continuing, Important, and Diverse

The teacher's role depends upon the experience, knowledge, and opportunities provided in the curriculum. The role is *always* important and can make a difference as to how activities and opportunities are received by children and other adults. In giving chores to young children, we need to convey that chores are important and that we value their work

Ways to Encourage Young Children

One of the important roles of the adult is to adapt to children of specific development: infants *(lap children);* toddlers *(knee children);* preschoolers *(yard children);* community children *(school agers);* taking into consideration the cognitive and socioemotional developmental stages, the children's roles, and the adult roles (Whiting & Edwards, 1988, p. 69).

Assurances, such as success, nurturing, self-awareness, willingness to take risks, natural curiosity, positive self-esteem, and others, help children believe that they can succeed. Wald (2000) has summed these characteristics into one word: *empowerment.* It is gained through daily activities of children wherever they may be. "Empowerment is not a subject in which teachers need extensive training." When they are aware of its importance, they find numerous ways to help empower the young children in their charge, such as a smile, a hug, verbal expression, and the like. Children need to feel they are loved because of who they are! They can settle their own arguments and help each other without teacher assistance. "Our job as teachers, once we have prepared the setting, was mainly to sit on the sidelines, watch, and take notes. . . . But while watching the kids, we came to realize that their free invention and intuitive thoughts were clearly assets" (Cartwright, 2000, p. 13).

From the writings of **Piaget** and other developmental theorists, we learn that children can be motivated to explore the world around them. Based on **Dewey's and Dewey's students'** writings and teachings, proponents of developmentally appropriate practice have for a century been refining ways of capturing this natural motivation to learn by involving children in project planning, "learning through doing" personally meaningful yet worthwhile concepts and skills. **Eriksonians** emphasize the industriousness of children

Reflection

As a dedicated, creative teacher of young children, consider providing new play "work" opportunities to involve the young children you teach. Possible suggestions:

Seasonal Activities: Weather: hot, cold, stormy, windy, arid, etc.
Holidays: Local, national, traditional.
Local Interest: Culture, building, landscapes, animals, agriculture, etc.
Inhabitants: Special groups (handicapped, culture), artists, athletes, musicians, occupations, etc.
Specific Interests: You add these.
Current Event/Activity Initiated in the Classroom: book, visitor, animal, weather, etc.

How do you intend to prepare the children, the environment, and parents for each event? What values are there in each event for children, teachers, and families?

in the preschool age group as having a strong innate urge to become competent and to motivate children to self-select challenging tasks that "make them think" (Hauser-Cram, 1998, p. 69).

Young children who especially enjoy pretending or who are given encouragement to engage in fantasy play:

➤ score higher on tests of imagination and creativity;
➤ use play objects in novel ways (objects seem to stimulate the discovery of new relationships and enhance children's ability to think flexibly and inventively);
➤ spend more time in sociodramatic play;
➤ are advanced in general intellectual development;
➤ show an enhanced ability to understand the feelings of others; and
➤ are seen as more socially competent by their teachers (Burns & Brainerd, 1979; Connolly & Doyle, 1984).

According to Frost (1992), teachers would be wise to remember that "insensitive, unskilled, excessive intervention in children's play by adults can interrupt the flow of play themes, block leadership roles of children, encourage dependency on adults, stifle self-confidence, and lead to the breakdown of play itself" (p. 34).

Throughout this book the theme of meeting the needs of children individually and in groups will be stressed. Children with special needs—whether it be developmental, cultural, racial, or whatever—are recognized and identified for the kind of help they require without putting undue attention or pressure on the individual children, the school, or the home. Some children will need experiences scaled down, and others will need them scaled up; some need to interact in small groups, and others benefit from action with large groups; some must remain inside the classroom (for health and safety reasons), and other react better in open spaces and fresh air. Teachers should make every effort to see that opportunities are open-ended—they can be terminated or expanded at any point. If a child has a disability, activities will be modified to fit individual needs and/or situations.

Parent participation with their developmentally delayed children builds a special bond between them.

Toys and Materials

Often parents buy toys too advanced for children, hoping the children will be ready for them early—almost like buying a pair of shoes that are too large now but hoping the child will get more use out of them as his feet grow! Perhaps parents lack buying knowledge of what is characteristic for different ages. Frequently parents buy toys that interest them (the parents) in hopes that their children will also be interested. The best advice to offer parents and to sustain a child's play is to buy toys that match the child's abilities and interests.

For the young child the best types of toys are those that offer a variety of uses. Wind-up toys may be interesting for the moment, but then what do you do with them? Building materials, art materials, and other versatile toys stimulate the imagination and provide many hours of pleasure and exploration. Toys have to be fun, evocative, and creative; interactive toys stretch the child's imagination.

Complex toys often hinder play; the simpler the toy, the more complex the play. As Albert Einstein once said, "Imagination is more important than knowledge."

Although computers can be educational, they don't teach children how to get along with people—the kinds of lessons you learn from a good old-fashioned board game or a box of building materials. (See the discussion in Chapter 8 about computers.)

Parents at home and teachers at school should be aware of the pressure they place on children to always be doing something, have something to show for their time, show positive changes in behavior, mature too rapidly in all areas of development, and be popular.

Teachers can obtain a current catalog from any manufacturer of toys for young children.

Outdoor Play

The role of the teacher outdoors is (but is not limited to):

➤ to provide for the individual child and her needs
➤ to "pace" the area to be inviting and stimulating
➤ to set up and maintain necessary limits
➤ to be flexible in her teaching
➤ to provide a variety of experiences in the fresh air
➤ to stimulate and encourage children to explore
➤ to appreciate the interests and enthusiasm of the children
➤ to enjoy being with the children
➤ to exhibit a positive attitude toward outdoor play
➤ to meet the needs of both girls and boys while removing superficial or real barriers related to gender, race, culture, or other destructive measures
➤ to see play as a fun but growth-stimulating opportunity for young children in all the developmental domains
➤ to enlarge children's vision of and participation in areas where they feel less secure (woodworking, climbing)
➤ to take some risks in activity planning and supervision, to respond to individual learning styles, and to initiate ways to combine interests and activities of the children
➤ "to act as a catalyst to help children experience and enjoy sociodramatic play and to improve each child's ability to extend and elaborate play themes" (Smilansky & Shefatya, 1990)
➤ to prepare "the environment and schedule blocks of time for play, intervening as matchmaker, peacekeeper, or coach" (Nourot & Van Hoorn, 1991)

Young children need time and equipment for developing motor skills.

Planning an Outdoor Play Area

The playground should provide large areas of space away from equipment. A garden or digging area provides many opportunities for children to use proper tools, to plant, and to harvest. Free-flowing paths are inviting to fast-paced youngsters, too. They resemble curves found on modern highways.

As a result of playing and building outdoors, a child adds to her experiences. Crates and large wooden cartons are fun to build with, as are old tires, wooden and metal frames, and boards. The weight of the object should challenge but not tax the ability of a child. She will also learn about cooperation, interdependence, independence, balance, size, and gravity. Through use of her body, she will develop skills and dexterity.

Following are suggestions for types of areas and items for an outdoor play area:

aesthetic design (color arrangement, variety)
animals
areas: domestic, open, private, planning, running
art materials
barrels
bedspread over box
blocks (hollow)
boards for crawling, jumping, bouncing
boxes (large packing)
cars (doors removed)
climbers (wood, metal), rings, ropes, poles, platform
clocks
cockpit
easels
fishing net
gardening equipment and plot
gas pump
housekeeping items (dolls, dishes, dress-up clothes)
inner tubes
ladders (horizontal or perpendicular; made of rope, wood, or metal)
levers
nets over frames
obstacle course
parachute

personal preferences
plants, flowers
playhouse
pulley
pumps (water, tire)
punching bag
radios
ramps
ropes (use with caution)
saddle
sand tools and toys
sawhorses
shovels
signs (road)
slides
sounds: pleasant, varied
stick horses
storage
storm drainpipe
surfaces: grass, dirt, asphalt
swing (tire)
tent
terrarium
trees
trucks, cars
trunk, suitcases
water and toys
wheel toys (wagons, tricycles)
woodworking equipment

Safety

Whether play materials are used indoors or outdoors, safety must be of utmost concern. Unbroken, nontoxic, well-fitting toys should always be used. Activities that include possible danger should be either closely supervised or not used at all. Woodworking is an example. It has so many developmental values for children that to exclude it would be unfortunate; however, when woodworking is used, the teacher must remain with the tools, must define the guidelines for participation, must provide tools that are appropriate and in good working condition, and must feel comfortable about working with the children.

Some areas or activities (indoors and outdoors) require more supervision than others. The teacher should make sure children have opportunities to get, use, and replace materi-

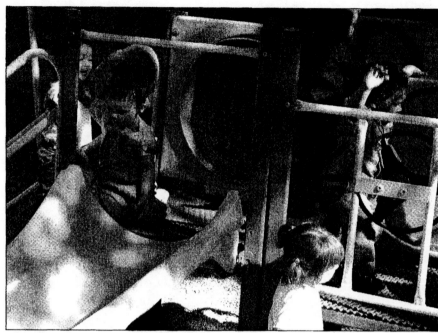

Motor skills are easily developed when proper equipment and supervision are available.

als independent of teacher direction. Occasional teacher contact or interaction may sustain children in an activity or may encourage them to try different methods. When a teacher has thought through the entire activity (preparation, availability, use, and cleanup), there is less chance of misuse of materials, inappropriate behavior, or danger. When children are climbing, running, or particularly activity, accidents may happen. Teacher awareness of these activities, or of particular children, can reduce possible problems. When accidents do happen, teachers must be quick, accurate, and calm in handling them.

Indoor Precautions

A number of safety factors inside the facility need the close attention of teachers and parents. They include but are not limited to the following:

Facilities

- Floor space, floor coverings and furniture
- Lighting and heating (including cords for cooking)
- Alarms (smoke, open doors, unsafe areas)
- Exits/entrances; emergency exit plan
- Water temperature (for water activities)

Personnel

- Adequate supervision; behavior limits

Classroom materials

- Art materials (see Table 6.1: Safety in Art Materials)
- Houseplants (may be poisonous) (See Alber et al, 1990; Taylor, 1997)
- Toys (some have small parts that could be swallowed)
- Pets (some may be unfriendly, have been mistreated, or carry diseases)

Outdoor Precautions

Two of the most important things to remember about play (whether it occurs indoors or outdoors, whether it is solitary or group, whether it is loud or quiet) are safety and supervision! Supervision has been defined as:

➤ being alert and attentive (moving around, eye contact, hazards, etc.)
➤ being aware of age-appropriate equipment (different ages and abilities)
➤ evaluating hazards (being aware, following up)
➤ observing signs (special ages for specific equipment)
➤ knowing safe playground rules (observing, enforcing)
➤ intervening when inappropriate behavior occurs (warning, following through)
➤ ensuring safe children's clothing (avoid strings and loose clothing)
➤ being prepared (first-aid kit, attention to injuries, supervision)

For government safety requirements, see Figure 3.5.

Values for Children

Dramatic Play

Children often reenact what they see or hear at home. To them, this reenactment is realistic living, not dramatic play, and helps them understand the adult world. Anything is possible: A child can be an adult, a child, a community worker, or whatever she likes. Roles change rapidly. Such play should be encouraged. Studies indicate that playful children are more advanced in their ability to think divergently than are their nonplayful counterparts. Note the learning young children can gain from dramatic play in Figure 3.6.

Outdoor Play

Often overlooked or underestimated, outdoor play is essential for the health and well-being of young children. The traditional school model contends that outside activities are to rejuvenate children (and teachers) and inside activities are for learning. How far from the truth! Anything that can be done inside a classroom can also be done on the playground—art, music, science, socialization, physical development, and on and on.

When weather permits, move easels and paint, dramatic play, music and movement, obstacle courses, wheel toys, and typically indoor activities onto the playground. In inclement weather, some climbing pieces, selected wheel toys, and open classroom space provide some of the opportunities often limited to the outdoor areas.

Typical *indoor* resources include furniture, art, music, dramatic play, block play, manipulative materials, movement experiences, food preparation, mathematics, science, language, resting areas, and sometimes water play.

Outdoor resource centers usually allow for greater action, more noise, sometimes an incline or hill, sand, water, swings, a climbing apparatus, playhouses, blocks, woodworking and carpentry, loose materials, a gardening area, animals, a group-activity area, a wheel-toy area, a quiet place, and a natural area. Creative teachers plan to integrate activities and areas to give greater flexibility and more interest to the children whether in indoor or outdoor areas. Materials for sensorimotor, construction, and dramatic play outdoors include those shown in Table 3.6.

Often teachers use outdoor equipment and space with less planning than for indoor activities. Stationary equipment is always available and may become the only activity on the playground unless some other focal point is provided daily, such as climbing apparatus arranged in a new or stimulating way, sturdy tools for gardening, games, musical activities, stick horses, and wheel toys.

Playground Safety

Check all the Soil on Playgrounds for Contamination

Playgrounds can be wonderful places for young children to play and learn. They can also be headaches for teachers. Well designed, appropriately placed climbing equipment, and sensitively arranged play areas can provide hours of exercise, camaraderie, growth, and enjoyment.

During the past two decades, Consumer Products Safety Council (**CPSC**) statistics have shown a dramatic increase in playground-related injuries. It is estimated that every two and a half minutes a child is treated in an emergency room for playground-related injuries. This does not include the children whose injuries receive treatment outside the emergency room. Clearly, efforts are needed to ensure safer play environment for the children of our nation's playgrounds. Statistics are based on the U.S. Consumer Product Safety Commission's National Electronic Injury Surveillance System (NEISS), which collects only playground-related injuries that are recorded in more than 90 hospital emergency room departments located in the United States. (Source: National Program for Playground Safety (**NPPS**) brochure *Working to Make America's Playgrounds SAFE*).

In updating guidelines for public playgrounds occupied after January 26, 1993, the **CPSC** made two changes that are significant for the child care industry: including child care facilities in its definition of "public" playgrounds and, even more important, including specific playground guidelines for preschool children ages 2 to 5. Title III requirements of the Americans with Disabilities Act (ADA) pertain to places of public accommodation, including more than five million private establishments—among them **private schools and day-care centers,** according to highlights from the law published by the Department of Justice.

"Public Playground Safety Checklist," available from **CPSC,** lists 10 important tips for parents and community groups. To obtain a copy, write: Playground Checklist, CPSC, Washington DC 20207; call **CPSC**'s toll-free hotline at 1-800-638-2772; or visit **CPSC**'s website at www.cpsc.gov. Another brochure, "Is your home playground a safe place to play?" is available from the same phone number and website.

The first mention of "age-appropriateness" by **CPSC** appeared in *Landscape Structures,* Fall 1992, p. 1.

The **NPPS** examined child care centers, schools and parks in a nationwide survey of playgrounds. The second half of their study from 1998–99 included 1,699 playgrounds in 23 states. The average grade for all 3,052 playgrounds in all 50 states reveals that the United States is still within the "C" range, earning an average grade of C. http://www.uni.edu/playground/report.html, 12-22-01. Call 1-800-554-PLAY (National Program for Playground Safety, 2001).

Child Injuries

Some children are accident-prone; some are more susceptible to accidents when they are hungry, fatigued, or inexperienced, or when equipment is new and challenging. Staff should be especially alert on the playground around climbing equipment, with tools (woodworking, cooking), with overstimulated children, and in crowded facilities. Young children **can** be taught how to use toys and equipment safely.

Through an awareness program, children and parents can learn and practice safety measures at school and home. Items to include are activities for children to hear, see, and practice, and articles sent to the home for parental awareness and implementation (pedestrian safety, poison safety, water safety, gun safety, pollution, and others).

"Each year, over 200,000 children are injured on America's playgrounds. That's one every 2½ minutes" (**NPPS** Safety School, http://www.uni.edu/playground/school.html, 12-22-01).

The American Academy of Orthopedic Surgeons (**AAOS**) says that nearly 270,000 children under age 15 were treated in hospital emergency rooms for injuries related to playground equipment in a previous year. Since then **AAOS** began a national public education campaign, "Play It Safe," based on the playground guidelines of **CPSC.**

Over a decade ago, the Centers for Disease Control (**CDC**) conducted a study of playground hazards at 58 child care centers in Atlanta, Georgia; identified the hazards at these playgrounds; pointed them out to the director at each center; and gave playground safety instruction to the directors. Licensing inspectors returned to the sites two years later and found that "the sites where directors had been shown the hazards and given information about them actually had higher hazard scores. . . . Playgrounds sites that had changed directors had fewer hazards." Pointing out hazards and providing information to directors was not enough to correct hazardous situations; therefore researchers suggested several interventions: more explicit regulations, better training of regulators, support for enforcement of regulations, more extensive training of child-care directors, increasing parental awareness, and posting of the inspection report in a conspicuous place at the center. A follow-up study has not be located.

Figure 3.5   Government Safety Programs

- To interact with other children (with age, ability, and interest differences): to develop personal relationships
- To cooperate: sharing and turn taking, being a productive member of society
- To experience different types of curricula: art, music, language, and so on
- To take and experiment with different roles
- To communicate: social skills, negotiation, expressing ideas
- To attain personal goals and act within appropriate limits
- To explore and experiment with their environment
- To exercise their imaginations and ideas
- To take responsibility (roles, preparation, cleanup)
- To understand others: gender roles, cultures, privileges, responsibilities, empathy, and so on
- To enjoy themselves, others, the environment, and so on
- To develop initiative, accountability, social competence, and so on
- To identify pleasurable activities; to find positive ways to release energy and ideas
- To play with other children, regardless of developmental delays or behavior advancement

Figure 3.6   What Do Young Children Learn from Dramatic Play?

Good planning is necessary for maximum use of the playground and its equipment. The area can be beautiful yet functional, with space for freedom of movement. Needs of the children can be provided for without a great deal of cost.

The children should play outside independently, but not unsupervised. Equipment and activities should provide opportunities to make decisions, try ideas, work, and play with others without fear of harm or destruction. The focal point should be obvious to the children and should attract them to it, either to use as provided or to stimulate their creativity.

Of course, the attractiveness of the playground is important for children to enjoy the area; however, the design and appearance will not ensure that the area will meet the needs of the young child. Adults who plan outdoor play areas must consider the goals and objectives for children's development. And in line with other learning areas, toys and activities should be age-appropriate for the development of the children, especially their large-muscle involvement. Some areas should be refined for social skills; there should be opportunities to solve problems using both physical and social skills; there should be enhancement of relationships (such as in/out, up/down, over/under, high/medium/low, heavy/light, hard/soft, and fast/slow); creativity should be expressed through art, carpentry, music, movement, and

Table 3.6   Props for Construction and Dramatic Play Outdoors

Type of Play	Props
Sandbox	Water, bottle caps for decoration, rocks and sticks, bowls, cups, wooden spoons; small trucks and cars; small people and animals
Art	Easel with paints, paper, and brushes; collage materials; dough
Music and movement	Record or cassette player, records or tapes, streamers, musical instruments, balls, hula hoops, scarves
Construction (exercise caution)	Large materials: wooden or cardboard crates, large blocks, large pieces of wood, vehicle tires, blanket or tarp, ladders, gardening tools
Dramatic play	Dress-up clothes, food cans, dolls, furniture, towels, drying rack, mirror, miscellaneous items
Water	Buckets, tubs, funnels, bowls, siphon, tubes, plastic containers, soap, washable items, brushes, towels
Wheel toys	Tricycles, wagons, carts, wheelbarrows, tires

*Toddlers
frequently engage
in solitary play.*

block building; opportunities should exist for physical knowledge about weather, growing seeds, animals, balance, distance and speed, and volume and shape; and the outdoor environment should be a comfortable place to eat, paint, read, and engage in other activities.

Teachers would be wise to remember that insensitive, unskilled, excessive intervention in children's play by adults can interrupt the flow of play themes, block leadership roles of children, encourage dependency on adults, stifle self-confidence, and lead to the breakdown of play itself.

Large-Muscle Development

The young child needs the proper equipment to help him exercise his large muscles. One of the most versatile is a good assortment of sturdy boxes and boards that can be moved easily and arranged in a manner stimulating to the interests and abilities of the children. Equipment constructed to take the abuse of energetic bodies should be brightly colored to attract attention. A board can be used directly on the ground for beginners, then raised to various levels as imaginations and skills dictate. One minute the board may be a road; the next, a bridge to crawl under. Boxes should be large enough for children to climb into, onto, or over. Boards and boxes can be combined into interesting obstacle courses. If funds are limited, large cardboard boxes can be obtained from floral, appliance, furniture, or grocery stores.

Outdoor play allows the children to connect with the community, to socialize, and to expand their horizons. On large, fixed equipment, children develop their bodies while experiencing basic physics (gravity, inertia, and optics [being upside down]).

A jungle gym or climbing apparatus of some kind (ladders, nets, trees, hills) that presents a variety of possibilities for activity is best. Such equipment stimulates imagination and exercises muscles as well.

A paved area should be provided for wheel toys. Tricycles and wagons can be used separately or jointly. Most pedal cars are difficult for preschoolers because the pedals and steering are not coordinated as they are on a tricycle. Some 5-year-olds are ready to ride a two-wheel bike but must constantly be reminded about safety (stopping, running into people and obstacles, going into traffic, and so on).

Swings have little to offer children between ages 2 and 5 (although the adult gets pushing practice). The 2-year-old is not coordinated enough to pump the swing; therefore, she gets no exercise and must depend on someone to push her. Accidents occur, also, because children walk into the path of the swing, or the swinging child decides to let go. Moreover, swinging takes a child away from group or active play. She has opportunities elsewhere (at home or in a park) for this type of experience. The 5-year-old, however, uses the swing in more advanced ways: pumping while sitting or standing, resting on her stomach, and twisting and turning in more cooperative and creative ways than the younger child.

Although large-muscle and cooperative activities are encouraged in young children, competitive games are best avoided, because the young child lacks the physical skills and emotional stability to make such competition a growth-promoting experience. Young children enjoy some appropriate outdoor games, but children should not be required to stay and play for a long period of time. Other activity suggestions include the following:

➤ A broom handle (or even a string) can be placed between two chairs or posts and the child encouraged to go under or over it at various heights.
➤ Tires or tubes help children release excess energy. Large truck or airplane tubes are exciting to roll in, climb through, jump on, and bounce on.
➤ Stick horses provide good exercise at a low price. They can be stored in tall garbage cans when not in use.
➤ Either blocks built for outdoor use or large barrels add interest to the playground.
➤ Large wooden or plastic carriers used by milk carriers make good stacking and storage units.
➤ Parachutes (or large sheets) provide fun and muscle practice.
➤ The play yard can be explored for such treasures as nests, insects, and rocks.
➤ Digging equipment of all kinds (sand, garden, and so on) encourages exploration and interest.
➤ Scientific equipment (pulleys, magnets, microscopes, and so on) takes on new challenges when used outdoors.
➤ The bottom and side beneath the handle of a gallon plastic container can be cut out to make a scoop for scoop ball. Partners throw and catch a ball or beanbag.

We like school; we like play; we like each other!

➤ A rope can be tied in a high place, such as a tree or the frame of a swing. Knots are made at 2- or 3-foot intervals so the child can sit on one knot while reaching for the next higher one and pulling himself up. Careful supervision is required.

➤ A steering wheel attached to a large wooden frame initiates interaction.

➤ Equipment can be put in different combinations or locations. In warm weather, materials and activities generally used inside can be taken outside.

More woodworking examples are discussed in Chapter 6.

Social Interaction or Dramatic Play

The theme and complexity of play depends on the age of the child. The 2-year-old child plays silently and alone. Variations continue up to the 5-year-old, who chatters incessantly, needs other children, and may initiate and continue elaborate play over a period of time lasting from minutes to days.

Much equipment discussed in this chapter stimulates socialization and group and dramatic play. Children often initiate an unusual use for a piece of equipment. For example, two children were building with large blocks when one discovered that his arrangement looked like a horse! (See Tables 3.4 and 3.5.)

Role playing takes on a new and vigorous light outdoors. The entire playground is the stage. A rowboat, for instance, provides hours of imaginative and co-operative play. It can be brightly painted and strategically placed, with some holes drilled in the bottom to facilitate drainage. Other similar possibilities are an old car frame, a tractor, or a cockpit from army surplus.

Strategically placed props can suggest and sustain dramatic play. For example, moving housekeeping items outside near a water outlet can encourage washing dishes or clothes, bathing dolls, pouring and measuring, and other activities that may be too messy to include indoors on a frequent basis. Or props such as a playhouse, a trunk, suitcases, occupational hats, and wheel toys bring new life, action, and practice for young children. Areas of partial seclusion (not unsupervised areas) bring excitement into the play of children (a small tent, large cardboard boxes, sheets or a parachute, low area dividers).

Sensory Experiences

Experiences with water are more fully undertaken outside than is possible inside. When weather permits, water makes an occasion special. Many parents object to their children's playing with water at home; opportunities should be provided at the center. Precautions are taken, of course, to see that children are properly dressed for this activity in bathing suits, boots, or cover-ups. Painting with water, sailing boats, or even watering plants can be fun. (See Chapter 6, Creative Arts, and Chapter 8, Science and Technology, for further suggestions about water experiences.) On a hot day, it is refreshing to let the hose run on the slide, cooling it and adding an extra zip as the children slide down. A wading pool filled with water at the end of the slide adds zest to the experience but must be closely supervised.

Sand is another item that is better used outdoors. It holds many possibilities, especially with the addition of props such as strainers, spoons, molds, buckets, shovels, cars, and various toys.

Creative art materials used outdoors can allow more freedom of movement and expression than materials used indoors. There need not be the degree of concern outside that there is inside—but if there is fear of spillage (of soap, which kills plants; paint that stains concrete; and so on) a cover of newspaper, plastic, or cardboard could be placed under especially messy activities. Placement of creative art materials outside should include

Toddlers rarely communicate with other children.

consideration of glare from the sun, disturbance or distraction by other activities, access to materials and cleanup items, sunburn of children, and the need for adult supervision.

Learning About Nature

The beauty and tranquility of the area will increase the children's enjoyment. A variety of flowers, a garden plot, an area for rest and relaxation, and a place to watch and listen assist children's learning.

The landscaping around the playground area can be planned to stimulate children's interest in nature. Shrubs of differing sizes, colors, and characteristics can be planted either in the ground or in large tubs. A large tree for climbing is desirable, if available. Check with a gardener or landscape architect to ensure that leaves, berries, shrubs, and other plantings are not poisonous or harmful to children if chewed, eaten, or touched. Planned experiences, such as feeders and animals, and unplanned ones, such as the weather and bugs, add to environmental learning.

Cumulative Value of Play (or the Child's Work)

Play is more than lining up to go outside and lining up to go inside. It is an opportunity for children to interact (work) individually or cooperatively, with ideas, materials, friends, activities, and time. Bronfenbrenner (1979) suggests that development occurs best in the context of an enduring, reciprocal relationship that is the basis for doing more—playing, loving, and working—and in which the balance of power shifts gradually in favor of the developing child. Readdick & Douglas (2000) say that we should be tending as much to providing legitimate work activities for our young charges as to providing chances for play and building strong positive adult-child relations (p. 63). They further state that "if we invite children to participate in the full spectrum of human activity, including work and play, developmental opportunities abound" (p. 64).

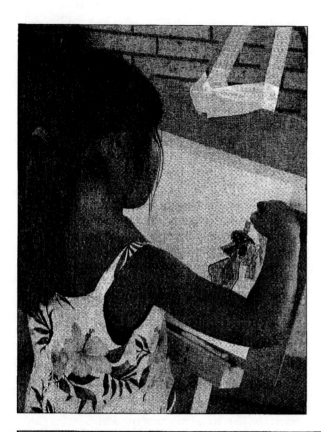

Having time, space, and proper materials, one can develop creative talents.

Notable Quotes

"Quite simply, *work* is the third necessary leg of the early childhood development stool." And "performance of tasks that are clearly related to the welfare and economy of the individual and the group appears to be a primary mechanism for learning to be responsible and nurturing" (Readdick & Douglas, 2000, p. 64). And further: "The more simple the society, the greater is the number of real work opportunities and the younger the age at which young children are assigned tasks to perform" (pp. 63–64).

John Dewey (1916) coined the word *occupation* to describe the focused doing of children. He declared:

"From an early age, however, there is no distinction of exclusive period of play activity and work activity, but only one of emphasis. There are definite results which even young children desire, and try to bring to pass. Their eager interest in sharing the occupations of others, if nothing else, accomplishes this. Children want to "help." They are anxious to engage in the pursuits of adults which effect external changes: setting the table, washing dishes, helping care for animals, etc." (1916, p. 239).

We may be "so dedicated to the importance of play in the child's life that we may be tempted to overlook the possibility that there are other avenues of development in addition to play that are important to encourage. One of these is experiencing pleasure in work" (Hendrick, 1992, p. 124).

Konner shares the following ideas about work:

Doing chores is not just about doing something necessary but also about feeling a part of something.

Developing skills and competence as a foundation for building self-concept and self-esteem and learning how to be helpful and to work well together are positive outcomes.

If the teacher does it all, it belongs to the teacher; if children do it, they feel it belongs to them too (1991, p. 65).

The "exercises of practical life" developed by Maria Montessori in her Casa dei Bambini acknowledged the centrality of work in young children's lives (Montessori, 1912; Standing, 1962). She emphasized real, as opposed to make-believe, activities performed with real tools in real environments, and exercises having to do with one's personal grooming and with one's environment (sweeping, chores). She wrote: "We teach the big ones to help the little ones, and so encourage the younger children to learn quickly to take care of themselves."

Violence and Children's Play

(Refer to Chapter 2 for additional information on violence and young children.)

Because of the importance of nonviolent play in early childhood education, additional information is presented here for careful thought and consideration.

One cannot discuss types of play (dramatic, skill, outdoor, solitary, and so on) without some focus on unacceptable, mainly violent, play that occurs when children get together. Parents as well as teachers need to know how to direct constructive, growth-promoting, and valuable play for young children.

Since the deregulation of children's media in 1984, there has been a steadily increasing amount of entertainment violence marketed to children, with the supporting linkup of toys to those TV shows. Manufacturers, who are driven more by profits than by what serves the best interest of children, have become a powerful influence over children, competing with teachers and parents in shaping children's values, behavior, and play. But a blanket disapproval of toys that glorify aggression and antagonism alienates children from their parents and teachers.

Adults have noted the increase of violence in the behavior of young children. Some adults (parents and teachers) have supported the behavior by providing certain toys, clothing, and activities to act out aggressiveness. Some teachers have banned such items from the classroom, only to find that while the banning gives children the strong message that violence is bad and that even pretending to hurt others is unacceptable, violent behavior continues to plague both parents and teachers. Banning such play also carries with it serious problems: it can encourage children to hide from adults the things that really interest or concern children. And more important, it prevents adults from having any direct influence on all the children are learning about violence and social behavior as they engage in unacceptable play outside the adults' view. Adults are faced with a new set of challenges.

Aggression occurs under normal circumstances, even with the presence of heroes. During the preschool years children are just learning to distinguish reality from fantasy (real victims and fictional ones) and how to act acceptably with peers and adults. Even normal play indoors and outdoors can degenerate into a hitting, negative, hurting situa-

 **Reflection**

One center was having trouble with games involving violent media heroes because some children were hurt and frightened while playing these games. The teachers had a discussion with the children; parents received a letter about the negative impact of the play along with suggested ways to downplay these heroes in selection of clothes, toys, books, and accessories, and in TV and movie watching (for example, de-emphasizing children's exposure to them, providing alternative toys and media viewing, suggesting more appropriate ways to play with toys, etc.).

What would be your plan of action and response as a teacher? As a parent?

tion. Strive to help children keep their negative feelings to a minimum and their positive ones to a maximum.

An alternate to banning classroom violence is to work directly with children's war play to counteract the messages children learn from media and toys (see Figure 3.7). It can also help them make meaning of the violence they have experienced in order to get some resolution or mastery over it. As teachers facilitate children's dramatic play, children develop better skills for working out the powerful issues in their lives, including violence, through play. But this choice, too, creates special challenges for teachers over how to maintain a sense of safety for all children in the classroom while beginning to work with difficult themes in children's play.

Aggressive play has been a topic over many years, and is certainly not just the result of more violent television programming or supporting toys (see Figure 3.8).

TV programming
Toys supporting violent TV programs, games, and so on
Video games
Books displaying violent themes or characters
Movies—including cartoons
Music (lyrics and gestures)
Games—group
Sports—participation or observation
Inappropriate expectations of adults
Peer reinforcement
Developmentally delayed behavior—immaturity
Adult models and encouragement (macho, powerful, dominant, possessive)
Lack of good models, lack of better ways of solving situations, or lack of cooperation skills
Status symbols—clothing, colors, insignias, hair styles, belonging
Allergies to food, fabrics, animals, toxins, and so on
Other things that may be "child-specific"— current world situations (oppression, war, terrorism, etc.) and others

Figure 3.7   Possible Causes of Violent Play in Young Children

Children need to feel safe. Experts describe the impact of violence on many children as *post-traumatic stress disorder* (Garbarino et al., 1992).

The younger the child, the greater the threat of exposure to violence poses to healthy development. Chronic exposure to violence can have serious developmental consequences for children, including psychological disorders, grief and loss reactions, impaired intellectual development and school programs, truncated moral development, pathological adaptation to violence, and identification with the aggressor (Craig, 1992; Garbarino et al., 1992).

Children exposed to violence have difficulty focusing on schoolwork or engaging in any of the other playful activities that should be reassured experiences of childhood (National Television Violence Study, 1996).

It is estimated that up to 80 percent of all children exposed to powerful stressors do not sustain developmental damage (Rutter, 1979; Werner, 1990). Most children are able to cope with dangerous environments and maintain resilience as long as their parents are not stressed beyond their capacity to cope (Garbarino et al., 1992).

Schools and child-care programs can be vitally important support systems by strengthening children's resilience and providing resources for parents so that they can serve as psychological buffers to protect their children (National Television Violence Study, 1996).

The National Association for the Education of Young Children (NAEYC), the nation's largest professional organization for early-childhood educators, is committed to actions (1) to decrease the extent of violence in all forms in children's lives by advocating for public policies and actions at the national level, and (2) to enhance the ability of educators to help children cope with violence, promote children's resilience, and assist families by improving professional practice in early-childhood programs (National Television Violence Study, 1996, p. 23).

Figure 3.8   Effects of Violence on Children

Bandura (1973), noted for using an inflatable child-sized doll in experiments, proposed a social-learning theory, which stressed that children who see aggressive acts performed by powerful models (adults) or similar models (peers) will be likely to also act aggressively. To control this type of behavior, teachers need to (1) convey to children and parents in their classrooms that violent play is not acceptable, and (2) remember that models who are rewarded for their violence increase their violent tendencies, and also those tendencies of others. Erikson (1977) supported a psychosocial viewpoint, which interprets aggressive actions in play as a way children can constructively deal with their emotions and gain a feeling of power and control over their environment. Thus, violent play is a natural and relatively harmless outlet for aggressive feelings within activities that the children control through their play, and can be expressed, mastered, and ultimately dissipated. This type of play allows children to feel more powerful and thereby express and master their natural anger in a "low-risk" manner; however, there must be limits.

See Figure 3.9 regarding aggressive and nonaggressive lessons learned from play.

A three-year effort to assess violence on television (1966) reported key findings and recommendations. The *findings* included the following: violence on television posed risks to viewers; perpetrators went unpunished in most violent scenes; negative consequences of violence were omitted from the programming; handguns were frequently used; programs contained a very limited amount of anti-violence; explicit or graphic violence was limited; different television channels showed different amounts of violence; children's programs were least likely to show long-term negative consequences; and violence was frequently portrayed in a humorous context (National Television Violence Study, 1996).

The study recommended:

For the television community: include less violence; increase portrayals of powerful nonviolent heroes and attractive characters; schedule high-violence shows in late-evening hours; establish codes for types of programs; provide advisory information in programming guides (revise frequently); give limited time devoted to sponsor, station, or network during public service announcements.

For parents: watch TV with the child; encourage discussion and evaluation of the program content; consider the child's developmental level when selecting programs; be aware of potential violence; recognize that different kinds of violent programs pose different risks for each person. (Parents are also encouraged to establish and follow rules for firearms within the home.)

For teachers: Safety is a prime guiding principle. Plan alternatives to meet developmental needs and inspire dramatic and artistic recreations; talk frequently with the chil-

Aggressive Play	Nonaggressive Play
Rewards aggressiveness. May or may not satisfy the child, but annoys teachers and children.	Encourages children to find better ways of interacting, working out feelings.
Gives the child a false sense of security or acceptance, negative self-perception.	Values each child: protects the rights of the shy child and shows the aggressive child better ways to control anger, desires, and so on.
Shows the teacher and others that the child needs attention.	Requires good teacher planning, classroom cooperation.
Involves much teacher time, sensitivity, and firmness.	Makes materials and props more flexible.
Makes other children feel insecure.	Helps teachers and children learn and work cooperatively; promotes productivity.
Focuses teaching/learning time on less important matters.	Attention can be shared with all class members.
Can consume much time and energy.	
Attention may be focused on a few students.	

Figure 3.9   Lessons Learned from Play

dren about different approaches, sharing your reasons, as a teacher, and listening to children's thoughts, feelings, and reasoning; involve parents in discussions about children's thoughts and feelings. NAEYC encourages members to commit to helping children cope with violence in their lives and promoting their resilience through partnerships with parents.

Note to Reader: If you are wondering why the play chapter is so long, it is because (1) play is important in the life and development of the young child (and all individuals); (2) there are so many different aspects of the topic; (3) it is frequently misunderstood and underrated; and (4) *foremost,* it is the basis for the entire book.

Application of Principles

1. Observe two or more children between the ages of 2 and 5. Note the type of play most frequently exhibited (solitary/with a companion, verbal/nonverbal, sharing/competitive, awareness/unawareness of others, and so on).
2. Discuss the motor, social-emotional, cognitive-language, and combined areas of development most common in children between the ages of 2 and 5. In which of the areas of development do you find it most difficult to see changes in the young child?
3. Through your observations of young children, describe how learning is manifested in play activities.
4. Discuss the role of competition for young children. Do you think it is a help or a hindrance in the child's development?
5. Name and implement ways to sustain children in their play without directing their activities.
6. Describe the stages and timing of play in young children.
7. Why is dramatic play important for young children?
8. What modifications need to be made for successful play of children with special needs?
9. How can children enhance their development through outdoor play?
10. How is violent play enacted by young children and how can a teacher or parent change it into productive, healthy play?
11. Carefully describe your personal feelings about play during the life cycle of an individual.
12. Prepare a hand-out for the parents of the children in your group outlining the possible causes of and probably solutions to violence in the home with young children.
13. Plan a meeting, individual conferences, a questionnaire, or home visit for the parents of the children in your group on a topic that is of **present concern to you and/or the parents:** appropriate behavior of young children; play, toys, and cooperation; health concerns in your community; questionnaire to parents about their concerns; anything timely and interesting. If possible, hold the meeting and then evaluate its effectiveness for you, the children, and the parents.

References

NOTE: Current References are used when available. Older references are classic, introductory, and important in development of later ideas, policies, and practices.

Alber, J. L., Alber, D. M., Santoliquido, D. R., & Allen, D. (1990). *Baby-safe houseplants and cut flowers.* Highland, IL: Genus Books. (Box 351, Highland, IL 62249)

Alliance for Technology Access. (2001). Splish-splash! Accessible water play. At www.ataccess.org/resources/wcp/enpdf/en20Water.pdf.

American Association for Leisure and Recreation. 1900 Association Drive, Reston, VA 22091. 800-321-0789. Website: http://www.aahperd.org/aalr/aalr.html. (Publications on child-care center and playground safety, injury prevention, and playgrounds for disabilities.)

Anselmo, S., & Franz, W. (1995). *Early childhood development.* Upper Saddle River, NJ: Merrill/Prentice Hall.

Bandura, A. (1973). *Aggression: A social learning analysis.* Upper Saddle River, NJ: Merrill/Prentice Hall.

Bergen, D. (1994, Annual Theme). Should teachers permit or discourage violent play themes? *Childhood Education, 300–302.*

Berk, L. E. (1994). Research in review: Vygotsky's theory: The importance of make-believe play. *Young Children, 50*(1), 30–39.

Berk, L. E., & Winsler, A. (1995). *Scaffolding children's learning: Vygotsky and early childhood education,* Vol. 7. Research in Practice Series. Washington, DC: NAEYC.

Bodrova, E., and Leong, D. J. (1996). *Tools of the mind: The Vygotskian approach to early childhood education.* Upper Saddle River, NJ: Merrill/Prentice Hall.

Bredekamp, S. (Ed.). (1987). *Developmentally appropriate practice in early childhood programs serving children from birth through age 8* (expanded ed.). Washington, DC: NAEYC.

Bredekamp, S., & Copple, C. (Eds.). (1997). *Developmentally appropriate practice in early childhood programs* (rev. ed.). Washington, DC: NAEYC.

Bronfenbrenner, U. (1979). *The ecology of human development: Experiments by nature and design.* Cambridge, MA: Harvard University Press.

Bronson, M. B. (1995). *The right stuff for children birth to 8: Selecting lay materials to support development.* Washington, DC: NAEYC.

Brosterman, N. (1997). *Inventing kindergarten: Nineteenth century children.* New York: Abrams.

Brownell, C. A., & Carriger, M. S. (1990). Changes in cooperation and self-other differentiation during the second year. *Child Development, 61,* 1164–1174.

Bruner, J. S. (1976). The nature and uses of immaturity. In J. S. Bruner, A. Jolly, & K. Sylva (Eds.), *Play: Its role in development and evolution.* New York: Basis.

Burns, S. M., & Brainerd. (1979). Effects of constructive and dramatic play on perspective taking in very young children. *Developmental Psychology, 15,* 512–521.

Caldwell, L. B. (1997). *Bringing Reggio Emilia home: An innovative approach to early childhood education.* New York: Teachers College Press, Columbia University.

Caplan, M., Vespo, J., Pedersen, J., and Hay, D. F. (1991). Conflict and its resolution in small groups of one- and two-year-olds. *Child Development, 62,* 1513–1524.

Caplow, T., Bahr, H., & Chadwick, B. (1989, May 26). Brigham Young University, *Y News, 14,* (p. 36).

Carlson-Paige, N., & Levin, D. E. (1992, November). Making peace in violent times: A constructivist approach to conflict resolution. *Young Children, 48*(1), 4–13.

Carlson-Paige, N., & Levin, D. E. (1995, July). Can teachers resolve the war-play dilemma? *Young Children, 50*(5), 62–63.

Cartwright, S. (1988). Play can be the building blocks of learning. *Young Children, 43*(5), 44–47.

Cartwright, S. (1990). Learning with large blocks. *Young Children, 3,* 38–41.

Cartwright, S. (1995, May). Block play: Experiences in cooperative learning and living. *Child Care Information Exchange, 30–41.*

Cartwright, S. (2000). Education is experience: The rest is only information. *Young Children, 55*(4), 12–13.

Connolly, J. A. & Doyle, A. B. (1984). Relations of social fantasy play to social competence in preschoolers. *Developmental Psychology, 20,* 797–806.

Consumer Product Safety Commission (CPSC). Washington, DC 20207. Toll free hotline: 800-638-2772. Website: www.cpsc.gov.

Cowan, P. A. (1978). *Piaget with feeling.* New York: Holt, Rinehart & Winston.

Craig, S. (1992). The educational needs of children living with violence. *Phi Delta Kappan, 74*(1), 67–71.

Cuffaro, H. (1986). The development of block building. In P. H. Sperr (Ed.), *Building block art.* Philadelphia: Please Touch Museum.

Cuffaro, H. (1995, May). Block building: Opportunities for learning. *Child Care Information Exchange,* 36–38.

Cuffaro, H. (1995). *Experimenting with the world: John Dewey and the early childhood classroom.* New York: Teachers College Press.

Dansky, J. L. (1980). Make-believe: A mediator of the relationship between play and associative influence. *Child Development, 51,* 576–79.

DeBord, K., Hestenes, L. L., Moore, R. C., Cosco, N., & McGinnis, J. R. (2002). Paying attention to the outdoor environment is as important as preparing the indoor environment. *Young Children, 57*(3), 32–35.

DeVries, R., & Kohlberg, L. (1987/1990). *Constructionist early education: Overview and comparison with other programs.* Washington, DC: NAEYC.

Dewey, J. (1916). *Democracy and education: An introduction to the philosophy of education.* New York: Macmillan.

Dewey, J. (1959). *The school and society.* In M. S. Dworking (Ed.), *Dewey on education,* ed. M. S. Dworking. New York: Teachers College Press. Out of print. (Original work published 1899).

Ditchburn, S. J. (1988). Conflict management in young children's play. *International Journal of Early Childhood (OMEP), 20*(2), 62–70.

Dunn, L., & Kontos, S. (1997). Developmentally appropriate practice: What does research tell us? *ERIC Digest.* (ERIC Document Reproduction Service No. ED413106).

Early Childhood Outdoors (ECO) Institute. *Earthworm.* Quarterly newsletter available from ECO Institute, Fontenelle Forest Assoc., 1313 Bellevue Blvd., Bellevue, NE 68005-4012.

Eberly, J. L., & Golbeck, S. L. (2001). Teachers' perceptions of children's block play: How accurate are they? *Journal of Early Childhood Teacher Education, 22,* 63–67.

Edwards, C. (1993). Partner, nurturer, and guide: The roles of the Reggio teacher in action. In Edwards, Gandini, & Forman, *The hundred languages of children* (pp. 151–170).

Edwards, C., Gandini, L., & Forman, G. (Eds.). (1993). *The hundred languages of children: The Reggio Emilia approach to early childhood education.* Norwood, NJ: Ablex.

Eibl-Eibesfeldt, J. (1970). *Ethology: The biology of behavior.* New York: Holt, Rinehart & Winston.

Erikson, E. H. (1950). *A healthy personality for your child.* Midcentury White House Conference on Children and Youth, December 1950. Washington, DC: U.S. Government Printing Office.

Erikson, E. H. (1977). *Toys and reason.* New York: Norton.

Flynn, L. L., & Kieff, J., (2002). Including everyone in outdoor play. *Young Children, 57*(3), 20–26.

Frank, L. K. (1968, March). Play is valid. *Childhood Education, 44,* 433–440.

Froebel, F. (1975). *The education of man.* New York: Appleton.

Frost, J. L. (1992). *Play and playscapes.* Albany, NY: Delmar.

Frost, J. L., Wortham, S. C., & Reifel, S. (2001). *Play and child development.* Upper Saddle River, NJ: Merrill/Prentice Hall.

FYI: How safe is your playground? (2000). *Young Children, 55*(4), 59.

Gandini, L. (1993). Fundamentals of the Reggio approach to early childhood education. *Young Children, 49*(1), 4–8.

Garbarino, J., Dubrow, N., Kostelny, K., & Prado, C. (1992). *Children in danger: Dealing with the effects of community violence.* San Francisco: Jossey-Bass.

Garvey. C. (1990). *Play.* Cambridge, MA: Harvard University Press.

Gillespie, C. W. (2000). Six Head Start classrooms being to explore the Reggio Emilia approach. *Young Children, 55*(1), 21–27.

Gillespie, C. W., & Chick, A. (2001, Summer). Fussbusters: Using peers to mediate conflict resolution in a Head Start class. *Childhood Education,* 192–95.

Glassman, M. (1994). All things being equal: The two roads of Piaget and Vygotsky. *Developmental Review, 14,* 186–214.

Goldstein, J. (1986). *Aggression and crimes of violence.* New York: Oxford University Press.

Granella, F. (1934). Blockbuilding activities of young children. *Archives of Psychology, 174,* 1–92.

Graue, E. (2001). Research in review: What's going on in the children's garden? Kindergarten today. *Young Children, 56*(3), 67–71.

Griffin, C., & Rinn, B. (1998). Enhancing outdoor play with an obstacle course. *Young Children, 53*(8), 18–21.

Gronlund, G. (2001). Rigorous academics in preschool and kindergarten? Yes! Let me tell you how. *Young Children, 56*(2), 42–43.

Gura, P. (Ed.). (1992). *Exploring learning: Young children and block play.* New York: Paul Chapman.

Hart, C. H., Burts, D. C., & Charlesworth, R. (Eds.). (1997). *Integrated curriculum and developmentally appropriate practice: Birth to age eight* (pp. 171–199). Albany, NY: State University Press.

Hauser-Cram, P. (1998). I think I can, I think I can: Understanding and encouraging mastery motivation in young children. *Young Children, 53*(4), 67–71.

Hendrick, J. (1967). The pleasures of meaningful work for young children. *Young Children, 22,* 373–380.

Hendrick, J. (1992). *The whole child* (5th ed.). Upper Saddle River, NJ: Merrill/Prentice Hall.

Hendrick, J. (1997). *First steps toward teaching the Reggio way.* Upper Saddle River, NJ: Merrill/Prentice Hall.

Henniger, M. (1987, Feb.) Learning mathematics and science through play. *Childhood Education, 63*(3), 167–171.

Henninger, M. L. (1994). Planning for outdoor play. *Young Children, 49*(4), 10–15.

Hestenes, L. L., & Carroll, D. E. (2000). The play interactions of young children with and without disabilities: Individual and environmental influences. *Early Childhood Research Quarterly, 152,* 229–246.

Hewitt, K. (2001). Blocks as a tool for learning: Historical and contemporary perspectives. *Young Children, 56*(1), 6–13.

Hill, D. M. (1977). *Mud, sand, and water.* Washington, DC: NAEYC. Order #310/$3.00. ISBN 0-912674-52-0. E-mail resource sales@naeyc.org.

Hill, P. S. (Ed.). (1915). *Experimental studies in kindergarten education.* New York: Columbia University.

Hill, P. S. (Ed.). (1923). *A conduct curriculum for the kindergarten and first grade.* Directed by Patty S. Hill. Compiled by Agnes Burke, Edith U. Conard, Alice Dalgleish, Charlotte G. Garrison, Edna V. Hughes, Mary E. Rankin, and Alice G. Thorn. New York: Charles Scribner's Sons.

Humpherys, J. (1998). The developmental appropriateness of high-quality Montessori programs. *Young Children, 53*(4), 4–16.

Hymes, J. L., Jr. (1981). *Teaching the child under six.* Columbus, OH: Merrill.

Jensen, B. J., & Bullard, J. A. (2002). The mud center: recapturing childhood. *Young Children, 57*(3), 16–19.

Johnson, H. (1972). *Children in the nursery.* New York: Bank Street College of Education. (Original work published in 1923).

Katz, L. G. (1997, April). A developmental approach to assessment of young children. *ERIC Digest.* (ERIC Document Reproduction Service No. #EDO-PS-97-18).

Konner, M. (1991). *Childhood.* Boston: Little, Brown.

Kramer, R. (1976). *Maria Montessori: A biography.* New York: Putnam.

Lally, J. R., Lerner, C., and Lurie-Hurvitz, E. (2001). Public Policy Report. National Survey Reveals Gaps in the Public's and Parents' Knowledge about Early Childhood Development. *Young Children, 56*(2), 49–53. Source of National Survey: "What Grown-Ups Understand about Child Development" was commissioned by Zero to Three, Civitas Initiative, and Brio Corporation (June & July of 2000).

Levy, A. K. (1984). The language of play: The role of play in language development. *Early Child Development and Care, 17,* 49–62.

Lindquist, B., & Molnar, A. (1995). Children learn what they live. *Educational Leadership, 52,* 47–51.

Locke, J. 1693. Some thoughts concerning education. Text available online at www.socsci.kun.nl/ped/whp/histeduc/locke/index.html. See § § 63, 74.

Marcus, R. F. (1987). The role of affect in children's cooperation. *Child Study Journal, 17*(2), 153–168.

McCracken, J. B. (1999). *Playgrounds: Safe and sound.* (Brochure.) Washington, DC: NAEYC.

McGinnis, J. R. (2002). Enriching the outdoor environment. *Young Children, 57*(3), 28–30.

Meisels, S. J. (2000). On the side of the child: Personal reflections on testing, teaching, and early childhood education. *Young Children, 55*(6), 16–19.

Moll, L. D., & Whitmore, K. F. (1993). Vygotsky in classroom practice: moving from individual transmission to social transaction. In E. A. Forman, N. Minick, & C. A. Stone (Eds.), *Contexts for learning.* New York: Oxford Press.

Montessori, M. (1912). *The Montessori method.* Cambridge, MA: Robert Bentley.

Montessori, M. (1964). *The Montessori method.* New York: Schocken.

Montessori, M. (1971). *Spontaneous activity in education.* Trans. F. Simmonds. Cambridge, MA: Robert Bentley. (Original work published in 1917).

National Association for the Education of Young Children (NAEYC). (1993). Position statement on violence in the lives of children. *Young Children, 48*(6), 80–84.

National Association of Early Childhood Specialists in State Departments of Education (NAECS/SDE). (2002). *Recess and the importance of play: A position statement on young children and recess.* Alexandria, VA: Author. Available online at http://ericps. crc.uiuc.edu/naecs/position/recessplay.html.

National Program for Playground Safety. (2001). Websites: http:www.uni.edu/ playground/plan.html; also: http://www.uni.edu/playground/home.htm, http://www. uni.edu/playground/school.html, http://www.uni.edu/playground/in_the_news.html, http://www.uni.edu/playground/report.html, www.uni.edu/playground/newsletter.html.

National Survey. (2000, June/July). What grown-ups understand about child development. Commissioned by Zero to Three, Civitas Initiative, and Brio Corporation.

National Television Violence Study: Key findings and recommendations. (1996). *Young Children, 51*(3), 54–55.

Nourot, P. M., & Van Hoorn, J. L. (1991). Research in review: Symbolic play in preschool and primary settings. *Young Children, 46*(6), 40–50.

Papert, S. (1999). *MindStorms: Children, computers, and powerful ideas* (2d ed.). New York: Basic.

Parten, M. (1932–33). Social participation among preschool children. *Journal of Abnormal and Social Psychology, 27,* 243–269.

Pepler, D. J., & Ross, H. S. (1981). The effect of play on convergent and divergent problem solving. *Child Development, 52,* 1202–1210.

Piaget, J. (1963). *The origin of intelligence in children.* New York: Norton.

Piaget, J. (1973). *To understand is to invent: The future of education.* New York: Grossman.

Piaget, J. (1979). *Play, dreams, and imitation in childhood.* New York: Harper. (Original work published in 1962).

Popham, W. J. (2000). *Testing! Testing! What every parent should know about standardized testing.* Boston: Allyn & Bacon.

Pratt, C. (1990). *I learn from children.* New York: Harper & Row, Perennial. (Original work published in 1948).

Quay, L. C., Weaver, J. H., & Neel, J. H. (1986). The effects of play materials on positive and negative social behaviors in preschool boys and girls. *Child Study Journal, 16*(1), 67–76.

Read, K., Gardner, P., & Mahler, B. C. (1987). *Early childhood programs: Human relationships and learning* (8th ed.). New York: Holt, Rinehart & Winston.

Readdick, C. A., and Douglas, K. (2000). More than line leader and/or holder: Engaging young children in real work. *Young Children, 55*(6), 63–70.

Readdick, C. A., & Park, J. J., (1998). Achieving great heights: The climbing child. *Young Children, 53*(6), 14–19.

Reifel, S. (1984). Block construction: Children's developmental landmarks in representation of space. *Young Children, 40*(1), 61–67.

Reifel, S., & Greenfield, P. M. (1982). Structural development in symbolic medium: The representational use of block construction. In G. E. Forman (Ed.), *Action and thought: From sensorimotor schemes to symbolic operations.* New York: Academic.

Reifel, S. & Yeatman, J. (1991). Action, talk, and thought in the block corner: Developmental trends. In B. Sales, M. Almy, A. Nicolopoulou, & S. Erwin-Tripp (Eds.), *Play and the social context of development in early care and education.* New York: Teachers College Press.

Rivkin, M. (2000). Outdoor experiences for young children. Online at *ERIC Digest* website: www.ael.org/eric/digests/edorc007.htm.

Rivkin, M. S. (1995). *The Great outdoors: Restoring children's right to play outside.* Washington, DC: NAEYC.

Roskos, K., & Christie, J. (2001). On not pushing too hard: A few cautionary remarks about linking literacy and play. *Young Children, 56*(3), 64–66.

Ross, H. S., & Lollis, S. P. (1989). A social relations analysis of toddler peer relationships. *Child Development, 60,* 1082–1091.

Rutter, M. (1979). Protective factors in children's responses to stress and disadvantage. In M. W. Kent & J. E. Rolf (Eds.), *Primary prevention of psychopathology: Social competence in children,* Vol. 3 (pp. 49–74). Hanover, NH: University Press of New England.

Seefeldt, C. (1997). Social studies in the developmentally appropriate integrated curriculum. In C. H. Hart, D. C. Burts, and R. Charlesworth (Eds.), *Integrated curriculum and developmentally practice: Birth to age eight* (pp. 171–199). Albany: State University of New York Press.

Smilansky, S., & Shefatya, L. (1990). *Facilitating play: A medium for promoting cognitive, socio-emotional and academic development in young children.* Gaithersburg, MD: Psychosocial and Educational Publications.

Snyder, A. (1972). *Dauntless women in childhood education (1856–1931).* Olney, MD: Association for Childhood Education International (ACEI).

Staley, L. (1998). Beginning to implement the Reggio philosophy. *Young Children, 53*(5), 20–25.

Standing, E. M. (1962). *Maria Montessori, her life and work.* New York: New American Library.

Stritzel, K. (1995, May). Block play is for ALL children. *Child Care Exchange,* 42–47.

Sutterby, J. A., & Frost, J. L. (2002). Making playgrounds fit for children and children fit on playgrounds. *Young Children, 57*(3), 36–41.

Taylor, B. J. (2002). Early childhood program management: People and procedures (4th ed.). New York: Macmillan.

Trawick-Smith, J. (1988). "Let's say you're the baby, OK?" Play leadership and following behavior of young children. *Young Children, 43*(5), 51–59.

Trepanier-Street, M., Hong, S. B., & Donegan, M. M. (2001). Constructing the image of the teacher in a Reggio-inspired teacher preparation program. *Journal of Early Childhood Teacher Education, 22,* 47–52.

Tudge, J. R. H., & Winterhoff, P. A. (1993). Vygotsky, Piaget, and Bandura: Perspectives on the relations between the social world and cognitive development. *Human Development, 36,* 61–81.

U.S. Consumer Product Safety Commission. (1997). *Handbook for public playground safety.* Office of Information and Public Affairs. Washington, DC 20207. Pub. No. 325. Website: www.ccpsc.gov.us. or at www.cpsc.gov/cpscpub/pubs.325.pdf.

Van Hoorn, J., Nourot, P., Scales, B., & Alward, K. (1993). *Play at the center of the curriculum.* Upper Saddle River, NJ: Merrill/Prentice Hall.

Vygotsky, L. (1987). Thinking and speech. In *The Collected Works of L. S. Vygotsky,* Vol. 1, *Problems of general psychology* (pp. 37–385). Eds. R. Rieber & A. S. Carton. Trans. N. Minick. New York: Plenu. (Original work published in 1934)

Werner E. E. (1990). Protective factors and individual resilience. In S. J. Meisels, & J. P. Shonkoff (Eds.), *Handbook of early childhood education* (pp. 97–116). Cambridge, England: Cambridge University Press.

Werner, H., & Kaplan, B. (1963). *Symbol formation.* New York: Wiley.

C H A P T E R

4

Curriculum Development

Main Principles

1. National accredited organizations provide guidelines for teaching young children (p. 118).

2. The teacher has specific training and is responsible to herself, the children, the parents, team members, the community, and her profession (pp. 119–141, 144–147).

3. To plan properly for young children, teachers follow guidelines but allow for some curriculum "negotiations" (p. 134–136).

4. Good planning includes preplanning, grouping, assessment, and commitment. (pp. 127–133, 136–149).

5. **Reflections** help students apply principles as they are discussed in each chapter (pp. 127–128, 137, 140, 142–143, 146).

6. Curriculum webbing is a very important way to plan and teach (pp. 141–145).

7. Flexibility and content help young children learn (pp. 125–126, 144–146).

8. Multicultural education is prevalent in our educational system and deserves attention (pp. 126, 127).

9. A good lesson plan provides information and continuity for the children and adults (pp. 127, 131).

10. Application of principles helps students apply overall information presented in chapter (p. 147).

Introduction

NAEYC and NAECS/SDE have identified some theoretical perspectives on developmental learning that acknowledge many theories of learning and development with various explanations of phenomena. Specifically, early childhood professionals have found some theories to be more comprehensive, explanatory, and useful than others, such as Piaget (1952), Vygotsky (1978), and Erikson (1963), and have used these theories to form their document (NAEYC & NAECS/SDE, 1992). (For information on theorists, see Chapters 1 and 3.)

It is somewhat unrealistic to think that there is a specific course of study in early childhood. Of course, there are some theories and programs that have specific lock-step study programs. But when one believes in developmentally appropriate curriculum for children of specific ages and interests, that is the curriculum. We look at children individually and collectively and discover that there are some common interests and some unique interests. So one begins thinking about curriculum by watching the children as they play and by listening to their comments and conversations. Curriculum is happening all around the home, the school, the playground, and wherever young children gather. Perceptive teachers can help enrich and enhance what is happening.

"In early childhood education, curriculum isn't the focus, children are. It's easy for teachers to get hooked on *curriculum* because it's so much more manageable than children. But curriculum is *what happens* in an educational environment—not what is rationally planned to happen, but what actually takes place" (Jones & Nimmo, 1994, p. 12). Teachers can set the classroom stage for different types of play and activities, but the children are the ones who make the production. Most preschool teachers do not write or expect typical school-type lesson plans to be effective with young children. They may follow a format (perhaps a theme, learning activities, classroom arrangement, sequencing, and so on) but these items should be skeletal and flexible. Writing the plan after the day's activities would be more productive than writing it before the action begins. *An emergent curriculum* is in continuous revision. What works one day, or with one group of children, may be entirely inappropriate another day or with another group of children. Flexibility on the part of teachers, availability of resources for quick revisions, and active children make for exciting and active classrooms.

Van Hoorn et al. identify three types of curriculum: (1) *play-generated curriculum,* which emerges directly from teacher observations of the interests and themes of the children; (2) *curriculum-generated curriculum,* which leads the teacher to include materials or techniques that he suspects will match the spontaneous interest of the children; and (3) *recasting the curriculum* through play, in which the teacher provides opportunities and asks questions that encourage children to use newly constructed knowledge derived from the curriculum in their play. This aspect of play is very important (1993, pp. 60–61).

Bruner (1963) coined the term *spiral curriculum* to represent the idea that at many stages of their development, children may grasp basic concepts, each time returning to the same ideas at a more sophisticated level of understanding. This aspect of play is important in children's development.

In her teaching, the teacher must attend to what she knows about the prior learning of children in the group so that she can teach in their *zone of proximal development (ZPD)* (Vygotsky, 1978), that is the range of tasks that the child cannot yet handle alone but can accomplish with the help of adults or more skilled peers (Berk, 1994).

The process of learning is complex and has been described in many ways. One helpful way of thinking about learning is to visualize the process as "a recurring cycle that begins in awareness and moves to exploration, to inquiry, and finally to utilization" (NAEYC & NAECS/SDE, 1992). "This cycle is not developmental in the pure sense of the word because it is similar for children and adults when they acquire new knowledge or skill" (Bredekamp & Rosegrant, 1995, p. 19). Curriculum decisions involve questions not only of *how* children learn, but also of *what* learning is appropriate and *when* it is best learned.

Our teachers provide interesting things for us.

Role of the Teacher

To plan properly for young children, a teacher needs to do the following:

➤ Understand the role of the teacher.
➤ Understand how and what young children should learn.
➤ Support good curriculum planning principles.
➤ Be able to define *webbing* and show how to effectively use it with young children.
➤ Know the developmental and individual characteristics of children at each age.
➤ Establish educational goals for the children and teacher.
➤ Respect and value each child.
➤ Perfect, execute, and evaluate good planning skills.
➤ Take teaching and planning as an important privilege and a serious responsibility.
➤ Value parents and keep them informed about their child and school activities.

Even though the teacher has training in curriculum, there are often hidden curriculum clues for children, such as the kinds of toys available; the room arrangement; the sequence and schedule of activities; the number and variety of opportunities; whether the child plays alone or with others; whether there is sufficient time for sustained or repetitive play; weather and/or temperature; indoor/outdoor flow; how and when the teacher interacts with the children and parents; the child's ability to gain trust in adults, peers, and the school environment; and other items.

Teaching is a great responsibility. Being a teacher of young children is even more important. Teachers should take their stewardship seriously by building good relationships with and among staff, parents, and children, being professional at all times, and keeping confidences. Judgments should not be made without facts. Frequent and friendly contacts with parents are essential.

The number of teachers required to operate a center efficiently depends on the number and ages of the children, physical facilities, experience of the teachers, and local regulations, when applicable; however, at least *two* trained teachers are needed per group. More are required when a group is composed of only 2-year-olds or more than 16 children. (State and local requirements vary, but the recommended maximum is 24 children per group, with the ideal number being between 16 and 20 for children ages 3 through 5.)

Why is one trained teacher insufficient to handle a group of young children? How can a center afford two trained teachers per group? *Trained* does not necessarily refer to a four-year college degree in early-childhood education. Training can be obtained through a trade/technical school, working for an associate degree or child development associate (CDA) credential, or on-the-job training.

Essentials in Planning

Emergent Curriculum

The term *emergent curriculum* was introduced by Betty Jones (NAEYC publication *Curriculum Is What Happens,* edited by Laura Dittman in 1970). Emphasis was given to *emergent* (indicating that planning comes from the children's own interests and spontaneity) and *curriculum* (conveys that planning occurs). And simply put, "emergent curriculum asks that we be responsible to particular people, in a particular place, at a particular time" (Dittman, 1970).

It would be difficult to identify the original source of most of our planning—it grows from every possible source as we try to invent functional systems for needed resources. Emergent curriculum is sensible but not predictable. It would be wrong to assume that everything simply emerges from the children—their ideas are extremely important but just one of many possible sources. Emergent curriculum is a continuous revision process of what is actually happening, but a responsible adult organizes, sets the stage, and keeps the production on track (Jones & Nimmo, 1994, p. 12).

The children are always the focus of attention in early-childhood education programs, and curriculum is what takes place in that environment. Teachers who prepare the physical environment to respond to children have the basis for interaction with materials, individuals, and ideas. To get your children acquainted with the outdoor playground or the indoor play areas, try a scavenger hunt, as described in Figure 4.1.

In your planning, include rules for behavior and rules for using materials and toys. Children need genuine rules for safety as well as opportunities for responding to the democratic rights of a group. "Taking into account individual and cultural differences may, at times, override the need to be universally consistent in the application of preset rules in group care and education" (Jones & Nimmo, 1994, p. 24). Unless we can look into a crystal ball and see how children and situations evolve, we need to anticipate revising rules as children mature, experience, and learn. This involves negotiation, risk taking, and willingness to deal with complexity. When safety is threatened, children need the security of clear limits, as well as when fairness and a sense of community call for a rule evenly applied (p. 24).

Look for things that:
- need repair (toys, equipment, swings, fences, and so on)
- are dangerous (open gates, nails, unattended swings, and so on)
- people can move (shovel, ball, boxes, toys, and so on)
- can move people (wagon, swing, wheels, and so on)
- are made of a certain material (wood, fabric, plastic)
- are favorite toys of children
- children can climb (slide, climbs, hill)
- water can be used with (buckets, washing equipment, water fountain)
- are shady (under tree, in shed, under bushes)
- have a certain texture (rough, smooth, soft, and so on)

Suggest some curriculum activities based on the hunt.
Try a spin-off for your indoor play spaces.

(The scavenger hunt idea is suggested by Jones & Nimmo, 1994, p. 21. This example is original.)

Figure 4.1   Scavenger Hunt on Your Playground

The program works best with two distinct teacher roles—the *lead* teacher and the *support* teacher. (A third teacher could also be assigned the role of support teacher.) As the name suggests, the lead teacher leads an activity, taking the major responsibility for planning, organization, and actual teaching. Support teachers assist the lead teacher. Although the roles differ in specific assignments, they are of equal importance. All teachers must have the training necessary to function competently in either role and to rotate roles easily and successfully.

For a brief clarification of the two roles, consider Teacher A (TA) and Teacher B (TB) in the same classroom. Both teachers have planned together for the day; however, TA takes the lead for the opening time, snack, and art, while TB takes the lead for the group theme time, outside activity, and language time. (See Appendix B.) A brief outline defining the two roles is shown in Table 4.1.

TA takes the initiative to set up free-play activities. Both teachers participate with the children as needed. At cleanup time, TA follows through; TB assists at the beginning and then moves to group time so he will be ready as the first children arrive. He begins some interesting activities. The children put away their toys and join TB. When TA is through with cleanup, she joins the children in the group and assists with incidentals while TB presents. At the conclusion of this period, both teachers help the children get ready to go outside. TB accompanies them while TA sets up the snack, with the help of two children, after which all three also go outside. To be ready when the children arrive at snack, TA precedes them into the classroom and assists them as needed. TB brings in the stragglers and joins the other children at the snack table. As this activity concludes, TB moves with the first children to another group time for stories and songs. TA clears away the snack, prepares the tables for art activities, then joins the group in progress. During art, both teachers move freely among the children, giving verbal support, physical help, or manipulating the materials when appropriate. At the end of the day, both teachers help the children make the transition from school to home.

The preparation of teachers of young children is extremely important. Some states have specific requirements for caregivers; some states have specific requirements for teachers or directors of preschool programs; and most (if not all) states require an additional certification for teachers of young children in public and private schools. (See Chapter 1.)

Clearly, two teachers are needed to work individually or cooperatively according to the needs of the children or the experiences planned. On another day, the teachers could change roles, with TA planning and presenting the curriculum areas that TB had done the previous day, or one teacher might keep the same role for a longer period of time. The best teaching occurs when plans are made well in advance of the teaching day; a week ahead gives plenty of time to gather materials, make contacts, and solidify ideas. This new two-teacher model eliminates the teacher-aide model, in which one person had the teaching responsibility and the other had a less important role. Each teacher now takes primary responsibility for some activities.

Table 4.1   Assignment Chart for Teacher A and Teacher B

Time	Activity Period	Description	Materials Needed	Teacher
_____	Opening	Free choice	(Complete this column according to activities planned)	A
_____	Gathering	Theme setting		B
_____	Activity	Outdoor		B
_____	Gathering	Snack		A
_____	Gathering	Language		B
_____	Activity	Creative art		A

The basic inner qualities of the teacher are more influential on the learning of the young child than any other single factor (Elkind, 1970); therefore, the teacher must accept the following responsibilities:

To Herself (Himself): growing professionally; maintaining good physical and emotional health; showing enthusiasm (being loving and patient); understanding self; developing and using good observational and reporting skills. Each teacher will have specific personal goals.

To Children: building a good relationship; valuing their uniqueness; meeting their individual needs through appropriate experiences; respecting their individualities, independence, self-control, and self-image; and assisting them toward reaching their individual potential.

To Parents: being a good listener and encouraging feedback from them; valuing their uniqueness, ideas, and goals; using their cultural and personal characteristics as a valuable curriculum resource; providing good counseling and/or appropriate referrals; providing information and materials at the developmental level for the child; keeping them informed about school practices and activities.

To Team Members: forming a good relationship with and among them by supporting high values and ideas; assisting in their personal growth; respecting them; being prompt (Have things organized and ready when the children arrive. Control is difficult to regain if children get ahead of you.); Keeping current by reading professional periodicals, books, and pamphlets and by attending professional workshops and conferences to aid you in becoming a more effective teacher; planning ahead (Make sure the next activity is ready before warning children to finish their current involvement.); refraining from interacting when another teacher is handling a situation or unless your help is requested; being a good housekeeper both indoors and outdoors (Keep the center clean and attractive; however, avoid being so involved in cleanup that children are unsupervised.); being totally aware of what is going on (Just furnishing a warm body is insufficient.); Striking a balance between giving needed one-to-one attention and keeping peripheral awareness of other activities; sharing your experiences and ideas with other staff members; being a good support and lead teacher; being honestly enthusiastic about being with the children; relaxing and smiling.

To the Community: being active in solving problems; participating in local early childhood organizations and local functions; communicating information about the importance of growth, development, and education for young children and families.

What to Plan?

One must find a way to bring relevant, appropriate experiences into the classroom. Several important questions must be considered:

➤ What are the children like? (See Chapter 1.)
➤ What is developmentally appropriate for the age levels and interests of individual children? (See Chapter 1.)

➤ What is the role and responsibility of the teacher? (See beginning of this chapter). Also consider five interrelated dimensions of early childhood professional practice: (1) maintaining a caring community of learners, (2) enhancing development and learning, (3) constructing appropriate curriculum, (4) assessing children's development and learning, and (5) establishing good relationships with families.

➤ What kinds of experiences should be included or excluded?

At the risk of sounding redundant, let me add some implications when working with children who have special (advanced or delayed) needs: Some adults (teachers, administrators, parents, or others) may want to place these children into classrooms where the opportunities will not complement their personal needs. Some need remedial experiences, while others need to be challenged. Careful planning for **all** children in your classroom is the basis for good teaching. For example, children without special needs tend to engage in more cooperative play and less solitary play and spend less time interacting with peers with disabilities Typically, developing children and those with advanced or delayed development spend less time interacting with their peers whose development is different from theirs. Adults (teachers and others) may want to place children with special needs into multi-age classrooms. Teachers might try to model new ideas or problem solve with all the children to promote successful interactions and learning for all children (Hestenes & Carroll, 2000, p. 244).

Here are some guidelines:

First—the Children. Consider each child individually and all children collectively—interests, knowledge, security, skills, and other known information.

Second—Experiences. Consider interpersonal relationships, sensory experiences, exploration of natural and physical surroundings, intellectual stimulation, muscle development, language opportunities, and other available information.

Third—the Curriculum. What do the children already know—and are the concepts true and on their developmental level? What are the most effective ways of teaching new information? How can curriculum areas be integrated, strengthened, and made more useful? How can teachers be most effective?

Fourth—Evaluation. How can teachers determine how effective the learning has been? What would be effective follow-up? Discussing events immediately after the

Teachers need to be well prepared when they teach young children!

1. Development	Have all domains of development been provided for?
2. Observation	Will teachers have an opportunity to observe and record (at least some of) the activities of (some of) the children?
3. Interaction	Has the environment been prepared so children learn through active exploration, through interaction with other children and adults, and across developmental domains and curriculum areas?
4. Interests/abilities	Are activities and materials interesting, slightly challenging, concrete, real, and relevant to the lives of young children?
5. Flexibility	Does the plan provide for activities with increasing difficulty, complexity, and challenge so children with either less or more developed skills will be interested and challenged?
6. Choice	Can children choose from among a variety of activities, materials, equipment, playmates, and time spent to become immersed, stimulated, and satisfied?
7. Balance	Is there provision for active and quiet, indoor and outdoor, individual and group play? (Equal time is not always the best plan.)
8. Diversity	Has there been concerted effort to avoid anti-cultural, biased, exclusive, and competitive play?

Figure 4.2   Daily Curriculum Checklist

departure of the children, an important responsibility, enhances planning skills, the ability to evaluate objectively, and relations with other staff members. Serious evaluation leads to better understanding of children and better planning (see Figure 4.2).

When teachers are aware of the individual characteristics of each child, they know which children are ready for new experiences, what will appeal to many children, what activities will support the experiences, and how to follow up on them. Rather than plan for a *specific,* nonflexible day, they consider attitudes and desire for participation as they are expressed by the children.

Teachers expect to clarify, increase, and stimulate the interests of children. They do so by being observant of children's actions and conversations. The written plan is merely a guide to assist teachers in providing breadth and depth experiences for the children, who are at varying levels of cognitive and physical development.

Try one of the following to acquaint children with the physical environment, safety rules, participation, or interaction:

➤ Introduce a new toy, game, procedure, field trip, and so on.
➤ Encourage the children to help set rules or limits. Consider appropriate praise or restrictions. What should we do when children follow the rules? What should we do when children do not follow the rules? Do we need to rethink our plan: too many things to consider, too many new things, or inflexible expectations of children's responses?
➤ Prepare some sensory stimulation experiences for the children. Include items that are hard/soft, wet/dry, cold/warm, pleasurable/annoying, odorous/non-odorous, loud/soft, sweet/sour, smooth/rough, movable/stable, and so on. Omit anything *harmful.* Stimulate various senses.

Sensory stimulation can help a child to learn about her environment. There are some qualities or textures that we want in a child-care setting. For example, softness can be in furnishings (furniture, wall hangings, floor coverings, toys, or other items). In the outdoors, there may be grass, sand, dirt, and so on. Manipulative materials may be messy, rough, soft, fluid, hard, or other textures. Quiet places are likely to have soft, cuddly materials; loud places may include blocks, riding toys, digging, or other activities. Objects and materials that the senses respond to are very important for young children.

*I wonder what I'm supposed to do
with these things!*

Flexibility in Planning

A truly appropriate curriculum will not look the same from one classroom of children to
the next, from one school district to another, from one year to the next, or for teachers
who have used the topic or information before—to be a duplicate would violate the philosophy of being developmentally appropriate for the children within the present classroom. However, early-childhood teachers can benefit from the experiences of other
teachers, classrooms, printed material, or strategies if proper adjustment has been made
for current children and classrooms. A curriculum is "grass roots" in the sense that it is
responsible to the "common people" (the children the teachers, the parents, and others)
(Cassidy & Lancaster, 1993, p. 47).

At the beginning of the school year, or at any time during the year, teachers may put
emphasis on the classroom atmosphere (attendance, playmates, rules, weather, playground, or other elements). Later, she may try to "web" earlier curriculum into additional meaningful experiences, such as rearranging the playground, creating new
combinations of friends, or providing additional cooking or other experiences. Or the
teacher may prepare (or substitute) new items for an "interest" table to encourage exploration by the children. Some materials and toys may remain in the classroom on a
semipermanent basis. Units and themes emerge from use of items rather than from a
pre-planned length of time. Popularity of ideas may change as children use or ignore
them.

Spodek (1973) made some interesting observations and concluded the following
about rigid or stereotyped planning:

1. Themes, as traditionally implemented, proved to be limiting and counterproductive to the task
   at hand.
2. The cookbook approach to curriculum planning was ineffective in planning developmentally appropriate curriculum.
3. Activities that were age appropriate existed within the teachers' repertoire of ideas . . . but the
   teachers didn't have specific information about what the individuals in the classroom needed or
   were interested in until they had an opportunity to observe and interact with the children on a
   daily basis.

4. Although child observation formed the foundation of the curriculum, the curriculum was neither prescriptive nor reactive in nature but rather interactive—a dialogue between teachers and children.
5. Observations were affected by teacher bias (p. 84).

Appendix A Suggested Curriculum Topics, and Appendix B Suggested Miniplans for Curriculum Chapters, are intended as "stimulators" or beginning points for classroom focus or webbing purposes.

To include flexibility in the curriculum, the teacher need look no further than observations of the children. They have some interests in common; yet at times they have totally diverse interests. At any rate, their use of materials, their conversation, their response to others, their sustained or divided interests, and their mortality add humor, seriousness, interest, and diversity. Children make a major contribution to the curriculum, but not the sole contribution. Teachers clearly are decision makers in this process.

Documenting comments of children, uses of materials, input from parents, spin-offs to other topics, better notes, or other information (a valued practice in Reggio Emilia classrooms) helps teachers have a more solid basis upon which to introduce or expand a particular topic at other times.

Multicultural Education

A multiculturally sensitive classroom has several advantages for children:

➤ They develop pride in and appreciation for their own culture.
➤ They increase their awareness of other cultural groups.
➤ They learn to promote diversity.
➤ Their activities are integrated into the curriculum.
➤ They begin a lifelong search about people who make up our world.
➤ They develop their own self-concept.
➤ They make new friends.
➤ They enlarge their view of families and the community.
➤ They develop sensitivity to others.
➤ They notice new and different ways to do things.
➤ They become curious about other aspects of family life.
➤ Their own lives are enriched and expanded to include issues beyond their immediate experiences.

For the teacher, incorporating a multiculturally sensitive classroom entails the following tasks and suggestions:

➤ Be curious about the children within your classroom regardless of their color, sex, or culture.
➤ Discover their interests and present knowledge.
➤ Seek out and bring materials into the classroom that will create interest in new and different ideas and things.
➤ Be patient and observant.
➤ Gradually, with authenticity and respectfulness, introduce cultures of children within your classroom.
➤ Ask parents for suggestions, resources, and assistance.
➤ Encourage curiosity and acceptance.

(Ideas that promote cultural sensitivity have been included at the end of each curriculum chapter.)

 **Reflection**

Using a multicultural theme of your choice, design an activity or daily theme. To make it successful, you will want to consider the following:

- Applicability (or interest) to the children
- Planning (before, during, and after)
- Preparation of the classroom and the children
- Ways to keep the activity child-centered
- Outside or special props or people
- Integration into known curriculum and familiar routines
- Any special instructions or restrictions
- Responses of the children: how to lengthen or shorten the activity
- Possible questions or concerns of the children
- Information for parents
- Follow-up/Other

Lesson Plan Guide

It may seem inconsistent to say that lesson plans should be flexible and then suggest a formal plan. In presenting the following information and format, it is assumed that the planner is always aware of the children he teaches, their interests, and their abilities, and is constantly aware of blending concepts together to aid children's learning. (See "Flexibility in Planning," p. 125.)

A good lesson plan is used as a guide and not as an end in itself. Planning is an ongoing procedure designed to meet the needs of young children. The process includes three general stages: preassessing, teaching, and evaluating. A complete lesson plan has seven components: theme, preassessment and findings, ideas to be emphasized, schedule of the day, items for special attention, evaluation, and follow-through for parents.

Prior to the day the lesson material is to be used, the teachers sit down together, before the children arrive, and review the activities and responsibilities so that everything is fresh in their minds. (See Figures 4.3 and 4.4.)

Theme

A theme may not always be selected; however, it does give some direction and continuity to activities provided. Teachers may get theme ideas from comments or play of the children—and may be surprised at play preferences or disinterests of children.

Some children might ask, "What are we talking about today?" and some may not pick up on a theme, but with a variety of open-ended opportunities the child is likely to gather subjective knowledge whether or not it is theme-related. The theme itself suggests the best ways to present the concepts.

Using the idea of webbing, consider (1) what led up to the selection of this topic and (2) how it can be expanded at a later date.

A theme is not used to impart knowledge that can be memorized or regurgitated. Nor is it taught once and forgotten. On their own, children will revive, elaborate on, or continue a theme while adding variety and dimension. Rather than being a one-shot overdose, the topic is used again later on, or frequently as the interest of children suggests.

For some suggested curriculum topics, see Appendix A.

Daily Planning Outline

———————————————   ———————————————
           Teacher/Planner   Date

THEME

PREASSESSMENT AND FINDINGS

IDEAS TO BE EMPHASIZED

SCHEDULE OF THE DAY
Time   Activity period   Description   Materials needed   Teacher

ITEMS FOR SPECIAL ATTENTION

EVALUATION

FOLLOW-THROUGH FOR PARENTS

Figure 4.3 Thumbnail Sketch of the Day

 *Reflection*

In order to get to the classroom, the children had to detour through a toy and supply area. Every day Alan spotted a package containing plastic dinosaurs, and every day he asked to use them. Thinking the dinosaurs would be of little or no interest to the 4-year-olds and forgetting to remove them before the next day, the teacher finally gave in. Alan spent most of the morning with the dinosaurs—and so did many of the other children. They would take a replica to the teacher and ask, "What's he called?" Unprepared, the teacher made a few excuses and then remembered a book about dinosaurs that was also tucked away in the storage room. Alan (and others—including the teacher) began matching the pictures to the replicas. In no time they could describe the animals, give their proper names, and tell something special about them (body, eating habits, and so on). Much learning, interacting, and excitement went on that day—and others. Thanks to Alan!

1. Theme	Consider ideas suggested by both children and adults, but make sure the topics are within the understanding of young children. Include ideas that have local, seasonal, or current interest, but also introduce new ideas when feasible.
2. Preassessment and findings	When questioning is used, be sure questions are thoughtful and open-ended. When using props or activities, make sure they are realistic and familiar. In reporting findings, use clear responses.
3. Ideas to be emphasized	Include the most important information related to the topic. Prepare simple, moderate, and advanced information to meet the needs of all the children. Assume that this information will be the basis for building on this topic.
4. Learning activities and tentative schedule of the day	Use ideas and activities that are realistic, are concrete, and teach the desired concepts. Include specific and detailed information about transitions, stories, outside activities, and so on, and when they occur. Have activities for all areas of the curriculum and provide for all domains of development. Provide large blocks of time—be prepared to lengthen or shorten periods depending on the interest of the children.
5. Evaluation	Reflect on how plan areas overlap and support each other (preassessment with activities, ideas and evaluation, and so on). Give specific examples of conversation and/or activities that show learning of individual children and the group as a whole. Consider how misconceptions can be corrected and how concepts can be used as a basis for future learning. Plan on using this topic at a later time, making appropriate modifications or additions.
6. Aids: books, records, other	List books on the theme and how they will be used. List books for diversion (include author, title, and publisher for future use). List records/tapes that will be used (include recording company and number). List other aids to be used (songs, visual aids, musical instruments, props, and so on).
7. Parental information	Give a brief overview of the day/week with brief and logical suggestions for parental follow-through. Include date and group. Make information neat, showing value for the teacher, child, and parent.

Figure 4.4   Lesson Plan Checklist

Preassessment and Findings

Once teachers know the interest of the children, the next step is to find out what the children already know about it, collectively and individually. Do have in mind some introductory, intermediate, and advanced ideas for children in different stages of learning. In this way the beginner will not be overwhelmed or the advanced learner demeaned. Some basic information can be used for review and some can be used for initial introduction of materials and activities. Children with prior knowledge are used to help inform the others, and each child is taken just beyond his present knowledge. Raw materials and unlimited time can help children find their knowledge and interest levels.

Preassessment is made before developing a plan and is done casually or formally. The casual approach yields general information; the formal, specific. The following are two examples of preassessment on shapes:

1. *Casual:* Approach individual children or a small group and ask them if they know any shapes. If so, which ones? On a table, place items in the different shapes you plan to teach. See what the children say about them or do with them. With this method you are trying to see if the children can name shapes without the shapes

Teachers and children share conversations about school, activities, and other things.

being present; then you are supplying the actual shapes and seeing if this gives the children clues. Observe, listen, and take notes.

2. *Formal:* Prepare some of the desired shapes. Then individually ask each child to hand you a specific shape. Also ask her to look around the room and tell you if she can see things in the room that are of the same shape. Can she give the right name for each shape and point out an example?

In the preassessment section of the planning checklist (Figure 4.4) are some guides. Preassessment is employed to acquire significant information. Teachers should pay close attention to the responses of the children, rather than deciding before the preassessment what they'll provide in the classroom and what they'll teach regardless of the present knowledge or interest of the children.

Several ideas or themes may be presented during an activity period. Materials planned with a certain child in mind may not be of interest to him at the time—but other children will probably join in.

Ideas to Be Emphasized

The central ideas, which are a direct result of the preassessment, bind the theme and the activities together. Known ideas are used as a foundation on which to add new ideas. The latter should be in the form of simple, true statements based on the developmental level of the children. The number of new ideas depends on the amount and depth of information to be taught without overwhelming the children.

Again, expect children to use materials in a variety of ways—some will be even better than the ones the teacher had planned. Be observant as the children interact with the materials and with peers. They don't have to respond as the teacher planned in order for the experience to be a success!

Schedule of the Day

This part of the plan can be in written or graphic form and reflects the teacher's creativity, thoroughness, and versatility (see Table 4.2).

The following are some suggestions for opening/activity play time:

➤ Creative art
➤ Books/flannel board and objects
➤ Manipulative toys
➤ Science table
➤ Dramatic play
➤ Music and movement
➤ Blocks
➤ Floor toys
➤ Water/sand table
➤ Outdoor climbing
➤ Outdoor wheel toys
➤ Food preparation and eating

Table 4.2 Suggested Daily Time Frames

Period	Setup	Particulars
Opening	Classroom is set up with a variety of centers. Children choose play situations and companions.	Transition from home to classroom. Flexible depending on the arrival of children. Teachers greet children. Parents depart. Child engages in activities.
Activity play time	Learning centers. In some cases materials are set out; in others, children get and replace toys of their choosing.	Can combine opening and activity play. Longest part of day. Flexible; avoid interruptions. Child-centered. Options in different areas and with peers. May recur throughout the day. Indoors, outdoors, or both. Teachers are available but do not direct play. Chance to encourage and broaden child's interests.
Gathering	Usually for stories, snack, music, language opportunities, a guest, special information, events important for the group.	Short and infrequent. Teacher/group-oriented. Indoors or outdoors. Social interaction: sharing, spacing self to see, turn taking, listening/speaking, instruction, information, peer relationships, participation, and so on. Drawbacks: child must leave what he was doing, may not be too interested, resent being directed, want more activity, and so on.
Closing time	Children replace toys, do wind-down activities, and gather personal items to take home.	Flexible—depending on arrival of parents. Teacher helps child prepare for departure as other teacher remains with other children.

Evaluation

Items for Special Attention

Items may or may not be listed here daily, but the reminder is invaluable when needed. The staff may need to carefully watch a certain activity (a transition, for example) or a certain child (perhaps one has been especially listless lately). A reminder to recontact someone for a future activity, such as a field trip or a visitor, can be written here. A note can be made to rearrange the indoor or outdoor areas, to order more supplies for an activity (wood for the woodworking table for Thursday), or to check the drain on the water table before filling it with water and boats. This space is not used for personal reminders (personal phone calls, errands, appointments, etc.).

Evaluation

This is how to determine how well the day was planned, how well the children responded, how well the staff performed, and what changes can be made before the plan is used again (webbed). Notes can be written right on the plan as reminders to make any additions, deletions, or modifications.

To be most effective, the evaluation is held as soon as possible after the children leave the center. All the staff who worked with the children that day are included, if possible. At times just the lead and support teachers participate.

On the lesson plan, valuable ideas evident during planning should be written in the form of questions, statements, or mere reminders. They give a starting point to the discussion and, it is hoped, help make the evaluation meaningful. Productivity of the evaluation, not the clock, decides the length.

To get the staff in a constructive mood, discussion should begin with things that went well. Open-ended questions, ones requiring thinking, recalling, observing, and interpreting, help make for effective evaluations. For example, compare these two questions: "Did the children like the activities today?" "Which activities did the children seem to enjoy the most today?" The first question calls for a yes or no answer; the second, for careful thought and response.

Things that did not go well are also discussed, continuing until ideas come up on how they can be done differently, avoided, or turned into learning experiences instead of failures.

The progress of each child should be assessed frequently. Looking at one or two children per week may be sufficient, or there may be a child who needs more consideration. The children should be the focal point of the center.

Follow-Through for Parents

This section gives space to consider, during planning, the parents and the home. Some teachers prefer to send home a note daily telling what has transpired during that day, and some prefer a weekly or monthly newsletter; still others post a lesson plan daily and remind parents to read it. Whatever the method, the closeness between home and center is vital, and the child is the connecting link.

A little time and effort are needed to prepare messages for the parents, but they are worthwhile. As the parent brings or picks up the child, a spontaneous or common topic can be shared. The teacher's message should never be a tool of interrogation. Rather, it should keep parents informed and encourage valuable feedback so that misconceptions, comments, or interests of the children can be used in future planning. (See the discussion in Chapter 2)

The teacher may find a skeleton plan helpful. Samples of miniplans will be found in Appendix A on selected curriculum areas.

Conclusions

The following paragraph receives my full support:

> NAEYC has devoted more than 60 years of activity to ensuring the best for children. We would never advocate subjecting children to inappropriate environments. At the same time, we cannot support policies such as readiness testing, transition classes, holding younger children out of school, or raising the entrance age, which we know at best are short-term solutions and at worst harm individual children and contribute to inappropriate expectations (Bredekamp & Shepard, 1989, p. 23).

Not all teachers have been trained in the developmentally appropriate practices (DAP) method. Some, hearing about it recently after university training and years of teaching in the field, have misgivings and frustrations. Consider the following report of Carter (1992):

> Not everyone is a believer in the discovery approach in early childhood education; some teachers still use the direct-instruction method. Interns can help bridge the gap that exists between the two philosophies. This will not be easy because everyone would rather resist change, especially if they have "*always* done it this way." Tenured teachers would benefit from seminars that would help them bridge the gap between the direct-instruction way they may teach now and developmentally appropriate practices. Teachers need to see the reward they would get for changing the way they teach now, and that reward is *children who can think* (p. 72).

Developing Curriculum

Of special concern when planning for young children (and also raised in the NAEYC guidelines) are:

- ➤ In the curriculum *all subjects are meaningfully addressed.*
- ➤ The *focus is on the whole child.*
- ➤ The activities, concepts, and materials *are age appropriate for **these** children.*
- ➤ The curriculum is planned around *the individual appropriateness* of the children in each classroom.

In each case, the zone of proximal development must continually be sought and incorporated in learning activities for young children (Krogh, 1997, p. 35).

Curriculum opportunities for children should include and integrate all areas of development. Children should have an opportunity to explore materials and activities as well as to interact with adults and other children. Learning activities should be real and relevant to the child's world. "Workbooks, worksheets, coloring books, and adult-made models of art products for children to copy are *not appropriate* for young children, especially those younger than 6" (Bredekamp, 1987, p. 4). Wise teachers plan periods of active play interspersed with more quite or restful periods so children do not become overly stimulated or bored. Teachers should always encourage children to participate both indoors and outdoors as weather, conditions, and interest dictate.

"Projects" in the Early Childhood Classroom

Frequently or seldom, depending upon the flexibility and/or the interests of the children, a child might bring an object or suggest an idea for classroom inclusion. Teachers would do well to consider such topics—thus encouraging children to generate ideas and questions about "coincidental" events. With roots in the work of Dewey (1916, 1938) and Kilpatrick (1925, 1936), projects allow for meaningful, hands-on learning (Sloane, 1999, p. 17). In this way, children are exposed to new ideas, are taught new skills, and have new experiences—their ideas and interests play a major role in shaping the curriculum. That *input* essential to a topic or project's success is what distinguishes a true project from a teacher-planned theme or unit (Katz, 1994).

Sometimes we work quietly at tables.

As teachers and children plan projects, "they generate questions and goals, engaging in learning experiences, summarizing and displaying what is learned (Chard 1997), and evaluation. The ways in which they differ include how they began, the type of goals they encompass, their length, and how much work they involve" (Sloane, 1999, p. 17). Based on the interests of the children, teachers will guide the breadth and depth of the experiences planned, which will become more complex and developmentally appropriate as the children mature and gain experience with project learning.

A developmentally appropriate (emergent) curriculum is a result of interaction between teachers and children, who both contribute ideas and react to them. "Units" in a developmentally appropriate classroom are not pre-planned activity segments with a standard time length.

Themes that emerge from brainstorming, an event, or introduction of materials interconnect and flow from one to the other as children ask questions and develop new interests.

Curriculum Negotiations

When teachers make a conscious effort to negotiate the curriculum, they are likely to plan between teachers, children, and sometimes parents. While they may not necessarily agree on what to provide, dialogue (a practice strongly emphasized in Reggio Emilia centers) can be a significant source of mutual and in-depth learning. Following are some ideas to consider.

Interests of the Children (Individual and/or Group)

➤ Something new, something based on a former topic (emergent curriculum), something children suggest, something they have always wanted to try, something "way out." Use table, floor, or wall space to display a number of replicas or real objects— for example, a plastic alligator, a large feather, real vegetables or fruits, hats, some straw, a piece of foam, seeds, a hula hoop, a peanut in a shell, a stuffed animal, a totally unfamiliar object, a holiday symbol (mask, basket, flag), a photograph of a person or location; you can add more.

➤ Ideas that are *open-ended* and are *starting points,* characteristics of emergent curriculum. Observe carefully, or better still, have someone record (tape or notes) the individual responses of the children (or adults). Always be alert to unexpected events. Documentation can be the driving force behind your curriculum development.

➤ Plan on webbing ideas so that the children will see ideas as connecting and supporting entities rather than just separate bits, pieces, or time consumers. (See section titled "Curriculum Webbing" later in this chapter.)

➤ Values of children that are at odds with the values of adults in their lives (violent play or war play, for example) may lead teachers to offer four options: (1) ban the play, (2) permit or ignore the play, (3) permit the play with specific limits, or (4) actively facilitate the play (Carlsson-Paige and Levin, (1987).

Requirements: (Suggested by Jones & Nimmo [1994, p. 77])

➤ canned (district, state, local, governing bodies)
➤ embalmed (from teacher's years of experience)
➤ accidental/unidentified or "inherited" (from "here and there")
➤ emergent (curriculum is more work, more fun, and a value choice)

In a speech given at and published by NAEYC, Margaret Mead (1973) described a preplanned, rational curriculum as

> the transcendent boredom—to be shut up in a room, away from anything that moves or breathes or grows, in a controlled temperature, hour after hour after hour—means that we are taking away from them any kind of chance of responsiveness. . . . When this occurs, it is a problem shared by teachers and children alike. Teachers shouldn't model giving in; they should model intelligent problem solving (Jones & Nimmo, 1994, p. 77).

"Open-endedness"

➤ These ideas can be used in daily teaching. Rather than overload the children with too many ideas, not enough time to use them, and cursory examination, some adults have to consciously let go of some ideas. There will be other times and other children who can benefit from new ideas (including those of the children).

➤ In the planning stages of the Reggio Emilia approach, adults discuss various possibilities, hypotheses, and potential directions that a project might take (Rankin, 1993, p. 192). "Isolating a teacher in a classroom and giving her or him a prescribed curriculum that presents only one hypothesis at a time is the opposite approach to ensuring quality in education. It assumes the possibility of 'teacher-proof' canned curriculum rather than reliance on teachers' continuing growth as the source of quality" (Jones & Nimmo, 1994, p. 51).

"Emotion Producing"

➤ At Reggio Emilia, teachers actually plan activities and experiences knowing that they may worry or frighten some children. When asked why they would purposefully provide such an experience, the simple explanation was that children need opportunities, within the safety of the group setting, to understand and learn how to cope with their own and others' feelings. "The American preoccupation with protecting young children from experiencing negative emotions is a marked contrast to this practice," says New (1993, p. 226).

➤ Instead of intensifying a fear (of darkness, animals, water, people, or whatever) adults can help children to understand other aspects of the fear: What is interesting, different, useful, beautiful, and so on. How could one harmoniously deal with the fear? If one pays close attention, what will one find out?

"Touchy" Topics   No matter what the subject, the educational setting, or the political or religious orientation of the locality, some topics will raise "red flags" for some parents, students, teachers, and others. Refer to Chapter 10, Social Studies, Anti-Bias curriculum, and Field Trips. Teachers are always cautious about teaching subjects that may need discretion, sensitivity, poise, accuracy, and other considerations. Some particular topics may be special occasions (holidays), religion, race, violence, food habits, and customs. When or if the topics are taught, they should be done with respect and accuracy and geared to the level of the children in the immediate setting. Some topics can be taught separately; some must include a combination of ideas to give a complete picture. Most of the teaching decisions will be determined by school or government policies, personal feelings of teachers and parents, allotted classroom time, community pressure, or other limitations.

Some values of children may be at odds with the values of the adults in their lives (violent play or war play, for example). When this happens, Carlsson-Paige and Levin (1987) offer four options: (1) ban the play, (2) permit or ignore the play, (3) permit the play with specific limits, or (4) actively facilitate the play. They further suggest that the teacher might try to

> bring in new content for the play, such as new props, roles, and physical settings, which grow out of current content and will help children vary and elaborate the play. This is especially important for those children who seem to be following a television script or acting out the same theme over and over in the same way.

For a discussion on violence and war play, see the section title "Violence and Children's Play" in Chapter 3. How many teachers tried (and in what ways) to calm the fears of young children following the World Trade Center attack on "9–11"? How successful were they in handling their own feelings?

Some teachers fill their walls with commercial or teacher-made patterns, thinking they will stimulate interest in learning. Rather, children's creative work, documentation of prior activities, and items of interest (another important feature of Reggio Emilia classrooms) should adorn the classroom for child pleasure, parent awareness and support, and further stimulation for teaching.

Example:
I was working with university students in the child development labs on our campus, and the student was ready to take over the role of "lead teacher." The next step was that she/he *casually* preassessed what the children already knew, were interested in, misunderstandings, and so on. After this information was carefully considered, a tentative lesson plan was outlined. Some of the student teachers were surprised about the present knowledge of some of the children, how some of them were uninformed or misinformed, and varying amounts of interest in the subject. Using more knowledgeable children to assist less knowledgeable children (scaffolding) was interesting, productive, and rewarding. In addition to measuring what the child currently knows, the examiner actively tries to facilitate performance in order to gauge the breadth of the child's ZPD (zone of proximal development: the hypothetical, dynamic region in which learning and development take place; or the child's *readiness* to profit from instruction).

Grouping

Levenstein, in line with Vygotsky's theory, concluded that "responding to children with lighthearted, pleasurable conversation that promotes involvement and imaginative thinking during play is especially well suited for fostering the effectance motivation and self-regulatory capacities necessary for success in school" (Levenstein and O'Hara 1993).

When I am stumped, my teacher helps me think things through.

 Vygotsky emphasized the importance of mixed-age groupings of children, which gives each child:

➤ more knowledgeable companions;
➤ more complex play;
➤ more challenge to master new skills;
➤ an opportunity to serve as an expert resource for others (scaffolding);
➤ more complex and goal-directed play;
➤ more gender interaction;
➤ more diverse and socially integrated play experiences; and
➤ an opportunity to improve self-regulatory skills (Berk & Winsler, 1995, p. 135).

Reflection

When I first started teaching at the university, each head teacher had a half-day group of children within a somewhat narrow age range, and each insisted that her age group (whatever it was) was the hardest to teach. We wondered why personal preference, time of day, influence of student teachers, the particular parents, other teaching assignments, and on and on made a difference in teacher attitudes. Later on we began multi-age groups of children from ages 2 ½ to 5. While some teachers still preferred the narrower age range for various reasons, we found that our teaching of wider-age groups was much easier than the narrower-age groups. Why was this so? Because we could see growth in the individual children, we could use "scaffolding"—although we didn't call it that! Some of our older children felt more comfortable with younger classmates because the competition was lessened. Some of our younger children "blossomed" as they followed the lead of the older children. As teachers, our education, training, and teaching were greatly enhanced and enlarged!

The benefits of mixed-age interaction in early childhood programs also depend on the classroom context and the amount of teacher-provided structure. For example, in one study, the prosocial and cognitive benefits of mixed-age peer interaction seemed to be strongest during classroom activities only moderately structured by the teacher (Winsler 1993). "In sum, mixed-age classrooms can provide unusually rich social experiences for preschool children. However, the benefits of mixed-age interaction depend on how well teachers organize and support children's classroom activities" (Berk & Winsler, 1995, p. 36).

Three questions to help teachers decide how much guidance to offer children during play with peers are outlined by File (1993) and displayed as Table 3.2 in Berk & Winsler, 1995, p. 74. These include (1) focusing on the skills of individual children, (2) determining what level of (adult) support is necessary, and (3) intervention.

Because of various (sometimes uncontrollable) reasons, some groups of children are close in age while others have wide age spans; grouping these children may be easy or difficult, mandatory or voluntary.

Assessment

How do you know when a child has learned something? Children differ in the breadth and depth of their of ZPDs—their zone of *readiness* to profit from instruction.

> Whereas static assessment procedures emphasize the child's previously acquired knowledge in terms of intelligence or achievement scores, *dynamic assessment* involves purposeful teaching within the testing situation. It attempts to distinguish a child's apparent level of development, as might be measured by a standardized test, from the child's potential level of development—the performance the child is capable of attaining with support (Berk & Winsler, 1995, p. 138).

One contemporary assessment approach for preschool through third grade asks teachers to use checklists to enhance the process of observation and make it more reliable (Meisels, 1993, p. 35). It covers the domains of personal and social development, language and literature, mathematical and scientific thinking, social studies, art and music, and physical development. Each child has a summary report completed during fall, winter, and spring that includes brief summaries of the child's classroom performance, based on teacher observations and records, and is transformed from the checklists into easily understood and interpreted documents for parents, teachers, and administrators.

In order to make any assessment meaningful, teachers must learn to become astute observers—knowing what to look for, what it means, and how to interpret it to others. Parents also become a part of the assessment process. They can be guided to see that standardized tests and typical report cards are poor substitutes for observations and participation of teachers and parents. Parents can also become more involved in their children's school behaviors, activities, and accomplishments.

Standardized tests, especially for young children, have been under fire currently, periodically, and continually. Some teachers devise their own methods of evaluating children and have difficulty in administering mandatory tests. What do they mean anyway? The condition of the room, the health and attitude of the child, external pressures (parents, peers, school, geographical location), and many other variables determine the child's performance. Tests for young children cannot be watered-down versions of tests for older children. NAEYC and NAECS/SDE have identified assessment measures for use with young children.

Testing can be a very powerful tool; it has "the power to change teachers' and children's perceptions of themselves and their view of the entire educational process. Teachers and researchers have studied this phenomenon extensively but our daily experience provides the most convincing evidence about how powerful tests have become" (Meisels, 1993, p. 35). And further, group-administered tests focus on the acquisition of simple facts, low-level skills, superficial memorization, and isolated evidence of achievement. Of

Listening to the teacher helps me learn new things!

greatest concern, they rob teachers of their sense of judgment—of how to help children develop to their optimal potential (Jerris, 1991).

> Vygotsky-inspired dynamic assessment differs from traditional assessment in that it focuses on process rather than product—identifying the strategies the individual child already uses to master academically relevant tasks and the instructional procedures most likely to help that child learn more effectively. In addition to measuring what the child currently knows, the examiner actively tries to facilitate performance in order to gauge the breadth of the child's ZPD (Berk & Winsler, 1995, p. 139).

Different methods of assessment, other than standardized testing, are being used as an outgrowth of the constructivist perspective in early childhood education, as a means of implementing developmentally appropriate practices in classrooms, and as an avenue for integrating assessment with curriculum. Based on these changes, the field of early childhood education advocates assessing young children through formal or informal methods of observation and interview, which must be systematic and ongoing (Fleege, 1997, p. 331).

The most appropriate methods for recording observations and interviews conducted with children would include: checklists, rating scales, photographs, audiotapes, videotapes, work samples, anecdotal records, running records, time sampling, and event sampling.

Assessing knowledge of school age children and adults can be more sophisticated than that of nonreading and language-limited young children. So how do we know what young children have learned? I had some very interesting experiences when inquiring of young children about different types of pictured situations (my dissertation on "The Ability of 3-, 4-, and 5-Year-Old Children to Distinguish Reality from Fantasy"). Most of the children could not verbalize the differences, but most of them were more than willing to demonstrate to me.

 **Reflection**

You have a student teacher (or an aide, or a parent, or friend) who recently traveled to a remote location to examine a coal mine. He (she) was so impressed with the mine that she/he wants to share this experience (or one that is outside the everyday experience of most preschoolers). Reluctantly, but curiously, you quiz the person about what he/she will tell (show, etc.) to the children, and ask for some general plans. This is done, but the information to present is extensive, demonstrations are abstract, time is restricted, and vocabulary is unfamiliar.

What do you do?

1. Let the person proceed as outlined (expecting the children to be bored and the "presenter" to be frustrated and/or disappointed)?
2. Completely reject the presentation?
3. Insist upon certain modifications (such as terms, ideas, props, etc.)?
4. Have only "advanced" children participate?
5. Have the person select an alternate presentation—from your selected list?
6. Other (you indicate the options).

Further consider:

1. What do you want individuals (presenter, the children, the head teacher, parents, others, etc.) to learn from a classroom "project"?
2. Ask yourself (and your teacher) what is the likelihood the children will have firsthand contact with a coal mine or be able to relate its role in society today?
3. Do you ever teach about anything that has no immediate relevancy? Be careful: this is a "loaded question."

Choosing a documentation method appropriate for an individual child depends on several factors: . . . the characteristics of the child, the developmental domain to be assessed, and the teacher's level of comfort and expertise with a particular method. An assessment plan should be individually tailored to each child (Fleege, 1997, p. 331).

Remember:
Take cues from the current children you teach!

As teachers consider topics for classroom use, they should carefully value the school, community, families, culture, and other aspects of their particular setting. The children themselves initiate play or suggest ideas that may be timely and urgent, temporary and fleeting, or misleading and inappropriate. Their ideas should be considered and valued; however, teachers should carefully justify topics for group exploration. For example, some Reggio Emilia teachers actually plan activities and experiences knowing that they may worry or frighten some children, while others express defiance through mass media or toys that expose unwholesome themes (see section titled "Violence and Children's Play" in Chapter 3). Teachers need to assess the potential of any interest or in-depth learning by both the individual child and other members of the adult-child classroom community. Teachers of young children also need to contemplate topics that support hands-on experiences (local geography, current events, family values) and leave more abstract teaching (outer space or unfamiliar land/water phenomena, for example) until the children are better able to handle them. In other words, focus on the child, the family, the school, the community, and the immediate environment before introducing topics avoided by some adults. If something is of particular interest, such as the discovery of the world's largest spider in the fall of 1996, address it and the children's questions and interest, and then move on.

Watch for those who are uninterested in available topics or materials. What hands-on activities could bring interest to him/her? Does any child in the group have something of interest or value to share with the other children? Watch also for the interest of chil-

Teacher, how many is this?

dren as individuals and as group members. Plan activities in which they can take active part: find a book, bring in items for dramatic play, combine activities and materials, encourage group activities, or provide props where the child can independently explore without disturbing others.

Curriculum Webbing

Consider Bromley's definition of *webbing* (1991):

> In nature, a web is a network of fine threads that a spider weaves. This network forms a complicated structure, the means by which the spider snares its prey. A web can also be a complicated work of the mind that represents objects or concepts and their relationships a person perceives among them. In a classroom, the term *web* borrows something from both definitions. A semantic web, used as an instructional tool in a classroom, is a graphic representation or visual display of categories of information and their relationship (p. 3).

Curriculum webbing will help to emphasize the importance of written and spoken language in relating concepts, in personal relationships, in everyday life, and in making sense of the world to the young children we teach.

Literacy development is a continuous process that begins in infancy. Literacy is learned through oral and written language. Its roots are found everywhere in the environment, beginning in the home and spreading as the child's literacy learning grows out of a variety of experiences.

Semantic webbing, especially the integration and connections among webs, may become the central feature of any curricular approach. Developmentally appropriate activities and outcomes for children are based on a well-used concept in early-childhood education circles: building on interest of children and their present knowledge. The preschooler thinks about the world primarily in limited terms of actions that can be performed, so the choice of concepts must provide for action-oriented, child-initiated plans and activities. When working with several webs simultaneously, children are encouraged to see connections among concepts.

Reflection

In preparing your preschoolers for a band concert on school grounds, during class time, with parents and siblings invited, where do you start your planning? Consider: visitors, noise, kinds of instruments and music you'll hear, length of time, and—believe it or not—unexpected things like bathroom trips, weather, supervision, and so on. You are making a WEB regarding the outcome of this experience!

Creating a curriculum web is based on a well-used concept in early-childhood education circles: building on interests of children and their existing knowledge. Basic concepts should include topics that are manageable, related to one another, part of a cycle, and universal (Workman & Anziano, 1993). The natural interrelations among these webs support the developmental interaction approach of Biber (1977), who, along with others, has advocated for preschool curricula in which cognitive, affective, and social processes are all interdependent.

For example, suppose a child brings a cocoon to school. Beginning with the cocoon, diagram the many events and ideas that could lead up to the cocoon in its present form.

Recall the beautiful thoughts by Carson (1956, pp. 42–45):

"If a child is to keep alive his inborn sense of wonder without any such gift from the fairies, he needs the companionship of at least one adult who can share it, rediscover with him the *joy*, excitement and mystery of the world we live in. . . . [I]t is not half so important to *know* as to *feel*."

My friend helps me when I need him.

Notable Notes about Play and Curriculum Development

"From the very beginning their educational experiences must enable children to:

- be knowledgeable, be able to learn, and continue to learn even more about themselves and the world in which they live;
- think, learn to make decisions, and experience the consequences of these decisions; and
- learn to become a member of a group and to feel a oneness with others" (Seefeldt, 1993, p. 4).

A curriculum that does not originate from the children, their interests, their needs, or their "own environment, whatever or wherever it may be" (Mitchell, 1934, p. 16) has little chance of being meaningful for children.

Without meaning, children are ill able to construct the type of knowledge that promotes freedom of mind. "Knowledge needs to be made meaningful in order to be made critical and transformative" (Giroux, 1992, p. 9).

Curriculum that enables children to construct knowledge that will free them to learn today and tomorrow stems from knowledge of each child and the environment in which he lives, as well as knowledge of subject matter. Teachers "study relations in the environment into which children are born and watch children's behavior in their environment to note when they first discover relations and what they are" (Mitchell, 1934, p. 12).

Teachers must study the goals of the classroom to determine the best ways to introduce experiences to the young children. They will find ways to introduce the key concepts of a given discipline (Bruner, 1966) through their experiences with the environment.

"Each teacher and each school will make its own curriculum for small children," records Mitchell (1934, p. 12).

When curriculum addresses the culture and heritage of the children, their interests and needs, it also addresses their environment. Thus they make sense of their world and their personal lives. Meaningful knowledge satisfies children's need for mastery today and may be the only knowledge that will enable them, in the future, to "reach beyond themselves, to wonder, to imagine, to pose their own questions" (Greene, 1988) and to continue to want to learn (Workman & Anziano, 1993, p. 6).

From Berk & Winsler, 1995, pp. 66–68, 79:

- Play can be looked at from diverse vantage points. Children can reverse roles with adults and compensate for unpleasant experiences in real life.
- Piaget and Vygotsky recognized that pretense allows children to become familiar with social roles, with wider society, and that it is vital for adults in early childhood setting to engage in joint play with children.
- Vygotsky's analysis of curriculum offers a convincing argument for why make-believe is the "ultimate activity for nurturing capacities that are crucial for academic as well as later-life success."
- Personal goals, becoming responsible and productive members of society can be realized through fantasy play.

From Vygotsky, 1930–1935, 1978, p. 102:

- Play helps children understand the meaning and function of significant cultural roles while promoting the formation of voluntary intentions . . . real-life plans and volitional motives.
- Several reoccurring themes apply Vygotsky's ideas to the education of young children.

Then sketch what will happen to the cocoon as it matures. How many ideas can be created that would be developmentally appropriate for 2-, 3-, 4-, or 5- year-old children, or children of mixed ages?

How many different curriculum areas could be involved (language, creativity, music/movement, science, social studies [visitors or field trips], mathematics, food, and so on)? After brainstorming by yourself ask an adult to contribute, and then ask preschool children to "think" with you. How do the ideas expand or change as other individuals share their ideas? What ideas could be tried in your classroom?

Now think of an item that has been brought to school by a child or contributed by an adult. How did you go about incorporating it into your classroom curriculum? How did you expand upon it—or did you use it just once—possibly without prior planning or follow-up? What happened when you ignored an item or event completely?

Think of a few ideas (topics) you would like to teach young children. Where do you start? At the results you wish? With the interim steps? With the props you have available? With the final results you desire? Why was this topic of such interest to you?

Those who work in early childhood programs with other adults find collaboration very helpful; however, those who work in isolated family child care, one-classroom sites, or centers have no interaction and often find planning difficult and challenging.

Sources of emergent curriculum include the interest of children and teachers; developmental tasks; things and people in the physical environment; curriculum resource materials; unexpected events; relationships with others; and values held in the school, community, family, and culture. Many sources of stimulation, encouragement, and support come from the children and parents.

When selecting classroom curriculum, teachers should ask themselves questions about the worth of the content. Is it meaningful and relevant; firsthand or vicarious; accurate and credible according to recognized standards of relevant disciplines? Are goals realistic and attainable expectations? Is the timing better now or after other skills have been acquired?

Narrowing the curriculum to those basic skills that can be easily measured on multiple-choice tests diminished the intellectual challenge for many children. Such intellectually impoverished curriculum underestimates the true competence of children, which has been demonstrated to be much higher than is often assumed (Bredekamp & Copple, 1997, p. 20; Edwards, Gandini, & Forman, 1993; Gelman & Baillargeon, 1983; Resnick, 1996).

Values for Children

There are times when children need to depend on adults to guide their thinking, decisions, and actions; however, under the right circumstances, children need to make decisions for themselves. In quality education programs, young children are given at least partial responsibility for making personal decisions and the opportunity to experience the consequences of their decisions. This enables them to develop the ability to think and decide for themselves through the day. Yet Dewey (1944) believed that another type of decision-making experience was necessary if children were to develop minds that would enable them to be free. In an attempt to push children into true decision making and thinking, Dewey called for classroom use of raw materials (those without any predetermined end or goal, such as blocks, clay, paper and paints, sand, water, boxes, and so on— which he labeled "stuff"). The children were to decide what to do with the materials and when their goals with the materials had been achieved. Achievement of their goals, determined only by themselves, brought joy and satisfaction; failure meant personal adjustment to their plans and actions.

Workbook sheets, workbooks, computer-assisted instruction, even units of group projects that are determined and directed by a teacher do not permit thinking because often much of the doing has been completed by someone else. There is little left for the child to decide or think about.... [W]ithout a solid foundation of decision making built during early childhood, children will be ill prepared to set goals for themselves and achieve these but may be ready and prepared to achieve goals established for them by others (Workman & Anziano, 1993, p. 7).

Classrooms should be arranged to sustain greater individualization on one hand and a broad sense of community on the other (Dewey, 1944; Greenberg, 1992). Opportunities for formal give-and-take with others are arranged "because one cannot share in intercourse with others without learning—without getting a broader point of view and perceiving things of which one would otherwise be ignorant" (Dewey, 1944, p. 123). Through naturally occurring interchanges, children are challenged to adjust their egocentric thoughts, assimilating and accommodating different points of view. "If they are to get along at all, children must consider the ideas, thinking, and wishes of others" (Dyson, 1988).

Group experiences, planned and informal, bring children together where they learn to value the perspectives of others. Spontaneous play, field trips, group interactions (lunch, outdoors, or wherever) provide opportunities for children to listen to, talk to, and interact with each other. They begin to share their thinking with others. And even though the children share the same experience, it has a different perspective for each child. Reflection, considering others' views, and sharing one's own views all further the thinking process and modify each life.

Through raw materials, play, stories and books, music and dance, and science and social studies, young children can have many opportunities to make decisions, interact with others, and develop values. The entire curriculum is important to their later attitudes about education, relationships, and themselves. Teachers can set a healthy learning stage for the children and offer them the type of education that "brings together the need for wide-awakeness with the hunger for community, the desire to know with the wisdom to understand, and the desire to feel with the passion to see" (Greene, 1988, p. 23).

The NAEYC and NAECS/SDE (1992) document identifies specifically:

1. *How* children best learn:
   a. when their physical needs are met and they feel psychologically safe and secure (p. 25)
   b. when they construct knowledge
   c. through social interaction with adults and other children
   d. when learning reflects a recurring cycle that begins in awareness and moves to exploration, to inquiry, and finally, to utilization (p. 26)
   e. through play
   f. when their interests and "need to know" motivate learning
   g. by individual variation (p. 27)

2. *What* children should learn (most important or worthy): The foundation for developmentally appropriate practice advocated here and elsewhere relates to at least two of Eisner's conceptions of curriculum (1990): (a) it promotes the development of cognitive processes and (b) it also emphasizes the role of personal relevance in curriculum decisions.

3. *How* definitions clarify (summarized in NAEYC and NAESC/SDE):

   Curriculum is an organized framework that delineates the content children are to learn, the processes through which children achieve the identified curricular goals, what teachers do to help children achieve these goals, and the context in which teaching and learning occur. The early childhood profession defines curriculum in its broadest sense, encompassing prevailing theories, approaches, and models.

   Assessment is the process of observing, recording, and otherwise documenting the work children do and why they do it, as a basis for a variety of educational decisions that affect the child, including planning for groups and individual children, and communicating with parents. Assessment encompasses the many forms of evaluation available to educational decision makers. Assessment in the service of curriculum and learning requires teachers to observe and analyze regularly what the children are doing in light of the content goals and the learning processes (pp. 21–22).

However, the dominant rationale for the kind of child-centered, experiential learning advocated here is its consistency with democratic values. NAEYC clearly acknowledges that the principles of practice it espouses have their roots in Dewey's vision of school and society (Bredekamp, 1987, p. 66).

Creative planning for young children is essential. Opposing the belief that children waste time until they are old enough to enter formal school, research in the field continues to indicate the importance of formative years. Early educators and researchers such as Montessori and Gesell felt that (1) development was a process of "unfolding" related to maturation, and (2) the rate of unfolding was determined genetically. More recently, educators and researchers have come to believe that a stimulating and planned environment can influence the learning capabilities of young children, especially those from deprived environments.

Although some children are prepared for group experience earlier than others, there is some general agreement that children are ready for peer contacts around the age of 3; however, more and more children are being placed in group care at age 2 or younger. Factors other than chronological age must be considered in evaluating the total social, emotional, spiritual, physical, and intellectual needs of each child. How secure does the child feel in the home? How well does his physical development fall within the expected range for his age? What opportunities does he have to be with children his own age? How does he respond to strangers (peers, adults)? What is the relationship between the child and his parents? What significant happenings in the home (new baby, recent move) may disturb his security or insecurity? What could the child gain from a group experience that he could not get at home? How would costs or arrangements change the family budget or routines? As these questions suggest, a group experience must be entered into with caution: the child must be given time to adjust, whether he does it slowly or rapidly.

Either daily or frequently, the young child should participate in various curricula on a developmental level that is appropriately challenging and interesting. Other provisions include individual concentration and play as well as group involvement; periods of activity and periods of quiet; indoor and outdoor play; and opportunities for physical, social,

 **Reflection**

Balls of play dough were placed in front of each child. Without delay, it was tasted, pinched, and smelled. This wasn't too exciting or interesting. As two children started to leave the table, the teacher brought out some flour sifters and flour. The children turned back to the activity. Sifting flour was fun for a few minutes: rolling the flour into the dough also took some concentration. Again a couple of the children were ready to leave. The teacher placed a small rolling pin in front of each child. Nothing was said, but eager hands reached for the pins. Now the children were tasting, pinching, flouring, and rolling. This continued for several minutes. Then, as lack of interest began to set in, the teacher placed cookie cutters and a pan on the table. Again, the eager fingers and minds were diverted back to the activity. All in all, the children stayed at the activity for a length of time that was notable, especially considering their age and short interest span.

What was it that kept the children interested? New and varied materials, attention from the teacher, peers, or success? Each of these components must have added to the experience.

emotional, intellectual, and moral development. The focus should ever be on helping each child to acquire a healthy self-concept and to reach her potential more fully.

Goals for teachers and children should be short- and long-range. Whatever the duration, careful planning and foresight are necessary. Good teaching does not just happen.

Application of Principles

1. Define *curriculum* and how it applies to young children. How can one blend flexibility and content into the planning?
2. Describe some of the "myths" of developmentally appropriate practices as they apply to young children.
3. Describe *webbing*. Using the topic of air, brainstorm some themes that could be presented to young children. Remember that webbing leads up to and provides follow-up for ideas.
4. Compare and contrast the general characteristics of children between the ages of 2 and 5 years to assure that you plan accurately for children of different ages.
5. Outline the role of the teacher in planning curriculum for young children. What are the differences between lead and support teachers?
6. When planning for young children, what are the four aspects to consider?
7. Using Figure 4.2, evaluate a day in preschool.
8. Write a lesson plan (using the seven elements listed in the chapter) and compare it with the outline in the chapter. Identify the areas that are *easiest* and *most difficult* for you to plan. Ask a teacher or classmate for assistance.
9. Explain how relations between home and school can be strengthened.
10. Make a floor plan of your present classroom and suggest some possible options in space and activities. Discuss your ideas with a teacher or classmate. (If possible, try some of them.)

References

NOTE: Current references are used when available. Older references are classic, introductory and important in development of later ideas, policies, and practices.

Berk, L. E. (1994). Vygotsky's theory: The importance of make-believe play. *Young Children, 50*(1), 30–39.

Berk, L. E., & Winsler, A. (1995). *Scaffolding children's learning: Vygotsky and early childhood education,* Vol. 7. Research into Practice Series. Washington, DC: NAEYC.

Biber, B. (1977). A developmental interaction APPROACH: Bank Street College of Education. In M. D. Day, & R. K. Parker (Eds), *The preschool in action* (2nd ed.) (pp. 434–460). Boston: Allyn & Bacon.

Bredekamp, S. (1991). Redeveloping early childhood education: A response to Kessler. *Early Childhood Research Quarterly, 6*(2), 199–209.

Bredekamp, S. (Ed.) (1987). *Developmentally appropriate practice in early childhood programs serving children from birth through age 8* (expanded ed.). Washington, DC: NAEYC.

Bredekamp, S., & Copple C. (Eds.). (1997). *Developmentally appropriate practice in early childhood programs* (rev. ed.). Washington, DC: NAEYC.

Bredekamp, S., & Rosegrant, T. (Eds.). (1995). *Reaching potentials: Transforming early childhood curriculum and assessment,* Vol. 2. Washington, DC: NAEYC.

Bredekamp, S., & Rosegrant, T. (Eds.). (1992). *Reaching potentials: Appropriate curriculum and assessment for young children,* Vol. 1 (pp. 9–27). Washington, DC: NAEYC.

Bredekamp, S., & Shepard, L. (1989). How best to protect children from inappropriate school expectations, practices, and policies. *Young Children, 44*(3), 14–24.

Bromley, K. D. (1991). *Webbing with literature.* Boston: Allyn & Bacon.

Bruner, J. (1966). *Toward a theory of instruction.* Cambridge, MA: Belknap Press of Harvard University Press.

Bruner, J. (1963). *The process of education.* Cambridge, MA: Harvard University Press.

Carlsson-Paige, N., & Levin, D. E. (1987). *The war play dilemma: Balancing needs and values in the early childhood classroom.* New York: Teachers College Press.

Carson, R. (1956). *The sense of wonder.* New York: Harper & Row.

Carter, G. J. (1992). How can the teaching intern deal with the disparity between how she is taught to teach and how she is expected to teach in "real world" primary grades? *Young Children, 47*(6), 68–72.

Cassidy, D. J., & Lancaster, C. (1993). The grassroots curriculum: a dialogue between children and teachers. *Young Children, 48*(6), 47–51.

Chard, S. C. (1997a). *The project approach: Making curriculum come alive.* New York: Scholastic.

Chard, S. C. (1997b). *The project approach: Managing successful projects.* New York: Scholastic.

Dewey, J. (1916). *Democracy and education: An introduction to the philosophy of education.* New York: Macmillan.

Dewey, J. (1938). *Experiences and education.* New York: Collier

Dewey, J. (1944). *Democracy and education.* New York: Free Press.

Dittman, L. (Ed.). (1970). *Curriculum is what happens.* Washington, D.C.: NAEYC.

Dyson, A. H. (1988). The value of time off task: Young children's spontaneous talk and deliberate text. *Harvard Educational Review, 57,* 396–420.

Edwards, C., Gandini, L., & Forman, G. (Eds.). (1993). *The hundred languages of children: The Reggio Emilia approach to early childhood education.* Norwood, NJ: Ablex.

Eisner, E. (1990). Who decides what schools teach? *Phi Delta Kappan, 71*(7), 523–26.

Elkind, D. (1970, January). The case of the academic preschool: Fact or fiction? *Young Children, 25,* 132–140.

Erikson, E. (1963). *Childhood and society.* New York: Norton. (Original work published 1950).

Ferguson, C. (2001). Discovering, supporting, and promoting young children's passions and interests: One teacher's reflection. *Young Children, 56*(4), 6–11.

File, N. (1993). The teacher as guide of children's competence with peers. *Child and Youth Care Forum, 22,* 357–58.

Fleege, P. O. (1997). Assessment in an integrated curriculum. In C. H. Hart, D. C. Burts, & R. Charlesworth (Eds.), *Integrated curriculum and developmentally appropriate practice: Birth to age eight* (pp. 313–334). Albany, NY: State University of New York.

Gelman, R., & Baillargeon, R. (1983). A review of some Piagetian concepts. In P. Mussen (Ed.), *Handbook of child psychology,* Vol. 3 (pp. 167–230). New York: Wiley.

Giroux, H. A. (1992). Educational leadership and the crisis of democratic government. *Educational Researcher, 21*(4), 4–12.

Greenberg, P. (1992). How to institute some simple democratic practices pertaining to respect, rights, roots, and responsibilities in any classroom (without losing your leadership position). *Young Children, 47*(5), 10–17.

Greene, M. (1988). *The dialectic of freedom.* New York: Teachers College Press.

Hestenes, L. L., & Carroll, D. E. (2000). The play interactions of young children with and without disabilities: Individual and environmental influences. *Early Childhood Research Quarterly, 15*(2), 229–246.

Hyson, M. (2000). Is it okay to have calendar time? Look up to the stars . . . Look within yourself. *Young Children, 55*(6), 60–61.

Jervis, K. (1991). Closed gates in a New York City school. In V. Perrone (Ed.), *Expanding student assessment* (pp. 1–21). Alexandria, VA: Association for Supervision and Curriculum Development.

Jones, B. (1970). In L. Dittman (Ed), *Curriculum is what happens.* Washington, DC: NAEYC.

Jones, E., & Nimmo, J. (1994). *Emergent curriculum.* Washington, DC: NAEYC.

Katz, L. (1994). *The project approach. ERIC Digest.* (ERIC Document Reproduction Service No. ED368509)

Katz, L., & Chard, S. (1989). *Engaging children's minds: The project approach.* Norwood, NJ: Ablex.

Katz, L. G., Evangelou, D., & Hartman, J. A. (1990). *The case for mixed-age grouping in early education.* Washington, DC: NAEYC.

Kessler, S. A. (1991). Alternative perspectives on early childhood education. *Early Childhood Research Quarterly, 6*(2), 183–187.

Kilpatrick, W. H. (1925). *Foundations of method: Informal talks on teaching.* New York: Macmillan.

Kilpatrick, W. H. (1936). *Remarking the curriculum.* New York: Newson.

Kostelnik, M. J. (1992). Myths associated with developmentally appropriate programs. *Young Children, 47*(4), 17–23.

Krogh, S. L. (1997). How children develop and why it matters. In C. H. Hart, D. C. Burts, and R. Charlesworth (Eds.), *Integrated curriculum and developmentally appropriate practice: Birth to age eight* (pp. 29–50). Albany, NY: State University of New York.

Levenstein, P., & O'Hara, J. (1993). The necessary lightness of mother-child play. In K. MacDonald (Ed.), *Parent-child play* (pp. 221–237). New York: State University of New York Press.

Mead, M. (1973). Can the socialization of children lead to greater acceptance of diversity? *Young Children, 28*(6), 329.

Meisels, S. L. (1993). Remaking classroom assessment with the work sampling system. *Young Children, 48*(5), 34–40.

Mitchell, L. S. (1934). *Young Geographers.* New York: Bank Street College.

National Association for the Education of Young Children (NAEYC) & National Association of Early Childhood Specialists in State Departments of Education (NAECS/SDE). (1992) Guidelines for appropriate curriculum content and assessment in programs serving children ages 3 through 8. *Young Children, 46*(3), 21–38.

New, R. (1993). Cultural variations on developmentally appropriate practice: Challenges to theory and practice. In C. Edwards, L. Gandini, & G. Forman (Eds.), *The hundred languages of children: The Reggio Emilia approach to early childhood education* (pp. 215–231), Norwood, NJ: Ablex.

Piaget, J. (1952). *The origins of intelligence in children.* New York: International University Press.

Rankin, B. (1993). Curriculum development in Reggio Emilia: A long-term curriculum project about dinosaurs. In C. Edwards, L. Gandini, & G. Forman (Eds.), *The hundred languages of children: The Reggio Emila approach to early childhood education* (pp. 189–211), Norwood, NJ: Ablex.

Resnick, L. (1996). Schooling and the workplace: What relationship? In *Preparing youth for the 21st century,* (pp. 21–37). Washington, DC: Aspen Institute.

Seefeldt, C. (1993). Social studies: Learning for freedom. *Young Children, 48*(3), 4–9.

Sloane, M. W. (1999). All kinds of projects for your classroom. *Young Children, 54*(4), 17–20.

Spodek, B. (1973). *Early childhood education.* Upper Saddle River, NJ: Prentice Hall.

Swanson, L. (1994). Changes—how our nursery school replaced adult-directed art projects with child-directed experiences and changed to an accredited, child-sensitive, developmentally appropriate school. *Young Children, 49*(4), 69–73.

Taylor, B. J., & Howell, R. J. (1973). The ability of three-, four-, and five-year-old children to distinguish fantasy from reality. *Journal of Genetic Psychology, 122,* 315–18.

Van Hoorn, J., Nourot, P., Scales, B., & Alward, K. (1993). *Play at the center of the curriculum*. Upper Saddle River, NJ: Merrill/Prentice Hall.

Vygotsky, L. (1978). *Mind in society: The development of higher mental processes*. Cambridge, MA: Harvard University Press.

Winsler, A. (1993). The social interactions and task activities of young children in mixed-age and same-age classrooms: An observational study. Paper presented at the Society for Research in Child Development, March, New Orleans, Louisiana. (ERIC Document Reproduction Service No. ED356 074)

Workman, S., & Anziano, M. C. (1993). Curriculum webs: Weaving connections from children to teachers. *Young Children, 48*(2), 4–9.

5

Language Arts

Main Principles

1. For the optimal development and learning of all children, educators (teachers and parents) must accept the legitimacy of the children's home languages. (pp. 154–155)

2. The four areas of language development (important in the life of each young child) discussed in this chapter are listening, speaking, reading, and writing (pp. 154–155).

3. Language may be responsive and/or restrictive (pp. 155–157).

4. Proponents of the whole-language approach (Vygotsky, Piaget, and many others) stress that it is not a single instructional strategy, or even a group of strategies, but a comprehensive theory of language learning and instruction (pp. 157–160).

5. Language and literacy learning are continuous processes (pp. 160–162).

6. Language serves the many needs of children, including those from linguistically diverse families (pp. 161–162).

7. The teacher's role is to encourage language development and use in young children through appropriate and integrated curriculum with stories and books (pp. 163–172), listening experiences (pp. 175–179, 182–183), and speaking opportunities and poetry (pp. 173–175, 179–183), and (*as each one is developmentally ready*) with reading (pp. 183–192) and with writing (pp. 192–195).

8. Alphabet learning is one part of learning to read (pp. 187–192).

Introduction

By design and because of its importance, this chapter on language arts follows the chapters on good environments, relationships and guidance techniques, play, and curriculum. Without language, none of the preceding or following chapters would have much meaning. But there need to be decisions and rationale. Young children are encountering language experiences from the day of birth; other curriculum areas fall into place with the opportunities and development of the child.

The goal in language arts is to help children develop and improve their ability to communicate. Language is oral, auditory, and visual and may be used to express personal or social ideas. One depends on it to clarify norms, to inform, and to transmit needs, feelings, and desires. Inability to communicate with another, whether due to a language barrier or to sensory impairment, impresses one with how much language is taken for granted and how much we depend on it in our daily lives.

This chapter is designed to emphasize the importance of the four areas of language (listening, speaking, reading, writing) and their interdependence, especially for children up to the age of 6. Not within the scope of this book are details about language acquisitions, problems related to each of the areas of development, possible referrals for diagnosis and treatment, and specific approaches to teaching and reading. However, it is intended that the information and activities herein will aid teachers in communicating with children from all backgrounds and language experiences.

Young children should be encouraged to actively participate in activities that allow for experimentation with listening, speaking, reading, and writing. When they participate with adults and peers in oral and written opportunities, they increase their awareness and understanding of their world. These early experiences lay a foundation and create interest for the child's later learning.

Poetry, an important part of a young child's life, can introduce language, rhythm, sounds, and concepts in a delightful way. Any topic can be highlighted, any time is appropriate, and humor is spontaneous with young children; however, some books or ideas that are humorous to adults fail to be so with children due to a mismatch with their learning ability and interest. Using humor can facilitate children's social, cognitive, and language growth. (See Jalongo, 1985.)

When language acquisition in young children is delayed, it may be caused by physical or structural deficits (such as hearing loss), physiological or neurological impairments (such as cerebral palsy), mental retardation, or emotional problems. Generally, early-childhood teachers are not trained to diagnose language problems or to prescribe therapy; however, they should be alert to hearing and speaking deficiencies and refer parents to appropriate agencies. Because of the complexity of hearing disorders, this topic is not within the scope of this text.

As discussed in Chapter 3, play is an important component in the healthy development of young children. Literature (language arts) helps provide familiar and vicarious experiences.

Language arts is a very broad category, for it includes verbal, written, pictorial, and performing media in all their forms for children and adults—it is much more than just children's literature or storytime. Language should be integrated into all areas of curriculum, with all individuals, and at all times. As you will discover while reading this chapter, language is one of the most important ways we communicate with each other—and sometimes our communication doesn't come out the way it was intended! So we use language for clarification, elaboration, justification, and personalization.

NAEYC. issued a position statement (1996) responding to linguistic and cultural diversity regarding young children. It states:

> For the optimal development and learning of all children, educators must *accept* the legitimacy of children's home language, *respect* (hold in high regard) and value (esteem, appreciate) the home cul-

ture, and *promote* and *encourage* the active involvement and support of all families, including extended and nontraditional family units (p. 5).

The report summarizes: Early-childhood educators can best help linguistically and culturally diverse children and their families by (1) acknowledging and responding to the importance of the child's home language and culture, (2) providing administrative support for bilingualism within the educational setting, (3) modifying the classroom to meet the individual needs of children, (4) learning and practicing ways to support children and families from linguistically or culturally different backgrounds, and (5) providing high-quality care and education for *all* children (p. 12).

To encourage literacy in young children, teachers can share books, poems, songs, and rhymes whenever and wherever they can throughout the day. These activities can be child- or adult-initiated, group or one-on-one. Teachers will want to initiate new selections periodically and invite *all* children to listen—not just the persistent, verbal ones. Some authors suggest the use of Big Books as children explore how print works. These books on nursery rhymes and song charts make pictures easily distinguishable from the well-spaced print. Signs and labels on children's cubbies, lockers, toy shelves, and other convenient places help children understand the function of the printed word, and convey information. Books and other print-related materials are valued and necessary ingredients for each day for the children. Through their intense involvement with literacy materials, the children are developing important concepts about print, an increasing ability to retell stories from illustrations, and a love of books.

The International Reading Association (IRA), with representatives from five national professional organizations (including NAEYC), has set forth recommendations for literacy before the first grade that call for the use of reading materials that are familiar or predictable, such as well-known stories, as they provide children with a sense of control and confidence in their ability to learn.

Children use language to communicate effectively and to facilitate thinking and learning. They become literate individuals who gain satisfaction as well as information from reading and writing.

Language Interaction

Responsive and Restrictive Language

Stone (1993) identifies two ways to interact with others, using either responsive or restrictive language:

Responsive Language	Restrictive Language
Shows regard and respect	Shows disregard and disrespect
Is democratic	Is authoritarian, intimidating, and disrespectful
Encourages give-and-take	
Uses alternates and choices, reasons and explanations	Uses threats, punishment, and criticism
Includes elaboration for understanding	Discourages independence
Shows sensitivity and caring	Is condensed and impersonal (Condensed from Stone, 1993)

Responsive language gives the individual options of what to do or how to do things better. Restrictive language is limiting and makes the individual feel inferior. In interacting with children, helping them to see a positive outlet (and to feel worthwhile) is far superior to being left hanging on a limb—when one often does not have the strength to hold on! Behavior problems can erupt.

Reflection

True or False: An Authentic Literacy Environment:

_____	_____	Has an abundance of printed materials.
_____	_____	Provides many opportunities for social interaction.
_____	_____	Is displayed in such a way that spontaneous literary learning can occur.
_____	_____	Has materials that support children as readers and writers.
_____	_____	Provides time for the children to experiment with reading and writing.
_____	_____	Has a teacher who reads to the children on a daily basis.
_____	_____	Provides a variety of opportunities for personal involvement (enacting, explaining, expanding, sharing, responding, creating, questioning, etc.).
_____	_____	Enables children to learn new information and to "act upon" present knowledge.
_____	_____	Considers the physical classroom space and arrangement ("to move, touch, experience variety, and make decisions") (Gareau and Kennedy, 1991, p. 51).
_____	_____	Expects teachers to know, use, and define terms such as "constructivism," "whole language," "emerging literacy," and others, and to incorporate evidence of these terms into her classroom.
_____	_____	Is a figment of the imagination and has no place in the classroom of young children.

(See Bobys, 2000, pp. 16–22.)

Emergent Literacy

Teachers should load their classrooms with award-winning books from many available sources. Not only should books *be* in the classroom, but they should also be used, reused, and overused. Verbal encouragement, time, and comfortable places will help young children become involved with print. Literacy begins with print awareness in children as young as 3 years old as a response to their experiences in a print-rich environment.

Enriching classroom play settings with message-bearing signs and labels and providing time for interaction among the children helps them develop the ability to read words, particularly when the print is embedded in its supporting context in a play setting and has important implications for classroom practice.

Providing print experiences means "awakening interest by providing continuous encouragement through positive discourse and by creating a warm and supportive atmosphere in which children can take risks without fear of failure" (Williams & Davis, 1994, p. 41).

Children are working on all aspects of oral and written language at the same time; therefore the term "emergent literacy" describes this learning as a continuum. There is

Good Usage of Classroom Language

1. Explain what is expected of the children.
2. Talk about various ways problems can be handled.
3. Combine words and actions when possible.
4. Check to see that children understand concepts and actions.
5. Encourage children to use verbal rather than physical actions to solve problems.
6. Combine verbal and written ideas during play and other activities.
7. Help children to control their verbal behavior (speak softly, slowly, friendly, etc.).
8. Suggest some ways adults can model verbal interaction.
9. Note some ways to improve your communication in the classroom.

significant evidence that children learn phonics from reading and writing as well as vice versa (Goodman, K. D., 1998). There is also evidence that children who are read to before entering school are more likely to succeed in school (Moustafa, 1997).

The emergent literacy focus is well grounded within popular developmental theories of both Vygotsky (1962) and Piaget (1967, 1983), supporting the idea that competence with using symbols (reading and writing) should predict skills in other areas of development. They also provide evidence that favorite play of young children (block building, dramatic play, creative art, etc.) greatly assists in the reading and writing process.

The work of Clay (1979/1991) and others has changed the focus of educators to think more of young children's literacy not in terms of "who *can* and *cannot* read," but as a long-term, ongoing process.

Children learn through social interactions. This learning consists of developmental and social processes; therefore, it is important that teachers and children talk to each

Notable Quotes

"Tell a child what to think, and you make him a slave to your knowledge. Teach him how to think, and you make all knowledge his slave" (Taitt, 1982).

The Vygotskian approach to language learning includes ideas such as "All humans in all languages have developed language [. . .] Once toddlers acquire language, their problem-solving ability improved dramatically" (Bodrova & Leong, 1996, p. 95). There is considerable evidence that high-quality early-childhood education programs for children from birth to age 5 can have long-lasting, positive consequences for children's success in school and later life, especially for children from low-income families; however, these programs may not be available for children who need them. The U.S. Department of Education released a study of skills and knowledge of a nationally representative group of kindergarten-entering children that suggests that kindergarten is too late to narrow the achievement gap. High-quality early-childhood education programs have great potential for preventing later school failure, particularly if teachers place a strong emphasis on language and literacy development (ERIC #ED447722).

From *What Early Childhood Teachers Need to Know about Language.* ERIC Digest 2000

other about classroom events and about personal activities. Ways that one teacher extended kindergarten children's learning included:

1. reading to the children and also encouraging the children to "read" together;
2. motivating the children to engage in "reading-like behavior";
3. sharing book experiences with others;
4. assisting the children to believe in themselves as readers (Moore 1998, pp. 72–75); and
5. encouraging children to learn in their own individual ways.

"Tips for Reading to Young Children," excerpted from *Teaching Our Youngest: A Guide for Preschool Teachers, Child Care & Family Providers* (limited free copies available from U.S. Department of Education, Issue No. 97, May/June 2002) include:

➤ make it an enjoyable experience;
➤ read frequently;
➤ help children to learn as you read by talking about the book;
➤ choose books to help you teach;
➤ reread favorite books;
➤ ask children questions as you read;
➤ encourage them to talk.

As you read with young children, you will know how to anticipate their questions, how to stimulate their thinking, and how to meet the needs of each.

Some interesting questions are asked in the article "What Are We Really Saying to Children?" It encourages adults to look for the messages in children's books, and specifically to ask for evaluation of the characters, the situation, the illustrations, the messages, the author/illustrator's credibility, and the selection as a whole. Too often these aspects are overlooked before books are purchased for or read to young children. We need to be EVEN MORE CAREFUL TODAY in the contents of books we purchase to read to young children (*Child Care Information Exchange,* March/April, 1987).

Performing for a group of peers encourages language development and cooperation.

Collaboration and *demonstration* are terms used to describe how children respond to one another while participating in individual and social situations. This collaboration is called "meaningful demonstrations" (Smith, 1984, 1992). The process of understanding text is always a social process (Applebee, 1978). According to Vygotsky (1978) *symbolic interactionism* is a theoretical assumption that people learn from social interactions as well as from their own experiences and that learning is developmental.

Teaching in a manner that enables children (Greenberg, 1992) is a practice highly valued by teachers who follow the works of John Dewey. Allowing children to make decisions about reading (with whom they read, what they read) encourages children to talk and laugh together.

Language and literacy learning is a continuous process. All children develop at their own rates and in their own directions in their sociocultural environments. Maturation and environmental experiences vary from child to child. It is *therefore virtually not possible, nor is it desirable, to provide a definitive sequence or age-regulated timeline for language and literacy development.* Children acquire a common fund of concepts, but the point of entry and the path of progress may be different for any two children.

Some researchers place more value on the social component of language development. For instance, Vygotsky states that "children solve practical tasks with the help of their speech, as well as their eyes and hands" (1978, p. 26) and that "language arises initially as a means of communication between the child and the people in his environment. Only subsequently, upon conversion to internal speech, does it come to organize the child's thought, that is, become an internal mental function" (p. 89).

At an earlier period, one approach to reading and writing instruction evolved that caused much interest and controversy among educators. Known as *whole language,* this approach was based on the premise that young children best learned language as a whole process using many reading, writing, and speaking skills and that they then gradually refined the different skills that made up the language process. The instructional focus was primarily on language meaning, rather than on specific skills (Heald-Taylor, 1989).

Sometimes it is relaxing to look at a book by yourself.

Figure 5.1 Symbols of the Four Areas of Language: Listening, Speaking, Reading, and Writing

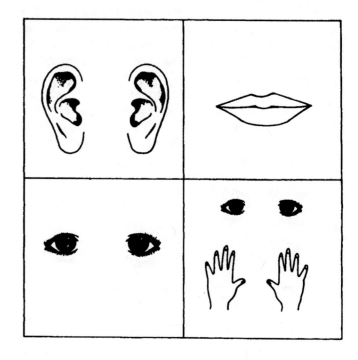

Implicit in the whole-language approach was the belief that children had already learned a great deal before they began school. The variety of backgrounds, cultures, and interests being brought into the classroom was considered a valuable part of whole-language learning by teachers, who often sought ways to incorporate these attributes into the curriculum in an effort to make learning more relevant to each child (Goodman, 1986, p. 10). In whole-language classrooms, children used the four classifications of language (speaking, listening, reading, and writing). See Figure 5.1. Classrooms often become flooded with abundant but frequently nonfunctional print that had no meaning for children but was provided by well-meaning teachers.

Studies of language development show that children do much more than imitate (Gallas, et al., 1996; Piaget & Inhelder, 1969; Weaver, 1996). Rather, they create their own theories about language (Fields & Spangler, 2000, p. 9). Chomsky's research demonstrated that children's drive to make sense of print is similar to their determination to utilize spoken language (1972). Understanding how youngsters learn to talk helps us understand how they master reading and writing too.

There is much disagreement about how children learn to read:

> The recent "reading wars" debate has polarized the issue, with each side citing its own research and accusing the other of flawed research. Teachers' unions, the PTA, and professional organizations for education administrators have signed onto a statement representing one side (Learning First Alliance, 1998); the professional associations composed of reading and writing experts and of experts on young children's learning defend the other side (IRA & NAEYC, 1998) (Fields & Spangler, 2000, p. 15).

One side says that phonics is the most important part of reading; the other side says that phonics is just one of many reading strategies learned *during* reading instruction. However, using phonics is one of several necessary reading skills, best learned during actual reading and writing practice. Keep in mind that it is children we are teaching—not just "language."

Everyday experiences are crucial in children's literacy learning, whether it is being read to, pretending to read, recognizing letters and/or words, or communicating with others. Learning to read and write are inseparable (Routman, 1996).

Print should serve as a real resource for children, as suggested in Figure 5.2.

Information:	*Useful* information, such as a schedule (for those who use one), special events, alphabet, lunch menu, date, weather, and so on
Integration:	Language and activities across areas of curriculum and throughout the day (math with play, literature with social studies, art with science, play with physical development, and so on)
Pleasure:	Printed literature (books, poems, songs), new books or activities
Recording:	Observations, weather logs, attendance, lunch count
Dramatic play:	Special props for various kinds of play
Home-school:	Information to share between home and school
Special events:	Field trips, celebrations, announcements, guests, new toys and activities
Follow-up:	Thank-you notes, recording of special events (visitors, field trips)
Curriculum:	Introduce new information, highlight a special activity for the day, recall former information, build on ideas
Notices:	Information of interest—especially on topics suggested by the children

Figure 5.2   Sources of Print for Classroom Use (from the child's-eye view)

Early-childhood educators are responsible for building on each child's knowledge from home, redefining the traditional relationship between schools and homes—based on partnership and communication, with the mutual goal of providing children with supportive and successful educational experiences.

Developing Programs for Linguistically and Culturally Diverse Children and Families

Most information about language and customs leans toward maintaining linguistic and cultural diversity in developing home languages (Tabors, 1998, p. 20). In the Head Start population, there "is only a fraction of the young children in preschool programs in the United States. One estimate (Kagan & Garcia 1991)—that may well be an underestimation by now—is that there will be 5.2 million other-than English-dominant preschoolers in the United States by the year 2000." This deadline has passed, but current figures are unavailable.

There are different language-types in our classrooms today: a first-language program (child's home language is the only language used in the classroom), a bilingual classroom (two languages are used regularly), and English-only classrooms (Tabors, 1998, p. 23). All three types have advantages and problems.

Support for second-language acquisition in the classroom is used in (1) classroom routines and organization; (2) language techniques (nonverbal communication); and (3) classroom activities (running commentary, songs, movements, outside activities) and other active play to increase the opportunity to hear and understand the new language.

The developmental sequence of second-language acquisition includes home language use; nonverbal period in the new language; telegraphic and formulaic (concise, often one-word use of the language such as naming people or objects); and productive use of the new language (Tabors, 1998, 21). Tabors concludes: "Serving linguistically and culturally diverse children and families in DAP classrooms is an ongoing process that will continue over time as teachers gain experience and expertise. Business-as-usual in early childhood classrooms serving linguistically and culturally diverse children and families is no longer preferable" (p. 26).

Creating Phoenemic Awareness in the Classroom

Working with children and families from all over our globe is challenging. Educators may have differing amounts of knowledge about these immigrant children. Regardless of circumstances of children, families, and educators, the teaching/learning environment must not include drills, or activities that put undue stress upon the children. Developmentally appropriate activities include: stories that include rhyming words, nursery rhymes, jingles, poems, finger plays, circle time, writing, and other activities familiar to the child and used often.

There are two ways of learning language: the natural way (learning the language of the home—called language acquisition: a process of making sense of things); and the "school way"—to teach about it rather than to use it (DeGaetano, Williams, & Volk, 1998) (a behaviorist view of memorizing, repeating, etc.).

The individual development of each child determines his/her instructional needs, which can be met by providing a variety of options for learning activities, considering the following:

1. Understanding of symbols develops during toddlerhood.
2. Reading "readiness": researchers and educators have characterized this as the ages 5–7. Hearn (1993) calls it *cracking the code.*
3. The term *emergent literacy* (popularized by Clay, 1979/1991, and others) highlights that learning to read and write is a developmental process, one that leads to much broader definition of literacy and occurs over many years with a minimum of instruction and as a natural part of cognitive development (Harste, Woodward, & Burke, 1984).
4. The symbolic thinking/emergent literacy connection is well grounded within child development theories. Vygotsky (1962) and Piaget (1967, 1983) both concluded that competence with using symbols in one area should predict skill in other symbolic areas such as reading and writing.
5. Classroom activities such as block building, dramatic play, creative and expressive arts, drawing, painting, scribbling, listening, oral language recognition and usage, and attending to printed materials (for example: books, magazines, postcards, letters, newspapers, etc.), as well as more commonly recognized preconventional reading and writing attempts (such as retelling events from memory, using contextual cues in telling the story, stringing together random letters, creating invented spelling, and other activities) contribute to literacy skills (Bredekamp & Copple, 1997; Harste, Woodward, & Burke, 1984; Hearn, 1993; Teale & Sulzby, 1996; and others).
6. Self-directed interaction with a variety of symbol systems to which children are exposed (Nowak-Fabrytkowski, 1992).
7. Child-directed exploration of the environment allows them to construct knowledge about the world of symbols more efficiently than most teacher-directed activities permit.
8. Many researchers have identified what they call "literacy behaviors" involving a variety of symbolic thinking activities that come before conventional reading and writing (Holdaway, 1979; Harste, Woodward, & Burke, 1984; Hearn, 1993; McMullen, 1998; Teale & Sulzby, 1996).
9. Problem solving has been associated with prereading/prewriting behaviors. McMullen states: "Once children become higher-level symbolic thinkers, they are able to piece together the mental processes used in everyday problem solving with the symbols needed for the reading and writing process" (1998).

Role of the Teacher

A teacher who wants to encourage language use and development in young children must be a good listener, a good model, and an interested and caring person. He must also provide for individual needs of the children by planning language experiences as an integral part of each day and each area of curriculum. To say, "Now it's language time," would be foolish and inaccurate. Language time is all the time. Nonverbal or body language is often better understood than verbal language. One can easily tell from a facial expression, movement of the body, or breathing whether the sender is pleased or annoyed.

Hendrick (1992) lists seven basic ways to foster language development: (1) listen to the children; (2) give them something real to talk about; (3) encourage conversation and dialogue; (4) use questions to generate and develop language; (5) provide auditory training; (6) seek professional assistance promptly, when necessary; and (7) become acquainted with and draw on research-based language development programs.

A review of additional references indicates that generally desired components for language development include favorable socioeconomic background, enriching experiences, sensory practice, respect for the child, interaction with other children, quality adult models, use of the same language at home and school, attentive listeners for the child, a noncritical attitude toward the child's language skills, flexibility in the child's life, and time to enjoy speaking and listening experiences.

If language is so much a part of living, why is it important to provide specific opportunities for children to just talk or listen? Consider these values of language:

1. It enriches or supplements firsthand experiences.
2. It enhances self-image and builds self-control.
3. It promotes diversity.
4. It helps establishment of social relations through sharing.
5. It facilitates accurate conceptualization, clarifies ideas and stimulates new ones, and presents information.

Conversation with a buddy encourages friendship in many activities.

6. It fosters aesthetic appreciation and stimulates creativity.
7. It provides literary experiences.
8. It acquaints children with another way of learning about their environment.
9. It provides auditory experiences and practice.
10. It provides opportunities for a change of pace and enjoyment of materials and people.

Thorough planning by the teacher is crucial if she is to utilize the many opportunities to foster language and identify and meet the needs of children individually and collectively. Following are some suggestions related to the four areas of language development: listening, speaking, reading, and writing. (Refer to Figure 5.3.)

Appropriate and Integrated Curriculum

If young children are to reach their potentials, the curriculum *must* be developmentally appropriate and begin with the individual characteristics of the children involved. They need firsthand experiences in exploration, practice, and learning. Consider the following:

➤ relevant (multicultural, nonsexist) and appropriate age-related materials
➤ opportunities for personal and social growth with children and adults
➤ sufficient and flexible play materials, work places, and companions
➤ specific and/or integrated curriculum areas
➤ individual and group experiences with language
➤ opportunities with curriculum areas
➤ child, teacher, parent suggestions

Stories and Storytime

The response of children to stories varies greatly. Some sit quietly during storytime; some make frequent comments; some do neither. If one child is disturbing the others, the teacher can say, "After we finish the story, I'd like to hear more about that. Could you tell me later?" She must then follow through and let him tell what he was thinking. The time lapse may or may not dampen his desire to talk. Although the teacher does not want to stifle one child's interest or imagination, she must also consider the rest of the children.

Books attractively displayed on a rack or table beckon children. Children like to sit quietly, undisturbed, while they look at books or have a story read to them individually or in a small, intimate group. A variety of books should be provided—some favorites, some new.

The teacher can be aware of the interests of the children and encourage them to spend time with books. One child may be fascinated with spiders, another with boats, another with weather. The teacher should point out to the individual child that she can learn more about her interests through looking at the books. The teacher might select one or more of these special books to use during group storytime.

The attitude and feelings of the teacher will greatly influence the children's interest in the story. One teacher felt sure the children would not enjoy the story she had prepared.

- **Listening—Teachers:**
  Pay attention
  Take time to talk with, not to, each child
  Plan environments that encourage questions and increase knowledge
  Provide appropriate listening experiences (records, tapes, visitors)
  Are aware of volume and intensity of conversations and the environment
  "Read" and react to the needs of individual children
- **Speaking—Teachers:**
  Speak with, not to, each child
  Help children establish rules and "reasons"—ways to help them resolve problems verbally rather than physically
  Speak clearly, positively, and happily (avoid baby talk, abstract words, talking "down")
  Give honest praise frequently
  Help children understand the message (explaining clearly, honestly, establishing rules, etc.)
  Talk about something of interest to the child while encouraging questions to increase his/her knowledge
  Speak at appropriate times (with one or more children, with parents, supervisors, etc.)
  Give full attention to person (child or adult) in conversations, questioning, seeking permission, conveying information, and so on
  Encourage responses ("What would happen if . . .?")
  Invite child participation (a poem, song, idea, or activity)
  Encourage a child to tell about . . . (maybe an experience or idea—or about his picture while the teacher writes about it on the **back** of the paper, etc.)
  Make verbal and nonverbal language (gestures, actions) compatible
- **Reading—Teachers:**
  Always have books and magazines readily available, and keep them in the classroom long enough for the children to become familiar and friendly with them
  Choose books that are physically appropriate to the age level, stage, and interest of the children (for example, cardboard for 2-year-olds)
  Provide quality listening experiences
  Take the children to the school or public library, when possible—helping them to select and check out books
  Purchase good books for the center
  Help children find out things by using books
  When children are interested and ready, have some alphabet or number cards for their exploration
  Provide magazines to be looked through, cut up, or written in
  Point out pictures and ideas in magazines, books, newspapers
  Talk about caring for books
  Provide a quiet, comfortable, well-lighted place to read, away from distractions
  When reading to and with the children, take time to look at the pictures
  Frequently let a child choose the book to read or look at
  Consider the role of parents regarding a child's interest in reading
- **Writing—Teachers:**
  Do note taking and recoding with a positive attitude
  Give each child some paper (or a booklet) and let him draw a story; the teacher writes down the comments
  Help the children write a letter or thank-you note to someone
  Provide good writing tools and time to write
  Appreciate attempts at writing
  Show each child how to write his/her name and other words as interest is indicated, and use capital and lowercase letters

Figure 5.3 Characteristics of Caring Teachers in Four Areas of Language

She was right; they picked up her attitude about it. On another day the same teacher was very excited about the story she had prepared. She was surprised when the children responded to her enthusiasm.

Storytime should be relaxed and leisurely, with the length depending on the children—not the clock! They should be comfortably seated on the floor. If they get restless but need to stay in the group, some activities can be started to involve them more, such as finger play, an exercise, or a song.

Thorough preparation of the story (whether it includes use of visual aids or just reading) will add interest for the children and flexibility for the teacher. When necessary, the teacher should be able to lengthen or shorten the story.

Storytime is when the two-teacher model works well. The lead teacher can begin and conduct the storytime while the support teacher assists with slow children, those who need quieting, or other interruptions. A child's attention may be regained by mentioning his name. When it is necessary to separate two children, the support teacher can move in casually but confidently and say, "I would like to sit by Denise and Michael today." He can then sit down and attend to the story. A support teacher can often reinterest a child merely by putting her hand on the child's shoulder or hand. If a particular child has an extremely difficult time enjoying storytime, it may be better for her to sit quietly in another area, not as punishment, but as preparation. She is always given the option of entering the group when she is ready.

Books are helpful to children who need time to assimilate the many facts thrown at them. Casually looking through a book may help children develop some concrete ideas or new concepts pertaining to their world. Occasionally they should be encouraged to act out a story.

Teachers should take advantage of teachable moments. One day, after a heavy snowstorm, the teacher told the children about the many things she had observed on the way to school. It sounded like a story! One child said: "Tell it again, teacher."

Storytelling

Most children (and most teachers) enjoy a quiet period where both can enjoy hearing (telling) stories. One day in a story group, the teacher had not yet gathered her materials and presented herself in front of the children. One 4-year-old boy said, "I'll be the teacher and tell you a story!" He placed himself in front of the other children, and began: "Once there was a little boy and he had a dog named Fido and that's the end of the story." He returned to his place among the children just as the teacher approached with her story.

Storytelling can be a wonderful experience for children and teachers. Theory tells us that such an opportunity is beneficial for language development, creativity, and brain development (memory, logical thinking, self-regulation). Using *story grammar*, children learn about general patterns common to all stories, such as "putting events in a logical sequence and understanding; imposing limits on content of the story, develop the idea of story grammar as children master basic logical concepts such as cause and effect, mutually exclusive events, and so on" (Bodrova & Leong, 1996, pp. 145–146).

Storytelling can help children make a transition from retelling familiar stories to creating stories of their own. Rodari developed and implemented storytelling techniques that were used in Reggio Emilia, Italy. He suggested combining two less compatible episodes or characters from different stories as a starting point for a new story (Edwards, Gandini, & Forman, 1994).

Vygotsky reminds us that storytelling is beneficial for at least language development, creativity, and mind development—where children learn about general patterns common to all stories, called *story grammar*—not to mention personal benefits of enjoyment, learning, sharing with others, and more. He also emphasizes the importance of play for all children—even beyond age 8—and its relationship to literacy. He determined that early writing evolves through play and gesture because it gives children the oppor-

Very young children like the closeness of others while enjoying stories.

tunity to experiment with uses of writing, to invent freely, and to practice approximate literacy behaviors in nonevaluative settings.

Individual and group language experiences are helpful. For a group of preschool children who are less attentive and rather disruptive during group storytime, one teacher found that the following suggestions recapture the children:

1. Spend a few introductory minutes discussing the story and making predictions.
2. Pause during the reading so children can join in with a familiar word or phrase.
3. Point to the pictures to emphasize the story.
4. Interject *brief* comments to help explain the text.
5. React positively to children's comments with a nod of your head or a short oral response.
6. Wonder aloud and invite the children to voice questions about pictures or text that might be difficult to decipher or understand, and ask open-ended questions.
7. Encourage the children to discuss and dramatize the story and to create art projects to enhance their enjoyment and comprehension of the story.

Criteria for Selecting Books and Stories

The materials should be *realistic and reported accurately*. Factuality helps children develop validity of concepts and form mental pictures for future use. Young children have difficulty distinguishing between what is real and what is fantasy. The younger the child, the more he needs realistic stories. Most children can more appropriately deal with abstract concepts after their fifth birthday. Human characteristics (talking, dressing, feeling) given to animals, objects, or things confuse young children. Some children handle abstract or inconsistent ideas at a younger age than do other children. Fantasy stories should be used in small proportion to such realistic stories as here-and-now experiences until the children can better distinguish real from unreal.

The question of telling fairy tales to young children always arises. During the preoperational stage of development, young children are unable to understand fairy tales.

Many fairy tales produce fear, deal with advanced concepts, or contain morals. They are better left until the school years (Kohlberg, 1966; Spock, 1976; Taylor & Howell, 1973).

DeVries (referred to by Bee, 1981) did an interesting experiment with 3- to 6-year-old children and a tame cat named Maynard. The children petted the cat and made friends with it. Then DeVries hid the front end of the cat behind a box and instructed the children to watch the tail end. Behind the box, DeVries put a very lifelike dog mask on the cat's head, showed him to the children, and asked if he could now bark, whether he would eat dog or cat food, whether the new animal would play like a cat or a dog, and so on. Young children thought the mask had essentially changed the animal into a dog and that he could bark and do other dog things. The 4- and 5-year-olds understood that the mask did not change the animal into a dog. This experience shows the level of belief in young children.

In *Island of Childhood* (1982), Griffin discusses animal disguises, animals smaller than children who need protection and security, animation of machines, competitive themes, extravagantly unreal happenings, bizarre creatures, imagination, hidden emotional problems, morals, and folk and fairy tales. This book is recommended to teachers of young children.

Another avenue of inquiry concerns the use of Mother Goose rhymes. These are often accepted because of the rhyme and rhythm, the humor, the suspense, and the repetition, but they should be used discriminately. Mother Goose rhymes, originally written as adult political satire, are usually enjoyed by young children. Avoid those that express or encourage aggression.

Books promote learning *by supporting firsthand experiences*. A book may be used to introduce a new idea, especially when followed by a direct experience, such as a field trip, a visitor, replicas, or other personal involvement.

Books help children clarify concepts about their environment. Books may also be used to stimulate dramatic play, give role models, define behavior, or encourage curiosity. Books often put into words and pictures things the children want to know about but lack skills to ask.

Young children like to hear stories *about familiar things* that they can also do, such as participating with the family, caring for a pet, visiting the community, developing new skills, or learning new information.

Young children like *visuals that are clear and fairly large and that clarify the text*. Books should have an appropriate art style and be aesthetically appealing. Abstract illustrations are generally confusing and annoying to young children.

Most adults prefer color in picture books, and so do most children; however, some favorite picture books are in black and white, sepia and white, or only two colors. Children consider clarity more important than color. The pictures should be uncluttered, yet contain some supportive detail. Children enjoy discovering a lady-bug or butterfly in the grass, but when the text calls for a brown-and-white cow and the picture is of a black one, the children are confused by the inconsistency.

Literature should *have value for the reader or listener* of any age. For young children, the following are important:

➤ A definite plot (ability to discern author's purpose and fulfillment)
➤ Interesting sounds or plays on words (catch phrases, repetition of incidents or ideas)
➤ A light element of surprise or suspense
➤ Language that is clear, descriptive, and understandable
➤ Direct conversation that adds interest and helps children develop respect for language
➤ An uplifting effect (A book that contains familiar elements and helps to promote sound concepts is generally appropriate. Elements that produce fear, nightmares, poor social relationships, or emotional upsets should be used with caution. Some excellent books depict children conquering fears of potentially upsetting situations. These help children learn to deal with normal experiences.)
➤ Accurate portrayal of gender, ethnic, and social models

➤ Interest for the age level of the children, reflecting their point of view in timeliness, problem solving, creativity, and so on
➤ A positive influence on language arts experiences in listening speaking, writing, and reading
➤ The ability to stimulate the imagination

Each year the John Newbery Medal is given for the best *literary contribution* to children's literature; however, it is not limited to books for preschool children. Librarians know the Newbery Medal winners and should be able to help determine their appropriateness for a specific group. Also check with local libraries, bookstores, and the Internet for lists of past and present Newbery Medal winners.

Some interesting questions are asked in the article "What Are We Really Saying to Children?" (*Child Care Information Exchange,* March, 1987). It encourages adults to look for the messages in children's books, and specifically asks for evaluation of the characters, the situation, the illustrations, the messages, the author/illustrator's credibility, and the selection as a whole. Too often these aspects are overlooked before books are purchased or read to young children.

To create extra interest in storytime, whether the group is large or small, methods of presentation should vary. Some examples are as follows:

1. Use the book.
2. Tell the story, with or without aids.
3. Use flannelboard aids.
4. Use only one picture and display it at an appropriate time.
5. Use flip-cards.
6. Use real objects or replicas.
7. Have the children dramatize the story after it is read or discussed.
8. Act it out as you tell it.
9. Use your own creative methods.

Teachers should be alert to children who have difficulty listening to books or stories; some children may need special placement in order to see or hear, and others may have physical difficulties in sitting on the floor or in a crowded area. For children to enjoy stories and social times, they need to be comfortable and interested in the proceedings.

Some benefits of reading aloud suggested by Conlon (1992) include closeness to an adult, attention to visuals and ideas expressed, opportunities to learn about the act of reading, a chance to practice making sense of stories with a deeper understanding through repetition, support of their own development (emotional, social, and cognitive), a love of books and reading, hearing language and ideas, and an individual or group social experience. See Figure 5.4 for a list of evaluation questions when considering picture books.

When planning a group storytime, consider the following factors:

➤ *Appropriateness of the story.* The teacher should know the children well enough to plan according to their needs, interests, abilities, interest span, and maturity level.
➤ *Variety.* Children are more willing to attend the group experience if it is interesting and challenging. They like some repetition but also some variety.
➤ *Length of time the children are expected to sit.* This depends on the children. Usually a 3-year-old sits quietly for a shorter period than a 4-year-old, but there can be differences among children, from day to day, or as weather changes. If the children grow restless, they can be allowed to participate more in the story; the teacher can also eliminate parts of the story or add interesting elements to it.
➤ *Visual aids.* Often these add interest, but should be used wisely.
➤ *Preparation of the teacher.* The teacher should be well prepared and have all of her materials before the story begins. Often, if a teacher leaves to get something, the children want to leave, too. The teacher should evaluate her personal actions, such as how often she reads instead of tells a story, her voice, her eye contact, and other techniques that add to the appeal of this experience for the children.

 *Reflection*

Because it is difficult to select stories and books for whole-group reading, the following are some possible considerations (adapted from Wolter, 1992):

1. *Grouping:* The activity may be divided by age or interest, or provided for all children; advance preparation is important. Some preschool and kindergarten teachers group children by listening levels and/or background knowledge; others include the whole group. The story area should be comfortable for the children.

2. *Selection:* Consider child development practices; backgrounds of children (ethnicity, cultures, diversity, family groupings); language ability of the children (domestic, bilingual, limited); timing of events; books brought from home; variety in topics (humor, science, relationships, support of classroom play, expanded knowledge, exploration); repetition; good visuals; and flexibility.

3. *Presentation:* Include different types of visual aids (original book, flannelboard, object, enactment, puppets, recording); use intonation, originality, and interest; have the children reenact the story; reread the book to individual children or at another group time.

4. *Children:* Consider individual and group interests and their ability to understand and sit still.

5. *Variation in literature:* Use children's books; poetry and other rhymes; nonfiction; letters, notes, and postcards; child participation; visitors; books made by the children; photographs with captions; items found while visiting the school or public library.

6. *Extension of storytime:* Use ideas that can be extended into other activities, such as art, dramatic play, and outdoor play. Books attractively displayed and accessible to children will increase their interest in and use of books.

Sources for selecting books for young children:

1. Check with the librarian of children's books at a local school or library.
2. Get acquainted with a buyer of children's books at a local bookstore.
3. Contact a teacher of children's literature courses at a local junior/community college or university.
4. Contact known reputable publishers of children's books for catalogs containing descriptions and recommended age levels.
5. Search the Internet for publishers of children's books, especially looking for Caldecott Award- and Newberry Award-winning books of current and past years (only some are appropriate for preschool children).

Evaluating Books for Young Children

[C]haracteristics of good picture books include the literary elements inherent in all literature: characterization, plot, theme, setting, and style. Rebecca Lukens (1995) and Donna Norton (1995) have addressed the following elements in their texts about books for children: characters should be portrayed realistically; story should unfold sequentially, theme should be related to children's needs, understandings, and interests; setting can be used to introduce culture or period in history, develop a mood, and stress symbolic meaning; style involved rhythm, repetition, and a very careful choice of words (James & Kormanski, 1999, p. 33).

Content Evaluation

1. How does the book compare with other picture books of its type (favorable, average, unfavorable)?
2. Do your colleagues, local educators, or librarian recommend or endorse the book? (Be very careful here. Some colleagues, educators, and librarians disagree on what is good literature or even what is popular. Not all good books can win awards or accolades of professionals.)
3. Is the story free from ethnic, racial, or gender-role stereotypes?
4. How could the story apply to or enhance the lives of the children in your group?
5. Are the pictures and text complementary?
6. From a literary standpoint, are elements of plot, theme, character, style, and setting used effectively?
7. Is the theme developmentally appropriate for the children?
8. How do preschool children respond to the story and pictures?
9. Does the book appeal to the parent or teacher?

Illustrations

1. Are the illustrations and text synchronized?
2. Does the mood conveyed by the artwork (humorous/serious, rollicking/quiet) complement that of the story?
3. Are the illustrative details consistent with the text?
4. Could a child get a sense of the basic concepts or story sequence by looking at the pictures?
5. Are the illustrations or photographs aesthetically pleasing?
6. Is the printing (clarity, form, line, color) of good quality?
7. Can children view and re-view the illustrations, each time getting more from them?
8. Are the illustrative style and complexity suited to the age level of the intended audience?

Note: Based on Huck (1979). No complete reference given.

Figure 5.4   Evaluation Questions for Picture Books for Young Children
Reprinted by permission, from M. R. Jalongo, *Picture Books and Young Children: Literature from Infancy to Six* (Washington, DC: NAEYC, 1988), p. 22. Copyright © by the National Association for the Education of Young Children.

Picture Books   Just because the visuals or text appeal to adults, it does not mean that they will interest young children. Watch the children, listen to the children, then select appropriate books for a particular individual or group of children.

Many old favorites and new books are available to interest and charm preschool children. Publishers, local libraries, many schools, and private institutions provide lists from which parents, teachers, and educators can choose good literature for classroom or home settings.

The word of caution is: READ AND EVALUATE EACH BOOK CAREFULLY BEFORE YOU READ IT TO ANY CHILDREN. Look for appropriate topics; thoughts, ideas, and feelings; realistic visuals; and themes that can be replayed in children's lives.

Alphabet Books   Children of all ages have been introduced to alphabet books. Associating letters with corresponding visuals is a beginning step in acquainting children with the alphabet.

These books create interest for one or more children and can be combined with other classroom activities (creativity, dramatic play, storytime, etc.) as children recognize shapes and letters in other parts of the environment.

The more current alphabet books do more than introduce the alphabet in a developmentally appropriate manner. Activities based on a book theme can be pursued independently by children, by small groups of children, or as a classroom project. These extended activities are recommended as an appropriate way to reinforce a book, theme, or concept (Canavan & Sanborn 1992; Raines & Canady 1992).

Characteristics of good alphabet books:

> meet the basic criteria of good children's literature;
> focus upon a central idea or concept;
> provide thoughtful features like bi-level text and addenda;
> invite the response or involvement of the child;
> provide teachers with a rich source of ideas for extended activities in the early childhood setting;
> can support young children's social development; and
> can invite high levels of physical activity (Rhoten & Lane, 2001, pp. 42–44).

These authors also explain:

> Recent publications, however, are highly sophisticated children's literature focusing on a single topic such as different languages, other cultures, ecology. . . . Many have received prestigious awards or recognition such as the American Library Association's Caldecott Medal, the *New York Times* Outstanding Children's Book Selection, and the Science Teachers Association Outstanding Science Book (p. 41).

Books help young children learn about the alphabet and topics in an interesting way, when the letters appear in a natural story sequence and the stories possess the attributes of good children's literature. (For further information, the reader is referred to *Books in Print*. [2000]. New Providence, NJ: R. R. Bowker.)

Intergenerational Books (Important, but often neglected.)   It is not uncommon for multiple generations to live together; therefore, it is important for children to learn about older family members and vice versa. All family members need to learn how to value diversity in race, religion, gender, age, and ability. Positive attitudes are learned over time; attitudes that children adopt early in life affect behavior throughout their lifetime (Jantz et al., 1977, p. 32). Teaching values to all family members includes discussing diverse characteristics, attributes, contributions, and appreciation of various ages.

Individuals with Advanced/Delayed Development   Frequently it is difficult to find good preschool literature that carefully and accurately discusses disabilities of children and/or adults. Children can form prejudices, fears, or mistaken thoughts about what disabilities are, how they occur, and why they occur, and other ideas that can lead to lifelong attitudes. "This fact highlights the need for the presence of similar feelings, experiences, emotions (Hall 1987) and characters with whom they can identify" (Rudman & Pearce, 1988). All children must be fairly represented in our daily curriculum.

Blaska and Lynch (1998) report that "[n]o group has been as overlooked and as inadequately presented in children's books, young readers' books, adult books, and the popular press as individuals with disabilities" (p. 36). They continue:

> Now (1998) in this time of heightened awareness and sensitivity to differences and to portraying people with mental and physical disabilities in more positive roles, it is distressing that the depiction of people with disabilities remains generally negative in the mass media (Keller et al. 1990) although the situation is improving. . . . Guided reading can bring about attitudinal change towards disabilities and exceptionalities (p. 36).

For a FREE LIST of award-winning books for the baby–preschool age: Go to computer and enter AMAZON.COM. The website has a list of these books and awards they have received. http://www.schoolratings.com/baby-preschool.htm.

And further: There is another group of books where the intent is not to inform about disabilities, but to present a person with a disability as a neighbor, a classmate, or a friend in a respectful yet realistic manner, just as all young children must be "routinely represented in the children's fiction and nonfiction we select in our classrooms, . . . just as we include books with people representing racial and cultural diversity" (Blaska & Lynch, 1998, p. 37). ALL individuals should be presented with respect and understanding.

Poetry and Young Children

Does poetry have a place in the preschool classroom? Yes, YES, **YES!**

Why bring poetry into the classroom? Because it stimulates the development of children in many ways (pleasant sounds to the ear, verbal expression, ideas for dramatic play, conversations with others, learning of new concepts, spontaneous recall, and many other uses). It can be recalled and used at any time of the curriculum. Reading poetry aloud, while displaying the written text, promotes emergent literacy, links sounds and symbols, helps children tie words and ideas together, stimulates and sharpens listening skills, provides opportunities for the child to be surrounded by spoken, written, and musical language, and is supported by recent brain development research (Shore, 1997). It also provides the child with a special kind of spoken and written language that can be easily duplicated, and offers many more advantages. Poetry encourages children to think, to problem solve, and to ask "What next?" (Andrews, 1988). "Children's excitement in poetry lies in the exercise of memory recall when they hear favorite poems repeated" (Geller, 1983). You think of additional benefits as you prepare to use poetry often with young children!

Children don't usually have to be encouraged to repeat or create rhyming words. Recall some of the rhyming songs and finger plays that children often request or repeat during their casual play (e.g., "Five Little Monkeys Swinging from a Tree" and "Five Little Ducks Went Out to Play" or others that children love and that tire teachers). A few repetitions and children request such songs or repeat them during individual play.

I compiled a book of poems which I thought young children would enjoy. It had a plain gray cover and no visuals in the book. I used it often with my preschoolers. Whenever I would take it into my classroom, the children would gather around and start requesting poems by content. The most frequent request was: "Read about me hiding!" (Dorothy Aldis' "Hiding"—"I'm hiding, I'm hiding and no one knows where"!).

(Source: Aldis, 1927, p. 5. EVERY teacher needs this delightful book! There are numerous poems to thrill children and excite teachers!

Notable Quote

"Although we push for more technology and efficiency in communication, one element of interpersonal relations that will never be replaced is the spoken and written word. Introducing children of all ages to poetry provides a positive experience of how language can delight, soften difficult moments, and transform the routine into something special" (Gable, 1999, p. 15).

Reading poetry with young children is consistent with recommendations from recent brain development research (e.g., Shore, 1997). Advocates recommend that for healthy and adaptive brain development, children need to be surrounded by spoken, written, and musical language (Shore, 1997). "Development of the brain relies on a multiplicity of learning opportunities that require children to actively think and respond," writes Gable (1999, p. 13). And further, "When children listen to poetry and see the written text, they hear letter and sound combinations and begin to recognize meaningful words (Bredekamp & Copple, 1997).

Through interactive exchange (taking turns, changing emotions, acting parts, etc.) children develop and improve their communicative abilities. "Thus, incorporating poetry into teacher-child interactions effectively stimulates children's delight in language and desire to read and write" (Gable, 1999, p. 13).

Seeing poetry displayed is as important as hearing it—children see a form of writing and relate it to the spoken word. "These opportunities allow children to become familiar with tools of literacy and to experiment with their use" (McLane & McNamee, 1990).

Using spontaneous poetry in the classroom can bring children and teachers together. Routine activities become a time of sharing, helping, cooperating, and enjoyment! Poetry encourages thinking, problem solving, and questioning while stimulating children in wanting to read and write!

 **Reflection**

Make (and keep handy) a list of poems to be used spontaneously or at planned times:

1. when children first arrive at school
2. during **ANY** play period: dramatic play, music, blocks, science, etc.
3. indoors/outdoors; field trips; rest activities
4. snacks, meals, cooking; special visitors; seasons/holidays
5. happy occasions; sad occasions

The children will say: "Read it again! READ IT AGAIN!"

Values for Children

Listening

Early-childhood teachers have long realized the importance of role playing and dramatic play for the children in their classrooms. These teachers reinforce and give firsthand meaning to stories, books, and everyday experiences by providing props and materials, replicas, pictures, flannelboard and flip-card stories, space, time, and a host of other necessities. Through these activities, children learn facts, concepts, and principles in addition to the literal and implicit content of the story.

Children within earshot of conversations, even if they appear not to be listening, learn about language. As reported by Garrard (1987): "Excellence in language does not come from a kit. It comes from children conversing with caring adults while busy playing and living in general, especially with adults who speak well and who encourage children to converse freely" (p. 17).

Too often, adults do not listen to young children, even though they can learn much about them and their concerns merely by doing so. Adults who expect children to listen need to model good listening. A child can be complimented by saying: "What a good idea!" "You thought of a different way to do it!" "You are a good thinker." Such approval tells the child that the adult can listen, too.

Because research reveals that auditory discrimination correlates positively with reading achievement, good listening experiences must be planned and executed often. A child learns to be selective by giving attention to others or to the task at hand (when important) rather than attending to the fly on the wall, other children outside, or thoughts within her head. Listening experiences help the child to increase her vocabulary, learn the structure of spoken language, add concepts and ideas, increase her speech accuracy, and interact with others. They also stimulate her imagination.

Some periods are natural for language development. One is during group time when stories, poetry, finger plays, and songs are used; another is during free play with friends and props or just spontaneously.

Developmental Characteristics

Age 2: Understands most simple words and sentences. Likes to hear commercial jingles and catchy tunes. Listens to simple stories. Likes nursery rhymes.

Age 3: Likes to hear familiar sounds (animals, transportation, household). Likes one-on-one reading experiences. Has rather short but attentive listening span.

Age 4: Listens longer to stories. Still likes one-on-one experiences. May bring favorite stories to be read. Follows simple directions.

Age 5: Seems content to listen for period of time. Enjoys stories, songs, finger plays, and rhymes. Can follow more directions. Carries on conversations.

Communication is an important part of friendships and learning.

We could all be better listeners: teacher-child, parent-child, husband-wife, sibling-sibling, employer-employee, and so on. A person may send a message in a particular way, and the receiver (based on former experience—or inexperience) receives the message in a logical (or illogical) way and acts upon it. Both sender and receiver may show confusion. It is particularly important for adults to carefully consider their information or request as a child may receive it, for a child responds from a limited background; the response could result in action that is inappropriate, unexpected, or unappreciated by the adult but perfectly natural or logical for the child.

Of all the language skills that human beings acquire, listening is the one they use the most throughout life, particularly during early childhood. The sense of hearing functions

 Reflection

The following story provides a *thought-provoking but poor example of teaching a concept—hopefully this will never occur in your preschool classroom!*

A preschool teacher wanted to teach the children about rain. She carefully prepared her visual aids and gave a lengthy demonstration about evaporation. A few of the children got a glimmer of the concepts, but in order to move on to an activity of individual selection, the teacher required each child to give her a verbal explanation, using some of her terms, of what she had just demonstrated. Some older children parroted back the teacher's words and moved on to other play. But, the younger, less verbal, less interested, limited-speaking children had a very difficult time. The children and teacher found the experience to be very frustrating.

Hopefully, the teacher will pledge to herself that she will be more careful in her future planning and requirements. As an observer of this experience, offer some constructive, but specific, suggestions to this teacher.

even before birth, and the typical child amasses extensive experience with listening long before he speaks, reads, or writes. But good listening is more than hearing. Listening is the process used to convert spoken language and sound into meaning in the mind (Lundsteen, 1979; Jalongo, 1996). At this point I would like to remind the reader that diagnosis, treatment, and special handling of children with hearing impairments will not be discussed in this text; however, these children can and should be included in regular classrooms.

Building children's listening skills is dependent upon creating a positive classroom communication environment. Jalongo (1996) suggests that teachers listen to themselves and use the following guidelines for self-assessment:

> Do I model good listening habits? Is there evidence that my classroom is a listening environment? Do I set a purpose for children's listening? Do I communicate clearly? Do I assess children's background knowledge and keep them actively involved in the lesson, project, or activity? Do I listen attentively to each child? (We can't expect children to listen to us if we don't listen to them.) Do I have projects and activities that are interesting to almost all children? Why should they listen if nothing worthwhile is going on? Do I work with parents to build listening skills at home? Are listening goals part of the curriculum?

Each question is followed by examples and dialogue.

To encourage listening, teachers must use clear, concise messages, use jargon-free language, consider what nonverbal communication says to children, and, above all, show respect for the children's home languages and cultures. "Listening is one of the primary methods by which children acquire the beliefs, norms, and knowledge bases of their society" (McDevitt, 1990, p. 571). When teachers build children's listening skills, they are making an important contribution that will serve the child well, not only during early childhood but also throughout life.

Language is frequently viewed as being spoken, but listening is a very important part of language development. If a person does not hear, she cannot respond. If she does

---

 Reflection

Teachers' Attitudes Regarding Language and Its Usage

Personal

Showing respect for (1) home languages and cultures; (2) culturally and linguistically diverse families and individual differences in second-language learning; (3) those who have language differences (are nonverbal, have speech/hearing problems, and so on); and (4) children who need extra time to express themselves or understand concepts.

Classroom Attitudes

Using (1) literature and activities that reflect the children in the classroom; (2) diversity in curriculum activities (music, art, and so on); (3) interpersonal relationships; (4) new languages and/or customs; (5) repetition; (6) information about language/hearing deficits; (7) specific guided information related to differences within the classroom; and (8) sensory deprivation as a positive teaching tool about others who are different from us.

(Some ideas suggested by Soto, 1995, p. 47.)

not respond, she may be inappropriately classified. And language can be used privately (reading, self-communication) or publicly.

Aimed at children who are slightly below the ages considered in this text but who will very shortly be in our focus, the National Institute for Child Health and Human Development (NICHHD) child-care study, the most comprehensive to date on child care in the United States to compare the progress of children in child care and those under their mother's care only, has identified linguistic interaction as a key to intellectual growth in infants (reported in 1997 in a local newspaper article. [This information is given here to alert the reader to research in progress on this topic.]) What researchers have found so far is simple, logical, and subtle: Quality and meaningful interaction between caregivers and children is a powerful influence on the children's intellectual progress—not the educational toys, the family's status, or even the security of home care, but caregivers who speak often and directly to children with respect, sincerity, and sensitivity. The right environment, in which children and caregivers can listen to each other, is critical—and that can be compromised in large groups in some child-care centers. "Quality interaction, apparently, can happen anywhere there's a motivated adult," says Huston, a professor of child development at the University of Texas at Austin and a researcher on the NICHHD study. "It doesn't matter what the topic of conversation, the trick is to speak to children at their level, and then open the door to two-way conversation by listening for their responses," adds Huston.

The sensitive and caring caregivers in the study who were adept at this used simple words, talked softly, and answered even babies' vocalizations—creating a language recognized by researchers as "Motherese."

If at all possible, purchasers of books for young children should *read the books before buying them or checking them out of a library.* Some publishers mail an annotated catalog with an age guide, but some books listed as appropriate for preschoolers may be too advanced or too simple or may cover too broad an age range for a particular group of children.

In addition to using stories and books as good listening experiences for young children, the value of poetry, finger plays, and Mother Goose should be taken into consideration (see Chapter 12).

Items in the following list are used to increase *listening ability:*

➤ Poetry
➤ Finger plays
➤ Mother Goose rhymes
➤ Sound boxes, tubes, and cans
➤ Tape recordings, commercial or classroom: Listen to a taped story. Play it again. Stop it at various places and ask what will happen next. Make a tape of children's voices and familiar sounds and have them guess who or what it is.
➤ Record player and records
➤ Listening walk
➤ Rhyming words and nonrhyming words
➤ Repetition in stories
➤ Rhythm: The teacher beats the rhythm and the children repeat it.
➤ Simple directions
➤ Sounds in the classroom: Have children imitate them.
➤ Sounds in the environment, such as those from a household, a playground, or transportation: Use sounds with and without pictures.
➤ Puppets: Have children listen and then repeat words or actions.
➤ Games: For example, "Simon Says" (the teacher says, "I am thinking about an animal and its name "sounds like *how*" and children guess); "Mother and Baby" (one child pretends to be a mother animal, makes the appropriate sound, then closes eyes, another child, pretending to be the baby animal, hides, and also makes the appropriate sound; the mother finds the baby); "Head, Shoulders, Knees, and Toes."
➤ Telephones (answering, dialing, etiquette)

Speaking

Young children should not be pressured to produce responses. Sometimes they lack understanding of what is required, sometimes they feel silence is safer than being incorrect, and sometimes their words just don't come out! The problem could arise if a teacher has expectations of, and demands, responses that are at a level beyond the child's development.

Adults may insist upon spoken language. Children who are reluctant to speak may feel uncomfortable, frightened, inexperienced, unaccepted, or coerced. French (1996) writes:

> There is much documentation of cultural differences in the extent to which children are encouraged to express themselves verbally at home. Also, considerable differences sometimes exist between children's language abilities at the comprehension level and at the production level; that is, children might be able to comprehend incoming language but still have difficulty in producing language expressing their understanding (p. 20).

Young children should be given frequent opportunities to express their affective and cognitive ideas. Mentioned previously in this chapter was the stimulating and beneficial use of poetry and nursery rhymes, either spontaneous or planned. Maclean, Bryant, and Bradley (1987) concluded: "The direct practical implication of our research is that an increase in the amount of experience that 3-year-old children have with nursery rhymes should lead to a corresponding improvement in their awareness of sounds, and hence to greater success in learning to read" (p. 280).

The Vygotskian approach to language learning includes such ideas as these: "All humans in all languages have developed language" and "once toddlers acquired language, their problem-solving ability improved dramatically" (Bodrova & Leong, 1996, p. 95).

Wordless books for young children have been appearing on the market. Do they have value for these children? Consider that stories told by young children using wordless

---

 Developmental Characteristics

Age 2: Has favorite word: "No!" Tries to say simple words: may use short sentences and carry on simple conversations. Names simple objects (body parts, pictures). Likes short responses.

Age 3: Can carry on a conversation. Uses simple words and short sentences (three to four words). May carry on a monologue. Asks "Why?" to gain adult attention.

Age 4: Is quick to pick up new words. Learns words for ideas, actions, and feelings. Combines more words. Is integrating rules of grammar; may have difficulty with irregular past tense or plurals. Is boastful and quarrelsome. May carry on a monologue. Talks about imaginary companion. Experiments with language. Asks "Why?" for knowledge.

Age 5: Has highly socialized speech. Is a continual talker. Uses "because" sentences. Has wide vocabulary, uses six- to eight-word, sentences. Can verbally compare two or more objects.

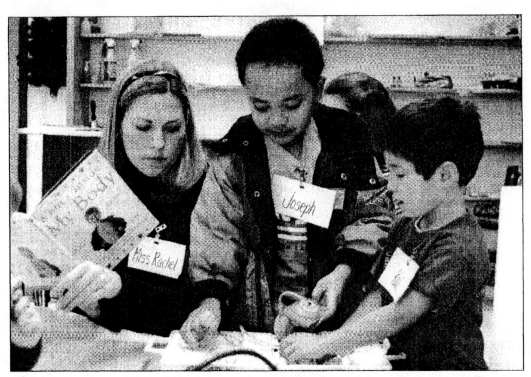

Hearing a story and then elaborating on it encourages creativity.

books are more elaborate in ideas and words than are stories they originate about a single picture, but less complex than original stories told by the children. Teachers and parents should encourage children to invent and tell their own original stories—with and without visuals.

Oral language is used to share, exchange, or test ideas; to express feelings; to gain new knowledge; to develop auditory acuity; to build relationships; to practice words and grammar; and to provide enjoyment. The younger the children, the less they verbalize; rather, they use physical methods for egocentric purposes. They take things, walk over others, bite, cry, kick, and scream. As children mature, they progressively use more verbalization.

Helping young children increase their speaking skills is desirable, but adults may do the opposite. When children receive too much attention, they do not need to speak; they can point, grunt, or cry. Children may use behavior below their developmental level just because it pays off. Adults may carry on their own two-way conversation by commenting and responding to themselves rather than giving the children a chance to respond. An adult may offer a choice to a child and when the child hesitates (or when the adult knows what he expects), the adult may respond as if making a democratic choice for the child.

Young children need attractive environments that are conductive to play, promote cooperation and enjoyment, and encourage verbal interaction. When they have thoughts, they want and need to express them. In some classrooms, however, teachers are known to talk 75 to 90 percent of the time to give instructions, keep order, and teach the children. When teachers use language in these ways, children speak infrequently. Frequent use of positive support comments decreases the need for disciplinary or negative statements and commands. In one study done by Serbin and O'Leary (1975), nursery-school teachers were found to reward boys for aggression and girls for passivity. In other words, they were "teaching girls to shut up"!

The teacher must learn how to establish rapport and a spontaneous flow of communication that provides comfort and security for each child. When teachers talk with children about interesting things, they get a rewarding response. The teacher can also help the shy child to verbalize by providing a variety of experiences, such as stories, songs, finger plays, new encounters, and friendly companions. Teachers, acting as resources for children's language, should be as precise as possible in their conversations, using many concept words, descriptions, and abstractions that help the child relate to the experience.

The teacher who shows sincere interest by getting down on the level of the children, by listening attentively and by making appropriate comments, can expect other "talking times" with them. The teacher further encourages language by expanding conversations ("Yes, I see your new shoes," when a child says, "New shoes") and by elaborating on what children say without controlling the whole conversation ("Your new shoes have two straps and two buckles."). The teacher may also need to assist very young children who are trying to use words and verbs that are irregular in forming plurals or past tenses.

Several authors discuss two popular myths about learning language: (1) that children learn by imitation and (2) that children learn by being corrected. Imitation by itself is insufficient, and correction does not occur with enough frequency to change verbal patterns. Many theories of language development agree that experience, conceptualization, and communication continuously influence the way children develop language.

Following are some suggestions teachers could use to increase the *speaking ability* of children:

➤ Poetry
➤ Finger plays
➤ Mother Goose rhymes
➤ Puppets—stick, sack, felt, cone, sock, glove, finger (A puppet stage is also useful. Remind the children that the puppets are kind and gentle, thus avoiding aggressive and loud behavior.)
➤ Telephone (for courtesy and conversation)
➤ Just talking about things that are of interest to the children
➤ Props: Put on various articles of clothing and ask the children to guess your occupation—firefighter, sports figure, doctor, skier, mail carrier, construction worker, nurse, baker, soldier. Stress that occupations can be for either males or females.
➤ Recordings, video or audio: Record original poems or songs and what the children say about their activities. Play back the recordings and try to identify voices.
➤ Stories: Discuss a story; let the children retell a story using visual aids; use a wordless book and let the children supply the story; tell a group story (each child tells part of it); have the children tell stories to each other.
➤ Television: Make a large cardboard TV set. Slip different pictures into its window and ask the children to tell about them. Provide a large box and let the children pretend they are actors.
➤ Naming, especially for younger children: The teacher points to a body part, and the children name it; the teacher shows an object or picture, and the children name it.
➤ Field trip: Discuss preparations and behavior with children, such as what they should ask, what they think they will see, and how they should act. Provide dramatic play as a follow-up.
➤ Songs
➤ Questions: Ask open-ended questions that require thought and verbalization rather than yes, no or one-word answers; propose questions—why, what, where, when, how—and help the children find out the answers.
➤ Food experiences: Let children help shop for, prepare, and eat different foods. Encourage conversation at snack time.
➤ Dramatic play: Provide an area in the classroom where the children can reenact a variety of themes.
➤ Show and tell: This may be less effective with younger children. Also, some children feel compelled to have something every time, so you may need a schedule. This is a time for children—not teachers—to talk.

➤ Spotlight: Have a place in your room where you display interesting science things. Rotate the display, but give the children enough time to enjoy and investigate. Use this area to stimulate curiosity and conversation.

➤ Microphone: Encourage the children to pretend they are talking through a microphone (use a small can, tube, or fist).

Drama

Young children can learn from dramatic play and also from informal drama—reenacting stories, making up situations, and using props that suggest activities. Through this type of play, children practice physical skills, social and emotional situations, cognitive and language development, and multisensory experiences as ideas unfold or are enhanced in the presence of others—actors and audience.

A supportive adult may need to be nearby to see that the dramatizations do not become negative, exclusive, or competitive. Teachers may also need special training, understanding, and confidence to make drama a delightful part of language development.

Child Participation

In the past, a more familiar name for child participation was "Show and Tell," which was popular in some homes and dreaded in others. In some early childhood programs it flourished; in others it has vanished. It sounds like a good opportunity for children to verbalize with a group of peers, but what often happens is that a child, as excited and desirous as he may be, becomes nervous, embarrassed, and nonverbal. The teacher does most of the talking—asking questions that can be answered with a nod, or repeating facts that the child has previously rehearsed at home.

If child participation is to be part of the classroom activities, guidelines need to be precise or the following problems may occur:

Inconsistency: A school policy of no toys coming from home, and then expecting child participation.
Taking turns: Some children want to participate *every* time; some never!
Embarrassment: Inability to speak in front of a group.

One can try out new ideas with a friendly puppet.

Parental/family fatigue: Always having to come up with something to take. One 4-year-old "sneaked" his little sister on the bus while the mother was in the shower; one child brought mother's diamond ring; still others brought brother's valued sport equipment, Dad's fishing gear, the neighbor's pet, worn-out shoes, and food stuffed into the child's pocket.

Concern for the item: A child may be so afraid of losing or having to share the item that she becomes very protective of it and loses interest in the activities and the other children.

Lack of interest of other children: Giving up valuable time for something that bores them.

There are, however, some advantages of having "S & T" time. When children share something of themselves with one and another, they gain confidence in becoming the focus of others' attention; they gain confidence in speaking skills; they find out that others can be interested in them; they discover that there are things they know about, and they feel good about themselves doing it!

A change of name to *sharing time* or *children's teaching time* encourages guidelines for parents and children to follow for things to show, such as something found in nature; exotic or little known food; safe hand tools; photo from newspaper, magazine, or book; or snapshot taken with a home camera; items the children have made themselves at home; a favorite book not available at school; and other timely and interesting items.

Parents and teachers need to carefully monitor items and amount of time spent in such group activities or they become boring/dreaded or pressure/competitive.

Reading

In the case of preschool children, reading more often consists of being read to than children actually reading.

Group storytime is an enjoyable experience.

Developmental Characteristics

Age 2: May recognize objects, turn pages in books, and point to or name objects.

Ages 3, 4, and 5: May learn to read simple words (some memorize or remember). May identify words that look alike or different. Recognize a few words (own name, logos, signs, television words, food containers).

Many young children are pressured to read by being subjected to drills or rigid, formal prereading programs. Both of these expectations are inappropriate for the experiences and skills of the children—but some adults (parents and educators) feel that early reading is possible and a sign of intelligence. In the home and in a preschool or kindergarten setting, many experiences prepare a child for learning to read. Children who are read to at an early age develop better reading habits and demonstrate significantly greater gains in vocabulary and reading comprehension than children who have not had this advantage.

Children who see adults reading observe eye movements (or finger movements) to follow the print, page turning, picture support, and enjoyment. Books become important to the children, too. Besides using books, adults can point out words and signs in the child's environment, assist the child in writing his name (using capital and lower-case letters, of course), and provide opportunities for eye-hand coordination and discrimination tasks.

Sensory experiences are vital in helping young children learn to read:

Visual discrimination: matching (buttons, colors, shapes, letters and/or pictures [cards, books, and so on]) and sorting (cans, groceries, clothes, pans, and so on)
Auditory discrimination: sounds, telephone experiences, hearing stories, singing songs, and conversations involving descriptive ideas or recalling information (loud/soft, same/different)
Tactile discrimination: feeling many objects (fabrics, plastics, wood, and so on)
Oral discrimination: tasting, smelling, chewing

Some adults become anxious about teaching alphabet recognition, naming, and writing. Read, Gardner, and Mahler (1987) issue this reminder: Learning to recognize and write the letters of the alphabet is not an appropriate activity for most three-year-olds, but it is often included in these programs" (p. 290). Smith (1985) states: "Of course, it does not hurt a child to have some acquaintance with the alphabet. . . . But learning the alphabet is not a prerequisite for learning to distinguish words."

Letter-name knowledge (not necessarily letter-name recognition) is frequently an important indicator of reading readiness. Children as young as 3 are capable of recognizing some letters, and some 5-year-olds have nearly mastered letter-name knowledge (Kontos, 1986, p. 62).

READING = written symbols + experience + meaning.

Many children learn to read before they come to school. Formal instruction is obviously not essential. Learning to read early is not determined by social or economic class, or by size of family, age, maturity, intelligence, an intact home, specialized programs and materials, or any specific geographical location or neighborhood (F. Smith, 1985). In order to read, children need to have reading experiences in a natural, nonpressured manner, with child and parents enjoying the process. See Figure 5.5.

---

1. Let children see an adult reading (modeling).
2. Arrange a comfortable reading area with magazines, newspapers, picture books, and so on.
3. Take children to the library: get a library card, choose books, and get acquainted with other media there.
4. Read road signs, store signs, package labels; find license plates for different states.
5. Reward children for reading achievement with *honest* praise, a trip to the library, or the purchase of a new book.
6. Make book projects: maps, special words, bookmarks, or other book-related activities.
7. Write down a story as a child tells it, then reread it.
8. Give children or help children make their own bookcases.
9. Limit television watching, or watch together.
10. Give books as presents.
11. As children draw and talk about their pictures, record descriptions and other information.
12. Show pictures and ask questions; prediction is an important reading skill.
13. Establish a daily pattern to read to your children (same time, same place). Talk about books you have read; anticipate what will happen next; recall a favorite thing or character. Talk about why the child liked the story. Ask the reader questions about the story; has something similar happened to the adult or the child?

Figure 5.5   Ways to Stimulate Reading in Young Children

There is concern that preschool programs have become too academic and are creating stress for children. This concern can easily apply to language arts, where stress may be on speaking frequently and fluently (in making one's needs and wants known, in getting along with others, in expressing one's feelings, and so on) or on learning to read and write.

Warnings about the dangers of including academics in preschool programs have appeared in both popular and professional literature. It seems that teaching methods and what is being taught have not been differentiated in these discussions.

There is some agreement that presently many preschool and kindergarten children are being subjected to inappropriate teaching methods in many settings. We don't want to keep academics out of preschool learning; home and school environments should be low in pressure and high in involvement.

The following elements help increase reading ability in children:

➤ Games where sound and listening are important
➤ A cozy place to read (loft or tent with pillows)
➤ A variety of good books appropriate for the child
➤ A discussion about the care of books
➤ Enrichment of the child's vocabulary
➤ Seriation (size, variation in color, or stacking of shoes, socks, sticks, cups, jars, ribbons, and so on)
➤ Classification: Have the children put objects into appropriate groups and then look for other ways of grouping.
➤ Card games (bingo and picture variations; old maid; go fish; matching pictures of shapes, sizes, and colors; combining two properties such as size and shape; large cards with numbers and letters the children can arrange)

➤ Poster or chart: Use a helper chart on which each child's name is placed by a picture with a word for an activity or an assignment. Make a word dictionary as children learn new words (include pictures).

➤ Visual discrimination opportunities (similarities and differences, missing items, comparison, shapes, sizes, and so on)

➤ Uninterrupted time

➤ Models who read and enjoy it

➤ Experiences and conversations that stimulate language usage.

➤ Food: Make a list, go to the grocery store, buy food for lunch or snack (observe labels). Make something using a recipe.

➤ Typewriter or computer

➤ Curriculum areas: (1) Have a pattern for toys that go in certain places. (2) Provide puzzles and rubber stamps of objects, letters, and numbers. (3) Supply sewing cards. (4) Have children reproduce designs with pegs, beads, or blocks.

➤ Symbols: (1) Place a sticker or design on each child's locker. (2) Wear name tags daily. (3) Write each child's name on the back of her artwork. (4) Use one picture of only boys, one of only girls, and one of both boys and girls; hold up one picture and have pictured children respond to actions or questions (no verbalization is used).

➤ Artwork: Ask children to tell about their artwork. On the back side or a separate page, write down what they say and read it back to them.

➤ Community: (1) Take a trip to the local library. (2) Observe safety and speed signs. (3) Go to some interesting places and observe signs. Write a thank-you note.

➤ Decentering: Help children focus on more than one aspect at a time. They will need to recognize parts and whole if they are to learn to read.

➤ Practice: Give the children opportunities to practice concepts of conversation, reversibility, seriation, whole-part relationships, and multiple and simultaneous classification. (Some examples are listed here and in Chapter 9.)

 *Reflection*

Ivan, a happy 5-year-old, sat looking at *The Wall Street Journal*. His mother had called him several times to prepare for dinner. Still he sat and looked. Finally, his mother became exasperated. "Ivan, if you don't come to dinner right this minute, I'll give your food to the dog!" Reluctantly, Ivan laid down the paper and strolled to the table. Still in deep thought, he finally said, "Mom, I just can't figure out why Dad likes that paper so much. It doesn't have any pictures, and it is all the same color!" Ivan was trying to equate his own reading experiences with those of his father. Ivan liked pictures, action, and color.

When young children are read to frequently and when parents are good models of reading, children begin their reading careers early. As Ivan and a parent sat down to read together, Ivan talked about the pictures, asked questions, and added new dialogue. He turned the pages when he was ready. Sometimes he or his parent made additions to the text and sometimes deletions. He memorized his favorite books and could tell when a word was misused or omitted. He figured out that the marks on the pages had something to do with the pictures, an important discovery in developing reading skill and comprehension. He also noticed that when he asked questions that his parents or teachers could not answer, they went to books, so, when he had questions, he looked at books. He did not always find what he wanted, but he knew the procedure followed by adults.

> ## Notable Quotes
>
> Esplin (2002) suggests some opportunities to help preschool children become readers:
>
> *For Parents and Children:* (a) daily conversations, (b) parents who read and write, (c) trips to the library, (d) daily reading together, (e) a reading and writing space, (f) attention to reading and writing in everyday activities, (g) printed and written materials easily available in the home.
>
> *For Children:* (a) a message board, (b) encouragement to "read," (c) displays of their writing, (d) a word bank or word file, (e) attention called to reading and writing in everyday activities, (f) television and technology used wisely (pp. 4–6).

Books for young children should be carefully selected bearing in mind the needs and interests of the individual child(ren) for whom they are intended. Remove those with undesirable messages, poor visuals, and the like. Be sure to include appropriate poetry. (See pp. 173–174.) Discuss children's thoughts, ideas, and feelings about stories you read them. Share *your* thoughts, ideas, and feelings after exploring *theirs*. Furthermore, we should encourage authors and publishers to create books that better reflect local and national customs as well as address the real issues children, parents, teachers, and principals face.

Children exhibit their literacy progress in situations that are meaningful to them. They need stimulating learning experiences based on contextual cues, encouragement, and opportunities to practice new words and ideas if they are to express themselves, build concepts, and enlarge their knowledge base. Familiarity with books and experiences (such as field trips, filmstrips or videos, books, discussions), adjusting content level, and using descriptive language—all based on the developmental level of the children involved—provide children with a sense of control and confidence.

The research of Emelia Ferreiro (1978, 1986, 1990) clearly documents children's thinking, watching, and listening as they work through various theories to make sense of a confusing system (Fields & Spangler, 2000, pp. 24–25) and as they spontaneously explore print in writing (Ferreiro, 1990). "After teachers learn about Ferreiro's research, many of them suddenly realize that they have been seeing this evidence of children's thinking all along, but didn't recognize it because they weren't looking for it" (Fields & Spangler, 2000, p. 26).

Children's play provides an important opportunity for children to practice using reading and writing skills through exploration, pretending, active play, games, manipulative materials, large and small-muscle coordination, art, and music, and personal interaction. (See Chapters 3 & 4.) Being read to regularly is the best way for children to become acquainted with written language.

Educators must make the distinction between constructing knowledge and learning facts. Young children need firsthand experiences to construct knowledge (Piaget, 1973). Adults who try to substitute secondhand experiences (pictures, films, lectures, etc.) for firsthand ones shortchange children's learning.

Teaching Children to Read

Research suggests that children who have advanced phonemic awareness are more ready to learn to read and are more successful at it. Learning to read is a complex process that begins long before first grade. Teachers of young children can facilitate the reading readiness process in a developmentally appropriate fashion by providing opportunities for children to comprehend the relation between sounds and words, as opposed to presenting concepts in isolation. Children need to learn phonemic awareness by engaging in *fun and motivating activities* that promote the recognition and manipulation of sounds in words (Wasik, 2001, p. 132).

The International Reading Association (IRA) and the National Association for the Education of Young Children (NAEYC) have issued a joint position statement (1998). These two organizations believe that goals and expectations for young children's achievement in reading and writing "should be developmentally appropriate, that is, *challenging but achievable,* with sufficient adult support" (p. 31). The document covers rationale for the position statement, the recommended age scope (birth through primary grades), recommended policies, and a conclusion:

> Developmentally appropriate practices (Bredekamp & Copple 1997) in reading and writing are ways of teaching that consider and meet each child's needs through . . . (a) learning that is challenging, but within personal limitations . . . (b) provides for individual improvement and advancement; and (c) personal, social, and cultural information is readily available to help each student "make sense of their learning experiences in relation to what they already know and are able to do" (p. 40).

The National Academy of Sciences (1998, copyright; 2000) has a publication, *Preventing Reading Difficulties in Young Children.* This information is also available online at http://www.nap.edu/openbook/030906418Xhtml/l.html. This committee recommends that all children, especially those at risk of reading difficulties, should have access to early childhood environments that promote language and literacy growth and that address a variety of skills that have been identified as predictors of later reading achievement.

Preschools and other groups available to lower-income families should be designed (1) in ways that support language and language development; (2) to provide optimal support for cognitive, language, and social development, within a broad focus; (3) to provide kindergarten instruction that stimulates verbal interactions; and (4) to generate familiarity with the basic purposes and mechanisms of reading (National Academy of Sciences, 2000, p. 9). The executive summary includes:

> If language-minority children arrive at school with no proficiency in English but speaking a language for which there are instructional guides, learning materials and locally proficient teachers, these children should be taught how to read in their native language while acquiring proficiency in spoken English and then subsequently taught to extend their skills to reading in English (p. 11).

Older children listen intently to stories for longer periods of time.

Notable Quotes

Washington Update: *Young Children,* July 2000, p. 44:

"Recent data show that by the fourth grade, 40% of children have not acquired basic reading skills. The 1998 joint position statement of the International Reading Association and NAEYC, *Learning to Read and Write: Developmentally Appropriate Practices for Young Children,* underscores the need for early childhood professionals to develop their knowledge of children's early literacy and to work with policymakers, parents, and community leaders to help prepare young children to learn to read and write" (Children's Champions section of website: www.naeyc.org.).

"A 1998 National Research Council study: *Preventing Reading Difficulties in Young Children,* recommended that policy makers target more funds for early literacy development." The one that pertains to young students is: Even Start Family Literacy grants (Elementary and Secondary Education Act). The Department also has an 'inexpensive book distribution' "to distribute, largely through school districts and libraries, free and low cost books to children birth to 11 years, many of whom are at risk of failing in school. In 1999 another nonprofit literacy organization, First Book, received a $2 million federal grant to work with local advisory boards to develop book distribution programs to reach the most needy children— for example, children living in shelters for homeless families."

"Two proposals are pending in Congress that would create federal grants specifically to support the reading readiness of children, ages birth to 5 years. For more information visit the newly designed **Children's Champions** section of NAEYC Website at www.naeyc.org" (*Young Children,* July 2000, Vol. 55, #5, p. 44).

Three potential stumbling blocks that are known to throw children off course on the journey to skilled reading are: "(1) difficulty understanding and using the alphabetic principle—the idea that written spellings systematically represent spoken words; (2) a failure to transfer the comprehension skills to reading and to acquire new strategies that may be specifically for reading; and (3) (which magnifies the first two) is the absence or loss of an initial motivation to read or failure to develop a mature appreciation of the rewards of reading" (pp. 4–5).

In yet another publication, Hargrave and Sénéchal (2000) report the benefits of regular reading and dialogic reading with preschool children who have limited vocabularies. Book reading occurred in groups of eight children, and all children were exposed to the same books, which were read twice. The results of this study revealed that "children in the dialogic-reading condition made significantly larger gains in vocabulary introduced in the books, as well as gains on a standardized expressive vocabulary test, than did the children in a regular book-reading situation" (p. 12).

Teaching the Alphabet

Some adults become anxious about teaching alphabet recognition, naming, and writing. Learning to recognize and write the letters of the alphabet is not an appropriate activity for 3-year-olds, even though it is often included. It doesn't hurt a child to have some acquaintance with the alphabet, but knowing it is not a prerequisite for learning to distinguish words, and the alphabet can be a handicap if adults use it to try to train children to sound out words before they are able to make sense of what the adults are talking about. Reading demands visual and auditory acuity, language ability, and the ability to learn. With regard to inventories of prerequisites for reading readiness, Smith calls them "shopping lists" of everything the compiler thinks might be relevant to reading, ranging from "knowledge of letters and sounds" to physical and emotional maturity and even "correct body-book posture."

"Although for many years we have had research telling us that knowing the alphabet helps children learn to read, many early childhood teachers have been opposed to teaching ABCs before kindergarten or first grade" (Wasik, 2001b, p. 35).

Some support for teaching the alphabet includes:

1. Early exposure to letters is a part of a rich literacy experience and helps build a strong literacy foundation for young children.
2. Advocates argue that many children who come to preschool from print-rich homes already have a great deal of experience with the alphabet.
3. Children from homes with limited literacy experiences need to be taught the alphabet.
4. Young children learn best when information is presented in context and when there are many opportunities to create experiences that allow the material to be meaningful (Bredekamp & Copple, 1997; Kagan, 1994).
5. "We know from the research in this area that alphabet knowledge is one of the best predictors of success in first-grade reading" (Adams 1990; Bond & Dykstra 1997; Wasik, 2001b).

Some opposition to teaching the alphabet includes:

1. Teaching letters is only one step removed from teaching reading.
2. Teaching methods (*skill* and *drill*) are not developmentally appropriate for young children (Kagan, 1994).
3. Unclear and inconsistent policies regarding the best learning experiences for young children.

The National Association for the Education of Young Children has been instrumental in defining appropriate practices for teaching young children. Their 1987 guidelines for 4- and 5-year-olds state that "stressing isolated skill development such as recognizing single letters or reciting the alphabet song" (Bredekamp, 1987, p. 55) is inappropriate early childhood instruction. Unfortunately, this advice was misinterpreted to mean that any teaching of the alphabet to young children is not developmentally appropriate. In the revised NAEYC guidelines (Bredekamp & Copple, 1997), the approach to teaching the alphabet is presented differently. The guidelines state that practices following a "rigid sequence of prerequisites" and taking a "single approach" (p. 31) for all children, regardless of what the children can already do, are developmentally inappropriate for young children. When "letters are introduced one at a time and with insufficient context in words," the guidelines point out, "some children are bored because they already know the letters, and other children are confused because they cannot make sense of isolate bits of information" (p. 131). The NAEYC guidelines do not recommend against teaching the alphabet; they address only the teaching methods for doing so. Furthermore, the recent position statement *Learning to Read and Write: Developmentally Appropriate Practices for Young Children* (1998), copublished by NAEYC and the International Reading Association, clearly states that "learning the alphabet plays an important role in the development of literacy skills" (p. 35).

Young children may be able to memorize the letters of the alphabet through drill and practice, but the letters may have no meaning to the children and may not facilitate the end goal of reading.

In teaching the alphabet to young children, begin with the familiar and work to the unfamiliar. Using direct teaching may be appropriate *only if it is done using language and experiences that are familiar to the children* (storybooks, center activities, signs in the classroom, etc.) and if used for short periods of time.

Symbol-Reading Exercises Just for Adults

Throughout this book, activities are suggested to increase skills and abilities in children. Figure 5.6 shows shorthand and Japanese symbol-reading exercises and Figure 5.7 shows music symbol-reading exercises just for adults.

As you approached each of these exercises, you probably looked for familiar signs. If you felt comfortable with one option more than the other two, you probably concentrated there. If none of the three exercises gave you any clues, you probably became frustrated and moved on to the next paragraph. Young children learning to read look for familiar symbols in their environment (names, road signs, designs) and then try to match them to symbols in written material. You just went through a similar experience.

Writing

One method of identifying an interest in reading in young children is by giving them access to important materials (e.g., books, paper, crayons), which helps stimulate interest and takes advantage of the important relationship between drawing and writing, and provides an outlet for children's natural curiosity about print as they see it being used.

To think that children under 6 years of age can maneuver writing implements with accuracy and precision or that they have mental organizational skills sophisticated enough to compose a short story indicates total ignorance as to how young children develop and learn. More realistic is the image of a young child crudely holding writing tools, making indistinguishable strokes at scattered locations on the page, giving first one description of his marks and then another, and combining unrelated ideas. Children do pretend to make up, write, and read stories of their own. They see adults do it, so why can't they?

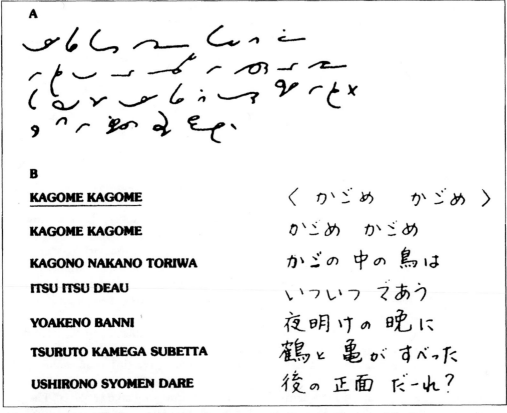

Figure 5.6 Shorthand and Japanese Symbol-Reading Exercises for Adults Only. Identify the individual words and meaning of the shorthand (A) and the Japanese (B).

Figure 5.7 Music Identification Symbol-Reading Exercises for Adults Only
Hum the music and identify the two songs (do not use a piano or other musical instrument).

Developmentally appropriate early writing stages include *scribbling* (written symbols that carry meaning and a message); the *linear mock writing stage* (left-to-right, single-line, top-to-bottom, sometimes reading written work to someone else); and *mock letter writing* (recognition of letters, imitation of the conventional alphabet) (Kuball, 1995).

It has been proposed that writing can be appropriately encouraged when children have exposure to items such as books, paper, crayons, and other objects that would stimulate their interest in print, help to build important relationships between drawing and writing, and serve as an outlet for the child's natural curiosity about print.

Learning to write can sometimes become a meaningless activity for children: The physical problems of trying to copy or trace the written word are tremendous. For example, watch a child who is beginning to write his/her name. Children who are encouraged to draw and scribble "stories" at an early age will later learn to compose more effectively and with greater confidence than children who do not have this encouragement.

Parents can stimulate and encourage children in writing experiences through (1) providing writing equipment (paper, pencils, crayons, envelopes, cellophane tape, staples, a comfortable place to work, and so on), so that the children can explore writing at any time; (2) providing blank forms, order forms, menu pads, and so on for play that stretches children's imaginations and broadens their experiences; (3) helping them write letters, cards, and so on to others; (4) putting notes in lunchboxes; (5) making books for children to write and draw (some folded sheets); (6) modeling writing—notes, lists, and so on; (7) praising their attempts and showing the relationship between print and speech; and (8) eliminating criticisms of neatness, spelling, or grammar.

Handwriting has several aspects: physical ability, organizational skills and idea presentation, and language skills (vocabulary, syntax, grammar).

Physical ability includes good use of hands and fingers. Writing requires more than a whole-hand grasp and uncontrolled large gross movements. The fingers need to have a good grasp of the utensil, and the arm needs to rest comfortably on a tabletop. The physical prerequisites are often lacking in 4- and 5-year-olds. Their control generally is still imprecise and awkward. Practice and some instruction are needed.

The second aspect of writing, *organizational skills* and *idea presentation,* is difficult for young children, who are still in the egocentric stage and have difficulty expressing ideas or seeing things from another's viewpoint. They think that others can see into their minds and know their thoughts and that others have the same view as they do. Expressing simple, often unrelated, ideas is the extent of their ability.

The third aspect of writing, *language skills,* is also difficult for young children. They know nothing about the use of capital letters, punctuation, placement of elements in the sentence, spelling, or the use of descriptive words. It will be some years before these attributes are developed.

Beginning writing experiences include the use of jumbo crayons and pencils, large sheets of paper, something interesting to draw, and motivation. When utensils and materials are readily available, the children are encouraged to use them.

Young children should learn manuscript letters (printing) before cursive ones for two reasons. First, when children have had extensive experience with drawing and painting, they may have already mastered the basic strokes required in handwriting. Second, as children begin their initial reading, manuscript letters more nearly resemble the print.

When a child expresses interest in writing, parents generally teach the capital letters only. When this occurs, the child must learn two different ways of writing. As a beginner, it is easier for the child to learn capital and lowercase letters in simple words such as his name and familiar objects and terms. Again, this type of writing looks like the type in books. When teachers in the classroom write names on possessions, they should start in the upper left-hand corner and use capital and lower-case letters. The adult should sit down by the children and make the letters neatly as a good model for the children to follow. Writing from across the table or in an awkward position distorts the letters.

Writing is not generally one of the regular curriculum areas for young children, but most preschools give help with writing as each child indicates interest. Individually, the experience can be one of joy and success. In some kindergartens, writing practice is one of the regular curriculum areas. Generally, teachers have a specific way of presenting the different letters that is not necessarily consecutive. Many preschool children memorize the alphabet before it has actual meaning to them.

 ## *Developmental Characteristics*

Age 2: Scribbles; repeats radial or circular pattern. Uses whole-hand grasp, whole-arm movement. Fills whole page. Is fascinated by markings.

Age 3: Prints large, single, capital letters anywhere on page. Likes to draw and paint (images are large, simple, and incomplete).

Age 4: May recognize a few letters, including own name. May write name or a few capital letters (large and irregular). Likes to draw and paint. Human figures are stick, drawings crude. Draws circles and squares.

Age 5: Prints first name (large, irregular letters increasing in size). Frequently reverses letters and numbers or writes from right to left. Prints numbers (uneven and medium-sized). Can write some capital and lowercase letters. Has better grasp on writing utensils. Likes to draw and paint. Pictures are more complex and complete. Combines squares and circles. Likes to copy a model. May ask about spelling.

The following activities are recommended to increase writing ability:

➤ Practice using and strengthening small muscles (pegboards, cutting, puzzles, stringing, lacing, zipping, drawing, painting).

➤ Use body movement: This helps children to observe; gives them a sense of high, low, and other directions; and teaches them shape and line. (For example, they can be told to swing their arms in a circle or to hold their legs straight.) The teacher can also ask the children to make their bodies into shapes shown on cards (see Chapter 12).

➤ Do your note taking and recording with a positive attitude.

➤ Give each child some paper (or a booklet) and let him draw a story; you write down the comments.

➤ Help the children write a letter or thank-you note to someone.

➤ Provide good writing tools and time to write.

➤ Appreciate attempts at writing.

➤ Show each child how to write her name and other words as interest is indicated (use capital and lowercase letters).

➤ Place names of individuals and objects around the room.

➤ Practice right-left concept ("Hokey Pokey"; body movement).

➤ Use manipulative toys (Tinkertoys, snap blocks, magnetic boards, blocks).

➤ Play games (Twister; "Do as I'm Doing"; circle games such as "Mulberry Bush" or Ring-Around-a-Rosy"); spinner games.

➤ Practice with letters (letters of the child's name to put together like a puzzle; letters and numbers to use on the flannelboard, or magnetic ones to use on magnetic boards; stencils to trace).

➤ Encourage drawing: This includes completing partially completed designs; reproducing designs; following patterns, making slanted, straight, and curved lines with crayons (teepees, boxes, a road); making designs and letters in the air; connecting dots or drawing lines to matching items (mother and baby animals, two shoes, go-togethers).

➤ Label things: Each child wears a label with her name that she can put into a chart to indicate an area she will play in, put into a helper chart, or use as a model when writing her name.

➤ Encourage art: The children can write in finger paint or sand; paste a variety of shapes to make letters and designs; weave paper, fabric, or yarn mats; stick golf tees into Styrofoam or pegboard (see Figure 5.8); and hammer small nails into fiberboard.

➤ Use sewing cards.

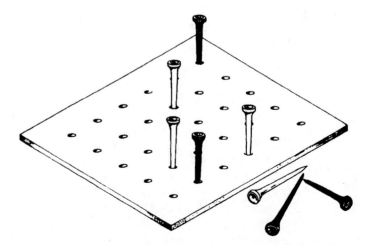

Figure 5.8 Sticking golf tees into styrofoam or pegboard helps increase abilities needed for writing.

Application of Principles

1. Briefly describe the four distinct but interrelated areas of language as they pertain to young children.
2. Walk around the classroom with the children and point out the many ways language is used (such as a calendar, books, notes from parents, daily schedule, lunch menu, singing songs, reading poetry, listening to each other, following directions, etc.). Talk to the children about "language interaction."
3. Using a storybook for visuals, tell the story to a group of children. What do you need to remember about your voice? Your eye contact? Interruptions from the children?
4. Ask the children about their favorite activities. How well can they describe them?
5. Give some criteria for books and poetry for young children. Would you use fairy tales? Why or why not?
6. Write and illustrate an original story for young children. Use it with a small group of children. Discuss the experience with another teacher.
7. Record the conversation of two or more children. Did their conversation contain more responsive or more restrictive language?
8. Briefly describe whole-language learning to a friend or colleague.
9. What precautions could you take to ensure that a group storytime would be interesting to all the children?
10. What would you say to a parent who *insisted* that you teach her 3-year-old to read?
11. Outline some activities that could help prepare "interested and ready children" to learn to write.
12. Engage three to five children in a spontaneous conversation. Talk about their interests.
13. During creative art time, note how children of different ages hold writing implements. Should you encourage a child who is using his left hand to change to his right hand? Why?
14. Display some meaningful words around the room, such as name tags for the children, labels on furniture, and words under pictures. Note which children comment, show interest, or attempt to write their own name or words.
15. If you have any bilingual children in your classroom, talk about the names of people or things in both languages.
16. Use games, toys, and so on to help children discriminate and describe colors, shapes, and sizes.
17. Note the specific interests of several of the children, then plan experiences to enhance their interests through books, activities, discussions, and so on.
18. Recall some of your favorite childhood books. Why did you like them and not others?
19. Do you recall any picture books that stereotype the characters? Were you ever in the minority? How do you feel about "questionable" children's books, such as *Little Black Sambo,* Indian folklore, or sexist or moralistic books? How do you think they make children feel?
20. Carefully observe the types of books children prefer. Are the pictures black and white or colored? Realistic or abstract? Is the plot one that children could reproduce and enjoy?
21. Go to the area where children's books are located at a local bookstore or library. Randomly select four to six books. Sit down and read them. Note whether the characters are correctly depicted—sex, age, ethnicity, culture. Note the publication date to see whether ideas are current with regard to portraying characters, roles, occupations, and other interests of young children
22. What would be your plan of action if you had a child in your classroom who had immature or delayed verbal skills?
23. Your supervisor has volunteered to give you $100 for new books for your classroom. What is your strategy in locating appropriate books and spending the money "wisely"?
24. You and your aide work with 20 preschool children. Four children do not speak English as their first language. What is your plan of action?

References

Adams, M. L. (1990). *Beginning to read.* Cambridge, MA: MIT Press.

Aldis, D. *Everything and anything* (10th impression). (1927). New York: Minton, Balch & Co.

Anbar, A. (1986). Reading acquisition of preschool children without systematic instruction. *Early Childhood Research Quarterly, 1,* 69–83.

Andrews, J. H. (1988). Poetry: Tool of the classroom magician. *Young Children, 43*(3), 17–25.

Applebee, A. S. (1978). *The child's concept of print, ages two to seventeen.* Chicago: University of Chicago Press.

Bee, H. (1981). *The developing child* (3rd ed.). New York: Harper.

Berk, L., & Winsler, A. (1995). *Scaffolding children's learning: Vygotsky and early childhood education.* Washington, DC: NAEYC.

Bhavnargi, N. P. (2001). The global village: Migration and education. *Childhood Education: Annual Theme,* 156–259.

Blaska, J. K., (1996). *Using children's literature to learn about disabilities and illness.* Moorehead, MN: Practical Press.

Blaska, J. K., & Lynch, E. C. (1998). Is everyone included? Using children's literature to facilitate the understanding of disabilities. *Young Children, 53*(2), 36–38.

Bloome, D. (1985). Reading as a social process. *Language Arts, 62*(2), 134–42.

Bobys, A. R. (2000). What does emerging literacy look like? *Young Children, 55*(4), 16–22.

Bodrova, E., & Leong, D. J., (1996). *Tools of the mind: The Vygotskian approach to early childhood education* (pp. 95–107, 145–47). Upper Saddle River, NJ: Merrill/Prentice Hall.

Bond, G. L., & Dykstra R., (1997). The cooperative research program in first-grade reading instruction. *Reading Research Quarterly, 32,* 348–427.

Books in print. (2000). New Providence, NJ: R. R. Bowker.

Bredekamp, S. (Ed.). (1987). *Developmentally appropriate practice in early childhood programs serving children from birth through age 8* (expanded ed.). Washington, DC: NAEYC.

Bredekamp, S., & Copple, C. (Eds.). (1997). *Developmentally appropriate practice in early childhood programs* (rev. ed.). Washington, DC: NAEYC.

Bruner, J. (1983). *Child's talk: Learning to use language.* New York: Norton.

Bruner, J. S. (1968). *Process of cognitive growth: Infancy.* Worcester, MA: Clark University Press.

Burrell, S. (1992). New ideas for "show and tell." *First Teacher, 13*(5), 30.

Canavan, D. D., & Sanborn, L. H., (1992). *Using children's books in reading/language arts programs.* New York: Neal-Schuman.

Carnegie Corporation. (1974). Racism and sexism and children's books. *Carnegie Quarterly, 22*(4), 1–8.

Child Care Information Exchange (1987, March/April). What are we really saying to children?

Chomsky, C. (1972). *Language and mind.* New York: Harcourt Brace Jovanovich.

Clay, M. M. (1991). *Reading: The patterning of complex behaviour.* Portsmouth, NH: Heineman. Originally published in 1979.

Committee on the Prevention of Reading Difficulties in Young Children. (1998). *Preventing reading difficulties in young children.* Washington, DC: National Academy Press.

Conlon, A. (1992). Give Mrs. Jones a hand: Making group storytime more pleasurable and meaningful for young children. *Young Children, 47*(3), 14–18.

Cunningham, A. (1990). Explicit versus implicit instruction in phonemic awareness. *Journal of Experimental Child Psychology, 50,* 429–444.

DeGaetano, Y., Williams, L. R., & Volk, D. (1998). *Kaleidoscope: A multicultural approach for the primary school classroom.* Upper Saddle River, NJ: Merrill/Prentice Hall.

Edwards, C., Gandini, L., & Forman, G. (1994). *Hundred languages of children: The Reggio Emilia approach to early childhood education.* Chicago: Teachers College Press.

Ehri, L. C. 1983. In Wasik, B. A. (2001). Teaching the alphabet to young children. *Young Children,* Jan., Vol. 56, #1, 34–40.

Esplin, A. S. (2002, Summer). *High / Scope Resource,* pp. 4–6.

Ferreiro, E. (1978). What is written in a written sentence? A developmental answer. *Journal of Education, 160*(4), 25–29.

Ferreiro, E. (1986). The interplay between information and assimilation in beginning literacy. In W. H. Teale & E. Sulzby (Eds.), *Emergent literacy: Writing and reading* (pp. 15–49). Norwood, NJ: Ablex.

Ferreiro, E. (1990). Literacy development: Psychogenesis. In Y. Goodman (Ed.), *How children construct literacy* (pp. 12–25). Newark, DE: International Reading Association.

Fields, M. V., & Spangler, K. L. (2000). *Let's begin reading right.* Upper Saddle River, NJ: Merrill/Prentice Hall.

French, L. (1996). I told you all about it, so don't tell me you don't know: Two-year-olds and learning through language. *Young Children, 51*(2), 17–20.

Gable, S. (1999). Promote children's literacy with poetry. *Young Children, 54*(3), 12–15.

Gallas, K., Anteon-Oldenburg, M., Ballenger, C., Beseler, C., Griffin, S., Papperheimer, R., & Swaim, J. (1996). Focus on research: Talking the talk and walking the walk: Researching oral language in the classroom. *Language Arts, 73*(8), 608–617.

Gareau, M., & Kennedy, C. (1991). Structure time and space to promote pursuit of learning in the primary grades. *Young Children, 46*(4), 46–51.

Garrard, K. R. (1987). Helping young children develop mature speech patterns. *Young Children, 42*(3), 16–21.

Geller, L.G. (1983). Children's rhymes and literacy learning: Making connections. *Language Arts, 60,* 184–193.

Gemma, M. (2001). Picture books and preschoolers' perceptions of school. *Young Children, 56*(1), 71–75.

Goodman, K. D. (Ed.). (1998). *In defense of good teaching.* York, ME: Stenhouse.

Goodman, K. S. (1986). *What's whole in whole language?* Portsmouth, NH: Heinemann Educational Books.

Goodman, Y. (Ed.). (1990). *How children construct literacy.* Neward, DE: International Reading Association.

Gottshall, S. M. (1995). Hug-a-book: A program to nurture a young child's love of books and reading. *Young Children, 45*(2), 29–35.

Greenberg, P. (1992). Why not academic preschool? (Part 2) Autocracy or democracy in the classroom. *Young Children, 47*(3), 54–64.

Griffin, E. F. (1982). *Island of childhood: Education in the special world of nursery school.* New York: Teachers College Press.

Hall, N. (1987). *The emergence of literacy.* Portsmouth, NH: Heinemann.

Hargrave, A. C., & Sénéchal, M. (2000). A book reading intervention with preschool children who have limited vocabularies: The benefits of regular reading and dialogic reading. *Early Childhood Research Quarterly, 15*(1), 75–90.

Harste, J., Woodward, V., & Burke, C. (1984). *Language stories and literacy lessons.* Portsmouth, NH: Heinemann.

Heald-Taylor, G. (1989). *The administrator's guide to whole language.* New York: Merrill/Macmillan.

Hearn, B. (1993). Literacy and reading development: A review of theories and approaches. *Early Child Development and Care, 86,* 131–146.

Hendrick, J. (1992). *The whole child* (5th ed.). New York: Merrill/Macmillan.

Hymes, J. (1965). *Grade Teacher,* 88–92.

International Reading Association (IRA) and the National Association for the Education of Young Children (NAEYC). (1998). Learning to read and write: developmentally appropriate practices for young children. *Young Children, 53*(3), 30–45.

Jalongo, M. R. (1985, Nov./Dec.). Children's literature: There's some sense to its humor. *Childhood Education, 62*(2), 109–114.

Jalongo, M. R. (1996, Jan.). Teaching young children to become better listeners. *Young Children, 51*(2), 21–26.

James, J. Y., & Kormanski, L. M., (1999). Positive intergenerational picture books for young children. *Young Children, 54*(3), 32–38.

Jantz, R., Seefeldt, C., Galper, A., & Serlock, K. (1977). Children's attitudes toward the elderly. *Social Education, 41*(6), 518–523.

John-Steiner, V., Panofsky, C. P., & Smith, L. W. (Eds.). (1994). *Sociocultural approaches to language and literacy: An interactions perspective.* Cambridge: Cambridge University Press.

Kagan, S. L. (1994). Early care and education. *Phi Delta Kappan, 76*(3), 184–187.

Kagan, S. L., & Cohen, N. (1997). *Not by chance: Creating an early care and education system for America's children.* New Haven, CT: Bush Center in Child Development and Social Policy, Yale University.

Kagan, S. L., & Garcia, E. (1991). Education of culturally and linguistically diverse preschoolers: Moving the agenda. *Early Childhood Research Quarterly, 6*, 427–443.

Keller, C., Hallahan, D., McShane, E., Cowley, E. P., & Blandford, B. (1990). The coverage of persons with disabilities in American newspapers. *Journal of Special Education, 24*(3), 271–282.

Kirk, E. W. (1998). My favorite day is "story day." *Young Children, 53*(6), 27–30.

Klenk, L. (2001). Playing with literacy in preschool classrooms. *Childhood Education,* Spring, 150–157.

Kohlberg, L. (1966). Cognitive stages of preschool education. *Human Development, 9,* Parts 1 & 2.

Kontos, S. (1986). What preschool children know about reading and how they learn it. *Young Children, 42*(1), 58–66.

Kuball, Y. E. (1995). Goodbye dittos: A journey from skill-based teaching to developmentally appropriate language education in a bilingual kindergarten. *Young Children, 50*(2), 6–14.

Kuptez, B. (1994). Ageism: A prejudice touching both young and old. *Day Care and Early Education, 21*(3), 34–37.

Kutiper, K., & Wilson, P. (1993). Updating poetry preferences: A look at the poetry children really like. *Reading Teacher, 47,* 28–35.

Lukens, R. (1995). A critical handbook of children's literature (5th ed.). New York: HarperCollins.

Lundsteen, S. W. (1979). *Listening: Its impact at all levels on reading and the other language arts.* Urbana, IL: National Council of Teachers of English.

Maclean, M., Bryant, P., & Bradley, L. (1987). Rhymes, nursery rhymes, and reading in early childhood. *Merrill Palmer Quarterly, 33*(3), 255–281.

McDevitt, T. M. (1990). Encouraging young children's listening. *Academic Therapy, 25*(5), 569–577.

McLane, J. B., & McNamee, G. D. (1990). *Early literacy.* Cambridge, MA: Harvard University Press.

McMullen, M. B. (1998). Thinking before doing: A giant toddler step on the road to literacy. *Young Children, 53*(2), 65–69.

Moore, L. M. (1998). Learning language and some initial literacy skills through social interactions. *Young Children, 53*(2), 72–75.

Moustafa, M. (1997). *Beyond traditional phonics.* Portsmouth, NH: Heinemann.

National Academy of Sciences. (2000). *Preventing reading difficulties in young children* (executive summary, pp. 1–13). Online at http://www.nap.edu/openbook/030906418xhtm.

National Association for the Education of Young Children/International Reading Association. (1998). NAEYC/IRA joint position statement: Learning to read and write: Developmentally appropriate practices for young children. *Young Children, 53,* 30–46.

National Association for the Education of Young Children. (1996). NAEYC position statement: Responding to linguistic and cultural diversity—Recommendations for effective early childhood education. *Young Children, 51*(2), 4–12. Online at NAEYC's website: http://www.naeyc.org.

Neuman, S. B., Copple, C., & Bredekamp, S. (1999). *Learning to read and write: Developmentally appropriate practices for young children.* Washington, DC: NAEYC.

Norton, D. (1995). *Through the eyes of a child* (4th ed.). Upper Saddle River, NJ: Merrill/Prentice Hall.

Nowak-Fabrytkowski, K. (1992). Symbolism, learning, and creativity. *Journal of Creative Behavior, 26*(4), 268–272.

Piaget, J. (1926). *The language and thought of the child* (M. Gawain, Trans.). London: Routledge & Kegan Paul. (Original work published 1923).

Piaget, J. (1952). *Play, dreams and imitation in childhood* (C. Gattegno & F. J. Hodgson, Trans.). New York: Norton. (Original work published 1945).

Piaget, J. (1967). *The psychology of intelligence.* London: Routledge & Kegan Paul.

Piaget, J. (1973). *To understand is to invent.* New York: Viking.

Piaget, J. (1983). Piaget's theory. In *Handbook of child psychology,* Vol. 1 (pp. 108–128). Ed. W. Kessen. New York: Wiley.

Piaget, J., & Inhelder, B. (1969). *The psychology of the child.* New York: Basic Books. *Preventing reading difficulties in young children.* (1998). The National Academy of Sciences. Online at http://www.nap.edu/openbook/030906418X/html/1.html, copyright 1998, 2000.

Raines, S. C., & Canady, R. J. (1992). *Story s-t-r-e-t-c-h-e-r-s for the primary grades.* Mt. Rainier, MD: Gryphon House.

Read, K., Gardner, P., & Mahler, B. C. (1987). *Early childhood programs: Human relationships and learning* (8th ed.). New York: Holt, Rinehart & Winston.

Rhoten, L., & Lane, M. (2001). More than the ABCs: The new alphabet books. *Young Children, 56*(1), 41–45. Also a listing of "ABC books for children." For permissions and reprints online: www.naeyc.org/resources/journal.

Routman, R. (1996). *Literacy at the crossroads.* Portsmouth, NH: Heinemann.

Rudman, M. K., & Pearce, A. M. (1988). *For the love of reading: A parent's guide to encouraging young readers from infancy through age 5.* Mount Vernon, NY: Consumer Reports.

Serbin, L. A., & O'Leary, K. D. (1975, Dec.). How nursery schools teach girls to shut up. *Psychology Today,* 113–116.

Shore, R. (1997). *Rethinking the brain: New insights into early development.* New York: Families and Work Institute.

Siemens, L. (1996). "Walking through the time of kids": Going places with poetry. *Language Arts, 73,* 234–240.

Smith, F. (1992). *Learning to read: The never ending debate. Phi Delta Kappa 73*(6), 432–441.

Smith, F. (1985). *Reading without nonsense* (2nd ed.). New York: Teachers College Press.

Soto, L. D. (1995). Children and language. *Scholastic Early Childhood Today, 10*(3), 47.

Spock, B. (1976, June). Are fairy tales good for children? *Redbook,* 136–138.

Stremmel, A. J., Travis, S. S., & Kelly-Harrison, P. (1997). Mutually beneficial activities for young children and older adults in dependent care. *Young Children, 52*(7), 29–31.

Strickland, D. (1990). Emergent literacy: How young children learn to read and write. *Educational Leadership, 47*(6), 18–23.

Stone, J. (1993). Caregiver and teacher language—responsive or restrictive? *Young Children, 48*(4), 12–18.

Tabors, P. O. (1998). What early childhood educators need to know: Developing effective programs for linguistically and culturally diverse children and families. *Young Children, 53,*(6) 20–26.

Taitt, H. (1982). *Thinking-learning-creating: TLC for growing minds.* Charleston, IL: Creative Learning Associates.

Taylor, B. J., & Howell, R. J. (1973). The ability of three-, four-, and five-year-old children to distinguish fantasy from reality. *Journal of Genetic Psychology, 122,* 315–318.

Teale, W. H., & Sulzby, E. (1996). *Emergent literacy: Writing and reading.* Norwood, NJ: Ablex.

Vygotsky, L. (1962). *Thought and language* (E. Hanfmann & G. Vokar, Trans.). Cambridge, MA: MIT Press. (Original work published 1934).

Vygotsky, L. S. (1978). *Mind in society: The development of psychological processes.* Cambridge, MA: Harvard University Press.

Wasik, B. A. (2001a). Phonemic awareness and young children. *Childhood Education,* Spring 128–133.

Wasik, B. A. (2001b). Teaching the alphabet to young children. *Young Children, 56*(1), 34–40.

Weaver, C. (1996). *Teaching grammar in context.* Portsmouth, NH: Heinemann.

"What are we really saying to children?" (1987, March). *Child Care Information Exchange.*

Williams, R., & Davis, J. K. (1994). Lead sprightly into literacy. *Young Children, 49*(4), 37–41.

Wolter, D. L. (1992). Whole group story reading? *Young Children, 49*(1), 72–75.

CHAPTER

6

Creative Arts

Main Principles

1. Individuals are creative in different ways.

2. Raw materials, uninterrupted time, and freedom to choose activities and playmates are valuable to both the child's development and her artistic expression.

3. Over time, educational theorists have advocated the important role of creative expression in the development of humanity.

4. Children need many different ways to express themselves that are healthy and acceptable to society.

5. Adults who are supportive and noncritical and are good listeners encourage a child's future experiences in self-expression and the child's good feelings about himself and his abilities.

6. Safety factors are as important in self-expression opportunities as they are in all other curriculum areas.

7. Children who share multicultural experiences with others establish their own identity and respect the differences in others.

Introduction

Creativity is defined differently by different people. Those who feel they have little creativity look at it as being negative and hard to come by and are spectators rather than participants in things viewed for their beauty, originality, or value. Those who have spontaneous or new ideas look at creativity as a gift, something natural, or just needing expression—whether through visual or performing arts. Then those in the middle, just neutral, feel they are creative sometimes and not others, do what they have to do under the circumstances, or feel their work is to be neither praised nor criticized. Too often the "creativity" is related to compositions of art or music when it should be seen as something much more broad. A creative idea may be a new way to do something (set the table, prepare food, solve problems, sew on a button, file materials, play a game). It may be a private or a shared experience.

One dictionary defines *creativity* as "artistic or intellectual inventiveness," and then defines *artistic* as "done skillfully aesthetically satisfying." This indicates that any and all of us can be creative—and we are creative in individual ways. Children are just beginning to explore art materials, movement to music, skill in manipulating their bodies, and interacting with others. They do it the best way they can—and for now it is through sensory, firsthand experiences. Perhaps adults should start there, too.

Nothing is quite so delightful as seeing a young child wholly absorbed in creative self-expression. She may be creative when she moves to music, engages in dramatic play, exercises large muscles, or prepares food. This chapter is devoted to creative, artistic, and sensory expression. Dramatic play and block building, forms of creative expression, were discussed in Chapter 3. Music and other forms of creativity are covered in later chapters.

Not all children enjoy things that are "messy," but the need for expression is still there. The teacher is responsible for seeing that children have many opportunities for self-expression, that these ways are acceptable in society and meet developmental needs, and that children feel good about them.

In order for a child to be creative, writes Schirrmacher (1988), he needs to choose (1) what he wants to make (content), (2) how he will go about making it (process), and (3) what it will end up looking like (product). Adults who are supportive and noncritical and are good listeners encourage the child's future experiences in this area and the child's feelings about himself and his abilities.

Davis and Gardner (1991) present an insightful illustration of the consequences of not understanding the knowledge embedded in early-childhood curriculum activities. They describe a classroom incident in which a young child has drawn figures representing her family during a classroom exercise. The teacher engages the child in conversation, asking her to tell about her drawing. The teacher then labels each figure in the drawing and writes the title, "Lucy's Family," at the top of the child's paper.

The teacher acted as most early-childhood teachers would. In doing so, Davis and Gardner argue, the teacher is telling the child that words are better symbol systems than are drawings. The teacher has also violated the child's compositional integrity by writing on the drawing. In addition, the teacher is sending a power message to the child: she can write on the child's work without fear of trespassing (Spodek, 1991). A separate page or the back of the picture could be used for comments made by the children while still preserving their masterpieces.

Too frequently one observes artifacts created during *art time* by children who have been taught to carefully follow directions. Each creation looks similar to all others and reflects themes and patterns from prior years (especially at holiday times and seasonal changes).

An example of the integration of art with content learning is an easy-to-envision *doing* example of the type of subject-integrated education going on in many classrooms across the country (Dever & Jared, 1996). It can be used with any topic. The primary goals of the unit are conventional and simple: to help the children enhance their understanding of the world and to meaningfully integrate art activities with other curricular areas.

"Inquiry learning is a generative process that encourages children to view life experiences as a continual process of building new understandings from their experiences" (Watson, Burke, & Harste, 1989). The teacher's role is (1) to provide many and varied experiences through primary resources: direct experiences to observe, interact, or manipulate, such as through dramatic play, art materials, field trips, oral discussions, and so on; (2) to provide many secondary sources, such as books, videos, visitors, storytellers, pictures, props, and so on; and (3) to provide ways for children to share what they have learned.

Whenever possible, teachers should ensure that children have real experiences before encouraging them to reproduce them through art or dramatization. Early on, teachers should make a distinction between arts (individual expression using a variety of materials) and crafts (product-oriented, pattern-directed activities) and their role in the lives of young children. "Crafts and expressive art are two different things," states Schiller (1995, p. 36). There will be more about this later in this chapter.

Art activities can serve as an expressive medium and a means of advancing the children's understanding of topic content, and there is an additional benefit as the children actively manipulate the art materials. They make discoveries about what they can make with the materials—perhaps unique shades or different images from the stroke of the brush. Colors created with paint, crayons, and markers are different and interact differently with different media, such as paste, dry ingredients, fabric, and others.

Teaching and learning must address the whole developing child. Art should be integrated into a curriculum for young children in ways that encourage them to express their ideas and feelings. Such activities provide children with the opportunity to experiment with various art materials as well as to express their ideas aesthetically. Creative expression should not isolate the child from other subjects; rather, it should be purposefully and meaningfully integrated into the curriculum, providing support for developing skills and for advancing knowledge about their world.

As I was sitting at my computer writing this chapter, we had one of the heaviest snowfalls in years. I wondered to myself, "How could I use this spontaneous event to stimulate young children to think about this wonderful occurrence?" I noticed the birds flying to their nests, the animals running to their holes, and the humans scurrying for shelter. I imagined myself with a group of children, as had happened many times over the years, and what this snowfall would mean to them: romping in the snow, heavy clothing, cold feet and hands. Snow means moisture—leading us into the water cycle and water sports, planting cycles, warm weather, and on and on. And what about the animals now and later? They grow heavier coats and need protection and access to food. Oh, where are the children when I need them most?

Theoretical Background of Art for Young Children

Art is not an automatic consequence of growth or development. It is the result of active exploration and inquiry that cannot occur without some adult assistance to draw, paint, and sculpt with interest and determination (Brittain, 1979; Vygotsky, 1978).

Teachers need to provide materials, space, and encouragement and realize that art is vital for all young children—not just a talented few. Children who are encouraged to pursue a medium or topic seriously for an extended period of time are capable of creating surprisingly complex and sophisticated works of art (Katz & Chard, 1989). Teachers and parents sometimes resort to highly directive methods of "teaching" young children to draw, which limit children's choices and encourage replication of an adult-produced model.

Art educators have become more directly involved in the preparation of early-childhood teachers and have shown increasing concern in creative activities for young

A Mental Checklist for Teachers of Young Children

Do I	Always	Seldom	Never
Attend to children who are doing routine art work?			
Attend only to children who show creativity and initiative?			
Make an extra effort to include different media and experiences?			
Use creative art as a time filler?			
Encourage and interact with the children during art time?			
Prefer to be in another activity?			

children. Art for young children is no longer considered an exclusively developmental phenomenon, but also a form of activity that deserves serious consideration as people experience art as part of their history and culture.

Art lessons for young children lead them to want finished products. A young child's progress is measured by the intensity of the child's involvement in art activities—her capacity to spend ever longer periods of time engaged in ever more ambitious projects and pursuits.

The arts can play a tremendous role in learning and may be more basic to the thinking processes than the more traditional school subjects. Every drawing demands a great deal of intellectual involvement: what to do, how to do it, what to use, where to place ideas, how much to include (or exclude), and so on. The procedure is the same for a scribbling child or a high school student at the peak of learning efficiency.

It is not unusual for many teachers to spend hours preparing parts, patterns, and activities for young children to glue together according to a specific pattern. They call this

Time and space to express oneself!

 **Reflection**

"The little girl who went to the park for a drawing lesson and drew a tree with a red trunk and blue leaves is a good example of how too many children are nudged away from art. When her grade-school teacher asked the supervisor what could possibly be done with such a child, and though great artists have painted blue leaves and great writers have described them as such, the supervisor said, "Take her back to the park.""

Source: Kellogg with O'Dell, 1967, p. 87.

art. One should know clearly the differences between art and crafts, as described earlier in this chapter.

In an interesting account of changing adult-directed art projects to child-directed experiences (and thus to an accredited, child-sensitive, developmentally appropriate school), Swanson (1994) reports the following: The children disliked coercion, threats, group "have-to" times, and directed periods. What they did like was being part of the planning, carrying through with their plans, and learning to be responsible for their actions. "By fall the art **projects** were out, and art **experiences** were coming in." The children were asking interesting, open-ended questions; participating in small groups; using materials and toys for extended periods of time; and being more creative. Circle times became lots of fun.

Teachers who are serious about children's art carefully consider their role seriously. They understand that talking with children about their art can foster children's ability to express themselves through the visual arts. "Talking to children about their art enriches their immediate experience and expands their understanding of the nature of visual forms and their own activity as artist" (Thompson, 1995).

Selected Early Childhood Educators' Influence on Creative Art for Young Children.

The selected educators and programs are described briefly here, for space considerations.

Cyril Burt (1883–1971)

British psychologist

Burt was one of the first to specify in detail a series of developmental stages. His aim was to establish norms of human intelligence for testing purposes. Some of his developmental stages are similar to contemporary formulations: scribble (ages 2–5), line (age 4), descriptive symbolism (ages 5–6), descriptive realism (ages 7–8), visual realism (ages 9–11), repression (ages 11–14), artistic revival (early adolescence) (Engel 1995, p. 15). Burt, a highly respected professional, falsified data in the 1970s to support his own beliefs about inherited intelligence (Engel, 1995, p. 51).

John Dewey (1859–1952)

American empirical philosopher and educator

Dewey was concerned with democratizing the arts: bringing them into everyday life and experience. In school, both fine arts and crafts (identified as woodworking and other hand skills) were to be available to all children as fundamental means of expression and communication. In his laboratory school at the University of Chicago, art was valued equally with other subject matter (Engel, 1995).

Artistic activity has been recognized as one of the primary ways that children can learn by doing and document what they learn (Dewey, 1934).

> Lack of an appropriate outlet for expressing strong feelings, no matter what their origin, results in frustration and unhappiness.... Psycho-analytically oriented educators became interested in mental health in schools and saw art as playing a crucial role in its maintenance—a way of providing access to, and allowing expression of expressed feelings" (Engel, 1995, p. 9).

Victor Lowenfeld

Known for his delineation of stages of development of art in children

In 1947 Lowenfeld published an important work on art and young children, *Creative and Mental Growth,* still important today (Lowenfeld, 1947; Lowenfeld & Brittain, 1967). The work emphasizes divergent thinking (original solutions) while denouncing coloring books, adult standards for judging children's art, and competition between children, who move from one stage to another at different rates, except for the abnormal or exceptional child. The stages follow one another, however, and "a description of each is valuable in understanding the general characteristics of children and their art at any particular time" (Lowenfield, 1987, p. 37).

Teachers who were concerned with manipulative skills put emphasis on products rather than on the process. For children, art is a way of learning and not something to be learned (Lowenfeld, 1987, p. 47). Their products often do not reflect the eye-hand coordination that one might expect.

In the 1940s, a number of books dealing with art for children were published—art began to be interesting in itself. Goals and purposes of including art in the curriculum for young children were established:

1. Children need the opportunity to be expressive.
2. They need to pass on some heritage in the area of arts.
3. They have an inborn drive to be creative.
4. Technical skills can be taught if there is a better understanding of children's growth—emotional, intellectual, physical, perceptual, social, aesthetic, creative, and so on (Lowenfeld, 1987, pp. 57, 59–71).

Art encourages divergent thinking (no single correct answer); intelligence tests stress convergent thinking (the *correct* response).

Also in the 1940's, education goals were viewed as therapeutic: a support of children's creative capacities, a release from anxiety and inhibitions, an outlet for aggression, and a means to depict fantasies (Lowenfeld, 1947). There was to be no direct intervention from adults, so children's natural abilities could unfold (Schaffer-Simmern, 1947). Lowenfeld, still a great influence on art education theory and practice (1947), felt that adult authority had negative effects on children's art learning in kindergarten through third grade (Zimmerman & Zimmerman, 2000.) He felt that every child had an innate capacity to make art, and that capacity was inhibited by society. Lowenfeld's values, promoting self-expression, creativity, and uniqueness, often were manifest in open-ended lessons not integrated into other aspects of the school curriculum, in which emphasis was placed on academic subjects and learning through direct teacher intervention. Influences such as adult artwork, copying from resources, observational drawing, and adult-prepared materials were to be removed from all educational settings as sources of inspiration for young children. This child-centered orientation has been challenged by many contemporary art educators (Zimmerman & Zimmerman, 2000, p. 87).

Lowenfeld's belief in children's natural creativity led to his important text, *Creative and Mental Growth,* which first appeared in 1947 and has influenced generations of teachers who prefer to allow a more natural unfolding of artistic development. Those holding the noninterventionist philosophical view of children's education and development in art champion beliefs that range from offering children stimulating experiences about art (Lowenfeld, 1947) to fear that adults have a vexing, negative impact on children and their work and should be essentially banned from the experience (Kellogg, 1970; Colbert, 1997, p. 202).

Further quotes from Lowenfeld:

"Preschool children learn in an active way. . . . Art is what they make themselves. However, nursery school children usually do not remember their own drawings or paintings after a few hours, and it could not be expected that they can develop any aesthetic awareness as adults understand it (1987, p. 120).

There is no place in the art program for those activities that have no meaning for the scribbling child. Occasionally a nursery school or kindergarten teacher may plan certain art activities such as pasting, lacing, tracing, folding, or cutting; these are designed for a particular end product. . . . Such activities are worthless and should never be included in a program planned for scribbling children because they only point out the inability of children to perform on a level foreign to their understanding and ability. . . . Any new material should be looked upon with a great deal of care to make sure that it can further the natural development of children. It must not obstruct their ability to gain control over the material; rather it should promote creative expression (1987, pp. 215–16).

At about the age of 2 every child begins to scribble . . . on paper . . . on fresh concrete. . . . To the adult, scribbling may seem senseless, but to the child it is as natural as eating a cookie; it is a natural thing to do with fingers and toes—and it is meaningful (Kellogg with O'Dell, 1967, p. 13).

Margaret Naumberg (1890–1983)

American art and education

In 1914 Naumberg founded and co-directed the Children's School (later renamed the Walden School) in New York City. She was one of the first educators to change classroom practice in response to the new psychology and encouraged free exploration and expression in all areas of learning. Children chose their own media and subject matter in art. Art lessons were eliminated, and adults were "reluctant to correct, judge, or react to children's work at all for fear of inhibiting spontaneous expression. Art as therapy came first and art as aesthetic experience second, although the two purposes were inseparable in practice" (Engel, 1995, p. 10). (Following their respective personal philosophies, Dewey emphasized art more as an aspect of community experience, while Naumberg used it as an outlet for the repressed feelings of the individual.)

Jean Piaget (1896–1980)

See Chapter 1 for more information.

Comparing Piaget's stages with his own, Lowenfeld states: "Although Piaget's stages are for intellectual development, it is not surprising to find the same stages in art" (1987, p. 45).

Reggio Emilia

Named after town in Italy. Founded by Loris Malaguzzi.

In the mid-1980s American educators became aware of an early-education program, The Reggio Emilia approach in Italy, which was based on art. Attention was brought to this approach through a traveling exhibit, "The Hundred Languages of Children," and an accompanying catalog (Commune of Reggio Emilia, 1987) explained that the pedagogy of the schools as "on the side of a genetic, constructivist, and creative perspective" (p. 18) and sees art as a language for which children have an inborn capacity. "Observing children's art works, both the process and product, allows teachers insight into how children are constructing their world" (Engel, 1995, p. 23).

The philosophy and operation of the Reggio Emilia (city-run) child-care centers, in the northern Italian city of the same name, is acclaimed as one of the best preschool education systems in the world (Edwards, Gandini, & Forman, 1993; *Newsweek,* Dec. 2, 1991, p. 52).

With goals in mind, teachers offer children sufficient experiential motivation so that they will have something to express and psychological safety in which to do so. Lacking in North American early childhood programs, but an essential part of the Reggio Emilia approach, is an art studio, or *atelier.*

Katz (1993) describes one of the primary lessons she learned from her visits to Reggio Emilia: young children can use graphic languages—paint, drawing, collage, construction, and so on—"to record their ideas, observations, memories and so forth . . . to explore understandings, to reconstruct previous ones, and to co-construct revisited understandings of the topics investigated" (p. 20). She concludes that "many of us in the United States seriously underestimate primary school children's graphical capabilities and the quality of intellectual effort and growth it can stimulate" (pp. 20–21).

There is understanding and psychological motivation in the Reggio Emilia approach. The role of teachers is more direct in Italy, as they model processes and products for the children and offer frequent praise and conversations about what is transpiring. The displays of children's art appear to be more like a museum presentation and therefore differ from the informal display used in other schools (Seefeldt, 1995, pp. 42, 43).

Art is viewed as serious work in Reggio Emilia. It represents the thoughts, ideas, and emotions of the children. With goals in mind, teachers offer children sufficient experiential motivation so that they will have something to express and psychological safety in which to do so.

"Reggio educators speak of projects that utilize children's symbolic languages, which include drawing, painting, constructing, clay modeling, and creative dramatics. These processes are imbedded in the total curriculum; they are children's way of making sense of the world through presentation" (Edwards, Gandini, & Forman, 1993, p. 4).

"Reggio Emilia programs in Italy demonstrate how art can be successfully integrated into a holistic early childhood program that includes child-centered, subject-matter-centered, and society-centered orientations. A number of early childhood education programs in the United States are adopting the Reggio philosophy" (Zimmerman & Zimmerman, 2000, p. 90).

In Reggio Emilia, young children (infants, toddlers, and children age 3 to 6) spend their day in the company of a small group of adults. Learning is a communal activity shared jointly by children and adults, and art is an integral part of their activities. The arts are not taught as separate disciplines; rather, they are integrated into the whole school curriculum. Art . . . is considered as one of the many *languages* available to children to express themselves (Edwards, Gandini, & Forman, 1993; Gallas, 1994), and each classroom has a place for children to engage in art activities (New, 1991).

In *general* the **teachers:**

1. have broad curriculum goals, but follow the lead of the children and accommodate to their interests (Schiller, 1995a);
2. construct/reconstruct environments that support learning and are aesthetically pleasing;
3. display children's work accompanied by words and photos of children engaged in activities;
4. observe children at work, and converse with them about their artwork;

5. plan for their future needs and interests;
6. see the children's interests as an opportunity to develop the perceptual and conceptual abilities that are so important for the "development of literacy";
7. create environments that are aesthetically pleasing; and
8. combine various areas of curriculum with art-making activities (music, dance, creative movement, etc.).

(Condensed from Zimmerman and Zimmerman, 2000.)

In *general* the **children:**

1. interact with other children and adults as a vital component of learning;
2. use symbol-making activities in art;
3. are encouraged to communicate their understandings; and
4. (very young ones) benefit from a socially constructive view of art-making activities in which the process of experience is valued.

Implication for practice: Early childhood educators *can* do a number of things to integrate art education into their programs, such as the following:

1. dedicate a space to art making;
2. create an environment that is aesthetically pleasing;
3. include resources not commonly considered art materials (photographs, postcards, colored lights);
4. encourage dramatic play;
5. provide for music, dance, and creative movement;
6. select books and pictures about various art forms; and
7. invite musical guests, and so on.

Lev Vygotsky (1896–1934)

Vygotsky's writings have been influential in emphasizing the social, cultural, and historical influences that surround the young child. He advocated teachers, parents, and peers as partners in learning processes and suggested that children learn more if they are exposed to directive instruction (Zimmerman & Zimmerman, 2000).

Vygotsky (1978) explained that learning occurs when a child interacts with people, including peers, in his or her environment. The child begins to develop a sense of self as part of a larger social and cultural environment and develops a desire to communicate through cultural symbols of significance. Vygotsky's writings have been influential in emphasizing the social, cultural, and historical influences that surround the young child. He advocated teachers, parents, and peers as partners in learning processes and suggested that children learn more if they are exposed to directive instruction (Zimmerman & Zimmerman, 2000, p. 90).

Role of the Teacher
Observation

Through the teacher's constant and casual observations of all children and activities, she will note the awareness, special interests, and developmental progress of each child in all areas of development. She will learn when to intervene, make a suggestion, ask a question, add new materials, or merely observe the process because of her increasing knowledge base of how children learn and develop. She will make mental or written notes about the types of play the children enjoy, when repetition of themes with or without new props would help the children clarify points in the environment, and activities and materials that discourage destructive or negative types of expression.

Notable Quotes

Various Perspectives about Art Education and Young Children.

Preschool teachers may expect each child to participate in the daily crafts activity but virtually ignore children when they are doing artwork on their own.
Bleiker (1999):

Young children can display their own works of art, meet local artists in their classrooms, "use manipulative materials, such as sand and water, that are aesthetically pleasing and designed for interaction" (p. 48).
Clark & Zimmerman (2000):

"When young children's own artistic heritages and those of their local communities are incorporated into art curricula, children learn to value many traditions, understand what art is, why it is made, differences in human experiences, and the variety of ways art is made" (p. 33).

"There are educators and psychologists who advocate that children's drawings are influenced by models available in their culture and that children often imitate the style of drawings they see" (p. 39).
Colbert (1997):

"Making art is something children do naturally, without adult instruction or intervention, yet others believe that children need to be instructed or assisted" (p. 201). Providing appropriate experiences for children promotes growth, gently moving children toward their potential in making art, looking at art, and talking about art (1992, p. 202). Most teachers find that most children need little help or encouragement before they take on a big, empty sheet of paper or a lump of unformed clay. "When teachers teach art badly, children would certainly be better off without their intrusions" (p. 202). "The visual arts are an excellent vehicle for integrating the curriculum. Through the proper use of the visual arts, literature, writing, social studies, mathematics, and science can be brought to life for children and made concrete and meaningful to them (Bredekamp & Copple, 1997). To do so while maintaining the integrity of the visual arts takes masterful teachers who are knowledgeable, flexible, and willing to collaborate" (Colbert, p. 207).
Discipline-Based Art Education (DBAE):

In the 1980s DBAE, a theory funded and disseminated by the Getty Center for Education on the Arts, was presented as a new approach to art education for children in kindergarten through grade 12. It emphasized the character of art and viewed it as a subject worthy of study itself (Clark, Day, & Greer, 1987), a drastic change from the previous pervasive emphasis on art as a means of freedom of expression, creativity, and studio art production in child-centered art curricula. DBAE now includes a wide range of art objects, an expansive view of how art is studied, an interdisciplinary focus, and authentic assessment procedures that have relevance to art education.
Feldman (1980):

Although children's first scribbles and drawings are almost entirely determined by universal forces, very little time passes before influences of culture begin to interact with these natural forces (p. 90).
Gardner (1980):

"Children's natural art abilities unfold if adults provide equipment and encouragement;. . . any adult intervention hampers the unfolding of their innate creative abilities." Gardner believes that young children between the ages of 2 and 5 will engage in art activities; any adult intervention hampers the unfolding of their innate creative abilities. Davis and Gardner (1993) view the "preschool child as glittering in a golden age of creativity" that, with too much adult intervention, can "too soon turn to lackluster" (p. 193). Teachers were not to intervene in children's art activities so children's natural abilities could unfold (Schaffer-Simmern, 1947).

Gardner has made some interesting observations about art education in the United States: it has been considered an unimportant part of a child's scholastic profile; it should be based in child-initiated projects; and "students learn best, and most integrally, from involvement in activities that take place over a period of time, that are anchored in meaningful production, and that build upon natural connections to perceptual, reflective, and scholastic knowledge" (1990, pp. 36, 46).

Lowenfeld (1947):

Child-centered art education has its roots in the 1940s . . . and was viewed as therapeutic, a support of children's creative capacities, a release from anxiety and inhibitions, an outlet for aggression, and a means to depict fantasies. . . .Adult authority had negative effects on children's art learning in kindergarten through third grade; every child had an innate capacity to make art, and that capacity was inhibited by society . . . Influences such as adult artwork, copying from resources, observational drawing, and adult-prepared materials were to be removed from all educational settings as sources of inspiration for young children. . . . This child-centered orientation has been challenged by many contemporary art educators (p. 88). Lowenfeld continues to have a great influence on art education theory and practice. His values, promoting self-expression, creativity, and uniqueness, often were manifest in open-ended lessons.

The National Art Education Association (NAEA):

The NAEA developed a policy statement, *Developmentally Appropriate Practices for the Visual Arts Education of Young Children* (Colbert & Taunton, 1992), which addresses the integration of the visual arts with other areas of the curriculum. This publication addresses "appropriate practice" (what art "is") and "inappropriate practice" (what art "is not"). The importance of interaction between the teacher and the children in regard to visual art is stressed. Teachers (experienced and new) may find it helpful to review this material often with other staff members and/or parents.

The NAEA's standards for the visual arts include goals of fostering children's ability to:

- effectively communicate ideas, attitudes, and feelings through the visual art form;
- innovatively express ideas with visual arts forms;
- interpret the meaning of works of art; and
- use art media, tools, techniques, and processes skillfully (Seefeldt, 1995, p. 49).

Newton (1995):

Beginning at about 3 years of age, children possess language to describe, discuss, and interpret works of art; they learn from each other; listen and respond actively; use body movements in responding to artworks, and invent stories such as pretending to take a walk in a painting (p. 83).

Parsons (1998):

Parsons describes two important issues of child development in art: (1) the socially constructive view, which emphasizes art processes rather than art products; (2) what Parsons terms an "interest in children's understandings, in their general expectations of art, or their interpretations of particular works" (p. 86).

N. Smith (1982):

Art education curricula for children ages 2 to 5 are beginning to be accepted as learning of body skills. Smith suggests that children should make art products that communicate their thoughts and feelings visually and have meaning. Through such instruction, children's thoughts, feelings, fantasies, and imaginations are broadened and enriched. (p. 89).

N. Smith (1982); Wilson & Wilson (1982); Stokrocki (1995):

Teachers of preschool-age children can: (1) encourage children to discuss and interpret their artwork with each other and talk about how they use media to create certain effects; (2) model manipulative skills, such as cutting and pasting techniques, when they are appropriate; (3) use examples of adult works and works of other children for discussion; (4) provide models of children's work as well as adult work, because young children learn naturally from each other; and (5) encourage metaphoric thinking and talking about how art can be used to express feelings and emotions.

Wilson & Wilson (1982):

There are educators and psychologists who advocate that children's drawings are influenced by models available in their culture, including popular culture, and that children often imitate the style of drawings they see around them.

Zimmerman & Zimmerman (2000):

"The nature of children's experiences with art depends on the adults guiding their art development and learning" (p. 87). And further: "A new focus is on in-depth understanding about the world of art and the objects contained within it" (p. 87).

Teachers with good observation skills are those who use the information about individual children as well as the group in providing successful, appropriate, and rewarding learning experiences for all the children.

Attitude

Some teachers have positive feelings toward messy and open-ended activities and time frames; others do not. But in order for children to gain experience, confidence, and joy from artistic expression, they need understanding and supportive teachers. Perhaps teachers need to ask themselves how they personally feel about participating in art activities. Are they enthusiastic or negative? Are they curious? Do they enjoy experimenting with materials? Do they think it is a wasteful or a good use of time? Do they enjoy or just tolerate "messes"? Do they realize the effect their attitude has on the children related to gender, personal characteristics, different cultures, and different types of play and expression, such as block, dramatic, and roles? Do they stimulate children's expressions?

Developing a positive attitude toward themselves, the children, and the activities is a beginning point for teachers. Those who display a positive attitude are personally secure and are confident in their interpersonal relationships.

Proper Materials

The teacher should clearly define the goals and objectives of creative activities, define and maintain necessary limits, be supportive of and available to the children, and know why certain activities are more enjoyed by and more developmentally appropriate for the children in the classroom.

Materials should be appropriate to the developmental level of the children. Large sheets of paper, large brushes, and jumbo crayons are easiest for children to use. They enjoy making large, free-arm movements, and they develop eye-hand coordination and show interest in the various uses of materials.

Reflection

In one center, a substitute teacher went to assist. As creative materials were being prepared for the day, she asked: "Why not use this bucket of earth clay, which is already prepared?" Several teachers agreed with the one who replied, "Our children don't like clay." The substitute persisted, volunteering to supervise, and the teachers agreed. As the children entered the center, they drifted to the clay table. There the substitute teacher was rolling and pounding the clay and remarking that it was cool, soft, and so forth. Many of the children sat down at the clay table and remained for a long period of time. Others stayed a short time, but during the period all of the children had been to the clay table. The conversation was delightful. At the end of the day, the teachers remarked, "We don't understand why the children went to the clay table. They haven't liked it before." The magical thing that drew the children was the attitude of the substitute teacher. The children felt her enjoyment and enthusiasm and wanted to share these feelings with her. At evaluation, the other teachers confessed that none of them enjoyed the messiness or the feel of clay. No wonder the children "didn't like it." Even though they had not expressed their dislike verbally to the children, the teachers had convinced them that something was wrong with the experience.

Covering the table with newspaper or plastic before an activity begins is a great aid at cleanup time. Simply roll up the paper containing the excess paint, clay, paste, or other spilled materials and place the roll in the waste container. A sponge quickly and easily cleans plastic; an old shower curtain or canvas under creative materials is also a time and energy saver.

Materials should help to release feelings, not create frustrations. At one center, several children were enjoying pegs and boards. Guido was not as adept as the others and soon became discouraged. Then he became frustrated and pushed the pegs and boards onto the floor. Painting at the easel or playing in the block area would have better met his needs.

The teacher provides a number of different materials, which the children use as their imaginations dictate. The number of different materials supplied at one time depends on the ages and development of the children involved. Young children adequately handle three or four materials, and older children delight in a larger selection. The children also need access to specific materials related to the activity they are engaged in (scissors, paste, something to paste on, and plenty of time when making a collage).

Placement and Use of Materials

The placement of equipment and materials for self-expression is most important. Messy materials should be placed near a water supply, in a well-lighted area out of the traffic pattern. Interruption by others passing by is discouraging to a child.

Materials placed on low shelves or cupboards are readily accessible and help children to be independent. Seeing materials often encourages their use. Of course, dangerous materials or activities require close teacher supervision.

The children should be allowed to help prepare the materials as much as possible. Children can easily make earth clay, dough clay, paint, and other media, and they should be expected to help clean up. Swishing a sponge around on a tabletop, a plastic cover, or a tray is fun.

Many creative ideas arise as children interact with each other.

Because most children like to take their creations home, a place should be provided where artwork can dry. If space is limited, a portable rack can be used and then folded out of the way. Some artwork can remain at the center overnight to dry; however, children do like to take it home the day they make it, if possible.

Creativity emerges from the process and the results of children's learning experiences. Their novel thoughts, solutions, and products are brought forth from the types of learning experiences that help them express themselves and represent the world around them as they explore, inquire, and engage their minds, hands, and bodies. Patterns, stereotype cutouts, and coloring books do not provide opportunities for young children to achieve these objectives.

 *Reflection*

Perception of Multisensory Activities

- Describe how indoor and outdoor activities fine-tune the senses of young children. Are there some precautions to take (pollution, safety, health)?
- Invite teachers to recall the activities of one day (or period) and note the numerous planned and spontaneous multisensory activities of the children. Why is it important to be aware of multisensory opportunities? Do teachers need to be more aware of combining sensory experiences for young children?
- Brainstorm how creative, expressive, sensory, and multicultural ideas and activities could enhance the learning and understanding of young children. For example, how do children express themselves in other cultures—art, music? Are tools used differently for cultural reasons?

Goals and Objectives

The objective of creative and expressive opportunities for young children is to help them expand horizons, while understanding and manipulating skills that may lie dormant within their maturing bodies. Benefits from such experiences are endless and priceless.

Creative experiences must be well planned and executed. Using an activity to consume a block of time is unacceptable. Goals and objectives should be clearly defined, flexible, and within the abilities of the children. Providing teacher-centered materials for children detracts from the experience and may even discourage further participation.

Besides other reasons, a creative art period can be provided just for fun or exploration! *Activities do not always have to promote the objectives of the day!*

See Figure 6.1 for ways to motivate creativity in young children.

Teachers should refrain from patterning for the children; they can manipulate the materials, encourage conversation, and give support, but their role should be minor. They should listen to enlightening and interesting conversation about the way the children think. They should not be the kind of teacher who thinks all pictures have to be done exactly the same or they won't be displayed!

Necessary limits must be clearly defined and consistently maintained. Each head teacher may designate different limits, so all teachers in a classroom must be aware of the limits of their individual group. One teacher may confine finger painting to paper; another may permit finger painting on table tops or the glass in windows or sliding doors.

Limits should be explained to and understood by the children. If each child is to clean up his own space when he is finished, he should be reminded in advance: "Here's a sponge to wipe up where you have been working." Also let the children know if the product is to be saved at school or if all materials will be placed back in containers for later use.

- A repertoire of experiences to think or feel about. Being able to think about something not present and then finding a way to express it is a major cognitive accomplishment for young children (Raines and Canady, 1990; Golumb, 1992).
- Time, opportunity, and encouragement to explore media. For an experience to be meaningful, children must "act upon it, do something with it" (Dewey, 1944, p. 139).
- Stimulation of all the senses:
     Visual—real objects, replicas, pictures, photographs, etc.
     Auditory—hearing about the item or its uses.
     Tactile—actually handling the item.
     Olfactory—smelling and/or tasting *safe* items.
- Teachers who understand the cognitive theories of art and who select motivational and teaching strategies appropriate for the age/interests/abilities of individual children (a Reggio Emilia and U.S. concept).
- Stunning displays of art, including that done by the children.
- Feeling secure, safe, and comfortable with themselves, teachers, other children, and their surroundings (Brittain, 1979; Moyer, 1990).
- Teachers who avoid "asking children to complete patterned artwork or to copy adult models of art, as far too many children are asked to do in the United States. . . . [It] undermines children's sense of psychological safety and demonstrates disrespect for children—their ideas, abilities, and creativity—more than anything else can" (Seefeldt, 1995, p. 42).

Figure 6.1 Experiences That Motivate Creativity in Young Children

Concern for Process/Product and Flexibility/Rigidity

In our complex society, it is possible to become too product- and time-conscious. Too often parents and teachers are heard outwardly encouraging their children to "make something" to account for at least part of their time.

One child received daily urgings from her mother to make something while at the center. This weighed heavily on the child's mind. On entering school one morning, she walked directly to the easel, grabbed a brush, dipped it in red paint, and made two large lines across the paper. As she left the easel, she was heard to say, "There, I've made a picture for Mother and now I can do what I want!"

One center was having difficulty with some product-minded parents. The parents were pressuring the children—and the center—into making something to take home each day. The teacher recognized that the children were not enjoying the materials as much as previously. She therefore arranged for the children to finger paint directly on the plastic tabletops. On another day, a large piece of butcher paper was placed on the floor, and the children made a group mural. (What conversation and cooperation!) When it came time to go home, the children had no products. Explaining the rationale to the parents helped them understand about pressuring their children. Shortly thereafter, the children again enjoyed the materials without feeling they had to "make something."

The focus of early childhood art *must* be on the process—something that is *theirs*. To encourage creativity in young children, teachers and parents should allow the children to enjoy the freedom that each basic material provides, let the children use their own ideas for selecting materials and themes, provide plenty of time for exploration and manipulation (they'll let us know when they are finished), and show honest appreciation for their efforts (see Figure 6.2). Patterning of any kind should be eliminated from art experiences for young children. It stifles rather than encourages creativity. Children draw things as they see them. Lines made by others are meaningless, and young children have difficulty staying inside lines created by someone else.

Coloring books stifle creativity in young children, cause frustration again because of the need to stay in the lines, discourage drawing because the child cannot draw as well as the model, require muscle skills that most young children do not have, and are often limited in size. Adults should never use coloring books or predrawn figures with young children and call them "art" projects. Coloring books may provide teachers with good sources for visual aids, however.

One mother was called to a conference with a kindergarten teacher because her child "refused to color anything" given to him by the teacher. Everything provided was stereotyped and provided no interest for the child, who had always been encouraged at home to draw his own pictures.

Some adults entertain children by drawing for them. Then when the child draws, he becomes easily frustrated because his pictures do not have the realism of the adult

---

- Relate the activities to the present knowledge and experiences of the children.
- Allow ample time, space, and permission to be fluent.
- Encourage new ways of experiencing the situation.
- Be flexible in your instructions and/or expectations.
- Value their originality.
- Repeat successful experiences by providing new, stimulating props.
- Help the children see how experiences build related experiences.
- Suggest and encourage new relationships.
- Listen to the children's ideas and responses. Give positive feedback.
- Offer positive suggestions if play turns destructive.
- Offer new opportunities based on positive aspects of previous play.

Figure 6.2   Ways to Encourage Children to Participate in a Variety of Wholesome Activities

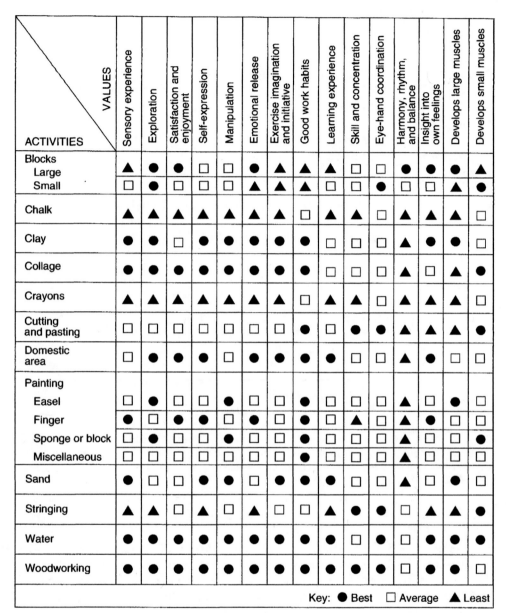

ACTIVITIES \ VALUES	Sensory experience	Exploration	Satisfaction and enjoyment	Self-expression	Manipulation	Emotional release	Exercise imagination and initiative	Good work habits	Learning experience	Skill and concentration	Eye-hand coordination	Harmony, rhythm, and balance	Insight into own feelings	Develops large muscles	Develops small muscles
Blocks Large	▲	●	●	□	□	●	▲	▲	▲	□	□	●	●	●	▲
Small	□	●	□	□	□	▲	▲	▲	□	□	●	□	□	▲	●
Chalk	▲	▲	▲	▲	▲	▲	▲	□	▲	▲	□	▲	▲	▲	□
Clay	●	●	□	●	●	●	●	●	□	□	□	▲	●	●	□
Collage	●	●	●	●	●	●	●	●	□	□	□	▲	□	▲	●
Crayons	▲	▲	▲	▲	▲	▲	▲	□	▲	▲	□	▲	▲	▲	□
Cutting and pasting	□	□	□	□	□	□	□	●	□	●	●	▲	▲	▲	●
Domestic area	□	●	●	●	□	●	●	●	●	□	□	▲	●	□	□
Painting Easel	□	●	□	□	●	□	□	●	□	□	□	▲	□	●	□
Finger	●	□	●	●	□	●	●	□	●	▲	□	▲	●	□	□
Sponge or block	□	●	□	□	●	□	□	●	□	□	□	▲	□	□	●
Miscellaneous	□	□	□	□	□	□	□	●	□	□	□	▲	□	□	□
Sand	●	□	□	●	●	□	●	●	●	□	□	▲	□	●	□
Stringing	▲	▲	□	▲	□	▲	□	□	▲	●	●	□	▲	▲	●
Water	●	●	●	●	●	●	●	●	●	□	●	□	●	●	●
Woodworking	●	●	●	●	●	●	●	●	●	●	●	●	□	●	□

Key: ● Best   □ Average   ▲ Least

Figure 6.3   Values of Specific Activities for Preschoolers

"artist." He refuses to attempt drawing because he compares his work to that of the adult. See Figure 6.3 for a list of the values of activities that are best suited for preschoolers. Table 6.1 shows safety tips when using art materials.

The movement in art education that questions a heavy emphasis on creative expression as the purpose for art-related activities with young children might appear to be in conflict with developmentally appropriate practices (DAP) (Bredekamp, 1987) as defined by the NA-EYC, a Piaget-based model of curriculum, which suggests that children have the opportunity "for aesthetic expression and appreciation through art and music. . . . (and that) a variety of art media are available for creative expression, such as easel and finger paint and clay" (p. 56). Some individuals advocate that this is not a complete experience and that art education should also be introduced without compromising the standards of NAEYC.

NAEA published a briefing paper addressing developmentally appropriate practices in art education for young children, focusing on three major themes in high-quality early art education, namely the need of children (1) to have many opportunities to create art, (2) to have many opportunities to look at and talk about art (which is most often neglected in pre-

Table 6.1 Safety in Art Materials

Media	Avoid	Use
Clay	Silica (in powdered clay) because of easy inhalation and harm to the lungs	Damp clay to avoid dust inhalation
Glazes	Those with lead content	Poster paints
Paints (requiring solvent cleaning)	Those requiring chemicals to clean brushes and other tools	Water-based paints
Paint	Powdered tempera because of additives	Liquid tempera or any nontoxic paint
Dyes	Chemical additives, cold-water or commercial dyes	Natural dyes from vegetables
Papier-mâché	Instant papier-mâché because of lead or asbestos	Newspaper (printed with black ink only) and library paste or liquid starch
Glue	Epoxy, instant or solvent-based glues because of chemical additives	Water-based white glue or library paste
Woodworking	Unwieldy or toy tools; tools that don't work; short nails or those with small heads; small or cluttered areas; unsupervised areas	Sturdy tools built for children; nails with large heads that are long enough to hold; workable tools; good supervision

For additional information, contact Art Hazards Information Center, 5 Beekman St., New York, NY 10038. Chart adapted from Kendrick, Kaufman, and Messenger (1988) and Aronson (1991). A list of arts and crafts materials that cannot be purchased for use in kindergarten through grade six is available from the California Department of Health Services, Health Hazard Assessment Division, 714 P Street, Room 460, Sacramento, CA 95814.

school classrooms), and (3) to become aware of art in their everyday lives (Colbert & Taunton, 1992).

Schiller (1995) found classroom environments that discourage an appreciation of art: cartoon-like images in the classroom, or exclusively photographic images. "These visuals give children little choice in what they view and what they have the opportunity to respond to. Providing books on art topics and opportunities to talk about art and artists supports and extends a rich art environment" (p. 34).

Although most preschool art activities are organized to have children interact and experiment with art materials in a non-teacher directed format, early-childhood classroom teachers can take art to another level, one of discussion and understanding, by fostering art appreciation through nondirective means.

As with other areas of the preschool curriculum, talking about art should spring from the interests of the children and be initiated, for the most part, by them through (1) frequent opportunities to use open-ended materials (paint, clay, markers) in original ways, (2) a variety of well-displayed, good-quality materials used every day with self-determined time frames and children seeing their work attractively displayed, and (3) crafts (product-oriented, pattern-directed activities) offered only occasionally. Many high-quality programs for young children include art appreciation (Epstein, 2001, p. 38) and aesthetic education, as well as an abundance of expressive art experiences (Schiller, 1995, p. 36). The goal of art education is to help children increase their capacity to create meaning and make sense of themselves and the world around them (Smith et al 1993, p. 3). It enhances areas of motor development, notably perception, cognition, fine motor skills, language, and social interaction; hopefully, appreciation for art in its own right is still maintained. By helping children grow from art producers to art appreciators, art can be appreciated for a lifetime.

Values for Children

Sensory experiences are very important to the young child; through these experiences, he learns about himself (herself) and the world. Some specific benefits include:

➤ *independence*—of retrieving and using materials and ideas
➤ *aesthetic appreciation*—wholesome attitude and atmosphere
➤ *satisfaction and enjoyment*—personal creation and ideas
➤ *emotional release*—slippery materials; pounding clay; dramatic play; separation anxiety; building trust
➤ *environmental awareness*—beauty in nature; changes in seasons
➤ *good work habits*—obtaining, using, and replacing items
➤ *muscle development*—small muscles in cutting, arranging; large muscles in block building, movement in activities
➤ *exploration and transformation*—trying new ideas; changing things. "Whether you call it fooling around with play dough or teaching physics, it's both!"
➤ *originality*—freedom and security in trying one's own ideas. Teachers in Reggio Emilia programs display the work of children; they call it "documentation."
➤ *expand personal horizons*—new friends, new opportunities, personal growth
➤ *time and space*—to enjoy and appreciate one's surroundings
➤ *miscellaneous*—originality, companionship, personal adaptation of environment

 Developmental Stages in Art

Scribbling: Ages 2-4: Children make random marks on paper; this is mainly a motor activity and can be considered a reflection of physical and emotional development (Lowenfeld & Brittain, 1967, pp. 196, 204). Materials suggested for this stage: large unwrapped crayons, white chalk on blackboard, fiber-tipped pen; old newspapers, wallpaper samples, wrapping paper; tempera or poster paint; clay; fingerpaint (p. 214).

Preschematic: Ages 4-7: Children make their first representational attempts, typical head-feet presentation; they begin to draw a number of other objects in their environment, randomly placed and varying in size.

"The ability to copy geometric forms is sometimes used as a measure of young children's developmental level. Although the circle can be copied by most children at the age of 3, it is not until 4 that a square can be copied successfully" (p. 205).

Schematic: Ages 7-9: Children develop a definite form; their drawings symbolize parts of the environment; children usually repeat with some variation the schema that they have developed; they arrange the objects they are portraying in a straight line across the bottom of the page; their works of art look quite decorative.

Dawning Realism: Ages 9-12: Children are interested in detail and no longer make the large free drawings made at a younger age; they hide their drawings from adult observation; their drawings symbolize rather than represent objects.

Adapted from Lowenfeld, 1987, pp. 38–39.

- Children can freely express themselves in design, color, and media.
- Competition and conformity are removed.
- Children may or may not select an art activity at a determined time.
- Their interests, choices, and abilities can be pursued.
- Creativity offers opportunity to express oneself constructively.
- Most children enjoy using the media; they may not have these experiences in other settings.
- Most materials and equipment can be set up permanently, or made easily accessible, for child selection.
- Valuable traits can be learned: responsibility (for getting and returning items), cooperation (sharing of items), respect (for others' space, accomplishment), socialization (conversations, questions), choice of activity, and more.
- Children learn to be resourceful and responsible.
- Children determine the amount of time to spend in the area.

Figure 6.4   Advantages of Raw Materials and Ideas over Patterned or Precut Materials

Ronald, 3 years old, was given several different opportunities at school to finger paint. He thoroughly enjoyed each experience. The request came from home to "quit finger painting at school because Ronald finger paints in everything at home—especially his food at mealtimes!" Here was a child who needed more, not fewer, sensory experiences.

Teachers who live in a community where paintings can be borrowed from a local source, such as a library or school, should plan to change the paintings in the classroom often, thereby teaching about famous artwork by pointing out the colors, the lines, and the meanings, but done on a level children understand and appreciate.

"Adults frequently show young children pictures of fruit or farms or families. Why not show them a lovely still life by Cezanne, a fine landscape by Corot, or a beautiful mother and child by Mary Cassatt?" writes Wolf (1990). She continues, "The early years, when children are so fascinated with picture books, are the natural sensitive years for them to become familiar with paintings" (p. 41). And rather than always showing large framed pictures, she encourages postcard-sized reproductions that fit easily in a child's hand and can be used for a variety of activities such as matching, pairing, sorting, and placing in chronological order.

Studies indicate that creativity increases in preschool children until the age of 5, when a sharp decrease begins, attributed to parental influence, need for conformity, patterning, adherence to unrealistic standards, peer pressure, and commercial materials—and the influence of television!

When children feel free to explore, they find many creative uses for "junk" or other items found in the environment—cardboard, candy papers, containers, eggshells, labels, string, tickets, and more. You be the supplier; let the child be the designer and builder! (See Figure 6.4.)

Over time, children's explorations become more organized and intentional. They begin to make events happen and reflect on the relationships among these events. Piaget (1976) refers to this kind of understanding of relationships among actions or events as *logicomathematical knowledge*. To build an understanding of how one event is related to another, a child must have countless opportunities to make events happen, to vary the related actions, and to reflect on the subsequent variations in outcomes.

Four characteristics of creativity have been identified by Torrance (1970), a pioneer in the study of the creative process. They include: (1) *fluency* in ideas and thoughts as children manipulate colors around the paper (body and material interaction); (2) *flexibility* in a purposeful activity, which gives the children freedom to experiment in their own ways with different approaches to changing colors and designs; (3) *originality* as children decide what designs to make and how to make them; and (4) *elaboration* as children add new colors, more details, or other elements to their activity.

Clay often represents cooking experiences the children have seen at home.

Include Everyone!

In all of the activities in this chapter, teachers should be sure to provide paints, paper, and other materials in skin-tone shades of different ethnic groups!

Clay

Clay can be used in many ways—for short or long periods of time, with or without utensils, alone or in the presence of others. It can represent a form or figure, can be changed, and can satisfy one's developmental needs—and through these characteristics, failure is eliminated.

Earth clay must be prepared in advance of its use, and the children delight in helping. Some teachers feel that a center cannot be successfully operated without a large bucket of earth clay readily available for experimentation and release of feelings.

Earth clay is most effective when the children use their hands freely. Cookie cutters, rolls, and other objects detract from the sensory experience with this type of clay.

With dough clay, however, the child may use her fingers, her hands, or cookie cutters and rollers. The medium closely resembles cookie dough, and the use of cutters and/or rollers makes the experiences more realistic because one often uses cutters and rollers with this type of food dough. Cookie dough provides sensory and manipulative experiences but does not stimulate the same kind of creativity as earth clay; therefore, it is not used as a substitute for earth clay.

Clay is an inexpensive medium for exploration, representation, language and social development, and personal development. When it is prepared, stored, and used properly, it will last for a long period of time and children can get and return it easily. Clay experiences can help children release their frustrations through pounding, twisting, rolling, and discussing, yet some teachers limit the frequency of its use, if they allow its use at all, for various personal reasons. It can come in a variety of colors, depending on where the clay was originally acquired. Clay is a safe medium, but some rules may need to be

Reflection

To stimulate the interests of the children in the clay area, one teacher discussed building a bird's nest and then helped the children gather leaves, twigs, string, and other materials. They took these materials to the clay table and there learned a great deal by making nests. (The clay will not be reusable because of the materials added.)

established until the children are more familiar with the experience. In providing an activity using clay, one teacher talked about it (and played with it), mentioning such things as where it comes from; that flowers, vegetables, and other plants grow in the ground; volcanic and earth changes over time; and how clay changes consistency when it is cooked (fired). During subsequent clay experiences, the teacher noted the appearance of universal themes (families, school and city life, transportation, food, natural phenomena, and other topics) as the children manipulated the clay (Neubert, 1991).

Example:

It will be difficult for a child to make a clay animal if she isn't familiar with the animal, the medium, the responses of teachers, or the time frame. Perhaps the experience would be more successful if the child (1) has a better introduction to the animal (sees one; uses books, pictures, or puzzles; talks about firsthand experiences); (2) can select from a variety of media and tools (clay, crayons, markers, and so on); (3) has special interest in making a specific item; (4) has been given prior encouragement for successful endeavors; and (5) knows that time is plentiful.

Caution: Provide opportunities for child growth by expecting results within the child's developmental abilities.

Suggestions Related to Clay

Multicultural Awareness

Display pieces of pottery made in different cultures for children to see and duplicate.
Use natural-colored clay (reds, browns) and let the children paint designs on them.
Display pictures of other cultures making and using clay items (pottery for cooking, eating, and so on).
Explore and share how clay is used in your community. Perhaps displaying and talking about tiles, slates, and other related materials would be of interest.

Special-Needs Children

Make sure that materials are nontoxic.
Provide objects that children can easily manipulate (size, weight, use, and so on).
Provide experiences that are open-ended so a child can feel success at any termination point.
Support the child physically, verbally, and socially without isolating her from other children or materials.

At times, children work quietly at creative endeavors; sometimes activity and conversation intermingle.

Collage

Webster's New Universal Unabridged Dictionary, deluxe second edition, 1979, printed by Dorset and Baber, defines *collage* as (1) "a kind of surrealist art in which bits of flat objects, as newspaper, cloth, pressed flowers, etc., are pasted together in incongruous relationship for their symbolic or suggested effect," and (2) "a picture so made."

Of serious concern is the question of using foodstuffs in creative art projects. Some people feel that food products enhance the experience (some children might not enter the experience if food were not a part of it); some say it broadens the child's acquaintance, reacquaintance, imagination, and exploratory ability with the products. Some feel it is unsanitary for children to "play with food." Others strongly feel that when people in our country (or worldwide) are hungry, foodstuffs should not be "wasted" as play materials (Jones & Nimmo, 1994). When edibles and non-edibles are used interchangeably, one can count on both items being placed in mouths—a rather hazardous situation. Keep in mind that objects small enough to be placed in eyes, noses, ears, or mouths should not be used around young children.

Food uses that might be objectionable include (but are not limited to) macaroni or breakfast cereals for necklaces; pasta and beans of different colors for collage; pudding for finger paint; flour and salt to make play dough; and rice, wheat, flour, or cornmeal in the sensory table. Some recipes call for some of the questionable ingredients. (For a clear statement of the view that food, a precious resource, is only for eating, see Holt, 1989, pp. 156–57.)

Individual teachers need to decide if and how they will use food in teaching. Young children need rich and varied sensory experiences. Raw foodstuffs, among other things, offer such experiences. Commercial products for art activities are also available; however, the purchaser is cautioned against buying any product that contains harmful elements, for the safety of the children. Substitutes include using birdseed, raw grains, and other nonharmful items. See Table 6.2 for suggestions of other materials to use in collages.

Junk can be made into beautiful pictures. Lots of boxes, tubes, and materials of all kinds and sizes should be on hand. Appropriate cutting tools are needed, as are good, strong ways to attach objects (glue, staples, and other materials). Let the children color and embellish the product. Through this kind of creative play, children learn skills, dexterity, scale, and balance. The intellect is stimulated in deciding what items to use, where to place them, and how to attach them. The following are suggestions for cultivating creativity:

 *Reflection*

Gigi, age 4, exercised her ingenuity with materials provided. She used straws for arms and legs, a sponge for a head, heavy twine for hair, different fabrics for a blouse and skirt, and small pieces of foam for shoes. Such imagination!

➤ Place materials between two sheets of waxed paper and then press with a warm iron to seal the design (especially good for crayon shavings and leaves).

➤ Paste materials on cloth or wallpaper instead of paper for a different experience.

➤ Apply colored tissue paper (with liquid starch as the adhesive) on nonwaxed paper plates for an interesting experience involving color.

➤ Using heavy paper and strong glue, let children make a collage with noodles, cornflakes, and similar materials.

➤ Glue small boxes (match, food, or other) together for an interesting design.

➤ Take small pieces of wood and let the children arrange and paste them onto another piece of wood or cardboard.

➤ Cut pictures out of magazines and let the children paste them on a sheet of paper. Encourage the children to do their own cutting when possible. You might have pictures for the children to arrange in groups (foods, colors, things to wear).

➤ Backgrounds can be of a number of surfaces: paper, cloth, cardboard, wood, plastic, wallpaper, or other surfaces.

➤ In preparation for a collage experience, tear, break, cut, or otherwise divide supplies into manipulative sizes.

Table 6.2   Suggested Teaching Aids for Collage Use

Suggested Teaching Aids for Collage Use	
Building materials	bark, Celotex, fiberboard, foam insulation, gravel, linoleum, Popsicle sticks, rocks, sand, sandpaper, sawdust and shavings, screens, tongue depressors, washers, wire, wood
Fabrics	burlap, carpet, chiffon, corduroy, cotton, cotton balls, denim, felt, fur, interfacing, knits, leather, muslin, net, satin, silk, taffeta, velvet, wool, yarn
Paper and paper substitutes	aluminum foil, blotters, boxes (small), cardboard (boxes, corrugated, food boxes, shirt forms), catalogs, cellophane, confetti, construction paper, crepe paper, cups (candy), doilies, egg cartons, gift cards, greeting cards, gummed labels, magazines, newspapers, plates, reinforcements, stamps, straws, tape, tissue, towels, tubes, wallpaper, waxed paper
Plastic	doilies, egg cartons, flowers, foam, food containers, hair rollers, straws, Styrofoam, toothpicks
Sewing	beads, buttons, elastic, lace, ribbon, rickrack, sequins, spools, string, tape, yarn
Miscellaneous	acorns, bottle caps, brads, cans, clothespins, corks, cotton balls, cotton swabs, excelsior, feathers, flowers (dried or fresh), glitter, hairpins, jars (lids and rings), jewelry, keys, leaves, net sacks, packing materials, paper clips, pipe cleaners, shells, shoelaces, sponges, twigs (and sticks), weeds, wrappers (gum, candy)

➤ If people are to be represented, have materials to represent different skin tones.

To help promote cultural awareness, select items familiar to different cultures:

Paper products (origami, rice, crepe paper, and so on)
Fabrics
Objects of different designs
Wood products
Pictures of people, objects, landscapes, and so on
Tools for cutting and pasting (brushes, tools, and so on)

Cutting and Pasting

Cutting is difficult for many young children; however, if they are provided with good scissors, they learn to use and enjoy them. Make sure the blades cut, are free from paste or other materials, and are the appropriate size for small hands and fingers. Every center should have some left-handed scissors, which are available from a number of sources. Manufacturers are also producing plastic scissors with inserted metal blades, handles with four holes for adult assistance, and scissors with a spring action. Try a number of

---

 Developmental Characteristics

Some activities discussed in this chapter require almost the same materials for children of any age (blocks, clay, domestic area, and sand, for example). Children participate with raw materials in a manner consistent with their interests and skills. The intensity and duration of any activity differ with age; younger children most often play alone and immaturely; older ones, cooperatively and in more complex ways.

Planning for some of the other activities (collage, cutting and pasting, drawing, painting, stringing, and woodworking) varies with age level, as shown in the following examples.

Cutting and Pasting

Age 2: Cutting is minimal. Use of scissors needs careful supervision. Lines to be cut must be simple. Children are more interested in squeezing the glue or brushing on the paste. The picture has few objects pasted on.

Age 3: Some children attempt to cut. Again, use of scissors needs careful supervision, and lines to be cut must be simple. Pasting is still fascinating, but most children still have few objects on their pictures. Color, form, and balance are informal.

Age 4: Many children pick up scissors first. Cutting is often crude, but the child attempts it. Lines can be varied; the child may prefer to cut pictures from magazines. Applying paste is a minimal part of the project. Pictures begin to have form and balance.

Age 5: Most children are adept at using scissors and can follow a simple pattern. Activity seems to balance between using the scissors and applying paste to make an aesthetic picture. Children may have preconceived notions of the final product.

Reflection

Here is a helpful hint when using glue: Place a blob of glue on a piece of paper towel glued to the tabletop on the right side of right-handed children and on the left side of left-handed children. The child can use a small brush or his finger to apply glue. When finished, the child can wrap up the paper and the excess glue and deposit it in the wastebasket. A damp sponge or paper towel helps in final cleanup (Clemens, 1991, p. 9).

kinds to see what features best meet the needs of your children: left- or right-handed, sharp or dull tips, metal or plastic blades, serrated or smooth blades.

Most 3-year-olds are unable to use scissors; some 4-year-olds can use them in rather immature ways; most 5-year-olds are able to follow lines and cut. Once Stephen, age 3, learned to cut, that was all he wanted to do. He was proud of the sack of scraps he had cut. Although it was still difficult for him to accurately follow lines, especially the curvy ones, he loved his own scissors and had some magazines that were just his own, but he could not cut up Mom's magazines, fabrics, books, or the evening paper.

The following activities are suggested to encourage cutting and pasting:

➤ Color dry salt with powdered tempera. Brush paste on paper, then sprinkle salt over the paste. A saltshaker makes a good container.
➤ Take a sheet of black construction paper and cut holes in various sizes, shapes, and places. Paste tissue over the holes to make stained-glass windows.
➤ Get fabric samples from a decorator or use remnants. Paste objects on them to make wall hangings.
➤ Cut designs from paper or fabric. Paste on cans or jars for gifts.
➤ Tear or cut strips from magazines. Have children paste them in interesting designs.

Each child seeks the easiest way to cut—often an extended tongue helps.

➤ Fold paper. Cut or tear designs in it.
➤ Make a mural of the community, having children make and cut shapes for their homes, churches, and other important landmarks.
➤ Provide scraps of paper and paper bags. Children can make paper-bag puppets or masks.
➤ Paste objects on paper plates.
➤ Use materials such as those listed for collage.
➤ Paste colored paper or magazine pictures on tubes, rollers, or boxes.
➤ Cut pictures from magazines and have the children make their family (determine how many children they need, what sizes, what color of hair, and so on).
➤ Have the children paste shapes, ribbons, or floral tape into a plastic meat tray. They can also paste textures in the bottom (straw for a cow, fabric for a cat, leaves for a bird) and then paste on a picture of an animal who would live there.
➤ Decorate large (gallon) plastic jugs with paper, fabric, or marking pens.
➤ Paste single-color objects on same-color paper (for snow pictures use white paper, wadded white tissue, felt, Styrofoam, popcorn, doilies, cotton balls, salt, and so on).
➤ Drip glue on dark paper. Sprinkle on salt or glitter.
➤ Draw a large body on a large brown bag and let the child use his imagination to decorate it (gingerbread boy; provide such items as rickrack and fabric scraps).

In order to stimulate multicultural awareness, provide pictures of people, clothing, situations, animals, and objects from different cultures.

Drawing

Young children spend a lot of time drawing. Whether this is the best experience for them is debatable. Art development has stages, and scribbling is an important beginning. Until children develop eye-hand coordination, muscle control, and the thought process, drawings will be scattered, unrecognizable, and primitive. By examining the drawings of selected children between the ages of 2 and 6 years, we can see progress in ability. One must remember that each child is unique and that experience also plays an important part.

Many drawing utensils are small, require pressure, or are messy. Adults give pencils, pens, and paper to children to keep them quiet and occupied. Most pencils are inappropriate for small, undeveloped fingers; if the child does use a pencil, a jumbo one with a soft lead is preferred.

Perhaps because of their attractiveness, availability, and inexpensiveness, most children have access to crayons. These come in regular and jumbo sizes, with the jumbo being easier for young children to hold. Pressure needs to be exerted if a dark color is desired. Often, the expenditure of energy tires the young hand before the child has had ample opportunity for self-expression. Some suppliers stock plastic crayons, which are less messy than wax crayons and are very colorful.

Crayons can be used in a number of different ways:

Crayon twist. Lay the crayon on its side and rotate it.
Shavings. Grate crayons. Place between two sheets of waxed paper and press with a warm iron.
Crayon melt. Heat a frying pan or griddle to warm. Place a piece of aluminum foil in the bottom. Have the child make a picture with crayon on the foil. Then apply a piece of newsprint or construction paper over the drawing and press gently. The paper will absorb the crayon design. Wipe off any remaining crayon from foil, and the next child can make his design.
Crayon texture. Place a flat object, such as a leaf, screen, or Popsicle stick, under newsprint. Color over it with crayon. Using a crayon directly on sandpaper is another sensory experience.

Large sheets of paper encourage large arm movements. Paintbrushes offer a much better experience for young children than do pencils, pens, and crayons. Standing at an easel, children can fully use their bodies.

Chalk provides many of the same experiences as crayons. Because of its dryness, chalk has a tendency to be messy and to rub off. It can be made more permanent if it is dipped into buttermilk or if the paper is rubbed lightly with buttermilk or water before the chalk is applied. Buttermilk brings out the color of the chalk and acts as a fixative. Chalk does not require much pressure but does soil the hands, which some children dislike.

Many adults supply *felt-tip pens* as substitutes for crayons; however, the pens can become messy. They often go into the mouths of children, and they mark anything they touch, such as fabric or bodies. Because such marks may be permanent, pens with ink that washes off hands and out of fabrics would be better for children to use. The pens do have the advantages of requiring less pressure and of being quite brilliant in color.

Children can be given blank sheets of paper or paper formed into a booklet to create their own books. They can make the pictures and dictate the text to an adult. With the child's permission, the book can be used at storytime (see Figure 6.5).

The following materials are suggested to use for drawing:

blackboard and chalk	oilcloth (use back side)
cardboard (lightweight)	poster paper
construction paper	sandpaper
fabrics	screens
manila paper	wallpaper
newspaper (want-ad section)	window shades
newsprint	wood

Painting

Painting can be done in different ways. Therefore, this section is divided into separate areas: easel painting, finger painting, sponge or block painting, and miscellaneous painting.

Easel Painting

A good easel is of sturdy wood or metal construction, has a place for paint jars and a clip for paper, and is easily cleaned. It should be the correct height for the child and portable, so that it can be used outdoors as well as indoors. Indoors, the easel should be out of the traffic pattern, under good lighting, and close to a sink, washroom, and sponges. Side-by-side use encourages children to cooperate and verbalize.

Paint   The children can help prepare the paint. Two to four colors are sufficient. Primary colors are most appealing and educational. Children learn to mix them to create secondary colors. White and black should be offered occasionally.

Dry powder paint and a small amount of water are shaken in a screw-top jar. Red and orange paint mix best in warm water. A small amount of wheat paste or extender is added to thicken the paint. A small amount of liquid detergent in the paint facilitates cleanup of hands, brushes, and clothing, and a pinch of salt keeps the paint from going sour in a warm room. The paint should be stirred well before using.

Paint keeps indefinitely if tightly covered and stored in a cool place. Improper storage greatly increases costs.

Jars   The following types of containers can be used:

➤ half-pint jars with lids for storage
➤ baby-food jars with lids for storage
➤ quart milk cartons washed out and cut down

➤ frozen-juice cans (6- or 12-ounce size)
➤ small food cans, such as those used for tuna and tomato paste
➤ muffin tins

Clothing   A cover-up of some kind should always be used. A smock, a large T-shirt, a fabric or plastic apron, or an old shirt worn backward will do. Use of a cover-up is one of the limits for participating in this activity, not because children are messy or infantile, but because it is good policy to protect their clothes.

Figure 6.5   Drawings of Similar Objects Done by Children Ages 3, 5, and 6 Years.

Techniques   The following recommendations are helpful:

➤ Using one brush for each color keeps colors true but does not provide much opportunity for the child to explore. Occasionally time should be allowed for experimentation.
➤ Before applying the brush to paper, the end should be wiped on the top of the jar.
➤ If easels are unavailable, paper can be placed on a large table or on the floor out of the traffic pattern. Paint is put in muffin tins and flat containers.
➤ A place nearby should be provided for hanging pictures to dry.

Cleanup   Children should be encouraged to cover unused paint and wash out brushes and empty jars. They should hang their pictures to dry. If space is limited, a large, portable, wooden clothes-drying frame can be used, or newspapers can be placed on the floor out of the traffic pattern. Spills on trays, easels, and the floor should be wiped up. A tarp, a plastic sheet, or newspapers placed on the floor before painting aids in cleanup.

The following are suggested materials for easel painting:

Brushes: bristles 1/2 to 1 inch wide
Paper: butcher, cardboard, cartons, construction, corrugated, finger-paint, magazines, newspaper, newsprint, sacks, towels, wallpaper
Fabrics: burlap, cotton, leather, nylon, oilcloth, plastic, vinyl
Other surfaces or materials: clay, metal, rocks, seashells, wood (boxes, branches, scraps)

When a child is making or painting a picture, one great disservice we can do is asking questions such as, "What is it?" or commenting on the quality of the work. Young children will be more encouraged to paint often if they feel they are free to create what is in their hand and head; if they are not interrupted by questions about the content, use of materials, or quality; and if they enjoy the use of a variety of materials.

The wise teacher or parent will carefully observe the child's progress and provide interesting and challenging opportunities as the child indicates readiness. Perhaps the child is ready to move beyond easels and tempera, to a different applicator (brush, eyedropper, sponge, spray bottle), a new surface (canvas, wallpaper, fabric), additional items (leaves, coins, keys, new materials, watercolors, finger paints, colored shaving cream, and so on), or even combining curriculum areas—science and art, for example (tinting water with food coloring, making secondary colors, changing consistency) (Demerest, 1996, p. 83). Stepping in when children are in exploratory mode, by telling them "how" to do this or that, will often sour their interest. They need to play, experiment, feel, and experience.

Finger Painting

Finger painting is a good emotional release. Children can express many moods, such as joy, concern, interest, curiosity, and sorrow. They can show fear, for example, and then quickly wipe it away.

Finger painting provides an excellent sensory experience. Adding different substances to the paint—sand, glitter, rice, or paper—can change the experience. To color the paint, powder paint is added to dry ingredients or food coloring to wet ingredients. (*Note:* Food coloring stains some surfaces. It can usually be removed from plastic surfaces by putting full-strength liquid detergent on the spot, leaving it a few minutes, then wiping it off with a damp sponge or cloth.)

Materials   A number of surfaces can be used, including paper (butcher, shelf, hard-surfaced wrapping), oilcloth, tabletops, wood, wallpaper, cardboard, glass, plastic, or vinyl. Sponges are provided to dampen the paper or tabletop and for cleanup, and racks

 **Reflection**

Betty carefully guarded her finger painting as she tenderly carried it to the car. A few moments later an angry young uncle stormed into the classroom with the painting and shouted, "If you think you're going to put that junk in my car and mess up the upholstery, you're sadly mistaken!" Betty ran after him with tears in her eyes but made no comment; she was heartbroken. One wonders how long it was before she tried finger painting again.

David sat quietly waiting for his father. As his father appeared, David proudly displayed his picture. The father studied the picture appreciatively, nodded his head, and smiled. After a short pause, the child looked at his father and asked, "Well, what is it, Dad?" as if the father saw much more in the painting than the child did. The father pointed out several appealing parts of the picture. Think how much more David was encouraged to pursue creative activities than was Betty.

are needed for drying the paintings. The children should wear cover-ups. (See the discussion about using edible products earlier in this chapter.)

Procedure   The following suggestions will ensure a pleasant finger-painting session:
➤ Define limits for children and teachers.
➤ Dampen the table or paper with a sponge so the paper is smooth and adheres to the surface.
➤ Put a heaping tablespoon of finger paint on the paper. (Colorless paint may be used; the teacher can sprinkle powdered tempera on paper. If children sprinkle tempera, cans become messy and hard to hold.)
➤ Play several types of music during the activity.
➤ Mention that the children can also make designs with their fists, knuckles, palms, and fingernails.
➤ Encourage children to clean up. Have sponges and water ready.

Finger painting can also be done directly on tabletops. When this is done, a design can be lifted onto paper.

Sponge or Block Painting

Sponge or block painting is done by dipping a sponge or other object into thick paint and then making a print on paper. The procedure is repeated in different positions and colors to make designs.

Sponges are cut into small pieces. A spring clothespin makes an excellent handle. Other objects include cork, pieces of wood, spools, string, potato mashers, sink stoppers, and plastic forks.

Paints should be quite thick. A small amount of wheat paste is used as a thickener. The paint is placed in staggered cups of a muffin tin or small aluminum pie pans.

The best paper for printing is butcher paper or cardboard. Absorbent paper can also be used.

Miscellaneous Painting

Brush painting. Different kinds of brushes can be used for paintings. Some unusual ones include tooth, bottle, hair, food, and straws from a broom.

Crayon painting. The child makes a design on paper with crayons and then "washes" paint over it. The wax resists the paint.

Ink-blot painting. Paper is folded in half and reopened. A few drops of paint are placed on one side of the paper. The paper is then refolded and pressed firmly. This creates a symmetrical design. Newsprint is best for this experience.

Mural painting. Children are provided with a long sheet of butcher paper, paint, brushes, and encouragement. They will do the rest.

Painting on different materials. A number of materials give experience in texture: cloth, paper towels, smooth paper, sponge, glass, plastic, leather, linoleum, egg cartons, aluminum foil, cone-shaped spools, corrugated paper, mailing tubes, paper bags, pleated muffin cups, waxed paper, tissue paper, metal, stone, rocks, and wallpaper.

Painting with water. Children can paint with water on boards, sidewalks, and other large surfaces that water will not damage. They should be given small pans of water and large brushes.

Snow painting. The child paints over a picture (greeting cards are good) with a mixture of 1 part Epsom salts and 1 part boiling water that has been cooled before painting. Evaporation leaves crystals.

Spool painting. The edges of a spool are nicked for design. A wire is inserted through the spool and twisted to make a handle. The spool is then dipped into thick paint and rolled on the paper.

String painting. A long piece of string is dipped into paint and rearranged on one half of a piece of paper. The other half is folded over the string and pressed. The string is pulled out, and the design appears on both halves of the sheet. Different strings and colors of paint can be used for colorful designs.

Tempera wash painting. Glue or paraffin wax is dripped on paper and allowed to dry overnight. A wash with tempera paint is done over the design.

Towel painting. A design is painted on a plastic tabletop or similar hard surface, and a paper towel is pressed on the painted surface. The towel is then removed and allowed to dry. This can also be done over a finger painting. A paper towel can also be painted directly with brush and easel paint.

Vinyl painting. Vinyl is applied to a wall or rolled out on the floor. Children paint on it and then wipe it off.

In order to promote multicultural awareness, ask children how colors are obtained for different uses (fabric, household goods, beauty, aesthetics, and other things) in different cultures and how patterns are made and if they have any special significance.

Puzzles

Puzzles are not considered as creative or artistic; however, they are frequently used during "table activities" but at different tables. Puzzles are seen as enhancing cognitive, perceptual, and motor development. Color, size, shape, and texture are experienced as the child learns the primary mathematical concepts (the sum of the whole is composed of many pieces). Puzzles require attention and concentration.

The teacher's role in puzzle making is to reinforce cognitive, language, problem-solving, and socialization skills in young children, who are learning to observe, analyze, share, and devise problem-solving strategies.

Characteristics of good puzzle-making situations include:

➤ appropriateness to each child's developmental abilities and needs
➤ attractive, interesting, or familiar designs
➤ puzzles designed and constructed at a high level of quality
➤ easy access and return
➤ time to ponder and place pieces

Puzzles may not be as creative as other materials, but their completion is just as satisfying.

 Reflection

The values of puzzles for young children include active participation, problem solving, learning, satisfaction in putting things together where they belong, and contentment as the child actively observes and detects likenesses and differences; physical manipulation; trial-and-error strategies; self-correction; making something "whole"; self-gratification; individual or cooperative participation; development of interpersonal skills and friendships (socialization and speech, for example); autonomy, competency, and success; concentration; color and shape matching; and other individual specific values (Maldonado, 1996).

Summary

Historically, one of the most commonly found materials in the early childhood classroom has been the table puzzle. Early childhood practitioners know that puzzles are an important tool in helping children engage in the problem-solving process. The use of table puzzles in early childhood programs has gone unchallenged and unchanged over the century due to continuing positive experiences of children and their teachers. This pleasurable activity is one of the best ways to work toward some of our educational goals (Maldonado, 1996, p. 10).

Sand

Most young children are delighted to play in sand. They run their hands through it, smooth out roads, construct tunnels and ditches, and make cakes. They socialize in sand: discussing, sharing ideas and materials, participating in collective monologue, and learning to cooperate.

Whether sand is used in a large area on the playground or in a sandbox matters little as long as space is sufficient for exploring. Props such as trucks, shovels, buckets,

Children enjoy sand, companionship, and the outdoors.

sifters, measuring spoons and cups, and containers stimulate the imagination of young children. Seashells make an interesting and lifelike addition.

Definite limits are set up so the children know how the *sand* is to be used. These are expressed as follows: "Keep the sand in the sand area," "Shovels, hoes, and rakes stay close to the ground," "Sand is for building."

During the winter, a sandbox can be used inside the school; however, some floors are easily scratched and require extra maintenance. For these reasons, some schools prohibit sand use in the classroom. Canvas, plastic, or newspapers can be spread to protect the floors.

Water changes the consistency of sand and makes it easier to manipulate. In summer, a hose stimulates creativity for children. Sand is dampened for pretend cooking and molding. A board nearby is convenient for dumping cakes and products or for children to sit on if the whole area is damp.

Sand toys are best stored near the sand area, separating them from other toys. Trucks, cars, measuring cups, sifters, gelatin molds, and so on are placed on low shelves; buckets and shovels are hung on low hooks or nails. A messy storage area discourages children from using the equipment and may cause accidents.

Stringing/Stitchery

Stringing and/or stitching encourages the use of small muscles and eye-hand coordination. Some children lack the control and concentration necessary to make the experience pleasurable; some are hesitant to use a needle because of previous warnings or experiences with sharp objects. It can be a useful and satisfying activity.

Helpful Hints

➤ Allow plenty of time for children to experiment.
➤ Make sure needles are large enough for the children to grasp, have blunt ends, and have an object tied on the end to keep objects from sliding off. Use a double thread so the needle will not become unthreaded. Yarn may be better to use.

Developmental Characteristics

Age 2: The child is not too interested in the activity. She may attempt to poke the string through a hole while the object is lying on the table, but does not try to steady the object or string (the other hand may not even be involved in activity). If an adult offers help, the child may turn away from the activity entirely, or after accepting help, may pull the object off and turn away.

Age 3: The child may observe activity with caution or attempt to string one or two objects. Large holes and objects are preferred. If the string becomes limp, the child becomes discouraged. He may accept help from an adult and watch as he is shown how to hold the tip of the string close to the hole and how to hold the object, but usually loses interest quickly.

Age 4: The child usually knows the relationship between holding the object and string and can string wooden beads easily. She now prefers a little challenge, such as a smaller hole or object, and may stay with the activity long enough to make a necklace or bracelet.

Age 5: The child enjoys stringing things and may ask for the activity or stay longer when it is provided. He introduces originality into the pattern and use of the finished string.

➤ If needles are not used, make ends of string or yarn firm by covering with transparent or masking tape, or by dipping in paste or wax and allowing to dry. A shoelace makes an excellent string because of the hard tip.

➤ Color dry macaroni with water and food coloring. Wood alcohol colors well and dries rapidly but may cause gastrointestinal upset if macaroni is ingested. When using food coloring, place small amounts of water and coloring in a small bowl and let the macaroni stand in the solution until the desired shade. Remove with a fork and place on paper towels until the excess moisture is absorbed. Spread individual pieces of macaroni on sheets of waxed paper and let dry overnight. If not separated, the macaroni will dry in clusters. (See discussion earlier in this chapter about using edible products as creative materials.)

Suggested Materials

Threading small objects can be a rather tedious task for inexperienced fingers; teachers may want to use larger objects as an introduction to stringing, such as the following:

Needles: sturdy (plastic or metal), blunt end, large eye
Paper: aluminum foil, construction, tissue, holiday, and others
Beads: clay; large wooden; plastic; and others
Spools: thread wire products, string, bubble wrap, and others
Plastic: spools, straws (1/2" pieces), and other object
Miscellaneous: foam packing materials, shredded packing, bubble wrap, dividers, plastic containers, fabric, and other appropriate materials

Woodworking

Very young children enjoy pounding and banging: preschool children obtain satisfaction from using tools and wood. Their first experiences are exploratory. They like to build simple structures and should be permitted to use their imaginations. The names they select for their objects should be accepted without comments indicating they look like something else, need some additions or changes, or are poorly done. To them, the objects are real. Patterning, as in other areas, has no place in woodworking.

Proper use of woodworking tools is much more difficult for young hands than scissors, paste, or string. The children need the coordination of eyes and hands and strength in fingers, hands, and arms. Saws, hammers, and other tools can cause immediate and serious injury to the yielder or receiver of the tool. The younger the carpenter, the simpler the experience. Young children need help to get the feel of a hammer or saw or the motion of using sandpaper attached to a block. With age, experience, and supervision, children can begin to take more responsibility for the use of tools. They'll want to make more complex projects and may even want to paint them.

Young children need experience and training in using tools. One can begin by telling stories while identifying the tools and their uses. One can show articles in various stages of completion. One can use pictures, storybooks, a guest, a field trip, and other methods convenient to the teacher and classroom. Advanced students might want to "draw" their project before they begin to "construct" it. From the use of tools, children can gain self-confidence, social skills, creativity, and physical abilities that might not be encouraged elsewhere.

Many children can learn to handle woodworking tools if they have proper instruction and encouragement. Some may be reluctant to enter the woodworking experience because it is too noisy, too dangerous, just for boys, or too scary, or for other personal reasons. But children who have been properly and carefully introduced to the equipment find it a very rewarding experience (See Figure 6.6.).

Teachers must feel comfortable in providing tools and wood for young children. There are hazards involved, but proper teaching and adequate supervision eventually pay off. Start off with one or two children and enlarge the group as others show interest and safety skills are exhibited. "The children need to experience and learn, at an age-appropriate level, the purpose and tools of planning in order to build what they want as they become more competent" (Sosna, 2000). Sosna continues:

> We teach young children science, music, and math without being scientists, musicians, or mathematicians ourselves. We need not be furniture makers or house builders to teach young children woodworking. A little knowledge, patience, passion for teaching, and good-quality tools are all we need. Let's work safely and have fun (p. 39).

Safety

An excellent experience for both girls and boys, woodworking requires close supervision. Precise limits must be set and maintained for obvious reasons—and the children will pay more attention to the limits if they help set them. Consider the following possibilities:

- ➤ Talk about and demonstrate the proper use and storage of the tools; for example, saws have a back-and-forth motion, hammers are used for pounding, sandpaper is a rubbing motion and helps smooth the wood, and so on.
- ➤ Besides careful supervision, the teacher has other roles (how much help to give, which children are more apt to need physical or verbal support, what if the teacher becomes distracted or needs additional help, and so on).
- ➤ What tools are appropriate for young hands?
- ➤ Are the tools sturdy and appropriate (weight, size, and so on)? Improper or poor tools (adult-sized tools are too heavy, toy tools are ineffective) are the cause of many accidents.
- ➤ How many children can participate at a time?
- ➤ How will a child know when it is her turn?
- ➤ What are the children to do with their finished products? Will they be painted, used for a later activity, or taken home?

Reluctance to use woodworking: too noisy, too dangerous, just for the boys, too expensive . . . any more?

Basic equipment: hammers; hand saws: crosscut, coping, keyhole, or compass; pliers; metal clamps; hand drills; brace and bit; rulers/ tape measures; pencils; scissors; paper; sandpaper; nails; screwdrivers: standard and Phillips; screws, vise grips; planes, levels; glue; safety goggles; files; crowbars . . . anything else?

Begin with a small group of children. Show and name each tool and tell of its use and care. Let them explore while an adult is there to guide them. Show pictures of construction or projects in progress. Take a field trip if possible—construction, lumberyard; bring in a guest; books for children and adults.

Buying pine at the store is well worth not having to sort through and identify donated wood. Teachers should cut large pieces of wood into manageable-size pieces for children.

It is important not to require the children to imitate models provided by others. Woodworking has not only a creative side but also a more structured side: following a design, pattern, instructions, or model. This is a very important aspect of woodworking, especially if teachers are going to have rules in the woodworking area and want to show why they are so important.

The children need to experience and learn, at an age-appropriate level, the purpose and the tools of planning in order to build what they want as they become more competent.

Help children work safely and have fun.

Summary:

Computers are important tools for learning, but only as a complement to such activities as woodworking, clay work, blocks, painting, and music, not as a substitute.

To establish and supervise a woodworking area requires a relatively small investment in time and money. The rewards for both children and teachers are many. Tools of high quality are necessary.

Woodworking can be challenging to a group of young children. Some of the benefits they gain are in self-esteem, social skills, creativity, and physical abilities. **IS WOODWORKING WORTH IT?** I say a wholehearted, "You bet!"

Books about Woodworking

Some adult/children books and articles regarding woodworking suggested by Huber (1999) include:

Adams, P. K., & Taylor, M. K. (1990). A developmental approach to woodworking. *Dimensions, 18*(3), 16–19.

Gibbons, G. (1982). *Tool Book.* New York: Holiday House.

Leithead, M. (1996). Happy hammering . . . A hammering activity with build-in success. *Young Children, 51*(3), 12.

Morris, A. (1992). *Tools.* New York: Lothrop, Lee & Shepard.

Robbins, K. (1983). *Tools.* New York: Four Winds.

Rockwell, A., & Rockwell, H. (1971). *The Toolbox.* New York: Macmillan.

Skeen, P., Garner, A. P., & Cartright, S. (1983). *Woodworking with young children.* Washington, DC: NAEYC.

Sosna, D. (2000). More about woodworking with young children. *Young Children, 55*(2), 38–39.

Figure 6.6   Helpful Suggestions in Starting a Woodworking Project.

➤ How can uninterested children be involved?

➤ Are there special considerations for your center?

Tree stumps (such as those normally cast off when cutting firewood), a hammer, and some nails (1 1/4-inch roofing nails have large heads that are not only easy to grasp, but also offer an easy target for a hammer) make a fun experience for children—provided they have good equipment and close supervision! After the stump is

Reflection

The values of a woodworking (hammering) experience include:

Social: Turn taking, predicting, discussing designs

Motor: Eye-hand coordination, strength

Intellectual: How hard to hit the nail; size of hammer to use; noise made when hitting the nail or wood; making designs; skills and procedures needed; math: measurements, number of nails for an area, number of strokes to bury a nail; using new tools; and so on

Emotional: "Venting" experience, sharing, cooperation

completely covered in nails, a slice can be cut off the stump with a chain-saw and the stump will be ready for another hammering experience. Expect the hammering to be random; however, some children may try to make recognizable designs as their skills develop (Leithead, 1996).

Woodworking is not used each day. Despite its many values and interests, the activity also has drawbacks—a limited number of children can participate at a time; constant, careful supervision is necessary; some children take a long time to finish a project—if they are hurried they become frustrated and careless, and if they take an excessively long time they deprive other children of the opportunity or miss out on other activities; tools and materials are expensive; and children can be easily injured.

Inexpensive substitutes for wood are Masonite, sheet rock, Celotex, acoustical tile, or a log of soft wood. (Avoid all materials containing asbestos!) The children can hammer small nails into them. Pounding boards and pressing golf tees into plastic foam are not substitutes for woodworking.

Suggested Woodworking Equipment

Workbench. A workbench can be purchased or made by cutting the legs off a wooden table. The correct height is a little shorter than half the child's height. Sawhorses with a sturdy plank may also be used.

Hammers. A claw hammer, the most practical for general use, should be well balanced, have a broad head, and weigh 7 to 13 ounces. It should be made with the same careful workmanship and durable materials as regular carpenter tools. A toy hammer is not acceptable.

Saws. Both ripsaws and crosscut saws should be provided, and the teacher should know the use of each. An 8- to 10-point crosscut saw, 12 to 20 inches in length, is desirable. A saw is held gently and used with long, even downward strokes. A groove that makes sawing easier is initiated by drawing the saw toward one on the first stroke.

Nails. A variety of nails creates interest. Roofing nails are useful because of the large heads; however, they may split the wood. Fourpenny, sixpenny, and eightpenny nails, 1 1/4 to 2 1/2 inches in length, are good.

Wood. A local lumberyard or carpenter will usually provide pieces of scrap wood. Soft woods, such as yellow or white pine or poplar, are easier for children to use. Wood of various sizes and shapes stimulates imagination. Wheels or dowels may be used as smokestacks, handles, and so on.

Plane. Many types and sizes of planes are available. The block plane is best for young children. They should be taught always to plane in an uphill direction and with the grain.

Vise. A vise mounted on the workbench holds the wood securely and allows the child to use both hands in sawing or hammering. Several vises may be mounted on the workbench.

Brace and bit. Children may need help in using a brace and bit. A 6-inch sweep is desirable for young children. Several different bits may be purchased. Recommended sizes are nos. 3, 4, 8, 12, and 16.

Sandpaper. Sandpaper can be used in a variety of sizes: fine 2/0, medium 1/0, and coarse 2 and 3. Sandpaper mounted on a wood block is easier for children to use.

Other tools and materials. Brushes, cans, carpenter's pencil, clamps (4- or 6- inch), fabrics, glue, leather, paint, paper, pliers, rasp, rubber, ruler, safety visor, screwdriver (4- to 6-inch handle, 1/4-inch blade), spools, square, string, tongue depressors, wire, yarn.

Sensory Experiences (Miscellaneous)

Feel or Texture

➤ In a table used for water or sand, use nonharmful substances of various textures.

➤ Place items of various textures on a table and let children feel them. Try wool, silk, cotton, corduroy, velvet, oilcloth, felt, screening, paper, sawdust, shavings, and fur.

➤ Dip colored yarn into a thick wheat-paste mixture. Shape it on waxed paper and let it dry to make interesting designs.

➤ Place various objects in a box or paper sack. Let the children feel them and try to identify them before seeing them.

➤ Ask the children to walk around the room and touch objects that are similar (for example, those made of wood or metal, those that are smooth or cold).

➤ Put cornstarch in a bowl and add enough water so that the cornstarch is semiliquid or runny. The mixture, sometimes called *ooblick,* feels both moist and dry. It runs through the fingers but becomes hard when the hand is clenched.

➤ Have a small picture and a replica of some object, such as a dog. Put a number of replicas in a "feel box." Have the child look at the pictures and try to locate replicas by feeling in the box.

➤ Show replicas or pictures of objects and ask children to describe how they would feel. Then provide real objects, if possible, and feel them.

➤ Make a mixture using equal parts of liquid glue and cornstarch (try 1 cup of each). The substance has an unusual feel and can be molded and rolled. It is called *glarch* or *glurch* (glue and starch).

➤ Let children help prepare creative media, using their hands to feel them in different stages of preparation (for example, dough clay as dry ingredients, when liquid is added, final use). It could feel warm, scratchy, smooth, cool, lumpy, and so on. Add the use of a garlic press, plastic knife, and so on and listen to the comments ("It's stringy," "Mine is globby," and so on).

➤ The skin is a sense receptor. Touch something with fingers, the cheek, elbows, or feet, and explore whether objects feel the same when touched by different body parts. Talk about the meaning of *receptor.*

➤ Make two identical feel boxes. Have a child place one hand in one box and the other hand in the duplicate box. Encourage him to find the same object with both hands simultaneously.

Smell

➤ In small containers, place small amounts of common liquids that have odors (for example, perfume, extracts, vinegar, household commodities). Let the children smell them and try to identify them. Be sure to avoid harmful odors!

Fingerprinting, introducing large and small muscles, is a "squishy" experience.

➤ Show children pictures of things and ask them to describe what they think the items would smell like.

➤ Ask children to name their favorite smells and tell why they like them.

➤ Talk about how smell helps us (for example, the smell of smoke means danger).

➤ In a water or creative activity, add scented bubble bath or food flavorings such as peppermint, vanilla, lemon extract, or others that would be somewhat familiar to the child. Is there more or less interest when a fragrance is added?

➤ Match two smells from fragrance containers. How easy is it for the children?

➤ Help the children learn and use only *safe* odors—avoiding those that are harmful to the body (glue, sprays, paint, and so on).

➤ Make and use sniff-and-scratch cards by putting small amounts of fragrances on sand paper. When the surface is scratched, the aroma becomes more evident.

Taste

➤ In small bowls, place staple items that look alike but have different tastes (white sugar, salt, flour, powdered sugar, tapioca, coconut). Taste them and talk about the differences.

➤ In small bowls, place staple items that have the same name but have different characteristics (white sugar, brown sugar, raw sugar, powdered sugar, sugar cane, sugar cubes, and others). Taste them and talk about the differences.

➤ Have plates of vegetables or fruits. Ask the children to taste and compare them (juicy, crunchy, sweet, sour).

➤ Have the same fruit or vegetable prepared in different ways (raw, cooked, peeled, unpeeled, as juice). Taste and compare.

➤ Have new foods as a snack or at lunch.

➤ Talk about vegetables that are generally eaten raw (lettuce) and those that can be eaten raw or cooked. Serve some of them at snack.

➤ Talk about nutrition frequently. Introduce the children to the current government pyramid chart.

➤ With and without food products present, ask the children to describe the tastes of their favorite foods and disliked foods.

➤ Talk about and taste food for babies (puréed, liquid, unseasoned, and so on).

Sound

- ➤ Fill containers with different items. Have the children shake them and try to guess what is inside.
- ➤ Have a group of duplicate containers with invisible contents. See if the children can correctly match them by shaking them.
- ➤ Play a record or tape and see if the children can identify the sounds. Pictures or replicas can go with the sounds. See if the children can match them.
- ➤ Make telephones with two empty juice cans and a string 10 to 20 feet long. Poke a hole in the bottom of a can, put string through the bottom, and tie a knot inside the can. Hold the string taut. Let the children talk and listen to each other.
- ➤ Borrow telephones from the telephone company (if available) to teach telephone courtesy and proper use.
- ➤ Record children's voices on tape. Play the tape back and see if they can identify the child who is speaking.
- ➤ Encourage the children to make poems or rhyming words.
- ➤ Have one child imitate a sound, such as an animal or vehicle, and another guess what it is.
- ➤ Behind a screen make sounds of common household items. See if the children can identify them.
- ➤ Tell a story of a child's day and have the children make the appropriate sounds (brushing teeth, turning on water, car starting, horns on the way to school, pet sounds).
- ➤ Have the children tell how they feel when they hear certain sounds, such as a dog, siren, band, familiar voice, or bell.
- ➤ Make the sound of an animal and have the children pretend to be that animal.
- ➤ Hide something that has a sound—ticking clock, rustling paper, squeaking toy, bell, musical instrument—and also some items that are soundless—flag, soft toy, hat. Inside an enclosed sack or box, make the item sound or soundless according to the item. Have the children guess the item.
- ➤ Why do some items make sound and others not? What can you do to silence items with sounds and make sound from items that are soundless?
- ➤ Use tapes or records of stories and/or music.
- ➤ Use a story/tape such as *The Listening Walk* by Showers (1991). Take a listening walk around the classroom or playground.
- ➤ Listen to different volumes of the same sound—perhaps use earmuffs or a mute on a stringed instrument to soften sounds.
- ➤ Explore sounds in different cultures that would be of interest to the children (music, chants, animal sounds, and so on).
- ➤ Read and/or use the "Noisy" books in Margaret Wise Brown's series (Harper Children's Books).

Sight

- ➤ Have the children look at various objects. Ask them to describe how the objects would feel before they touch them (hard, smooth, cold, and so on).
- ➤ Have the children look at a picture. Ask them to act out the scene.
- ➤ Have the children act out their favorite game or activity. See if the other children can guess it.
- ➤ Have the children put crayon shavings, things of nature (for example, flower petals, seeds, leaves), or small objects between two pieces of waxed paper and then press with a warm iron.
- ➤ Talk about the differences between opaque and clear things.
- ➤ Ask the children how they tell if something is hot just by looking at it.
- ➤ Have the children watch you complete a task and then model it.

- Show four to six objects. Have the children close their eyes while you remove one object. Have them name the missing object.
- From a variety of objects, have the children group items that are alike in color, size, or composition. Can the objects be grouped in other ways, such as by shape or use?
- From a group of objects, have the children select the things that would be used by a certain family member (father, mother, baby).
- Show a suitcase full of clothes. Have the children decide what articles are needed for different occasions or seasons.
- Be sure to have large and hand-held mirrors for the children to see themselves and in different activities (movement, dramatic play, and so on). This increases a child's self-awareness, self-esteem, interaction, and participation.
- Occasionally focus on a particular color in an activity or area of the room.
- Explain and show how and why animals camouflage themselves.
- Help the children identify and locate different shapes within the classroom.

Miscellaneous Ideas for Small-Muscle Development

- Pegboards
- Small, colored cubes
- Snap blocks
- Small plastic blocks representing bricks
- Puzzles (commercial or handmade)
- Tinkertoys
- Assorted table toys (small vehicles, people, animals)
- Geoboards: Use a piece of wood of any size but preferably about 4 by 6 inches or 5 by 8 inches. Hammer small nails into it about 1/2 inch apart. Give the children some small colored rubber bands and let them create their own designs by stretching the bands over the nails.
- Picture lotto or card games
- Mobiles: Use a coat hanger, string or yarn, and a variety of either purchased or handmade objects.
- Spool knitting
- Sorting buttons by size, shape, color, composition, and so on.
- Sewing cards (purchased or handmade)
- Sewing on burlap or soft fabrics
- Plastic objects that fit together (Multi-fits, Knoppers, Bristle Blocks)
- Creative arts (cutting, pasting, stringing, painting)
- Pipe cleaners: Let children make interesting shapes.
- Manipulation (zippers, buttons, snaps)
- Puppets (hand, finger, sack)
- Nesting objects (cans, boxes, barrels, containers)
- Objects (felt, metal) and appropriate boards (flannel, magnetic)

Water

Children need to have water experiences. Water has a soothing effect. It gives way to the motion of one's hands. At school, basins and sinks are generally low and available to the children. Water can be used daily or just for special occasions.

Water encourages action, as do props. When children participate in this activity, wearing a cover-up is a prerequisite. Sponges, towels, mops, and buckets should be close at hand and used by the children for spills and cleanup. The number of children at this activity is limited by providing only a set number of cover-ups.

If water is not desired in certain areas of the classroom, these areas should be separated by as much distance as possible and the rationale explained to the children:

"Water in the book area could ruin our books." They should be told where and when water can be used.

One preschool teacher had difficulty accepting water play. She felt water was for drinking and washing only. In her particular preschool group were several children who never passed the water to play in the other areas. As children measured, spilled, poured, wiped, and experimented with water, the teacher's dislike for it intensified. After a considerable length of time (and admitting she could not eliminate water from the room), she realized that the experience had a therapeutic effect on the children, and she began to recognize other values as well. Perhaps instead of fighting the presence of water, she should have joined the activity!

Teachers may consider the following suggestions for water use:

➤ Give children a bucket of clear water and a large brush and let them paint anything outdoors that water will not damage.
➤ Get a plastic container with a squeeze handle similar to that used with window cleaner. Let the children squirt at waterproof targets such as a fence or tree.
➤ Let the children bathe dolls or wash doll clothes.
➤ Have a box of water toys readily available for use in the water table.
➤ Provide containers, water, and food coloring. Children can make and mix colors. Eyedroppers and plastic egg cartons are easy to use and clean.
➤ Encourage water play in the domestic area.
➤ During the summer, have a hose running in the sand area or use a wading pool.
➤ If other sources of water play are not available, cut a tire in half and fill each half with water. Or use a jug, a large tub, or a 5-gallon plastic jug with a spout.
➤ Demonstrate the use of steam for cooking and pressing.
➤ Point out and make use of community resources, such as lakes, rivers, ponds, or fountains.
➤ Observe activities relying on water, such as fishing, logging, or boating.
➤ Tell how plumbing works and what repairs are needed.
➤ Go through a car wash or let the children help wash the car.
➤ Take a trip to the fire station and have the firefighters explain how water helps put out fires, how hoses are used, and so on.
➤ Explain or observe irrigation of crops.
➤ Visit a shipyard or dock and learn about it through use of books, pictures, and replicas.
➤ Watch the water wagon as it washes the streets.
➤ Encourage children to help water a garden, plants, or animals.
➤ Talk about the characteristics of water and evaporation.
➤ Talk about rain, snow, ice, and other weather conditions.
➤ Involve the children in cleanup using sponges and water.
➤ Provide containers and spouts for measuring and exploring water.
➤ Introduce new terms and characteristics of water (recycling, buoyancy, volume, weight, leveling).
➤ On a stormy day, watch the change in clouds, the darkness of the sky, the falling moisture (the bounce of raindrops, the floating of snowflakes, and so on), and the different types of clothing worn to accommodate the moisture and temperature.
➤ Talk about a rainbow. Use such books as Freeman's *A Rainbow of My Own* (1966).
➤ When using water in the classroom, encourage the children to help set and enforce limits for its use (type of clothing to be worn, cleanup procedures).
➤ Place some rocks or shells in a small fishbowl and let the children examine them through the glass, under magnifying glasses, or by removing them from the bowl.
➤ Mix water and dirt.
➤ Look for and use books about water and weather.

See also the section on water in Chapter 8.

Don't overlook the enjoyment of bubbles. Solutions can be purchased or made: Mix 1 gallon of water; 1 cup of dishwashing detergent (some are better than others), and 50 drops of glycerin. Anything with a hole is wonderful for making bubbles: plastic six-pack soda holders make six big bubbles!

Young children seldom have to be invited to join water or mud play. Water is adaptable, appealing, inexpensive, flexible, sometimes clean, mixable with other items (liquid and solid), abundant, and on and on. Frequently both mud and water play have a calming effect on children.

Multicultural Experiences

- ➤ *Art materials:* Designs, colors, textures; natural materials and colors; fabrics; pictures; experiences, patterns; tools; preservation; and so on.
- ➤ *Blocks:* To construct dwellings, buildings, activities; of different compositions, uses; and so on.
- ➤ *Dramatic play:* Materials and toys of different cultures and races and of both genders; dolls; communication devices; cooking and eating utensils; occupations; print or language of different cultures; games; replicas of food; storytelling materials; professions/occupations; fabrics; hobbies; and so on.
- ➤ *Manipulative materials:* Puzzles representing different cultures, activities, places, homes, and so on; counting and sorting pieces; typical sensory experiences; and so on.
- ➤ *Music:* Instruments (including construction: wood, metal, skin, and so on); recordings of cultural music; dance accessories; participation in movement and rituals; books and pictures of musical activities; and so on.
- ➤ *Pictorial media:* Picture/storybooks reflecting family, individual, and cultural diversity; illustrations (posters, cards, books, and so on) and objects related to culture; replicas of toys and play; clothing and food examples; and so on.
- ➤ *Science accessories:* Foliage used in home construction, toys, dress, and so on; measuring and building tools; pets (land/water/air); plants; weather and protection against it; food preparation and preservation; and so on. (Some ideas for this section were adapted from "Multicultural Materials," 1995.)

Parents, neighbors, relatives, community people, missionaries, foreigners, and people of all races and backgrounds can be valuable resources to the preschool teacher. When you contact them, give them some basic guidelines about the ages and backgrounds of the children in your classroom and give them some ideas about how *you* believe they can be of great value in enlarging and clarifying the importance of ALL people. You may even arrange for a future visit after you have had spontaneous and planned experiences with the young children in your classroom. You may want to set aside a certain day of a week or a month so the children can look forward to "visitor's" day—or whatever title you want to give to "cultural" opportunities. *Help the children to look forward to the "visits" and plan for follow-up activities!*

Some suggested beginnings:

- ➤ Prepare the parents, guests, and children so they will know what to expect, how to behave, and other criteria specific to your classroom, the guests, objects being shown, and the children.
- ➤ If possible, meet with your "guest/guests" and give them some ideas about why this experience would be of value to these particular children, what they may want to "show" or "tell," if it would be permissible for the children to handle objects, some "follow-up" visits or experiences for the children, and so on.

Make these special opportunities valuable and meaningful to each child!

 *Reflection*

Some teachers think that it reveals respect for a child's work to mount it, mat it, or frame it, or to cover a bulletin board with some interesting material before pinning up children's carefully arranged works. Does this procedure enhance or detract from the child's efforts?

Does it encourage or discourage young children from participating in "creative activities" when teachers provide:

- cookie cutters, rolling pins, etc., with clay
- cutouts to paste
- verbal monologue (unnecessary chatter, some "*do's*" and "*don'ts,*" etc.)
- time and unnecessary behavior restrictions
- equipment that doesn't work (dried brushes, blunt scissors, small materials)

Share some of the "encouragers" and "discouragers" you have noticed.

Application of Principles

1. Briefly describe creativity for young children.
2. List six ways that creative experiences can enhance the growth and development of young children. Include some personal examples.
3. If possible, observe children in the four different development stages of art suggested by Lowenfeld, as described early in this chapter.
4. Give some specific examples of how creativity can be webbed with other curriculum areas.
5. Describe the differences between creative and product-oriented activities.
6. From the ideas suggested in the chapter, what values for children most appeal to you? Why?
7. What role does the teacher play in helping young children express themselves through creative activities?
8. Observe which activities are most popular with the children in your center. Discuss with other adults how you could interest the children in a variety of creative materials.
9. Explain how you would set up an activity differently for the following:
   a. 2-year-olds and painting
      4-year-olds and painting
   b. 2-year-olds and sand
      5-year-olds and sand
   c. 3-year-olds and cutting
      5-year-olds and cutting
   d. 4-year-olds and woodworking
      5-year-olds and woodworking
   e. 2-year-olds and water
      5-year-olds and water
10. Plan and use two different sensory experiences with children between the ages of 2 and 5.
11. Role play with a partner. One of you plays a teacher who firmly believes in using food products in art experiences in the classroom; the other plays one who firmly believes that food products have no place in creative art. After three minutes, switch roles. Discuss your feelings in both roles.

 *Reflection*

Teachers: Look around your preschool/kindergarten classroom and see how many of the following opportunities are readily available for young children:

Clay: How many kinds and textures are available? Are other utensils and surfaces available for exploration? Can other items (wire, cookie cutters, transparent paper, candy papers, buttons, small objects, magazine pictures, etc.) be used?

Cutting and pasting: Are scissors sharp enough (but not too sharp) for cutting provided materials? How can children learn to use and enjoy cutting and pasting?

Drawing: Are there good-quality markers and colored pens of all colors and types?

Paper: Is there a selection (color, texture, size, transparent, etc.) from which to choose?

Other materials: Can children select preferred surfaces (fabric, wood, glass, mirrors, leaves, cones, shells, twigs, seeds, dried flowers, sand, etc.) for activities?

Paint: Is it freshly mixed? Is there a variety of colors (shades, tints, natural, etc.)? Are colors inviting; are they visible through the containers? What activities are available (finger painting, sponge or block, easel, miscellaneous, etc.)?

Brushes: Are there various sizes, shapes, and textures?

Woodworking: How frequently is this activity available in the classroom? Are tools properly stored when not in use? List precautions in using tools.

Water: What kinds of water activities are provided, and how frequently? What are some hazards and precautions?

Sensory experiences: How frequently are children exposed to sensory (or multisensory) stimulation? What kinds of activities do they like most/least?

Multicultural experiences: What kinds of experiences, and how frequently, are they provided to help the children: (a) learn more about their own culture, and (b) learn about the culture of others (preferably those in there immediate setting)?

Miscellaneous activities: Of what value are activities for building (a) large muscles (block building, wood working, climbing, riding, etc.), (b) small muscles (puzzles, stringing, cutting and pasting, etc.), and (c) creativity?

12. Explain how you can introduce safety factors in creative and sensory activities and why it is so important. Be specific.
13. Refer to the curriculum checklist in Figure 4.2 to see if *each item* can apply to an art experience as well as to the whole day. (Are there provisions for different areas of development, indoor/outdoor use, a wide range of skills and interests, repetitive or new play, and so on?)
14. Plan and use resources in your classroom to help promote healthy multicultural information and attitudes through creative expression.
15. Of all the suggestions listed in this chapter (or others), what are your favorite creative activities/materials to use with young children? Do you enjoy getting messy and making your own decisions about projects? Which experiences do you avoid? Why?

References

NOTE: Current references are used when available. Older references are classic, introductory, and important in development of later ideas, policies, and practices.

Aronson, S. (1991). *Health & Safety.* New York: Harper Collins.

The best schools in the world. (1991, December 2). *Newsweek,* 50–56.

Bleiker, C. A. (1999). The development of self through art: A case for early art education. *Art Education, 52*(3), 48–53.

Bredekamp, S. (Ed.). (1987). *Developmentally appropriate practice in early childhood programs serving children from birth through age 8* (expanded ed.). Washington, DC: NAEYC.

Bredekamp, S., & Copple, C. (Eds.). (1997). *Developmentally appropriate practice in early childhood programs* (rev. ed.). Washington, DC: NAEYC.

Brittain, W. L. (1969). Some exploratory studies of the art of preschool children. *Studies in Art Education, 10*(3), 14–24.

Brittain, W. L. (1979). *Creativity, art, and the young child.* New York: Macmillan.

Clark, G., Day, M., & Greer, W. D. (1987). Discipline-based art education: Becoming students of art. *Journal of Aesthetic Education, 21*(2), 129–196.

Clark, G., & Zimmerman, E. (2000). Greater understanding of the local community: A community-based art education program for rural schools. *Art Education, 53*(2), 33–39.

Clemens, S. G. (1991). Art in the classroom: Making everyday special. *Young Children, 46*(2), 4–11. Available online: http://home.earthlink.net/eceteacher/articles.html/#artart.

Clemens, S. G. (1998). Discussing the news with 3–7-year-olds: What to do? Reprints online at www.naeyc.org/resources/journal.

Colbert, C. (1997). Visual arts in the developmentally appropriate integrated curriculum. In C. H. Hart, D. C., Burts, & R. Charlesworth (Eds.). *Integrating curriculum and developmentally appropriate practice: Birth to age 8* (pp. 201–223). Albany, NY: State University of New York Press.

Colbert, C., & Taunton, M. (1992). *Developmentally appropriate practices for the visual arts education of young children.* NAEA Briefing Paper. Reston, VA: NAEA.

Cole, E., & Schaefer, C. (1992). Can young children be art critics? *Young Children, 45*(2), 33–38.

Commune of Reggio Emilia. (1987). *The hundred languages of children.* Reggio Emilia, Italy: Author.

Davilla, D. E. (1998). Bringing the Reggio concept to American educators. *Art Education, 51*(4), 18–24.

Davis, J., & Gardner, H. (1991). The arts and childhood education: A cognitive development portrait of the young child as artist. In B. Spodek (Ed.), *Handbook on Research on the Education of Young Children.* New York: Macmillan.

Demerest, K. (1996). Playing with color. *Young Children, 51*(3), 83.

Dever, M. T. & Jared, E. J. (1996). Remember to include art and crafts in your integrated curriculum. *Young Children, 51*(3), 69–73.

Dewey, J. 1934. *Art as experience.* New York: Putnam.

Dewey, J. 1944. *Art and experience.* New York: Free Press.

Dighe, J., Calomiris, Z., & Van Zutphen, C. (1998). Nurturing the language of art in children. *Young Children, 53*(1), 4–9.

Edwards, C., Gandini, L., & Forman, G. (Eds.). (1993). *The hundred languages of children: The Reggio Emilia approach to early childhood education.* Norwood, NJ: Ablex.

Edwards, L. C., & Nabors, M. L. (1993). The creative arts process: What it is and what it is not. *Young Children, 48*(3), 77–81.

Eisner, E. (1976). What we know about children's art—and what we need to know. In E. Eisner (Ed.), *The arts, human development and education* (pp. 5–18). Berkeley, CA: McCutchan.

Engel, B. S. (1995). *Considering children's art: Why and how to value their works.* Washington, DC: NAEYC

Epstein, A. S. (2001). Thinking about art: Encouraging art appreciation in early childhood settings. *Young Children, 56*(3), 38–43.

Freeman, D. (1966). *A rainbow of my own.* New York: Viking.

Gallas, K. (1994). *The languages of learning: How children talk, write, dance, draw, and sing their understanding of the world.* New York: Teachers College.

Gandini, L. (1993). Fundamentals of the Reggio approach to early childhood education. *Young Children, 49*(1), 4–8.

Gardner, H. (1980). *Artful scribbles.* New York: Basic.

Gardner, H. (1990). *Art education and human development.* Los Angeles, CA: Getty Center for Education in the Arts.

Gardner, H. (1994). *The arts and human development.* New York: Basic Books.

Golumb, C. (1992). *The child's creation of a pictorial world.* Berkeley, CA: University of California Press.

Greenberg, P. (2000). Display children's art attractively. *Young Children, 55*(2), 89.

Gross, T., & Clemens, S. G. (2002). Painting a tragedy: Young children process the events of September 11. *Young Children, 57*(3), 44–51.

Hohmann, M., & Weikart, D. P. (1995). *Educating young children.* Ypsilanti, MI: High/Scope Press.

Holt, B. G. (1989). *Science with young children* (rev. ed.). Washington DC: NAEYC.

Huber, L. K. (1999). Woodworking with young children, you can do it! *Young Children, 54*(6), 32–34.

Jones, E., & Nimmo, J. (1994). *Emergent curriculum.* Washington, DC: NAEYC. Order #207/$6. ISBN: 0-935989-62-5.

Katz, L. (1993). What can we learn from Reggio Emilia? In C. Edwards, L. Gandini, & G. Forman (Eds.), *The hundred languages of children: The Reggio Emilia approach to early childhood education* (pp. 19–37). Norwood, NJ: Ablex.

Katz, L., & Chard, S. (1989). *Engaging young children's minds: The project approach.* Norwood, NJ: Ablex.

Kellogg, R. (1970). *Analyzing children's art.* Palo Alto, CA: Mayfield.

Kellogg, R., with O'Dell, W. (1967). *The psychology of children's art.* New York: CRM, Inc.

Kendrick, A. S., Kaufman, R., & Messenger, K. P. (Eds.). (1988). *Healthy young children: A manual for programs.* Washington, DC: NAEYC.

Leithead, M. (1996). Happy hammering: A hammering activity center with built-in success. *Young Children, 51*(3), 12.

Lowenfeld, V. (1947). *Creative and mental growth* (3rd ed.). New York: Macmillan.

Lowenfeld, V. (1987). *Creative and mental growth* (8th ed.) New York: Macmillan.

Lowenfeld, V., & Brittain, W. L. (1967). *Creative and mental growth.* New York: Macmillan.

Maldonado, N. S. (1996). Puzzles: A pathetically neglected, commonly available resource. *Young Children, 51*(4), 4–10.

Moyer, J. (1990). Whose creation is it, anyway? *Childhood Education, 66,* 130–132.

Multicultural materials. (1995). *Scholastic Early Childhood Today, 10*(3) 46.

National Association for the Education of Young Children. Some Creative Arts aids available: Engle, B. S. *Emergent Curriculum.* Order #102/$8. ISBN: 0-935989-70-6. Jones, E., & Nimmo, J. *Emergent Curriculum.* Order #207/$6. ISBN: 0-935989-62-5. Lasky, L., & Mukerji-Bergeson, R. *Art: Basic for Young Children.* Order #106/$5. ISBN: 0-912674-73-3.

Neubert, K. (1991). *The care and feeling of clay.* Pasadena, CA: Pacific Oaks College.

New, R. (1991). Projects and provocations: Preschool curriculum ideas from Reggio Emilia. *Montessori Life, 3*(1), 26–28.

Newton, C. (1995). Language and learning about art. In C. M. Thompson (Ed.), *The visual arts in early childhood learning* (pp. 81–83).

Parsons, M. (1998). Book review: Child development in art. *Studies in Art Education, 40*(1), 80–91.

Piaget, J. (1976). *The grasp of consciousness: Action and concept in the young child.* Cambridge, MA: Harvard University Press.

Raines, S., & Canady, R. I. (1990). *The whole language kindergarten.* New York: Teachers College Press.

Schaffer-Simmern, H. (1947). *The unfolding of artistic activity.* Berkeley: University of California Press.

Schiller, M. (1995a). An emergent art curriculum that fosters understanding. *Young Children, 50*(3), 33–38.

Schiller, M. (1995b). Reggio Emilia: A focus in emergent curriculum and art. *Art Education, 48*(3), 45–56.

Seefeldt, C. (1995). Art—A serious work. *Young Children, 50*(3), 39–45.

Shirrmacher, R. (1988). *Art and creative development for children.* New York: Delmar.

Showers, P. (1991). *The Listening walk.* New York: Trumpet Club, 666 5th Avenue. (A cassette tape is also available here.)

Smith, N. (1982). The visual arts in early childhood education: Development and creation of meaning. In B. Spodek (Ed.)., *Handbook on research in early childhood education,* (pp. 295–317). New York: Free Press.

Smith, N. R., with Fucigna, C., Kennedy, M., & Lord, L. (1993). *Experiences and art: Teaching children to paint* (2nd ed.). New York: Teachers College Press.

Solter, A. (1992). Understanding tears and tantrums. *Young Children, 47*(4), 64–68.

Sosna, D. (2000). More about woodworking with young children. *Young Children, 55*(2), 38–30.

Spodek, B. (1991). Reconceptualizing early childhood education: A commentary. *Early Childhood and Development, 2*(2), 16.

Stokrocki, M. (1995). Understanding young children's ways of interpreting their experiences through participant observation. In C. M. Thompson (Ed.), *The visual arts in early childhood learning* (pp. 67–72). Reston, VA: NAEA.

Swanson, L. (1994). Changes—how our nursery school replaced adult-directed art projects with child-directed experiences and changed to an accredited child-sensitive, developmentally appropriate school. *Young Children, 49*(4), 69–73.

Thompson, C. M. (1995). Transforming curriculum in the visual arts. In Bredekamp, S., & T. Rosegrant (Eds.), *Reaching potentials: Transforming early childhood curriculum and assessment,* Vol. 2, 81–96. Washington, DC: NAEYC.

Torrance, E. P. (1970). *Encouraging creativity in the classroom.* Dubuque, IA: Wm. C. Brown.

Vygotsky, L. S. (1978). *Mind in society.* Cambridge, MA: Harvard University Press.

Watson, D., Burke, C., & Harste, J. (1989). *Whole language: Inquiring voices.* New York: Scholastic.

Wilson, M., & Wilson, B. (1982). *Teaching children to draw: A guide for teachers and parents.* Upper Saddle River, NJ: Prentice Hall.

Wolf, A. D. (1990). Art postcards—another aspect of your aesthetics program? *Young Children, 45*(2), 39–43.

Zimmerman, E., & Zimmerman, L. (2000). Art education and early childhood education: The young child as creator and meaning maker within a community context. *Young Children, 55*(6), 87–93.

7

Music/Movement

Main Principles

1. Music is an enjoyable art form that aids self-expression and personal development.

2. Movement education is a viable curriculum area because of its enjoyment and value for children.

3. Alert teachers and parents bring many spontaneous and planned music and movement opportunities into the lives of young children.

4. Young children need many and varied opportunities to develop their bodies and abilities.

5. Music is a good medium for teaching other curriculum areas.

6. Music and movement education are certainly a part of creative expression but are discussed in a separate chapter for emphasis and enjoyment.

7. Music and movement from different cultures enrich children's lives and help them to better understand different racial and ethnic backgrounds.

Introduction

Recall the following familiar nursery rhyme:

> *Jack and Jill went up the hill to get a pail of water,*
> *Jack fell down and broke his crown*
> *And Jill came tumbling after.*

Now try this new version of the same rhyme:

> *A whistling Jack and a singing Jill went skipping merrily up the hill.*
> *They filled their pail clear to the top and started home without a stop.*
> *They both were quick, they both were agile;*
> *Their bodies had developed so they were no longer fragile.*
> *They sang and played the whole day through; they liked themselves, and others, too.*

The feeling one has about his body and his abilities is very important in the development of a good self-image. One likes to feel confident in trying things, in interacting with others, and in exploring the environment.

From the time a baby is old enough to be aware of sounds, he attends to those that are rhythmic and melodious. Some of his first games are pat-a-cake, bye-bye, and peek-a-boo. Toddlers and young preschoolers readily sing and perform catchy commercials on the radio or television, while 4- and 5-year-olds enjoy songs, finger plays, and activities that have rhythm, repetition, and interaction of body parts as they play alone or with others. Music has a definite effect on the way one feels and moves.

The research in review by Andress (1991a) is an important and informative article, as it describes developmentally appropriate music experience for children, from birth through age 8, building on the framework of national music education standards established by the Music Educators National Conference (1994a, 1994b). Examples of typical behavior are cited to demonstrate how children at each stage of development may be expected to perform, create, listen to, describe, and value music as they sing, move, play instruments, read music, and write music (Andress, 1995, p. 99).

 **Reflection**

Consider the following helpful hints about music and movement education with young children (source: "Music for the Young Child," 1995):

"Dr. Benjamin Bloom from the University of Chicago states that 40 percent of everything we know we learn by age seventeen and 50 percent of that knowledge has been learned by age four. He suggests that the age from six months to four years may be the most important time in a person's life." (p. 2)

"Research suggests that the brain cells stop their dramatic growth after about age four. Brain cell growth is stimulated by *vibration* (singing is intensified vibration), *exploration,* and *experience with the senses.* In order to provide for the most possible growth of a child's brain cells, we must lay a rich foundation for learning before age four. That *does NOT mean teaching skills,* but, instead, offering rich environment and exposure." (p. 2)

"Young children need to learn through their bodies. Everything they do with their bodies to explore and make sense out of the world at this young age transfers directly to higher forms of thinking as they grow older. They can represent something internally if allowed to explore it with their bodies while very young. Young children need to *move* to learn." (p. 2)

An early childhood curriculum is based on the assumption that the learner (the child in this case) is more important than what is to be learned (music, in this case). However, music has the power to add importance to the child's life. The music curriculum must include an understanding of the child's cognitive, physical, and socioemotional development, and the planner must be familiar with good music education resources.

Characteristics of a child-centered music and movement program for young children include:

➤ Each child has musical potential and personal and unique interests and abilities.
➤ Children come from diverse backgrounds.
➤ Work is their play.
➤ Each child needs caring, effective, and knowledgeable adult models.
➤ They need exemplary musical sounds, activities, and materials.
➤ The best learning environment has pleasant and social settings.
➤ Very young children can develop critical thinking skills through musical experiences.
➤ They should perform at their own developmental level.
➤ They need diverse learning environments for individual growth (MENC, 1994b, p. 9).

Appropriate musical content can best be explored in an interactive environment that is rich in manipulative objects, instruments, quality musical examples, and adults effectively modeling music. Music learning experiences for young children should occur throughout the day and the curriculum, as well as in special-interest areas and guided group play (Andress, 1991a).

Music across the curriculum, in special-interest areas, when choices are available, and during guided group music times are appropriate and encouraged.

Young children demonstrate their music abilities when they perform, listen, create, and describe music, as well as when they respond to pictures of musical ideas.

Children of all ages should experience music daily in spontaneous and planned ways. Adults can encourage music experiences by:

➤ singing, humming, and chanting;
➤ using songs and rhymes representing a variety of meters and tonalities;
➤ imitating sounds (human, household, motorized, etc.);
➤ exposing children to a wide variety of vocal, body, instrumental, and environmental sounds;
➤ playing selected live and recorded music;
➤ rocking, patting, touching, and moving with the children to the beat, rhythm patterns, and melodic direction of music they hear;
➤ playing instruments;
➤ creating short pieces of music (improvising songs, instrumental accompaniments);
➤ responding to music (sounds, tempos, modes, styles);
➤ using the voice to imitate other voices and/or sounds;
➤ using vocabulary to describe sounds;
➤ demonstrating an awareness of music as a part of daily life;
➤ talking about music and its relationship to expression and feeling;
➤ providing safe toys that make musical sounds the children can control; and
➤ using other opportunities provided in the environment.

Music experiences for children from birth through age 8 must be planned to meet the needs of each child's unique learning style, interests, and abilities. It is recommended that a rich and diverse learning environment be provided for all children at various levels for a successful music experience in early childhood education. Be creative; engage children in relevant tasks that are real and familiar; help children to be safe and social in a real-world environment; and challenge children in problem-solving situations. See Figure 7.1.

Figure 7.1 Music and the Developing Young Child

In Neelly's comprehensive and valuable article (2001), she has written a section ("The child's brain and music") that is of particular interest to physicians, researchers, and *educators*. Some of the ideas in the article that point to the power of music's role in children's overall development include:

- Multisensory musical behaviors (aural-oral, visual, and tactile) are concurrent with critical brain growth spurts (Campbell, 2000; Fox, 2000). These musical behaviors activate both hemispheres of the young child's brain (Campbell, 1997) (the left hemisphere processes verbal, sequential, logical, and analytical information; the right hemisphere is more holistic, creative, and intuitive, regulating functions in language, signing, and memory).
- The brains synapses continue to increase and need experiences to strengthen them (Begley 1997).
- The time to lay the foundation for motor control circuitry in the brain is between the prenatal period and age 5 (Gabbard, 1998).
- From the writing of Jean Piaget and his interpreters, we have long known that the sensorimotor stage of development is the "bedrock on which the subsequent hierarchy of all intelligence is built" (Olds, 1994, p. 33).
- More than half of American children are inactive on a regular basis and are overweight. Active young children, in addition to undergoing brain development, are also forming habits for long-term health benefits (Miller 1999, p. 58).
- Some researchers suggest engaging children in regular, vigorous activities that take more forms rather than focusing on traditional fitness and training (Strand, Scantling, and Johnson, 1998).
- The 3- to 5-year-old age range is a period when the foundation of physical skills is laid (recognized by the American Medical Association, the American Academy of Pediatrics, the President's Council on Physical Fitness, the National Association for the Education of Young Children, and the American Alliance for Health, Physical Education, Recreation, and Dance) (Miller, 1999, p. 59).
- Active engagement in the organization of music sound while singing, moving, and listening influences the overall functioning of the body (Tomatis, 1997).
- Music influences how children experience their own individual space (Aldridge, 1998); can change a child's perception of time (Boyce-Tillman, 2000); can help the child's immune system as it regulates stress-related hormones . . . and can heal a child when healing is needed" (Neally, 2001, p. 35).
- "Whenever there is music, all kinds of levels of appraisals are going on at the same time" (Elliott, 1995).
- "[H]ands-on, direct, multisensory musical experiences in which children have opportunities to interact with others, to solve problems, to make decisions, and to reflect on their decisions": this is "developmentally appropriate music practice" and is a "collaborative learning process in which both adults and children can explore their own musical capacities through many kinds of musical contributions" and contribute new ways of thinking and doing (Neely, 2001, p. 36).
- When planning success-oriented opportunities for children's overall growth and development, "we must remember that music is not just another part of children's day, it is an essential part of their makeup. . . . Experiences are designed to stimulate children's music thinking and decision making, involve multisensory learning strategies, encourage creativity, and guide appropriate responses that they may not otherwise have experienced" (Neelly, 2001, p. 36). Musical opportunities should be adapted for a variety of children and their personal needs.

The Music Educator's National Conference (MENC)
The MENC has provided curriculum guidelines for beliefs about children's musical learning (Kenney, 1997, Table 1, p. 106), about teaching children (Table 2, p. 107, 1997) and for creating a curriculum in music (Table 3, p. 108, 1997). These MENC documents are consistent with NAEYC's position statement on developmentally appropriate practice, and reflect three basic principles: (1) age appropriateness, individual appropriateness, and context should be taken into account when planning music learning environments; (2) play is a primary vehicle

for musical growth; and (3) every student should have access to a balanced, comprehensive, and sequential program of study in music (pp. 106–107).

To meet the unique needs and interests of individual children:
- **Andress** (1995) suggests that appropriate early-learning classrooms must provide three kinds of music environments: (1) those that enhance teaching of other subjects, (2) those where children are free to interact with musical materials (instruments, recording, and personal interests), and (3) those where children come together for group activities in adult-guided music play (singing, playing instruments, listening, and learning in a cooperative setting).
- **Kenney**, discussing music for different age groups, summarizes music education as: (1) being a basic part of all human beings, (2) requiring the mind to behave differently from logicomathematical thinking, and (3) being important for total child development (1997, pp. 107–108). There should be freedom and time for each child to construct his/her own musical knowledge in an environment that provides for individual expression, as well as group activities to help children sense the social values of music and to facilitate blending music with other curriculum areas.
- **James** uses music to foster children's language and math development, which allows children to add to their understanding of the rhythm of language in a joyful, natural way (2000, p. 36). "You're not going to explain the intricacies of notes and scales to a three-year-old, but exposing a child to music now will help him learn these concepts later (Gill, 1998a, 40). . . . The more rhythms a child hears and moves to, the more patterns he will be able to recognize in math" (James, 2000, p. 37).
- **Wolf** (2000): "When I think of the impact that songs, rhymes, chants, and even singing games have on young children, I become overwhelmed. Educators at all levels tout the benefits of singing and playing musically with young children (Adachi 1994; Birkenshaw-Fleming 1997; Cave 1998; Chenfeld 1993; Feirerabend 1996; Honig 1995; McDonald 1979)" (p. 29).

How can you use the ideas of Andress, Kenney, James, Wolf, and others in your teaching?

"If we can explain music, we may find the key for all human thought—failure to take music seriously weakens any account of the human condition."
—Howard Gardner

Concerns have been raised about the music educator's approach to teaching prekindergarten children. Andress (1989) proposes a prekindergarten music curriculum model based on a synthesis of theories about the learning environment with the contributions of learning/play theorists and music educators. Music is primarily the discovery of sound. It should include purposive action or involvement, and should consider social, environmental, and procedural conditions (Wolf, 1992). Teachers will find that environmental conditions, such as space and attitude, are important components of successful music experiences.

Reassuring words and helpful ideas from Wolf (1992) give some comfort to music-shy teachers:

> A reasonable range (C to G or A) and uncomplicated rhythms add to the appropriateness. . . . Singing from the heart and setting aside any insecurities about singing will also boost the confidence of those early childhood teachers who shy away from singing with their classes. Children are not critics and actually learn best by hearing an unaccompanied voice. A child's ability to hear through harmony does not become sophisticated until after the age of five or six. . . . [M]usic can happen and often *does* spontaneously outside the group time we call *music time*. It is during these moments that the child appears to express the music from within himself (p. 58).

Props can introduce cultures through music!

 Reflection

Do the following two-part exercise:

1. From the previous discussions, select from the following list the music and movement opportunities that would be appropriate (DAP) and ones that would be inappropriate (DIP). Give rationales for your selections.

    _____Mixed ages of children riding stick horses

    _____2- and 3-year-olds skipping outdoors

    _____5-year-olds climbing on a jungle gym

    _____A teacher introducing a new song while using a tape recorder for the melody

    _____Toddlers singing a song, playing an instrument, and marching around the room—all children and all three activities at the same time

    _____4-year-olds matching the beat of different rhythms

    _____Preschool children singing rounds

    _____Preschool children imitating the sounds and/or movements of animals, household items, transportation vehicles, and objects

    _____4-year-olds throwing and catching a ball

    _____A teacher teaching math concepts (or other curriculum areas) to toddlers through singing and movement; to a mixed-age group

    _____5-year-olds using props (scarves, streamers, and so on) while moving to different types of music

    _____3-year-olds learning a folk song and dance

2. Now, for all the activities you identified as being inappropriate, state a more appropriate age for the activity, or a more appropriate activity for the age given.

Role of the Teacher

The role of the adult in structuring an environment that fosters and facilitates music and language growth in young children includes the following:

1. Increasing their own awareness of the range of musical opportunities
2. Providing a wealth of music experiences
3. Making music an integral part of the day
4. Building a strong and varied repertoire of rhythms, finger plays, poetry, and movement exercises
5. Fostering a sharing, verbal atmosphere surrounding young children
6. Recognizing the individual differences reflected in each child's musical preferences
7. Delighting in music with young children
8. Interacting with children as they sing or speak
9. Helping young children put their own nonsense rhymes, riddles, and verses to music
10. Using music to expand memory
11. Playing a supportive role as young children experiment and discover music

A wise teacher discovers the developmental stage of each child and then plans beneficial experiences, avoiding activities that are too complex or frustrating. Andress (1984) states that when planning an age-appropriate music curriculum, adults need to observe (1) how the child thinks ("often illogically, with single focus"), (2) how natural language acquisition influences the child's response ("from babbling, global properties of song, to more accurate pitch and rhythmic matching"), (3) how spontaneous the child's songs may be ("nurture these experiences as a means toward maintaining the child's creative tendencies"), (4) how play styles change as the child grows ("using settings that allow for playing alone, playing beside others, and with others") and also must (5) avoid exploiting the child ("provide experiences important and appropriate for the child, never for the ego-satisfaction of the adult") and (6) acknowledge that children "are capable of interacting with and learning about basic musical concepts" (p. 61). When we use a child-centered approach in teaching young children in all areas of curriculum, the children have opportunities to solve problems, be creative, make decisions, interact with materials and people, and enjoy the lighter side of music.

The teacher should provide some type of music every day and encourage spontaneous expression both indoors and outdoors, using a variety of methods and activities. She can pick up and encourage the rhythmic movements of the children. She must value individuality and plan accordingly for the children. If she is not musically inclined herself, she can arrange for another person to assist her, or use records, tapes, or a guest rather than eliminate music from the daily curriculum. She provides experiences that help the children release their feelings constructively, whether the feelings are of anger and hostility or of joy and excitement. She may even need to provide props that encourage creative expression, such as long, full skirts, crepe paper streamers, scarves, yarn balls, and the like. Children develop a lifelong appreciation for music as a result of a pleasant introduction.

When we use a child-centered approach in teaching young children in all areas of the curriculum, the children have opportunities to solve problems, be creative, make decisions, interact with materials and people, and enjoy the lighter side of learning. A wise teacher discovers the developmental stage of each child and then plans individual and beneficial experiences.

The "music person" has the responsibility and opportunity to bring music into the lives of the children with whom she interacts. Music and language have similar roots. Early vocalizations are the precursors of song and musical understanding just as they are the precursors of speech and language. There is a critical phase for the development of language, therefore, it seems logical that the abilities to sing and to respond musically have their roots in early childhood experiences. Teachers can help children feel good

Reflection

As a former student, teacher, trainer, and coordinator of early childhood programs, I am very aware of how structured and "teacher directed" most music activities are. We (the adults) select the songs, the music/exercise activities, the rhythm instruments, the amount of time spent, the listening activities, and so on that are used inside our classrooms and on our playgrounds.

Outline some specific plans to involve the children more in planning and executing child-centered music/movement activities!

Use some of their ideas. Note whether child participation increases, whether the children are more interested in the activities, whether they continue to make requests and suggestions, and so on.

Note your personal reactions to enlisting the ideas of children! Are we encouraging young children to be "puppets" or "original thinkers"?

about themselves and their participation in musical activities at appropriate age levels (Moravcik, 2000, p. 27).

Teachers may reflect on their own feelings when they hear various types of music (different tempos, favorites, past experiences, first-time exposure, etc.) and try to relate personal feelings with the feelings of children as they are exposed to new types of music. Does it make one feel happy, sad, excited, apprehensive? How can we use music to stimulate or quiet children? How can we encourage children to interpret, invent, or appreciate different types of music? What is our goal and what kinds of responses are we teaching children when we always use a certain tune or rhythm to remind them when it

Children with less music experience may need suggestions from teachers.

is time to . . . (line up, go to the restroom, prepare for lunch, clean up, be quiet or active, etc.)? Compare those responses to helping children become spontaneous, creative, thinkers, and more.

Background music has the same positive effect on children in any activity in the classroom. "The important thing to remember is that most kids function very well with music in the background, and that the right music at the right time can make them less stressed, more relaxed, happier, and more productive" (Giles, 1991, p. 44).

Music is an important part of the early-childhood education program. It can be appropriate in any setting (group or solitary play; types of curriculum; indoor or outdoor; spontaneous or specially planned; child or teacher initiated; to teach concepts; for relaxation; during transitions; to increase or decrease energy levels; to teach specific concepts; ANYTIME!)

Learning Through Music and Movement—General

By now the reader may be questioning why music and movement education are not a part of Chapter 6, Creative Arts. Consider the following:

1. Music and movement are certainly classed as creative and artistic expression; however, they deserve more attention than can be given in that chapter.
2. Teachers may need extra encouragement to include music and movement in their curriculum. Many feel inadequate to teach music or are self-conscious when singing or dancing with the children because of lack of formal training in either music or movement education. Although this training can add much to this area, many activities can be easily and inexpensively used, are growth-promoting, and have great benefit for children—and adults.
3. Music and movement are so much a part of the daily lives and activities of children. They enjoy music and rhythm.
4. Music and movement are great tools for integrating language, mathematics, science, social studies, art, nutrition, and health and safety subjects with children's natural and spontaneous interests.
5. Music and movement help children increase their self-esteem and their personal relationships with others.

Generally, music is thought of as a pleasant, enjoyable experience. Most young children are not exposed to practicing an instrument or performing in music competitions; to them music and movement are natural, spontaneous, and fun. Music is as respectable a curriculum area as any other, but doesn't appear to have the rigor or to inspire the fear often associated with math, reading, or science, for example. Still, there are many opportunities for music to interact with all other curriculum areas and to provide practice for personal skills and attributes.

Music can be easily used to help children think divergently—or creatively. For this to happen, they need adults (teachers and parents) who stimulate their thinking: "How else could a dog run?" "How would a tree bend in a slight breeze? In a strong wind storm?" "Could you show us another way to dance with the scarf?" But it is interesting to note that very few teachers ask children divergent-thinking questions automatically or consistently— and that training is necessary for teachers to use such questioning (Shaw & Cliatt, 1986). Goodlad (1984) found that less than 1 percent of time in school was devoted to open questioning that calls for skills other than simple memory, such as reasoning, problem solving, or forming opinions. Indeed teachers do talk 70 percent of the time giving instruction, but part of this time could be used to gain—not always give—information.

Use familiar (or new) songs to help children solve problems. For example, "Eensy Weensy Spider" is loved and enjoyed by a particular group of toddlers. After singing the regular version using hand movements, they love to mouth the sound (no sound) and make the hand movements. Then they pretend to put their spiders in a quiet, safe place while other songs are sung. In another group of preschoolers, the teacher was singing "Do as I'm Doing" and then called up various children to lead a verse, but instead of letting them express their own ideas, the teacher would hold the child's hands and make the motions she thought were appropriate. The children quickly tired of this activity. How much more exciting it would have been for each child to present an action for the other children to model. Do things *always have to be done* a certain *way, or don't some* teachers trust children's ideas? An eternal favorite of young children is "The Wheels on the Bus." Sometimes the children will say, "Let's do it different this time. Let's make the daddy snore!"

It takes all the enjoyment out of an activity if it has to be done a certain way, with a certain amount of proficiency, and for a designated period of time. Take for example fundamental motor patterns: running, walking, jumping, throwing, catching, kicking, and combinations of these activities (skipping, running and jumping; catching and throwing a ball; and so on). Teachers can preassess the abilities of children just as well when they are performing these patterns in a group or when music is added as they can standing with a pad and pencil and testing each child individually. Music helps add beat, tempo, and meter to the activity. Balls, hoops and tires, ropes, beanbags, balance beams and boards, mat activities, and climbing apparatus are challenging and exciting while music is heard. Besides varying the movements in games, children can also solve problems such as how to involve more children, how to keep score, ways to use scarves or other props, or possibilities for accompanying singing with instruments.

As in other curriculum areas, children need "the security of having certain decisions made for them, of knowing the limits beyond which they may not go" (Riley, 1984, p. 8). Are the dancing drums to be used only by teachers? Will mishandling the instruments cause forfeiture of a turn to use them? Is jumping on and off the furniture permitted during music time but forbidden at other times? Are there certain drums to be played with mallets and some only tapped with hands? Not only are there rules, but if children can help establish those rules, they have greater understanding of the rules and greater respect for them.

When planning for young children, regardless of their ages or the curriculum area, adults should carefully study the research of developmental theorists and movement specialists in order to better understand the predictable movement characteristics of various age groups.

Since the 1980s, there have been increased emphasis and research on brain development and the functions of each half of the brain—the left for verbal and analytic thought, the right for intuition and understanding of patterns. The verbal-analytic half is extremely important in dealing with the object world and in learning spoken language as well as reading and writing. The right hemisphere is used to perceive and express novel and complex visual, spatial, and musical patterns. Both brain halves are specialized and complementary, but may be in conflict. The left hemisphere tends to be dominant (Galin, 1976). Therefore, specific experiences must be provided to exercise the right hemisphere. Creativity is one way, whether through music, art, science, or other means. "People with strong right-hemisphere processing skills seem to have their own sense of time and rhythm" writes Cherry, Godwin, and Staples (1989, p. 243). (See also Taylor, 2002.)

Each person needs to find acceptable ways of expressing herself openly without fear of ridicule or embarrassment. Music or movement is more comfortable than verbalization for some individuals.

A child's acceptance or rejection of music depends on his age, his past musical experiences, cultural awareness, and attitude within his home. Children whose parents appreciate music and have musical talents are indeed fortunate, because parents share things they enjoy. A father who sings will sing with his children. A mother who plays the piano will play it with her children. Some families form their own musical groups—either

How can we encourage exploration and experimentation between children and music?

Are teachers and children taught to follow instructions and ignore creativity?

Are some teachers known to use music to control children's behavior by always selecting the kinds, the time, the limits, the acceptable behavior, and so on?

When given freedom, opportunity, interesting props, encouragement, and time, will the creativity and humor of the children come forth?

Is it a wonder that some children dread music/movement experiences?

What could we be doing to increase the spontaneity and creativity of music and movement in our classrooms?

How could you teach about: (a) musical patterns, and relations between each; (b) sound (pitch, loudness, timbre, duration); (c) making and using musical instruments; (d) developmentally appropriate music experiences; and (e) success-oriented opportunities for children's overall musical growth?

singing or instrumental—and spend many delightful hours together. They also attend concerts and share their talents with others.

Movement Education

Movement experiences are a vital part of the music education program because they represent the sensing-doing stage of learning, which is a means to understanding more abstract musical ideas. How the child responds to the experience depends on the child's disposition, developmental stage, and environmental factors (Andress, 1991b).

The following suggestions were made by Andress (1991b) in encouraging movement experiences for young children:

The goal of a music educator is to build musical understanding through movement experiences rather than strive for highly refined performance. Consider the activities within a classroom for 3- to 5-year-old children. Some are experimenting with a computer, others are at the carpentry table, some are playing unorganized circle games, some listen to a story, some check on pets, some are at the easel, some are preparing for snack, and others are doing numerous other activities. Each is involved in his/her own interest and skills in concepts of force, direction, balance control, and other motor skills. Lack of adequate movement experiences may contribute to disinterest, clumsiness, risk taking, and inactivity.

Movement experiences are very important in the early years of the child's development. Lack of these experiences can lead to bad habits, self-consciousness and embarrassment, fear of learning new skills, fear of injury, and other hard-to-overcome behaviors (Miller, 1999, p. 59). Some activities that are fun and growth promoting use balloons, blankets, parachutes, and/or balls. Miller concludes that movement should be at the center of a young child's learning environment. It is essential to the physical and cognitive development of young children (Paglin, 2000). By providing appropriate opportunities to move in a variety of ways, we're helping children become skilled movers. Gallahue (1996) encourages adults to focus on the process and quality of a child's movement (quantitative product) and to remember that exploration and repetition take time, that there is wide variation in skills, and that the child has a vivid imagination regarding his abilities and accomplishments. The child needs much encouragement and many opportunities to find joy in his movement, in healthy activities, and in opportunities to become a competent mover. See Figure 7.2.

Figure 7.2 How
Music and Movement
Educate Young
Children

The following elements are important in that they stimulate movement education.

1. **A combination of skills:**

   Kinesthetic activities and props (scarves, streamers—ideas familiar to the children) are basic concepts. Music can be used as a companion to *all* curriculum areas. Adults must make sure that the concepts, activities, and materials presented to the children are well within the range of individual children and the group as a whole, and somewhat familiar to the children, in order for the experiences to be meaningful.

   From my personal experience with toddlers in the past, I would be cautious about saying children of *any age can or cannot do* certain things. My professional training told me to include or avoid certain types of activities with young children, only to have these children prove it right or wrong—it's abilities and interests of the children you are working with at the time that count. Be willing to try different ideas—but be just as willing to discard them if they are too difficult or not well accepted at the time.

2. **Creativity:**

   . . . guides imagery or make-believe; combines curriculum areas (stories, dramatization, movement and environment, language and action, social studies and interaction, and so on); provides artistic and expressive avenues.

3. **Cultural development:**

   . . . brings an awareness of music, instruments, folk songs, clothing, dances, games, and traditions of other cultures. "In our pluralistic society, music is a valuable way to linking different people together: I may not be familiar with your culture, but I like to hear and sing your songs" (Wolf, 1992, p. 58).

4. **Environmental awareness:**

   . . . brings on awareness of the community and people, of health and safety needs (pollution of water, land, and air; recycling); provides exploration of surroundings (walk in the community), different types of weather; landscapes, vegetation, and needs.

5. **Intellectual development:**

   . . . promotes learning basic concepts (music and other), memories (recall), descriptions, problem solving, and is the foundation for later skills (reading).

   Learning musical concepts such as rhythm (steady and melodic pattern), tempo (fast, slow), pitch (high, low), timbre (tone quality of different instruments), dynamics (loud, soft), melody and related words, phrasing, accent, and mood promotes intellectual development.

6. **Language development:**

   . . . is encouraged by verbalizing (describing movements, tempo, rules, prepositions), learning and using symbols; imitating sounds (objects, animals, household, transportation, and so on); putting rhythm with familiar activities and objects (clipping rhythm of names, activities, and so on). A sensory approach to song learning that includes visual, kinesthetic, and aural stimulation increases children's vocabulary.

7. **Perceptual Awareness:**

   . . . includes being aware of one's senses, body space, and directionality (prepositions, obstacle courses, size, shape), and sharpens auditory discrimination skills (listening).

   For young children, music is primarily the discovery of sound—focused listening means helping children zero in on specific sounds or words that give direction. Listening is the basis of all musical learning. Early-childhood educators are very aware of the value of helping children sharpen auditory discrimination skills, but many have never considered it a part of music education.

8. **Physical/Motor Development:**

   . . . releases excess energy, reduces stress, increases strength and coordination; uses body in individual and group activities; teaches new skills; improves self-esteem; encourages leadership/followership, balance, one's own space, management of one's own body, indoor and outdoor activity.

   "Clapping, chanting, and playing simple instruments help children to develop basic motor coordination and control over simple body movements" (Kranyik, 1993, p. 25).

9. **Social development:**

   . . . increases self-concept/body awareness—success, self-esteem, security to risk one's ideas, releases stress, and provides for interactive singing and games

Doing group music activities can be fun—or boring—depending on teacher and child participation.

Music Education

Concerns have been raised about the music educator's approach to teaching prekindergarten children. Andress (1989) proposes a prekindergarten music curriculum model based on a synthesis of theories about the learning environment with the contributions of learning/play theorists and music educators. Music is primarily the discovery of sound. It should include purposive action or involvement, and should consider social, environmental, and procedural conditions (Wolf, 1992). Teachers will find that environmental conditions, such as space and attitude, are important components of successful music experiences.

Reassuring words and helpful ideas from Wolf (1992) give some comfort to music-shy teachers:

> A reasonable range (C to G or A) and uncomplicated rhythms add to the appropriateness. . . . Singing from the heart and setting aside any insecurities about singing will also boost the confidence of those early childhood teachers who shy away from singing with their classes. Children are not critics and actually learn best by hearing an unaccompanied voice. A child's ability to hear through harmony does not become sophisticated until after the age of five or six. . . . [M]usic can happen and often *does* spontaneously outside the group time we call *music time.* It is during these moments that the child appears to express the music from within himself (p. 58).

In early-childhood settings, teachers need to meet musically teachable moments with confidence by organizing music experiences to enhance the lives of young children and the total curriculum, while promoting good music education goals. Teachers with less musical education or background should not shy away from these important experiences, but should make a concerted effort to learn more about the basics of music and plan to include an abundance of focused listening, singing, and instrumental activities that encourage hearing and moving to the beat as well as music appreciation. Beat competency reflects the ability to keep time with or feel the pulse of the music (McDonald, 1979). As children grow they begin to go beyond their own personal sense of timing and develop the ability to relate to the timing of others. Keeping time with music is a skill that is gradually developed (Wolf, 1992).

Singing is a complex skill. In order to sing, children must listen, remember what they hear, and then control their voices to imitate the sounds they hear (Wolf, 1992). In selecting music for young children, pay attention to the range of notes and tempo within the song—some songs are pitched too high, some are monotonous because of limited range of notes, and others may be too complicated because of wide range or tempo.

For singing games, see Landeck (1950), Seeger (1980), and Glazier (1973, 1980). Other good sources are available at music stores or early-childhood education publishers.

Children love to sing their own improvised songs as well as structured songs of the culture. The developmental sequence as the young child grows in ability to sing alone or in a group involves (1) engaging in voice-inflection play, (2) singing her own rambling tunes, (3) listening to traditional songs of the culture, (4) singing global properties (most obvious words/melodic patterns) of traditional songs, and (5) displaying increased skill in performing lyrics with rhythmic and melodic accuracy (Andress, 1995, p. 102).

> The goal of the music educator . . . is to build through movement experiences toward musical understanding, rather than strive for the highly refined performance skills achieved by the movement educator. Movement experiences are a vital part of the music education program because they represent the sensing-doing stage of learning, which is a means to understanding more abstract musical ideas (Andress, 1991b, p. 22).

How the child responds to the experience depends on the child's disposition, developmental stage, and environmental factors.

The following suggestions were made by Andress (1991b) in encouraging movement and music experiences in young children:

1. A child-centered developmental approach: "As early childhood educators, it is important that we prepare young children to perform fundamental movement skills at an appropriate developmental level in order that they may feel and be physically competent" (Seefeldt, 1984, p. 35).
2. Modeling, imitated by 3- and 4-year-olds
3. Beat-keeping experiences for 4-year-olds: rather than clapping hands together to a given song, the teacher *should* beat the drum to the children's natural walking tempo (Andress, p. 25).
4. Arranging the environment for *enactive* (movement: such as swaying, bouncing, walking, and turning in response to the expressive whole of the music) and *iconic* (visual concrete representation using small props, including flowing scarves, streamers, and so on) levels of learning
5. Teacher interaction: combining modeling, describing, *and* suggesting so that the child's own creativity is allowed to flourish as awareness of music and movement is extended (p. 26)
6. Teachers who use types of interactional behaviors that reinforce music-related responses (p. 26)

Using Recorded Music

Based upon her study, early-childhood music specialist Gharavi (1993) identified five basic problems with preschool teachers' current practices in using music with young chil-

 *Reflection*

How could you teach about:

- musical sounds, patterns, and relations between each?
- sound (pitch, loudness, timbre, duration)?
- making and using musical instruments?
- developmentally appropriate music experiences?
- the role of children as composers, lyricists, orchestrators, choreographers, instrument makers, musicians?
- making new lyrics (or movements) to previous creations?
- music and movement of other cultures? ("Like the *whole language* approach to literacy, a *whole* music approach includes a broad range of music from other cultures and the use of music across the curriculum" (Hildebrandt, 1998).
- "creativity" without infringing upon or deleting traditional forms? (See Choksy, et al., 1986; McDonald & Simons, 1989; Peery 1993.)

dren. Her major findings and some recommendations and ways that recorded music can help include the following:

1. Sing at a comfortable pitch for children's voices.
2. Expand your musical repertoire by borrowing a songbook from the library and/or by asking a friend who can sing and play to make a tape for you.
3. Become familiar with the best music available for young children.
4. Provide a wide range of musical styles, particularly ethnic music.
5. Provide opportunities for quiet listening (p. 27).

Music is particularly important in the early-childhood program; leading theorist and Harvard professor Howard Gardner, who calls music one of the eight forms of multiple intelligences, has concluded, "Of all the gifts with which individuals may be endowed, none emerges earlier than musical talent" (1993, p. 99).

Too often, teachers reserve music for just a few minutes each day during circle time because they lack confidence in their own musical abilities. Yet, as we know, children form enduring attitudes about music during the early-childhood years. Thus, teachers of young children—regardless of musical talent, training, and performance skills—have a special responsibility for developing young children's musical abilities. Some good references about books and journals, recorded music, sound recordings, sources for children's music, and big-book song/picture books are listed at the end of the Jalongo (1996) article.

When high-quality musical recordings are used effectively, they will make a powerful, positive influence on children during their lifetime (see Figure 7.1).

Activities to Increase Music Abilities

Music is often limited to singing songs. Singing is fun and a good musical activity but is only one of many possibilities. Suggested activities in other chapters could be enhanced or varied with the addition of music. The following ideas are submitted as being useful; however, it is hoped that the reader will be creative when planning music experiences for young children.

Reflection

When you listen to live or recorded music, what kind of music makes you:

1. want to bond with individuals near you?
2. feel comfortable in the situation?
3. feel aggressive and/or irritated?
4. want to get active and/or expressive?
5. want peace and quiet?
6. feel relaxed, happier, more productive?
7. have a better understanding of (or appreciation for) other cultures?

What changes could you initiate in your classroom to help **you and the children** more fully enjoy and appreciate music experiences? ("[A]dults who willingly and flexibly infuse music in children's routines are nurturing powerful learning connections, . . . are engaging in developmentally appropriate practices," which "can have decisive, long-lasting impact on children's well-being and ability to learn" (Neelly, 2001, pp. 32, 35).

➤ Use finger plays, chants, and poems.
➤ Provide experiences with a variety of musical instruments.
➤ Make and use rhythm instruments, or pretend to play some.

Singing

Singing, an important benefit from music, greatly enhances vocabulary. Sometimes children sing words that just don't make sense, but they sing them anyway. Teachers need to note when children are having difficulty making sense of words and to help them more easily form a link from auditory, to oral, to print through rhyme, rhythm, repetition of vocabulary, and repetition of story structure. Language is natural and overlaps *all* curriculum areas, providing students with yet another opportunity to express themselves and learn from others.

Lyrics of Songs and Literacy   Singing with children should always be fun. It *is* fun! Singing is a natural form of expression for young children. Teachers need to assume a posture of confidence, apply their newfound knowledge, use the tools and secrets, and enjoy. Many wonderful musical moments are ahead.

1. Language of song is natural for children.
2. Help children to more easily form a link from oral to printed language through rhyme, rhythm, repetition of vocabulary, and repetition of story structure.
3. Lyrics overlap into curriculum areas, such as science, math, social studies, art, music, and others (see Figure 7.3).
4. Integrate skills. Karnowski (1986) encourages the integration of writing with music and art because "writing flourishes in a social environment where young children are free to use oral language, art, music, and drama to explore and enhance their writing" (p. 60).
5. Encourage language fluency or "meaning makers."
6. Use picture books to tie music and language together. Music and reading go together because singing is a celebration of language—consistent with the purposes of language—and puts readers in touch with satisfying meanings (Harp, 1988). Place the books in the book racks for children to explore and enjoy.

- Teach the song: Use music, sing words, invite children to join in the repetitions of the song. Talk about the meaning, discuss special words, and encourage motions; then add all the elements together.
- Link the song to print: Use a song picture and ask the children to discuss the pictures; read the book; reread the book with children adding information and asking questions; show lyrics written on a chart; invite children to "read" along as you point to each word in the song; highlight repetitious phrases.
- Involve the children in extension of literature activities: Dramatize the song; tape and replay the song; help children identify the printed word with the spoken word; create big books; make the book available for children's exploration and enjoyment.
- Encourage children to find other appropriate songs: Help them to make a printed and pictorial chart using original ideas, other song books, storybooks, and experiences.

Figure 7.3   Steps in Introducing Song Picture Books in the Classroom
Adapted from Barclay & Walwer, 1992, p. 78.

Teaching Songs   A few general suggestions help teachers prepare for singing with the children. First, be enthusiastic! Learn the song well before presenting it to the children (and teach it to support teachers). Select songs that have appeal for you and the children (their interests, their abilities, their stage of development). Children especially like using their own names, nonsense, body parts, and familiar experiences. Sing slowly and clearly, repeating the song several times. Then invite the children: "Sing along with me when you are ready." Use appropriate visual aids (which can be optional).

Songs are to be sung, not to be talked about. Pitcher et al. (1974) remind us as follows:

> The teacher should not expect a response on the first day or the second. It takes time for a young child to understand and remember the words and longer still to gain a clear conception of a melody. . . . Encourage him to sing, even if he isn't singing your tune. Vocal cords need exercise, and he needs vocal expression. Drill on either words or music is harmful for preschool children. Sing the song, straight through, and let him catch what he can, even if it is only the last note. Pitch will come on the wave of rhythm (p. 47).

If teachers do not read music, play an instrument, or have access to a songbook or cassette, they can ask a suitable person (music teacher, friend) to make them a recording so they can learn the song by singing with the recording.

Teachers often mistakenly believe that a piano or guitar is necessary to accompany singing with young children. Only a skilled musician can sing, play a difficult instrument, and watch the children rather than their music. Your voice is your most important musical instrument. An ordinary voice is quite adequate. It is your enthusiasm that will make the difference.

Start your singing time with familiar songs so the children will get comfortable and join in. At times it may be interesting to record a music session, then later evaluate the responses, the attention span, and requests or comments of the children. Young children learn songs best through repetition. They do not read, their experience is limited, and they cannot remember new long sentences and phrases. The song should be short (no more than two phrases of words), easy to sing, and have familiar ideas, repetition, a distinct rhythm, and a limited range of notes.

Chants   Chants and other oral repetitions (poems, games, sayings, and so on) are beneficial for most young children—providing they are done in a voluntary, enjoyable manner. Research shows that children's success in reading and writing depends upon a solid

Children usually like singing familiar or new songs in the presence of other children.

background in the development of oral language skills (Hennings, 1990). With an increased awareness of whole-language philosophy, educators are realizing that meaningful, interactive experiences with language provide the most effective curriculum for developing speaking as well as reading, writing, and listening skills (Sampson, Sampson, & Van Allen, 1991). Teachers are trying to incorporate as many interesting language experiences into each day as they can (Buchoff, 1994, p. 26).

According to Anderson & Lapp (1988), a *chant* is any group of words that is recited with a lively beat. Through chanting, all children speak together in unison and need not fear intimidation. They learn the importance of clear and expressive pronunciation as their voices combine to make the message of the chant come alive.

The values of chants can include all the following:

➤ perfection through repetitious or rhyming words
➤ success to even a shy child, a poor speaker, or a reluctant reader
➤ experience with and perfection of listening and writing skills
➤ introduction to poetry and rhyming
➤ cooperation and participation in a group
➤ rhythmic patterning
➤ supplementation to curriculum areas
➤ introduction to new cultures and situations
➤ humor
➤ practice in hearing and seeing words (on a chart)
➤ body involvement (snapping fingers, tapping toes)
➤ expanding curriculum (reading with speaking, body motions, and so on) and ways to learn a concept
➤ combining senses (seeing, hearing, playing instrument or clapping, dramatizing)
➤ thinking up new chants or dramatizing current ones

 **Reflection**

Should we wait for children to become verbal before we sing, chant, or verbalize with them? If we do, the child *may miss* these important benefits:

- being soothed and feeling that someone cares
- having a focal point
- feeling a closeness with a caregiver
- learning about daily routines and cooperativeness
- building trust and self-esteem
- comforting during times of separation
- poetic experiences and visual imagery
- opportunities to model or mimic sounds and phrases
- stretching his mental abilities
- experiences in humor and incongruities in verse
- opportunities to practice large and small motor skills (rhythm, bouncing, whole-body movement, hand and finger manipulation)
- eye-hand coordination and exercise
- important language experiences
- attentiveness to the human voice
- listening experiences
- many other benefits that affect children personally

Introducing Rhythm Instruments

Because of frustrating experiences with rhythm instruments, some teachers include this experience infrequently or never in their curriculum. Suppose someone placed in front of you a very exciting and new object—and told you not to touch it? Wouldn't that be frustrating? Now, also suppose that you knew what to do with the object and your body was saying, "Pick it up and see what you can do with it!" and somebody kept saying, "I'll show or tell you how to do it." The minute you got the go-ahead, wouldn't you do as much, as fast, and as loud as you could? Does it make sense to place something like a rhythm instrument in front of a child and then tell him not to touch it?

Teachers may want to introduce one kind of instrument at a time. They should try to have enough of the same kind so that each child can explore it on the same day. When first introducing the instrument, they may want to talk about its properties or use. Then they should identify a signal of when to start and when to stop playing and let the children try it. If the number of instruments is limited, the children take turns so that each child knows he will get a chance. On other days, different instruments are introduced. After the children are exposed to several kinds, the instruments are combined for a more advanced experience. Each child should have an opportunity to use all the instruments—even if for a short time.

On return use of the instruments, the children are allowed to select the instruments they want to play, with the understanding that there will be trading. The children can be responsible for passing out and gathering in the instruments.

Playing Musical Instruments   Instruments can be used in the learning environment to explore shape, size, and sound relationships; to organize, order, and classify sounds; to use sounds to express musical ideas (loud and soft composition created with a wood block) and nonmusical ideas (the wood-block sound of galloping ponies); or, when developmentally appropriate, to play simple accompaniments for songs and perform rhythmic and melodic ideas.

Weikart (1985), a pioneer in teaching rhythm to children, suggests that children pat the beat in a bilateral or parallel movement by simultaneously tapping their hands on their knees. This is conveniently done during chants, rhymes, or music that has a very evident pulse or beat. Until a child is ready to pat the beat, the teacher can pat the steady beat on the child's knees or shoulders as music is played or sung. The more experience the child has, the quicker the competency develops. Experiences with different types of music (marches, waltzes, polkas) encourage the child's ability to keep time with the music.

Values for Children

To develop in young children a variety of skills:

➤ Play a variety of records, tapes, and music—classical, contemporary, instrumental, rhythmical, tempo, participation, listening, and so on.
➤ Teach the children how to use tape recorders. Tapes with songs, instrumentation, and stories can be checked out from many libraries. They make great individual or group listening opportunities. They last better than records; they don't scratch as easily, can be used in the car or outdoors, and are more available. (CDs are more expensive and may not have as appropriate a selection of music for young children at present.)
➤ Sing songs (with and without aids, with and without actions).
➤ Sing scale songs ("I Love Little Pussy," "Do, Re, Mi").
➤ Encourage children to sing while they play.
➤ Often, let the children choose songs to sing.
➤ For children who are reluctant to suggest songs, make a large cube with a picture for a song on each side. Roll the cube like a die and sing the song that comes up on top. Or make a singing tree. Pick a leaf off the tree. Turn it over for the song title. Or make a flower out of construction paper. Print the name of a song on it. Attach it to a straw and plant it in a clay pot of dirt. Let a child select a flower and then sing that song. Or place objects that represent certain songs in a basket. A child selects an object to sing about.
➤ Record and replay the children's voices (singing, talking, playing).
➤ Over a period of time, teach about three groups of instruments: woodwinds, percussion, and strings.
➤ Invite guests who sing, dance, or play musical instruments on the level of the children.
➤ Plan an activity around high/low, fast/slow, or loud/soft music.
➤ Identify natural rhythm in the classroom or play yard, such as clocks, squeaks, drips, bouncing balls, and swaying trees.
➤ Go on a walking field trip to hear and identify rhythm.
➤ Go places where music can be heard (band or orchestra practice, parade, sporting event, stores, television studio, dance studio).
➤ During each season, go for a walk and listen to different sounds (for example, crunch of ice and snow, snap of a twig, rustle of leaves, pattern of rain, blowing of wind, stepping on stones or in puddles).
➤ Combine experiences so the children can listen, create, sing, move, and experiment with sounds (based on the developmental level of the children).
➤ Use music with other curriculum areas (art and science) and activities (free play and snack).
➤ Be constantly aware of opportunities for spontaneous music.

Developmental Characteristics

Age 2: Moves up and down to music, tries to imitate sounds, and is fascinated by simple songs.

Enjoys bouncing motion, swaying, swinging arms, nodding head, tapping feet, clapping hands, but demonstrates little or no rhythmic accuracy for any length of time.

May walk with arms outstretched for balance.

Primarily a listener; jabbers.

Loves action songs and finger plays. Sings (or hums) parts of songs spontaneously with or without an adult but matches few tones correctly.

Experiments with rhythm. Walks on tiptoes. Pushes and pulls toys. Actively explores his environment.

Climbs stairs with both feet on each step; jumps immaturely (2-foot takeoff). Stands on low balance beam. Walks forward, sideways, and backward.

Rarely still—wiggles and toddles, bounces and waves, jumps and claps, springs and chases, hides and seeks.

Age 3: May or may not sing, but likes songs and rhythm.

Walks a 10-foot line, heel to toe. Hops two to three steps. Walks on balance beam for short distance. Climbs stairs with alternating feet. Throws ball about 10 feet.

Rides tricycle.

Is excited about walking backward without peeking.

No longer walks with arms outstretched. Gallops, jumps, runs, and walks in *fairly* good time to music.

Age 4: Creates own rhythm and keeps it somewhat. Enjoys singing, especially action songs. Is more observant of sound and rhythm around him.

Walks easily up and down stairs; runs well, jumps, and walks on a balance beam.

Likes to be independent; resists many instructions.

Feels quite confident about body skills; notes abilities of other children.

Has good balance; likes to carry liquids without spilling them.

Can throw objects at a target.

Enjoys climbing and obstacle courses.

Begins to kick large balls. Shows more controlled balance: swings back and forth, stands on one foot.

Fine movements are better differentiated.

Age 5: Enjoys singing; has large repertoire of songs.

Likes rhythm instruments; can keep time. Participates to records and tapes; is coordinated.

Has interest in musical instruments; enjoys guests.

Learns to skip. Has boundless energy; wiggles, runs, hops, jumps, and climbs with proficiency.

Attempts roller-skating, rope jumping, stilt walking, and swing pumping. Is more coordinated at throwing and catching.

Broad jumps two to three feet.

Rides a two-wheel bike.

Plays games with simple rules; enjoys company.

➤ Have some specific listening experiences. Make sounds and then have the children repeat and identify them.

➤ Clap rhythm patterns to names, poems, and nursery rhymes and have the children repeat them or do them with you.

➤ Use body actions to music ("Head, Shoulders, Knees, and Toes").

➤ Exercise to music (aerobics are popular with children).

➤ Provide props that encourage rhythm and music (blocks, sticks, coconut shells, shakers, bells).

➤ Use a piano often, if available. You can vary the tempo and rhythm for exciting activities.

➤ Obtain an Autoharp, an excellent instrument to use with children (available in different sizes and prices).

➤ Fill matching film cans for identifying sounds.

➤ Use visual aids to create interest in music (objects, posters, charts, pictures, movie boxes, transparencies, costumes, flip charts, drawing on a chalkboard).

➤ Play circle games ("Mulberry Bush," "Ring Around-a-Rosy," "Hokey Pokey," "This Is the Way We . . . ").

➤ Practice body sounds (hum, click teeth, snap fingers, blink eyes, clap, slap, rub, tap, shake).

➤ Use music outdoors often.

➤ Provide guidelines so children will know what is expected of them in various activities. Can they play the autoharp, or is it just for teachers? How about the new dancing drum? Do the instruments stay in a certain area? Who can operate the record player and tape recorder?

➤ Provide opportunities to support musical concepts such as rhythm, tempo, timbre, dynamics, and melody.

➤ Sing and hum in the presence of children.

➤ Put bells on different body parts—experiment.

➤ Play music boxes that feature different tunes.

➤ Use timers and clocks that produce unusual dings and ticks.

➤ Use books with sounds: *Old MacDonald Had a Farm, This Old Man,* Margaret Wise Brown's series on sounds, and so on.

➤ Play quiet background music.

➤ Chant ideas (repetition).

➤ Adapt familiar songs ("Mary Wore Her Red Dress").

➤ Encourage parents to have music at home. Give simple ideas.

➤ Play rhythm games.

➤ Move or dance to music.

See the activities in the section titled "Listening" in Chapter 5.

"The wonderful result of including a lot of musical experiences in programs for young children—whether teachers view themselves as musical or not—is that children *learn* a lot about music, and also about language arts and much more, even if teachers can't itemize what it all is exactly" (Wolf, 1992, p. 56).

The Pillsbury Foundation Studies of 1937–1938 (Zimmerman, 1985), set up to discover the principles that govern children's relationship to music, resulted in four significant insights still meaningful today:

➤ For young children, music is primarily the discovery of sound.

➤ Music time with children should include their purpose, action, or involvement.

➤ In planning music time, it is necessary to consider social, environmental, and procedural conditions.

➤ Spontaneous music making should be carefully observed.

Some things to consider are developmental stages of the children; environmental considerations of the room; meeting musical and curricular objectives; focused listening, singing accuracy, beat competency, and music appreciation.

Helping children zero in on specific sounds or words that give direction is called *focused listening* and includes singing games, walking/running/skipping music, and songs that provide vocabulary for movement and silence for stopping. Careful listening is the basis for musical learning; it is the ability to focus the mind on sounds perceived. Activities that focus on auditory activity meet the same objective.

Auditory-discrimination skills are important in learning; however, some teachers have not considered music as one of the avenues for helping children develop these skills. Keeping time to music, keeping in tune, or maintaining a steady beat heighten listening skills. Recordings that give directions or sound cues, songs that have movement cues, and games that require a response are examples of appropriate musical listening activities. Children (and adults) can learn to recognize patterns, cues, and interactions from musical listening activities—live or recorded. Thus, their focused attention is helping them develop accurate listening skills. See Table 7.1 for ideas about young children and development through music.

Expecting young children to sing with accuracy is premature. This accuracy is basically established by age 8 (McDonald, 1979); therefore, before we can assume the responsibility of teaching singing skills, we need to understand how young children learn to sing. Music educators have determined various stages of singing development. For instance, Smale (1985) organized these stages into a sequential list: (1) musical babbling; (2) tagging on; (3) talking/singing; (4) increased accuracy (ages 3–4); (5) accurate

Table 7.1 Music and Young Children

Characteristics of Young Children	How to Support their Development Through Music, Movement, and Sound Experiences
They are active	Provide ways for them to touch, move, and manipulate their bodies (rhythm instruments, a song manipulative; a firm, steady beat; active participation).
They learn through play (specific developmental stages)	Encourage them to watch, play alone, play with others, play musical instruments, march, sing and hear music.
They are inquisitive	Expose them to a rich environment of singing, playing instruments, listening to music, and creating music; be involved with them.
They have a limited voice range	Select and use songs that have a reasonable range.
They like to mimic	Give them many listening experiences so they can reproduce a song, an experience, or an activity.
They like repetition	Even after you tire, give the child an opportunity to *re*-experience the music, the movement, and the experience.
They have a limited vocabulary	Introduce and verbalize music and language experiences and give children plenty of opportunities to repeat, repeat, and repeat.
They learn from models	Be a model (singing, movement, and so on) but encourage them to express *their own ideas*. A child copies what she sees. If models are excited, interested, and expressive, so will the child be.

*Young children respond differently to music activities: some are eager, some reluctant,
some distracted.*

singing of simple songs, alone; and (6) accurate singing with a group. Wolf (1992)
states:

> First the child listens to sounds. Babies are likely to first hear musical sound through the human
> voice, although TV, radio, records, and music boxes are also usually part of their environment early
> on. As a result, the child invents musical sound sometimes referred to as musical babbling. This in-
> vention precedes imitation, or copying what has been sung. . . . Imitation is observed as toddlers lag
> behind a bit or tag on to the end of a song. From the age of three or so, children progressively increase
> their ability to join in song. First they join in a little, and by school age they sing at group time with
> enthusiasm. Our job is to provide a repertoire of singable songs through recordings as well as
> teacher-sung songs (p. 57).

Young children learn songs best by hearing an unaccompanied voice, when the
range is reasonable (C to G or A), and when they listen attentively before trying to join
in the singing. Their ability to keep time on their own often has no relationship to others (Wolf, 1992).

Movement Education

"Movement, in addition to singing and playing instruments, continues to be one of the
most important instructional tools available to the educator for setting an environment
in which children learn to perform, describe, and create music," writes Andress (1991b,
p. 22). To be developmentally appropriate, free choice and games without rules are more
usable than structured music activities for this age group. Simple opportunities such as
clapping or playing simple instruments help children to develop basic motor coordination
and control over simple body movements. Children with more advanced gross motor coordination enjoy musical instruments and large muscle movements as they move isolated body parts, practice and control their movements, and respond to rhythm using
their entire bodies. But a child's response to music depends on disposition, developmental stage, and environmental factors.

Reflection

Observing a group of teachers in training, one notes that they are participating to "This Is a Song about Colors" (Hap Palmer record; check supply catalogs for ordering information). It has good rhythm, it makes one think and act simultaneously, it is fun to participate with others, it's exhilarating, and it's popular with adults. But then adults have learned to recognize colors in shades and hues beyond the abilities of children—and if one doesn't get to participate because he is wearing lavender, magenta, or chartreuse rather than the basic colors, one either enjoys the participation of others or pretends to have the right color. Now, look carefully at using the same experience with the following groups:

- 3-year-olds (2-year-olds would be a disaster!)
- 4-year-olds
- 5-year-olds
- special-needs or bilingual children
- older children and adults

Consider the background of the individuals who would most benefit from the experience. Consider the feelings of children who had not learned their colors yet. Consider children who need more time to put together two ideas before acting (color and action). Now consider the preparation necessary for a color-song experience to be stimulating and successful for each of these groups.

Example: for 3-year-olds, you may use one or two colors only, and give each child a prop of that (or one other) color. You would surely want to slow down the tempo of the action—you could just say a color name and mention an action: "Red stand up." "Blue turn around." "Red smile." "Blue wiggle your toes."

Teachers need to modify ideas and activities so the children will enjoy the activities and find joy and success in them. You don't just use them because they are there or because others have enjoyed them. You modify and adapt!

Readers should not assume that children know how to move. That is, if the teacher wants the children to hop like a bunny, she should first talk about bunnies and how they move. Someone could demonstrate (before group hopping) how a bunny might hop. This way each child will have his definition of hopping (and all definitions are accepted) prior to the activity.

Movement exploration, a method of teaching that considers the development of the total child, encourages children to apply problem-solving techniques and to explore fantasies and relationships with others, while experiencing natural development of motor skills and knowledge of the operation of their own bodies. The self-concept of the children can grow in positive directions because the teacher establishes nonjudgmental techniques while demonstrating respect for each child's abilities (Sullivan, 1982, p. 1).

The Sullivan book (1982), available from NAEYC, provides countless movement activities mainly for working with 3- and 4-year-olds, but does extend through 8-year-olds. Activities allow for creativity with adult support and modeling. Different types, tempos, and instruments can add challenge or success to activities. The purposes of movement sessions include complementing free play, concepts to be taught, relaxation, interaction, change of pace, self-image development, and others.

Stretching muscles to musical rhythms is fun.

Some of the equipment, materials, and activities that might be included in outdoor areas at various times during the year are included in Chapter 3, The Value of Play, in the section titled "Outdoor Play."

> The young child's movement is an important musical response because it is non-verbal and allows the observer to better understand what aspects of the music the child is sensing. Early movement activities center on the body (body touch, finger plays, song games) and responses to the wholeness of the music heard. The child begins to refine gestures to perform and describe introductory-level music information as heard in timbre, expressive controls, rhythm, melody, and form (Andress, 1991a, p. 103).

For some reason, children's play is associated with noise and outdoor space. But much valuable play goes on within the classroom, provided there is time and space to do it. Both indoor and outdoor play are valuable. Movement and action are essential to children's development in general and to intellectual development in particular. Through it, children sense and act upon their environment.

Piaget (1974) called the first stage of children's intellectual development the *sensorimotor* stage, indicating the importance of experiencing the world primarily through their senses and motor abilities. He argued that the sensorimotor stage is the bedrock on which the subsequent hierarchy of all intelligence is built. Between birth and age 5 or 6, children's bodies, as much as their minds, are the organ of intelligence.

From Olds (1994) we read:

> A facet of learning to read may illustrate the relationship between movement and learning. Until children have experiences orienting their bodies in space by going up, on, under, beside, inside, and in front of things, it is possible they will have difficulty dealing with letter identification and the orientation of symbols on a page. The only difference between a small "b" and a small "d," for example, both of which are composed of a line and a circle, depends upon orientation, i.e., which side of the circle is the line on? Zeller found that 98% of the 500 learning disabled children she tested were characterized as being physically *clumsy*. Similarly, Jean Ayres demonstrated that learning disabled children respond more readily to symbolic tutelage after being trained in the use of fundamental motor patterns that promote sensory integration—crawling, falling, rocking, and spinning. Thus, learning disabilities may be caused or exacerbated by immature or improper development of children's sensorimotor systems (p. 33).

Movement is very important in the learning of a child, who must be personally and physically involved. It can only be done *by* the person, not *for* the person: her movements,

Reflection

Off-limits use of facilities includes:

- Climbing on tables
- Jumping off furniture (tables, beds, cupboards, and so on)
- Crawling under low furniture
- Sliding down banisters
- Balancing on ledges
- Hiding in closets
- Climbing in high or dangerous places
- Standing on moving objects (swings, wheel toys, and so on)
- Using ropes in an unsafe way
- Playing near hot equipment (heater, furnace, and so on)
- Using flame without adequate supervision
- Other hazards that may appear in *some* settings

Take a careful look around your indoor and outdoor spaces and add other specific "off-limits" activities. (For safety information, see Taylor, 2002, pp. 322–354.)

her manipulation of materials. Overprotective caregivers must make the environment safe for the actions and interactions of *all* children. Movement is essential to the maintenance of the body's integrity. Adults should be aware of the rules, admonitions, and confinement they place upon children. True, adults need to take responsibility for the safety and protection of children, but they must plan for and accept the curiosity and exploration of children. Too many restrictions make children insecure rather than secure. Space is important and should be fully utilized. The requirement in many states is 35 square feet per child indoors to support gross motor play; others feel that is too cramped. Caregivers should carefully evaluate the amount of space they have available and the best use of it. At home some children must live in cramped spaces, but the center should find ways to make space for active indoor play. Limiting active play to the outdoors is not an option. "Failure to meet children's varied needs for movement prevents them from having experiences fundamental to their intellectual, social, and physical development," cautions Olds (1994, p. 33).

Activities should be based on available time and on equipment that is sturdy, safe, and well maintained. Activities should be supervised, developmentally appropriate, and stimulating. (See Figure 7.4.)

Other activities to consider and plan for (according to the child's developmental abilities, safety, supervision, and other applicable conditions): hanging (to strengthen arms) and sliding (for coordination). Prepositions that encourage movement include *on (above), under (beneath), over, around, through, by, between,* and so on.

"Physical fitness refers to the level of health development and functional capacity of the body. A person needs to develop and maintain an adequate level of cardiovascular endurance, muscular strength, muscular endurance, flexibility, and body leanness to be deemed physically fit" (Seefeldt, 1984, p. 35).

Children move because it is essential to their development; they explore, discover, and interact with the world. They develop and strengthen muscles, refine motor skills, learn vocabulary and concepts, better understand their world, work out problems, and improve communication. Movement is in all areas of the curriculum and should not be limited to a certain time, place, or activity. The ability and flexibility to move freely in

Balancing	*Balance beam:* vary width of board, adjust height, adjust slope. *Rope:* vary width, vary length. *Experiences:* vary body usage (one or two feet, on your back, on your stomach, seated, on knees, on hands, on head), balance on a stationary object.
Jumping	*Off* low (but stable) objects, from one object to another (such as colored paper shapes), on one or two feet, from a running or stationary position, *up* onto a safe object, onto something soft, *across* objects (small rope, a stuffed toy, ribbons, balls, puddles), *through* things (hoops, an inner tube, a large opening), *on* an old mattress, partially inflated inner tubes, or small trampoline.
Swinging	Seated in a swing, on study bars, using one or both hands, by knees (for children who are developed enough), holding onto ropes with knots to secure hands.
Throwing	Space, incentive, balls, beanbags, targets, companionship, challenge.
Body movement	Space, interesting props (streamers, ribbons, balloons—using caution with balloons—and so on), stories, music, companionship, dress-up clothing, encouragement, attention, experiences.
Climbing	Appropriate equipment, space, time, supervision.
Crawling	Interesting places, tunnels, suggested activities, reenacting stories, imitating (babies, animals).

Figure 7.4   Activities That Encourage Movement

the classroom create an atmosphere that encourages interaction, divergent thinking, and individuality.

Teachers need to think in terms of movement as they plan their physical facilities and prepare their curriculum activities. They must be flexible to the needs, responses, interests, and abilities of the children they teach. Movement interests of children may be spontaneous, planned, short-lived (seconds or minutes), or continued over a period of time (hours, days, weeks). Activities may be initiated by children (excited about a trip or experience) or teachers who are perceptive to spontaneous stimuli, interests of children, or the need for a change of pace.

All teachers and children move from location to location, activity to activity, or child to child. Transitions to facilitate these changes can be smooth, incidental, planned, or purposeful. (See the discussion of transition activities in Chapter 12).

Fundamental movement skills and combinations of movements that a child is neurologically ready to develop and refine during the preschool years include locomotor, manipulative, nonlocomotor, and perceptual-motor development skills (see Figure 7.5).

Recent research reveals that many young children have not developed their perceptual-motor skills, especially in the areas of visual awareness, auditory awareness and time awareness (Weikart, 1985).

> Many educators believe that children will automatically develop fundamental movement skills when they are ready. This is only partially true. Maturation provides a young child with the ability to perform a specific movement skill at a very low level of performance. It is only with continuous practice and instruction that a child's level of performance will increase (Seefeldt, 1984, p. 35).

Helping Young Children Develop Their Bodies Properly

> Designing and implementing a developmentally appropriate movement curriculum will take time and effort. But it is worth it. If we are concerned with the whole child, we need to plan and implement appropriate activities that will facilitate the development of young children's motor skills (Seefeldt, 1984, p. 35).

Locomotor	Walking, running, leaping, jumping, hopping, galloping, sliding, skipping, climbing, and propelling a wheel toy, such as a tricycle, scooter, or wagon
Manipulative	Throwing, kicking, punting, striking, volleying, bouncing, dribbling (hand), dribbling (foot), rolling, catching, and trapping
Nonlocomotor (balance)	Bending, stretching, twisting, turning, swinging upright and inverted balances, body rolling, dodging, and beam walking (Gallahue, 1982)
Perceptual-motor	Involves monitoring and interpreting sensory data and responding in movement. It is generally accepted that this type of development includes awareness of each of the following: *Body skills:* Ability to name, locate, and identify the function of the body parts *Time skills:* Ability to move to a steady beat, perform a series of movements in a coordinated manner, speed up or slow down movements, and freeze movements without falling down *Spatial skills:* Ability to know internally how much space the body occupies and to control the body as it moves through space *Directional skills:* The internal ability to identify the dimensions of external space—up, down, in, over, under *Visual skills:* Ability to perceive and copy demonstrated movements *Auditory skills:* Ability to attend to verbal directions and discriminate between a variety of sounds.

Figure 7.5 Fundamental Movement Skills
Adapted from Poest et al., 1990.

We can do this through:

1. *Fundamental movement skills:* Teachers and parents cannot assume that young children will get enough of the age- and individual-appropriate motor activities to provide them with adequate motor skills.
2. *Physical fitness:* Daily fitness activities, good models, good stress-reducers, outdoor (walk, run, gallop, climb, jump) and indoor (music, imitate animals, variety of stationary movements) activities. Encourage children to try more challenging things and to do them longer, according to time, space, and interest.
3. *Perceptual-motor skills:* Activities such as "Simon Says" for body awareness and visual clues; moving (tapping, marching, skipping, and so on); nursery rhymes, chants, songs; obstacle courses, directions in space: over, around, through.

Andress (1991b) states:

> We, as practitioners, tend to think from an activity base, constantly searching for "fun" ways to use movement and music in circle time sessions. We must abandon this practice now and use a child-centered approach wherein materials and activities reflect concerns for the various stages of development (p. 27).

Young children are doers, talkers, and movers. Their bodies are not naturally still; however, movement should be encouraged in the right places and in the right ways, with time, space, ideas, and props.

When children discover the great potential in their body movements, they want to explore the possibilities. They test, try to understand and accept their bodies, and begin to feel confident and to lose self-consciousness. They feel joy and pleasure in free movement. Movement exploration can lead directly into a creative dance or a cultural experience. As such, it is the process, the solving of a problem, and the discovering of a new way, rather than an end product, that are important.

Listening is an important part of music.

Movement may take place in a quiet and solitary setting or in an active group. Moha, a quiet 3-year-old, sat listening to a record. Then he commented: "It goes around and around!" His head began going around and around, then his arms, and finally his whole body. He was transferring the motion from the record to his body and finding it to be a delightful experience.

Movement is a viable and important part of the daily curriculum—not an add-on. It can easily be integrated as an expression medium. It is natural, essential, and valuable for physical and mental health and can also enhance academic learning; it aids in problem solving, exploration, and success. It helps to encourage inquisitiveness and creativ-

 Reflection

Little research has been done in the area of preschool fitness. We know, however, that:

[T]he first signs of arteriosclerosis are now appearing at about age five. Children need to exercise aerobically at least three times a week and eat properly to reduce this disease process.

[C]hildren are not engaging in the moderate- to high-intensity physical activity necessary to increase cardiovascular fitness.

[C]ardiovascular fitness is not enhanced during most childhood sport and recreation activities, recess, or play time since the movement is not continuous.

[F]or every 100 children, at least 16 are obese (Mayer, 1968); the prevalence of obesity increased by approximately 40 percent from the 1960s to the 1970s in both children and youth.

[Y]oung children are especially weak in the areas of muscular strength, cardiovascular endurance, and body leanness. The research seems to show that children are in worse physical condition now than 20 years ago.

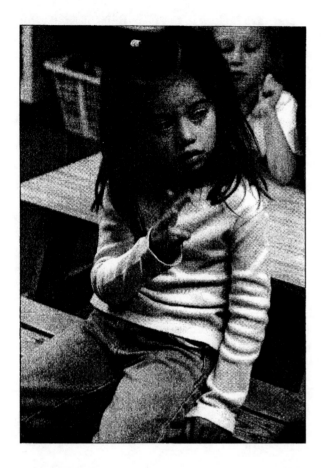

Small muscles can be developed through music activities.

ity in children, who have an innate drive to master their environment through sensori-motor activities. Through space exploration, they can develop body control; ease and confidence in movement; motor skills of coordination, strength, flexibility, balance, laterality, and directionality. Their bodies move in time (fast, medium, sudden, or sustained), in force (strong or light), in flow (bound, free, or a combination), in tension/relaxation, and in such relationships as near and far, front and back, over and under, lead and follow, or unison and contrast.

Factors that affect movement are: (1) body awareness and actions (what is moved), (2) space (where one moves), (3) effort, or quality, of movement (how), and (4) relationship (with whom or what). Appropriate experiences can be provided so children can practice and become more proficient in the use of their bodies. Competition, such as pitting boys against girls or children against each other, is avoided. Rather each child tries to improve his own physical skills and abilities.

Children who are restricted or forbidden to explore are at a definite disadvantage. One young child was given an ample number of playthings and good physical care and attention, but was restricted in space. She soon became listless, subject to illness, overweight, and insecure. Becoming concerned, her mother sought professional help, only to be encouraged to "open up the child's world." The child soon returned to her usual happy self when she was allowed more freedom to explore, find toys of her interest, interact with other children, and become more independent.

Activities to Increase Movement Skills

➤ Place a series of footprints on the floor. Ask the children to walk or skip on them, jump from one to another, roll over them, and so on. Have footprints spaced at varying intervals that lead to another activity, a neglected area, and so on.

➤ Provide a balance beam. For beginners, have it close to the floor. Raise it as the children develop skill.

➤ Encourage the children to act out their feelings (stamp, pound, yell, glide, skip, dance).

➤ Tell them to act out movement in nature (sway, bend, tap).

➤ Encourage each child to move in her own way.

➤ Give mental images and have the children imitate them (rowing a boat, walking in wind, flying like a bird, walking with a broken leg, pulling a heavy load, carrying a vase on the head, and so on).

➤ Use records or tapes that encourage gross movement, listening, interpreting, and moving.

➤ Provide props that encourage movement, such as scarves, balls, clothes, and streamers.

➤ Make obstacle courses both indoors and outdoors. Verbally tell the children what is expected, or have indicators for *over this, around that, under this, between those,* and so on.

➤ Encourage the children to explore space by running, rolling, jumping, swinging arms, and so on. At times have them confined to a small area; at other times let them move as far as they desire.

➤ Provide a mat for tumbling, jumping, and rolling.

➤ Do activities using various body parts (touch your elbow; touch your elbow to your toe; put your hand on your knee; put your nose on your knee).

➤ Encourage the children to make their bodies tall, small, straight, or crooked.

➤ Provide many opportunities to practice locomotor skills (walking, crawling, hopping, jumping, running, leaping, skipping, galloping, rolling, climbing, sliding).

➤ Provide many opportunities to practice nonlocomotor skills (bending, swaying, rocking, stretching, turning, pulling, pushing, twisting, curling, standing, sitting, kneeling, reaching).

Music is a great transition to move children from one area or activity to another!

➤ Go on a walk; jump over cracks, straddle a rock, balance on a curb, skip around a fountain, and so on.

➤ Play the sponge game. Each child has a sponge (approximately 1 by 4 by 6 inches). The children follow the directions of a teacher or another child: Put your sponge on your head. Walk without letting it fall off. Put it on your shoulder, your arm, your shoe. Crawl with it on your back. Jump over it. Sit on it. Roll on it. Length of this activity is determined by the interest of the children.

➤ Dramatize stories or activities.

➤ Sing songs that encourage actions (for example, "Wiggle Song," "Head, Shoulders, Knees, and Toes," "Do as I'm Doing," "The Bus Song").

➤ Ask the children to go to various parts of the room without using their feet, like a ball, backward, and so on.

➤ Have the children pretend to be Raggedy Ann and Raggedy Andy (no bones).

➤ Use body cards and have the children model poses. (See Chapter 12.)

➤ Plan activities during which the children use their bodies to learn about location (especially good for learning about prepositions).

➤ Pantomime different activities.

➤ Help children see movement in everyday things such as animals, people, or objects (clocks, faucets, cars, trains).

➤ Suggest ideas to children and let them express their individuality (colors, moods, holidays). Be prepared for nonresponses. These ideas may be too advanced for young children.

➤ Do simple aerobics with the children.

➤ Make and use equipment (hula hoops out of plastic tubing, scoops out of plastic bleach bottles, and balls from yarn).

➤ Use a hula hoop. Move inside of the hoop, roll it, jump into it, crawl through it, or share it with a friend.

➤ Combine activities using a rope, hula hoop, beanbag, and ball.

➤ Play games such as Twister, "Mother, May I?," "What Can You Do?," and tag.

➤ Make body shadows.

➤ Pretend to jump across a stream, narrow at first, then wider and wider.

➤ Follow a rhythm chart. Picture of a hand indicates when to clap; a picture of a foot indicates when to stamp.

➤ Practice ball handling as the children develop such skills as rolling, catching, throwing, bouncing, and kicking.

➤ Use beanbags to throw at a target (bucket, box), kick them, or balance them on the head or back.

➤ Provide rope experiences. Rope can be made into shapes, jumped over, crawled under, or used to circumscribe space.

➤ Get a small parachute (a tablecloth or sheet may also work) and have children try the activities in the following list. Original activities are also encouraged.
Marshmallow: Hold parachute waist high. On signal, throw arms and parachute as high as possible. Let parachute float down softly.
Waves: Gently wave parachute up and down and observe rippling motion.
Cover-up: Hold parachute waist high. On signal, extend arms upward and, while still holding on to parachute, turn around and squat on ground. Chute covers participants.
Bouncers: Place two yarn or other small balls in center of parachute. Try to keep them bouncing by shaking parachute up and down.
Catchers: Space teachers and children around the outside of parachute. Slowly move parachute up and down. On count of three, the teacher calls either "boys" or "girls." The called group runs under parachute, and others try to catch them.

➤ Show pictures of animals and have children imitate their movements, such as sliding like a snake, jumping like a kangaroo, flying like a bird, and hopping like a bunny.

Reflection

Some adults try so hard to include music in the lives of children that they greatly overdo it: Take for example the adult (teacher, parent, other) who insists that all instructions and interactions be carried out in a musical or rhythmical manner: One must sing all instructions, stories, songs, responses, requests, and communications to one another. How long would you last in their environment? Rather than stimulate language, movement, and rhythm, it would frustrate and discourage anyone who wanted to communicate with another.

➤ Have an animal walk. Imitate a bear, seal, crab, frog, duck, or monkey.
➤ Take a field trip to a gymnasium, sports arena, or dance studio.
➤ Have the children move as they would in different occupations (sanitation worker, engineer, baker, mountain climber, forest ranger, and so on). Note that occupations can be for both sexes.
➤ Tell each child to form a circle with his body; then add a partner to form a circle; continue to add more children to form still larger circles. Do the same with other shapes such as a line, square, or triangle.
➤ Show pictures of a circus. Have the children pretend to be dancing bears, prancing horses, stalking tigers, trunk-and-tail-holding elephants, and performing lions.
➤ Let the children practice coordination skills by walking first on a piece of string or yarn placed on the floor, then on the wide side of a balance beam placed on the floor, then on the narrow side of the beam. Begin to raise the beam slightly from the floor as skills develop.
➤ Make a number of pictures of animals and tape them to the floor. Bunnies mean *hop;* frogs *jump;* and ducks *sway.* Start with a series of the same animal; later mix up the pictures so the actions will vary as the child moves around.
➤ Demonstrate flexibility and stretching to children by using a large rubber band. Ask the children to use their bodies in the same way, stretching and flexing in various ways.
➤ Take a make-believe ride in an elevator, stretching high, higher, highest as the elevator goes up and low, lower, lowest as it comes down.

Multicultural Music and Movement Activities

In addition to the previous activities, which provide multicultural music and movement activities, you might want to focus on the following:

➤ records and songs with international ties
➤ movement (games) and dances of different countries
➤ costumes (clothing) for dancing
➤ different instruments—for example, kalimbas, maracas, bells, gongs, castanets, guitars, and drums

Application of Principles

1. Make an effort to use more music with young children. Sing, hum, or move to music outdoors as well as indoors.
2. Encourage the children to use their large muscles by imitating animals, feelings, objects, or people, sometimes with and sometimes without musical accompaniment.

3. Over a period of a few weeks, learn and teach three new songs to young children. Use visual aids for one of the songs.
4. Use rhythm instruments, first without accompaniment and later with a record or piano, using a steady beat.
5. Invite a guest who has musical talents. What suggestions would you offer to that person?
6. Originate an outdoor game that involves the use of a ball, a parachute or small sheet, or an obstacle course.
7. Make a list of the five records and five songbooks you would like to own personally.
8. Sketch some possible obstacle courses. If possible, set them up and watch as the children participate.
9. Note the differing ages and physical abilities of the children. Are they within a "normal" range for their ages?
10. Consider how to modify suggestions for music and movement education for children of different ages or abilities.
11. Ask someone to help or coach you if you don't feel self-confident in music and movement experiences.
12. Refer to Figure 4.2, Daily Curriculum Checklist. Which of the areas (1–8) have been planned for the day or period?
13. Does physical ability (or rhythm, sound, and so on) influence learning? Look over the information in the section titled "Values for Children" and the chapter discussion for important relationships between curriculum and development.
14. Using the information in the section on developmental characteristics, design some movement activities appropriate for each age group. (Play follow-the-leader as children march around the room, down the hall, outdoors, and so on.)
15. Young children love to dance. Encourage them to create original dance steps to any musical selection.
16. Pick up the rhythm of children at play or tap out rhythm patterns (steady for walking, quick for running, uneven for skipping or galloping, slow for jumping). Change rhythm and see if the children can change their activities.
17. Take a familiar song (or one you are going to teach the children) and see how many curriculum areas are being taught through the words and actions of that song (science, social studies, creative art, language, math, music, reading, and so on).

References

NOTE: Current references are used when available. Older references are classic, introductory and important in development of later ideas, policies, and practices.

Achilles, E. (1999). Creating music environments in early childhood programs. *Young Children, 54*(1), 21–26.

Adachi, M. (1994). The role of the adult in the child's early musical socialization: A Vygotskian perspective. *Quarterly Journal of Music Teaching and Learning, 5*(3), 26–35, as reviewed in *Early Childhood Connections,* Spring 1999, 40–44.

Aldridge, D. (1988). *Music therapy with children.* London: Jessica Kingsley.

Anderson, P. S., & Lapp, D. (1988). *Language skills in elementary education.* NY: Macmillan.

Andress, B. (1984). The practitioner involved young children in music. In Boswell, J. (Ed.). *The young child and music.* Reston, VA: Music Educators National Conference.

Andress, B. (Ed). (1989). *Promising practices: Prekindergarten music education.* Reston, VA: Music Educators National Conference.

Andress, B. (1991a). Developmentally appropriate music experiences for young children. In National Dance Association (Ed.), *Early Creative Arts* (pp. 65, 73). Reston, VA: American Alliance for Health, Physical Education, Recreation and Dance.

Andress, B. (1991b). From research to practice: Preschool children and their movement responses to music. Research in review. *Young Children, 47*(1), 22–27.

Andress, B. (1995). Transforming curriculum in music. In S. Bredekamp, & T. Rosegrant (Eds.), *Reaching potentials: Transforming early childhood curriculum and assessment,* Vol. 2 (pp. 99–107).

Ball, W. A. (1991). Music: An avenue for cultural literacy. Paper presented at the Annual Conference of the Southern Association on Children Under Six (SACUS), March 15, in Atlanta, GA. (ERIC Document Reproduction Service No. ED332799)

Barclay, K. D., & Walwer, L. (1992). Linking lyrics and literacy through song picture books. *Young Children, 47*(4), 76–85.

Bayless, K., & Ramsey, M. (1982). *Music: a way of life for the young child.* Upper Saddle River, NJ: Merrill/Prentice Hall.

Begley, S. (1997, Spring/Summer). How to build a baby's brain. *Newsweek Special Edition, 28–32.*

Birkenshaw-Fleming, L. (1997). Music for young children: Teaching for the fullest development of every child. *Early Childhood Connections, 3*(2), 6–13.

Boyce-Tillman, J. (2000). *Constructing musical healing: The wounds that sing.* London: Jessica Kingsley.

Bredekamp, S., & Copple, C. (Eds.). (1997). *Developmentally appropriate practice in early childhood programs* (rev. ed.). Washington, DC: NAEYC.

Buchoff, R. (1994). Joyful voices: facilitating language growth through the rhythmic response to chants. *Young Children, 49*(4), 26.

Campbell, D. (1997). *The Mozart effect: Tapping the power of music to heal the body, strengthen the mind, and unlock the creative spirit.* New York: Avon.

Campbell, D. (2000). *The Mozart effect in children: Awakening your child's mind, body, and creativity with music.* New York: Morrow.

Cave, C. (1998). Early language development: Music and movement make a difference. *Early Childhood Connections, 4*(3), 24–29.

Cherry, D., Goodwin, D., & Staples, J. (1989). *Is the left brain always right? A guide to whole child development.* Belmont, CA: Fearson Teaching Aids.

Choksy, L., Abramson, R. M., Gillespie, A. E., & Woods, D. (1986). *Teaching music in the 20th century.* Upper Saddle River, NJ: Prentice Hall.

DeVries, R., & Kohlberg, L. (1990). *Constructivist early education: Overview and comparison with other programs.* Washington, DC: NAEYC.

DeVries, R., & Zan, B. (1994). *Moral classrooms, moral children: Creating a constructivist atmosphere in early education.* New York: Teachers College Press.

Elliot, D. (1995). *Music matters: A new philosophy of music education.* New York: Oxford University Press.

Fox, D. B. (2000, September). Music and the baby's brain. *Music Educators Journal, 23–28.*

Gabbard, C. (1998). Windows of opportunity for early brain and motor development. *Journal of Physical Education, Recreation, and Dance, 69*(8), 54–55, 61.

Galin, D. (1976). Educating both halves of the brain. *Childhood Education, 53,* 17–20.

Gallahue, D. L. (1982). *Developmental movement experiences for children.* NY: Wiley.

Gallahue, D. L. (1996). *Developing physical education for today's children* (3rd ed.). Madison, WI: Brown & Benchmark.

Gardner, H. (1993). *Frames of mind.* New York: Basic Books. Originally published in 1983.

Gharavi, G. J. (1993). Music skills for preschool teachers: Needs and solutions. *Arts Education Policy Review, 94*(3), 27–30.

Giles, M. M. (1991). A little background music, please. *Principal, 71*(2), 41–44.

Gill, J. (1998a). Add a little music. *Parent and Child, 5*(4), 40.

Gill, J. (1998b). Jim Gill on music in the classroom. *Early Childhood Today, 12*(4), 36–39.

Gilliam, T., Freedson, P., Geenen, D., & Shahraray, B. (1981). Physical activity patterns determined by heart rate monitoring in 6–7 year old children. *Medicine and Science in Sports and Exercise, 13*(1), 65–67.

Glazier, T. (1973). *Eye winker; Tom Tinker; chin chopper: Fifty musical fingerplays.* New York: Doubleday.

Glazier, T. (1980). *Do your ears hang low? Fifty more musical fingerplays.* New York: Doubleday.

Goodlad, J. I. (1984). *A place called school.* New York: McGraw-Hill.

Harp, B. (1988). Why are your kids singing during reading time? *The Reading Teacher, 41,* 454–456.

Hennings, D. G. (1990). *Communication in action.* Boston: Houghton Mifflin.

Hildebrandt, C. (1998). Creativity in music and early childhood. *Young Children, 53*(6), 68–73.

Jalongo, M. R. (1996). Using recorded music with young children: A guide for nonmusicians. *Young Children, 51*(5), 6–14.

James, A. R. (2000). When I listen to the music. *Young Children, 55*(3), 36–37.

Karnowski, L. (1986). How young writers communicate. *Educational Leadership, 46* (3), 58–60.

Kenney, S. H. (1997). Music in the developmentally appropriate integrated curriculum. In C. H. Hart, D. D. Burts, and R. Charlesworth (Eds.), *Integrated curriculum and developmentally appropriate practice: Birth to age eight* (pp. 103–144). Albany, NY: State University of New York Press.

Kranyik, M. A. (1993). Body music. *First Teacher, 14* (1), 25.

Landeck, B. (Ed.). (1950). *Songs to grow on: A collection of American folk songs for children.* New York: Edward B. Marks Music & Wm. Sloane Associates.

McDonald, D. (1979). *Music in our lives: The early years.* Washington, DC: NAEYC.

McDonald, D. T., & Simons, G. M. (1989). *Musical growth and development: Birth through six.* New York: Schirmer.

Miller, S. E. (1999). Balloons, blankets, and balls: Gross-motor activities to use indoors. *Young Children, 54*(5), 58–63.

Moore, T. (2002). If you teach children, you can sing! *Young Children, 57*(4), 84–85.

Moravcik, E. (2000). Music all the livelong day. *Young Children, 55*(4), 27–29.

Music Educators National Conference (MENC). (1994a). *Opportunities-to-learn standards for music instruction: Grades preK–12.* Reston, VA: Author.

Music Educators National Conference (MENC). (1994b). *The school music program: A new vision.* Reston, VA: Author.

Music for the Young Child. (1995). *Staff notes for LD.S. church missionaries and staff, 7*(2). Salt Lake City, UT: Church of Jesus Christ of Latter-Day Saints.

Neelly, L. P. (2001). Developmentally appropriate music practice: Children learn what they live. *Young Children, 56*(3), 32–37.

Neelly, L. P. (2002). Practical ways to improve singing in early childhood classrooms. *Young Children, 57*(4), 80–83.

Olds, A. R. (1994). From cartwheels to caterpillars: Children's need to move indoors and out. *Child Care Information Exchange, 97,* 32–36.

Paglin, D. (2000). Dance like a caterpillar: Movement is a big part of learning for little kids. *Northwest Education, 6*(1), 26–35. (ERIC Document Reproduction Service No. EJ616922).

Peery, J. C. (1993). Music in early childhood education. In B. Spodek (Ed.), *Handbook of research on the education of young children.* New York: Macmillan.

Piaget, J. (1974). *The child and reality: Problems of genetic psychology.* Trans. A. Rosen. New York: Viking.

Pitcher, E. G., Lasher, M. B., Feinburg, S. G., & Braun, L. A. (1974). *Helping young children learn* (2nd ed.). Columbus, OH: Merrill.

Poest, C. A., Williams, J. R., Witt, D. D., & Atwood, M. E. (1990). Challenge me to move: Large muscle development in young children. *Young Children, 45*(5), 4–10.

Riley, S. (1984). *How to generate values in young children.* Washington, DC: NAEYC.

Sampson, M., Sampson, M. B., & Van Allen, R. (1991). *Pathways to literacy.* Fort Worth, TX: Holt, Rinehart & Winston.

Seefeldt, V. (1984). Physical fitness in preschool and elementary school-aged children. *Journal of Physical Education, Recreation, and Dance, 55*(9), 33–40.

Seeger, R. C. (Ed.). (1980). *American Folk Songs for Children.* Garden City, NY: Doubleday. Music Sales Corporation. (Originally published in 1948.)

Shaw, J. M., & Cliatt, M. P. (1986). A model for training teachers to encourage divergent thinking in young children. *Journal of Creative Behavior, 20*(2), 81–88.

Smale, S. (1985). *Music—basic for the young child.* Edina, MN: LEA/DECE Publications.

Strand, B., Scantling, E., & Johnson, M. (1998). Guiding principles for implementing fitness education. *Journal of Physical Education, Recreation, and Dance, 69*(8), 35–39.

Sullivan, M. (1982). *Feeling strong, feeling free: Movement exploration for young children.* Washington, DC: NAEYC.

Taylor, B. J. (2002). *Early childhood program management: People and procedures* (4th ed.). Upper Saddle River, NJ: Merrill/Prentice Hall.

Tomatis, A. (1997). *The ear and language.* Trans. B. M. Thompson. North York, CA: Stoddart.

Torbert, M., & Schneider, L. (1998). *Follow me too: A handbook of movement activities for three- to five-year-olds.* Washington, DC: NAEYC.

Weikart, P. (1985). *Movement plus music.* Ypsilanti, MI: High/Scope Press.

Wolf, J. (1992). Let's sing it again: Creating music with young children. *Young Children, 47*(2), 56–61.

Wolf, J. (2000). Sharing songs with children. *Young Children, 55*(2), 28–30.

Yinger, J., & Blaszka, S. (1995). A year of journaling—a year of building with young children. *Young Children, 51*(1), 15–20.

Zimmerman, M. (1985). State of the art in early childhood music and research. In J. Boswell (Ed.), *The young child and music: Contemporary principles in child development and music education* (pp. 65–78). Reston, VA: Music Educators National Conference.

8

Science and Technology

Main Principles

1. The general feeling of some students about science is that it is hard to understand, boring to learn, and easy to forget. We must work diligently to change these attitudes (p. 294).

2. Science includes both knowledge about specific phenomena and the general strategies or process to collect and to evaluate such information (p. 294).

3. Experiences must be individually appropriate for each learner. Checking the learning environment is a prerequisite for science learning (pp. 294–296).

4. The role of the "teacher" (whether at school or home) is very important for children to learn about themselves and the world in which they live (pp. 297–302).

5. An overview of developmentally appropriate science helps the teacher to plan well and children to learn more effectively (pp. 298–302).

6. Based on the developmental characteristics of individual children, each child can learn about and appreciate science (pp. 299–303).

7. Some subjects are "touchy" and should be handled discreetly (p. 307).

8. The general behaviors of science learning include: observation, communication, comparison, organization, relationships, inferences, and application.

9. The role of the teacher (whether at home or school) is multi-faceted and of vital importance (pp. 297–303).

10. Biological science, the study of plant, animal, and human life, is valuable and interesting to children. This aspect of science gives the child a positive view of his/her environment (pp. 308–315).

11. Awareness of the physical environment can be introduced according to the perspective and readiness of young children. The following suggestions are over-simplified to introduce ideas for young children: **astronomy** can help them learn about space, stars, warmth from the sun, darkness that emphasizes the stars and moon (p. 318); **chemistry** teaches about mixtures and properties (pp. 318–320); **geology** teaches about rocks and playgrounds, and introduces field trips (pp. 320–321); **physics** teaches about force, machines, shapes, wheels

(pp. 315–321). Most all children show interest in the above topics—even if it is in a primitive way. Now use your own ideas, "favorite topics," or local "environment." You will learn right along with the children!!

12. **Technology** introduces children to computers, jargon, experimentation, and so on (pp. 322–326). If your classroom doesn't have some of the items you need, see if you can borrow them from other classrooms, homes, or friends, or make a personal investment. If you are not convinced about young children using computers, for example, talk to someone—a teacher, a friend, a merchant, a parent. See what introducing computers would mean to the children in your classroom. Make sure you know what you are teaching!

13. Integrating curriculum topics give children a wider view of learning. Some information and ideas can help expand a teacher's experience with computers (pp. 322–326).

14. Reviewing Gardner's theory of multiple intelligence helps teachers and parents see a broader picture of young children's learning (p. 327).

Introduction

In the year 2000, it was estimated by the Bureau of Labor that statistics would report these facts:

➤ The United States would have a 1,000,000-person shortage of trained scientists and technicians (estimated by the National Science Foundation).
➤ More than 80% of all jobs would require proficiency in math and science.
➤ Between 60 and 80% of career fields would be closed to those with poor skills in math and science.
➤ More than 40% of the college-age population would be African American and Latino/Latina.

Now, in 2003, how close did we come to these predictions?

"Is it true that the easier subjects should precede the harder ones? On the contrary, some of the hardest must come first, because nature so dictates, and because they are essential to life," stated Alfred North Whitehead.

Students compare most, give more excuses, and feel more threatened in science than in any other curriculum area. Why is this so? On quizzing, one frequently gets answers such as "I hate science!" "I don't understand it myself, so how can I teach it to children?" "Please, please, let me do extra assignments in other areas instead." This is where toughness comes in—and usually pays great dividends. Offer assistance, but insist that the learner follows through.

Science is a most vital subject, for it encompasses all other topics. It is knowledge and is found in relationships, in the environment, in art and the senses, in verbal and written communication, in music and movement, in living and physical things, and in aspects of daily living such as nutrition, health, and safety. It is discovered through play and one's interaction with the environment. But opportunities for science must be based on the individual developmental level of each child.

Two reasons I feel so strongly about science is that it is so exciting, and it is so much a part of our daily living. A third reason is that knowledge helps us live happier and more productive lives. And still another reason is that there is a negative or fearful attitude in some circles toward anything scientific. I am speaking about learning scientific concepts in realistic, meaningful, and growth-promoting ways. I reject learning scientific facts merely to recite or write them to pass tests or because they are requirements. I encourage learning facts because they are interesting, useful, and satisfying.

A "crisis in education" was reported and discussed by Fisher 10 years ago in a two-part article (August and September 1992) by the National Science Foundation regarding

Reflection

It is curiosity, the drive to make sense out of something in our surroundings, that causes children to reach out, touch, and wonder and it is curiosity that moves scientists to do the very same thing. (Abruscato, 1992, p. 3; see also Carson, 1956, p. 112.)

an earlier 10-year prediction about U.S. elementary and secondary education in science and math being "premier in the world by 1995, as measured by achievement scores and participation levels." (1992, August, p. 58). But instead, 300 reports attested to the fact that the scores of American children had gotten significantly worse. The Americans flunked the science test—taking thirteenth place—and in math the 13-year-olds from the U.S. "landed in the next-to-the bottom slot." Fisher concluded that the students would have performed better if they had access to more reading materials (books, magazines, newspapers, and encyclopedias, read more than five pages for school each day) and spent at least some time on daily homework, had both parents living in the home, and watched less television (1992b, p. 51). The Third International Mathematics and Science Study (TIMSS, July/August, 1997) reported a more positive note: "Our nation's fourth-graders are near the very top in science achievement in the world, and better than ever in mastering the basics of arithmetic."

TIMMS is the most thorough international study of math and science education ever conducted, comparing the performance of a half million students, including 33,000 Americans, at levels corresponding to U.S. grades 4, 8, and 12.

For learning possibilities in the classroom, see Figure 8.1.

Teachers and children can make science happen any time and with any subject.

Note to teachers: Look around yourself, your classroom, and your community to determine how many science activities are already available. Make an effort to use them in incidental and planned ways.

1. Is there a center for science and mathematics?

2. Are there libraries and other resources for science and mathematics?

3. Are there live plants and animals?

4. Are there hands-on/minds-on exploration opportunities: construction materials, supplies, running water, time allowances, peers, projects, books, and other equipment (calculators, microscopes, hand lenses, computers)?

5. Is there time to explore? Research indicates that young children require 30 to 50 minutes of free play/ independent exploration time in order to fully engage in these types of environments. NAEYC and the National Council for Teachers of Mathematics support the strategy of providing large blocks of time for children to engage in meaningful learning, which includes play and exploration of materials as well as structured learning experiences. "Allowing children to move freely about the classroom, initiating learning experiences in a variety of ways, requires a movement away from rigid scheduling of discrete, subject-driven activities to an integrated, holistic view of curriculum, development, and learning" (Patton & Kokoski, 1996).

6. Is there encouragement for in-depth study rather than fleeting interests?

7. Are other subject areas combined with science and mathematics (literature, dramatic play, outdoor activities, and so on)?

8. How do you encourage some of the ideas for this "center" to come from the children? "A strategy for ensuring that every child has access to science, mathematics, and technology disciplines is for teachers to use an inclusive planning process" (Nelson & Frederick, 1994).

9. How do you encourage less-interested or shy children so that the area is utilized by *all* children?

10. Is this "center" available at all times for new or continued exploration?

11. How could you use webbing to include children and science in a variety of fun, meaningful experiences? (Construct a web and label only parts of it. Ask the children to help you fill in the blanks.)

12. Teachers: *Think and get excited!* Example: "What could you tell me about _____?" The teacher asks leading questions, and the children supply information. Then combine the information into a teacher-child web: language arts, music, art, dramatic play, social studies, sensory play, field trips or speakers, math, parent involvement, science, food/nutrition leading up to a tasting party. (Specific information, related to each curriculum area, can provide interesting choices for the teacher to consider.)

13. How do you tie indoor activities with an outdoor or natural habitat (playground, field trip, and so on) to make it more meaningful? Is there a local "real" experience?

14. How do you keep parents informed as to classroom activities and how do you encourage them to further the experience? Is there provision for follow-up (classroom or community exhibits), home use, outside resources (books, pictures), and spin-offs?

15. How do you handle questions that you cannot answer immediately? (This requires careful, honest, and resourceful answers! Think about it very carefully!) Do you try to bluff you way? Do you say, "Let's find out together"—and then do so? Do you say, "I'm not sure but I will find out and let you know,"—*and then do so?*

Figure 8.1 Checking the Learning Environment

Role of the Teacher

Early-childhood educators should not feel intimidated by nature education. If they think they know too little about it, they can prepare in such simple ways as bringing in different items of nature (especially those that pertain to their area); growing plants from seeds, bulbs, or sprouts; posting interesting pictures; acquiring good books; taking walks around the center—stopping to examine trees, bark, insects, and foliage; picking up trash; visiting with a gardener or groundskeeper; watering and caring for plants and animals; and other things of local interest (a busy spider, tadpoles transforming into frogs, the rain forest, exploring the five senses, etc.).

Through observation, interaction, and study, the adult can determine appropriate kinds of activities for young children. The following should be considered:

➤ the adult's personal attitude toward science
➤ activities that are neither too hard nor too easy—but are safe
➤ activities that interest particular children
➤ some activities that are done individually (one's own way and pace) and some that are best done in small groups (cooperation without intimidation)
➤ choices between two activities
➤ timely interests (holidays, community, personal, seasons)
➤ amount and kind of supervision needed, including safety factors—not to taste unless approved, use of safety equipment, preventing and/or handling accidents
➤ the purpose, goals, and benefits of the activity (possible follow-up)

Attitudes in adults (teachers, parents, friends, others) can certainly stop, slow down, or encourage children's science inquiries. Taking cues from adults, children can feel excited or frightened about happenings in their environment. An atmosphere of wonder can be created, nourished, and sustained in young children when adults do the following:

A quiet, friendly teacher helps children as they show interest.

➤ respond to voiced and unvoiced needs
➤ lovingly hold and cuddle a child so they feel mutual comfort and joy
➤ show (model) surprise, interest, novelty, and attraction to natural happenings
➤ interact with the child with interest, spontaneous humor, and joy
➤ encourage children to freely experiment with their senses in safe ways
➤ learn from mistakes they and children make as they grow and learn
➤ are flexible enough to let a child's creativity or direction lead the way
➤ ask probing questions to encourage children to be successful observers
➤ assist children as they *communicate* and describe observations
➤ introduce multisensory, spontaneous, integrated, concrete, relevant ideas
➤ construct an environment that supports scientific inquiry and experimentation
➤ let children design curriculum through a collaborative effort (sharing ideas, planning activities, collecting materials, exploring resources, etc.)

Getting started on good science for children and teachers may contain three phases: teacher-planned tasks, child-initiated learning (exploratory), and application (Perry and Rivkin, 1992). Sometimes teachers and children explore roles as both "learners" and "teachers."

Overview of Developmentally Appropriate Science

Science is more than a collection of facts. **Young children must live it!** It builds on children's curiosity and willingness to explore the things around them. It entails investigating phenomena, facilitated by open-ended questions that encourage children to organize information and to reach their own conclusions.

Things that appeal most to them are situations that allow them to figure out what happens—in short, things they can see, touch, manipulate, modify. Older children and adults can learn about science in a more mature or abstract way (observation, predicting, testing predictions under controlled conditions, and interpretation). Younger children use these steps in a more primitive way and can be easily discouraged in trying something new. The important thing is that they try, make modifications, and try again: the very essence of science.

Science is a vital part of our daily lives—through natural resources, medicine, production and consumption of goods and services, and more. It is so much a part of us, why do some adults find it intimidating, frustrating, and to be avoided? Young children are interested and excited about their environment. They need to keep their curiosity alive!

In the rest of this section are a few suggested ideas. Use only those that are appropriate for the ages and/or interests of the children you are currently teaching. Add local areas of interest.

Astronomy and Meteorology

Astronomy is especially difficult to teach young children. Most observable activity occurs at night; however, children are very interested in the sun, moon, and stars because of the warmth and light from the sun, the shining moon and stars at night, the beautiful sunsets, and the changes in weather.

Ecology

Young children are natural naturalists. All one needs are curiosity, joy of exploration, and a desire to discover firsthand the wonders of nature.

People have a fundamental need to care for things outside themselves. This need can be met—and human life enhanced—by caring for the natural world. A genuine concern for wild creatures and their habitats can promote great fulfillment in one's individual life and a sense of caring for others.

Using good conservation policies in classrooms and centers can help children form environmentally sound lifestyles. Suggestions include using durable dishes for food service rather than disposable ones; using personal cloth towels instead of paper ones; saving paper scraps and other items for collages; turning off unneeded lights; promptly repairing toys and equipment; and protecting our resources many other ways. Involving children in caring for living things (in gardening, composting, harvesting, and using food products) helps them practice responsibility and nurturing.

Books on the environment and ecology for children have greatly increased over the last decade. We should encourage children to be aware of environmental problems in conserving our resources, in loving nature, and in celebrating our earth. Walks in different types of weather, colors at different times of year; animals all around us, foliage in different stages, and other types of experiences are there for the taking. What are the assets and liabilities of nature around us? Are daily necessities such as farming, weather, water, and climate serious concerns? What are the most serious industry problems? Just look around the school, home, and community to see how children could be encouraged to appreciate and protect what is there.

Home-School Partnership

To achieve a good home-school connection, all involved need to know what types of experiences are appropriate for the child, what good science and math experiences are, and what strategies to use in engaging children. (**Note:** Many authors and educators use the word *experiences,* not *experiments*. The former connotes involvement; the latter, observation.)

Overall goals in providing appropriate science experiences for the young child (at home or at school) are defined by Kilmer and Hofman: "to lay a solid foundation for the continuing and development of an interest in and an understanding of science and technology with active participation for *every child*" (1995, p. 44).

A good science and mathematics program fosters the development of lifelong skills and attitudes in children. The most appropriate place and time to begin such learning is in a well-developed early-childhood program or in a comfortable home setting where parents know and appreciate the importance of the learning years.

Parent and child attitudes about school become more positive through academic interactions at home, affecting the child's self-esteem. Theoretically, acknowledgment of these benefits should lead to a more positive attitude toward and interest in science and mathematics (Kokoski & Downing-Leffler, 1995, p. 35). Parents and educators need to know what types of experiences are appropriate for the child, what good science and mathematics experiences are, and what strategies to use in engaging with children at home as defined by the following:

1. "a solid foundation for the continuing and development of an interest in and an understanding of science and technology with active participation for *every child*" (Kilmer & Hofman, 1995, p. 44); and
2. a general framework recommended for kindergarten through sixth grade, yet broad enough to serve as guidelines for planning experiences for preschool children as well (NCISE, 1990, p. 9).

Specifically, the National Center for Improving Science Education recommends: (a) developing each child's innate curiosity about the world; (b) broadening each child's procedural and thinking skills for investigating the world, solving problems, and making decisions; and (c) increasing each child's knowledge of the natural world (NCISE, 1990, p. 9). (Objectives and ways to achieve these are in the referenced article.)

Home-school partnerships are important in a young child's education.

Living Things

Young children are very curious about living things: people (including themselves), animals, creeping things, birds—you name it, they are interested in it! Helping them to understand themselves and other living things is fascinating and enlightening!

Self-expression

The arts are an extension of nature, culture, and education. Encouraging children to express their interests and discoveries using art, music, dance, movement, and storytelling are ways to support and extend environmental learning and at the same time extend the child's learning environment and education.

Transportation/Machines (Technology)

Children in different parts of our world use different modes of transportation and different machines in their daily lives. Informing young children about using water, air, land, animals, and other sorts of transportation can be exciting and puzzling. Machines in various countries can be exciting and mind stimulating; frequently young children even use their own bodies as machines!

Elkind (1991), a contemporary and respected early-childhood education leader, provides his cautionary note and viewpoint regarding young children and technology:

> [Regarding the] growing prevalence of computers in our schools as well as in our homes and in our workplaces . . . I have no doubt that computers will indeed change the way in which teachers teach, particularly at the elementary and secondary level. But when I read about the goals to be reached through having computers in the classroom, I was amused to discover that these were goals early childhood educators had attained long before computers, such as teachers:
>
> > are still responsible for students' learning but rather than being dispensers of become guides to the learning process,

act as facilitators and organizers of learning activities,
are free to focus on small groups and individuals who need more specialized attention, helping them to make choices and validate their learning (Van Dusen & Worthen, 1995, p. 32).

Elkind reports in an earlier reference:

If computers and educational software encourage primary and secondary school teachers to operate more like early childhood educators, these machines most certainly bring about a miraculous transformation in teaching. Well before computers, many of us argued that teaching at all levels should follow the early childhood model. If the computer, with its high-tech image and authority, can bring about what all our efforts to disseminate developmentally appropriate practice has yet to achieve, I don't think any of us will complain or lament (1966, p. 22).

NAEYC's guidelines for early childhood curriculum accept the Piagetian notion that children construct knowledge through interaction with materials and people (NAEYC & NAECS/SDE, 1991). Are computers to be included among these materials? Some critics think computers are not concrete and that even shape drawings should not be included until children reach elementary-school age; others say that preschool children can use *appropriate* computer programs. Some drill-and-practice programs produced significant *losses* in creativity. Children using open-ended software made significant gains in intelligence, nonverbal skills, structural knowledge, long-term memory, complex manual dexterity, and self esteem (Haugland, 1992).

Personal Relationships

An important environmental relationship must exist between the needs of the student and the total environment of the social context in which teaching and learning take place. Children generally prefer to work in dyads or triads rather than alone; in small groups, they spontaneously teach, help, and encourage each other. Preschoolers were found to spend 63% of their time at the computer when working with a peer, compared to only 7% when working with puzzles. In another study, the frequency of cooperative play at the computer was comparable to that exhibited during a fishing game (96% and 98%, respectively), but was much higher than that exhibited in other traditional preschool activities such as blocks (27%), play dough (14%), and art (8%) (Clements 1993, p. 302).

As with any area of curriculum, thematic units of study can include many different activities (blocks, sand, outside play, movement experiences, mathematics, and on throughout the entire day). Teachers can also enhance units by using computers at one or more levels:

1. with specific software using unit-related information,
2. with tool software—for specific areas,
3. with computer-related activities designed to build specific skills/concepts,
4. in building a "network" of related topics,
5. in locating resource material (Davidson, 1994).

Water Play

Water play is basic raw material. It fosters curiosity, imagination, and experimentation (see Chapter 6 for other uses). The child has a natural affinity for water play indoors and outdoors.

Weather

When children study weather, informally or formally, they have many opportunities to use science-processing skills and to construct mathematical understandings in developmentally appropriate ways. They learn to integrate science, math, and literacy in discovering and exploring the environment. Some activities they might participate in include gathering data and organizing study topics (rain and rainbows, clouds and precipitation, air and wind, the sun, and so on).

No matter where they find it,
water is a delight and a
fascination for children.

Summary

How do all of these introductory topics (ecology, life, machines, transportation, and weather) blend with the learning of the children in your classroom? What other topics would be of more interest or value to them at their particular stage of growth? See Figure 8.2.

 Developmental Characteristics

The amount of intellectual development in children is often difficult to determine. Their lack of language and the adult's inability to determine precisely what and how to measure are both limiting factors. The age and size of the child can mislead adults into thinking children know more or less than they actually do.

Essentially, young children participate in many scientific activities. They may stay for long or short periods of time and feel joy or frustration. They are self-centered, seeing their own point of view, and center on only one aspect at a time. They are limited in their ability to handle abstract ideas.

Young children play alone or alongside another child. Eventually they join a small group; later they enjoy the companionship and ideas of others. They tend to judge others by their own acts. Not until later are they able to consider motives behind actions.

Intellectually, children begin by repeated experimentation with objects. They believe that natural phenomena are created by human beings and that inanimate objects have life and human characteristics.

To make science exciting and meaningful for young children, activities are based on familiar ideas. Children are encouraged to explore and discover; however, adults should be willing and able to assist when appropriate.

Values for Children

What Is Science?

Science is usually defined by delineating the content, procedures, and assumptions of the field. Science includes both knowledge about specific phenomena (characteristics, classifications, and principles that explain the universe) and the general strategies or processes used to collect and to evaluate such information (Kilmer & Hofman, 1995, p. 43).

But what is science for children under the age of public school admission? Can they comprehend any scientific data? If so, how can it help them in their future personal and educational goals?

Developmentally appropriate science builds on children's curiosity and willingness to explore the things around them. It entails investigating phenomena facilitated by open-ended questions that encourage children to organize information and to reach their own conclusions.

Science kits and curricula, with their attractive advertising and brilliant colors, should not give educators and parents a false sense of teaching "nature or the right way to teach young children" (Fenton, 1996, p. 10). Also, it is our job to be sure that each child's interactions with nature are safe and sensible.

Take your cues from the children: when appropriate, repeat familiar experiences; introduce new information; or combine familiar and new information.

Who gains from science learning? See Table 8.1.

In review: Through science experiences, children build confidence in themselves and in their environment; gain necessary firsthand experiences; develop basic concepts;

---

1. Make science an everyday, exciting event. Provide many hands-on experiences.

2. Remove the stigma that science is hard and only for the bright students.

3. Encourage *all* children (regardless of gender, socioeconomic status, culture, age, or any other category) to be curious, to investigate, to explore, to revise and retry, to question, to seek solutions, and to understand their environment and the people around them.

4. Inform parents of ways to involve young children in activities and actions that help children protect and enhance their environment rather than destroy and distrust it.

5. Instill in children that science is a way of life and, therefore, understanding it will bring joy and satisfaction in daily life.

6. Help teachers and parents be aware of science opportunities in the daily environment—*not make learning (especially science) something that is separate, distasteful, boring, regimented, difficult, and competitive.*

7. Carefully planned curricula that includes opportunities for children of all interests and abilities to become interested in spontaneous and/or planned scientific exploration—resulting in better understanding, more willingness to explore, and an increased feeling of self-worth.

8. Increase language opportunities for young children—exposure to print (books to look at and hear, magazines to peruse), listening experiences (others, tapes, stories), and casual and formal discussions with peers and adults. Adults can initiate conversations, but would probably be more useful if they provide a stimulating environment and respond to the children's needs vocally and physically.

Figure 8.2 How to Change Attitudes Toward Science

Table 8.1 Gains from Science Experiences in Early-Childhood Curriculum

Who?	How?
Children can gain:	Experiences in problem solving, social skills, creative thinking, spatial relations, decision making, observation, sorting, categorizing, curriculum knowledge, estimating—all essential skills for later success in science
	Self-confidence when they can successfully manipulate objects in the physical world
	Skills in adaptive behavior to outdoor settings (balance, walking through different areas—snow, mud, fields)
	Survival skills
	Aesthetic development: sensitivity to beauty, seasonal changes, moisture, birds and animals; "Beauty is not just in what can be seen but is present, also, in what can be touched, felt, and listened to" (Wilson, 1995).
	Cognitive development
	Skills in observing, listening, and responding to divergent information
	Communication skills: something to talk about
	Sensorimotor development: natural sights
	Understanding of space relationships (crawl under, jump over, slip through)
	Socioemotional development: caring for things outside themselves
	Improved personal and social behaviors
	(Sources: ideas from Sprung, 1996; Wilson, 1995, and present author)
Teachers can gain:	A sense of empowerment (overcoming a fear of science)
	Sharing of knowledge with children
	Security of not having to have all of the "right answers"
	Confidence: "It becomes apparent how interdisciplinary the activities are and what a boost they can give to the entire curriculum. New science activities can be a wonderful remedy for the midyear doldrums" (Sprung, 1996, p. 31).
Parents can gain:	An understanding of the importance of science for their children's futures and their role as teachers within the home
	Awareness that the science they know and use every day can become home-learning activities to do with their children
	Awareness of how their involvement plays an important role in children's success in school
	More involvement in their child's school education
	Satisfaction in everyday home activities, which are full of science learning: greasy pots become an experiment in how oil floats on top of water; storage (conservation); recycling; waste disposal; wheels, motors, and so on
	"Parents should know that their children's livelihoods may depend on how much math and science they know. Now, while the kids are in school, is the time for them to learn" (Sagan, 1989, p. 6).

Who?	How?
Everybody wins because of:	Better-trained individuals
	More confidence in "science" activities
	More knowledge and security in everyday lives
	More trust in each other to be better citizens (recycling, product uses, better use of their money and environment)
	Solutions to home/work problems
	"We live in a society exquisitely dependent on technology, in which hardly anybody knows anything about science and technology. This is a clear prescription for disaster" (Sagan, 1989, p. 6).
	Reread the statistics at the beginning of this chapter. Then apply them to the information in this table. How could we further improve our lives, our society, and our world?

increase observation skills; receive opportunities to use tools, equipment, and familiar materials; receive aid in problem solving; stimulate their curiosity for exploration and discovery while increasing basic knowledge; develop sensory, physical, emotional, intellectual, spiritual, and social attributes; develop language through increased vocabulary and an opportunity to ask and answer questions; and obtain many unnamed or child-specific values.

Schultz (1985) adds:

We cannot expect children to grow up valuing trees, spiders, and snakes without positive experiences that touch them personally. Young children's direct contacts with nature awaken them to its beauty and the pleasure it offers. . . . And the children who had this (science) hands-on experience improved 80 percent in the area of science concepts, 167 percent in science vocabulary, and 15 percent in perceptual skills over their pre-instruction scores. Informally, I noticed that both teachers' and children's fear of animals decreased as their interest rose (p. 49).

Still another value is perceived by Henniger (1987): "Young men and women with sound math and science understandings have many job opportunities and career choices unavailable to others" (p. 167).

Piaget (Elkind, 1981) effectively summarizes the challenge as follows:

The principal goal of education is to create men who are capable of doing new things, not simply repeating what other generations have done . . . men who are creative, inventive and discoverers. The second goal of education is to form minds which can be critical, can verify, and not accept everything they are offered. The great danger today is of slogans, collective opinions, ready-made trends of thought. We have to be able to resist individually, to criticize, to distinguish between what is proven and what is not. So we need pupils who are active, who learn early to find out by themselves, partly by their own spontaneous activity and partly through materials we set up for them. We learn early to tell what is verifiable and what is simply the first idea to come to them (p. 29).

Smith (1987) reports Piaget's findings concerning young children and science:

For Piaget, the foundation upon which all intellectual development takes place is physical knowledge, knowledge that comes from objects. This includes information about the properties of objects (their shape, size, textures, color, odor), as well as knowledge about how objects react to different actions on them (they roll, bounce, sink, slide, dry up). Children construct physical knowledge by acting on objects—feeling, tasting, smelling, seeing, and hearing them. They cause objects to move—throwing, banging, blowing, pushing, and pulling them, and they observe changes that take place in objects when they are heated, cooled, mixed together, or changed in some other way. As physical knowledge develops, children become better able to establish relationships (comparing, classifying, ordering) between and among the objects they act upon. Such relationships (logicomathematical knowledge according to Piaget) are essential for the emergence of logical, flexible thought processes (p. 35).

Teaching science to young children can be easy, inexpensive, and rewarding. For example, a teacher could have a portable science kit ready to take out with the children on walks, on field trips, or just in the play yard. Contents of the kit depend on where the children are going, their ages, and what you are trying to investigate. Some suggestions are a magnifying glass, a tape measure, a flashlight, string, binoculars, plastic bags and ties, clear jars and other unbreakable containers, a small garden trowel or large sturdy spoons, plastic bags for treasures, and paper and pencils for note taking.

Science is a part of our daily lives. It is of vital importance to each and every one of us—through natural resources, through medicine, through production and consumption of goods and services, through life itself. If it is so much a part of us, why do some parents and teachers find the subject one that is intimidating, frustrating, and to be avoided? Young children are interested and excited about their environment. They need to keep that curiosity alive.

Science is the process of inquiry. Young children are natural scientists with spontaneous and ingenious ideas. They are, at this stage, egocentric. They see no reasons for things except for their benefit (parents make cookies because children are hungry, or the sun comes out so children can play). As they grow and have experiences, they become less egocentric; they look for physical, magical, or psychological reasons as causes for events. While in the preoperational stage, they live in the here and now. They believe all they see. "It's true! I saw it on television" is a common response. Then children try to duplicate some feats, only to end up injured or disappointed. They have limited ability to understand causality, reason logically, or predict consequences.

Young children often have misconceptions about their world; these need to be clarified and revised. By listening to or watching young children, adults receive clues as to when they need to offer a firsthand experience to get the child thinking in the right direction.

While setting up some guidelines for a science curriculum, see that all children are included—regardless of sex, race, age, or any other criteria. All children should have equal access to all areas of curriculum. All of them will be interested and ready for opportunities within their developmental and skill abilities. Because science encompasses their entire world, children will want to participate—maybe cautiously or hesitantly at first, but they will be interested. (Review, at least in your mind, the emphasis John Dewey [See Chapter 3] placed on the importance of self-directed activity [active involvement]—he viewed children as scientists whose major occupation was problem solving.) Holt

 Reflection

A teacher demonstrated the principle of rain in the classroom. The children asked no questions, so the teacher assumed they had learned the concepts as she had planned them. The next day, a mother reported her daughter's comments: "Mother, God doesn't make the rain; I learned how to make it at school." Without this vital feedback, the teacher would have assumed the children had gained correct concepts. Instead, she was back to the drawing board for another attempt to teach about rain.

Adults have many opportunities to help young children understand the fascination of science. For example: Why is salt used in freezing ice cream? What makes popcorn pop? What is the principle of gravity? How can heavy airplanes stay up in the air, or heavy boats float? If you do not know answers, take the child to a book, or other resource, and find out together. Keep the information simple and on his level of understanding. Complicated lectures will discourage him from asking questions in the future.

(1989) says: "I believe we are passing, to children, responsibility for a 21st Century Earth in shameful condition. Science and technology can only aid us if we all work at preserving, conserving, and sharing resources."

Life . . . and Death

It may be a touchy subject, but when one deals with life in science, one needs to also consider death—of plants and animals at first. The attitude, information, and method of presentation will all carry great importance.

On this topic Furman (1990) writes,

> [C]oping with death depends on first knowing what dead means. A basic concept of death is best grasped, not when a loved one dies, but in situations of minimal emotional significance, such as with dead insects or worms. Since all children encounter such deaths very often and since even toddlers notice and ask about them, we can help them by utilizing their experiences and interest instead of averting our or their eyes. Dead means the lasting end to signs of life (p. 16).

> Plants provide the most prevalent, accessible and emotionally neutral opportunities to learn about life and death . . . sweet potato in water, orange and grapefruit seeds, popcorn, top of carrot, beans in wet cotton (p. 17).

With plants, children can learn about isolated experiences (planting seeds, watching plants grow, appreciation of product) and about the whole life cycle. With insects, young children can learn about their birth, care, habits, protection, and functions without needing to destroy them or be afraid of them. Of course, caution needs to be exercised when safety and health are involved. We also need to help young children value life—why pull every flower or stomp on every bug?

Adults must be very careful with the words and ideas they use when discussing death with young children, for, as just stated, children use their own experiences as references. Words like *old, sleeping, sick, tired,* and so on mean very different things to children. "Grandma is old." "If I go to sleep (or get sick or tired), will I not wake up (or will I

 **Reflection**

Ned's father had just returned from a trip to the desert and had brought Ned a horny toad. He excitedly put it into a shoebox and brought it to school one morning. Every time he showed it to someone, it jumped out of the box and ran. The children would run after it and try to catch it, a successful procedure at first. The teacher told him to keep the lid on the box until she could bring a small cage from the storage shed—but while she was gone, another child asked to see it. Proudly, Ned took off the lid and away went the horny toad again. The children ran after it and an unfortunate accident occurred: It ran in front of Del, and Del's inability to avert it caused him to step on it! The children ran to the returning teacher and said, "We don't need a cage. Del stepped on the horny toad and killed it—and we don't like Del anymore." The teacher tried to console the children and wondered just how much involvement she should exhibit. In an instant, and without the teacher's participation, one child said, "Well, I guess we had better bury it." Another one said, "We'll need some flowers." Still another said, "I'll get a shovel from the shed to dig a hole." Before the eyes of the speechless teacher, the children had organized and initiated ideas from their own experiences. A spot was selected, a hole was dug, the horny toad was buried, and flowers were placed on the grave.

die)?" How do young children relate to ideas such as *discard, replace, unwanted*? Do they apply to concepts about death?

Activities to Increase Awareness of Biological Science

Biological science is the study of plant and animal life. In this chapter, for ease in planning, the activities are divided into four areas: people, animals, plants, and food. Examples of these four areas are also found in other chapters as they relate to different curriculum topics. Emphasis is placed on making experiences meaningful and appropriate for children who participate.

People

See also Chapter 10 for more information.

➤ Focus on helping the children increase their self-image: draw an outline around each child's body and let him color or finish it; let the children make a "me" puppet; provide a place to make a mural of handprints and footprints; let the children participate in a group experience, such as holding visual aids for a story or song, introducing a toy, or choosing an activity.

➤ Discuss things the children can do now that they could not do when younger or smaller.

➤ Make a chart and show how the human body works.

➤ Display photographs of the children at their eye level.

➤ Weigh and measure each child. Post the chart.

➤ Observe different characteristics of people (for example, hair, eye, and skin coloring; height, weight, sex). Talk about special characteristics of each child.

➤ Give children some enjoyable, stimulating sensory experiences.

➤ Help children recognize and appreciate different physical characteristics of children and adults. Discuss skills. Encourage development of a positive self-attitude.

➤ Give children some quality experiences with older people (for example, grandparents, community workers, and so on).

➤ Use a real skeleton or a replica to talk about bones (unless a culture would find this unacceptable).

➤ Learn about such different parts of the body as the digestive tract, heart, tongue, hair, and eyes.

➤ Stimulate the five senses (see Chapter 6).

➤ Use a large hand mirror for the children to see their facial expressions for different emotions. Have at least one full-length mirror.

➤ Talk about the importance of good mental hygiene: thinking good thoughts, positive relationships, helpfulness instead of negativity.

➤ Visit a local health center, doctor's office, or hospital.

➤ Invite a resource person, such as a doctor or nurse.

➤ Visit community helpers or invite them to your classroom.

➤ Discuss the different places people live, such as apartments, houses, trailers, and dormitories, and then visit some of them.

➤ Discuss ways to stay healthy (for example, proper nutrition, clothing, rest).

➤ Observe someone with a cast on. Discuss the healing process.

➤ Observe a mother bathing, feeding, or dressing a baby.

➤ Discuss and enact roles of various family members.

➤ Make a family portrait by cutting pictures from magazines and pasting them on construction paper or paper plates.

➤ Throughout the day, help children solve problems through verbalization, cooperation, and sharing.

Sample Miniplan Involving People

Theme

Sounds around us

Ideas to Emphasize

1. We hear through our ears.
2. Sounds are all around us.
3. Sounds help us identify people and things.

Learning Activities

1. Have the children place their hands over their eyes. Talk to them. Ask them if they can hear you. Ask them to put their hands over their mouths. Can they hear you? Have them put their hands over their ears. Can they still hear you? Discuss the use of ears.
2. Play a tape of familiar sounds while the children listen. Include sounds that are normal in the home, such as an alarm clock, brushing teeth, going downstairs, preparing breakfast, running water, beating or mixing, setting the table, a crying baby, pet noises, radio or television, a ringing telephone or doorbell, opening and closing a door, a running car, typing, and so on. Arrange the sounds in logical sequence so they can easily be used as part of a story. The second time the tape is played, stop it after each sound while the children discuss it. Be accepting of their ideas. Encourage them to make sounds they heard earlier in the day and let the other children guess what the sound represents. Also talk about how certain sounds protect us, such as those from smoke alarms, horns, sirens, or bells.
3. Play a game making and identifying the sounds of animals, transportation, occupations, and so on.
4. Write and use a similar plan on sounds for hearing impaired children/adults.

➤ Involve the children in establishing guidelines for behavior.
➤ Talk about common emotions. "How did it make you feel?" "How did it make someone else feel?" "What can we do to help someone feel happy?" "What should we do when someone is unhappy?"

Help each child learn about and appreciate himself/herself as well as others. *Avoid overloading the children with information and/or experiences.* Caution: are there some children/adults in your group who cannot hear as well as others or who speak a different language? How would you teach children about these differences?

Animals

➤ Have a small box with pictures of animals and also a duplicate of each cut into a silhouette from black paper. Children match the animal with its shadow.
➤ Make animal shadow pictures on a screen, using a strong light and imagination.
➤ Sing "Over in the Meadow."
➤ Make or purchase an ant farm or observe ants in their natural setting.

All varieties of life are fascinating to young children.

➤ Have animals in the classroom often. Teach about the care and characteristics of each. Some good classroom pets are ants, butterflies, caterpillars, earthworms, frogs, gerbils, goldfish, guinea pigs, hamsters, and hermit crabs. On special occasions, hatch eggs or bring in baby animals (a goat, lamb, rabbit, or other available animals).

➤ Build an insect collection in boxes or jars. Discuss local insects (bees, mosquitoes, fleas, and so on).

➤ Collect ants, ladybugs, caterpillars, earthworms, and butterflies from the play yard.

➤ Take a walk and observe birds, insects, and animals common to the community.

➤ Make a bird bath or feeder (using a milk carton).

➤ Make self-correcting card games: (1) the same animals on two different cards for matching; (2) pictures of an animal and its habitat for matching; and (3) classifications of animals, such as those that fly or have four legs.

➤ Make a net out of a nylon stocking. Go bug-catching.

➤ Borrow a pet from a family, a farm, or a pet store. Make sure the animal is tame and free of disease. (A pet show of animals from home may be inadvisable because some animals do not get along!)

➤ When possible, bring in a guest who has an unusual pet or raises animals.

➤ Observe or discuss the characteristic movement of animals (some swim, some fly, some hop, and so on).

➤ Observe or discuss physical characteristics of various animals (for example, flippers, wings, webfeet, claws, or number of legs).

➤ Observe or discuss the diet of various animals (for example, hay, grain, milk, carrots, or nuts).

➤ Observe and discuss birth, nutrition, and habits of animals or insects.

➤ Observe frogs in various stages, from egg to tadpole to frog.

➤ Observe and discuss various housing for animals, such as a nest, hole, house, or cage.

➤ Observe animals with their young (care and feeding).

➤ Imitate animal sounds.

➤ Learn the names of adult male and female animals and babies.

➤ Discuss how animals protect themselves through camouflage, hibernation, claws, odor, horns, or stingers.

Sample Miniplan Involving Animals

Theme

    Covering of animals

Ideas to Emphasize

1. Animals have specific body coverings.
2. Each type of covering feels different when touched.
3. These coverings help the animal.

Learning Activities

If possible, take the children to a nearby farm to observe animals. If this is not possible, bring tame caged animals to school. Talk about different coverings: hair on a horse or dog, fur on a rabbit, feathers on a chicken or other bird, wool on a lamb, a shell on a turtle, and scales on a fish. (If animals are not available, be sure to have some good samples of these coverings for the children to feel and examine.) Use the number of coverings you feel are appropriate for the children you are teaching— you can use this theme for several days. Discuss each type of covering, its color, how it helps the animal, how it feels, how it differs from other coverings, where the animal lives, uses of coverings to people, and other facts. Give the children time to ask and answer questions and make comments. At the end of the discussion, have pictures of animals with both similar and dissimilar coverings. Let the children group the pictures according to similar coverings.

➤ If possible, feel the covering of various animals (for example, shell, fur, wool, skin, feathers).
➤ Observe animals at work (mule, bee, ant, spider, beaver, squirrel, or horse).
➤ Care for animals at the center or home by cleaning cages, feeding, and watering (this increases self-reliance). Discuss ways animals are cared for and limits in handling them.
➤ Using heavy paper, make a series of pictures about an animal, with each picture emphasizing a different part of the animal, such as the head, ears, or feet. Make identical pictures on cards for the children to match, to chart, or to form a puzzle.
➤ Observe wild animals at a park or zoo, if possible.
➤ Visit a ranch or farm to see poultry, sheep, cattle, or dairy animals.
➤ Rather than discussing general characteristics of animals, such as habitat, coverings, and diet, discuss many characteristics about one animal at a time (for example, where a cow lives, information about its calf, and sounds it makes).
➤ Make feeding places for birds in your play yard.
➤ Bring in a variety of bird nests.
➤ Catch a caterpillar, then watch it spin a cocoon and eventually emerge as a butterfly.

Plants and Nature

➤ Talk about using plants for food, clothing, protection, beauty, and health.
➤ Talk about different ways to start plants from bulbs, seeds, sets, slips, or parts of the produce (potato).
➤ Observe and discuss trees and shrubs during different parts of the year.

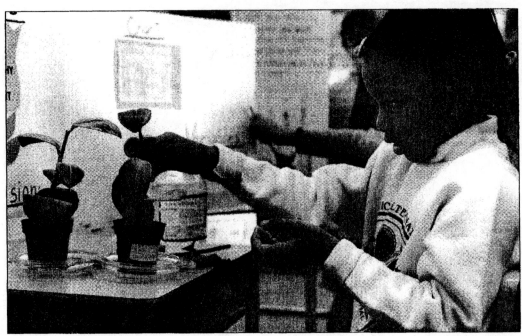

Plants within the classroom help children ask about and appreciate their environment.

➤ Prepare soil and plant a garden. Seeds for beans, melons, pumpkins, grass, and radishes germinate easily.

➤ If outdoor space is unavailable, plant a garden inside the classroom in a water table, pots, milk cartons, cans, jars, egg cartons, or paper cups.

➤ When possible, harvest, prepare, and use produce grown at school.

➤ Use *The Carrot Seed,* a story and record by Ruth Krauss.

➤ Soak bean seeds overnight, then open and examine them with a magnifying glass. Plant some beans against a glass container. Watch them grow, roots down, stem up.

➤ Observe how plants grow from seeds inside fruit (avocado, orange, apple). Note that they require light and water and grow toward the source of light. Also observe how some seeds grow faster than others. Sprout seeds for snacks, such as alfalfa, mung beans, soybeans, and wheat.

➤ Seal seeds and a picture of the produce in a small plastic bag. Have a second bag of the same seeds and picture separately. Have the children match them.

➤ Observe landscaping in your play yard.

➤ Put a stalk of celery in a bottle containing water and food coloring. Observe how the water is carried to the leaves.

➤ Purchase fresh cobs of popcorn. Let it dry; then pop it.

➤ Purchase and observe Indian corn.

➤ *Multicultural experience:* Provide a means of learning about different types of growth and climates—tropical (jungle), arid (desert), mountainous (forest), oceanic (rivers, seas, lakes), the local conditions, and others of interest.

➤ Prepare a nature table using plants and produce. Change often, or use produce for snacks or lunch.

➤ Gather different kinds of seeds (fruit, vegetable, weed).

➤ Observe changes in nature during different seasons.

➤ Discuss the cycle of a tree and its uses for lumber and paper.

➤ Plant and observe growth of seeds in a terrarium.

➤ Have plants in the classroom. Let the children help care for them.

➤ Talk about and eat the different parts of the plant, such as seeds (peas, beans, corn, peanuts), roots (carrots, radishes, beets, onions, potatoes), stems (celery, asparagus,

Sample Miniplan Involving Plants

Theme

Beans

Ideas to Emphasize

1. Bean seeds are usually larger than other seeds.
2. Beans grow on a vine or stem.
3. Beans are prepared for eating in different ways. Sprouts are eaten fresh while green beans are usually cooked. Dried beans need to be soaked and cooked before eating.

Learning Activities

Bean seeds, along with a variety of other seeds, such as beet, radish, carrot, and tomato, are placed on the science table. The teacher points out characteristics of the various seeds, and the children look at the seeds through a magnifying glass. During art, the seeds are used in a collage. An appropriate bean dish (for example, chili or string or lima beans) is served for lunch, and sprouts or bean salad for a snack. Bean seeds for sprouting and planting are soaked overnight. The children plant the beans in a terrarium or in paper cups to take home. Seeds for sprouting are placed in wire or plastic containers. The children care for the plants, noting daily changes.

rhubarb), leaves (lettuce, cabbage, spinach), blossoms (broccoli, cauliflower), and fruit (apples, berries, grapes). Watch for allergies when using seeds and food.

➤ Observe the growth of plants in water (tops of carrots or turnips, bird seed on a damp sponge, sweet or white potato in a jar).

➤ With heavy paper or tag board make a series of pictures about a plant, each picture emphasizing a different part (blossom, root, leaf, or stem). Place pictures on a chart, and make individual cards identical to those on the chart. Children match the cards to the chart or form a puzzle.

➤ Go on nature walks often. Take a sack for gathering treasures to make a collage.

➤ Visit a plant nursery or greenhouse.

➤ Provide a variety of nuts. Let the children sort them by kinds and learn their names. Help them crack and taste the different kinds of nuts. Some may need to be roasted. Watch for allergies when serving nuts.

➤ Grow herbs and seasonings.

Food

➤ Discuss the different tastes of food, such as sour, sweet, bitter, and salty. Show a picture or replica of the tongue and point out where these different tastes are located.

➤ Discuss different ways food grows—fish, shrimp, crab, oysters, and rice in water; apples and pears on trees; potatoes, carrots, and peanuts underground; and tomatoes and corn aboveground. (See the preceding section, "Plants and Nature.")

➤ Let the children help prepare fruits and vegetables for lunch or a snack.

➤ Observe differences in fruits and vegetables (color, taste, peeling, texture, and moisture).

➤ Taste fruits and vegetables in various forms (raw, cooked, or as juice).

➤ Experiment with coconut (husk, shell, liquid, chunks, shredded, toasted).

➤ Prepare food using dairy products (ice cream, butter, pudding, cottage cheese, cheese).

➤ Bake cookies, bread, and pies.

➤ Use water to make soup and gelatin and to boil corn.

➤ Observe a raw egg and see the difference when eggs are soft-boiled, hard-boiled, or fried.

➤ Pop popcorn. Discuss how heat makes the kernel expand.

➤ Make something for lunch or a snack (applesauce, spaghetti, sandwiches, fruit or vegetable plate).

➤ Provide empty food containers to stimulate interest in the domestic area.

➤ Use the food pyramid to discuss nutrition.

➤ Provide a certain food commodity in various forms, such as sugar (raw, refined, brown, powdered) or wheat (grains, cracked, flour).

➤ Examine food in various stages (for example, potato as seed, potato for eating, potato sprouting).

➤ Purchase (or grow) squash or pumpkins. Eat the produce but save and dry the seeds. Roast and eat some of the seeds; plant others.

➤ Purchase some raw peanuts. Shell and roast them. Make peanut butter. Watch for allergies when serving nuts.

➤ Make a drying frame and dry some fruit. Make fruit leather.

➤ Involve the five senses with food (smell different fruits and vegetables both raw and cooked; touch the various peelings; touch the food after it has been cooked; taste food as ingredients, and then cooked; sample foods that look alike but taste different, such as apple, pear, onion, turnip, radish, and white potato; compare peelings and meat of fruit and vegetables).

➤ Use household tools (grinder, peeler, beater, mixer).

 Sample Miniplan Involving Food

Theme

　Apples

Ideas to Emphasize

1. Apples are prepared for eating in different ways.
2. Apples are green, yellow, or red.
3. Apples grow on trees.
4. An apple has different parts.

Learning Activities

Pictures of apples in different forms are placed on the bulletin board. A low table nearby, washed and covered with butcher paper, contains apples of different colors and sizes. With the children, the teacher discusses how apples are grown, their various colors, different ways they are eaten, and the kind of covering. Children wash their hands. Under careful supervision, the teacher and children peel, core, and cut the apples. The apples are placed in an electric saucepan, cooked, and served for a snack.

➤ *Multicultural experience:* Provide a sensory table that features textures and smells from around the world (cinnamon, curry, pepper, extracts). Include coffee beans, grains, whole nuts, bark, dry leaves, kinds of flour, and raw cotton.

See Chapter 11 for further information on food.

Activities to Increase Awareness of Physical Science

Physical science is the study of material things and their properties and reactions when they are changed or combined. It includes areas such as astronomy, chemistry, engineering, geology, physics, and other related fields. These subjects are difficult to teach to young children because they are more abstract than other sciences; nevertheless, children should be exposed to physical science. Children are natural explorers and are curious about many things. It is appropriate for the teacher to utilize the scientific method: observe the children, provide experiences to which they can relate, help them ask and answer questions, encourage their exploration, help them come up with alternate solutions, and introduce good terms and help the children practice them. Be excited yourself!

As mentioned earlier in this text, the field of education is embracing a constructivist approach to early-childhood education. It moves children at all levels away from "one right answer" into the inquiry-based process, in which they construct learning through experience, research, and working cooperatively with others. Trained early-childhood educators provide children with a stimulating environment with opportunities and objects from which to "construct" learning. So it is with physical science. By handling, manipulating, reacting, combining, questioning, and other methods, children learn about their world. They experience, discover, and learn that while there may be one "right answer," this answer can lead them to further knowledge—memorization and rote answers are no longer conclusive.

Nor is physical knowledge limited to the science table. It happens in many ways, in many places, and in combination with other things. Every day, teachers can help children focus on exploration of the physical world by asking open-ended questions, extending children's thinking, and helping them build upon their experiences in developmentally appropriate ways.

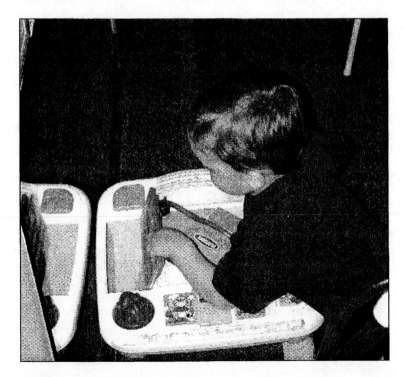

Mirrors add a new dimension to one's environment.

Sample Miniplan Involving Physical Science

Theme

  Crystals

Ideas to Emphasize

  1. Crystals are clear and angular in shape.
  2. Crystals are found in the earth or can be made (jewelry, candy).

Learning Activities

  1. The teacher shows the children different crystals and rocks. He explains what a crystal is and what things are crystals (sand, sugar, salt). Then he shows some crystals previously made. The children examine the crystals using a magnifying glass.
  2. On another table are many objects. Some are crystals, some are not. The teacher helps the children identify the crystals.

The word *physics* itself brings fear into the hearts of many teachers and children. But it is fun and important, and it belongs in the early-childhood curriculum. It's true! The pioneers in experiential learning through play—Lucy Sprague Mitchell, Caroline Pratt, Harriet Johnson, and John Dewey—were encouraging young children to explore objects in their physical world before the first half of the twentieth century (Dewey, 1938; Johnson, 1972; Pratt, 1924). Through the use of unit blocks, invented by Caroline Pratt, children gained experience with gravity, weight, balance, trial and error, the properties of matter, and the interaction of forces. Lucy Sprague Mitchell understood in the 1920s that children hone their spatial-relations skills by interacting with their environment. In *Young Geographers,* she writes about how children develop knowledge of their world through a process of discovery based on the relationships among facts of their physical environment (Mitchell, 1921/1971).

Sprung writes:

> In most classrooms, science, particularly *physical* science, is not given equal importance with other areas of the curriculum. In too many classrooms the 'science area' is a table on which some shells or leaves are set out at the beginning of the year and remain, collecting dust, when summer vacation rolls around. For the most part, early childhood science curriculum revolves around plant and animal activities. While these activities are a very important part of science and are comfortable for most early childhood teachers to carry out, they are far too limited in scope to be considered a full-bodied curriculum (1996, p. 30).

Activities of physical science that are part of the curriculum include activities for children to discover the physical properties of objects using a process approach (Piaget, 1970). They are activities that encourage exploration through the manipulation of familiar everyday objects, such as water, sand, blocks, and rolling things. There is nothing esoteric about these activities. In fact, they are part of a long tradition in progressive early-childhood education (Sprung, 1996).

Here are some suggested activities. Use, modify, or discard them as you feel appropriate for your children.

➤ Use woodworking tools and materials.

➤ Discuss occupational tools and their uses.

➤ Bring in a camera (a box camera is good). Take pictures of the children. Talk about how the camera works.

➤ Bring in and explore lenses (a magnifying glass, an old box-type camera, binoculars, eyeglasses, a telescope, a jar with water in it).

➤ Investigate how water or air can cause pressure, as in a balloon, bottle, can, or parachute.

➤ Use a straw or medicine dropper to illustrate a vacuum being created as air is removed and another substance rushes in to fill space.

➤ Introduce vibration by using rubber bands, strings on a piano or other instrument, or a tuning fork.

➤ Go to a children's museum or aquarium.

➤ Build dams and canals.

➤ Provide scales, thermometers, prisms, and color paddles.

➤ Have an outdoor science area with boards and boxes, levers, wheels and axles, pendulums, and pulleys (clotheslines).

➤ Provide wind-up toys and objects (clocks) so that children can explore their workings.

➤ Help the children work with batteries, switches, bells, and lights.

➤ Provide gears and springs for exploration (alarm clock, gear-driven toys, music boxes).

➤ Acquire empty plastic gallon containers. Cut and use them as funnels, scoops, pots, vases or other containers, sieves, bug catchers, and so on (see Figure 8.3).

➤ Make a discovery chart. Through exposure, children will discover different things about physics. Help them make and post a chart of their new findings. Use the chart in a group setting.

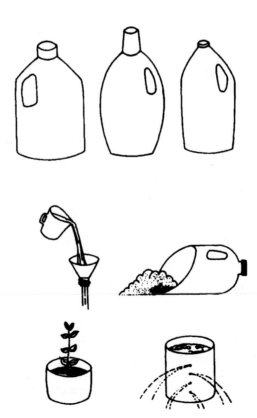

Figure 8.3 Empty Plastic Gallon Bottles Can Be Cut for Funnels, Scoops, Pots, or Sieves

 *Reflection*

Bess-Gene Holt (1930–1992) was a lifetime promoter of science with young children and a woman whose love for and dedication to science will influence teachers forever. Best-known in her field for her book, *Science with Young Children* (NAEYC, 1989), her enthusiasm for children drew packed rooms at her frequent workshops.

Holt felt that science education of the young child is crucial to the preservation of our world. As she saw us approaching the 21st Century with Earth in a disreputable condition, she communicated that it was crucial to teach science to children in a developmentally appropriate way so that they can understand and enjoy their lives as part of our present and future environment. Science and technology, she felt, should only be used to the benefit of our environment—conserving, preserving, and sharing resources.

Holt wanted people—children and adults alike—to experience science as a source of wonder and discovery, as a way of life as they interact with their world both mentally and physically. She believed that young children come with open minds to science inquiries and urged adults to avoid the passing on their own mental obstacles to this discovery—obstacles that can contaminate effective science education.

Another of Holt's ambitions was to promote a nonsexist approach to science for young children. She encouraged clear, sensible and happy science experiences, noting that "knowledge makes for more sensible behavior than ignorance." She fostered the idea of "personal ecology" for the child as the child interacts with, relates to and weaves together the reality that makes up his or her environment.

Above all, she cared about young children, our earth, and science as a way of life that can promote joy, excitement and beauty.

For further information about this influential teacher and scientist, see her book, *Science with Your Children* (Washington, DC: NAEYC, 1989).

Astronomy and Meteorology

Astronomy is especially difficult to teach at school because most observable activity occurs at night; however, you may want to discuss the warmth and light from the sun and encourage the children to notice sunsets and the stars and moon at night.

A visit to a planetarium is not the best for young children; they are often fearful when lights are turned off in an unfamiliar place. However, they may be interested in watching television reports about space exploration.

Cloud formations can be discussed and observed.

Chemistry

➤ Have the children mix things together and see the results. Even sand and water interest them.
➤ Provide experiences to see how heat affects cooking, wearing apparel, and activities.
➤ Observe how light changes things (growth, warmth, appearance).
➤ Discuss the use of light (flashlight, lamp, sun, candle, sundial, shadows).

➤ Talk about the seasons and how people and animals prepare for them; note how the landscape changes.

➤ Observe the difference in temperature in the shade and in the sun, or during different seasons of the year.

➤ Investigate water. (See also Chapter 6.) It evaporates, cleans, changes things (rocks, sand), comes in different forms (liquid, gas, solid), is used for many purposes (mixing paint, drinking, play), and can be an excellent emotional release. Following are some suggested uses of water:

Siphon from one container to another.

Float objects (soap, toys, wood, metals); show effects of size and weight.

Pour water into different-shaped containers and note that the water takes the shape of the container.

Colored water could be poured into different clear containers and the children can note how the water changes color when they are poured together.

Pour warm water into four different small jars and provide bowls with sugar in one, salt in one, sand in one, and oil in one. Spoon one ingredient into each jar, shake the jar and let it set 30 seconds. Spoon another ingredient into another jar and repeat the procedure until all four items have been used. Note the differences in the four solutions (salt and sugar dissolve, sand sinks, oil forms droplets which then rise to top). Introduce appropriate terms about what is happening.

Water absorption: Give each child a sponge on a plate, an eyedropper, and a small container of water. The child drops water onto the sponge. When she is ready, she squeezes the water to measure how much water has been absorbed by the sponge, repeating the process as long as the child wishes. It appears that the sponge is drinking the water.

Blow bubbles:

> *Bubbles* are bits of air or gas trapped inside a liquid ball. The surface of a bubble is very thin. Bubbles are particularly fragile when a dry object touches them. That's because soap film tends to stick to the object, which puts a strain on the bubble. So if you want your bubbles to last longer, keep everything wet, even the sides of the drinking straw (Paulu & Martin, 1992, p. 17).

Observe reflections.

Wash and dry doll clothes (evaporation).

Build dams and canals.

Feel the force as water comes from the tap.

Observe evaporation by marking the water level in a pan and checking it daily.

Build a snowman; make snow angels.

Freeze ice, then watch it melt; use ice to set gelatin.

Stretch various materials (fabrics, plastic, paper, rubber) over a can and pour water over it. Show that water goes through some things easier than others.

Introduce the terms *porous* and *nonporous*. Allow experimentation.

Water plants.

Discuss wearing apparel for water (boots, umbrella, cover-ups).

Clean with water. Talk about absorption.

Observe the moisture on a glass of ice water on a hot day.

Boil water to produce steam.

Pour water through a funnel or from one container to another.

Prepare creative materials.

Drink water.

Prepare food and cook it.

Change the consistency of materials by changing the amount of water.

Play in water (sail boats, wash self or toys).

Talk about conservation, pollution, recycling.

Using different-sized cups or containers, have children pour water back and forth for experience in varying volume.

With different amounts of water in glasses or jars, have a child gently tap the glass with a spoon for different musical tones.

Have the children determine objects that would sink or float.

➤ Make crystals (see "Sample Miniplan Involving Physical Science" p. 316).

➤ Make a discovery chart. As children are exposed to chemistry, they will discover different things about it. Help them make and post a chart of their new findings. Use their ideas in a group setting.

Geography

See Chapter 10 for more information.

Geology

➤ Discuss various kinds of rocks.

➤ Discuss various fuels and methods of heating (coal, oil, gas, electricity, steam, solar).

➤ Provide a museum or nature shelf with rocks, shells, and cones.

➤ On a science table, provide different kinds of soil, such as sand, clay, and volcanic ash. Place a magnifying glass nearby.

➤ Bring in a collection of rocks. Note how the rock changes color when it is wet.

➤ Examine pieces of coal with a magnifying glass.

➤ Point out and discuss the topography of your area (hills, mountains, valleys).

➤ Examine the properties of sand (varying volume, consistency with and without use of water).

Things in nature help young children develop meaningful concepts about the world around them.

➤ Notice the different surfaces of the play yard (sand, dirt, grass, asphalt, concrete). Discuss their uses.

➤ Take local field trips noting various geological formations.

➤ Make a discovery chart. As children are exposed to geology, they will discover different things about it. Help them make and post a chart of their new findings. Also use the chart in a group setting.

Physics

➤ Observe machines at work (dump truck, street sweeper, steamroller, garbage truck, derrick, steam shovel, farm, home).

➤ Familiarize children with gravity by placing a car on an inclined board or a wagon on a slope. Talk about roads.

➤ Talk about balance through use of blocks, a teeter-totter, and weights. Let children use their bodies in balancing.

➤ Discuss and have children participate in activities involving friction.

➤ Use a magnifying glass to examine various materials and objects.

➤ With the children, discover the use of a magnet and show things that are attracted and things that are not. Introduce, define, and experiment with new terms, such as *attract* and *repel*. Sprinkle pepper or lightweight visible material over water and watch it float. Dip small pieces of soap into the water and watch the material go away from (be repelled by) the soap. Sprinkle sugar into the water and watch the material float to (be attracted by) the sugar.

➤ Explore the uses of household tools and appliances (vacuum, eggbeater, mixer).

➤ Talk about various methods of communication (telephone, telegraph, radio, television, newspaper, magazine, letter).

➤ Use a magnifying glass to see what's hidden in soil or under leaves, what's on both sides of leaves, different patterns of snowflakes, and butterfly wings (Paulu & Martin, 1992).

➤ Make a game. Have the child focus on one dimension (color). When he knows this, add another dimension (shape). When he understands these, look for something that contains both the shape and color. Add another dimension, such as density (thick, thin). Have the child look for something that includes all three. Then add another (size), and look for all four. ("Look for something that is red, square, thin, and large.") Use only when the child is ready to combine dimensions.

➤ Observe shapes (round, square, oblong, triangular, hexagonal, octagonal, free-form); look for objects that are these shapes.

➤ Use a lever (for example, a claw hammer).

➤ Use wheels. Show how they aid in work, in play, and in the home (motors, pulleys, roller skates, toys, sewing machines, clocks).

➤ Provide substances and their opposites (wet and dry, long and short, hard and soft, hot and cold, sweet and sour, rough and smooth).

➤ Explore the weather (seasons, time of day, changes, temperature).

➤ Discuss how weather is influenced by sun, clouds, and wind.

➤ Observe and discuss fog (watch it move, lift); mist; rain (moisture it provides, appearance of sky, temperature); sun (warmth, light); frost; hail; snow. Talk about appropriate wearing apparel for different types of weather.

➤ Dress dolls or flannelboard characters of children for different types of weather.

➤ Investigate the characteristics of snow (taste, feel, appearance).

➤ Make a simple chart that shows snow, rain, sun, and wind. An arrow can be turned to indicate the current weather.

➤ Discuss wind. Use kites, pinwheels, or balloons (with caution). Watch smoke. Observe dry leaves when the wind blows. Watch a weather vane or wind sock. Discuss the strength of wind.

➤ Explore air (movement made by a fan, how air occupies space but is unseen). Use a paper bag, balloon (with caution), pinwheel, whistle, parachute, weather vane, tire pump, and bubbles.

Technology and Young Children

The use of computers with young children is a sensitive and controversial issue. The basic question appears to be: Will the addition of computers to the classroom add to or detract from the desired development of the young child? The question involves performance, skills, language, socialization, self-image, interest and creativity. "In one study only children using drill-and-practice programs had significant *losses* in creativity. Children using open-ended software made significant gains in intelligence, nonverbal skills, structural knowledge, long-term memory, complex manual dexterity, and self-esteem" (Haugland, 1992, p. 18).

Some education specialists say that young children definitely should not be involved with computers; some advocate computer exposure in all classrooms as a means of developing intimate contact with an individual's thinking. Still others take the middle-of-the road approach. Researchers list and discuss key issues regarding the cognitive stage of the child: socialization, isolation, real-life experiences, and the "pushing" of children.

Many adults use computers on an individual or solitary basis. Would computer use by children:

➤ Encourage fewer language and physical skills than in other activities?
➤ Be used as a means of entertainment or to seek the "one right answer"?
➤ Be another means of pressure and preparation for future schooling?
➤ Emphasize a narrow or inappropriate view of the abilities of young children?
➤ Encourage less personal interaction?
➤ Be less or more of a threat to work with precise information or open-ended information?
➤ **BE** the program rather than a part of the program?

Many examples of developmentally appropriate programs have been given throughout this text. But how do they apply to computer use? First, a refresher about the DAP programs being age- and individual-appropriate. Sitting at a computer is a stationary, usually solitary, highly structured, and academic approach—somewhat uncommon for children under 6. Drill programs are not compatible with NAEYC curriculum guides.

Some individuals have a difficult time in preserving ideas and privileges for themselves (adults), while others think that if it is good for one segment of the population, it is good for ALL—which includes young children. Those who work with young children must answer these questions for themselves about using computers with the children:

1. Is the presence of computers in the classroom disruptive or enriching?
2. Do computers provide one or many values for young children?
3. How does computer use help enhance personal qualities in young children (self-esteem, autonomy, persistence, decision making, creativity, cooperation, socialization, and so on)?
4. When computers are available in the classroom, is there a decrease in the amount of time children spend in other activities?
5. Through familiarity with computers, are pre-reading and reading skills increased in young children?
6. If you were offered *one* choice, which would you select and why?
   a. A computer in the classroom for young children.
   b. A computer for teacher use.
   c. A classroom aide.

Ever since computers have been introduced to children, there have been many debates about whether or not they belong in early classrooms. Depending on how ideas and

One needs time to contemplate and figure out the next move.

tools are used, there could be a convincing argument that computers are an asset or that they are a detriment to young children.

Computers enhance children's self-concept, and children demonstrate increased levels of spoken communication and cooperation. Children share leadership roles more frequently and develop positive attitudes toward learning (Clements, 1994; Cardelle-Elawar & Wetzel, 1995; Adams, 1996; Denning & Smith, 1997; Mathews, 1997). (For a detailed description of developmentally appropriate/ inappropriate computer experiences, see Haugland & Wright, 1997, p. 27).

Potential *positive* elements for kindergarten and primary grade children include:

➤ Use of developmentally appropriate software
➤ Time to experience, explore, seek information, ask probing questions, and build memory skills
➤ Personal interaction, integration of knowledge, delegation and acceptance of responsibility
➤ Improved motor skills
➤ Enhanced problem solving, mathematical and creative thinking, higher scores on tests of critical thinking and problem solving
➤ Well-trained teachers: practical experience, mentors, supervisory follow-up
➤ Use of high-quality software (list by Haugland and Wright, (1997, p. 90)
➤ Responsible use at computer, such as time allotment ("Maximum of 20 minutes at the computer, with control of the mouse for 10 minutes" before child makes another activity choice [Anderson, 2000, p. 90], sign-up list, other guidelines

Potential *negative* elements for kindergarten and primary grade children include:

➤ Developmentally inappropriate software
➤ Too many restrictions on the children (rushing, strict rules)
➤ Demanding answers and results

> Not having sufficient knowledge or assistance to make the program useful
> Warning of "significant losses in creativity" (Elkind, 1996)

Computer use for children younger than 3, who are full of movement (their eyes, ears, mouths, and bodies), frequent change, and focus is not recommended (Haugland and Herzog, 1998; Haugland and Wright, 1997; Elkind, 1998).

To maximize children's learning and to integrate computers into the lives of young children, (making sure that programs have been screened for developmental appropriateness), Haugland lists four critical components:

1. selecting developmental software;
2. using the website http://childrenandcomputers.com: the Haugland/Herzog Developmental Scale for Web Sites (1998) is a tool for evaluating the appropriateness of websites before exposing children to them;
3. integrating these resources into the curriculum; and
4. selecting computers to support learning experiences (2000, p. 12)

Haugland also makes the following points:

> Children should be introduced to computers early in life.
> The challenge to teachers is to find ways to use electronic technology that sparks the learning process.
> Research has shown that 3- and 4-year-old children who use computers with supporting activities to reinforce the major objectives of the programs have significantly greater developmental gains than children without computer experiences in similar classrooms—gains in intelligence, nonverbal skills, structural knowledge, long-term memory, manual dexterity, verbal skills, problem solving, abstraction, and conceptual skills (1992, p. 28).
> "What we as early childhood educators are presently doing most often with computers is what research and NAEYC guidelines say we should be doing least often" (1999, p. 33). It should be a process of exploration and discovery for teacher and child.
> Providing children with minimal helps, plenty of time, and a teacher who observes what they are doing while asking probing questions enhances and expands the children's computer experiences (1999, p. 28).
> "Most parents believe that computers can have a positive effect on children's learning, as dramatically illustrated in a national study done by the Milken Exchange on Education Technology and Peter D. Hart" (1999, p. 27).
> "In 1996 NAEYC published the 'NAEYC Position Statement: Technology and Young Children—Ages Three through Eight,' which provided important guidelines regarding technology with young children." Many teachers still question whether they should use computers with young children: do computers teach important developmental skills, and what is the teacher's role in the computer-integrated classroom? (p. 27)

She concludes her article with these thoughts: (1) computers empower young children and enable them to become totally immersed in the joys of learning, (2) computer experience must be developmentally appropriate or should not be used with young children, and (3) parent collaboration is important to increase computer access and a child-empowering experience at home and at school (1996, p. 18).

Computers have a positive impact on children when they provide concrete experiences, children have free access to control the learning experience, children and teachers learn together, peer tutoring is encouraged, and computers are used to teach powerful ideas (Haugland, 1998; O'Riordan, 1999; Papert, 1999).

As reported in *Young Children*, NAEYC (1996) has issued a position statement on technology and young children. According to the statement, early-childhood educators must take responsibility to influence events that are transforming the daily lives of children and families. This statement addresses several issues related to technology's use

Notable Quotes

"Integrating, assessment, and individualization of curriculum using discover centers, project and small-group work with lots of choices to facilitate high engagement, and opportunities for scaffold of skill development are the heart of our family studies preschool program" (Anderson, 2000, p. 90). Anderson concludes that children learn to cooperate and verbalize more freely at the computer, especially when they were observers and not in control of the action on the screen. And outcomes and benefits included enriched project-based, hands-on curriculum, which allowed the inclusion of computers as a discovery center with minimal adult supervision (p. 93).

"Rich in tradition of a play-centered approach to discovery": The cautionary voice of David Elkind (1996) also warned of "significant losses in creativity."

"A child exposed to developmental software had significant gains in intelligence, nonverbal skills, structural knowledge, long-term memory, and complex manual dexterity" (Haugland, 1992, p. 15).

with young children: (1) the essential role of the teacher in evaluating appropriate uses of technology; (2) the potential benefits of appropriate use of technology in early childhood programs; (3) the integration of technology into the typical learning environment; (4) equitable access to technology, including children with special needs; (5) stereotyping and violence in software; (6) the role of the teachers and parents as advocates; and (7) the implications of technology for professional development (p. 11).

Although now there is considerable research that points to the positive effects of technology on children's learning and development, the research indicates that, in practice, computers supplement and do not replace highly valued early-childhood activities and materials, such as art, blocks, sand, water, books, exploration with writing materials, and dramatic play. Computers can be used in developmentally appropriate ways beneficial

Young children learn about computers in an environment that is based on their needs and interests.

to children and also can be misused. Educators must use professional judgment in evaluating and using this learning tool appropriately by weighing the cost of technology against the costs of other learning materials and program resources to arrive at an appropriate balance for their classrooms.

Some schools continue to place computers in isolated labs where children are taught "computer literacy skills," which Papert (1993) states is the most useless thing we could teach children, as technology skills they learn today will not be the same skills needed in the future (p. 18).

What to Consider in Evaluating Software

Child features: one's own ability to manipulate on the screen; accurate representations; expanding complexity of various developmental levels; self-directed exploration.
Teacher features: interchangeability; control over customizing software for the classroom and the individual child.
Technical features: compatible with your computer; aesthetically pleasing; easy for children to use. Educators today are being challenged to create educational activities and environments that are attentive to the needs of different communities. It has been found that software in one's native tongue enhances self-concept, personalizes learning experiences, and reaffirms culture.

Conclusion   The problems and solutions of computer inclusion can be common or unique to any classroom. Therefore, teachers and administrators need to carefully consider the benefits and liabilities. After careful and thorough study of current information about computer/young child issues, study these concerns and reach your own conclusions:

Children What is the composition of the group (age, interests, abilities)?
  Would a computer promote socialization and cooperation?
  What rules would be needed?
  How would a computer support the varied developmental levels within the classroom?
  Would its use be just for your classroom or would it be shared with staff and/or other classrooms?
Adults How many adults would be available for assistance?
  How knowledgeable are the adults about computers?
  Are other adults pressuring for computers?
  Does it lighten or increase the teacher's responsibilities?
  Specifically, how would you use it with one or more children?
Computer What could it offer these children that the teacher (adults) could not?
  What guidelines would you establish with the children?
  Would it displace or supplement firsthand experiences with the children?
  Would its use be disrupting or enriching?
  Is the software structured or flexible?
  Is there software that would be appropriate for your group?
Classroom Where could it be placed for best use?
  Would it cause unreasonable financial adjustments?
  Would there be upkeep problems—delays, costs, and so on?
  Are opportunities abundant in the classroom for sensory experiences, construction, language, raw materials, firsthand experiences, choice of activity and playmates, and so on?
  Is it an "aid" to your classroom or an extra "burden" for you?

Gardner's theory (1993):

- was proposed as a way to "broaden conceptions of intelligence to include not only the results of paper-and-pencil tests but also knowledge of the human brain and sensitivity to the diversity of human cultures (Krogh, 1997, pp. 29–48).

- was designed as an alternative means of preassessing preschool children's cognitive abilities (Fleege, in Hart, 1997).

- supports the notion that some children learn best in ways other than the verbal, mathematical, or logical approach, including bodily kinesthetic, interpersonal, and spatial ways of learning (Gardner, 1983).

- places mathematics in the area of *logical-mathematical intelligence.*

- "should be integrated with the other areas of intelligence in order to reach children through their strongest areas of learning" (Charlesworth, 1997, p. 51).

- applies to curriculum development and the visual arts education of young children in a positive way.

- is designated *Project Spectrum* (Krechevsky & Gardner, 1990) and was designed as an alternative means to standardized testing of preschool children's cognitive abilities.

- furnishes richer and more complex portraits of children in context-sensitive ways, emphasizing the integration of alternative assessment with integrated instructional practices (Fleege in Hart, et al., 1997, p. 15).

- includes "music which requires the mind to behave in ways different from linguistic or mathematical thinking . . . which development is essential to the growth of the whole child" (Kenney in Hart, 1997, p. 210).

- implies his work in relation to curriculum development and the visual arts education of young children has been positive (Kantner, 1990).

- began with six components but has been extended to eight.

Figure 8.4   Notes and Quotes About Gardner's Theory of Multiple Intelligences.

Application of Principles

1. Considering the Bureau of Labor statistics at the beginning of the chapter, give some curriculum suggestions for teachers *and* parents of young children.
2. Briefly outline your feelings about (a) science and (b) technology. Have your experiences been positive or negative? How can you reinforce positive feelings and eliminate negative feelings about science and technology in yourself and others?
3. Considering science as a whole, what are your favorite areas? How could you teach these topics to young children?
4. Identify some negative attitudes toward taking science classes or planning some areas for young children. Make several plans where-by you can change those attitudes into positive, exciting experiences for yourself and children.
5. How do you think young children can learn to appreciate themselves and their immediate and extended environment?

6. Plan and take a nature walk with several children. What did you expect them to learn? What did you learn?

7. Identify and plan two simple, exciting activities to teach children about physical science. The first activity should include areas of your interest; the second should include an area that you feel less sure about.

8. Brainstorm with a friend or colleague about the many ways an outdoor experience involves science. How about an indoor experience?

9. Quietly contemplate your personal experiences learning to use a computer (or why you have not learned to use a computer). Could you be a good example to others? Do you use a computer frequently or resist using one? Could you strengthen your positive attitude or diminish a negative one?

10. Briefly discuss multiple intelligences. In order of strength, identify different intelligences in yourself or someone else.

11. Describe a scene where young children could have an enriching experience using a computer.

12. If you were responsible to decide whether a computer would be part of a home or classroom experience for young children, *how* and *what* would you decide? Give reasons.

13. Have the children place their hands over one sense organ at a time (eyes, ears, mouths, noses). Discuss the use of each different sense organ. Caution: are there some children/adults in your group whose sensory organs are impaired or who speak a different language? How do different circumstances affect learning?

14. What conditions exist in your classroom or community that would help you teach good science/technology principles to young children? (Weather, climate, food production?)

15. What is your attitude toward scientific events? Do you need to change?

16. Dewey viewed children as scientists whose major occupation was problem solving. How can you use this view in your classroom?

17. How do you help the children learn about weather or seasons when that kind of weather does not occur in your locality? For example: wind (do you use kites, pinwheels, balloons—with caution, parachute, weather vane, or wind sock?), drought, flooding, etc.? Do you ever use a thermometer, pinwheels, whistles, weather vane, or tire pump?

18. Science kits and curricula, with attractive advertising and brilliant colors, should not give adults a false sense of the right way to teach young children. All interactions with nature must be safe and sensible.

19. Talk about the importance of good mental hygiene, thinking good thoughts, positive relationships, helpfulness instead of negativity.

References

NOTE: Current references are used when available. Older references are classic, introductory and important in development of later ideas, policies, and practices.

Abruscato, J. (1992). *Teaching children science* (3rd ed). Boston: Allyn & Bacon.

Adams, P. (1996). Hypermedia in the classroom using earth and science. CD-ROMs. *Journal of Computers in Mathematics & Science Teaching, 15*(1/2) 18–34.

American Association for the Advancement of Science. (1989). *Science for all Americans: A Project 2061 report on literacy goals in science, mathematics and technology.* Washington, DC: Author.

American Association for the Advancement of Science. (1993). *Benchmarks in science literacy.* Washington, DC: Author.

American Association for the Advancement of Science. (1995). Common ground: Benchmarks and national standards. *2061 Today, 5*(1), 1–3.

Anderson, G. T. (2000). Computers in a developmentally appropriate curriculum. *Young Children, 55*(2), 90–93.

Berk, L. E., & Winsler, A. (1995). *Scaffolding children's learning: Vygotsky and early childhood education.* Washington, DC: NAEYC.

Black, S. M. (1999). HIV/AIDS in early childhood centers: The ethical dilemma of confidentiality versus disclosure. *Young Children, 54*(3), 39–45.

Bredekamp, S. (Ed.). (1987). *Developmentally appropriate practice in early childhood programs serving children from birth to age 8.* Washington, DC: NAEYC.

Bredekamp, S., & Coppel, C. (Eds.). (1997). *Developmentally appropriate practice in early childhood programs* (rev. ed.). Washington, DC: NAEYC.

Bredekamp, S., & Rosegrant, T. (Eds.). (1992). *Reaching potentials: Appropriate curriculum and assessment for young children.* Washington, DC: NAEYC.

Caperton, G., & Papert, S. (1999). *Vision for education: The Caperton-Papert platform.* Online at http://www.mamamedia.com/areas/grownups/new/education/papert_001.html.

Cardelle-Elawar, M., & Wetzel, K. (1995). Students and computers as partners in developing students' problem-solving skills. *Journal of Research on Computing in Education, 27*(4) 378–401.

Carson, R. (1956). *The sense of wonder.* New York: Harper & Row.

Char, C., & Forman, G. E. (1994). Interactive technology and the young child: A look to the future. In J. L. Wright & D. D. Shade (Eds.), *Young Children: Active learners in a technological age* (pp. 167–177). Washington, DC: NAEYC.

Charlesworth, R. (1997). Mathematics in the developmentally appropriate integrated curriculum. In C. Hart, D. Burts, & R. Charlesworth, *Integrated curriculum and developmentally appropriate practice: birth to age eight.* Albany, NY: State University of New York Press, pp. 51–73.

Clements, D. H. (1993). Computer technology and early childhood education. In J. L. Roopnarine & J. E. Johnson (Eds.). *Approaches to early childhood education* (pp. 295–316). New York: Macmillan.

Clements, D. (1994). The uniqueness of the computer as a learning tool: Insights from research. In J. L. Wright & D. D. Shade (Eds.), *Young children: Active learners in a technological age.* Washington, DC: NAEYC.

Davidson, J. (1994). Using computers to support thematic units. In J. L. Wright & D. D. Shade (Eds.), *Young children: Active learners in a technological age* (pp. 178–180). Washington, DC: NAEYC.

Denning, R., & Smith, P. (1997). Cooperative learning and technology. *Journal of Computers in Mathematics and Science Teaching, 16*(2/3), 177–200.

Dewey, J. (1938). *Education and Experience.* New York: Collier.

Edwards, C., Gandini, L., & Forman, G. (1995). *The hundred languages of children: The Reggio Emilia approach to early childhood education.* Norwood, NJ: Ablex.

Elkind, D. (1966). Viewpoint: Young children and technology: A cautionary note. *Young Children, 51*(6), 22–23.

Elkind, D. (1981). *Children and Adolescents* (3rd ed.), New York: Oxford University Press.

Elkind, D. (1991). Developmentally appropriate practice: A case study of educational inertia. In S. L. Kagan, (Ed.), The care and education of America's young children: Obstacles and opportunities. *Ninetieth yearbook of the National Society for the Study of Education. Part I,* 1–16. Chicago: University of Chicago Press.

Elkind, D. (1996). Young children and technology: A cautionary note. *Young Children, 51*(6), 22–23.

Elkind, D. (1998). Computers for infants and young children. *Child Care Information Exchange, 123,* 44–46.

Family Forum. (1999). *Computers in the home.* Online at http://www.parenting.qa.com/cgi-bin/detailcomputers/5203.core.tipsfact.

Fenton, G. M. (1996). Back to nature's classroom. *Young Children, 51*(3), 8–11.

Fisher, A. (1992a). Crisis in education, Part 1: Science + math = F. *Popular Science, 241*(2), 58–63, 108.

Fisher, A. (1992b). Crisis in education, Part 2: Why Johnny can't do science and math. *Popular Science, 241*(3), 50–55, 98.

Fitzsimmons, P. (1995, Fall). Kindergarten conversations: Butterflies, crystals, and babies. *Connections: Newsletter of the Vermont Association for the Education of Young Children.* Available from VAEYC, P.O. Box 5656, Burlington, VT 05402-5656.

Fleege, P. O. (1997). Assessment in an Integrated Curriculum. In C. Hart, D. Burts, & R. Charlesworth, *Integrated curriculum and developmentally appropriate practice* (pp. 313–334). Albany, NY: State University of New York Press.

Forman, G. (1994). Different media, different languages. In L. Katz & B. Cesarone, (Eds.), *Reflections on the Reggio Emilia approach* (pp. 41–53). Urbana, IL: ERIC Clearing House on Elementary Education.

Forman, G., & Kuschner, D. (1983). *The child's construction of knowledge: Piaget for teaching children.* Washington, DC: NAEYC.

Furman, E. (1990). Plant a potato—learn about life (and death). *Young Children, 46*(1), 15–20.

Gardner, H. (1991). *To open minds.* New York: Basic Books.

Gardner, H. (1991). *The unschooled mind.* New York: Basic Books.

Gardner, H. (1993). *Frames of mind: The theory of multiple intelligence.* New York: Basic Books. (Original work published 1983)

Gardner, H. (1993). *Multiple intelligences: The theory into practice.* New York: Basic Books.

Gardner, H. (1994). *The arts and human development.* New York: Basic Books.

Goldhaber, J. (1998). Oh, Miss Jones! Where did you get that beautiful butterfly? *Young Children, 53*(4), 60–63.

Haugland, S. W. (1998). *Children and computers.* Online at http://childrenandcomputers.com.

Haugland, S. W. (1992). *Science experiences for early childhood years* (5th ed.). New York: Merrill/Macmillan.

Haugland, S. W. (1999). What role should technology play in young children's learning? Part 1. *Young Children, 54*(6), 26–31.

Haugland, S. W. (2000). What role should technology play in young children's learning? Early childhood classrooms in the 21st century: Using computers to maximize learning. Part 2. *Young Children, 55*(1), 12–18.

Haugland, S., & Herzog, G. (1998). *The developmental software scale for web sites.* Cape Girardeau, MO: K.I.D.S. & Computers.

Haugland, S. W., & Wright, J. L. (1997). *Young children and technology: A world of discovery.* New York: Allyn & Bacon.

Henninger, M. L. (1987). Learning mathematics and science through play. *Childhood Education, 63*(3), 167–171.

Holt, B. G. (1989). *Science with young children* (rev. ed.). Washington, DC: NAEYC. Order #309.

Johnson, H. (1972). *Children in the nursery school.* New York: Agathon.

Kantner, L. (1990). Visual arts education and multiple intelligences: Before implementation. In W. J. Moody (Ed.), *Artistic intelligences, implications for education.* New York: Teachers College Press.

Kenney, S. H. (1997). Music in the developmentally appropriate integrated curriculum. In C. Hart, D. Burts, & R. Charlesworth (Eds.), *Integrated curriculum and developmentally appropriate practice* (pp. 103–144). Albany, NY: State University of New York Press.

Kilmer, S. J., & Hofman, H. (1995). Transforming science curriculum. In S. Bredekamp & T. Rosegrant (Eds.), *Reaching potentials: Transforming early childhood curriculum and assessment,* Vol. 2 (pp. 43–66). Washington, DC: NAEYC.

Kokoski, T. M., & Downing-Leffler, N. (1995). Boosting your science and math programs in early childhood education: Making the home-school connection. *Young Children, 50*(5), 35–39.

Krauss, R. (1989). *The carrot seed.* New York: Harper Children's Books.

Krechevsky, M., & Gardner, H. (1990). The emergence and nurturance of multiple intelligences: The Project Spectrum approach. In M. A. A. Howe (Ed.), *Encouraging the development of exceptional skills and talents.* Leicester, Eng.: British Psychological Society.

Krough, S. L. (1997). How children develop and why it matters. In C. Hart, D. Burts, & R. Charlesworth (Eds.), *Integrated curriculum and developmentally appropriate practice.* (pp. 29–48) Albany, NY: State University of New York Press.

Kupetz, B. N., & Twiest, M. M. (2000). Nature, literature, and young children: A natural combination. *Young Children, 55*(1), 59–63.

Lenhoff, R., & Huber, L. (2000). Young children make maps! *Young Children, 55*(5), 6–11.

Lind, K. K. (1997). Science in the developmentally appropriate integrated curriculum. In C. Hart, D. Burts, & R. Charlesworth (Eds.), *Integrated curriculum and developmentally appropriate practice: Birth to age eight* (pp. 75–101). Albany: State University of New York Press.

Malaguzzi, L. (1987). *The hundred languages of children.* Catalog. Reggio Emilia, Italy: Department of Early Education, Region of Emilia Romagna.

Mathews, K. (1997). A comparison of the influence of interactive CD-ROM storybooks and traditional print storybooks on reading comprehension. *Journal of Computing in Education, 29*(3), 263–273.

Milken Exchange. (1998). *West Virginia Study Results.* Online at http://www.milkenexchange.org/research/wvirginia_article.html.

Milken Exchange on Education Technology, & Hart, P. D. (1999). Public opinion poll, 1998. Online at www:milkenexchange.org/publications.

Mitchell, L. S. (1921, 1971). *Young geographers.* New York: Bank Street College of Education.

NAEYC Resource Sales. Call 800-424-2460 or 202-232-8777, ext. 604 or NAEYC catalog at www.naeyc.org.

National Association for the Education of Young Children. (1996). NAEYC position statement: Technology and young children—Ages three through eight. *Young Children, 51*(6), 11–16.

National Association for the Education of Young Children and National Association of Early Childhood Specialists in State Departments of Education (NAECS/SDE). (1991). Guidelines for appropriate curriculum content and assessment in programs serving children ages 3 through 8. *Young Children, 46*(3), 21–38.

National Center for Improving Science Education (NCISE). (1990). *A report from the National Center for Improving Science Education.* Colorado Springs, CO: Author.

National Council for Teachers of Mathematics. (1989). *Curriculum and evaluation standards for school mathematics.* Reston, VA: Author.

Nelson, L., & Frederick, L. (1994). Can children design curriculum? *Educational Leadership, 51*(5), 71–74.

O'Riordan, K. (1999). *Report reviews current research on education technology.* Online at http://www.milkenexchange.org; click on articles.

Papert, S. (1993). *The children's machine: Rethinking school in the age of the computer.* New York: Basic.

Patton, M. M., & Kokoski, T. M. (1996). How good is your early childhood science, mathematics, and technology program:? Strategies for extending your curriculum. *Young Children, 51*(5), 38–44.

Paulu, N., & Martin, M. (1992). *Helping your children learn science.* Washington, DC: U.S. Government Printing Office. GPO Stock #065-000-00520-4.

Perry, G., & Rivkin, M. (1992). Teachers and science. *Young Children, 47*(4), 9–16.

Piaget, J. (1952). *The origins of intelligence in children.* New York: W. W. Norton.

Piaget, J. (1970). *Science education and psychology of the child.* New York: Grossman.

Pratt, C. (1924). *Experimental practice in the city and country school.* New York: Dutton.

Ross, M. E. (2000). Science their way. *Young Children, 55*(2), 6–13.

Sagan, C. (1989, September 10). Why we need to understand science. *Parade,* p. 6.

Schultz, C. (1985). Early childhood. *Science & Children, 22*(8), 49–51.

Seefeldt, C. (2000). *Social studies for the preschool-primary child* (6th ed.). Upper Saddle River, NJ: Merrill/Prentice Hall.

Shade, D. D., & Watson, J. A. (1990). Computers in early education: Issues put to rest, theoretical links to sound practice, and the potential contribution of microworlds. *Journal of Educational Computing Research, 6*(4), 375–392.

Sible, K. P. (2000). Water, water everywhere! *Young Children, 55*(1), 64–65.

Smith, R. F. (1987). Theoretical framework for preschool science experiences. *Young Children, 42*(2), 34–40.

Sprung, B. (1996). Physics is fun, physics is important, and physics belongs in the early childhood curriculum. *Young Children, 51*(5), 29–33.

Third International Mathematics and Science Study (TIMSS). (1997, Jan.). Stronger focus needed in improving math education, study shows. *Community Update,* #43, U.S. Dept. of Ed.

Third International Mathematics and Science Study (TIMSS). (1997, July/Aug.). Americans beat international averages in science and math. *Community Update,* #49, U.S. Dept. of Ed.

Van Dusen, L. M., & Worthen, B. R. (1995). Can integrated instructional technology transform the classroom? *Educational Leadership, 53*(2), 28–33.

Wadsworth, B. (1996). *Piaget's theory of cognitive and affective development: Foundations of constructivism* (5th ed.). New York: Longman.

Wells, G. (1994). The complementary contributions of Halliday and Vygotsky to a "language-based theory of learning." *Linguistics and Education, 6,* 41–90.

Wilson, R. A. (1995). Nature and young children: A natural connection. *Young Children, 50*(6), 4–11.

Woods, C. S. (2000). A picture is worth a thousand words: Using photographs in the classroom. *Young Children, 55*(5), 82–84.

CHAPTER

9

Mathematics

Main Principles

1. Teachers and parents need to reflect a positive attitude toward mathematics (pp. 336–337).

2. Two nationally recognized educational organizations provide goals and standards for teaching mathematics to young children: National Association for the Education of Young Children and the National Council of Teachers of Mathematics (pp. 338–339).

3. Children have a natural curiosity regarding mathematical knowledge (pp. 339–340).

4. Teachers provide appropriate mathematical concepts to young children (pp. 340–346).

5. Appropriate mathematical experiences for young children: one-to-one correspondence, teaching about sets, time concepts, and spontaneous experiences (pp. 346–348).

6. Mathematical values for young children include: stages of development, literature and mathematics, classroom activities, and spontaneous activities (pp. 348–354).

7. Activities to increase mathematical conceptualization include: sorting and classifying, counting, measuring, exploring space and shapes (pp. 354–359).

8. Suggestions for student application of the principles in this chapter (pp. 360–361).

Introduction

How often have you heard a child or an adult say, "I don't like math! I'll do anything to get someone else to do it for me"? Many teachers don't like one subject or another (reading, outdoor activity, etc.). Isn't part of our job to help children understand and enjoy the many facets of education? Mathematics is just one part of our job. It isn't a matter of whether we think different subjects are important, it's a matter of giving each child a fair start and a love for all aspects of learning! If adults dislike math because of earlier experiences that left them feeling less than confident, here is their golden "second chance" to learn the rewards of math through positive and rewarding experiences with children!

Early childhood teachers need to keep a keen eye for opportunities to integrate mathematics into other curriculum areas in order to help students understand that mathematics is useful, enjoyable, and challenging! It is not isolated, boring, difficult, and frustrating. These teachers must have flexible expectations of young children and their mathematical concepts. Children relate objects and activities as a means of putting their world into perspective. They should be allowed to practice mathematical concepts; allowed to discover things for themselves through concrete, sensory, familiar, useful, and exploratory ways; and then helped to move forward one step at a time.

Some attainable goals, based on the developmental abilities of individual children in a relaxed atmosphere, are as follows:

1. to stimulate an interest in numbers and their uses
2. to show how number concepts can aid in problem solving
3. to increase worldly knowledge through mathematics
4. to introduce number symbols and terms as the children indicate readiness
5. to stimulate an interest in numbers and their uses

Unlike the curriculum of older children and adults, mathematics for young children is an integrated topic. In fact, interest in the topic is created when these young children have a manipulative experience, when concepts are within their level of understanding, when learning is related to familiar things, and when there is an integration of curriculum—such as number learning through music, art, food, science, language arts, and other areas.

Math can be taught through many different curriculum areas. For example, it can be easily taught through children's storybooks, music, outdoor activities, free play, and other

---

 **Reflection**

How can the following examples be meaningful to young children?

"We need two more blocks to make this stack as high as that one." This is later followed by subtraction: "If I give you two of my cars, we will both have the same number of cars!"

Count the number of children and chairs for snack time and determine whether to get (add) more chairs or children, or have some of the children move to another setting (subtract).

When one wants (or needs) more of something, one adds (gets more); when one wants less (or not as many), one subtracts (or takes away). Some children understand what *equal* means: illustrated by placing the same number of children or objects on one side of a line as on the other side.

Using children or familiar objects helps the children see relationships.

times. All are readily available resources. Teachers must carefully review any sources to enhance math education, and should select books in which illustrations portray correct mathematical ideas, are attractive, appeal to young children, and are appropriate in size and detail for the child's developmental characteristics. The text should be easily understood and interesting to young children. A number of resources are available; however, some counting books are inappropriate for young children because of unclear illustration, advanced concepts, or the misuse of cardinal or ordinal numbers. For a refresher, cardinal numbers indicate how many (1, 2, 3); ordinal numbers indicate the relationship with another item or event (first, second, third).

Teachers should take caution to encourage children to explore and enjoy mathematics—avoid making such comments as "I don't like it, either," or "It's hard for me, too—I never can balance my checkbook," or discouraging "child-invented" problem-solving techniques that work and/or seem right to children, such as counting on one's fingers. Teacher discouragement of such techniques makes mathematics seem arbitrary, convention-bound, and counterintuitive. On the contrary, good mathematics is *intuitive*. Teachers who know how counting skill develops know when to notice, applaud, and appreciate the progression of young children's numerical concepts one step at a time.

We need to teach our children, from early life, to be thinkers and solvers—a concept whereby our youngest children can have experiences and opportunities to use their minds creatively, instead of being mere repeaters of facts. This chapter shows how activities and attitudes can influence the young child in beginning and continuing productive thinking—not just in math, but in all topics.

For decades, early childhood educators have advocated the hands-on approach, and more recently they have emphasized the need for activities, materials, and relationships to be built on what is developmentally appropriate for each child. Activities grounded in the experiences of the individual child increase his/her interest, attention to details, and future use of these skills.

Time to contemplate about size, shape, color, and use.

Importance of Math Learning for Young Children

Two nationally recognized educational organizations, the **National Association for the Education of Young Children (NAEYC)** and the **National Council of Teachers of Mathematics (NCTM),** provide goals and standards for teaching mathematics to young children. They say that early-childhood educators should use a constructivist theoretical view of both Piaget and Vygotsky. The *Piagetian* view places the major focus on the child's inner maturation, making his own discoveries, and constructing knowledge independently (Charlesworth & Lind, 1995a). Young children have a natural curiosity and an inherent desire to find patterns and resolve problems, the essence of mathematics; however, very young children are not capable of abstract concepts or logical thinking. They construct their mathematical knowledge by interaction with their physical and social worlds. Teachers of preschoolers need to engage young children in appropriate and challenging mathematics activities. The work of Vygotsky recognizes the importance of developmental and environmental factors in learning and teaching (Cobb, 1994). *Vygotskians* are especially concerned with children reaching their full potential (Charlesworth & Lind, 1995a). The NCTM (1989, 1991, 2000) has recommended shifting from a traditional instructional approach to an approach that better fosters the mathematical power of children. This new approach is consistent with the teaching guidelines outlined in the revised edition of *Developmentally Appropriate Practice in Early Childhood Programs* (Bredekamp & Copple, 1997).

NAEYC and NCTM also suggest these standards:

➤ Promote an integrated curriculum and practices that emphasize exploration.
➤ Value the process rather than the one-correct-answer end product.
➤ Include skills and concepts that are both individually and age appropriate.
➤ Integrate mathematics into other content areas, cultural backgrounds, and interests.

According to the **NAEYC** guidelines (Bredekamp, 1987; Bredekamp & Copple, 1997) "mathematics begins with the exploration of materials such as building blocks, sand, and water for 3-year-olds." For 4- and 5-year olds, "learning about math, science, social studies, health, and other content areas are all integrated through personal and meaningful activities." For 5- through 8-year-olds, "the goal of the math program is to enable children to use math through exploration, discovery, and solving meaningful problems. Math activities are integrated with other relevant projects, such as science and social studies" (Bredekamp, 1987, pp. 52, 56, and 71).

The **NCTM** standards for prekindergarten through grade 12 (2000, ch. 3) are "ambitious and required to achieve a society that has the capability to think and reason mathematically." And in chapter 4, "Standards for Grades Pre-K-2," considerations "such as high-quality educational settings and experiences become paramount." Building on curiosity and enthusiasm, children's mathematical learning is more than "getting ready" for school. It challenges young children to increased sophistication through ideas related to patterns, shapes, numbers, and space.

The **NCTM** believes that mathematics education for children aged 3–8 should

➤ be developmentally appropriate through "exploration and interaction with materials and people" (NCTM, 1994–95, p. 16): Assessment and data should be collected through observations and interviews as children engage in mathematics problem solving and investigations (not through timed arithmetic fact tests); observations should be recorded as anecdotal records, documented with drawings, painting, graphs, and the like (p. 66); and
➤ develop and expand language acquisition while structuring, restructuring, and connecting mathematics.

Each standard comprises a small number of goals that apply across all grades—such as a commonality that promotes a focus on the students' knowledge and sophisti-

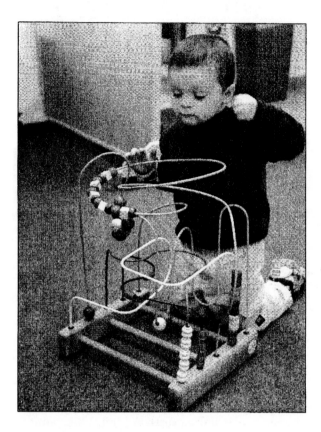

Contemplate the many math skills this young boy is encountering (number, speed, comparisons . . .).

cation as they progress through the curriculum. Standards for grades pre-K–2 include nurturing and supporting an innate desire for learning. Recommended mathematics learning can help parents and educators give children a solid affective and cognitive foundation.

The curriculum standards emphasize five goals for students:

1. Learn to value mathematics.
2. Become confident of one's own ability.
3. Become a mathematical problem solver.
4. Learn to communicate mathematically.
5. Learn to reason mathematically.

After reviewing *Principles and Standards for School Mathematics* (2000), *Professional Standards for Teaching Mathematics* (1991), and *Curriculum and Evaluation Standards for School Mathematics* (1989), all by the NCTM, Murray (2001) concluded that math would be best understood and appreciated by children and teachers alike if it followed his five-C formula. (shown graphically in Figure 9.1).

Notable Highlights of Mathematics for Young Children

➤ Children have a natural curiosity regarding mathematical knowledge and are ready to learn mathematics through *informal experiences.*
➤ Teachers need to know what mathematical foundation children already have.
➤ Children as young as 3 years old can understand simple addition.
➤ Treat children as valuable members of learning; build upon their strengths.
➤ Combine language, action, and mathematics; use "good" questions or problems.
➤ Use various means of assessing each child's mathematical knowledge.

Figure 9.1 A Graphic
Representation of Murray's
Five-C Formula

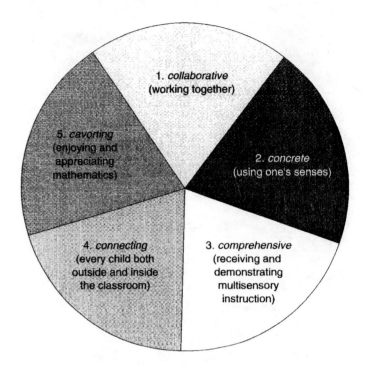

> Make the classroom interesting, varied, and challenging.
> Young children acquire mathematics concepts through interacting with the environ-
> ment (naturalistic); through informal means (suggestions, questions, comments);
> and through preplanned activities (structure) (Charlesworth & Lind, 1995a, unit 2).

Websites

Helpful websites for teaching math to young children include:
   Conference on Standards for Preschool and Kindergarten Mathematics Education:
      www.gse.buffalo.edu/org/conference/
   National Council of Supervisors of Mathematics:
      (NCSM): http://ncsmonline.org/
   National Council of Teachers of Mathematics (NCTM):
      http://nctm.org and www.standards.nctm.org
   U.S. Department of Education, Office of Educational Research and Improvement
   (OERI) National Institute on Early Childhood Development and Education:
      www.ed.gov/pubs/EarlyMath/

Role of the Teacher

Teachers, having flexible expectations of young children and their mathematical concepts,
should capitalize on spontaneous events to the degree that the experience is meaningful
to the children. Many opportunities should be provided for children to see, manipulate,
and test ideas in a friendly atmosphere. Children relate objects and activities as a means
of putting their world into perspective, and should be allowed to practice mathematical
concepts and to discover things for themselves through concrete, sensory, familiar, useful,
and exploratory ways, and then should be helped to move forward one step at a time.

Mathematical terms can be introduced to children as long as these terms are defined
and the children have opportunities to practice their meanings. When one wants (or
needs) more of something, one adds (gets more). When one wants less (or not as many),
one subtracts (or takes away). Some children understand what *equal* means.

Maria Montessori devised games, activities, and materials for teaching number concept to young children. She thought the concept of *zero* (or nothing) was worth special

 *Reflection*

Through your prior knowledge and understanding about the learning of young children, and based on **NCTM** standards, *cited on p. 339*, indicate which of the following statements is **TRUE**:

_____ 1. All children have an innate desire for learning to be nurturing and supportive.

_____ 2. Standards can help parents and educators give children a solid affective and cognitive foundation in mathematics.

_____ 3. Appropriate mathematical experiences challenge young children to explore ideas related to patterns, shapes, numbers, and space with increasing sophistication.

_____ 4. Children's long-term success in learning and development requires high-quality experiences during the "years of promise."

_____ 5. Mathematics learning builds on the curiosity and enthusiasm of children and grows naturally from their experiences.

_____ 6. Adults support young children's diligence and mathematical development when they direct attention to the mathematics children use in their play, challenge them to solve problems, and encourage their persistence.

_____ 7. Children learn through exploring their world; thus, interests and everyday activities are natural vehicles for developing mathematical thinking.

_____ 8. When children recognize a stop sign by focusing on the octagonal shape, adults have an opportunity to talk about different shapes in the environment.

_____ 9. Through careful observation, conversations, and guidance, adults can help children make connections between mathematics in familiar situations and new ones.

_____10. Children learn mathematical concepts through everyday activities: sorting, reasoning, representing, recognizing patterns, following directions, music, using spatial visualization, and taking other advantages of their environment.

_____11. "Not knowing" more often reflects a lack of opportunity than an inability to learn.

_____12. Schools and/or parents should furnish materials and allow young children to continue to learn mathematics through counting, measuring, constructing with blocks and clay, playing games and doing puzzles, listening to stories, and engaging in dramatic play, music, and art.

_____13. Teachers need to determine what students already know as they prepare their classrooms and learning experiences for young children.

_____14. Mathematical learning must be active, rich in natural mathematical language, and filled with understanding rather than built around preconceptions about children's limitations.

_____15. Assessment data on children should be collected through observations, interviews, and anecdotal records as children engage in mathematics problem solving and investigations, and not through timed arithmetic fact tests.

Note: You were probably aware enough to know that all of the above (and many more) statements are "true." Some statements were adapted from NCTM standards, 2000, ch. 4.

Adults need to exercise caution to guide children within the child's interest and level of understanding.

teaching, and she taught numbers in a series of zero to nine just to give special emphasis to zero.

The importance of auditory skills in learning to read is discussed in Chapter 5. The best preparation for successful math experiences, however, is visual development. If the child is unable to discriminate visually, learning mathematical concepts will be a problem.

Chapter 7 contains a short discussion on the two brain hemispheres: The left side controls verbal and analytic functioning and the right side controls intuition and understanding patterns. Piaget says that young children deal with intuition; yet the child must also be able to analyze if she is to perform mathematical tasks. Both hemispheres are utilized in learning mathematics.

Math is not something that waits until a child enters a formal classroom at a prescribed age. From birth children have a desire to make sense of what is going on. Teachers can encourage a good attitude about math through the experiences and successes provided for preschool children. And for later and continued success, the National Council of Teachers of Mathematics has set curriculum standards for grades K–4, 5–8, and 9–12. Each standard within the grade division is copiously illustrated with examples. The standard emphasizes the development of children's thinking and reasoning abilities from kindergarten on, calls for the appropriate use of calculators and computers, and specifies what should be known at each stage for a broad range of content: measurement, computation, geometry, algebra, and—in what will be startling to many parents and teachers—statistics and probability, beginning in kindergarten. Shirley A. Hill, professor of mathematics and education at the University of Missouri and a key player in the development of new standards, described them this way:

> There has been a long-time consensus about making mathematics-learning more about thinking and engaging the intellect and less about memorizing; more a task of the mind than a test of rote memory. That basic philosophy is now manifested in detailed and specific terms in a document that is the centerpiece of the profession's reform efforts in mathematics. (Fisher, 1992, September, p. 55)

For decades, early childhood educators have advocated the hands-on approach—and more recently they have emphasized the need for activities, materials, and relationships to be built on what is developmentally appropriate for each child.

As teachers of young children, we need to show enthusiasm for life and its challenges! In math, as in all other curricula, teachers also need to do the following:

- know each child personally
- apply ourselves and our knowledge wisely
- provide stimulating (but not frustrating) experiences
- take advantage of spontaneous questions and situations
- plan open-ended activities so children at all developmental levels can experience success
- prepare an environment of math-rich and math-related experiences
- pose situations in which children can contemplate, try (modify when necessary), and enjoy their surroundings
- use math and thinking in other curriculum areas
- promote a healthy, positive attitude toward math
- help children learn different ways to solve problems (by actually manipulating objects but also brainstorming)
- find activities to interest particular children (dinosaurs, transportation, insects, books, curriculum areas, and so on) in math experiences
- provide large blocks of uninterrupted time for thinking
- place more quiet activities out of the traffic flow
- discover math opportunities in daily living and playing
- put emphasis on thinking and solving rather than table work or completion
- encourage children to solve problems individually or with others
- help a child move beyond present knowledge (and then what?)
- place themselves strategically so they can interact physically or verbally *when necessary*
- have a math-lush (but not overwhelming) environment—indoors and outdoors
- encourage children to select activities and time frames that help them enjoy and understand their environment (democracy)
- encourage use of all parts of the body in learning math concepts (large and small muscles, listening and speaking, seeing and touching, alone or with others, and so on)
- be receptive to different interests and moods of children
- assume with confidence that during meaningful, move-around activities, children will encounter problems and may need some assistance
- continually review where children are in their mathematical thinking, the importance of concrete experiences, and how all curriculum areas support thinking and problem solving

Teachers should note how individual children respond to mathematical situations. This is far more important than whether they reach a "correct" answer. Constructivist teaching involves an understanding of each child's thinking in order to plan further learning opportunities that will take that child to higher, more inclusive levels of understanding; knowing how each child thinks in various cognitive domains is vital for the teacher in planning for each child. Teachers also need to consider how interesting each topic is and how the experience can be related to other experiences in each child's life.

When the teacher accepts and encourages a variety of answers and procedures, the children will respond in individual and creative ways. To reach a consensus (when important), the constructivist teacher helps children reach higher levels of understanding and learn more efficient procedures, as well as helping them clarify their thinking.

Seeking to understand students' points of view is essential to constructivist education. The more we study the learning process, the more we understand how fundamental this principle is. Students'

Reflection

Rather than having sequenced, planned math activities, note that young children can use math concepts in various ways, depending on the development and experience of the child:

- communicating, reasoning, and problem solving (How can I get a turn with the toy?)
- one-to-one correspondence (How many cookies do we need so each child can have two?)
- recognizing and writing numerals 0 to 20 (How many is "3"?)
- communicating (How can I get a turn?)
- sets, classifying, comparing, and matching (Does the button go with the color, the number of holes, or the composition?)
- whole-number operations (How can we each have the same number of blocks?)
- spatial relations, shapes, and geometry (How can you fit things together when they are different shapes?)
- sequences (What happened first, next, last?)
- measurement (Which one is longer or weighs more?)

(Topics suggested by Greenberg, 1993; examples by the present author.)

points of view are windows into their reasoning. Awareness of students' points of view helps teachers challenge students, making school experiences both contextual and meaningful. Each student's point of view is an instructional entry point that sits at the gateway of personalized education. (Brooks & Brooks, 1993, p. 60)

Within the last decade educators, cognitive researchers, and professional organizations have stressed the importance of children using their own procedures to arrive at a solution to promote true understanding. The traditional method of teaching one procedure for getting an answer is increasingly seen as harmful for children. It encourages distrust of children's own thinking and discourages the development of number sense.

Teaching Mathematical Concepts

If counting is going to be meaningful to children, it must have a solid foundation upon which they can build.

There is some general expectation that kindergarten children can understand addition and subtraction up to 10, but *only* if they understand the relationship between numbers—that any number plus one (n + 1) = the next higher number; any number minus one (n − 1) = the next lower number. Any number has a relationship to its neighbor numbers (the one just below it and the one just above it). This is its ordinal relationship.

A criticism of teaching numbers to young children is that adults hastily and repeatedly teach each number up to 10 but fail to relate each number with actual objects: They concentrate on the number name and sequence. Those who want to help children mathematically must spend a great deal of time giving children concrete opportunities and verbal prompts to help them relate the number name with an actual object. It would be more productive to teach numbers through play (how many wheels on the cart), daily activities (one sock or two), curriculum components (music, stories), outdoor activities (buckets and shovels), and typical early childhood education themes (pets, toys, family). Math is about thinking, figuring things out, and reasoning.

Some of the implications that flow from the research are that number understanding can be greatly enhanced when teachers:

➤ are sensitive to children's thinking in relation to stages of learning of key elements;
➤ plan and assess programs that reflect these learning stages;
➤ engage children in collaborative problem-solving situations as the basis for exploring, developing, and applying multidigit-number concepts and relationship;
➤ pay astute attention to how children treat each others's responses and mistakes;
➤ break free of chalkboards and workbook, create great curriculum;
➤ be more effective educators; and
➤ have much more fun!

From her extensive research and writing about numbers, Kamii (1995) organized the teaching of numbers into three areas: (1) kinds of relationships (objects, events, and actions); (2) quantification of objects (thinking about numbers, logical comparison of sets—rather than counting—and movable objects); and (3) social interaction with peers and teachers.

She cautions: "Just as there are many ways of getting the wrong answer, there are many ways of getting the right answer" (p. 42).

> I would like to remind the reader once more that the child does not construct number outside the context of thinking in general throughout the day. The teacher must, therefore, encourage the child to put all kinds of things, ideas, and events into relationships all the time rather than focusing only on quantification (Principle #2a) (p. 42).

> Educators unfamiliar with Piaget's theory may believe in the importance of the child's manipulating objects. However, they are stumped when asked *how* children learn number concepts by manipulating objects. Most answer the question by referring vaguely to empirical abstraction. The most original and fundamental idea in Piaget's theory of number is that of reflective abstraction and the child's construction of the numerical structure through reflective abstraction (p. 68).

Recall the statement in Chapter 6 in which Lowenfeld said that some things cannot be taught until a child is cognitively able to grasp the concepts, illustrated when Brittain (1969) unsuccessfully attempted to teach preschool children the concept of copying a square. Lowenfeld's follow-up was: "If we really expect to develop an inquiring mind in a child, one that is eager to tackle the problems of today, a mind that is flexible, inquisitive, and seeks for solutions in unusual ways, then the attention that we have paid to the so-called basic learning areas may be ill-placed" (1987, p. 53).

The cycle of teacher learning from children who are learning for their own experiences empowers children to make their own connections between experiences. They learn

 *Reflection*

Greenberg offers some helpful, specific hints about involving young children in successful math experiences: provide equity in gender, encourage participation, set a good example, help each child feel successful, play fair (equal turns and time), compliment each child's accomplishment (not effort), encourage child-child cooperation (including boy/girl), avoid letting one child dominate the group, encourage female and male participation in all sciences, and educate parents against sex stereotyping in the sciences (1994, p. 18).

about the *process* of connection-making between ideas. Mathematical problems and projects that lend themselves to investigations into a variety of curricular areas are seen as opportunities to make learning more relevant. "Big ideas" within the math curriculum are important in organizing ideas.

Obviously, autonomy (or the lack of it) changes the nature of classroom learning. Researchers have examined communication within the classrooms and have provided some important conclusions. One of the challenges of constructivist teachers is to find ways to facilitate and build on their students' ideas. This requires listening to children's explanations and developing an understanding of the underlying conceptual operations that underscore children's thinking. When teachers provide autonomy and questions to understand children's mathematical thinking, this is constructivist math education.

Appropriate Mathematical Experiences

Teaching One-to-One Correspondence

One to one correspondence: If you add another number, you have to touch another object; you can't skip over objects, and you can't say the same number twice. Each number name means another object.

Most 3-year-old children understand *singular* and *plural* and groups of things (sets) better than they understand one-to-one correspondence and accurate counting. If we can, we should really further develop 3-year-olds' understanding of sets *before* introducing them to counting (assigning number words to things); it's children's interest in comparing sets (more crackers than, less crackers than, the same amount of crackers as) that stimulates interest in learning to count elements to ascertain the answer.

Math is about the relationships between things and numbers. The concept of a set is the basis of other mathematical concepts.

> The best early childhood teachers teach largely through playing purposefully with children. Three-year-olds should be developing:
> the idea of and ability to create sets (of blocks, sand toys, balls, fish in the tank, etc.),
> the ability to compare whether sets have an equal or unequal number of elements; and
> the ability to group sets according to different attributes (shape, color, etc.) (Greenberg, 1993, pp. 79, 81).

For 4- and 5-year-olds, Greenberg states: "Number recognition, while prematurely and inappropriately stressed by many adults, *is* one of the many aspects of math we want fours and fives to learn, and being able to help themselves to these learning-through-play materials does facilitate learning" (1993, p. 83). Using Cuisenaire rods, counting individually or within a group, and looking at books or playing games are all helpful practices.

Young children can learn one-to-one correspondence through various areas of the curriculum during dramatic and free play, music and movement, storybooks, transitions, theme-based units, math centers, and wherever they go.

Teaching About Sets

As children gather casually or deliberately and play begins, the children frequently select and distribute objects: "I want the red one, you can have the green one," or "You have more than me!" They are working with "sets" of objects and are in the beginning stages of addition and/or subtraction. Adding is joining things together, usually *sets* of things, and subtracting is taking things away. Most children younger than 6 or 7 don't add by counting on; they count *all* the objects.

Before they can count, add, or subtract, 18-month-old toddlers know something about numbers. They collect objects, remove and arrange them, and then rearrange them again.

You are so BIG and I am so small! (Learning to make comparisons helps in mathematical understanding.)

In mathematics a set is defined as a collection of objects considered as a whole. Much as they are enamored of sets, very young children can't see the single whole unless the set consists of an extremely small number of things in a predictable place (two eyes, two ears, five fingers, five toes) or unless two or three objects are close together in a line. If the objects in a group (set) *aren't* arranged in a line, a two- or three-year-old will have great difficulty determining how many there are even if she counts; she can't judge by assessing, and she becomes confused when she tries to count unaligned objects.

If the objects in the "set" are not near each other, two- and three-year-olds don't recognize them as a set. . . . Three-, four-, five-, and six-year-olds need a lot of experience with small sets of people and things, too. *Keeping in mind the principle that a young child learns more if she constructs something than she does if she merely looks at something constructed by somebody else, we can see that a child will learn more about sets if we frequently ask her to make them, than if the teacher (or worksheet author) makes them and the child is only asked to compare them* (Greenberg, 1994, p. 13).

Personal involvement with objects (touching them, moving them) is as essential a part of a child's learning about sets as it is of his learning about counting.

There is a firm conclusion that instruction for small children should begin not with counting using number words but by having children actively create sets themselves and compare them by the techniques of superposition and association, so that the children gradually become familiar with equal and unequal aggregates. . . . Linear arrangements promote the most distinct visual perception of a set as a whole and of its elements (Leushina, 1991, p. 87).

Teaching Time Concepts

In helping preschool and primary children understand time concepts, teachers often ask them to recite the name of the day of the week, then the month, and then the year. ("Today is Tuesday, January 13, 2003"). They are being given an opportunity to construct *social knowledge* about time, which is an arbitrary set of symbols that will eventually help them develop an understanding of the passage of time.

Reflection

A 4-year-old was patiently waiting to go on errands with his mother. He kept saying, "What time is it?" and the mother would answer, "10:30," "noon" and so on. But the child was persistent, and asked even more frequently. The mother became impatient and responded with, "Quarter to one." The child, also becoming impatient said, "No, I mean what time is it? Tell me what we have to do before we can go." To him sequencing was more important—not the actual time! Then the mother explained, "We need to get lunch, rinse the dishes, feed the dog. . . . before we can go." "Oh," said the child, "now I know what time it is!"

Piaget (1969) described the construction of two other types of knowledge—*physical* (knowledge of objects that are observable) and *logicomathematical* (a relationship that the subject creates and introduces into or among objects).

To help children understand the passage of time, we must relate time to physical objects and/or events that are meaningful to the children, by using innovative calendars, recording the passage of time, and discussing shared experiences or individual experiences.

Diagnosing children's levels of understanding of time and providing appropriate, personally meaningful learning experiences is challenging for teachers.

One useful way to help very young children determine the passage of time is to tell them a sequence of events ("We'll go outside, then have our snack and clean up before it is time to go home"). For older preschool children, a teacher may show a clock and talk about the numbers and placement of the hands and how they will change before "time to go home." At home we had a modernistic clock hanging on the wall. It was difficult for our children to learn to tell time because they didn't even have numbers for referents! Parents, beware—even digital clocks may confuse young children.

Adults live in a time-conscious world! But children understand the passage of time when it is related to their firsthand experiences or events that already have meaning to them.

And some adults teach children about placement of the hands on the face of the clock, so a child can relate, "The long one is at 6 and the little one is on 2," but the meaning is not there. And children who learn to tell time with a digital clock and then are expected to transfer that learning to a "regular" clock often find it difficult and frustrating. Our actions help them better understand the urgency of the moment. If you say, "We have to go," and then just sit, they just sit! If you say, "We have to go," and then get going, so do they!).

Values for Children
Stages of Development

The same question asked about reading could be asked about mathematics. Should it be taught to the young child? The answers range from an absolute *yes* to an emphatic *no*. The question is rather unfair without defining the term *mathematics*.

Mathematicians disagree as to what mathematics is. The higher the level, the more complex the definition. Some suitable definitions include: "an agreed-upon system for describing objects, time, and space in terms of quantity or magnitude"; "a study of relationships that exist between and among sets of quantity"; "assistance toward mathematical understanding by learning how to solve problems, becoming successful with activities of a mathematical nature, understanding the utility of mathematics, and having fun with it"; "to compute with facility as children learn to see how objects in their own environment are placed into a quantitative context"; and others—including ones you might originate. The experience should be of a *sensorimotor* nature, with the child using his senses and moving himself and objects about in space. As in other areas of curriculum, Piaget advocates teaching mathematics through the sensorimotor approach as preparation for logical operations; *logic* is based on coordination of action even before the development of language.

Piaget's second stage of mental development—*preoperational*—coincides with the ages from 2 through 6, just slightly older than the focus of this text. Broman (1982) says it is

> during this stage that children reason and explain through intuition rather than logic. They have difficulty expressing the order of events, explaining relationships, understanding numbers and their relations, understanding what others say accurately, and understanding and remembering rules.

Piaget (1965) states that mathematical learning takes place in three stages: (1) coordination within the field of perception, (2) operations that go beyond the field of perception, and (3) transition from perception to deduction, progressive coordination of operations, and gradual development of reversibility. Young children begin at stage one and move gradually into stage two. Not until they are in the *concrete operational* stage (ages 7 through 11) of Piaget's stages of mental development do they comprehend concepts of numbers, relationships, and processes.

Young children progress in mathematical knowledge if the activities and expectations match their abilities. In the preoperational stage, young children are very egocentric and generally incapable of seeing a situation from more than one perspective. However, they learn to discriminate color soon after shape and then become:

Solitary and parallel play are important components in gaining mathematics skills.

increasingly adept at working with progressively more difficult concepts of size, classification, seriation, and patterning. A child can work with numerals (chanting them, recognizing them, writing them) long before numeration can be comprehended appropriately. The abilities to use numerals in chanting or recognizing situations does not imply that a child can understand numberness. When the child can conserve, he or she moves from the preoperational to the concrete operational stage of the number concept (Richardson et al., 1980).

When young children enter school, they have some mathematical skills. They can count some numbers and can classify and compare; most know the meaning of ordinal positions through *fifth;* they can recognize numerals from 1 to 10; they can answer simple addition and subtraction combinations; and most have some knowledge about coins, time, simple fractional concepts, and geometric shapes (Payne, 1975, 1990). They also are developing concepts of one-to-one correspondence, number, shape, space, parts and wholes, sequence, and measurement, and relating symbols and sets and applying basic knowledge through hypothesis testing and problem solving (Kamii, 1986; and others).

Literature and Mathematics

Many counting and number books are available; many opportunities arise in the home/classroom every day where numbers are appropriate. They can be helpful if they are used in combination with other learning—not just counting on fingers, but including live people, familiar objects, and everyday living.

Topics that teachers discuss with children on a regular basis include: the calendar, celebrating birthdays, the daily schedule, taking attendance, and the lunch menu. But number experiences can include all areas of the curriculum and can be used in planned or spontaneous situations.

Books, stories, pictures, field trips, and unplanned activities generally include opportunities for young children to become involved with numbers. That's the way it should be. However, before selecting books and planning events, teachers should make sure that the books and activities meet good literature criteria and that they are developmentally appropriate for these particular children. Most children enjoy stories about the passage of time (events, calendars, birthdays) with some modifications to meet the needs of different children.

Because books are in and out of print frequently, check with your local librarian, early childhood teachers, or bookstore for current and favorite books about mathematics and time. Teachers often tire of favorite books and stories long before children do. What ways can you think of to keep your enthusiasm and storytelling at a high level?

Whiting has an interesting article in *Young Children* (1994) to help children learn from an enjoyable source:

> Many children view mathematics as a series of rules to follow or facts to memorize; they do not see the relevance of mathematics to their own lives. . . . One way that teachers might use these books is to connect literature to some of the daily events that naturally occur in their classrooms. This article suggests using children's books pertaining to five topics that teachers discuss with children on a regular basis: the calendar, celebrating birthdays, the daily schedule, taking attendance, and the lunch menu (p. 4).

Areas of the curriculum can be considered individually or in combination with other areas, for example: books, songs, stories and mathematics; snack and mathematics; outdoor play and mathematics, and so on. As in selecting all books for young children, language experiences need to be thoughtfully selected, easily available to the children, and frequently used by teachers and children. (See Chapter 5.)

Thatcher (2001) asks five pertinent questions for teachers who are selecting a mathematical book for young children:

1. Does it have value besides teaching math concepts (enjoyment, good illustrations, natural language, etc.)?
2. Does it stimulate curiosity and a sense of wonder?

3. Is it meaningful to the children? Can they make personal connections?
4. Are the math connections natural (time, life cycle, environmental impact) so that the children have opportunities to question and pursue solutions?
5. How accurate is the information?

In addition, could you, the teacher or parent, stimulate children's interests in mathematics (graphs, charts, timelines, diagrams, drama, music, poetry, stories, etc.)? Are you aware of "KWL" charts (what do you **K**(now), **W**(onder) about, **L**(earn))? (Thatcher, 2001, p. 24).

When children have little experience with a concept or topic, there is little they want to know. They need experiences to build upon. Here are three guidelines to help teachers stimulate children's mathematical questions:

1. Select a good book and pose natural mathematical questions.
2. Use both fiction and nonfiction books.
3. Ask "what if" questions (Thatcher, 2001, p. 23).

I would add one more:

4. Have an inquiring mind and make your classroom conducive to exploring and investigating!

As with books on other topics, not all mathematical books are of high quality. Use the same high criteria as suggested for all books for young children (see Chapter 5). Some authors are more concerned about the subject content, others about visuals, still others about having a publication; some lack good literary concepts. **Some are excellent in both facts and visuals.** Take time to visit a local children's library or bookstore and note the number of books that teach accurate mathematical concepts, have good clear visuals, and portray science as natural, interesting, and **exciting!**

Activities to Increase Mathematical Concepts

Some teachers have tried to teach conservation and other number concepts to children younger than 7 years, but most have failed. However, an appropriate atmosphere and materials can help facilitate the development of concepts of conservations as well as number. Instead of planning specific number experiences and expecting the children to learn them, the teacher should plan a variety of opportunities whereby the children can manipulate objects and practice problem solving.

The involvement of mathematics provides excellent vocabulary experiences, with many new words to learn, meanings to explore, descriptions to use, solutions to discuss, and ideas to relate. There are times to contemplate silently and times to seek companions or assistance.

One of the earliest math experiences children have is in counting. They may count as high as 3 (depending on their age); use randomly selected numbers up to 20; or express an astronomically large number, such as 271. The introduction is through the number's cardinal name (how many). Children do not recognize symbols yet, but they have heard their names, so repetition follows, in or out of order. The next step will be in learning each ordinal name (or position, such as first, second, and so on). This often comes from hearing older children select positions or turns. Rote counting has value in repeatedly hearing the names and sequence of numbers; however, when the children are stopped in recitation, they return to the first number. The value of drilling young children in number sequence is questionable, because as yet numbers mean nothing to them.

Piaget has outlined the following concepts as appropriate when they correspond to the preschooler's development:

1. Classification (grouping by some common characteristic)
2. Seriation (ordering by a common characteristic)

3. Spatial relationships (distance, movement, and so on)
4. Temporal relationships (time)
5. Conservation (permanence of materials or objects)

Relationship is an important aspect of mathematics. A relationship is necessary to classify, order, and measure space or time, and also in the permanence of things. Relationship between sizes, such as small, smaller, smallest, is one of the more difficult concepts for young children to learn. For example, when given five items of mixed sizes, most young children cannot easily arrange them in appropriate sequence.

Young children may not be able to add or subtract, but their relationships with people and their interactions with a stimulating environment set the stage for the development of mathematical concepts (Sinclair et al., 1989).

Small-Group Activities in the Classroom

Play is beneficial for arithmetic learning in young children. Worksheets can be harmful in that they require children to do multiple tasks at once (think of solutions, write with immature young fingers, concentrate on answers rather than on solutions, try to please the teacher, observe what is going on in the classroom), teach children to count mechanically when they don't know a sum, and so on. Direct teaching cannot build concepts of conservation or of number. These concepts must be developed by the children themselves.

I used this example in an earlier publication, but repeat it here because of its applicability.

Example:
A 3-year-old was asked to count to 5. With his left index finger he counted the fingers on his right hand—"1, 2, 3, 4, and 5." He was then asked, "Can you count higher?" "Yes," he said, and climbed up on a chair, raised his hand, and began pointing to his fingers and counting, "1, 2, 3, 4, and 5." He was further asked, "Can you count backwards?" "Oh, yes," he replied. He climbed down off the chair, turned his back, pointed to his fingers, and counted, "1, 2, 3, 4, and 5."

From her extensive research and writing about numbers, Kamii organizes the teaching of numbers into three areas: (1) kinds of relationships (objects, events, and actions); (2) quantification of objects (thinking about numbers, logical comparison of sets—rather than counting—and movable objects); and (3) social interaction with peers and teachers. She cautions: "Just as there are many ways of getting the wrong answer, there are many ways of getting the right answer" (1995, p. 42).

Here are some suggestions that could be used in the home or in the classroom:

Shopping: newspaper and magazine ads, comparing prices, weight, quantity, using a calculator, preparing a shopping list, working with a budget, managing one's allowance, collecting and sorting coupons
Traveling: directions, maps, street maps, speed limits and distances, time to get to place, fuel cost and amount, counting cars or items, license plates, road signs
Gardening: what to plant and when, growing period, harvest, height and distances between plants, garden spot needed
Cooking and eating: measuring ingredients, cooking times, temperatures, amount needed, size and amount needed for each person, using measuring utensils, how to do things (chop, crush, roll)
Personal aspects: sorting clothing, family sizes (height, weight, clothing), time for activities, estimating measurements

Games and friends help young children to learn mathematics principles.

Play: games that involve counting, finding patterns, and solving problems (tic-tac-toe, crossword and jigsaw puzzles, checkers, and chess). Buy your child a calculator and encourage playing with it to explore numbers and number facts. Relate sports to mathematics (player numbers, scoring, timing).

The involvement of mathematics provides excellent vocabulary experiences, with many new words to learn, meanings to explore, descriptions to use, solutions to discuss, and ideas to relate. There are times to contemplate silently and times to seek assistance.

While most young children are solitary or parallel players, some short group activities and games can enrich mathematical experiences in the classroom through the use of spinners, card numbers, counting, or dice. Games also provide an opportunity for children to become more autonomous or self-directed. A variety of types of games enforce mathematical experiences in the classroom through the use of spinners, number cards, counting, dice, and bowling. These games can provide an opportunity for children to become more autonomous or self-directed. Children can learn the rules of the games with the help of a teacher, who then can become a facilitator. Children think about the games and rules; ask pertinent questions; clarify thinking for themselves and others; and observe, assess, and evaluate the interaction. Also involved is rule negotiation, score keeping, counting, reaching agreement on how to approach a mathematical situation posed by a game, and successful resolution of problems.

> In addition to encouraging children to combine sets and to separate out subsets as we play with individuals and small clusters of children in the math center, natural math opportunities through which we can help children learn the rudiments of adding and subtracting abound in every classroom, waiting for us to think of them (Greenberg, 1994, p. 12).

As mentioned previously, mathematical experiences are divided into four areas: sorting and classifying, counting, measuring, and exploring space and shapes.

Teachers should think spontaneously, integrate ideas into the curriculum when it is most valuable *(spontaneous),* and help the children see that the curriculum is expansive, exciting, and useful. When a teaching incident occurs and the teacher feels threatened or

Recognizing the different sizes and shapes is an important understanding for mathematics learning.

unprepared, it should be a warning and a challenge to commit oneself to reading, researching, or whatever it takes to fill this void. It may be a written plan that is implemented soon; it may be discussion with other adults; it may be more experience and practice.

Sample miniplans are included in each of the following mathematical areas and should be used as *idea givers, teacher builders,* and *mind expanders.* Learn to think ahead and respond to current needs.

Sorting and Classifying

When children are asked to put things that belong (or go together) in a certain place, they may group them differently than an adult would. Before responding to their appropriateness, or inappropriateness, seek further clarification from the children.

➤ Ask the children to sort a variety of objects by a common characteristic. Then ask for a different grouping. At first have two or three different possibilities. Use buttons as examples. Sort by color, size, number of holes; composition (wood, glass, plastic, fabric); use (men's, women's, children's); design; and so on. Also useful for this task are animals, cans, clothing, dishes, flowers, food, fruit, jars, leaves, marbles, rocks, seeds, and toys.

➤ Have objects in sets of four (three belong together, one is different, such as three animals and a pillow or three wheel toys and a shovel). Present the objects to the children and have them select the one that is different. This is an important experience.

➤ Let the child sort familiar objects (socks, shoes, boxes, and so on).

➤ Use commercial toys that have different-shaped objects to put in correspondingly shaped holes.

➤ Play or sort cards (old maid, go fish, and so on).

➤ Have the children place pictures or cards in the proper sequence and tell a story about them.

Sample Miniplan Involving Sorting and Classifying

Make a set of 40 number cards of light cardboard or heavy paper, 3″ × 4″ in size, individually numbered from 0 to 9, in four different colors. Along with the number, the card should show the number of dots represented by the card's number. Laminate the cards for longevity. (You may want more than one set to encourage interaction.)

Theme

Number, color, and symbol recognition.

Ideas to Emphasize

Give few instructions to the children. If necessary, suggest they look for something the cards have in common (color, numerals, design).

1. Each card has number symbols, colors, and a design. The cards can be put in stacks of things that are alike (color, symbol, design).
2. The cards can be put in order of quantity (low to high).
3. The cards could be used for playing games (taking turns, singing about colors or numbers, and so on).
4. The cards can be matched to other things in the room.

Learning Activities

1. Give few instructions to the children. If they can't figure out a way to use the cards, suggest they look for something the cards have in common (color, numerals, design).
2. Help them establish a name for each pile (color, number).
3. After familiarization with the cards, suggest that the children take a card and match it to something in the room (toy, numbered object, another activity, and so on). (Prior to the activity the teacher should be sure there are a number of easily accessible "matches" in sight.)

➤ Provide many opportunities to develop visual discrimination (for example, sizes, shapes, similarities, differences, symbols, and designs).
➤ Have a display of coins. Discuss characteristics and amounts of each.
➤ Use math vocabulary: and (more), subtract (less); wide, narrow; large, larger; largest; middle; and so on.
➤ Have duplicate cards showing a certain number of objects or dots on one and a corresponding written symbol on the other.
➤ Make sandpaper shapes and written symbols.

Counting

➤ Provide many counting-out experiences (number of people for snack, cups for measuring, trikes to ride, and so on).
➤ Do number finger plays and nursery rhymes.
➤ Sing number songs.
➤ Use books about numbers.

➤ Recite poems containing numbers.
➤ Focus on one number at a time (make a book about *four;* that is, talk about animals with four legs, involve four children in an activity, and so on).
➤ Make and use a daily calendar.
➤ Count items (number of buttons on a shirt; number of children wearing tie shoes; number of trees in the yard; spools, boxes, shovels, instruments).
➤ Bring in and use a calculator or adding machine.
➤ Talk about and show objects that have numbers: bottles, boxes, a calendar, cards, a cash register, a clock, flash cards, license plates, measuring spoons and cups, money, a phone, road signs, a ruler, scales, a speedometer, a sports player, tickets, a timer, a watch, a yardstick.
➤ Make a store. Provide cans, boxes, money, and a cash register. Write numbers (cost) on articles and amounts on money. Make it fun and simple.
➤ Earn and use tokens.
➤ Relate numbers to activities: how many times the ball bounced, the clock struck, the teacher clapped.
➤ Keep attendance records of the children.
➤ Make and post a class directory with addresses and phone numbers of the children and teachers.
➤ Use counters and containers (for example, an egg carton and poker chips; numbers written on a small juice can and Popsicle sticks to go in it).
➤ Talk with children about the difference between cardinal (1, 2, 3) and ordinal (first, second, third) numbers.
➤ Show how grouping helps in counting things.
➤ Go on a picnic. How much and what will you need to take?
➤ Play games with number symbol spinners.
➤ Use a die (dots represent numbers: numerals can be included on each face of the die).
➤ Count objects in a book or in the environment.
➤ Teach each child his or her phone number and how to use the telephone.
➤ Talk about numbers on athletic clothing.
➤ Point out numbers in the environment (speed limits, costs, quantity, and so on).
➤ Tell a story and have the children supply number parts (of legs on animals, distance, and so on).
➤ Count the number of children with a certain color of clothing, type of shoes, or physical characteristics. Count and name the parts of plants or objects.
➤ Set the table for snack or lunch. Decide how many things are needed.
➤ Have tickets for snack or lunch.
➤ Have a variety of clocks (number, digital, modernistic).
➤ Sell something for snack or lunch.
➤ Write numbers on spring clothespins. Hang a clothesline, yarn, or string at the child's level. Have the child take a clothespin from a box and hang it on the line in proper sequence (clothespins are easily moved around if errors occur).

Measuring

➤ Provide opportunities for various methods of measurement (length, width, time, size, amount).
➤ Provide opportunities for linear measurement (use string, stick, measuring tape, yardstick). Introduce the metric system for those who are ready for it.
➤ Weigh each child, measure her height, and post information about her on a chart or wall.
➤ Provide scales for weighing objects (this activity could also be used in a store).
➤ Introduce a thermometer and have ways for the children to use it (hot and cold).

Sample Miniplan Involving Counting

Theme

　　Numbers

Ideas to Emphasize

　1. Numbers are all around us.
　2. Numbers can help us in work and play.
　3. Numbers are represented in different ways.
　4. Numbers are in a certain sequence.
　5. Numbers can be fun.

Learning Activities

　1. Prepare the environment so there are many opportunities to observe, count, and use numbers throughout the day.
　2. Prepare number opportunities throughout the day—some to be spontaneous (suggested by the children) and some to be planned.
　3. Take a planned or "pretend" field trip. We have _____ children, _____ teachers, and _____ cars. How can we take the trip without being overcrowded or understaffed?
　4. Periodically throughout the day, involve children and numbers together (chairs for snack, toys to play with, instruments for music, and so on). Compare timers (clocks, watches, others) that use symbols and/or numbers.
　5. Take children on a casual walk through your facilities. Gather up or make a list of all the things that have numbers on them (phone, clock, attendance list, toys, and so on). Talk about how numbers help us.
　6. Show individual number cards and help the children arrange them in a numerical sequence.
　7. Use your own imagination! Numbers are everywhere! Numbers are important to adults and children!

➤ Introduce the concepts *zero, equal,* and *half* as the child is ready.
➤ Cut an apple. Ask how many pieces are needed to give each person a slice. Ask what the various pieces are called (half, quarter, eighth).
➤ Pack a sack. Talk about putting heavier things on the bottom.
➤ Use a compass, barometer, or speedometer.
➤ Relate measurement to an activity: how long you can stand on one foot, how far you can jump, and so on.
➤ Talk about center activities that are in the recent past or the near future (yesterday, today, tomorrow).
➤ Measure ingredients and make an art medium (such as clay).
➤ Measure: heel-toe across room, for woodworking, or the amount of space in the block area.
➤ Follow a recipe for food.
➤ Compare size and number of objects.
➤ Balance objects in a scale, on a board, or on your head.

Sample Miniplan Involving Measurement

Theme

   Measurement

Ideas to Emphasize

1. There are different kinds of measurement: weight, size, time, amount, and so on.
2. Measurement can help us do things faster.
3. It is fun to measure things.

Learning Activities

1. Set up the classroom to stimulate children to participate in measurement activities: scales, tapes, art activities, measuring cups and spoons with a recipe, timing (cooking, endurance), new jargon, timing devices, new ideas suggested by children, and so on.
2. Help the children see how measurement is beneficial (saves time, better product, coordination, and so on).
3. Provide a container and objects of different sizes. How can you determine if the objects will fit?
4. Help the children determine a routine or schedule for the day (things they want to do before lunch or going home).
5. Talk about different sizes of things (clothes, houses).
6. If possible, have an artisan (carpenter, tailor, baker, and so on) come to class and construct something of his or her trade.

➤ Using measuring cups and spoons, see how many times you need to fill a smaller container to fill a larger one, or how many times a larger one will fill a smaller one.

Exploring Space and Shapes

Suppose you were going to introduce different shapes to young children and help them begin to distinguish shapes. Which of the following would you do?

1. Trace the shapes on a piece of paper and give the children cutouts to place over the traced shapes.
2. Give them three-dimensional shapes to place over traced shapes.
3. Talk with the children about different shapes, what their uses are (so they will roll—or not roll), and ask children to get examples from a set of blocks as the adult describes them or asks for them by name.

Use only a few, most familiar shapes. Help the child verbalize the names and shapes. Make sure the child does not identify the color of a cutout with its shape (all "rounds" are red). Encourage the child (verbally or physically, if necessary) in placing shapes into a composition. Is it easier for the child to use cutouts or real objects? How were the child's senses and developmental ability shown in each case? What did you learn from this experience?

Sample Miniplan Involving Space and Shape Exploration

Now it is your turn to plan and implement this topic. Make it spontaneous, important, and fun! You may want to walk into your classroom and see how many readily available things are already there.

Theme

   Space and shapes

Ideas to Emphasize

Learning Activities

How would you change (or build on) each option to take the child further in shapes learning? Under what conditions would you display the child's work (if it was correct, if it was neat or complete, if the child at least initiated the task, if the child wanted to keep it, if the child showed creativity, if parents value "products")?

"If we are to view the development of mathematics as emergent, we must understand the construction of mathematical concepts begins the day a child is born . . . without much interference or direct teaching from adults. The understanding of these concepts is not something that *can* be taught to children; they must construct it for themselves. The role of a teacher is to facilitate learning by offering infants, toddlers, and preschoolers opportunities and materials to promote their construction of mathematical thinking" (Geist, 2001, p. 19.).

Trying different ideas and methods increases a child's thinking ability and confidence.

Application of Principles

1. Using the children in the classroom as "subjects," how many ways could we "classify" (or group) them—in constructive and complimentary ways (colors they are wearing, kinds of shoes, sex, favorite animal, food likes, etc.)? Does classifying children in various ways mean that some are better than others? (NOTE TO TEACHERS: AVOID WAYS THAT WOULD BE DESTRUCTIVE: race, uncomplimentary characteristics such as weight, popularity, smart, disposition.)

2. Using **items** in the classroom, can the children guess which objects would weigh more, weigh less, combine to equal another item, work best in water or dry settings, and so on? How could you make this a more hands-on experience (charts, bar graphs, scales, time, energy, etc.)?

3. Encourage children to sort items according to some criteria they select.

4. What could you do in your classroom to make math a favorite activity? Are you willing to make the necessary preparations, follow-through, and learning experiences for individual children as well as the whole class?

5. Would you be willing (and able) to create a "mathematical experience," make visuals, and present it in your preschool/kindergarten classroom? What kinds of hands-on experiences would you provide for the children (literature, field trip, nature objects, creative arts, music, etc.)? How would you evaluate the effectiveness with the children? What would you plan differently if you were to present this same "experience" again—now or much later? What kinds of follow-up would you do?

6. For experiences combining math and other curriculum areas, try the following:
    a. *Math and creative and artistic expression:* Help the children make a recipe for creative arts (finger paint, glue, clay).
    b. *Math and cooking:* Help the children make a favorite recipe for snack time.
    c. *Math and music:* Select one of the number songs or finger plays in Chapter 12, or one of your (or their) favorites.
    d. *Math and field trips:* Let the children help plan the trip (how many children and teachers, what to take for snack (napkins, cups, juice, crackers), time to go and return, and so on.
    e. *Math and literature:* Tell one of their favorite number stories, or read a book about numbers. Involve them in the counting.
    f. *Math throughout the day:* Carefully plan activities where numbers will be used: number of children in an area, chairs for snack, number of paintbrushes and scissors, games using spinners and counting, a broad schedule of activities, child/child and child/teacher ratios in certain activities; weigh and measure children and make an individual or group chart; involve all curriculum activities (songs, stories, outdoor play, creative activities, and so on). Make it fun—not just an assignment filler.
    g. *Make a reflection of your own:* It may be a game, a story, physical involvement, a food experience, or an idea of your choice to illustrate math opportunities for young children. Consider the following ideas:
        1. *Daily living:* distribution of materials (even one-on-one); division of objects (equal snack items); collection of things (parental slips, number present or absent)
        2. *Keeping records:* attendance, books; cleanup (number of items that go in each box); voting (comparison of quantities)
        3. *A guessing game:* removal of a numbered card.
        4. *Board games:* Candy Land, Chutes and Ladders, or an original game
        5. *Card games:* many available—choose for developmental level
    h. Originate an enjoyable method of determining which children in your center can correctly identify number symbols.

i. Using materials in your classroom, or those suggested in the chapter, provide experiences for children in classification, seriation, and conservation. Observe closely the responses of each child. Which experiences need to be modified or repeated? Why do some of the children have difficulty in understanding some number concepts?

References

NOTE: Current references are used when available. Older references are classic, introductory and important in development of later ideas, policies, and practices.

Anderson, A. (1997). Families and mathematics: A study of parent-child interactions. *Journal for Research in Mathematics Education, 28,* 484–511.

Austin, P. (1998). Math books as literature: Which ones measure up? *The New Advocate, 11*(2), 119–133.

Bereiter, C., & Englemann, S. (1966) *Teaching disadvantaged children in the preschool.* Upper Saddle River, NJ: Prentice Hall.

Blevins-Knabe, B., & Musun-Miller, L. (1996). Number use at home by children and their parents and its relationship to early mathematical performance. *Early Development and Parenting, 5*(1), 35–45.

Bredekamp, S. (Ed.). (1987). *Developmentally appropriate practice in early childhood programs serving children from birth to age 8.* Washington, DC: NAEYC.

Bredekamp, S., & Copple, C. (Eds.). (1997). *Developmentally appropriate practice in early childhood programs* (rev. ed.). Washington, DC: NAEYC.

Bredekamp, S., & Rosegrant, T. (Eds.). (1992). *Reaching potentials: Appropriate curriculum and assessment for young children.* Washington, DC: NAEYC.

Brittain, W. L. (1969). Some exploratory studies of the art of preschool children. *Studies in Art Education, 10*(3), 14–24.

Broman, B. L. (1982). *The early years in childhood education.* Chicago: Rand McNally.

Broody, A. J. (2000). Does mathematics instruction for three- to five-year-olds really make sense? *Young Children, 55*(4), 61–67.

Brooks, J., & Brooks, M. (1993). *In search of understanding: The case for constructionist classrooms.* Alexandria VA: Teacher Association for Supervision & Curriculum Development (ASCD).

Charlesworth, R. (1997). Mathematics in the developmentally appropriate integrated curriculum. In C. H. Hart, D. Burts, & R. Charlesworth (Eds.), *Integrated curriculum and developmentally appropriate practice: Birth to age eight* (pp. 51–73). Albany: State University of New York Press.

Charlesworth, R., & Lind, K. K. (1995a). *Math and science for young children* (2nd ed.). Albany, NY: Delmar.

Charlesworth, R., & Lind, K. K. (1995b). Whole language and the mathematics and science standards. In S. Raines (Ed.), *Whole language across the curriculum: Grades 1, 2, and 3* (pp. 156–178). New York: Teachers College Press.

Chomsky, N. (1999). On the nature, use, and acquisition of language. In W. D. Ritchie & T. K. Bhatia (Eds.), *Handbook of child language acquisition* (pp. 33–54). San Diego, CA: Academic Press.

Cobb, P. (1994). Where is the mind? Constructivist and sociocultural perspectives on mathematic development. *Educational Researcher, 23*(7), 13–20.

Colbert, C. (1990). The visual arts: Multiple ways of knowing, in W. H. Moody (Ed.), *Artistic intelligences, implications for education* (pp. 102–108). New York: Teachers College Press.

Copley, J. V. (2000). *The young child and mathematics.* Washington, DC: NAEYC. #119. $10.

Copley, J. V. (1999). *Mathematics in the early years.* Washington, DC: NAEYC. #109. $30. Copublished by the National Council of Teachers of Mathematics (NCTM) and NAEYC.

Davis, R. B., Maher, C. A., & Noddings, N. (Eds.). (1990). Constructivist views on the teaching and learning of mathematics. *Journal for Research in Mathematics Education Monograph, 4.*

Durkin, K., Shire, B., Reim, R., Crowther, R., & Ritter, D. (1986). The social and linguistic context of early number use. *British Journal of Developmental Psychology, 4,* 269–288.

Edwards, C., Gandini, L., & Forman, G. (Eds.). (1993). *The hundred languages of children: The Reggio Emilia approach to early childhood education.* Norwood, NJ: Ablex.

Fisher, A. (1992, Aug.). Crisis in education, Part 1: Science + Math = F. *Popular Science, 241*(2), 58–63, 108.

Fisher, A. (1992, Sept.). Crisis in education, Part 2: Why Johnny can't do science and math. *Popular Science, 241*(3), 50–55, 98.

Fromboluti, C. S., & Rinck, N. (1999). *Early childhood, where learning begins, mathematics: Mathematical activities for parents and their 2- to 5-year-old children.* U.S. Department of Education. (ED Pubs, P.O. Box 1398, Jessup, MD 20794-1398).

Gardner, H. (1993). *Frames of mind.* New York: Basic Books. (Original work published in 1983).

Geist, E. (2001). Children are born mathematicians: Promoting the construction of early mathematical concepts in children under five. *Young Children, 56*(4), 12–19.

Ginsburg, H. P., & Baron, J. (1993). Cognition: Young children's construction of mathematics. In F. J. Jensen (Ed.), *Research ideas for the classroom: Early childhood mathematics* (pp. 3–21).

Ginsburg, H. P., Klein, A., & Starkey, P. (1998). The development of children's mathematical knowledge: Connecting research with practice. In W. Damon, I. E. Sigel, & K. A. Renninger (Eds.), *Handbook of child psychology.* Vol. 4. *Child psychology in practice* (5th ed.) (pp. 401–476). New York: Wiley & Sons.

Greenberg, P. (1993). Ideas that work with young children. How and why to teach all aspects of preschool and kindergarten math naturally, democratically, and effectively (for teachers who don't believe in academic programs, who do believe in educational excellence, and who find math boring to the max)— Part 1. *Young Children, 48*(4), 75–84.

Greenberg, P. (1994). Ideas that work with young children—Part 2. *Young Children, 49*(2), 12–18, 88.

Helm, J., & Katz, L. (2001). *Young investigators: The project approach in the early years.* New York: Teachers College Press. Available from NAEYC.

Hinnant, H. A. (1999). Growing gardens and mathematicians: More books and math for young children. *Young Children, 54*(2), 23–26.

Hyson, M. (2000). "Is it okay to have calendar time?" Look up to the stars. . . Look within yourself. *Young Children, 55*(6), 60–61.

Jensen, R. J. (Ed.). (1993). *Research ideas for the classroom: Early childhood mathematics.* Reston, VA: NCTM.

Kamii, C. (1982, 1995). *Number in preschool and kindergarten.* Washington, DC: NAEYC. #103. $8. ISBN 0-912674-80-6.

Kamii, C. (1985). *Young children reinvent arithmetic: Implication of Piaget's theory.* New York: Teachers College Press.

Kamii, C. (1986). Cognitive learning and development. In B. Spodek (Ed.), *Today's Kindergarten* (pp. 67–90). New York: Teachers College Press.

Kamii, C., & DeVries, R. (1980). *Group games in early education: Implications of Piaget's theory.* Washington, DC: NAEYC. #317. ISBN: 0-912674-71-1.

Katz, L., & Chard, S. (2000). *Engaging children's minds: The project approach* (2nd ed.). Stamford, CT: Ablex.

Koechlin, E., Dahene, S., & Mehler, J. (1997). Numerical transformations in five-month-old human infants. *Mathematical Cognition, 3*(2): 89–104.

Krechevsky, M., & Gardner, H. (1990). The emergence and nurturance of multiple intelligences: The Project Spectrum approach. In M. J. A. Howe (Ed.), *Encouraging the development of exceptional skills and talents*. Leicester, Eng.: British Psychological Society.

Lang, F. K. (1999). What is a "good guess" anyway? Teaching quantity and measurement estimation. *Young Children, 54*(4), 78–81.

Lave, J., Murtaugh, M., & de la Rocha, O. (1984). The dialectic of arithmetic in grocery shopping. In B. Rogoff and J. Lave (Eds.), *Everyday cognition: Its development in social context* (pp. 67–94). Cambridge MA: Harvard University Press.

Leino, J. (1990). Knowledge and learning in mathematics. In L. Steffe & T. Wood (Eds.), *Transforming children's mathematics education* (pp. 41–46).

Leushina, A. M. (English translation, 1991). The development of elementary mathematical concepts in preschool children. *Soviet Studies in mathematical education* (Vol. 4) Reston, VA: National Council of Teachers of Mathematics.

Lowenfeld, V. (1987). *Creative and mental growth* (8th ed.). New York: Macmillan.

Meriweather, L. (1997). Math at the snack table. *Young Children, 52*(5), 69–73.

Murphy, S. (1997). *Just enough carrots.* New York: HarperCollins.

Murray, A. (2001). Ideas on manipulative math for young children. *Young Children, 56*(4), 28–29.

National Council of Teachers of Mathematics (NCTM). (1989). *Curriculum and evaluation standards for school mathematics.* Reston, VA: Author.

National Council of Teachers of Mathematics (NCTM). (1991). *Professional standards for teaching mathematics.* Reston, VA: Author.

National Council of Teachers of Mathematics (NCTM). (1994–95). *Handbook: NCTM goals, leaders, and positions.* Reston, VA: Author.

National Council of Teachers of Mathematics (NCTM). (1995). *Assessment standards for school mathematics.* Reston, VA: Author.

National Council of Teachers of Mathematics (NCTM). (2000). *Principles and standards for school mathematics: Prekindergarten through Grade 12* (chs. 3 and 4). Reston, VA: Author. Online at http://standards.nctm.org/document/chapter3/index.htm and http://standards.nctm.org/document/chapter4/index.htm.

Nodelman, P. (1996). *The pleasure of children's literature.* White Plains, NY: Longman.

Payne, J. M. (Ed.). (1990). *Mathematics for the young child.* Reston, VA: NCTM. (Original work published in 1975).

Piaget, J. (1965). *The child's conception of number.* New York: Norton.

Piaget, J. (1969). *Science of education and the psychology of the child.* New York: Viking.

Reggio Children. (1997). *Shoe and meter. Children and measurement. First approaches to discovery, function, and use of measurement.* Reggio Emilia, Italy: Author.

Richardson, L., Goodman, K., Harman, N., & LePique, H. (1980). *A mathematics activity curriculum for early childhood and special education.* New York: Macmillan.

Richardson, K., & Salked, L. (1995). Transforming mathematics curriculum. In S. Bredekamp & T. Rosegrant (Eds.), *Reaching potentials: Transforming early childhood curriculum and assessment,* Vol. 2 (pp. 23–42). Washington, DC: NAEYC.

Rogoff, B. (1990). *Apprenticeship in thinking.* Oxford: Oxford University Press.

Saito, N. (1999). *Dynamics in play.* Albany, NY: Delmar.

Saxe, G., Guberman, S., & Gearhart, M. (1987). Social processes in early number development. *Monographs of the Society for Research in Child Development, 52*(2).

Simons, M. A. (1995). Reconstructing mathematics pedagogy from constructivist perspective. *Journal for Research in Mathematics Education, 26,* 114–45.

Sinclair, H., Stambak, M., Lezine, I., & Rayna, S. (1989). *Infants and objects: The creativity of cognitive development.* San Diego, CA: Academic Press.

Skinner, P. (1990). *What's your problem?* Portsmouth, NH: Heinemann.

Starkey, P., & Cooper, R. G., Jr. (1980). Perception of numbers by human infants. *Science, 210*(4473), 1033–1035.

Steffe, L. P., & D'Ambrosio, B. S. (1995). Toward a model of constructivist teaching. *Journal for Research in Mathematics Education, 26,* 145–159.

Thatcher, D. H. (2001). Reading in the math class: Selecting and using picture books for math investigations. *Young Children, 56*(4), 20–27.

Unglaub, K. W. (1997). What counts in learning to count? *Young Children, 52*(4), 48–50.

Vygotsky, L. (1968). *Thought and language.* Cambridge, MA: MIT Press.

Whiting, D., & Wilde, S. (1992). *Read any good math lately?* Portsmouth, NH: Heinemann.

Whiting, D. J. (1994). Literature and mathematics in preschool and primary: The right connection. *Young Children, 49*(2), 4–11.

Wynn, K. (1995). Origins of numerical knowledge. *Mathematical Cognition, 1*(1), 35–60.

10

Social Studies, Anti-Bias Curriculum, & Field Trips

Main Principles

1. Some adults have unrealistic expectations of children's thoughts and actions. (pp. 368)

2. Diversity in children needs to be recognized; however, there are some types of diversity that we do not tolerate, such as abuse in any of its many physical, verbal, social, emotional, and intellectual forms. (pp. 368–369)

3. Teachers have a very important role in building upon the experiences parents provide for their children as well as introducing new experiences to enrich the learning of young children. (pp. 369–376)

4. Through "social studies" children learn about anthropology, ecology, economics, current events, geography, history, political science, psychology, sociology, and other related fields. (pp. 369–371)

5. The values of learning for young children include (but are not limited to):

   ➤ learning about oneself (pp. 376–382)

   ➤ learning about others (pp. 380–384)

6. Several theories provide information about children's growth and behavior:

   ➤ social behavior (pp. 377–379)

   ➤ special needs of individual children (pp. 385–390)

   ➤ anti-bias curriculum (pp.390–398)

Introduction

Do adults expect young children to act, feel, and respond as adults do? Do adults realize that "until about age four children have a tendency to act as if everyone knows and believes what they themselves know to be true" (Lillard & Curenton, 1999, p. 55)? Studies suggest that engaging in pretend play (Youngblade & Dunn, 1995) and having conversations about mental states (Dunn, Brown, & Beardsall, 1991) may support the development of children's social understanding.

Lillard and Curenton (1999) suggest that pretend play may help children understand the mental states of others by talking about those emotional states, a view that Piaget would endorse. It is a major development of the preschool years when a child understands that others have different beliefs. Lillard and Curenton summarize their article with these thoughts:

> Generally, research suggests that children who understand others' minds at an early age may be more able to get along well with others and that parents and teachers can support the development of this understanding by encouraging pretend play and discussing mental states with them from storybooks or real-life encounters. . . . Every child develops ideas about minds and behaviors, but the ideas individual children have may be different depending on their cultural millieu" (p. 57).

It should be noted early in this discussion that although we are recognizing and accepting many types of diversity, there are some types of diversity that we do not tolerate, such as abuse in any of its many physical, verbal, social, emotional, and intellectual forms. Nor do we tolerate adult or societal behaviors that may cause bodily harm to young children. In these cases we recognize (as in the cases of abuse, AIDS, and drugs), we teach (adults and children), we report to the proper authorities, and we do whatever is necessary for young children to grow up in a healthy, happy, growth-promoting environment.

> In 1997 more than three million children were reported to child protective services (CPS) for child abuse and neglect, and 1,054,000 cases were confirmed by authorities (Prevent Child Abuse America 1998). This number represents 15 out of every 1,000 children in the United States. Approximately 8% of all cases of confirmed victims of maltreatment were child sexual abuse. Since 1985 the fatalities rate as a result of abuse has increased by 34% (Wang & Daro, 1998) (reported in Nunnelley & Fields, 1999).

As mentioned in Chapter 8, social studies are a part of the science curriculum. They are a part of our daily lives, a process of inquiry, and more than a collection of facts. Because of the strong influence social studies have on the child and his view of himself and his world, information is extended to this chapter, which consists of three parts, each one equally important in the lives of young children and families: (1) learning about oneself, (2) learning about others using an anti-bias curriculum, and (3) awareness of social science.

Teachers can build on the experiences parents provide for their children. It may be easier for a child to understand and interact in dramatic play when she has seen or heard things related to that play (real animals on a farm, or a visit to a fire station). Teachers need to know the children and families well so they can reinforce family values, build understanding and acceptance, and support cultural heritage.

Parents take their children to more places in the community than do teachers, so parents play an important role in familiarizing their children with activities, occupations, resources, and functions. They may take their children to the fire station, police station, post office, hospital, or an interesting landmark. They also may take their children to places of significance to the family, such as a church, a cemetery, the home of a relative, or a cultural event. As parents do daily errands, they should briefly tell the child how the people they see can help us (service-station attendant, cleaner, baker, banker, grocer). Children can learn firsthand about their extended families, or parents can invite guests into their homes or do something nice for a neighbor, relative, friend, or a new-found acquaintance.

Role of the Teacher

Teachers can build on the experiences parents provide for their children. It may be easier for a child to understand and interact in dramatic play when she has seen or heard things related to that subject.

Teachers can provide new experiences for the children or they can build on the experiences parents provide for their children. Teachers need to know the children and families well so they can reinforce family values, build understanding and acceptance, and support cultural heritage.

There will be opportunities for each teacher to broaden experiences in the child's environment by giving personal attention, providing a healthy environment, and selecting and using appropriate activities in a healthy classroom setting, while helping each child adjust to cultural, physical, emotional, and social environments.

Activities to Increase Awareness of Social Science

The study of social science includes anthropology, ecology, economics, current events, geography, history, political science, psychology, sociology, and other related fields. Some of these fields are more appropriate than others for teaching young children. A few ideas are given here; the teacher can develop activities of interest and value to the children he teaches.

Notable Quotes

"Social studies educators would say there is no doubt that the social studies are the true integrator of the curriculum. Nevertheless, those who are experts in mathematics, the sciences, language, visual, or musical arts, or any other discipline, would say the same thing, for there really is no way to separate the curriculums for young children into separate subjects. Life is whole, children are whole, learning is whole" (Seefeldt, 1997, p. 195).

It is often distressing that many of today's early childhood students have not become acquainted with dedicated "early pioneers" in the field! (See Chapter 1 of this text.) One of my favorites, **Lucy Sprague Mitchell** (1934), first suggested key concepts from the field of geography.

"By matching the key concepts of children's cognitive development, Mitchell believed, the study of geography could be made meaningful for children of any age. Starting with infancy and ending with the 12-year-old, Mitchell specified the interests, drives, orientation, and tools of children, and matched these with key concepts from geography" (Seefeldt, 1997, p. 175).

Vygotsky thought it would be unlikely for children to gain conventional concepts without a foundation of everyday personal experiences. He states:

"An everyday concept clears the path for the scientific concept.... It creates a series of structures necessary for the evolution of a concept's more primitive, elementary aspects that give it body and vitality. Scientific concepts grow down through spontaneous concepts; spontaneous concepts grow upward through scientific concepts" (1986, p. 109).

Children can learn many social ideas and behavior while in the classroom.

➤ Experiences with *ecology*: Talk about such natural resources as water and energy. Talk about the care of the center and the community. Have a general cleanup.

➤ Experiences with *economics*: Provide activities that teach the children the principle of supply and demand (number and amount of creative materials, for example, and who will use them; care of unused materials). Give the children weekly or daily opportunities to help with center responsibilities. Teach care and respect for property and rules for behavior, such as sharing, replacing all toys and parts in proper places, and cooperating in play and ideas.

➤ Experiences with *current events*: Know what is going on locally, nationally, and personally within families. Help children verbalize happenings and the impact on them.

➤ Experiences with *geography*: Give the children experiences with various maps (for example, road, community, center, play yard). Have a fabric or plastic printed community with props, a farm with animals and equipment, a dollhouse and furniture, or a floor plan of a room or outdoor area, and ask for the children's help in rearrangement. Talk about concepts of direction, location, distance. Talk about the earth (land, sea, air, the solar system). Talk about geographic features in the community such as rocks, rivers, and mountains. Walk or ride on field trips around the school or community, noting routes, buildings, and landmarks. Make a mural showing important landmarks in the community such as homes of children, places of worship, stores, and parks.

➤ Experiences with *history*: Talk about the changes in the children. What are they able to do that they could not do earlier? (Use the book *The Growing Story* by Ruth Krauss [1947].) Talk about families and holidays.

➤ Experiences with *sociology*: Provide opportunities for children to participate in group living and learn cooperation, responsibility, courtesy, and sharing. Discuss ways people help each other. Help the children accept and appreciate peers who are of a different race, culture, size, or sex; those who have a disability; and those with diverse beliefs and ideas. Include nonsexist curriculum experiences. Provide props for dramatic play about families and careers. Ask the children what they want to be when they grow up; provide props (clothes, books, and games) for practice. Provide artistic materials for each child to make a picture about her family (she can draw, paint, or cut and paste pictures). Invite resource people to tell stories, share hobbies and interests, demonstrate skills, and bring objects from the past. Talk about behavioral guidelines. Let the children help establish and enforce necessary rules of safety, protection, and responsibility for the classroom, field trips, care of animals, and so on. Invite a safety guard or police officer to tell how she helps the children and the community. Make and post a helper chart for snack time, cleanup, and watering plants. Provide opportunities for children to select playmates, materials, and activities, and allow time to enjoy them. Invite community helpers and parents to share their occupations.

Geography (Field Trips)

Do some "pre-thinking" before planning field trips.

1. Consider some hypothetical statements about geography. Geography is:
   a. too advanced for preschool/kindergarten children.
   b. uninteresting.
   c. too risky (liability).
   d. inappropriate for preschoolers.
   e. a waste of time, money, and effort.

   Do you agree with each? Disagree? Why?

2. How could you make a geographic activity without leaving the room or premises?
   a. Outdoor area
   b. Field trip
   c. Another classroom

3. How could you take a "trip" without a map? Would a map of the school be helpful? Would a road map be helpful? Would a globe be helpful?

   Now get serious about planning and taking field trips. The following are considered worthwhile reasons for taking young children on field trips:

   ➤ to gain firsthand experiences on their developmental level
   ➤ to see career models (most occupations can be done successfully by males and females)
   ➤ to increase and clarify concepts
   ➤ to increase language skills by learning and associating new words with experiences
   ➤ to increase their frame of reference and sense of observation
   ➤ to develop initiative and creativeness in dramatic play
   ➤ to help build good relationships with other children and adults through a group experience
   ➤ to give parents an opportunity to participate
   ➤ to have fun

One of the prerequisites of a successful field trip is a visit to the location in advance. Many a field trip has ended in failure because the person conducting it directed the information to the teachers rather than to the children. A successful field trip is one that involves the children and stimulates them to learn more about the particular subject.

At the advance visit, the teacher should insist on discussing the visit with the person who will conduct it when the children come. She should not accept the statement that "anybody who is here can take you through." It just does not work. The teacher needs to explain about the interests and abilities of the children—an informed person should meet the children.

Successful field trips depend on appropriate planning.

During the advance visit, the teacher should inquire about bathrooms, drinking fountains, and any other things that may be important to or distract from the excursion (for example, change of shift, everybody out to lunch, special clothing to be worn, limits).

In the early stages, decisions are made regarding method of travel (bus, car, foot), cost, and how much supervision is required. Written permission is obtained from the school official. Unattended details can prevent a trip at the last minute Depending on one's location and school policies, some of the best and cheapest field trips are made on foot, followed up with a thank-you letter. For children who ride a school bus, teachers can design activities, present information, and role play situations that help the children feel secure and safe on their daily trip while becoming aware of environmental changes—the bus ride is not just a period before and after school.

Be sensitive to nature and the needs of living things as you complete your walk. Teach the children to be good observers and listeners. Patterns developed early can give a lifetime of enjoyment. Encourage children to make discoveries and to bring things back to the classroom when appropriate. Help them to combine development and curriculum areas—a good physical activity, science, art, music—depending on where you go and what you see.

Children can observe and study in the natural setting when trips outside of the familiar classroom meet their needs and interests. However, the frequency of the trips needs careful consideration; some children enjoy going often and others need the security of the classroom. Rather than continually going to new and different places, the teacher might well consider returning to a successful and well-liked location, particularly during a different season or when activities are different.

The decision for a field trip must be carefully made. Perhaps the children have been some places many times; in other places, danger, loud noise, or unexpected activity may be encountered. There are also places to which parents want the privilege of taking their own children. See Figure 10.1 for a checklist to use for a field trip and Figure 10.2 for a suggested permission form.

CHECKLIST FOR FIELD TRIP

1. Destination _____
2. Proposed purpose _____
3. Pre-planning (check and record information) _____
   a. School policies _____
   b. Readiness of children _____
   c. Advance visit _____
      1. Person who conducts visit _____
      2. Safety _____
      3. Restrooms/fountains _____
   d. Mode of travel _____
   e. Supervision _____
   f. Permission of center official _____
4. Actual trip
   a. Time of departure and return _____
   b. Supervision (list people) _____
   c. Parental permission (check for each child) _____
   d. Transportation (list mode) _____
   e. Preparation of children (list ways) _____
   f. Assignment of children (give specifics) _____
5. Follow-up (informal discussion, art, food, dramatic play, pictures, classroom project, and so on)
   a. _____
   b. _____
   c. _____
6. Evaluation after trip
   a. What went well on the trip?
   b. How did the children respond to the experience and follow-up activities?
   c. How were problems solved?
   d. What changes are recommended for a future visit? (for example, preparation of children, follow-up, time)

Figure 10.1 Checklist for a Field Trip

Dear Parent:

We are conducting a field trip for the children. We will be visiting _____
_____ *(place)* _____ on _____ *(date)* _____.
We will go by _____ *(foot, car, bus)* _____.
If you give permission for your child to go, please sign below.

_____
(Child's name)

_____   _____
(Date)   (Signature of parent or guardian)

Figure 10.2 Field Trip Permission Form

Reflection

Be aware of the season and the reason for the walk. Perhaps in the spring you will look for new growth and color; in the fall look for seeds and color. Recently we took our 2- to 3-year-olds for a walk around the building. We looked for flowers and insects; to see if the wind was blowing our flag; birds; and seed pods. The thing that interested them most was large heads of milkweed seeds. Each child held and examined a seed. One said it looked like a parachute, another said it looked like an umbrella. After examination, they watched as the wind gently blew it away. Great follow-up activities could include examining seeds with a magnifying glass, covering the children's legs with stockings and letting them walk through weeds—then examine the different kinds of seeds, making a seed collage, sprouting then eating seeds, the cycle of seed growth, acting out the sequence from seed to plant, and other ideas suggested by the children.

Bring to the children's attention some activities you used in preparation for the field trip. Now expand their geography into the real world.

Many methods increase and stimulate knowledge of a field trip. A bulletin board, for example, with pictures and materials conveys information before the visit and reinforces it afterward.

Dramatic play clarifies and increases concepts. One teacher provided small cots and bandages and placed doctor and nurse kits strategically throughout the classroom. Many of the children wandered about aimlessly, paying no attention to them. That morning the class toured a nearby health center. When the children returned to school, there was

Important follow-up of field trips/visitors can occur within individual classrooms.

much activity. They now had firsthand ideas about nurses, doctors, and a hospital. It was fascinating to see how their ideas had increased.

Because dramatic play after a field trip is important, the children should have sufficient time and props to work through their ideas. For example, large blocks can be used to make a bus after a bus ride, instruments can be played after a parade, or a cooking experience can be provided after a trip to the grocery store or bakery.

Stories, pictures, songs, and creative materials add to the learning experience of a trip. Children need more than one exposure if they are to develop correct concepts and a sound foundation. Relaxed talk about the trip elicits information from the children, but they should not be expected to spit back specific or detailed information.

The children are invited to help prepare a thank-you note and picture for the privilege of visiting a certain place. This will help the children express appreciation and also use some of their artistic and language skills.

As soon after the field trip as possible, the experience should be evaluated. What were the strong points? What were the weak ones? What concepts were learned by the children? Was the experience of interest to them? How could the trip have been improved or planned differently? What teaching aids could be employed to increase the children's knowledge and understanding? When could the topic be used again to the children's advantage?

Suggested Field Trips

You do not have to leave your classroom to have a field trip! Consider having self-contained experiences, such as (1) a sensory trip (look for things that stimulate each of the senses, preferably one at a time, or have some children look for "smell" things and others look for "feel" things), (2) a shape trip, (3) a color trip, (4) things made of similar materials (wood, for example), or (5) a "living" trip (plants, animals).

Keep in mind that a field trip should be on the *developmental level* of the children involved and should be *fairly close* to the school. Some places may be familiar to some children and unfamiliar to others. For example, Juan's parents operate a restaurant, and he spends a great deal of time there. He may have a special interest in visiting a restaurant or may be totally uninterested.

Know your community and special attractions. You might consider some of the following:

airport terminal	community specialties	fire station
animal show	(cave, livestock show,	fish hatchery
apartment house	cheese factory)	fish market
aquarium	construction site and	flower garden or show,
artist's studio	equipment	florist, or greenhouse
athletic field or building	dairy	foundry
aviary	dance studio	garbage dump
bakery	dentist's office	grocery store
bank	department store	hairstylist
beach or seashore	dock	harbor
bird watching	doctor's office (also eye	hobby shop
boat ride	doctor)	hospital
body paint shop	dog kennel	house
bus depot	dormitory	junkyard
bus ride	elevator/escalator	laundry
car dealer	factory (food, clothing, fur-	library
car wash	niture, toy, other)	livestock show or auction
collector (rock, insect, coin)	farm	lumberyard

lunchroom
manufacturer (car, household)
marching band
museum
music department or rehearsal
newspaper
nursing home
office
orchard
park
pet shop
photo studio
planetarium

police station or car
post office
pottery factory
poultry farm
recreation areas (bowling alley, gym, hobby display, skating rink, swimming pool)
repair shop (bike, car, shoes, watch)
restaurant
road construction building
road equipment
school
seed store

service station
sewage disposal plant
stable
streetcar ride or station
subway
television, radio, or recording studio
trailer park
train depot
truck terminal
upholstery shop
water (dam, lock, lake, stream, river)
woods
zoo

Values for Children

Studying social aspects for young children can help them do the following:

1. learn about themselves, their family, and their environment;
2. prevent feelings of inferiority or prejudice toward others;
3. become more productive members of society; and
4. enlarge their horizon of knowledge and understanding of other people.

Learning About Oneself

Young children learn about themselves before they learn about others. From birth they are learning to adjust to and accept themselves through their interactions with others and their environment.

Some children and families face problems not experienced by other children and families (for example, homelessness, poverty, illness, violence, financial insecurity). The homeless child, for example, through no fault of his own, finds himself and his family living in a car, a tent, a box, or even an open park. There is little or no food, clothing, or shelter. Although the McKinney Act, which passed in 1987 with amendments passed in 1988, provides states with funds to assist the homeless, including assistance to schools to assure that each child of a homeless family has access to free public education, these children and families face problems not conceived by other families and need some special understanding and support if they are to maintain self-respect and survival. Parents of homeless children want teachers and other staff to know that their children are embarrassed about their homelessness; their families face multiple problems (such as spouse abuse, depression, desertion, illness, etc.). Children from these situations, or others equally discouraging, need extra love and attention if they are to feel they are worthwhile and competent people.

The young child, even under the best of circumstances, has much to learn about herself, her family, her environment, and her extended world. Children who are raised in a loving, secure home where their developmental needs are met, and who feel good about themselves, have a head start in life. At first, young children depend on others to provide their care and to fulfill their needs; later, they learn how to meet many of their own needs; the success of this depends on how they feel personally and in the presence of others. (Refer to Chapter 1 and Erikson's steps to a healthy personality [1950b].)

Self-esteem is a crucial aspect of human dignity, and it requires home and school cooperation to help a child build and feel worthiness. The school can enhance self-esteem by helping children to cope with ambiguities and discontinuities in their lives and to avoid self-destructive behaviors that are symptomatic of such conditions. For schools to play their contributing role, Beane (1991) writes:

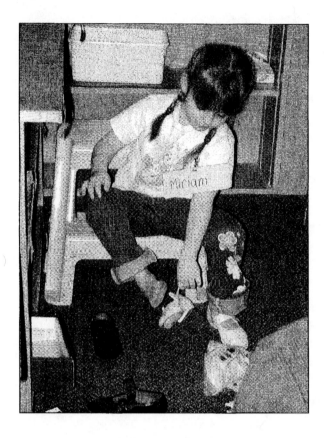

Children like to repeat new and familiar activities.

[W]e might expect to observe a humanistic climate, participation of children in school and classroom governance, heterogeneous grouping, cooperative learning, thematic units that emphasize construction of personal and social meanings, self-evaluation multi-cultural content, community service projects, and activities that involve making, creating, and doing things. We would not expect to see an autocratic, adult-dominated environment, either explicitly displayed or thinly veiled behind gimmicks, gadgets, and coupons that are meant to insidiously seduce children into prizing someone else's agenda over their own.

. . . [N]o truly authentic project for self-esteem can proceed without a vision of a socially transformed world and a critique of the current status of our society (Ladewig, 1990). Many will recognize this as the language and politics of social reconstruction and they will be correct in doing so. But if "developmental" interests are sincere about the quality of life for children, then this is the direction they must take. Anything short of this will continue the superficial, culturally detached, utilitarian, and self-protective definition of self-esteem, a version that clearly does not serve the self-esteem of children (pp. 159–160).

Social Behavior

According to Cartwright (1993), "We now know that it's not so much competition as cooperation that ensures survival in our fragile environment. . . . Cooperative learning in the classroom is not only relevant to life; it may be childhood learning at its best" (p. 12). Teachers can stage classrooms so they promote or destroy cooperation. Consider Table 10.1. (See also Chapter 2.)

Socialization is an integral part of children's normal growth and development by directing the development of their personalities. It also guides their learning of how to interact with other people. The main goals should be to:

➤ assist children in discovering personal ways of interacting with peers;
➤ ensure that they feel good about their personal interactions;
➤ help them develop social competence;
➤ help them maintain positive relationships with others over time and across situations;

Table 10.1   Classroom Behaviors Depend on Teacher Preparation

Cooperation	Contention
Kinds of activities selected	Limited kinds of activities selected
Placement of materials for child use and replacement	Materials unaccessible for child use—no responsibility for replacement
Variety of opportunities	Few opportunities for personal selection
Adequate spaces	Cramped or traffic-pattern spaces
Uninterrupted time frames	Interruptions and time limitations
Types of toys and activities	One-of-a-kind toys or activities
Congenial and supportive attitudes of adults and children	Poor attitude of adults and children
Challenging, new, or repetitive activities	Broken, difficult, or one-turn toys
Sharing or trading toys and ideas	Limited use of toys and ideas (sharing means "losing")
Happy and secure children	Possessive or insecure children
Companionship—a sense of belonging	Isolation—a sense of rejection
Adults help children resolve conflicts in nonviolent ways (negotiation and conflict resolution)	Adults leave children to resolve disputes without giving them the skills or support to do so

Greenberg, 1992a, p. 14.

➤ help them acquire skills essential to decision making, problem solving, working together, and handling conflicts; and
➤ predict academic success.

Bandura's social cognitive theory, Piaget's cognitive developmental theory, Dodge
and Rubin's social information processing model, and Erikson's psychosocial theory are
helpful in explaining how children develop social skills in the context of environmental
factors. An eclectic approach provides a means of encompassing many complexities of social development (DeWolf & Benedict, 1997, p. 259).

Research and theory support the integration of the young child's learning. "The interre-
latedness of developmental domains virtually dictates an integrated approach to programming" (Bredekamp & Rosegrant, 1992). Learning is an interactive process where teachers:

➤ make observations and recording of special interests and progress or children
➤ prepare the environment for active exploration/interaction
➤ provide concrete, real, and relevant activities and materials
➤ provide for opportunity in difficulty, complexity, and challenge
➤ meet the needs/interests/skills of individual children (Bredekamp, 1987, pp. 3–5)

 Reflection

Consider having a camera in your classroom for spontaneous pictures of children
and activities that are meaningful to class members and even stimulate adding
to prior experiences. Personal photographs, displayed frequently, provide incen-
tives for language, activities, relationships, self- and social awareness, recall,
creativity, and many more growth-promoting experiences. (See Woods, 2000,
pp. 82–84.)

Children ask for assistance in carrying out individual projects.

Individuals, as well as organizations, have developed position statements that define and organize social studies (Seefeldt, 1997). Three of them are:

1. National Council for the Social Studies (NCSS)— geography, history and economics;
2. National Council for Social Studies in the Schools (NCSSS)— breadth and depth;
3. California State Board of Education (CSBE)— the discipline of history.

 Reflection

Social studies of history, geography, and economics must be on an elementary level before young children can build upon them. What could you teach about history? How is time important to young children? How can we integrate language arts with mathematics, art, or physical activities? What do young children know about change? Can we talk with them about yesterday, today, tomorrow, next week? How important are time concepts?

How do you plan to introduce social studies into your daily, weekly, monthly schedule so that young children find security (rather than insecurity) and look forward to holidays/celebrations (rather than ignore or dread them)? Make up some alternatives you can use in your classroom with your present students. Consider time, geography, history, economics (such as consuming, producing, and bartering), field trips, direction and location, relationships. Would the same options meet the needs of all students?

What are the roles of "community helpers"? Could we help children be more aware of those around us? How can we assist and/or appreciate them? Do we invite them into the classroom—or do we go where they are?

How can you involve the children in planning, integrating, and evaluating social studies experiences?

Democracy

Greenberg (1992b) offered this account:

> My classroom is not child centered. It is not curriculum centered. It is not centered around research-
> ing the child's mind. It is developmental for each child, I hope—in other words, based on each child's
> physical, psychological, and social accomplishments, issues, needs, and readiness, as well as intellec-
> tual and academic accomplishments, issues, needs, and readiness. Isn't that what *development*
> means? (p. 10)

Let there be no doubt that parents and teachers are *always* responsible for the
health, safety, and teaching of young children. It is the way they exercise these responsibilities that makes for a democratic or autocratic classroom. (See Chapter 2.) Democratic adults create and maintain necessary guidelines (with input from children),
but the adults do not demand or command! They set the tone of the group and classroom through room arrangement, materials and equipment, enforcement of the philosophy of the center, and personal interaction with children and adults. They also
allow ample time and opportunities for spontaneous or child-initiated ideas. (See
Figure 10.3)

Seefeldt (1993) reminds us that quality programs for young children (1) "recognize
that children are dependent on adults. At the same time, however, they realize that children must not learn the *habit* of being dependent on others but must learn to think and
make decisions for themselves to develop independence"; (2) give children the responsibility of taking "at least partial responsibility for solving problems that arise from living,
learning, and working with one another in a group"; and (3) also give children the opportunity "to experience the consequences of their decisions . . . determining which action

Teacher-child	Provide a safe, trusting atmosphere where children will verbalize their feelings.
	Talk directly about issues and feelings.
	Role play if appropriate.
	Use terms and situations that are age-appropriate.
	Jointly establish goals and methods so children feel understood and accepted.
	Try to see problems and solutions from both points of view.
	Carefully listen to children's views and suggestions.
	Ask and answer questions in a responsive way.
	Talk at a special time that does not interfere with activities and child/child relationships (Armstrong, 1994, p. 22).
	Organize the environment to minimize stress and pressures put on children (noise, time, choices, interaction with others, special needs, curriculum).
	Be aware of each child's personal needs and interests.
	Invite children's input into the classroom.
Teacher-parent	Help parents to see the particular needs of their children (separation, unfinished activities, late arrival, and so on).
	Point out developmental progress in various areas of behavior.
	Be considerate of the stress and demands life makes on parents.
	Invite parent participation when appropriate.
	Respectfully seek information from parents and listen to parental concerns and input.

Figure 10.3   Ways to Establish Good Social Relationships in the Classroom

they would change and how, or why the decision was or was not effective," helping them develop the ability to think and decide for themselves (p. 6).

Dewey (1944) believed another type of decision-making experience was necessary if children were to develop a mind that would enable them to be free. He called for more "stuff" in schools and encouraged teachers to use raw materials so children could develop the ability to think. He believed that raw materials, such as wood, clay, and paints—without any predetermined end or goal for their use—push children into true decision making and thinking. Seefeldt (1993) discusses Dewey's philosophy:

> Children are the ones who must figure out not only what to do with the materials but how they will do it and when they have achieved their own goals. . . . And when they reach their end goal, determined only by them—not by another—they are the ones who experience the joy of achievement and the satisfaction of developing a mind (p. 7).

In line with this thinking, Seefeldt adds:

> Worksheets, workbooks, computer-assisted instruction, even units of group projects that are determined and directed by a teacher do not permit thinking because often much of the doing has been completed by someone else. There is little left for the child to decide or think about. . . . Whenever the end goal of some activity has been predetermined by someone else, children only have to follow . . . but they will fail to develop a mind that could free them from the authority of others. Without a solid foundation of decision making built during early childhood, children will be ill prepared to set goals for themselves and achieve these but may be ready and prepared to achieve goals established for them by others (p. 7).

Young children benefit from group experiences where they can try, test, share, and evaluate their ideas. They can listen to the ideas of others and compare them to their views. The child will find that some ideas may be better than his, support his, or be in total conflict with his. Until "individuals are able to identify with others, to empathize with

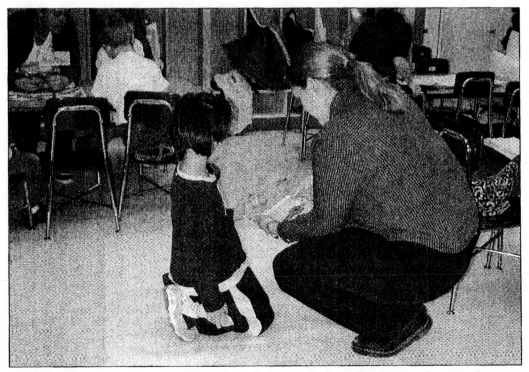

When a child and teacher have the same eye level, messages are sent and received more clearly.

others' thoughts and feelings and to develop the capacity for ethical respect, the world may never be free of tyranny and suffering" (Giroux, 1992, p. 7).

When teachers have these same opportunities as children (freedom to try, test, share, and evaluate their ideas), they provide settings for freedom, human dignity, individual rights, and responsibility toward others.

Moral Understanding

According to Buzzelli (1992),

> As early as the second year of life, children begin to use standards in evaluating their own behavior and the behavior of others, an achievement that marks the beginning of moral understanding. . . . Most parents expect their children to have an awareness of behavior standards by age three and to regulate their behavior according to the standards by age seven (p. 48).
>
> During the one- to three-year age period, conflicts involving opposing motives between parent and child first arise. It is no mere coincidence that as the toddler becomes more willful and able to say "No!" more often and more emphatically, parents become increasingly focused on teaching standards, enforcing rules, and using other types of discipline. Conflicts between children and caregivers take on special meaning not only because they represent constraints on the child but also because the conflicts are emotionally charged. Through such encounters, pride, shame, and guilt emerge (p. 50).

In Buzzelli's research of moral development, the following implications are suggested for parents and teachers:

1. Adults must acknowledge and value young children's emerging morally relevant abilities, including increasingly sophisticated cognitive and language skills, which provide the foundation for moral understanding.
2. Adults need to set clear and appropriate standards and expectations for young children's behavior.
3. Parents and teachers support children's moral understanding when they respond to children's transgressions in ways that are consistent with the type of transgression.
4. Children in the constructivist classroom (DAP) were more cooperative with one another and used more negotiation strategies to solve conflicts than children in other types of classrooms.
5. Early-childhood educators know that from their earliest years, impressionable young children possess sophisticated abilities and understandings of their social world; therefore, they look to adults.

Diversity

A discussion regarding diversity was introduced in Chapter 1. Children with different backgrounds, genetics, cultures, physical characteristics, personalities, and expectations require teachers and parents to look for these differences and handle them in ways that meet the needs of individual children. Some parents have very definite and particular goals for their children—some parents have similar goals for their children. As educators of young children, we must see that the needs of all children are met in the very best way for each child. We can do this if we recognize that children utilize experiences and information in ways that may be vastly different for each child. See Figure 10.4 for different ways to respond to different situations.

A very useful list of children's books about diversity is found in the article "Enriching Classroom Diversity with Books for Children, In-Depth Discussions of Them, and Story-Extension Activities" (1993). It has a three-page list of books including children with special situations, cooperation, diverse abilities, diverse families, special relationships, diverse gender behaviors, environment, anti-animal stereotypes, low income and job loss, misuses of power, and general multicultural/anti-bias themes.

Say . . .	Instead of . . .
The children are restless today (have lots of energy).	The children are wild as Indians today (downgrading a culture).
Tell her with your voice that you would like a turn.	You can't take that away from her (not promoting cooperation, peace).
If you ask in a friendly way, he'll let you have a turn in a minute.	You're just a bully and he doesn't have to share with you (downgrading a child).
This activity will be fun for all the children.	Just boys can play here (sexist).
Try to make it (or do it) yourself, and if you need help, I'll be here to help you (encouraging self-reliance).	Only strong (or smart) children can do this task.
Everyone has a different kind of family.	The best kind of family is white and has a mother, a father, two children, and a dog (insensitive to different family patterns).
Most children can do some things better than other things.	Children who can't hear stories and people talking (or can't run and jump) are not very smart (insensitive to abilities/handicaps).
It's nice to have grandmas and grandpas come to our classroom to see what we are doing and to help us out (valuing age).	Old people are grumpy, make trouble, and get in our way.
Let's think of ways men and women (boys and girls) could do the same job.	Let's think of all the jobs just men do and all the jobs just women do (sexist).
Which children in our group have blond hair? (Repeat for each hair color in the group, naming the children and counting them.)	Only children with black hair can swing today (segregating children, promoting competition, or indicating that one characteristic is better than another).
Find an activity you would like to do or a place to play until lunchtime (allowing choice of activity, time span, individual skills, and interest).	You may play wherever you like *after* you have completed *the* flower picture and written your name on it—but you have to hurry or you won't have time to do a good job.
In different families and places, people eat different kinds of food, wear different kinds of clothing, and do special activities (recognizing and learning about different cultures).	Children and families who eat different food than we do, dress differently than we do, or do different activities than we do are not as good as we are.
It is a good idea to take turns being the leader (democracy in choosing roles).	Paul is always the leader and Jennifer is always the caboose.
Sometimes parents get angry at children for the things they do or don't do (alternate discipline vs. abuse).	Parents have the right to hit or punish their children for bad deeds.
Tell her what it is you want or what she did to upset you (giving child a more appropriate response).	It is all right to hit children who get in your way or don't give you what you want.

Figure 10.4   Diversity in Response to Situations

NAEYC has produced recommendations effective for early-childhood education that respond to linguistic and cultural diversity (1996). These recommendations include specific guidelines for (1) working with children; (2) working with families; (3) professional preparation of early-childhood educators in the areas of culture, language, and diversity; and (4) recommended programs and practice. Their position reads:

> For the optimal development and learning of all children, educators must *accept* (hold in high regard) and *value* (esteem, appreciate) the home culture, and *promote* and *encourage* the active involvement and support of all families, including extended and nontraditional family units.

The article concludes that early-childhood professionals—by responding to the importance of the child's home language and culture—and families—by working toward the

Reflection

A 4-year-old boy from India asked his teacher one day, "Are we going to have any other children like me?" Not knowing the point of the question, the teacher asked for clarification. Pulling up his sleeve and pointing to his arm, the child replied, "You know, some children like me." The teacher knew he was asking about children of color, and quickly pointed out a Native American and several children with olive skin. The boy replied: "No, I mean *brown* like me!" What a golden and spontaneous moment to talk about the similarities and differences of the children in the group.

"school culture"— can provide a wholesome education for linguistically and culturally diverse children.

Multicultural Education

Multicultural education is a daily, ongoing process, and reaches beyond the typical food and dress in different cultures. It helps children to develop pride and appreciation for their own culture and to become sensitive to others. It is integrated into the curriculum and not merely added to it. It may be an initial cultural introduction for some children and should be done in a casual and accepting way.

But don't wait for children to ask questions about cultural differences. Be aware of opportunities that are always there. Some young children have exposure to cultural differences and others do not. As children develop their self-concepts (during the preschool

Sharing one's ideas and feelings with a friend provides comfort and security.

years), they do so as they make friends and interact with families and other individuals within their environment. When these interaction opportunities are not there, children become fearful of others—especially if others are different from themselves. They have a tendency to believe things they see and hear about others (collectively and individually). Even when there is cultural homogeneity, adults or children can talk about differences and encourage discussion without introducing competition, fear, dislike, or other negative aspects, such as comparing children against each other, family differences, physical characteristics, things people do, or kinds of clothing they wear, foods they eat, their housing, and so on.

Teachers in early childhood can implement multicultural education by being curious themselves, without being negative or judgmental, about the children in their classrooms. How do the children show affection or emotion? What are their attitudes toward school, themselves, and others? What materials can be brought into the classrooms that will introduce different ideas, expose the children to new things, and add an awareness and concern for others? Start where the children are now and focus on them. Change inappropriate things in the classroom and seek information and help from parents and others. Be sincere and respectful in your actions and dealings with children and adults. At the end of each curriculum chapter are some general suggestions to stimulate adult awareness of items and activities to incorporate in the classroom for a multicultural curriculum.

Caution: To begin with an extended exposure to many people at the same time, or to bombard the children with multicultural experiences, may just confuse or annoy them. Use wisdom in your planning—and make sure the children are the focus of your curriculum planning!

The suggestions can help creative positive relationships among different groups of people and help children gain interest in and concern with issues outside of their immediate experiences. Young children are usually more tolerant of changes if they meet them in a comfortable setting and if they have time to investigate and find out for themselves. Some teachers may feel that getting authentic information (dress, food, clothing, activities) on several different cultures is laborious and nonproductive. Begin with cultures or groups most likely to be in the lives of children within the classroom, then gradually broaden out to people who are in the community.

Children with Varied Needs

Children with Special Needs   Special laws regarding care and education have been adopted to protect the rights of young children with handicaps:

➤ PL 94-142, the Education for All Handicapped Children Act of 1975, mandates that educators provide special-education and related services within the lest restrictive environment.

➤ PL 999-457, the Education of All Handicapped Children Act Amendments of 1986 (amended by PL 101-476), requires all states to offer educational services to children between the ages of 3 and 5 who have handicaps.

The Americans with Disabilities ACT (ADA), signed into law on July 26, 1990, by President Bush, prohibits discrimination on the basis of disability in a wide range of areas. Specific application to early-childhood education programs (for children and their parents/guardians with disabilities) include:

1. *acceptance of children* with disabilities (each individual child considered on a case-by-case basis);
2. *accommodations* (perhaps some architectural changes that are reasonable and readily achievable, and/or subtle changes in the daily program);
3. modification of *behavior procedures* as needed;

Reflection

At our university preschool, many of our student teachers have spent time in other cultures or have close friends who have done so. Many student teachers want to share their excitement and objects with the young children. Most experiences end up with adults talking to adults and uninterested children.

A head teacher and four graduate students found a need to plan a cultural demonstration in one classroom. They decided on Japan because of firsthand knowledge, authentic materials, and parental support. The morning consisted of child-sized kimonos and clogs in the housekeeping area (furnished by a parent of one of the children in the group), teachers wearing kimonos and clogs, cooking rice and eating it with chopsticks for snack, Japanese and English books in a quiet area (a simple picture book was read in Japanese and translated into English—noting the different way the book is printed and used), pictures of the teachers in Japanese settings and clothing, tasting Japanese food, hearing Japanese music, and learning to count to five in Japanese.

The children were fascinated with the clothing, toys, activities, and participation. One child mastered chopsticks—eating four bowls of rice! They talked about the different clothes, shoes, books, and food. Nobody wanted to go home, and they asked for assurance that we "could do this another time, too." It gave reassurance to our Japanese child, and relationships blossomed.

Contrast the preceding experience with that of a group of 4-year-old boys who continually played together at the center following a series of World War II movies playing on television nightly. One boy was Japanese. After several days of reenactment of fighting, the Japanese boy said, quite fairly, "Why do I always have to be the Jap?" It appeared that the other boys recognized his features as being of the "enemy," but he could see no difference and wanted to know why he was singled out. How did he feel about himself? His heritage?

4. *staff training;*
5. *termination of a child* (for reasons other than prejudice—failure to progress, incompatible program, health or safety risk for others—applied equally to all children); and
6. *cost*—no additional cost to serve the child.

Russell-Fox (1997) has some very good suggestions on working with children who have *health* needs, *hearing* needs, *learning* needs, *visual impairments, communication* needs, and *physical* needs. It would be well for anyone working with young children, inexperienced children, or special-needs children to review this article.

Not being trained in special education, not wanting to take on the field, and not trying to be narrow-minded or directive, but having an interest in all children and having worked with young children with special needs over the years, Mahoney and Robinson (1992) proposed goals that are appealing and closely fit the ECE (or DAP) curriculum. See Table 10.2 for specific differences between the two programs as identified by Mahoney and Robinson.

Depending on the circumstances of the individual child, the classroom facilities, and the training of the teacher, some groups of young children include one or more children with "special needs." In one study the primary goal of including special-needs children was to give providers information and support to accept these children into their family child-care settings and to be able to work effectively with them. From their experience

Notable Quotes

A few words about diversity are offered by d'Entremont:

- "Weave a particular culture into a curriculum to offer more depth . . . and present aspects of the culture other than its holidays."
- "Consistently offer a variety of languages, books, stories, music, and all decorations that represent a cross section of our society."
- "Focus on the cultural, socioeconomic, and lifestyle differences represented within the families in the program."
- "React comfortably and appropriately to children's questions and observations about the diversity that exists around them" (1998, pp. 72 & 73).

And a note about ecology:

"We cannot expect three- and four-year-old children to understand the direct consequences of overconsuming or not recycling, but they are the perfect age to learn habits that will become part of their lives. Let's act on our belief that we need to respect the earth" (Shantal, 1998, p. 71).

What could you do in your classroom to help children and families become more aware of tolerance toward others and conserving our resources? **START NOW!!!**

the teachers valued outside assistance and confidence to work with these children (Crowley, 1999).

Crowley concluded that there is a current need for, and lack of, quality child care for special-needs children; the program is extremely cost effective; and benefits are received by children with and without disabilities in a mainstreamed classroom.

Table 10.2   Differences Between ECSE and ECE Programs

Early-Childhood Special Education (DIP)	Early-Childhood Education (DAP)
This model more closely represents developmentally inappropriate programs (DIP) in that it does the following:	This model conceptualizes development as being driven by the child's introduction to and interaction with the environment, and does the following:
Emphasizes teacher-directed activities.	Is child-centered.
Views development as being driven by the acquisition of new skills.	
Tends to ignore or disregard children's interests.	Places high priority on supporting and encouraging children's interests and on
Acknowledges performances of the behaviors required of children.	accepting children's behavior as legitimate and worthwhile.
Is based on the notion that children need direction and guidance to perform desired developmental behaviors and activities.	Encourages the development of self-esteem, self-discipline, curiosity, and problem solving.
Encourages teachers to be directive and structured in their interactions with children.	Encourages teachers to be warm, available, and nonintrusive.

There is an often asked question about enrolling a child with a developmental delay in a regular classroom. Stewart (1999) lists five questions to ask a parent about: medical/ physical issues; special services through the school district; IFSF (family education plan) and IEP (individualized plan); services the child receives outside the school district; and parental expectation of the child in this classroom.

The following information was retrieved from the Internet, December 12, 2002:

In 1975, Congress passed Public Law 94-142 (Education of All Handicapped Children Act), now codified as IDEA (Individuals with Disabilities Education Act). In order to receive federal funds, states must develop and implement policies that assure a free appropriate public education (FAPE) to all children with disabilities. The state plans must be consistent with the federal statute, Title 20 United States Code Section 1400 et seq. (20 USC 1400). (For more information on IDEA, legislative history, implications, see the other files in forum libraries, especially those that relate to the Shannon Carter case which was argued before the US Supreme Court on October 6, 1993.)

H.R. 1912: Sponsor: Rep. Simmons, Rob (introduced 5/17/2001)

Latest Major Action: 7/20/01 Referred to House subcommittee. Status: Referred to the Subcommittee on Education Reform.

Websites relating to these issues:

Family & Advocates Partnership for Education: www.fape.org.
Spanish: www.fape.org/search/query.asp.
Ideapractices.org: thearc.org/faqs/dueproc.html—Procedural Safeguards in 94-142

Summary as of 5/17/2001—Introduced: "Keeping Our Promise to Special Education Act of 2001—Amends the Individuals with Disabilities Education Act (IDEA) to specify mandatory minimum levels of Federal grant payments to States for assistance for education of all children with disabilities. . . . Requires local educational agencies, if they choose to treat certain IDEA funds as local funds, to use them to provide additional funding for programs under the Elementary and Secondary Education Act of 1965."

A new program called "New Friends" was designed to teach preschoolers about differences, similarities, and impairments of hearing, physical ability, and learning. Results indicated that exposure to the program led to positive changes in attitudes and to increased knowledge of disabilities. Thios and Foster (1991) noted that "no behavioral changes in social interaction patterns were observed. It is concluded that 'New Friends' appears to provide a useful curriculum for use in conjunction with other procedures designed to enhance the acceptance of children with disabilities by their non-disabled peers"

Children in School Before Kindergarten   The question, "Who is responsible for early childhood services for children before kindergarten?" is asked often. In a Public Policy Report, Clifford, Early, and Hills (1999) report the following information:

1. Schools and school districts are becoming increasingly more involved.
2. The U.S. Department of Education's National Center for Educational Statistics (NCES) compiles information on pre-kindergarten children.
3. Using data from *National Household Education Survey of 1995* (Department of Education NCES 1996), it was estimated that some 900,000 pre-kindergarten children (mostly 4- and 5-year-olds) were served in programs at public elementary, junior high, and senior high schools in 1995.
4. The roles of various levels of government in financing, regulating, and delivering services requires a comprehensive review.

Until there is agreement or responsibility taken, "many families will continue to be faced with a patchwork of service, and many children will spend their early years in settings of unknown quality" (Clifford, et al., 1999, p. 51).

 *Reflection*

It was summertime and a group of disabled children was housed next door to a group of nondisabled children—an arrangement heretofore not done. At first each head teacher scheduled a time for her group to be outside—therefore nondisabled children and disabled children were not on the playground at the same time. The disabled children had a joyous time indoors and outdoors, but the nondisabled children began to change. They pressed their noses to the glass when the disabled children were outside; they asked serious questions about the disabled children. They became quiet and fearful—of becoming the same way, of the unknown, of losing friends, and so on. The teacher of the nondisabled group began to notice these changes and the seriousness and lethargic response of the children. As they talked within the group, the children began to verbalize their concerns. The teachers began to bring things into the curriculum that the children were noticing—how would it be to be blind? Could a game with a blindfold ease or increase concerns? Would a wheelchair and crutches help the children to know how it felt to be injured or crippled? How would it be if you couldn't hear—or climb? Gradually, the children became less fearful and more curious. Disabled children were invited into their classroom. As tension eased, more and more children of each group were on the playground together. The nondisabled children wanted to ride in wheelchairs, try crutches, and assist the disabled children in many ways. By the end of the summer, the two groups were well integrated, had fun doing things for and with each other, and even had a parade and circus on the playground. What had started out as a fearful and negative situation turned into a cooperative and understanding experience for both groups of children.

Teachers can plan activities and materials to meet the interests of individual children.

Children in Child Care   "The National Institute of Child Health and Human Development (NICHD) has released findings from its Study of Early Child Care, a seven-year longitudinal study on the effects of child care on children's development and mother-child relations. The findings show:

> Children cared for in settings with several other children have fewer behavior problems than those cared for alone or with one or two other children.
> Children in higher-quality child care programs have greater language abilities than those in lower-quality programs.
> Children in child care for more than 10 hours per week perform better on cognitive and language measures when quality caregiver-child interaction takes place in the care setting.
> Higher-quality caregiver-child interactions predict greater maternal involvement and positive engagement between mother and child (*Young Children*, May, 1998, p. 29).

"One of the most dramatic changes in American family life in recent years has been the increased participation of young children in nonparental child care and early education settings. Between 1970 and 1993 the percentage of children regularly attending these types of arrangements soared from 30 to 70% (Department of Health, and Human Services, n.d.)" (NAEYC, 1998, pp. 43–50).

Anti-Bias Curriculum

A filmstrip by the Council on Interracial Books for Children (1980) defines *stereotyping* as follows:

> A stereotype is an oversimplified, generalized image describing all individuals in a group as having the same characteristics, that is to say, in appearance, in behavior, in beliefs. While there may be a germ of truth in a stereotype, the image usually represents a gross distortion, or an exaggeration of that truth, and has offensive, dehumanizing implications.

Children benefit from learning about other people and cultures if activities and concepts are appropriately planned. The following criteria should be considered:

1. developmental level of each child and of the total group, including interest, attention span, and skills;
2. possibility of increasing existing knowledge or of clarifying concepts;
3. activities that are child-centered but may be adult-initiated;
4. possibility of increasing independence;
5. inclusion of many different aspects—examples: food, customs, music, and so on; and
6. opportunity to increase understanding about and relationships with other cultures and people.

Teachers of young children can do many things to avoid stereotyping. In their classrooms they can give wholesome examples of people of different races, ethnic groups, and family composition, and of people of both sexes doing the same and different things. The toys and activities planned for the classroom should include opportunities for children to learn about ethnic groups through books, dramatic play, written and spoken language, music, art materials, guests, manipulatives, blocks, food experiences, and other means. An excellent resource section on children's books (including publishing information; age recommendation; family, gender, people of color, and disabilities; work; prejudice; activism; comments; curriculum materials; and stereotyped worksheets) is found in Derman-Sparks and the A.B.C. Task Force (1989, pp. 119–145).

Teachers want the children in their classrooms to know that people of both sexes, different races, ethnic groups, and family composition can do the same and different things. Some things can be done more casually than others. Instead of making name tags (when used on lockers, for example), the teacher could let the child choose from a variety of pictures—not arbitrarily placing feminine symbols on girls' lockers and masculine symbols on boys' lockers. The classroom should include areas and activities that typically have been classed masculine (woodworking, trucks, and so on) and feminine (dramatic play, art, and so on), but **ALL** children should be encouraged to participate in all areas and feel that it is acceptable. One parent would almost threaten her son not to dress up, play with girls, or get messy. The more she pushed her idea, the more Nick wanted to do these things—and the more guilt he felt when he did. The teacher and the mother discussed the problem, and the mother finally stopped making an issue. Nick found more pleasure from various activities and then moved into other areas of play. Why shouldn't boys be nurturing, domestic, and creative? The mother's reasoning was she "didn't want him to be a sissy"!

Conversations and ideas such as this inspired a mini-study with the children presently in our early-childhood lab. Each child (age 3-1/2 to 5 years) was asked: "What do you want to be when you grow up?" Following a response, each one was asked, "If you were a boy (girl) rather than a girl (boy), what would you want to be when you grow up?" The answers were diverse. Many of the children of one sex just couldn't imagine being the other sex—or stated, "I don't want to be a (person of the opposite sex)." Some answered quickly and surely about each sex. Most of the children (especially the younger ones) selected a familiar role (parent, community helper, or television character) for both roles, but there were a few different ones: pumpkin, snake, dinosaur, or pirate of one's own sex; and for the opposite sex: nothing, chicken, climb up rainbows, Superman, witch, and gremlin. Joshua said, "I hate to grow up—they never have any fun!" and no comment about being a girl. Michael just wanted to be "myself" for both answers.

The Council on Interracial Books for Children (1980) outlined ten quick ways to check for sexism in *Guidelines for Selecting Bias-Free Textbooks and Storybooks*:

1. Check the illustrations (stereotypes, tokenism, leadership/passive, males/females).
2. Check the story line (success, resolution of problems, role of women).
3. Look at lifestyles.
4. Weigh the relationships between people (whites/African Americans, dominant/ subservient).
5. Note the heroes (minorities).
6. Consider the effects on a child's self-image.
7. Note the background of the author or illustrator.

 Reflection

In one preschool, the mother of one child was a nurse and volunteered to show the children what she did at work. She also mentioned that many men where she worked were also nurses—and doctors were women or men. A teacher and a group of 4-year-olds were having a spontaneous discussion about the occupations of the parents. One boy said, "Well, my dad's a doctor!" and another one said, "Mine is, too." The teacher told the children that she was also a doctor. The response came back quickly and strong: "Oh, no, you can't be a doctor. You're a girl!" The teacher told them she was not a doctor who gave shots and took care of sick people, but she was a teacher-doctor. The first little boy responded: "Nope! You can be a teacher-nurse but you can't be a teacher-doctor!"

8. Check the perspective of the author.
9. Watch for loaded words (sexist).
10. Look at the copyright date.

Children begin to label people around them according to their gender. It is still not clear to them what constitutes gender at this stage because clothing, hair length, names, toy choices, and other means are not as clearly differentiated as they have been in the past. Gender constancy develops around age 6 or 7, when:

➤ children begin to understand that their sex is determined by their anatomy;
➤ gender identity and gender constancy leads to children's development of healthy, gender-fair attitudes; and
➤ children begin to feel capable and confident in their abilities (Wellhouse, 1996, p. 83).

Young children need to know that fathers (males) can be nurturing (have characteristics generally given to females); mothers (females) can be breadwinners (have characteristics generally given to males). Dramatic play with appropriate props, field trips, literature, music, and other curriculum segments can help reinforce these ideas.

Celebrations

Celebrations may include **ethnic customs, holidays, and/or other special occasions** and should be integrated into the regular routine. The focus is kept simple and low-key, and a few appropriate concepts are selected. Attention can be centered on a special child, on a visitor, or even on a fire drill. Children need to know how to handle a variety of situations. Experiences in the classroom reduce fear and frustration in future happenings.

Children look forward to celebrations.

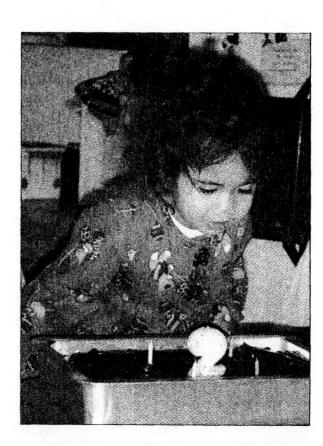

In planning holiday celebrations, the teacher must consider what value the holiday has for these particular children. Is it a cultural tradition? Is it developmentally appropriate for them? Will it give them a better understanding about their culture, values, and so on? Will it teach stereotypes or prejudices? Is it just a time consumer, or something everybody else is doing? Is it more commercialized than useful? If you don't celebrate it in the classroom, how will the children learn about it?

Some questions about holiday celebrations outside the home are posed:

If some families have religious prohibitions against celebration of holidays with pagan roots (including traditional religious holidays), should we eliminate them from a school setting or should we promote them to give greater understanding to the children? Don't we need shared celebrations in order to create a better community understanding? What can we do about the formidable differences among us? Is it important to honor the rich cultural traditions of the families in an early-childhood program? How can this be done without trivializing symbolic meanings on the one hand, or offending people with different beliefs on the other? Would it be appropriate to downplay specific holiday-identified celebrations and look instead for the universally shared meanings underlying the holiday traditions of different cultures? Is there provision for dialogue between teachers and parents, or does the school have the final word?

Should there be no formal celebration of traditional holidays in the classroom? Perhaps a child-care program is an inappropriate place to celebrate holidays—end of discussion. While children love anticipation and planning and all the excitement that goes with festivity, consider the following:

1. It's extremely difficult to give holidays meaning that is developmentally appropriate for very young children. Most holidays are based on abstract concepts that are beyond their comprehension.
2. It's difficult to be inclusive. Are we going to celebrate holidays based in cultures represented in our program? What if there is little diversity? What if there is a great deal? What if some parents object to all holidays? Do we have the time and resources to do justice to them all? How much of our curriculum do we want to devote to holidays? What important activities are being displaced?
3. Many holidays are overdone anyway. Children see signs of the major commercialized holidays everywhere, so they'll be asking questions and their families will be making choices. If families are celebrating, why do we need to celebrate too?

When we make choices about what to celebrate, let us be very conscious of who we are doing it for. . . . If we are doing it for the families, we must choose carefully what to celebrate so that we are inclusive. If we are doing it for the children, let us be conscious of all the subtle messages inherent in what we do and choose things to celebrate that are meaningful, developmentally appropriate, and healthy for them (Neugebauer, 1990, p. 42.).

Alternatives in a diverse classroom could be:

➤ Integrate December holidays from several cultural groups, identifying common themes and observations.
➤ Do December holidays other than Christmas.
➤ Don't do December holidays at all in the classroom (Derman-Sparks & the A.B.C. Task Force, 1989, pp. 91–93).

Age

Children not accustomed to being around elderly individuals (especially ones with disabilities) may be frightened, but once they understand that these individuals are nurturing and caring, the fears gradually dissipate. Talking with elderly people can help

Very young children feel more secure around loving/caring adults and in familiar places.

generate values in young children. They like to hear about "Tell about when you were little," and "Tell me about when I was a baby and the things I could do and say." This interaction can enhance the self-confidence and self-esteem of the children and enrich the lives of children and elderly individuals.

It has been noted in settings outside the classroom, such as being with senior citizens, that some children begin to express themselves verbally, begin to feel their own capacities, and smile more. The same may be true of the seniors.

Race/Culture

Not only must one be careful to include diversity in the curriculum and to plan for children of varied needs and background, one must also take precautions against ideas and attitudes that show bias toward some children and against others.

Throughout this book there is a focus on anti-bias curriculum. In some settings this will be easier to accomplish than where a strong bias feeling exists—but even in such settings, attempts should be made to reduce the negative or competitive feelings.

Racial prejudice, societal stereotyping, and bias can begin during the preschool years through lack of contact with and information about people of diverse backgrounds. See Figure 10.5 for multicultural educational goals.

Teachers can talk with children about the different cultures represented in their classroom or community, use authentic visuals, invite visitors, remove stereotypes, value differences, feel what it is like to be in a minority, and provide other "here and now" experiences from which children can learn and in which they can participate.

By 2 years of age, children not only notice, they also ask questions about differences and similarities among people. How we answer their questions and respond to their ideas is crucial to their level of comfort when learning about diversity (Derman-Sparks & ABC Task Force, 1989; Taylor, 2002, p. 10).

To teach all children and adults:
1. To respect his/her (their) own culture as well as that of others.
2. To function successfully in a multicultural, multiracial society.
3. To develop a positive self-concept—especially those most affected by racism.
4. To experience in positive ways both their differences as culturally diverse people and their similarities as human beings.
5. To encourage children to experience people of diverse cultures working together as unique parts of a whole community.

Figure 10.5   Goals for Multicultural Education

Parts of our country are more monocultural than others, and children there do not have daily contact with people of other races or ethnicities or other cultural differences. Rather than thinking it is not their problem to teach multicultural ideas, adults (teachers and parents) can find ways to introduce diverse ideas. Perhaps they can team up with a companion school in another part of the country and exchange photographs, books, weather and natural conditions, songs, curriculum activities and other ideas, exercising caution that ideas are not too abstract for young children to grasp. Nevertheless, concepts of acceptance, uniqueness, self-identity and esteem, cooperation, democracy, and other principles can be taught within a classroom. The more realistic the experience (good props, visuals and stories, understanding and patient teachers), the more the children can gain from the experience.

There are two tremendous resources in *Young Children* (1993, March) about diversity (Seefeldt and "Enriching Classroom Diversity with Books for Children. . . . "). Topics have been identified and references are clearly labeled and readily available. Some are resources for adults; others are books to be used with children. A description reads: "Think what a difference it would make in your classroom if you merely bought, often read and discussed, and sometimes did story-extension activities related to a number of

 Reflection

Using age-appropriate props, language, and time frames, try some of the following activities to inform young children about different cultures within the classroom or community (Boutte, LaPoint, & Davis, 1993):

- Read and talk about pictures, books, and artifacts of many cultures.
- Use music: sing songs, dance, imitate behaviors.
- Examine photographs and drawings.
- Provide replicas of clothing.
- Acquire appropriate props and encourage dramatic play.
- Provide cultural toys and games.
- Invite diverse visitors and resource people.
- Provide raw materials for exploration (wood, clay, paper, crayons, markers, paints, and so on—include opportunities to note various skin colors).
- Talk about interaction between people of similar and different cultures.
- Prevent such comments as preservice teachers label[ing] children of color "the quiet one" or "the maladjusted one," or [saying] "talking about race is not polite" when (actually, *not* discussing it is impolite) (p. 20).

Understand your own feelings and issues.
Treat persons as being concerned about their children.
Avoid stereotyping interracial children and families.
Seek help from parents in dealing with derogatory comments from others.
Feel love, support, and acceptance for each child.
With openness, discuss physical differences and similarities, feelings, and negative reactions.
Help the children protect themselves from verbal and physical abuse.
Encourage children to share and be proud of their heritage.
Help each child define his or her identity.
Provide materials, activities, and interactions among religions, heritages, races, and ethnic
    backgrounds.
Be sensitive about racial differences.
Help children to intermingle.

Figure 10.6   Suggested Guidelines for Working with Interracial (and All) Children
Adapted from Wardle, 1987.

these books! Buying and frequently using diversity books with your children can make the most homogeneous group more familiar with human diversity!" (p. 10).

A child's race is an intimate part of her self-esteem, a fact that teachers must realize. How one reacts to this aspect of a child has a tremendous effect upon her—racial issues in the classroom must be recognized and addressed! Teachers are the most powerful influences that young children encounter; these teachers can perpetuate or discourage racial problems within their classrooms. See Figure 10.6 for guidelines concerning race.

> Unless educators provide encouragement and a nurturing environment in which all children and older students can learn and excel, negative misconceptions about their academic, communication, and social abilities will be perpetuated. In a diverse society, we as educators must learn to recognize subtle negative racial attitudes. Prejudice is no joke—it is ignorance! (Boutte, LaPoint, & Davis, 1993, p. 23)

Native Americans

This group is selected here for emphasis because it has been underrecognized and misrepresented, and is easy to identify. They are scattered throughout the United States and belong to many different nations and bands, each having similarities and differences with others.

The first thing should be to remove existing misconceptions and begin teaching true and accurate concepts. Unfortunately, written and visual media have portrayed Native Americans as warlike, uncivilized, and fearsome people. Teachers of young children can stop being culturally assaultive to these people by carefully selecting songs, books, activities, and references. Some teachers (and parents) teach concepts and promote ideas that are offensive and inaccurate without giving it a second thought because they learned and repeated these ideas from childhood. Now is the time to begin analyzing words to songs, examining text and pictures in media, thinking about activities prepared, and challenging erroneous, insulting, and discriminatory behavior—not only to Native Americans but to all cultures and races.

Although many Native American children adjust to the dominant society's school world, many of them experience a high degree of inner turmoil and lack necessary coping skills because of differences in child-rearing practices, indifference to material goods, acting out of need rather than by clock or plan, and inappropriate teaching methods currently used.

Figure 10.7 shows a letter written by a concerned parent, regarding the concepts being taught about Native Americans.

Dear Teacher:

I applaud the music experience the children have had in nursery school and the note of explanation you sent. I am very concerned, however, about the focus song on the handout:

I'm a great big Indian chief
With feathers in my cap
I play my tom-tom all day long
Now what do you think of that! Hmmmm

A study[1] by the League of Women Voters has shown that kindergartners have the following misconceptions:

1. All Indians are alike (no tribal or cultural distinctions).
2. Indians lived long ago.
3. Indians are threatening.
4. Indians live in teepees, wear headdresses, and are led by male "chiefs."

Sadly, by the sixth grade there is no significant change of perception.

You can see how this little song, with instructions to "chant" it, contributes to the described stereotypes. This concerns me for two reasons. First is my child's self-perception. [Name] knows his grandfather is Indian (Native American is a better term), but he has trouble connecting with all the scary or inane images projected by media—cartoons, picture books, songs, and Thanksgiving art projects. These incorrect and unpleasant ideas have been a source of inner conflict for [Name] that he certainly does not need.

Secondly, for children and parents who do not make the effort to distinguish between reality and stereotype, ignorance is perpetuated. This ignorance sows the seeds of racism. To fail to object to false images, to fail to properly educate is a racism more subtle, insidious, and dangerous than open bigotry.

I realize that there is no malicious intent of the little song or the teachers. I know music is a wonderful medium for teaching. I am merely afraid of the underlying message of generalized falsehood in this song.

Sincerely,

[1]See Gretchen M. Betaille and Charles L. P. Silet, *The Pretend Indians*, Iowa State University Press, 1980.

Figure 10.7 Parental Concern About Heritage

For those not directly involved in a particular point, or those who say, "Oh, it's only a fun little song," the parent's point of view is well taken. The little song may be unconsciously causing prejudice or stereotyping. How seriously does a teacher (or parent) need to take such things? And how can the teacher use curriculum ideas to promote positive attitudes toward different ethnic groups?

Different Families

The past image of the typical American family needs to be updated. Today there are many different family compositions: one parent (headed by either a male or a female), two parents (headed by a male and female, or two same-sex parents), interracial parents, stepparents, adoptive parents, extended families, no parent (raised by older sibling), and others. Children need to know that many family compositions exist. Some are harmonious and others experience difficulty of many kinds. "Educators must provide for children not living with their natural parents, children from abusive families, children who rarely see their parents, and children from single-parent homes," states Wardle (1987, p. 53).

Early childhood educators are expected to create an environment of tolerance and justice for all people, including those unlike us in some way (religion, color, sexual orientation, family format, ability, socioeconomic status), and to promote tolerance and justice even for people with whom we disagree and of whose behavior we disapprove. This is the way of democracy, and democracy is the ideal of our country" (Wickens, 1993, p. 25).

There are over ten million children in three million gay and lesbian families in this country (American Bar Association, 1991). When parents disclose their same-sex parenting, usually when children are ages 3 to 7, teachers who have previously dealt with similar situations or who have had prior instruction usually handle the information better than teachers who are experiencing the situation for the first time or have strong feelings about the topic. Instruction on the topic helps teachers and parents handle the situation without trauma and shame on the part of either one.

> The inclusion of diverse family structures and family patterns in what we offer the children in our classrooms is important, whether the class has a child with lesbian or gay parents or not. In fact, teaching diversity of any kind is even more complex when diversity is *not* represented in the school (Wickens, 1993, p. 26).

In addition,

> some teachers seem to be examining their curriculum; modifying stories and songs to present parents of both sexes in protective and nurturing roles, and creating a climate in which children can talk about their family structure, regardless of how conventional or unconventional it is (p. 28).

One must not always conclude that because there are two male or two female parents that these parents are gay or lesbian. There are cases where two sisters, two brothers, or two unrelated same-sex adults are guardians of underage children.

Individuals working with young children should be caring and secure enough to discuss different types of families (single-parent, adoptive, extended, traditional, same-sex, homeless, abusive) without being judgmental. Corbett (1993) states:

> If we can learn to believe that gay people are meaningful, productive, equal members of our society, we will start thinking about the little ones we nurture who will one day join their ranks (p. 30).
>
> How must the scores of children living with gay parents feel, never to see any representation of their lives in any book, any song, or any television program? The paucity of appropriate materials is admittedly great, but we owe these children and their families the same sensitivity we show everyone else we serve . . . some pictures of families with same-sex parents, a single parent, a grandparent as parent, two sets of parents/stepparents, and so on. Our attitude can be such that no child need feel ashamed to draw or discuss her family (p. 31).

Application of Principles

About Oneself: Help the children learn about their bodies and build self-esteem by doing the following:

1. Acquire a skeleton—preferably a replica of the human body—from a library, university, museum, or other available source. Introduce it in an informal, nonfrightening way. Help the children feel their own bones and match those bones to the skeleton. Note that there are large and small bones. Place the skeleton where children can refer to it at their leisure or interest. Concepts you could introduce include the following: A skeleton is made up of many bones of different sizes; it provides shape to the body (human or animal); it gives strength to the body (ability to stand, play); it helps protect parts of the body (internal organs and brain); bones connect to each other through joints and enable movement; and the children will likely suggest others.

2. Following information on bones, help the children learn that muscles help humans (and animals) move in different ways—gallop, hop, crawl, reach, jump, run, carry, climb. Encourage children to think of all the ways they can move. Add rhythms of music that might suggest different ways to move.

3. Help the children discover and discuss a particular part of the body (head, arm, foot). How does this body part function individually and in concert with the other parts of the body or the body as a whole? (How are body parts similar to and different from those of someone else—shape of teeth or ears?)

4. Taking each one of the five senses individually (and later combining senses or all of them collectively), help the children discover how their bodies help them in different ways.

5. Combine curriculum ideas to help the children better understand about their bodies—cutting and pasting body parts, comparing the growth of their bodies to that of an animal or plant, singing songs, doing physical activities, cooperating with someone on a project, hearing activity stories, taking a walk through the playground, counting and naming body parts, nutrition, health and safety in activities, things they can do now that they could not do when younger, and so on.

About minorities:

1. Before planning and teaching concepts about Native Americans or any other minority group, learn true concepts and carefully plan activities. Correct any misconceptions or partial truths you currently have so you know and understand the particular culture.

2. Look through visual aids, materials, books, pictures, music, and other teaching materials to determine which ones teach true, accurate, and useful concepts about Native Americans and other minority groups. Discard inaccurate materials or modify them so they portray accurate concepts.

3. Purchase materials that are accurate and provide opportunities for children to learn and discover information about other peoples.

4. When teaching about minorities (cultures), involve ideas in addition to the food, clothing, and music of each group.

5. Are there some ethnic, religious, or cultural occasions that would be of value or interest to the children in your classroom? If so, select one and make plans to implement it. List some people and activities that could help the children gain a better understanding of the occasion.

6. Correct any misconceptions the children may have, such as "Indians are bad," "Indians scalp people," sitting "Indian style," "Cowboys kill Indians because Indians are bad," "Indians live in teepees," and so on.

7. Teach through a variety of media: photographs, dress-up clothes, miniature people, puzzles, visitors and resource people, creative media (including all sorts of skin colors), field trips (when possible), and so on. Have props available so children can replay the themes over again as their interest indicates.

8. Talk about similarities and differences between the families of children within the group and those of other cultures. Point out things that are especially good about the culture (music, family relationships, art, housing, and so on).

9. Avoid teaching stereotyped ideas or using traditional projects (headbands, tomahawks, totem poles, Thanksgiving feast) that teach inaccurate concepts.

10. How do you personally feel about using nonsense songs or those that do not teach true concepts—especially those that might offend other races or cultures?

General:

1. Make a list of topics you think can appropriately be classed as "social studies" for young children.

2. Determine the social/ethnic problems in your area (gender, race family composition, and so on). How can you help combat them? Focus on the young children.

3. Make a sociogram by casually asking children with whom they like to play (or by observing children over a period of time). Avoid making choices for children.

4. Explain how special occasions can be overemphasized. How would you handle a situation when parents objected to the celebration of a particular cultural or religious holiday?

5. List appropriate field trips near your center.

6. With another adult, select and plan a field trip. Fill out the checklist in Figure 10.1 (p. 373). If possible, take the trip, being sure to evaluate it properly on your return.

7. Why is it important to make a visit before taking a field trip with young children? What are the values of follow-up activities?

8. Devise a method of informing parents about field trips and of getting parental permission.

9. How appropriate are the center's present field trip policies for children, parents, and staff? Make constructive suggestions.

10. Evaluate the legal and moral responsibilities related to taking field trips. Are there state or federal laws related to transporting children (for example, liability, seat belts) that apply to your center?

11. Refer to the curriculum checklist in Figure 10.1 to make sure your planning covers the suggested points.

12. Write a lesson plan on some aspect of society—"Hats for My Head," "Shoes for My Feet," "Food for My Lunch"—and help the children learn about the people in their community.

References

NOTE: Current references are used when available. Older references are classic, introductory and important in development of later ideas, policies, and practices.

Armstrong, J. L. (1994). Mad, sad, or glad: Children speak out about child care. *Young Children, 49*(2), 22–23.

Bandura, A. (1977). *Social learning theory.* Upper Saddle River, NJ: Prentice Hall.

Beane, J. A. (1991). Enhancing children's self-esteem: Illusion and possibility. *Early Education and Development, 2*(2), 153–160.

Betaille, G. M., & Silet, C. L. P., (1980). *The pretend Indians.* Ames, IA: Iowa State University Press.

Boutte, G. S., LaPoint, S., & Davis, B. (1993). Racial issues in education: Real or imagined? *Young Children, 49*(1), 19–23.

Bredekamp, S. (1987). *Developmentally appropriate practice in early childhood programs serving children from birth through age 8.* Washington, DC: NAEYC.

Bredekamp, S. (1997). Social studies in the developmentally appropriate integrated curriculum. In C. H. Hart, D. C. Burts, & R. Charlesworth (Eds), *Integrated curriculum and developmentally appropriate practice: birth to age eight* (pp. 171–199). Albany: State University of New York.

Bredekamp, S., & Copple, C. (Eds.). (1997). *Developmentally appropriate practice in early childhood programs* (rev. ed.). Washington, DC: NAEYC.

Bredekamp, S., & Rosegrant, T. (1992). Reaching potentials through appropriate curriculum: Conceptual frameworks for applying the guidelines. In S. Bredekamp & T. Rosegrant (Eds.), *Reaching potentials: Appropriate curriculum and assessment for young children,* Vol. 1 (pp. 28–42). Washington, DC: NAEYC.

Brophy-Herb, H. E., Kostelnik, M. J., & Stein, L. C. (2001). A developmental approach to teaching about ethics using the NAEYC code of ethical conduct. *Young Children, 55*(1), 80–84

Bureau of Indian Affairs, Office of Indian Education Programs. Washington, DC 20240.

Buzzelli, C. A. (1992). Research in review: Young children's moral understanding: Learning about right and wrong. *Young Children, 47*(6), 47–53.

California State Board of Education (CSBE). (1989). *History social science framework.* Sacramento, CA: Author.

Carron, D. T., & Scott, K. G. (1992). Risk assessment in preschool children: Research implications for the early detection of educational handicaps. *Topics in Early Childhood Special Education, 12*(2), 196–211.

Cartwright, S. (1993). Cooperative learning can occur in any kind of program. *Young Children, 48*(2), 112–114.

Chambers, B. (1983). Counteracting racism and sexism in children's books. In O. Saracho, & B. Spodek (Eds.), *Understanding the multicultural experience in early childhood education* (pp. 91–105). Washington, DC: NAEYC.

Clark, L., DeWolf, S., & Clark, C. (1992). Teaching teachers to avoid having culturally assaultive classrooms. *Young Children, 47*(5), 4–9.

Clifford, R. M., Early, E. M., & Hills, T. W. (1999). Almost a million children in school before kindergarten: Who is responsible for early childhood services? *Young Children, 54*(5), 48–51.

Cobb, P. (1994). Constructivism in mathematics and science education. *Educational Researcher, 22*(7), 4–5.

Corbett, S. (1993). A complicated bias. *Young Children, 49*(3), 29–31.

Council for Exceptional Children. 1920 Association Drive, Weston, VA 22091-1589. 800-328-9272, TDD: 703-264-9449. Division for Early Childhood: http://www.dec-sped.org.

Council on Interracial Books for Children. (1980). *Identifying racism and sexism in children's books.* New York: Racism and Sexism Resource Center for Educators (distributor). Filmstrip.

Crowley, A. L. W. (1999). Training family child care providers to work with children who have special needs. *Young Children, 54*(4), 59–61.

Curry, N. E., & Johnson, C. N. *Beyond self-esteem: Developing a genuine sense of human value.* NAEYC order #143. ISBN: 0-935989-39-0.

d'Entremont, L. (1998). Food for thought: A few words about diversity and rigidity: One director's perspective. *Young Children, 53*(1), 72–73.

Derman-Sparks, L. (1999). Markers of multicultural/antibias education. *Young Children, 54*(4), 43.

Derman-Sparks, L., & A.B.C. Task Force. (1989). *Anti-bias curriculum: Tools for empowering young children.* Washington, DC: NAEYC.

Derman-Sparks, L., & Phillips, C. B. (1997). *Teaching/learning anti-racism.* New York: Teachers College Press.

Dewey, J. (1944). *Democracy and education.* New York: Free Press.

DeWolf, M., & Benedict, J. (1997). Social development and behavior in the integrated curriculum. In C. H. Hart, D. C. Burts, & R. Charlesworth (Eds.) *Integrated curriculum and developmentally appropriate practice: Birth to age eight* (pp. 257–284). Albany: State University of New York Press.

Dodge, K. A. (1986). A social information processing model of social competence in children. In M. Perlmutter (Ed.), *Cognitive perspectives on children's social and behavioral development. The Minnesota Symposia on Child Psychology,* Vol. 18 (pp. 77–126). Hillsdale, NJ: Erlbaum.

Dunn, J., Brown, J., & Beardsall, L. (1991). Family talk about feeling states and children's later understanding of others' emotions. *Developmental Psychology, 27,* 448–455.

Enriching classroom diversity with books for children, indepth discussions of them, and story-extension activities. (1993). *Young Children, 48*(3), 10–12.

Erikson, E. (1950a). *Childhood and society.* New York: Norton.

Erikson, E. (1950b). *A healthy personality for your child.* Washington, DC: U.S. Government Printing Office.

Fu, V. R., Stremmel, A. J., & Treppte, C. (1993). *Multiculturalism in early childhood programs.* Urbana, IL: ERIC/EECE. Online at: http://eric/eece.org/pubs/books/multicul.html.

Giroux, H. A. (1992). Educational leadership and the crisis of democratic government. *Educational Researcher, 21*(4), 4–12.

Greenberg, P. (1990). Why not academic preschool? Part 1. *Young Children, 45*(2), 70–80.

Greenberg, P. (1992a). Why not academic preschool? Autocracy or democracy in the classroom? Part 2. *Young Children, 47*(3), 54–64.

Greenberg, P. (1992b). How to institute some simple democratic practices pertaining to respect, rights, roots, and responsibilities in any classroom (without losing your leadership position). *Young Children, 47*(5), 10–17.

Gullo, D. F. (1994). *Understanding assessment and evaluation in early childhood education.* New York: Teachers College Press.

Hannon, J. H. (2000). Learning to like Matthew. *Young Children, 55*(6), 24–28.

Happe, F., & Firth, U. (1996). Theory of mind and social impairment in children with conduct disorder. *British Journal of Developmental Psychology, 14,* 385–398.

Heintz, K. E. (1987). Examination of the sex-role and occupational-role presentations of female characters in award-winning children's picture books. Paper presented at the 37th Annual Meeting of the International Communication Association, May 21–25, in Montreal.

Hendrick, J. (1992). Where does it all begin? Teaching the principles of democracy in the early years. *Young Children, 47*(3), 51–53.

Hohensee, J. V., & Derman-Sparks, L. (1992). *Implementing an anti-bias curriculum in early childhood education.* (ERIC Document Reproduction Service No. EDO-PS-02-8).

Hosfield, D. (1998). A long day in care need not seem long. *Young Children, 53*(3), 24–28.

Hunt, R. (1999). Making positive multicultural early childhood education happen. *Young Children, 54*(5), 39–41.

Krauss, R. (1947). *The growing story.* New York: Harper Children's Books.

Lalonde, C. E., & Chandler, M. J. (1995). False belief understanding goes to school: On the social-emotional consequences of coming early or late to a first theory of mind. *Cognition and Emotion, 9,* 167–185.

Leeham, S. (1993). Children's understanding of mind. In M. Bennett (Ed.), *The development of social cognition: The child as psychologist* (pp. 26–61). New York: Guilford.

Krough, S. L. (1997). How children develop and why it matters. In C. H. Hart, D. C. Burts, and R. Charlesworth (Eds.), *Integrated curriculum and developmentally appropriate practice: Birth to age 8* (pp. 29–48). Albany: State University of New York Press.

Kuperschmidt, J. B., Coie, J. D., & Dodge, K. A. (1990). The role of poor peer relationships in the development of disorder. In S. R. Asher & J. D. Coie (Eds.), *Peer rejection in childhood* (pp. 273–305). New York: Cambridge University Press.

Lillard, A., & Curenton, S. (1999). Do young children understand what others feel, want, and know? *Young Children, 54*(5), 52–57.

Little Soldier, L. (1992). Working with Native American children. *Young Children, 47*(6), 15–21.

Mahoney, G., & Robinson, C. (1992). Focusing on parent-child interaction: The bridge to developmentally appropriate practices. *Topics in Early Childhood Special Education, 12*(1), 105–120.

Mitchell, L. S. (1934). *Young geographers.* New York: Bank Street College of Education.

National Association for the Education of Young Children (NAEYC). 1996. *Responding to linguistic and cultural diversity—recommendations for effective early childhood education.* Washington, DC: NAEYC. Order #550.

National Association for the Education of Young Children. (1997). NAEYC position statement on the prevention of child abuse in early childhood programs and the responsibilities of early childhood professionals to prevent child abuse. *Young Children, 52*(3), 42–46.

NAEYC position statement on licensing and public regulation of early childhood programs, Adopted 1997. (1998). *Young Children, 53*(1), 43–50.

National Child Abuse Hotline: 800-422-4453.

National Council for the Social Studies (NCSS). (1989). *Social studies for early childhood and elementary school children: Preparing for the 21st century.* Washington, DC: Author.

National Council for Social Studies in the Schools (NCSSS). (1989). *Charting a course: Social studies for the 21st century.* New York: Author.

National Council for Teachers of Mathematics (NCTM). (1989). *Curriculum and evaluation standards for school mathematics.* Reston, VA: Author.

National Research Council. (1994). *National science education standards* (draft). Washington, DC: National Academy Press.

National Science Teachers Association. (1992). Outstanding science books for young children in 1991. *Young Children, 47*(4), 73–75.

Neugebauer, B. (Ed.). (1987). *Alike and different: Exploring our humanity with young children.* Redmond, WA: Exchange Press.

Neugebauer, B. (1990, Aug.). Going one step further—No traditional holidays. *Child Care Exchange, 74,* 42.

Nunnelley, J. C., & Fields, T. (1999). Anger, dismay, guilt, anxiety—the realities and roles in reporting child abuse. *Young Children, 54*(4), 74–79.

Parker, J. G., & Asher, S. R. (1987). Peer relations and later personal adjustment: Are low-accepted children at risk? *Psychological Bulletin, 102,* 357–389.

Piaget, J. (1970). Piaget's theory. In P. H. Mussen (Ed.), *Carmichael's manual of child psychology* (pp. 703–732). New York: Wiley.

Piaget, J., & Inhelder, B. (1969). *Psychology of the child.* New York: Basic Books.

Prevent Child Abuse America. (1998). *Child abuse and neglect statistics.* Chicago, IL: Author. (Http:www.childabuse.org/facts97.html). National Child Abuse Hotline: 800-422-4453. Parents Anonymous: 800-421-0353.

Ramsey, P. G. (1991). *Making friends in school: Promoting peer relationships in early childhood.* New York: Teachers College Press.

Riley, S. S., *How to generate values in young children: integrity, honesty, individuality, self-confidence, and wisdom.* NAEYC Order #202. ISBN: 0-9126674-88-1.

Russell-Fox, J. (1997). Together is better: Specific tips on how to include children with various types of disabilities. *Young Children, 54*(3), 81–83.

Seefeldt, C. (1993). Social studies: Learning for freedom. *Young Children, 48*(3), 4–9.

Seefeldt, C. (1997). Social studies in the developmentally appropriate integrated curriculum. In C. H. Hart, D. C. Burts, and R. Charlesworth (Eds), *Integrated curriculum and developmentally appropriate practice: Birth to age 8* (pp. 171–199).

Shantal, R. (1998). Age appropriate ecology: Are you practicing it? *Young Children, 53*(1), 70–71.

Sloan, M. W. (1999). "All kinds of projects for your classroom." *Young Children, 54*(4), 17–21.

Stewart, S. L. L. (1999). Good questions to ask: When a child with a developmental delay joins your class. *Young Children, 54*(5), 25–27.

Sussman, C. (1998). Out of the basement: Discovering the value of child care facilities. *Young Children, 53*(1), 10–17.

Taylor, B. J. (2002). *Early childhood program management.* Upper Saddle River, NJ: Merrill/Prentice Hall.

Thios, S. M., & Foster, S. B. (1991). Changing preschoolers' attitudes toward children with disabilities. Paper presented at the Annual Meeting of the American Psychological Association, August 16–20, in San Francisco, CA. (ERIC Document Reproduction Service No. ED340516)

Third International Mathematics and Science Study (TIMSS). (1997, Jan.). Stronger focus needed in improving math education, study shows. *Community Update, 43,* U.S. Department of Education.

Third International Mathematics and Science Study (TIMSS). (1997, Aug.). Americans beat international averages in science and math. *Community Update, 49.* U.S. Department of Education.

Vygotsky, L. (1986). *Thought and language.* Cambridge, MA: MIT.

Wang, C. T., & Daro, D. (1998). *Current trends in child abuse reporting and fatalities: The results of the 1997 annual fifty state survey.* Chicago, IL: Prevent Child Abuse America.

Wardle, F. (1987). Are you sensitive to interracial children's special identity needs? *Young Children, 43*(2), 53–59.

Washington Update. (1998). Positive interactions in early childhood settings support children, teens, families, staff, and seniors. *Young Children, 53*(3), 29.

Wellhouse, K. (1996). Girls can be bull riders, too! Supporting children's understanding of gender roles through children's literature. *Young Children, 51*(5), 78–83.

West, J., Denton, K., & Reaney, L. M. (2002). The kindergarten year: Findings from the Early Childhood Longitudinal Study, Kindergarten Class of 1998–99. *Education Statistics Quarterly, Elementary and Secondary Education. NCES.* Online at http://nces.ed.gov/pubs2001/quarterly/winter/elementary/e_section1.html.

Whitebook, M., Sakai, L., & Howes, C. (1997). *NAEYC accreditation as a strategy for improving child care quality, executive summary.* Washington, DC: National Center for the Early Childhood Work Force.

Wickens, E. (1993). Penny's question: "I will have a child in my class with two moms— What do you know about this?" *Young Children, 48*(3), 25–28.

Woods, C. S. (2000). A picture is worth a thousand words—using photographs in the classroom. *Young Children, 55*(5), 82–84.

Young Exceptional Children. Division for Early Childhood of the Council for Exceptional Children. 303-620-4576. 1444 Wazee Street, Suite, 230. Denver, CO 80202.

Youngblade, L. M., & Dunn, J. (1995). Individual differences in young children's pretend play with mother and sibling: Links to relationships and understanding of other people's feelings and beliefs. *Child Development, 66,* 1472–1492.

11

Nutrition and Health

Main Principles

1. The teacher has many important roles in planning for the nutrition and health of each enrolled child (pp. 408–415).

2. Food should be high in nutritive value (p. 410), selected from the Food Guide Pyramid (pp. 410–413), and served in a wholesome environment (pp. 414–415).

3. Good eating habits are to be developed; harmful ingredients (sugar, caffeine, chocolate, additives, etc.) are to be avoided (pp. 416–420).

4. Food experiences offer many learning values to young children (pp. 415–427).

5. Children can be encouraged to participate in food experiences (pp. 424–427).

6. Nutrition and health can be promoted through experiences in the classroom, on field trips, with resource people, through curriculum areas, and other appropriate means (pp. 425–428).

7. Indoor and outdoor exercise is important for children and adults (p. 430).

8. Immunizations are an important part of the young child's health (pp. 429–430).

9. Teachers can assist parents with good health procedures; parents can assist teachers with knowledge about their particular children (pp. 434–435).

Introduction

It is agreed and understood that nutrition and health are not curriculum areas and could easily be part of other chapters (science, social science, or others); however, because of their importance in the learning of young children, they are singled out and addressed here.

Some children do not have opportunities to participate in food preparation because some adults feel time pressure, do not understand the abilities of children, or are unwilling to involve them. Nevertheless, this area offers additional experiences in becoming independent, in learning about nutrition, in feeling accomplishment and satisfaction, and in contributing a service.

This chapter is intended to (1) give an overview of nutrition and its importance to young children, (2) discuss the involvement of children in food preparation, (3) give suggestions as to how to make eating more enjoyable for children, and (4) identify some important health factors for young children. Further reading is encouraged in the area of nutrition, especially as it applies to the growth and development of the young child. Local libraries, state departments, or welfare or social agencies can offer assistance. The National Dairy Council, with local offices in most states, has reference material, films, slides, and transparencies available at low or no cost to help in teaching about nutrition. Check for an office in your area or state.

Over 11 million children attend day care centers in the United States. These centers typically serve two meals a day plus snacks to children ranging in age from 6 weeks to 5 years old. The nutritional needs of these children should be a serious concern.

When malnourished children are mentioned, one commonly pictures children from low-income homes or impoverished countries. Some of these children do come from such settings; some parents with limited food budgets lack good spending knowledge. But some children of the affluent are also malnourished; some of these parents also lack knowledge as to effective use of their money—they spend freely on junk foods, do not consider nutritional value, or fail to plan well-balanced meals.

Basic nutrients to be included in the daily diet are carbohydrates, fats, protein, minerals, vitamins, and water. Amounts vary according to a person's age. Most nutrition books give proper amounts, as well as height and weight charts based on body structure.

A familiar way of identifying daily food requirements is the pyramid food groups. Departments within the U.S. government have proposed a nutrition guidance and child nutrition program, which has been adapted in Table 11.1. The U.S. Department of Agriculture has presented the basic four food groups in a food guide pyramid for young children. Note the categories and suggested daily amounts in Figure 11.1.

Menus should meet one-third to one-half of the recommended dietary allowances (RDAs) of key nutrients and energy. Menus can be recycled as long as there is variety within each meal component: color, textures, temperatures, and flavors. Eliminate the use of added fats, salts, and sugars. Encourage children to drink adequate water and milk. It is hoped that most young children eat breakfast before going to school. Lately there has been more focus on breakfast and school performance and behavior. Children who are hungry are not as alert, often misbehave, and find attention and learning difficult. For many children, the choice is not between breakfast at home or at school; it is a choice between breakfast and no breakfast. (It is alarming that one of every eight children in America suffers from hunger.) A nutritious breakfast also can have a positive impact on cholesterol levels, weight control, and learning. Nutrition has a strong physical, emotional, and intellectual impact on a child's ability to learn.

Dietary guidelines provide for a variety of foods; a way to maintain ideal weight; avoidance of fat, sugar, and sodium; and food with adequate starch and fiber.

Humans need a variety of foods to obtain adequate nutrition. Their ability to adapt readily to eating substances that are available in their environment plays a central role

Table 11.1 Nutrition Guidance for Child Nutrition Programs

Goals	Notes	Examples
Offer a variety of foods prepared in different ways	Nutrients important for good health: vitamins, minerals, water, carbohydrates, amino acids from protein, and certain fatty acids from fat	Milk for calcium; some bread, meat, and their alternatives for iron; fruits and vegetables for vitamins, minerals, and fiber
Serve meals that help maintain a healthy body and weight	For fun and relaxation; a healthy heart; develop positive attitudes; strengthen bones and muscles; healthy weight; develop motor skills, balance, and coordination; increase energy; and improve self-esteem	
Offer meals low in fat, saturated fat, and cholesterol	*Dietary Guidelines for Americans* suggests goals of 30 percent or less of total calories from fat, and less than 10 percent of calories from saturated fat to decrease obesity and certain types of cancer.	Butter, margarine, vegetable oils, salad dressings, cream, lard, egg yolks, and organ meats. In general, foods from animals (milk, meat poultry, and fish) are naturally higher in fat than foods from plants. *Saturated fats* are found in animal products and some vegetable oils such as coconut, palm, and palm kernel.
Serve plenty of vegetables, fruits, and grain products	Foods differ in the kinds of fiber they contain. Carbohydrates from vegetables, fruits, and grain products are important parts of a varied diet. (A research team from Johns Hopkins University School of Medicine has identified a potentially potent cancer-fighting substance called sulforaphane, found in broccoli, kale, cauliflower, brussels sprouts and greens. *AICR Newsletter*, Fall 1992, Issue 37)	Include a variety of fiber-rich foods, such as whole-grain breads and cereals, fruits, vegetables, and cooked dry beans, peas, and lentils.
Offer and use sugars only in moderation	Main reasons for limiting sugar intake in children: excess calories, can lead to tooth decay	Sugar-coated cereals, candy, gum, cookies, ice cream, sweetened drinks.
Offer and use salt and sodium only in moderation	Table salt contains sodium and chloride essential to the diet; however, most Americans eat more than needed—much is added during processing and manufacturing. Reduce or omit salt during food preparation and help children avoid high blood pressure as adults.	Added salt includes cured and processed meats; cheeses; most snacks, ready-to-eat cereals, breads, and bakery products; prepared frozen entrées and dinners; packaged mixes; canned soups; and salad dressings.
Promote an alcohol- and drug- free lifestyle	Children and teens should not drink alcoholic beverages because of risks to health and other serious problems.	Some preschools and homes actively campaign to deter children and teens from using alcohol, especially among families and areas where alcohol abuse is a problem.
Build lifetime eating habits	Nutrition awareness is an essential part of education.	Education takes place during meals with the foods that are offered. It also happens throughout the day.

Developed jointly by U.S. Departments of Agriculture and Health and Human Services, 1992, April. Washington, DC 20250.

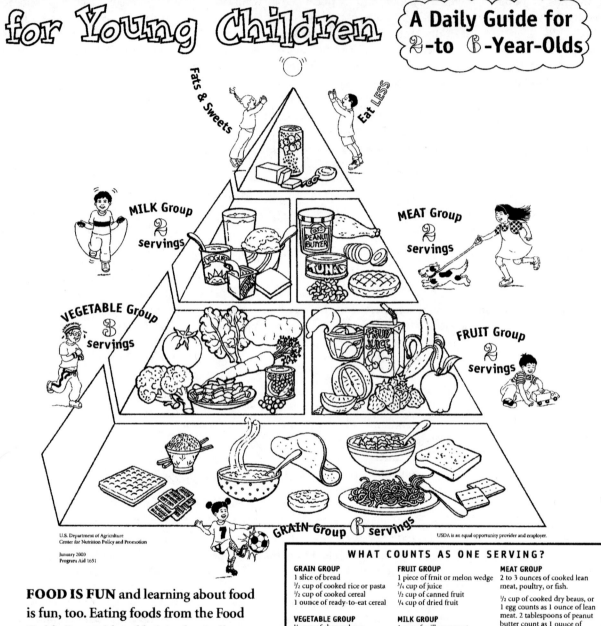

FOOD IS FUN and learning about food is fun, too. Eating foods from the Food Guide Pyramid and being physically active will help you grow healthy and strong.

WHAT COUNTS AS ONE SERVING?

GRAIN GROUP
1 slice of bread
½ cup of cooked rice or pasta
½ cup of cooked cereal
1 ounce of ready-to-eat cereal

VEGETABLE GROUP
½ cup of chopped raw or cooked vegetables
1 cup of raw leafy vegetables

FRUIT GROUP
1 piece of fruit or melon wedge
¾ cup of juice
½ cup of canned fruit
¼ cup of dried fruit

MILK GROUP
1 cup of milk or yogurt
2 ounces of cheese

MEAT GROUP
2 to 3 ounces of cooked lean meat, poultry, or fish.

½ cup of cooked dry beaus, or 1 egg counts as 1 ounce of lean meat. 2 tablespoons of peanut butter count as 1 ouuce of meat.

FATS AND SWEETS
Limit calories from these.

Four- to 6-year-olds can eat these serving sizes. Offer 2- to 3-year-olds less, except for milk.
Two- to 6-year-old children need a total of 2 servings from the milk group each day.

Figure 11.1 USDA Food Guide for Young Children
From U.S. Dept. of Agriculture

Reflection

Read through the rest of this chapter and see how you could make "nutrition" an important and enjoyable part of each child's day. Jot down some notes to share with other teachers and parents who may be having difficulty with meals and snacks for young children.

For information about the nutritional needs of all young children, obtain a copy of *Dietary Guidelines for Americans* from the Consumer Information Center, Pueblo, CO 81009 (#320E, $.50) or download at http://www.pueblo.gsa.gov.

in shaping food-acceptance patterns. Within each culture, people develop individual patterns of food likes and dislikes. Repeated exposure enhances children's acceptance of foods only when they actually taste the foods.

Many child-care professionals understand the need for adequate nutrition and the role it plays in healthy child development; however, many have had little nutrition training and few feel competent in planning menus. Even some trained dietitians can plan well for the needs of adults but fall far short of the mark for good nutrition planning for young children. Still others can plan adequate basic menus for young children but have no concept of quantities consumed or the eating behaviors involved during meals (ability to manipulate utensils, size of food easiest to handle and eat, seasoning of food, fat content, restlessness, distraction, and so on).

It is interesting that the daily suggested requirements from the Cancer Research Foundation of America (www.preventcancer.org) are similar to those listed in the USDA food pyramid for vegetarian meal planning. See Figure 11.2.

For some snack suggestions from the pyramid, see Table 11.2.

Alan Meyers, M.D., of the Boston University School of Medicine, conducted a school breakfast and school performance study in which he examined the standardized test scores of 1,023 Lawrence, Massachusetts, schoolchildren in grades 3 through 6. Results showed that increases in achievement test scores were significantly greater for school breakfast participants than for nonparticipants. Also, absenteeism and tardiness rates decreased for participants and increased for nonparticipants. The importance of school breakfast has also been substantiated by related studies. This study found that children who eat breakfast are less likely to suffer from fatigue, irritability, and inability to concentrate. A school district in rural West Baton Rouge, Louisiana, received a USDA grant targeting the district's 4,000 students and their families in topics such as nutrition units tied into science curricula and reinforced in the cafeteria; field trips to links in the food chain, such as a dairy or strawberry farm; billboard advertising; television and radio talk-show appearances; and even the publication of a breakfast recipe book.

Some schools and administrators decline to have breakfast programs for reasons such as the following: belief that it's the parents' responsibility—not the school's; lack of money; inadequate school facilities; mass confusion in scheduling; and belief that breakfasts are geared just for disadvantaged children.

Role of the Teacher

The teacher has many roles. In addition to planning for and working with the children, she is also responsible for others who do important supportive tasks, such as planning and serving the food each day. She must see that the food is carefully planned, prepared, and served to support the growth and health of strong bodies and minds.

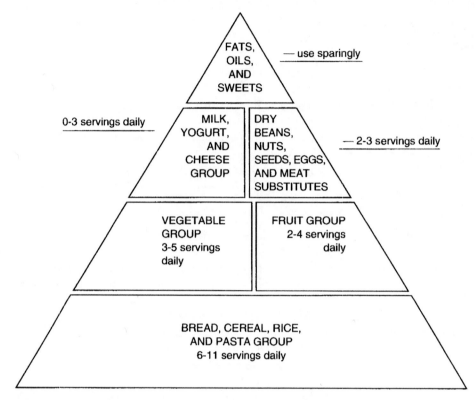

Figure 11.2 Food Guide Pyramid for Vegetarian Meal Planning
From U. S. Dept. of Agriculture

Table 11.2 Snack Suggestions from the Food Guide Pyramid

Group	Suggested Foods
Milk, yogurt, and cheese group (2–3 servings daily)	Butter for crackers and bread
	Cheese chunks
	Cottage cheese
	Kabobs (cheese and lunchmeat)
	Milk (whole, powdered, canned)
	Puddings
	Sauces
	Yogurt
Meat, poultry, fish, dry beans, eggs, and nuts group (2–3 servings daily)	Creamed meat sauces (chicken, tuna)
	Dried beans
	Eggs
	Fish
	Lunchmeat (limited)
	Meatballs
	Meat loaf
	Meat sandwich fillings
	Nuts and nut butters
	Poultry
	Soy products (including tofu)

Table 11.2 Snack Suggestions from the Food Guide Pyramid

Group	Suggested Foods
Vegetable group (3–5 servings daily)	Cooked, raw, juice, and a variety for finger foods, salads, dips, soups, dried (peas, corn, popcorn)
Fruit group (2–4 servings)	Cooked, dried (or leathers), fresh, juice (low in sugar), sauce, and a variety for finger foods, salads, dips, kabobs, frozen treats
Bread, cereals, rice, and pasta group (6–11 daily servings)	Bread (preferably whole-wheat or enriched; occasionally biscuits, bran muffins, bread sticks, melba toast, fruit and nut breads) Cereal (enriched, cooked or prepared, granola) Cookies (low in sugar and fat) Crackers (whole-wheat or grain) Pasta (macaroni, noodles, spaghetti, other) Pizza (child-made) Rice (unpolished) Sandwiches (enriched bread) Tacos
Combinations	Apple wedges with cream cheese, nut butter, or other spread Bacon and eggs Baked potato with cheese Cabbage, corned beef, and rice Carrot, raisin, apple, and pineapple salad Cheese melted on wheat crackers or enriched bread Chicken, dumplings or noodles, and vegetables Cottage cheese with fruit or vegetables Creamed meat sauce on toast Creamed peas and new potatoes Creamed tuna with rice or toast Custard with or without fruit Dairy dip with vegetables or fruit Macaroni and cheese Meat and vegetable soup Meatballs and spaghetti Milkshake (fruit) Nut butters on crackers Pocket sandwiches Puddings (rice, tapioca, and so on) Trail mix (nuts, seeds, fruit) Tuna casserole Yams baked with apple slices Yogurt pops (orange juice concentrate and yogurt, frozen on a stick)

Add a variety of ethnic foods in each category, as appropriate.

Young children need plenty of liquids.

Planning menus for a diverse group of children is not easy—it becomes as complicated as trying to please all family members, or planning a luncheon or dinner for a group of adults! Some like this food; others won't taste it. But the teacher's job isn't all frustration! She can listen to the children, ask questions of the parents, talk with others who feed groups of young children, read literature, and learn through experience. Some of her best teaching will be through other areas of the curriculum with the children—stories about food, creative arts ideas using pictures of food, music and movement, science, interesting snack and meal settings, introduction of familiar and/or ethnic foods, and the children's help in food preparation. One child even offered to prepare snack saying: "If you would just get some [particular item], I could make the snack!"

Nutrition

Nutrition of the children should be of high priority. Maybe they won't eat a certain food the first time it is introduced—maybe not the second or third time! But don't give up! Someone might suggest, "You might just want to taste it," or "I didn't like it at first, but now I do." Some children will eat anything—some won't eat anything.

There are many reasons why children won't taste new foods. Maybe it doesn't have anything to do with the food, but perhaps an incident that happened earlier in the day, or at home, or elsewhere. Teachers can watch for opportunities to help children eat a variety of foods—especially the ones important for their growth and development—vegetables, fruits, dairy products.

Some government (and private) centers serve breakfast, lunch, and one or two snacks a day. Some children think that food is used to interrupt their activities. If it is pleasurable, the children will look forward to it, to visiting with friends, and to replenishing their energy.

For many children, the choice is not between breakfast at home or at school. A nutritious breakfast can have a positive impact on cholesterol levels, weight control, and learning. Nutrition has a strong physical, emotional, and intellectual impact on a child's ability to learn.

Values for Children

Food

When we think about treats and snacks for children, we frequently focus on juice and cookies—maybe because of ease in preparation or availability. One should note that most of the cookies available in supermarkets today are high in fat and that many juices have additives and excessive sugar.

The *American Institute of Cancer Research Newsletter* (1992) states: "Let's face it, cookies will never go for a good-for-you snack. But you can avoid the monsters that are packed with fat and still satisfy your sweet tooth" (p. 4). Purchasers of snack foods (including cookies) are encouraged to *check labels and make wise choices.* Cookies vary greatly in their fat content, even though packages brag "no cholesterol" or "no tropical oils." "Generally speaking," continues the Newsletter,

> vanilla wafers, graham and animal crackers, and fruit cookies, have the least fat. Creme-filled sandwich, butter and oatmeal cookies fall in the middle. Fudge, nut, and short-bread cookies usually have the most fat. . . . Remember, moderation is the key. It's fine to indulge every once in a while, but with cookies, fat and calories add up quickly (p. 4).

Wise choices for children's snacks include foods that are nutritious and contain complex and unprocessed carbohydrates—fresh fruits and vegetables (including juices) and whole-grain products such as breads, cereals, and crackers.

One component of the Head Start program has been nutrition and health. This has been designed to help children develop positive food attitudes and eating habits, to provide nutrition education, and to increase parents' awareness and ability to meet the nutritional needs of their children and families.

Many disadvantaged preschoolers are hungry or poorly nourished, but severe malnutrition is rare. A Harvard University study notes that "silent undernutrition" is common in the United States, causing anemia, stunted growth, and failure to thrive.

Some goals for nutrition education programs, include meeting total nutritional needs of the child while preserving and considering cultural and social needs of the child and family; encouraging healthful good habits promoted by a pleasant eating environment and increasing the variety of foods served; and continuing an educational program for children, parents, and staff regarding nutrition and health through making good choices and taking appropriate responsibility.

Some children have a group experience for four or fewer hours per day, during which they likely have a snack. Children in all-day care should have two snacks and a meal, appropriately spaced. In the latter case, the center would undoubtedly come under local, state, or federal regulations. Caution must be exercised to see that the children receive at least part of their daily nutritional requirements.

The most important time of life for the child, nutritionally, is before birth; the next most important time of the baby's life, nutritionally speaking, is immediately following birth. The first "growth spurt" comes from early infancy until around the child's first birthday. Even though they seem to be burning up considerable energy in their daily routines, children do not require large quantities of food until they begin another growth spurt.

A nutrition writer testified before a Senate subcommittee, spelling out some of the objectionable aspects of television promotion of food products to children. She and others monitored 388 network commercials during a week of viewing children's TV programs and learned that 82 percent of the commercials involved food, drink, and vitamin pill ads directed at children. They urged children to eat the worst type of food and swallow the

Table 11.3   Contrast Between Well-Nourished and Poorly Nourished Children

Well-Nourished	Poorly Nourished
Full of energy	Lethargic
Attentive	Attention lags
Good concentration	Concentration wanes
Happy	Irritable
Curious	Uninterested
Healthy	Frequent and prolonged illnesses
Verbal, cooperative	Nonverbal, uncooperative
Usually completes tasks	Frequently leaves tasks
Benefits from school	Dissatisfied with school
Plays with peers	Solitary play
Positive correlation of intelligence/learning	Negative correlation of intelligence/learning
Good sleep habits	Poor sleep habits

worst type of drinks. Eating wrong foods could be corrected by eating daily vitamins. Conclusions noted that "we can expect a continued growth of heart disease, hypertension, and poor dental health—the diseases that result from poor eating habits established in childhood which cripple and kill in adulthood." See Table 11.3.

It has been suggested that a critical period for the formation of food preferences is between ages 2 and 5. The factors that affect the development of food preferences have been identified as "familiarity (i.e. exposure to food); age; parents; peers; teachers and other significant adults; and programs that are designed to influence food habits." Food presented as a reward enhanced the acceptance and preference for that food item.

Toddlers learn good health habits.

In the past 10 years, several studies have examined the effects of **sugar** on children's behavior. Here are the aspects of the studies that make them credible:

➤ Known quantities of sugar in the diets were studied.
➤ The studies compared the effects of sugar with those of a placebo (a substance without any active ingredients).
➤ The children, parents, and researchers involved in the studies never knew which children were given which diets.
➤ Conclusions: Sugar in the diet did not affect the children's behavior. The authors did point out, though, that the studies didn't rule out completely that sugar might be having a slight effect on a small number of children. (Analysis was published in the November 22, 1995 issue of the *Journal of American Medical Association*.)
➤ Some researchers suggest that simply expecting sugar to affect your child can influence how you interpret what you see.
➤ If you still feel food is causing an adverse reaction, consult with your child's doctor.

In an earlier study of children's food acceptance at nursery school and then later, it was found that earlier acceptance of foods does persist and that non-nursery-school attenders selected sweets more often than former nursery-school children. This study indicates the importance of creating an atmosphere in which children are encouraged to try a variety of new and nutritious foods—whether at home or school. Recommendations to increase the child's interest in and acceptance of new foods and development of good eating habits (listed in Figure 11.3) may include a discussion about the foods when they are introduced; preparing familiar foods in different ways; repetition of new foods; behavior at the table (adults eating with the children, encouraging the tasting of new foods, showing acceptance of the food, and acknowledging sampling); and serving familiar and new foods at the same meal.

Preference for a food has a great deal to do with how it smells. The nose knows what the palate may expect. Some people are more sensitive to one taste; taste varies among people and from time to time, with acuteness being the lowest just after meals and before breakfast.

- Give children many opportunities to participate in food experiences: preparing, tasting, shopping, growing, cleaning up. These experiences provide children with a greater opportunity to develop healthy lifetime eating behaviors.
- Encourage good health habits when preparing and eating food (wash hands, clean surfaces, use safe tools and sturdy utensils).
- Engage in interesting conversation—frequently initiated by the children.
- Eat with the children, eat what they are eating, and model the kind of behavior you expect from them. In a positive way—including pleasant facial expressions and positive conversation—provide frequent exposure to new foods and encourage (never force) them to taste the foods.
- Bake rather than fry meats and other items.
- Eliminate foods that are highly seasoned or have high fat or sugar content.
- Encourage variety in children's diets. Be aware of taste, color, and texture combinations.
- Make preparation and eating times pleasant.
- Serve a variety of foods.
- Allow children to serve themselves, encouraging a portion of each food.
- Talk about differences in the color, taste, and smell of the food as it is cooked.
- Provide finger foods.
- Check each child's personal records for allergies and prohibitions.

Figure 11.3 Hints for Developing Good Eating Habits

Harmful Ingredients

The research on food additives and behavior remains inconclusive. Studies suggest that a small number of hyperactive children may be sensitive to food additives. Special diets (including Feingolds' K-P Diet), however, have not consistently improved symptoms. The only recommended diet for hyperactive children is one that provides the energy and nutrients required for normal growth (Spoon, n.d.).

Nutritionists, medical people, educators, and others in supporting fields urge adults to monitor children's diets. They recommend a diet low in sugar, salt, and fats, and warn about foods containing caffeine, chocolate, additives, and foods that may cause allergies or reactions in particular children. Alcohol should never be served to young children or teenagers!!

Sugar Sugar may be harmful to children in two identified ways: development of dental caries and consumption of empty calories. Tooth decay results from the stickiness of sugar containing food, the frequency of eating, and oral cleanliness; and the severity depends partly on whether the sugar is consumed with other foods or is accompanied by a beverage.

Feingold's Diet (1973) advocated a diet free of salicylates, food colorings, and artificial flavoring for treating hyperactivity. His study was interpreted as advocating the *elimination* of sugar and other additives. Refined sugar soon came under scrutiny as causing behavior problems. Some parents and health organizations believe there is a link between a child's diet and behavior, even though the majority of studies so far don't agree:

> The latest group to join the debate is the nonprofit Center for Science in the Public Interest, which recently released a report charging that the government, professional agencies and the food industry have been ignoring evidence that diet affects behavior. However, the majority of studies between sugar and hyperactivity so far haven't found a connection, and most in the medical industry maintain there is no known link" (Regalado, 2002).

In the last decade several studies examined the behavior of children given sugar with those given a placebo (a substance without any active ingredients). Researchers found that sugar in the diet did not affect the children's behavior; however, they do point out that the studies didn't rule out completely that sugar might be having a slight effect on a small number of children (Regalado, 2002).

If a child "acts-up" after eating sweets, there may be several explanations: (1) sweet foods and celebrations often go together—excitement may stimulate the behavior; (2) when parents expect a change in a child's behavior after consuming "sweets," they may be more sensitive to specific kinds of behavior, such as restlessness; and (3) "hyperactivity may cause children to eat more sweets, rather than sweets causing hyperactivity." Additional facts from this source: "Eating too much sugar can cause tooth decay, a major health problem in this country. . . . [G]et in the habit of reading food labels. Limit foods that have sugar listed among the first few ingredients" (Spoon, n.d.).

Food containing empty calories dulls the appetite. Therefore, food served at snacks and meals should contribute to the child's balanced diet. Some sugar substitutes have been introduced on the market; however, their effect on children has also left questions unanswered. Candy or gum labeled sugar-free may contain calories and in some cases may cause the preschooler gastric distress and diarrhea. Reducing sugar consumption may prevent childhood obesity (often difficult to reverse), and psychological abuse of food—where it is used as rewards—has symbolic meanings.

Adults can limit children's sugar intake by avoiding obvious high-sugar or "hidden" sugar foods, reducing amount of sugar in recipes, and providing better food substitutes (fruits, vegetables, and natural foods) or nonedible items as treats (combs, soaps, jewelry, stickers, privileges, etc.).

Caffeine Caffeine is suspected of causing or increasing hyperactivity. Caffeinated drinks are readily available, well advertised, and addictive, but drinks have been introduced on the market with reduced or no caffeine. If adults realized the harmfulness of these drinks, they would restrict children's—and their own—intake.

> Caffeine stimulates the nervous system. Some say it is the most widely used drug in the U.S. . . . found in many foods including coffee, tea, cocoa, soft drinks, chocolate and some medications. . . . There is no evidence that small amounts of caffeine, on occasion, are harmful to children (Spoon, n.d.).

Chocolate   Chocolate should be considered with foods in the caffeine category, but because of its popularity it is singled out for emphasis. It has been suggested that chocolate interferes with calcium metabolism and also places a great burden on the liver. The cocoa bean, from which cocoa and chocolate drinks are made, contains a chemical (an alkaloid) very similar to the one in coffee and is a stimulant.

Pure chocolate contains 20 milligrams of caffeine per ounce. Carob, a substitute available in health food stores, is very similar to chocolate but is devoid of theobromine and other objectionable features of the cocoa bean.

Additives   Salt has been linked with hypertension. Some researchers have successfully reduced blood pressure in hypertensive patients by using a low-sodium rice diet. Others feel that reduced sodium intakes may or may not be beneficial to children, but suggest the salt-shaker not be placed on the table. Children generally do not like their food seasoned as much as adults do. However, when salt is used, iodized salt is highly recommended.

Allergies   If allergies are not listed on the intake form, the teacher should ask the parent if a child has allergies, and if so, what they are, how the child reacts, and how the situation should be handled if the child has an allergic reaction at the center.

Many children have allergies, ranging from slight to violent reactions. Children can be sensitive to pollen, mold, dust, wind, animals, food, household products, and many other things. Frequently these allergies lead to various symptoms such as runny nose, itchy eyes, sneezing, redness, swelling, or others. Asthma can result in serious and even fatal reactions if not handled properly. Some foods that cause allergic reactions include candy, cookies, and pastry that contain peanuts, nuts, eggs, and milk. A study at Johns Hopkins University reported: "Dangerous anaphylactic reactions to food occur in children and adolescents. The failure to recognize the severity of these reactions and to administer epinephrine promptly increases the risk of a fatal outcome."

Some children, aware that certain foods cause itching or tingling in the mouth, constricted throat, cramps, vomiting, hives, or other unpleasant responses, may avoid these products, and some children will need constant reminders and supervision.

Example:
At a birthday celebration at preschool, a child brought cupcakes. One child, especially allergic to chocolate, asked what kind of cake it was. Assured that it was white, she accepted one, looked very carefully at the colored sprinkles on the icing, and proceeded to pick out any dark pieces. Unfortunately, there were a few minute chocolate pieces, and even though the child knew what her reaction would be—and carefully picked off those pieces—she became ill just from the chocolate *barely* melting on the icing.

Children and adolescents with food allergies should be evaluated and educated about those allergies by a knowledgeable physician, and the parents of these children should be taught ways of ensuring rapid response by schools and other public institutions in the event of the accidental ingestion of a food allergen. How fast the children receive medical attention has much to do with whether or not they survive their allergic attack. Anaphylaxis to food may not be as rare as many people think. Teachers of young children should be especially conscious of common reactions in many children or specific reactions in specific children.

Additional Precautions   Cleaning supplies, plants, toxins, paints, and other harmful substances should be kept in locked cupboards and under the strict supervision of responsible people.

Food Preparation

Through participation in the preparation of food, young children learn much about their world, their environment, and themselves. They have psychomotor experiences (coordinating eyes and hands and in spatial relationships), cognitive experiences (planning, sequencing, discriminating, deciding), and affective experiences (working and sharing with others, being persistent, feeling satisfaction). They develop and increase language skills through asking, answering, and listening. Academic opportunities lie in reading (interpreting the symbols of measurement and ingredients), in science (seeing how ingredients react to heat, moisture, and so on), in math (combining the right amounts of ingredients), in motor skills (stirring, beating, rolling, chopping), and in social skills (taking turns, verbalizing, eating, and sharing cultural experiences).

Food is not a separate or infrequently used topic and is included in all areas of the curriculum. Food of some type is prepared every day in the center and is a vital part of the children's activities. At snack time, food is used for nourishment as well as a socializer. The children have an opportunity to prepare and serve food and learn proper etiquette. Food is used as a science experience, in growing, harvesting, preparing, or eating. It is used in an art activity. It is used successfully and interestingly in math. It is used in a social-studies theme or a movement activity. It is frequently used as the topic of music, stories, or spontaneous conversation. Thinking and speaking are a part of each of the preceding activities, thereby stimulating verbal expression.

The greatest benefit from experience with food appears to be the change in the attitudes of children toward themselves. After preparing, cooking, and eating applesauce at nursery school one day, Pia asked her mother if she would buy a bushel of apples so that Pia could make more applesauce that afternoon. After another cooking experience, Joseph informed his mother, "I am going to make spaghetti for Dad for dinner tonight because I learned how to do it at school today." Still another child, Val, pleaded, "If you'd just let us make doughnuts at school, I'd show you how."

As with any activity, certain precautions are taken. When children use sharp knives, for example, the teacher must instruct and supervise. When they use cords, utensils, and other apparatus, the teacher indicates precautions or limits to encourage safety, and stays close by.

Some children have frequent opportunities at home to help with food preparation and cooking and find different ways of doing things. For example, some mothers mix bread with their hands, others with an electric mixer, and others with a hand-turned mixer. Some children aid in the process of bread baking from grinding the wheat through tasting the warm, fragrant product. But even these experiences take on new dimensions when done with a group of peers.

In food preparation, new terms and definitions are added to the vocabulary of the children, and opportunities provided for practicing them. Consider some of these terms—*measure, ingredients, recipe, beat, stir, fold*—or these processes—*dipping, scrubbing, shaking, spreading, rolling, peeling, cracking, juicing, cutting, grinding, blending, grating,* and *scraping.*

Different products have different characteristics: some are soft, others hard; some smooth, others textured; some crunchy, others "quiet." In bread, gluten is desired, so it is mixed a long time; in muffins, gluten is not desired, so the dry ingredients are stirred in quickly.

To aid children in independence and learning, a picture recipe (Figure 11.4) can be prepared and the children assisted in using it. If the cups, spoons, and so on are depicted actual size, the children hold them up to the recipe to "measure" whether they have the

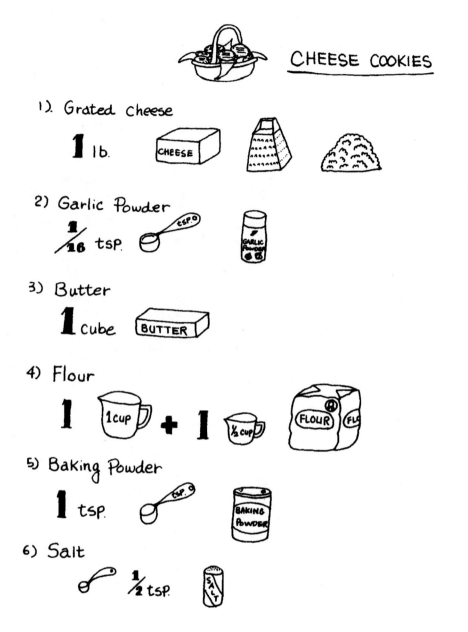

CHEESE COOKIES

1). Grated cheese
1 lb.

2) Garlic Powder
1/**16** tsp.

3) Butter
1 cube

4) Flour
1 1 cup + **1** ½ cup

5) Baking Powder
1 tsp.

6) Salt
½ tsp.

Mix cheese and garlic. Then add it to softened butter. Sift baking powder, salt, and flour together. Add to cheese mix. Make balls and mash with fork. Bake at 350° for 20 minutes.

Figure 11.4 Picture Recipe for Children to Follow in Preparing Cookies

right cup or spoon. Pictures from labels of the ingredients (when available) also aid the children in getting the correct amount of the right ingredient. Making and eating the product takes on significance because of personal involvement.

All children are allowed to participate, even though several may have to be involved at a time or the process repeated several times. The group is divided into two parts, with the lead teacher working with one group and the support teacher working with the other group, or a parent can be invited in to assist. Each child should have several opportunities to participate.

Sometimes teachers serve children; sometimes the children serve themselves.

At the time of actual preparation, health and safety are emphasized by (1) making sure each child washes and dries his hands thoroughly and puts on food-handler gloves and a cover-up, and (2) washing all surfaces and utensils that will be used. Then:

1. Show the recipe, utensils, and ingredients.
2. Explain why the recipe is read in its entirety before beginning to measure.
3. Talk with the children about what they can do and the sequence that will be used.
4. Be perceptive to the questions and feelings of each child. Be an observer and facilitator as much as possible. Be sure to mention when the food is to be eaten! They'll want to know!
5. On completion, involve the children in cleaning up the table and area as a normal part of the experience.

While assisting the children in food preparation, the teacher makes the experience calm and comfortable. She avoids hovering over the children and giving them too many strict instructions: A relaxed atmosphere, with the teacher entering into the action and verbalization when necessary, provides an enjoyable interaction. Encourage the children to use their senses, when appropriate: "Smell that aroma." "You can taste _____." "Did you see how he cracked the egg?"

Some special preparations are needed, depending on the type of food experience (washing fruit or vegetables, supervising dangerous tools such as knives and graters, getting proper equipment and ingredients). The recipe should have been tried beforehand, all tools should work properly, and all necessary equipment and ingredients should be available. The teacher can avoid a negative experience by being well prepared.

The teacher can be adventurous but secure in what is planned. When proper supervision is available, some different kinds of equipment and methods of preparation can be tried; children need and want some safe opportunities to try knives, for example. They should be helped to cut, spread, and slice. Grinders, choppers, peelers, graters, blenders, and other available appliances can be used, but with constant promotion of safety and proper use of tools.

CHECKLIST FOR A FOOD EXPERIENCE

1. Food experience (name) _____

2. Date to be used _____

3. Approval (if necessary) _____

4. Materials needed (list each ingredient) _____

   _____

   _____

5–6. Equipment needed and preparation _____

   _____

   _____

7. Responsibility of adults _____

   _____

8. Participation of children _____

   _____

9–10. Any possible problems _____

   _____

11. Disposition of food product _____

   _____

12. Evaluation of experience _____

   _____

   _____

Figure 11.5   Checklist for a Food Experience

Discussion of Checklist

See Figure 11.5 for a checklist for a food experience.

1. Decide on the specific experience.
2. Record the date. Avoid conflicts with holidays, other curriculum plans, or other teachers.
3. If necessary, discuss the experience with the appropriate person and get approval.
4. List all materials needed. Check to see that all supplies are fresh and available. Order necessary supplies, bring them from home, or have children bring them, if necessary.
5. List all equipment needed, including the equipment inside the classroom, such as tables, chairs, and cover-ups. Kitchen equipment might include bowls, appliances, pans, tools, hot pads, and cleaning supplies. Check all equipment for usability and safety.
6. Double-check both the list of materials and the equipment needed. Failure of the experience could be attributed to poor planning.
7. Write down how you expect the adult to contribute to the experience (crack the eggs, encourage children to participate, get cover-ups, actually cook food). Discuss this with the adult.

8. List the specific participation of the child (cracking eggs, putting on a cover-up, measuring ingredients, cooking food).

9. Anticipate problems. Discuss possibilities with both adults and children so problems can be reduced or eliminated. Unexpected problems may still arise.

10. Check children's health records to be sure no one is allergic to the ingredients or end product.

11. Inform the children when the product will be eaten. Is it for snack time today or a picnic tomorrow? Can they take it home? Is it all right for them to taste during the experience? Eating the product is the highlight of the experience.

12. Be sure to evaluate the total experience and record your thoughts and feelings. Then you will have a foundation for planning similar experiences. Do not be discouraged if the experience had some drawbacks or did not go the way you planned.

Teaching and Encouraging Good Nutrition Habits

Try some food combinations that provide healthy choices: (1) Instead of serving bologna and cheese on white bread, serve turkey, lettuce, and tomato in a whole-wheat pita. Why? Because the turkey combination contains less sodium and has fewer calories, and wheat bread has more fiber and vitamins. Of course, the dressing deserves consideration. Mayonnaise on either sandwich adds fat and calories. (2) As a side entree, serve vegetable sticks or fruit chunks instead of something sweet or high in fat and calories (potato chips). (3) Instead of punch, serve milk because it is low in fat and supplies calcium and iron.

It is possible that the only nutritionally balanced meals children eat are at school. Children may have specific food biases or habits. Listen to their concerns. Watch how they respond to the food that is presented to them. Place some attention on manners, but focus on helping the children develop healthy attitudes toward food and eating. Make gradual changes—and introduce new foods slowly and individually. Give them tasty and interesting food choices.

Food preparation is fun for boys and girls; therefore, it follows that good health and the making of tasty cuisine result in its enjoyment. Good health and safety habits begin early in the child's life; however, adults must provide information and supervision.

Food and eating habits may be heavily laden with emotion. If the child is to utilize the food she eats, she must do so in a loving atmosphere. Force, anger, hostility, and other unpleasantness should be absent from meals.

Here are some techniques to promote good attitudes toward food and eating:

➤ Understand the background of the children with regard to their culture and personal food preferences. Help the children enjoy a wide variety of foods—and the same food in a variety of forms to add interest to meals and snacks. Avoid the rut of serving the same foods prepared in the same way just because you know that the children will eat them. Feature new foods or food combinations at least monthly.

➤ Introduce new foods slowly, always in the presence of a known, and preferably liked, food. Even if the child only asks about it, fingers it, or ignores it, the food will be more familiar another time. Encourage her to taste it, but do not force her to eat it.

➤ Use family style as appropriate. Children often eat more when they serve themselves; however, some take more than they can or want to eat.

➤ Encourage small portions. Letting children ask for more gives them a sense of satisfaction rather than of failure for not being able to eat all their food.

➤ Serve finger foods and expect children to be more adept with fingers than utensils.

➤ Be sure a liquid is available to drink when dry foods are served, even if you can provide only water. Dry foods are hard for young children to swallow.

➤ Serve food separately rather than in casseroles, stews, and mixtures.

➤ Serve the food in bite-sized pieces.

➤ Vary the consistency of food served at each meal (soft, crisp, and chewy).

➤ When possible, let the children choose (for example, between two fruits or two vegetables).

➤ Use peer influence in a positive way. Encourage children to bring their favorite fruit or vegetable. Let the group prepare them all, cut into bite-sized pieces, and have a tasting snack session. Be aware of the nutritional value of each food served.

➤ Provide opportunities to taste food at times other than snack or lunch (tasting table, science).

➤ Serve foods that are mild and natural in flavor; young children reject strong flavors. Dilute strongly flavored juices (grapefruit, grape, pineapple) with water.

➤ Encourage the children to drink water frequently.

➤ Most young children prefer food served at room temperature; hot food may frighten them, and they often stir hard ice cream until it becomes liquid.

➤ Never use food as a weapon, such as refusing to serve dessert until after all other food is eaten. A nourishing dessert should be as important as other foods.

➤ Precede all eating situations with a calm, quiet activity. Excited or overstimulated children do not enjoy their food as much as tranquil children.

➤ Require children to wash and dry their hands before eating or working with food. Let the children serve themselves when possible. Use child-sized pitchers, glasses, and utensils.

➤ Make sure the children are comfortably seated, with feet touching the floor.

➤ Let children assist in setting the tables.

➤ Make the area attractive and peaceful.

➤ See that the food is attractively presented in color, variety, and consistency. (Popular food colors for young children include green, orange, yellow, and pink.)

➤ Meet children's social needs by providing time and association with peers.

➤ Help the children use this experience in an educational way. Make it a time to learn about, identify, and talk about the food.

➤ Assist the children in developing and using good table manners and etiquette.

➤ Help build a bridge between home and the center in behavior during eating and in promoting and understanding about food habits in different ethnic groups.

➤ Help the children become more conscious of nutrition and eating proper foods.

➤ Be patient and understanding about the different rates at which young children eat. Often eating takes less priority than socialization and exploration. Handle table accidents calmly and reassuringly (have sponges close at hand). Let the children resolve the situation as much as possible.

➤ If a child refuses to eat, invite him to the table to enjoy the conversation rather than going to another activity.

Make this nutrition program a part of the total school or child-care curriculum. Talk about food at noneating times—during stories, during a planting experience, while feeding animals, and at other spontaneous and planned times. Work closely with parents and others in the school program and within the community—visit a garden or farm, pick and prepare foods for meals, talk about the color of foods or different ways plants grow. Set small but successful goals.

For additional safety and sanitary concerns, see Figure 11.6.

Ways to Encourage Child Participation with Food

Have a tasting table with fruit or vegetable (carrots, broccoli, cauliflower, cucumber, cherry tomatoes, pepper strips) chunks. A dip could be made from sour cream, cottage cheese, or yogurt.

1. Avoid foods that could cause choking: hot dogs, grapes, popcorn, peanuts, foods with small bones, and hard candies. *All staff must be trained in the Heimlich maneuver.*
2. Nutritionists recommend that meat, fish, and poultry products be cooked to an internal temperature of 160°F or until all the pink is gone.
3. Cool cooked foods to avoid burned mouths and tongues.
4. Avoid holding foods between 40 and 140°F for extended periods of time.
5. Plan carefully for supervision of classroom cooking experiences: sanitation, heat, utensils, cords, sharp tools, and so on. *NEVER* LEAVE A CLASSROOM COOKING EXPERIENCE UNATTENDED.

Figure 11.6   Monitoring Safety and Sanitary Concerns in Child Settings

Have a sight and/or touch experience: use raw veggies and/or fruit. Encourage the children to describe the skin of the food before they touch it (peach is fuzzy, cucumber is prickly, cherry is slick, squash is firm, and so on). Talk about the covering of each. How does the touch differ when a food is peeled and unpeeled? Which ones are generally peeled before eating, and which ones are not? Talk about where the food is grown (bush, underground, tree, vine, and so on).

Have a smell table: See if the children can identify fruit and vegetables by their smell only. Which ones have strong odors and which have little or no odor? What is the difference between the smell of raw and cooked food (cabbage, for instance)?

After reading the story *Stone Soup,* by Marcia Brown (1986), ask the children how you could make soup at school. Through volunteers or assignment, the children could each bring one ingredient for making soup at school. Assist the children in cleaning, cutting, and cooking the vegetables. Serve the soup for snack or lunch.

For information about using food for art activities, see the section titled "Collage" in Chapter 6.

Boys like to help with food experiences.

Food-Related Experiences

Make sure all sources are safe!

Field Trips

bakery	flour mill
berry patch	food processing plant
bottling plant	garden
butcher shop	grain field or mill
cannery	greenhouse
cheese factory	grocery or local market
cold-storage plant	kitchen (restaurant or home of a teacher or
dairy farm	child)
dairy processing plant	natural food store
farms (animal, produce)	nut store
fields (corn, potato, peanut, pumpkin)	picnic orchard (seasonal)
fish hatchery or market	pizza parlor
fishing at a local lake or river	poultry or turkey ranch
(close supervision is mandatory)	restaurant (specialty, ethnic)

Resource People (use appropriate aids)

baker	fisher
beekeeper	grocer
butcher	milk carrier
chef	miller
cook at your center or local school	parent to demonstrate preparation and
farmer with produce to tell how food	use of products
is prepared for market and how he	poultry rancher
sells it (crate, truckload, pound)	others particularly interesting to the
	children

Songs   Many good songs concern food. Check your favorite songbooks.

Health

The health of young children is not an isolated or unimportant factor; however, an in-depth discussion about the growth and development of young children is not appropriate here. Nevertheless, it is important to note that the integration of hereditary and environmental influences, attitudes and actions, and opportunities and deprivations will have a bearing on their health.

Strong bodies can be strengthened or weakened, as can weak bodies. The genetics of the child sets limits for her potential, but external forces (disease, pollution, poverty, and so on) influence the child's attainment.

In recent years forces have been pulling against each other; health, nutrition, and well-being have been stressed by some and resisted by others (reduction in physical-education emphasis and financial backing, increased availability of drugs, inaccurate and inappropriate media advertising, fewer educational and career opportunities for the poor, reduced food and social programs, increased environmental pollution, and others).

It is during the early developing years that children adopt models, establish patterns, and set goals. Adults who interact with these children have the responsibility and opportunity to influence them in happy, healthful, and productive ways by planning activities to increase and encourage physical development; being aware of and preventing harmful environmental effects; reducing disease through research, immunizations, and education; and increasing their awareness of harmful agents and activities.

Learning sanitary bathroom procedures helps to maintain healthy children and pleasant surroundings.

Always practice good health habits: proper purchase, preparation, storage, and disposal of food items; hand and body cleanliness; proper disposal of waste; avoidance of contagion or infection by using rubber gloves for certain procedures; knowledge and practice of good first-aid procedures for accidents and other emergencies; and others of general or specific nature. Some state laws mandate procedures for training or interaction with young children or those in groups.

Children with Chronic Illnesses

Children with chronic illnesses need not be restricted from group participation unless it is recommended by a physician, even though it is difficult for some children to stay healthy in a schooling setting or among peers. Not only may chronically ill children be absent more frequently than other children, they also may experience more injuries.

Dramatic play and other experiences that help ill children deal with their experiences help them, and other classmates, understand and accept health problems. See References at the end of this chapter for resources on chronic illnesses.

Hyperactivity and Other Behavior Problems

According to a study published in the *Journal of the American Medical Association* (February 2000), the number of preschool children receiving stimulants, antidepressants, and other psychiatric medications "rose drastically from 1991 to 1995." This raised concerns because few of the drugs are "approved by the U.S. Food and Drug Administration for prescription to young children." "Treatment programs can take many forms and are best when specifically tailored for the child" (American Psychological Association). Email: mail to: public.affairs@apa.org. Website: http://www.apa.org/pubinfo/kidsmed.html.

Lead pollution is believed to cause hyperactivity, a symptom seen in persons with acute lead poisoning. Other environment factors, such as noise (both audible and inaudible), fumes (including odorless), and light (natural and artificial), have been shown to cause hyperactivity in some children and adults.

Examples of Health Care

The most common health problems in school can be divided as follows:

➤ chronic conditions, such as allergies and asthma;
➤ mishaps, such as scrapes and cuts, bumps on the head, sand in the eyes, and splinters
➤ infections, such as conjunctivitis, head lice, chicken pox, strep throat, and lingering coughs (Needleman and Needleman, 1995, pp. 22–23).

Practical health-related exercises are outlined and discussed by Werner, Timms & Almond, 1996):

➤ Children may have boundless energy and move constantly, but they also may be less than healthy.
➤ Coronary heart disease may have its origins in childhood. Data show that only 2% of adults who were inactive as children become active as adults, according to a national fitness survey conducted in England, and it is suspected that patterns are similar in the United States.
➤ The best guideline for young children is to offer them both a mixture of free play and guided exploration or discovery, such as music and movement and vigorous games— both types of play promote health.
➤ Activities must be fun for each child.
➤ Some children are absorbed in activities for long periods of time; others have relatively short attention spans.
➤ Healthy atmospheres include both indoor and outdoor play (pp. 48–55).

Check with local health authorities if you have any concerns about health care for children and for families. See Figure 11.7 for a suggested curriculum that can help address and prevent health problems.

Immunizations

Immunization is the most effective way to prevent many infectious diseases in children.

The American Academy of Pediatrics recommends that children be immunized according to a schedule they have established. Child care providers in centers or family day care homes can help reduce these risks. They can: (1) get training in health and safety; (2) maintain current immunization records on all staff and children in their center or home; (3) identify health resources in the community that families can use to get immunizations; (4) encourage low-income families to explore eligibility for medical coverage under Medicaid; (5) require full immunizations for all staff and children in the center and home; (6) develop a written procedure to keep families informed when infectious disease occurs in the center or home.

See Figure 11.8 for the immunization schedule recommended and approved by the Advisory Committee on Immunization Practices (www.cdc.gov/nip/acp), the American Academy of Pediatrics (www.aap.org), and the American Academy of Family Physicians (www.aafp.org).

An essential resource for family day care homes and centers is *Caring for Our Children: National Standards for Health and Safety in Out-of-Home Child Care,* published by the American Academy of Pediatrics and the American Public Health Association. To obtain this manual, contact the American Academy of Pediatrics, 141 NW Point Boulevard, Elk Grove Village, IL 60009-1098.

Those who care for or teach children in groups have concern about HIV infection (AIDS) as well as common childhood diseases. Although new information may be coming frequently, it may be overshadowed by myth, rumors, fears, and speculation. For the latest facts, contact your local or state health department. Basically, "studies continue to show lack of transmission from HIV-infected individuals by nonsexual contact, even

Priority	Major Topic	Subtopics
	Physical health	Senses
		General hygiene
		Dental hygiene
		Nutrition
		Exercise, relaxation, sleep
		Illness and prevention
		Substance-abuse prevention (drugs, alcohol, tobacco)
		First aid
		Abuse (physical, mental, sexual, other)
		Handicaps
		Environment (pollution, disasters)
		Other (identify)
	Mental health	Self-esteem
		Identifying and expressing one's feelings
		Identifying and accepting others' feelings
		Emotional neglect
		Abuse
		Disabilities or gifts
		Other (identify)
	Family living	Diversity within families
		Cultural diversity
		Socioeconomic differences
		Prenatal development
		Problems (death, divorce, illness, diverse parenting styles)
		Sibling rivalry
		Moving
		Other (identify)

Figure 11.7 Proposed Health Curriculum for Young Children

under conditions of close contact such as occurs among children and staff in group programs." Cleanliness and precautions are always in order.

Exercise

When one approaches a situation with enthusiasm and a good attitude, the positive feelings spread—but the opposite could just as well be true: A bad attitude, lack of enthusiasm, and a negative feeling can cause even the best ideas to fail! So it is with exercise; however, it does seem that children have boundless energy for activity.

You don't have to provide formal fitness training for enjoyment and benefit. Start out slowly and with skills the children can already do (most of them are more limber than adults, but they still must begin slowly). Remember that young children need to move often; when they have been sedentary for a period, introduce some fun movement activities. They can help initiate ideas.

Music, rhythm, and feeling and enjoyment. Just keep the activities within the abilities of the children. A group of 2- and 3-year-olds enjoyed a story about a parade. They even liked playing instruments, but when they were asked to play their instruments and march at the same time, their confusion increased and their desire decreased.

Obstacle courses take on a new twist when children are asked for suggestions and help in arranging the items. What could we do with this box? Who can do a different thing with the ball?

Recommended Childhood and Adolescent Immunization Schedule -- United States, 2003

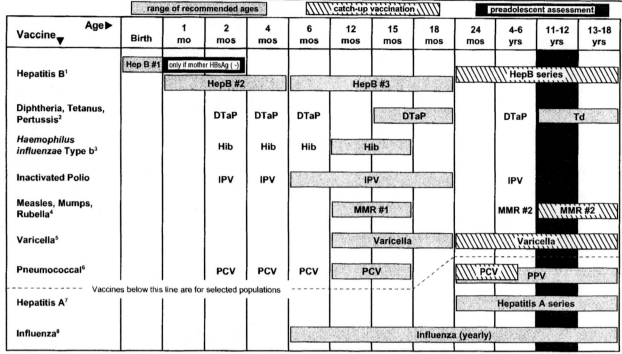

Vaccine ▼ / Age ▶	Birth	1 mo	2 mos	4 mos	6 mos	12 mos	15 mos	18 mos	24 mos	4-6 yrs	11-12 yrs	13-18 yrs
Hepatitis B[1]	Hep B #1	only if mother HBsAg (-)									HepB series	
			HepB #2			HepB #3						
Diphtheria, Tetanus, Pertussis[2]			DTaP	DTaP	DTaP		DTaP			DTaP	Td	
Haemophilus influenzae **Type b**[3]			Hib	Hib	Hib	Hib						
Inactivated Polio			IPV	IPV		IPV				IPV		
Measles, Mumps, Rubella[4]						MMR #1				MMR #2	MMR #2	
Varicella[5]						Varicella					Varicella	
Pneumococcal[6]			PCV	PCV	PCV	PCV				PCV	PPV	
Hepatitis A[7]										Hepatitis A series		
Influenza[8]						Influenza (yearly)						

Legend: range of recommended ages / catch-up vaccination / preadolescent assessment

Vaccines below this line are for selected populations (Hepatitis A, Influenza)

This schedule indicates the recommended ages for routine administration of currently licensed childhood vaccines, as of December 1, 2002, for children through age 18 years. Any dose not given at the recommended age should be given at any subsequent visit when indicated and feasible. Indicates age groups that warrant special effort to administer those vaccines not previously given. Additional vaccines may be licensed and recommended during the year. Licensed combination vaccines may be used whenever any components of the combination are indicated and the vaccine's other components are not contraindicated. Providers should consult the manufacturers' package inserts for detailed recommendations.

1. Hepatitis B vaccine (HepB). All infants should receive the first dose of hepatitis B vaccine soon after birth and before hospital discharge; the first dose may also be given by age 2 months if the infant's mother is HBsAg-negative. Only monovalent HepB can be used for the birth dose. Monovalent or combination vaccine containing HepB may be used to complete the series. Four doses of vaccine may be administered when a birth dose is given. The second dose should be given at least 4 weeks after the first dose, except for combination vaccines which cannot be administered before age 6 weeks. The third dose should be given at least 16 weeks after the first dose and at least 8 weeks after the second dose. The last dose in the vaccination series (third or fourth dose) should not be administered before age 6 months.

Infants born to HBsAg-positive mothers should receive HepB and 0.5 mL Hepatitis B Immune Globulin (HBIG) within 12 hours of birth at separate sites. The second dose is recommended at age 1-2 months. The last dose in the vaccination series should not be administered before age 6 months. These infants should be tested for HBsAg and anti-HBs at 9-15 months of age.

Infants born to mothers whose HBsAg status is unknown should receive the first dose of the HepB series within 12 hours of birth. Maternal blood should be drawn as soon as possible to determine the mother's HBsAg status; if the HBsAg test is positive, the infant should receive HBIG as soon as possible (no later than age 1 week). The second dose is recommended at age 1-2 months. The last dose in the vaccination series should not be administered before age 6 months.

2. Diphtheria and tetanus toxoids and acellular pertussis vaccine (DTaP). The fourth dose of DTaP may be administered as early as age 12 months, provided 6 months have elapsed since the third dose and the child is unlikely to return at age 15-18 months. **Tetanus and diphtheria toxoids (Td)** is recommended at age 11-12 years if at least 5 years have elapsed since the last dose of tetanus and diphtheria toxoid-containing vaccine. Subsequent routine Td boosters are recommended every 10 years.

3. *Haemophilus influenzae* type b (Hib) conjugate vaccine. Three Hib conjugate vaccines are licensed for infant use. If PRP-OMP (PedvaxHIB® or ComVax® [Merck]) is administered at ages 2 and 4 months, a dose at age 6 months is not required. DTaP/Hib combination products should not be used for primary immunization in infants at ages 2, 4 or 6 months, but can be used as boosters following any Hib vaccine.

4. Measles, mumps, and rubella vaccine (MMR). The second dose of MMR is recommended routinely at age 4-6 years but may be administered during any visit, provided at least 4 weeks have elapsed since the first dose and that both doses are administered beginning at or after age 12 months. Those who have not previously received the second dose should complete the schedule by the 11-12 year old visit.

5. Varicella vaccine. Varicella vaccine is recommended at any visit at or after age 12 months for susceptible children, i.e. those who lack a reliable history of chickenpox. Susceptible persons aged≥ 13 years should receive two doses, given at least 4 weeks apart.

6. Pneumococcal vaccine. The heptavalent **pneumococcal conjugate vaccine (PCV)** is recommended for all children age 2-23 months. It is also recommended for certain children age 24-59 months. **Pneumococcal polysaccharide vaccine (PPV)** is recommended in addition to PCV for certain high-risk groups. See *MMWR* 2000;49(RR-9);1-38.

7. Hepatitis A vaccine. Hepatitis A vaccine is recommended for children and adolescents in selected states and regions, and for certain high-risk groups; consult your local public health authority. Children and adolescents in these states, regions, and high risk groups who have not been immunized against hepatitis A can begin the hepatitis A vaccination series during any visit. The two doses in the series should be administered at least 6 months apart. See *MMWR* 1999;48(RR-12);1-37.

8. Influenza vaccine. Influenza vaccine is recommended annually for children age≥6 months with certain risk factors (including but not limited to asthma, cardiac disease, sickle cell disease, HIV, diabetes, and household members of persons in groups at high risk; see *MMWR* 2002;51(RR-3);1-31), and can be administered to all others wishing to obtain immunity. In addition, healthy children age 6-23 months are encouraged to receive influenza vaccine if feasible because children in this age group are at substantially increased risk for influenza-related hospitalizations. Children aged ≤12 years should receive vaccine in a dosage appropriate for their age (0.25 mL if age 6-35 months or 0.5 mL if aged ≥ 3 years). Children aged<8 years who are receiving influenza vaccine for the first time should receive two doses separated by at least 4 weeks.

For additional information about vaccines, including precautions and contraindications for immunization and vaccine shortages, please visit the National Immunization Program Website at www.cdc.gov/nip or call the National Immunization Information Hotlinet 800-232-2522 (English) or 800-232-0233 (Spanish).

Figure 11.8 Recommended Childhood and Adolescent Immunization Schedule—United States, 2003

*Outdoor play is an important part
of health and nutrition.*

Children are in constant motion and don't often need encouragement to run, climb, jump, or combine motor skills. Records with and without instructions can be used over and over again.

Developmentally Appropriate Exercise for Children Because young children have small bodies and limited muscular endurance, they easily and quickly tire—three to five minutes may be the limit of their endurance during lively play. Within minutes they are back at the activity.

Active play need not be limited to outdoors or a certain time period during the day. Refer to Chapter 7, Music and Movement Education, and Chapter 12, Transition Activities, where discussions and/or activities are suggested for both locomotor and nonlocomotor actions.

Preschool and child-care teachers are always expected to include lots of vigorous physical activity in their daily programs; however, there is seldom a physical education or music/movement education specialist on the staff; therefore, planners of physical activity often have little or no physical-education training for working with the young child.

A simple set of guidelines that both physical-education specialists and early-childhood teachers can use is provided by Werner, Timms, and Almond (1996):

1. Allow Children to make individual decisions about when to join or terminate an activity.
2. Creative simple fitness activities that allow everyone to succeed.
3. Suggest actions—many young children are visual earners.
4. Keep directions simple. Use cue or key words in your verbal descriptions.
5. Change activities often.
6. Allow maximum practice opportunity—provide a piece of equipment for everyone.
7. Encourage more active play; show enthusiasm and play actively with the children yourself.

Exercise is an important part of nutrition and health.

And I would like to add:

1. If necessary, limit the number of children participating at one time due to lack of equipment, space, endurance, interest, safety, or other limitations.
2. Use props (music, scarves, hats, and so on) that enhance the experience.
3. Review Chapter 7, Music and Movement Education.

 Reflection

Keeping in mind the interests and skills of preschool children, make some guidelines for use in an exercise program for young children. Consider the following items:

1. The physical abilities and endurance of the children (the need of some to settle down and the need of others to liven up)
2. How exercises enlarge, stretch, or strain developing muscles and other parts of their bodies.
3. Ways to encourage children and their personal satisfaction
4. Amount of time (daily/monthly, spontaneous/planned)
5. Warm-up and cool-off activities and times
6. How to build endurance
7. Sequence and routine
8. Special clothing or equipment
9. New or more complex activities or uses of equipment

"Quick Notes" About Cultures, Nutrition, Health, Learning, and Young Children

Cultures

Look around your classroom. How many different cultures are represented by the children? What foods are used most in their diets? Why are these so important? Ask parents if they would be willing to help you teach these preschoolers more about their classmates by introducing foods of different kinds, different methods of preparation, and why these foods are so valued in their culture! Encourage children to "taste" small portions of new foods.

Poverty/Nutrition/Health Care

Research tells us that poverty during the first five years of life has especially deleterious effects on children's future life chances (FYI, 2000, p. 66). Yet:

➤ 42% of children under age six in the United States *live in or near poverty* in families with income near the poverty line ($23,684 for a family of three);

➤ 22% of children *live in poverty* in families with incomes below the poverty line ($12,802 for a family of three); and

➤ 10% of America's young children *live in extreme poverty*—well below the poverty line ($6,401 for a family of three) (FYI, 1998, p. 47).

"All children need good nutrition every day to be ready to learn! New research provides compelling evidence that *undernutrition*—even in its 'milder' forms—during any period of childhood can have detrimental effects on cognitive development. Even nutritional deficiencies of relatively short term influence children's behavior, ability to concentrate and to perform complex tasks" (FYI, 1998, p. 47).

Continuous malnutrition can produce lasting cognitive damage—improving children's nutrition (together with other qualities of their impoverished environments) can modify harm that has already occurred. Children who live in poverty (14.5 million U.S. children in 1996) are highly likely to suffer from inadequate nutrition and other environmental insults that impede their opportunities to grow and learn.

Undernourished children are typically fatigued, become more apathetic and less able to establish relationships or explore and learn from their surroundings. "Hungry children have a decreased attention span and are not able to perform tasks as well as their nourished peers." (FYI, 2000, p. 66). A public policy report on the new children's health insurance program was issued by O'Connor (1999). Among other points, it includes:

"Today across America 11 million preschoolers and school-age children do not have health insurance, although 92 per cent of them have at least one parent who works and 66 percent have a parent who works full-time (Bureau of the Census 1997).. . . These children—most of whom are likely to be in child care or after-school programs every day while their parents work—suffer needlessly from preventable health problems" (p. 63).

Now families can get help from their state. While few parents know about it, Congress passed in 1997 a new Children's Health Insurance Program (CHIP) designed to provide free or low-cost health insurance to children in uninsured families with low or moderate incomes. CHIP is the most significant funding increase for children's health coverage since Medicaid began in 1965" (O'Connor, 1999, p. 63).

The Children's Defense Fund can be a valuable source of assistance and information. Project coordinator: Jeannette O'Connor. Phone: 202-662-3653. Website: www.childrensdefense.org. Phone: 800-CDF-1200 and press "2" for information.

Dietary Guidelines for Americans, 2000, Home and Garden Bulletin No. 232, provides patterns for healthful eating, a variety of food hints, advice for today (a healthy base for keeping food safe to eat; choosing food sensibly; selecting beverages and foods to moderate sugar intake, choosing prepared foods with less salt; aims for fitness; and other valuable food information for children and families). Obtain a copy of the bulletin from the Consumer Information Center, Pueblo, CO 81990 (#320E, $.50) or download at http://www.pueblo.gsa.gov.

Curriculum

Cooking is an ideal topic for introducing **reading** (following a recipe); **math** (quantity); **science** (combinations and reactions); **mathematics** (counting and measuring); **multicultural activities** (about others); **creative activities** (extended, modified, changed); **social skills** and **independence** (satisfaction, following directions, taking turns, sharing, cooperation, initiative); **literature** (directions, highlights of the experience, drawing, telling); **nutrition, health, and safety** (food groups, strong bodies, etc.); and others.

A food pyramid is available on the Internet at www.usda.gov/cnpp/KidsPyra/index.htm.

Enjoyment

Researchers and teachers believe that it is easier to learn to like all foods during the first five or six years of life than it is in later years (Nakikian-Nelms, Syler, & Mogharrehan, 1994).

➤ Encourage children to "taste" small portions of new foods.
➤ Snack time is an intimate, comforting break where children can gain physical, social, and emotional nourishment.
➤ Teachers can organize snack routines where they sit at eye-level with the children; respect and care about social skills; offer food choices; teach independence; encourage child participation and preparation; nurture and enjoy children; and "embrace the occasion to nourish the body, mind, and spirit of each child" (Murray, 2000, p. 32).

In 102 day care centers, data were collected on nutritional content of menus, compliance with guidelines, children's food consumption, and safety/sanitation. Although menus exceeded recommended daily allowances, quantities of food were below recommendations. No menu components were consumed by more than 65% of children. Sanitation problems were also identified (Kuratko et al., 2000).

Application of Principles

1. Make a list of foods typical of your area, such as fruit, vegetables, meat, and seafood. Tell how you could utilize each of these in your center.
2. Design a lesson plan based on nutrition. Use it in your center.
3. Provide materials and opportunities for your children to practice good sanitary procedures such as washing hands, cleaning nails, and covering clothes.
4. Make a chart of basic nutrients and their sources. Check the information against the food served in your center over the past week. What nutrients need to be included more often in foods you serve? How often are "harmful" ingredients (sugar, caffeine, chocolate, salt, and other additives) served? Should a specific attempt be made to reduce their use?

5. If possible, provide weekly opportunities in food preparation. Use the checklist in Figure 11.5.

6. Make a nutritious snack schedule for one month. Also make a quantity and price list. Compare the various menus for food value and cost.

7. Check each child's personal record to see if she has food allergies, dislikes, or cultural restrictions. How do you handle these limitations?

8. Using a week's menu from a child-care center or recalling your own food intake for one week, record the number of times the following foods were eaten in a chart like Figure 11.10

9. Make a weekly meal schedule in which you introduce a new food, outline hygiene and mealtime behavior, encourage sensory enjoyment of foods, and provide for child participation daily. Indicate child-oriented goals, preparation of the teacher, materials needed, and anticipated results.

10. Make a list of the most common fruits in your locality, specifying whether or not they are seasonal. Then list at least four ways each fruit could be served to increase its familiarity and versatility. (Remember to use different combinations.) In how many of these methods could children assist in preparing and/or serving the fruit?

Now, compare the food intake for one week with the Department of Agriculture Food Guide Pyramid (Figure 11.1 p. 410) to see if the intake was in accordance with their recommendations.

	Mon.	Tues.	Wed.	Thurs.	Fri.
Fruit citrus other					
Vegetables green/yellow starchy other					
Dairy products milk cheese yogurt cottage cheese other					
Meat/alternatives meat fish poultry eggs other					
Grains bread nuts/seeds pasta rice other					

Figure 11.10   Food Intake Chart

11. Make a list of favorite snacks of young children. Make a list of your favorite snacks. Evaluate both. Make a substitute list of more nutritious foods for young children and yourself. Plan and serve these snacks for a two-week period.

12. Using the curriculum checklist in Figure 4.2, see how many ways food can be integrated into the curriculum.

13. Design and present a lesson on health care or personal grooming that would be appropriate for the children in your classroom.

14. Prepare a lesson on first aid or health. Present it to the parents.

15. What health conditions need to be improved in your area? How can you assist?

16. Check with local clinics or health departments as to immunization information and dates. Encourage parents to have their child's immunizations current.

17. Design and implement a day (or week) lesson plan related to health and/or safety for young children.

18. Provide a one-week exercise plan that includes daily locomotor activities to be used (a) indoors, (b) outdoors, and (c) spontaneously without props. If possible, implement your plan. Note the responses of the children. Would you need to revise your plans? If so, how?

19. How do you personally feel about health and exercise? Do you make them a part of your daily living? How could you use one or both to a better advantage?

     For a miniplan on nutrition and health, see Appendix B.

References

Nutrition & Health References.

American Academy of Pediatrics (AAP). 141 Northwest Point Boulevard, P.O. Box 927, Elk Grove, IL 60009-0927. E-mail: childcare@aap.org. Phone: 708-228-5005.

American Psychological Association. Online at http://www.apa.org/pubinfo/kidsmed.html.

Bureau of Census. (1997). *Current population survey.* Washington, DC: Author.

Children's Defense Fund. (1996). *The state of America's children.* Washington, DC: Author.

Children's Defense Fund. (1998). *CHIP checkup: A healthy start for children.* Washington, DC: Author.

DeBord, K., Hestenes, L. L., Moore, R. C., Cosco, N., & McGinnis, J. R. (2002). Paying attention to the outdoor environment is as important as preparing the indoor environment. *Young Children, 57*(3), 32–34.

Dooling, M. V., & Ulione, M. S. (2000). Health consultation in child care: A partnership that works. *Young Children, 55*(2), 23–26.

Dietary Guidelines for Americans 2000 (5th ed.). Home and Garden Bulletin No. 232. Consumer Information Center, Pueblo, CO 81009 (#320E, $.50) or download at http://www.pueblo.gsa.gov.

Flynn, L. L., & Kieff, J. (2002). Including everyone in outdoor play. *Young Children, 57*(3), 20–26.

Fuhr, J. E., with Barclay, K. H. (1998). The importance of appropriate nutrition and nutrition education. *Young Children, 53*(1), 74–79.

FYI. (1998). Nutrition and cognitive development. *Young Children, 53*(4), 47.

FYI. (2000). The faces of poverty—our young children. *Young Children, 55*(2), 66.

Gesell, A., & Thompson, H. (1934). *Infant behavior: Its genesis and growth.* New York: McGraw-Hill.

Greenman, J. (1988). *Caring spaces, learning places: Children's environments that work.* Redmond, WA: Exchange Press.

Henderson, G. (1993). Diversity or divisiveness. *Dimensions, 21*(2), 19–20.

Howell, N. M. (1999). Cooking up a learning community with corn, beans, and rice. *Young Children, 54*(5), 37–38.

Jensen, B. J., & Bullard, J. A. (2002). The mud center: recapturing childhood. *Young Children, 57*(5), 16–19.

Kurato, C. M., Martin, R. E., Lan, W. Y., Chappell, J. A., & Ahmad, M. (2000). Menu planning, food consumption, and sanitary practices in day care facilities. *Family and Consumer Sciences Research Journal, 29*(1), 81–91.

McGinnis, J. R. (2002). Enriching the outdoor environment. *Young Children, 57*(3), 28–30.

McGraw, M. B. (1935). *Growth: A study of Johnny and Jimmy.* New York: D. Appleton.

Murray, C. G. (2000). Learning about children's social and emotional needs at snack time—nourishing the body, mind, and spirit of each child. *Young Children, 55*(2), 43–52.

Nakikian-Nelms, M. L., Syler, G., & Mogharrehan, C. M. (1994). Pilot assessment of nutrition practices in a university child care program. *Journal of Nutrition Education, 26*(5), 238–240.

National Association for the Education of Young Children. Public policy section online at http://www.naeyc.org.

National Association of Child Care Resource and Referral Agencies (NACCRRA). 1319 F Street, NW, Suite 810, Washington, DC. 20004-1106. Phone: 202-393-5501. Online at www.naccrra.net.

National Association of Early Childhood Specialists in State Departments of Education (NAECS/SDE). (2002). *Recess and the importance of play: A position statement on young children and recess.* Alexandria, VA: Author. Available online at http://ericps.crc.uiun.edu/naecs/position/recessplay.html.

National Association of Pediatric Nurses and Practitioners (NAPNAP). 1101 Kings Highway, N., Suite 206, Cherry Hill, NJ 08034-1912. Phone: 609-667-1912. Online at www.napnap.org.

National Institute of Child Health and Human Development (NICHD). Online at http://www.nih.gov/nichd/html/news.html.

National Resource Center for Health and Safety in Child Care. University of Colorado Health Science Center School of Nursing. 4200 E. Ninth Avenue, Campus Box C287, Denver, CO 80262. Phone: 800-598-KIDS. Online at http.://nrc.uchsc.edu.

O'Connor, J. (1999). Public Policy Report. New Children's Health Insurance Program: Early childhood professional outreach efforts can make a difference. *Young Children, 54*(2), 63–65.

Payne, V. G., & Rink, J. E. (1997). Physical education. In C. H. Hart, D. C. Burts, & R. Charlesworth (Eds.), *Integrated curriculum and developmentally appropriate practice: Birth to age eight* (pp. 145–170). Albany: State University of New York Press.

Needleman, R. & Needleman, G. (1995). Ten most common health problems in school, *Scholastic Early Childhood Today, 10*(3), 22–23.

Rabinovich, B. A., Lerner, N. D., & Huey, R. W. (1994). Young children's ability to climb fences. *Human Factors, 36*(4), 733–744.

Readdick, C. A., & Park, J. J. (1998). Achieving great heights: the climbing child. *Young Children, 54*(6), 14–19.

Regalado, M. (2002). Busting the sugar-hyperactivity myth. *LYCOS Health with WEBMD.* Online at http://webmd.lycos.com/content/article/1739.50032.

Rivkin, M. S. *The great outdoors: Restoring children's right to play outside.* NAEYC order #108/$7. ISBN 0-935989-71-4.

Spoon, M. (n.d.). *An apple a day: Do food additives affect children's behavior?* Fact Sheet 92-59. University of Nevada Cooperative Extension and the University of Nevada School of Medicine. (775/784-4848).

Sutterby, J. A., & Frost, J. L. (2002). Making playgrounds fit for children and children fit on playgrounds. *Young Children, 57*(3), 36–41.

Swadener, S. (1995). Nutrition education for preschool children. *Journal of Nutrition Education, 27*(6), 291–297.

U.S. Consumer Product Safety Commission. (1997). *A handbook for public playground safety.* Washington, DC: Author.

Websites on accessible playgrounds. (2002). See *Young Children, 57*(3), 26.

Werner, P., Timms, S., & Almond, J. (1996). Health stops: Practical ideas for health-related exercise in preschool and primary classrooms, *Young Children, 51*(6), 48–55.

12

Transition Activities

Main Principles

1. Periods between activities or locations require careful planning, variety, and cooperation. (pp. 442–443)

2. Good transition periods accomplish the following: (pp. 444–460)

   ➤ provide good learning opportunities

   ➤ reduce random and disruptive behavior

   ➤ promote confidence, independence, and inner control

   ➤ meet individual and group needs

   ➤ increase participation

   ➤ add variety to the curriculum

Advantages of Smooth Transitions

Looking at a group of young children absorbed in a curriculum area, such as art or music, and then later looking at these same children absorbed in another curriculum area, perhaps now in language arts or science, one wonders how the teacher moves these children from one topic (or area) to another so the children will again find interest and motivation. Or does the change involve chaos, undesired behavior, noise, and frustration for both the teacher and the children?

When a teacher plans the daily schedule, are there provisions for the in-between periods (described by Berk [1976] as periods between activities, generally involved in reading, wandering, exploring, and waiting)? In studying several different kinds of nursery schools Berk reported that transitions occupy from 20 percent to 35 percent of activity time in nursery school (depending on the school, the particular day, and the skill and planning contributed by the teacher). These periods consume a sizable amount of time, which can either be utilized or wasted. Those who make teaching look so easy and flow so smoothly attend to both transition and curriculum components.

It has been suggested that a number of factors contribute to difficulties around transition time, including boredom, the insistence on conformity, the absence of a future orientation in some children, the absence of clearly defined tasks, and a possible fear of failure (Hirsch, n.d.). Careful planning on the part of teachers at these times can reduce the negative behavior and attitudes that may occur.

Transition periods can make the day flow smoothly, or they can make the day seem choppy and out of control. Once the children get ahead of the teacher and the schedule, it is difficult for the teacher to regain control.

Times when schedules need attention are when children change activity or location. Activity changes include arrival of the children, opening time or free play, completion of an activity, moving between activities (sometimes from more desired to less desired ones, such as napping), waiting for an activity to begin (such as waiting for a ride, a visitor, or a group member), and preparing for departure. Change of location includes going outside or to another room, lunchtime, napping, field trips, and departure. Separation of the children from the parents or from the center to home may cause some children to feel anxious. A wise teacher will have several available techniques for working with children under these circumstances.

At times children may see transitions differently than do adults and will delay, resist, refuse, or ignore interruptions to pleasurable or interesting activities. Teachers should show respect for the children at these times by discussing with them the changes and expectations. Ordinarily the children will want to take responsibility when they know what is to be done, what is expected, or what comes next. Cleanup can be an enjoyable activity and a good learning experience for the children. They should be involved in it, and teachers can encourage their participation by giving them attention and honest approval. Situations where children just wait while the teacher cleans up the present activity and prepare the following one are inappropriate.

Well-planned transitions, those that are of interest to and meet the needs of the children in a particular group, add much value to a classroom. Lest there be a misunderstanding, transitions are not to be interpreted as another period for academic performance. True, knowledge and opportunities are there, but transitions are used for a change of pace and place, even though learning occurs simultaneously. Consider the following as advantages.

Misbehavior Can Be Reduced or Avoided

Informed children (those who know what is expected of them and what to expect from the program, the schedule, and the teachers) become involved in undesirable behavior less frequently. With a little warning (first to those at the activities that require the most time or effort in cleaning up, or to the children who are dawdlers), the children can finish a present task and move easily to the next one.

Children Grow Individually

When teachers believe children are competent, dependable, and trustworthy, the children act in these ways. Children can learn and practice independence ("I can do it myself"), gain confidence, and build inner control through good transition planning on the part of the teacher. Children like to help make decisions (when feasible), to feel some control over their actions and lives, and to be independent. These traits can be developed at school because of their knowledge of the program and environment.

Development Occurs

Transitions can enhance areas of skill and personal development.

Physical Activities can be provided to exercise large and small muscles through perceptual-motor and eye-hand coordination, balance, body movement, self-help, and other opportunities.

Cognitive Children exercise memory and recall in cleanup, in refreshing previous concepts, in imaginative and creative thinking about old and new concepts, and in understanding their world.

Emotional Children take pride in the appearance of their classroom and in developing good work habits.

Social During transitions, children learn how to work cooperatively with others and to see each other's views. They learn how to build and strengthen relationships with peers and adults.

Learning Is Increased

Young children need firsthand, or concrete, experiences; therefore, transition activities that focus on sensory development are essential. Numerous opportunities to hear, smell, feel, see, and taste are especially good learning reinforcers for young children.

Rather than use transition times as stallers, one can use these periods productively to disseminate new information, to review and reinforce old information, or to build personal relationships.

Language Can Be Practiced

Some teachers use a particular sound (bell, chords on piano, lights flickered, record, and so on) to warn children about the impending change of activity. When they do this, they do two things: (1) they forfeit an opportunity to practice language skills, and (2) they teach children to respond to external stimuli. The practice of using sounds could be used as a shaping tool until the children get the routine, but should then be replaced by verbal interaction and by the children taking more responsibility for their own behavior.

Teachers Can Be Better Prepared

Teachers use the physical environment in planning movement and participation activities so children will not be restricted by furniture or people. Teachers organize their teaching materials to be easily accessible, appropriate, and interesting. Teachers schedule activities and routines to meet the needs of individual children, small groups, and the whole group.

Good Transition Activities

A good transition activity will accomplish one or more of the following: enable the child to see the conclusion or completion of an activity; allow for child involvement and independence; set the mood for the next activity; reinforce ideas already learned; preassess the present knowledge of the child; serve as a valuable teaching time in all areas of development; help the child build good relationships with others; and add interest and variety to the daily schedule. Thus, the activity should:

1. Provide a variety of experiences. Using the same finger play or song day after day may discourage children from coming. Make it so exciting that the children will be there in order not to miss something!

2. Encourage self-control. When moving from one room or location to another, try putting something on the floor for the children to follow (yarn or paper objects such as footprints) or give them a particular way to go (for example, jumping like a frog) *until* they have established the routine. *Then* try saying that all those wearing shoes (or green, or stripes) can go to the next activity or place. Still later on, just tell them what is expected ("We're going to lunch now"), and let them take responsibility for getting there. It removes the external control and helps them build internal control, independence, and self-confidence—very important steps. To reiterate this point: At first give the children a specific idea of how to go and where they are expected to go; then move to verbalization and independence building. Teachers who must always tell children what to do and how to do it do not have confidence in the children or themselves.

3. Prepare the children for what is to follow (snack, story, going outside). A transition period may be used as specific preparation for an activity or as a quieting time for the children.

4. Meet the needs, interests, and developmental abilities of the children. Transition time should encourage participation, provide some learning, and be enjoyable and flexible. The teacher should watch the children for clues as to length, type of activity, and expectations.

5. Be started by the teacher when the first children arrive in the area. Other children will finish their activities and join the group. If a teacher waits until all the children are there before she begins, there is no incentive for the children to get there. "Why hurry so you can wait?"

Tips for Better Transitions

➤ Have the next activity or location prepared before terminating the present activity.

➤ Allow a realistic amount of time for the transition.

➤ Give sufficient warning about the impending change.

➤ Avoid having all children move at once. Forming lines and waiting for others create noise, crowded situations, competition, frustration, and aggression.

➤ Have a positive attitude and act in a calm, respectful way with a conviction in your voice that the children will follow the requests.

➤ Allow for requests of and suggestions by the children.

➤ Use planned and spontaneous transitions to preassess new concepts to be taught or to reinforce knowledge previously taught.

➤ Avoid transition periods that are too long or too short, too boring, or too demanding.

➤ Use the same careful planning and considerations as for other activities. Appropriate transitions help children move through the routine with ease.

➤ Plan some transitions to quiet the children (to relax, to settle down, to think and reason, to apply and reinforce concepts); plan others to stimulate participation, cooperation, or activity.

If a teacher of young children is asked what part of the day is the most troublesome or frustrating, the answer is generally, "When we're changing from one activity to another!" This is especially true with an inexperienced teacher. A bit of organization and planning, however, can change a dreaded period to one of pleasure and reward.

Webster's Tenth New Collegiate Dictionary defines transition as "a passage from one state, stage, subject, or place to another." When one works with young children, transitions occur frequently, from the time they enter the door until they leave for home. It is not like a formal high school or college class where students enter at a specified time, hear a lecture on a designated topic, and then leave at the sound of a bell. Young children can be interested in an activity for a long period of time—in fact, they sometimes need to be reminded that it will soon be time for another activity. In a developmentally appropriate program, individual children move more frequently than those in more traditional or academic programs.

In an effort to find ways to reduce random behavior during transition from one activity to another, the teachers should review the plan for the day before the children arrive. A few extra minutes spent on transition activities will be well worth the effort. During the meeting, a song can be reviewed, any activities using props readied, and specifics discussed with other teachers if their assistance is needed. A few extra activities should be ready to use when needed. Preparation before children arrive pays off while they are there.

How can children be encouraged to clean up their toys and materials before moving on to the next activity? Possibly by observing when they begin to lose interest and then stepping in to suggest that the blocks be put on the shelf or to assist in clearing up the art materials and putting things away; possibly by giving a few minutes' warning; possibly by having something of interest planned and started before the children begin random or running behavior. What happens at transition times really depends on the teacher. If she stops to clean up or get involved with a single child, or is not ready for the next activity, the children usually go right on past her. Then she has difficulty regaining her lead. In a developmentally appropriate program, children may replace their personal work materials but leave the area or activity ready for other children.

Several studies have focused on the amount of time teachers and children spend in transitions. Berk (1976) found that for children under the age of 6, transitions were the most prominent activity in all schools studied, ranging from 20 percent of the time in the community day care center to 30 percent to 35 percent in all settings, including a Head Start program and a Montessori preschool. That is a lot of time when children may not know what is expected of them, and can increase aggression, class disruption, or deviant behavior. Reporting on the behavior of passive and aggressive children who were not provided with positive transitions, Wolfgang (1977) observed that the passive child (1) remains stationary, showing no response to commands, (2) withdraws to some quiet place, or (3) silently does what he or she is told. Meanwhile, the aggressive child responds by (1) destroying materials, (2) throwing objects, (3) becoming verbally aggressive, or (4) running and forcing the teacher to chase him or her.

In the daily activities, most teachers plan for curriculum areas, such as art, free play, and music, but neglect transition times—and then wonder why they are so difficult to manage. When teachers do not know what to expect, how can the children know? Teachers who write into their lesson plan the specific activities to be used at transition times find control of the children much easier. Teachers should also try to delay unnatural breaks in classroom activity, minimize interruption of activities, and, when possible, allow completion of an activity before introducing another.

Transition times are not merely time consumers; they can be very valuable teaching times. Much learning and feedback comes at times when the group is small and time is available for informal conversation. Transition can be a time of relationship building or a time for relaxation or emotional or physical release.

Routines

Children who know the routines and expectations find it easier to make changes from activities or locations—even though some changes flow more smoothly than others. It is when children are unsure that problems occur. Some of the daily routines are arrival, washing and toileting, resting, eating, and departing. In a developmentally appropriate program, there are fewer routines as a whole group and more individual changes.

Arrival   In a regular, short-day program, many of the children arrive simultaneously. Sometimes this creates confusion and sometimes it gives each child an opportunity to obtain desired toys, join playmates in a small group, and initiate an activity.

In full-day or long-hour programs (day care, for example), children are coming and going throughout the day. Interruptions must be tolerated by both children and adults.

As children arrive for any length of program, there will be a certain amount of confusion and time expended before they settle into play or activities.

Washing and Toileting   Some centers have specific times they encourage children to wash and use the toilet (before eating, resting, or outside times). Some children need to be reminded frequently to use the toilet and wash their hands; other children recognize and meet their own needs.

When children use the restroom for washing/toileting as a group, confusion may result. Children may need help in finishing their tasks and moving out to make room for other children. Some children may use the excuse of having to wash or use the toilet when they are expected to be in a group time (storytime, meals, or outside). If they need to be a certain place for a specific reason or length of time, remind these children beforehand to take care of these necessities.

Resting   Children enrolled in short-day programs usually do not have an organized or specific time or place for resting. Usually they move between active and quiet periods, so resting, per se, is not suggested; however, tired children are encouraged to rest when and if they need to.

In long-day programs, children may be expected to rest on a cot or bed (for a short time each morning and each afternoon with an actual sleeping time for younger children). Some teachers have found that "resting" is more of a frustration for them and the children than providing other options—a quiet activity or listening to a story or music. In some states, an individual place to rest and a specific time (or length of time) is required. Centers must conform to this requirement.

Eating   Eating can be a social time, but it also provides a time for relaxation and nourishment. Short-day programs may provide only a snack; however, long-day programs usually provide a morning snack (or breakfast), lunch, and an afternoon snack, providing part of the total daily nutritional requirements for each child.

Eating experiences can help the child become familiar with different kinds of food, practice group living (manners), and learn about foods and customs of other people. (See Chapter 11.)

Departure   It is just as important to give children attention and time to wind down school activities as it is to get them involved when they arrive. Sometimes parents are in a hurry and expect their children to drop everything and leave. A wise teacher helps the children finish tasks and be partially ready to depart when parents or car-pool drivers arrive. For security reasons, the center should require and have on file the names and/or identification of the people who are authorized to pick up each child. An authorized person should daily sign the child into the center and sign him out when he leaves.

Parents and teachers need to have personal contact often, and it may be at the beginning or the end of the child's day. Leaving the center should be as relaxed and joyful as possible.

Teaching Suggestions

Following are some suggestions that could be used as transition activities. Use only those that are appropriate for your group of children and add other ideas of your own.

Animal

Have an animal concealed until group time. Then bring it into the group or take the children to the animal, whichever is more appropriate. Discuss, touch, and enjoy the animal.

Ball Toss

As each child (for example, John) comes to the group, the teacher says, "John is ready." Toss or roll a soft ball to the child, who returns it. Repeat as each child arrives.

Body Cards

The teacher shows large cards on which have been drawn different positions (see Figure 12.1). The children use their bodies to represent the symbols.

Figure 12.1   Body Cards with Stick Figures Representing Different Positions That Children Can Imitate

Figure 12.2 Body Cards with Silhouette Figures That Children Can Imitate

Another way to use body cards is to have individual silhouette figures cut out of tag board (see Figure 12.2). The teacher holds up an example, and the children form that position with their bodies.

Chalkboard

With the teacher drawing stick figures, the children supply a story. It is surprising how rapidly the story content changes. Some children who do not ordinarily express themselves become verbal in such a setting. Accept the children's ideas and let the story flow freely. If children are able, have them draw some of the story on the chalkboard.

Children's Original Stories

Without Props or Aids   One day a group of children was waiting for storytime before the teacher was ready. One child volunteered, "I'll tell you a story." The other children agreed; so Dell moved to the place usually occupied by the teacher and told his story. It was short and to the point: "Once there was a dog." Then he returned to his place in the group. Other children wanted a turn. Some of the stories were familiar ones; some were make-believe. The children thoroughly enjoyed participating. Children who wanted to tell a story were given the chance, but those who did not were not forced to do so.

With Props or Aids   Paste pictures into an old book (for example, a dress pattern book) with a stiff back and heavy pages. (Children or teachers may do this.) At storytime, show the pictures and let the children make up a story. This can be used over and over.

Provide the children with flannel board cutouts and let them make up a story, or let them use visuals that teachers have previously used. The stories may be traditional or original.

Cognitive Concepts

Suppose you want to see how children respond to certain situations. "I want to buy some oranges. Where do I go to get them?" "Where can I get a new collar for my dog?" This gives the children an opportunity to think. Before you respond, "No, you can't buy it there," ask for further clarification. The child may be perfectly correct!

Teach about prepositions by using an object in relationship to another object. "Where is the spoon?" (*over, under, beside, on,* or *in* the box). Then give the child a chance to place the object and tell its relationship. A better activity would be for the child to use his body in relationship to an object; however, space may be a limitation.

Enforcing Themes

Example 1   When a theme concerns air, use a canister vacuum with the hose attached to blow rather than suck air. Place the opening directly up, put a Ping-Pong ball on the opening, and turn on vacuum. The ball bounces up and down.

Example 2   For a theme on magnets tell the story *Mickey's Magnet* (Branley & Vaughan, 1956). Demonstrate how Mickey kept spilling and picking up pins. Then divide children into groups and give them objects and magnets. Let them determine which objects are attracted by the magnet.

Exercises

Exercises such as "Head, Shoulders, Knees, and Toes" help to reduce some of the tensions and physical needs of children. Many exercises can be used.

- With children sitting on the floor, legs outstretched, have them touch the opposite knee with their fingers. Try it with an elbow, then the nose.
- Have the children pretend they are rag dolls. Help them relax by first hanging their heads, then moving their arms limply, then their legs, and so on until they are on the floor.
- Have the children walk around the room as they think animals would walk, using their own creative imaginations without patterning from teachers.
- Use some of the movement activities suggested in Chapter 7.

When stimulating activity occurs just before a quiet period, it is important to provide an activity immediately after it to relax the children. Some of the finger plays on the following pages work nicely for this purpose.

Feel Box

Take a small cardboard box (about 16 × 8 × 8 in. or a size that can be easily handled by a child) and cut out one side. On each end make holes large enough for the child's hands. Have the child put his hands in the ends and hold the open side away from himself so that he cannot see inside the box, but so that the other children can. The child closes his eyes while the teacher places an object through the open side into the box. The child feels the object and tries to guess what it is.

Films

Films should never take the place of actual experience, but they can be used infrequently as supplements to firsthand experiences. Carefully evaluate each film as to length, concepts taught (including vocabulary), interest for the children, and value to be gained from the film. Consider also *whether this is the best way to teach a particular topic.*

Finger Plays

Fingerplays allow children to do as well as see. They have been favorites of young children and their teachers for many years. They should be short and of interest to the children. Teachers should know the finger plays well before attempting to teach them to the children, and all teachers in the group should do them the same way. Following are some favorites of mine and of many others that I have learned as a child or later as a teacher of young children.

One Little Body
Two little hands go clap, clap, clap!   (Do actions as mentioned.)
Two little feet go tap, tap, tap!
Two little hands go thump, thump, thump!
Two little feet go jump, jump, jump!
One little body turns around;
One little body sits quietly down.

Hands
On my head my hands I place,
On my shoulders, on my face.
On my waist, and by my side;
Quickly at my back they hide.
I can wave them way up high,
Like the little birdies fly.
I can clap them; one, two, three.
Now see how quiet they can be.

Little Hands
Open, shut them; open, shut them;
Give a little clap.
Open, shut them; open, shut them;
Lay them in your lap.
Creep them, creep them slowly upward
To the rosy cheek;
Open wide the shining eyes,
Through the fingers peek.
Open, shut them; open, shut them;
To the shoulders fly;
Let them like the birdies flutter,
Flutter to the sky.
Falling, falling slowly downward,
Nearly to the ground;
Quickly raise them, all the fingers
Twirling round and round.
Open, shut them; open, shut them;
Give a little clap.
Open, shut them; open, shut them;
Lay them in your lap.

Creep them; creep them; creep them
Right up to your chin;
Open wide your little mouth,
But do not let them in!

Ten Little Fingers

Ten little fingers, and they all belong to me.
I can make them do things, would you like to see?
I can shut them up tight, or open them wide.
I can put them together, or make them all hide.
I can make them jump high. I can make them jump low.
I can fold them quietly, and hold them just so!

Where Is Thumbkin?

Where is Thumbkin? Where is Thumbkin?	(Hide hands behind back.)
Here I am. Here I am.	(Show one thumb, then the other.)
How are you today, sir?	
Very well, I thank you.	
Run away. Run away.	(Return each hand to back.)
Repeat song using:	(Repeat actions showing appropriate finger, then return hands to back.)

"Pointer" (index finger);
"Tall Man" (middle finger);
"Ring Man" (ring finger);
"Baby" (little finger);
and "All the Men" (all fingers at once).

Night and Morning

This little boy is going to bed;	(Place first finger of right hand on palm of left hand.)
Down on the pillow he lays his head;	(Thumb of left hand is pillow.)
Pulls the covers up round him tight,	(Fingers of left hand close.)
And this is the way he sleeps all night!	
Morning comes, he opens his eyes;	(Open and blink eyes.)
Back with a toss the cover flies;	(Fingers of left hand open quickly.)
Up he jumps, is dressed and away.	(Right index finger is up and hopping away.)
Ready for frolic and play all day.	

Bunny Song

Here is my bunny with ears so funny,	(Right fist forms bunny, and two fingers the ears. Left hand is closed to make a "hole.")
And here is his hole in the ground.	
When a noise he hears,	
He pricks up his ears	
And jumps in his hole with a bound.	

Quacking Ducks

Five little ducks went out to play,	(Hold up five fingers.)
Over the hills and far away.	(Fingers run away.)
When the mother duck said,	(Make quacking motion with both hands.)
"Quack, quack, quack,"	
Four little ducks came waddling back.	(Four fingers return.)
Four little ducks went out to play.	(Four fingers run away.)
(Continue words and motions until . . .)	

No little ducks came waddling back.
BUT, when the mother duck said,   (Make deliberate quacking motion.)
"QUACK, QUACK, QUACK!"
Five little ducks came waddling back!   (All fingers return.)

Five Little Squirrels
Five little squirrels sitting on a tree.   (Hold up hand.)
The first one said, "What do I see?"   (Shield eyes with hand.)
The second one said, "A man with a gun."   (Take aim.)
The third one said, "Oh! Let's run!"   (Hands run away.)
The fourth one said, "Let's hide in the shade."
The fifth one said, "I'm not afraid!"   (Thumbs under armpits.)
Then "BANG!" went the gun   (Clap hands loudly.)
And away they all run.   (Hands go behind back.)

The Beehive
Here is the beehive.   (Close fist, thumb inside.)
Where are the bees?
Hidden away where nobody sees.
Soon they'll come creeping out of the hive;
One, two, three, four, five.   (Bring out finger with each number.)
BZZZZZZZ, BZZZZZZZ.   (Fingers and hands fly around.)

Five Little Kittens
There were five little kittens.   (Hold left hand up; with right hand
                                                 fold the left-hand fingers into the palm,
                                                 one by one, starting with the little finger.)

One little kitten went to sleep.
Two little kittens went to sleep.
Three little kittens went to sleep.
Four little kittens went to sleep.
Five little kittens went to sleep.
All the kittens were fast asleep.

My Little Kitten
My little kitten ran up a tree.   (Fingers run up arms.)
And sat on a limb to look at me.   (Hands are placed on opposite shoulders.)
I said, "Come, kitty," and down he ran,   (Fingers run down arms.)
And drank all the milk   (Hand is cupped, opposite hand drinks.)
I poured in his pan.

Eensy, Weensy Spider
Eensy, weensy spider   (Opposite thumbs and index
                                                  fingers climb up each other.)

Climbed up the water spout.
Down came the rain   (Quickly lower hands and arms.)
And washed the spider out.
Out came the sun   (Make circle of arms around head.)
And dried up all the rain.
So eensy, weensy spider
Climbed up the spout again.   (Repeat thumbs and finger motion.)

Here Is a Ball
A little ball,   (Make ball with fingers.)
A bigger ball,   (Make ball with both hands.)

A great big ball I see.	(Make ball with both arms.)
Now let's count the balls we've made.	
One, two, three!	(Repeat previous three circles.)

My Dolly

This is how my dolly walks,	(Walk around a circle stiff-legged and arms raised.)
This is how she walks, you see.	
This is how my dolly runs,	(Run stiff-legged.)
This is how she runs, you see.	
This is how my dolly talks,	(Bend over, say, "Mama, Mama.")
This is how she talks, you see.	

The Fruit Tree

Way up high in the apple tree,	(Extend arms up high.)
Two little apples smiled down on me.	(Put hands around eyes.)
I shook that tree as hard as I could,	(Pretend to shake tree.)
And down came the apples;	(Arms move to ground.)
M-m-m-m, were they good!	(Rub stomach.)

Repeat poem and motions using different kinds of fruit: pears, peach, banana, orange, cherry, and so on. For last verse, use a lemon tree. Last action is pulling a sour face and saying, "U-u-u-uh! They were sour!"

Jack-in-the-Box

Jack-in-the-Box, all shut up tight,	(Close fist with thumb inside and cover with palm of other hand, or curl up body on floor with arms around head.)
Not a breath of air or a bit of light.	
How tired he must be, all folded up.	
Let's open the lid, and up he'll jump.	(Thumbs pop out of fist, or child jumps up, extending arms.)

Guessing Games

Say: "I am thinking of something that _____ (give a couple of clues). Can you guess what it is?" (Use animals or transportation vehicles; describe a child.) Children can also take a turn giving clues.

Guests

Often bringing a guest into the school is easier than taking children on a particular field trip. By bringing the guest to school, the children can enjoy the experience in a familiar setting. This is often helpful.

A doctor, father of one child in the center, came to the school with his black bag. Rexene backed off, saying, "But I don't want a shot today." She was assured by the teachers and the doctor that he had not come to give shots that day. This particular doctor was a bone specialist. After showing the children all the things he carried in his bag, he asked, "Have any of you ever known someone who had broken a bone?" Some did, and some did not. He went on to explain how he helped people when they had a broken bone. He applied a cast to a teacher's arm for demonstration—none of the children would be his patient! How real the experience was to the children! They expressed sympathy to the teacher, as if she really had a broken arm. After the cast was dry, the doctor removed it. Many of the children were concerned, thinking he would cut off the teacher's arm with the cast. He took care to explain away all their fears and questions. After the cast was removed, the children said how glad they were that the teacher's arm was better. The children examined the cast, tried it on, and explored it in every way. This was an excellent experience for them because the doctor could communicate with them on their level. One child commented, "My dog has a broken leg, but he doesn't have a cast on." Shortly after this classroom experience, the teacher's own young son broke his arm, and she had information to make the experience less frightening for him.

A carpenter also paid a visit to a group of preschool children. The visit had been pre-arranged and well planned. Through his conversation, he helped the children to understand his occupation better. He brought a small door that was nearly completed and let the children finish it by putting screws in predrilled holes. He explained the use of all his tools, and, on departing, gave each child a carpenter's pencil. How busy the woodworking bench was that day!

A musician invited as a guest should be asked to explain about the instrument briefly and then play tunes that are familiar to the children. The children can listen to some selections, but they also enjoy participating. If the children are not allowed to touch or use the instrument, they may be able to sing or dance with the music. Although a guest may be very talented and want to display his or her skills, young children are easily bored and may walk out on the guest. The experience should be kept simple, therefore, with the length of the presentation varied according to the interests of the children.

Mirror Image

The teacher shows a mirror, and the children see how it reflects their movements and expressions. The mirror is removed and the teacher or a child makes movements for the others to reflect.

Musical Experiences

Children enjoy expressing themselves—verbally or physically—through music. Free, spontaneous movement should be encouraged. Occasional honest praise helps to motivate the quiet child.

A number of records and tapes encourage children to participate. When selecting this material, see that they give ideas, but do not restrict freedom to interpret actions. (See music catalogs for possible selections.)

Use the piano from time to time, sometimes to accompany songs, sometimes to teach specific concepts (high and low, loud and soft, fast and slow); sometimes encourage child participation (marching, moving to various rhythms).

Some of the ideas under the section titled "Exercises" could be used with the addition of music. For other specific suggestions, see activities listed at the end of Chapter 7.

Number Experiences

With the aid of a flannel board, chalkboard, bulletin board, finger plays, games, songs, and other methods, provide some relaxed and enjoyable but meaningful experiences with numbers. Many preschool children can do rote counting but still do not understand number symbols. For example, when interrupted in counting, they must return to the beginning—they cannot continue where they left off.

For some specific ideas, see finger plays listed previously that include numbers, see Chapter 9, or try some of the following (*Note:* It is generally easier for young children to count forward than backward.)

This Old Man
This old man, he played one,
He played knick-knack on his thumb;

With a knick-knack, paddy-whack, give my dog a bone,
This old man came rolling home.
This old man, he played two (shoe); three (knee); four (door); five (hive); six (sticks);
seven (up to heaven); eight (gate); nine (vine); ten (hen).

One Red Valentine
One red valentine, two red valentines,
Three red valentines, four;
I'll snip and cut out, color and paste
And then make twenty more.

Over in the Meadow (Southern Appalachian Folk Song)
Over in the meadow in the sand in the sun
Lived an old mother turtle and her little baby one.
"Swim," said the mother; "I swim," said the one,
And he swam and was happy in the sand in the sun.

Over in the hollow in a pool in the bogs
Lived an old mother froggie and her two polliwogs.
"Kick," said the mother; "We kick," said the wogs,
Then they kicked and kicked into little green frogs.

Over in the meadow in a nest in the tree
Lived an old mother birdie and her little babies three.
"Sing," said the mother; "We sing," said the three,
And they sang and were happy in the nest in the tree.

This song has 10 verses. For another version, see *Over in the Meadow* by John Langstaff (1957).

One Elephant (Chilean folk song)

One elephant went out to play,	(Children extend arms down,
All on a spider's web one day.	clasp own hands, pretend
He had such enormous fun,	to walk like an elephant.)
He called on another elephant to come.	

Continue counting as "elephants" (children) are added to group. "Two elephants went out to play . . . Three elephants . . . Four elephants," and so on.

Three Blue Pigeons (American folk song)
Three blue pigeons, sitting on the wall,
Three blue pigeons, sitting on the wall.
One flew away. Whee-ee-ee-ee!
Two blue pigeons, sitting on the wall,
Two blue pigeons, sitting on the wall.
One flew away. Whee-ee-ee-ee!

Repeat, using one blue pigeon, then no blue pigeons.

Five Little Buns (Traditional English song)
Five little buns in a baker's shop,
Nice and round with sugar on the top.
Along came a little boy (girl) with a penny to pay,
And bought a sugar bun and took it right away.

Repeat, using four, three, two, one, and no little buns.

Five Little Chickadees (Old counting song)
Five little chickadees peeping at the door,
One flew away and then there were four.

Refrain:
Chickadee, chickadee, happy and gay,
Chickadee, chickadee, fly away.
Four little chickadees sitting on a tree. (refrain)
Three little chickadees looking at you. (refrain)
Two little chickadees sitting in the sun. (refrain)
One little chickadee left all alone,
He flew away and then there were none. (refrain)

Nursery Rhymes

Young children enjoy the play on words, repetition, and nonsense that are incorporated in nursery rhymes. Pictures add to the enjoyment. Through repetition they learn the rhymes without formal training. Nursery rhymes should be selected by the same criteria used for books. Avoid those that are violent or encourage aggression.

Following are some nursery rhymes familiar to most young children:

Curly Locks	Little Boy Blue
Hickory, Dickory, Dock!	Little Miss Muffett
Jack Be Nimble	To Market, To Market
Mary Had a Little Lamb	Little Jack Horner
Old King Cole	Simple Simon
Peter, Peter, Pumpkin Eater	Lucy Locket
Rub-a-Dub-Dub	Mary, Mary, Quite Contrary
Twinkle, Twinkle Little Star	Pease Porridge Hot
Deedle, Deedle, Dumpling	Rock-a-Bye, Baby
Humpty Dumpty	Seesaw, Margery Daw
Little Bo Peep	Wee Willie Winkie

Original Stories from Adults

Perhaps you have written a story, or would like to, and are interested in the reactions of the children. You do not want to use it as your main story, but you do want to try it. Use it as the children are assembling for a group time. (Maybe a parent, a friend, or someone else has written a story and would like response from a group of young children. Try it for them, if you think it would be appropriate.)

Writing for young children is challenging. You need to know their interests, their needs, and some of their growth characteristics. Your story should be short, simple, and realistic. Writing in poetry form is stimulating and exciting. (See Chapter 5.)

Pantomime

Read a favorite story to the children. Briefly talk about it with the children. Help them identify some key concepts or characteristics. Encourage them to act it out. Sometimes they are better at pantomiming than at reciting.

Paper Bag

Give each child a paper sack and tell him to go around the room, putting into her sack objects of a certain color or shape (or other description). Examine the contents with the group.

Have two sacks or boxes with identical contents. Have a child feel in his sack and name an object in it. The second sack is handed to another child, who is requested to find the same object. Sacks are passed around until all the children have had a turn.

Give each child a paper sack. Go into the play yard or on a walk and ask them to either pick up garbage or bring back some things for making a picture. At group time, examine the contents and then proceed with the appropriate activity (keeping the community clean or appreciating things of beauty in nature).

Show a paper bag. Ask the children how many ways the bag can be used. Brainstorm. Try some of the ideas.

Pictures

Select with care the pictures you use with young children. Avoid confusion and distraction.

A teacher can show an interesting picture and start talking about it—the children will generally join in—or a teacher can hold up a picture and stimulate verbal responses by asking questions such as, "What do you think these children are doing?" "Would you like to do what they are doing?" "What time of year is shown in the picture?"

A bulletin board with selected pictures can also be very effective for discussion.

Do not hesitate to get quality (perhaps, famous) artwork from the local library or other available sources. Help the children appreciate aesthetic values.

Poetry

Listen to the conversation of children; it is truly poetic! The play on words, the fun sounds, and the humor are delightful. Too often adults think that poetry has no place in the lives of young children. How wrong they are! An excellent introduction to poetry when a child is young is a priceless experience that will add greatly to his future enjoyment of it.

Young children thoroughly enjoy the rhythmic quality of poetry (nursery rhymes included). They can often be heard reciting a line, phrase, or entire poem as they play. It encourages them to sharpen their hearing perception. They begin to discriminate between similar sounds, they enjoy the sense and nonsense of poetry, and they learn new things.

Poetry should be a part of the teacher's repertoire. When appropriate, she can recite a poem, expressing her enjoyment of the verse and also showing the children that she values it.

Select poetry as carefully as you do other language experiences. Use it in a similar way: for a transition, to support areas of curriculum, to create interest, and to verbalize with the children. You can dramatize it or use it spontaneously or as a planned activity, with or without visual aids. If the children seem interested, use more verses; if they become restless, only a first verse or the first and last verses may be sufficient.

The teacher's attitude toward poetry will be influential. A teacher who enjoys and appreciates it will select and share it enthusiastically and will use different types: poems related to children's everyday experiences, nonsense verses for fun, poems that bring melody and rhythm to the ear, poems with special meaning, and poems that stimulate and encourage verbal exploration. Through repetition, not through rigid memorization, children learn and enjoy poetry.

As you can tell, using poetry with young children is one of my great favorites. When I was required to use poetry as a student in a children's literature class, the experience started off on a reluctant note. The children responded so well, my timidity vanished, and now it is impossible to get along without using it often in the classroom. If you cannot find a poem on a specific topic, you might even try writing your own.

Among the many excellent sources of poetry for young children are favorite authors such as Dorothy Aldis, Dorothy Baruch, Polly Chase Boyden, Marchette Chute, Rachel Field, Rose Fyleman, Josette Frank, Kate Greenaway, A. A. Milne, Elizabeth Madox Roberts, Carl Sandburg, Robert Louis Stevenson, and James S. Tippett.

Preparation for a Field Trip

Tell the children about an excursion just before you go. Help them to understand why you are going and what you will see and do. Set up the guidelines and make necessary stops at the bathroom and water fountain before leaving the center.

After a field trip, use transition time to discuss what happened, to ask and answer questions, or to draw or write a story of the group's experience.

For additional information about field trips, see Chapter 10.

Puppets

Several kinds of puppets are available and add interest to activities. Sack, finger, hand, sock, tube, and clothespin puppets can be easily made and used by either children or teachers. Making something for later use (perhaps at group time) adds an element of anticipation for the children.

Make sure the puppets are realistically represented and that correct concepts are taught. This should be a learning experience as well as a fun one.

Some shy children who do not respond to a person will respond to a puppet. Use this experience to encourage verbalization, or have the puppet give instructions for the children to follow: "Lester, please hold a picture while we sing." "Mindy, please put the cow on the flannel board." "All hop like bunnies."

Set the guidelines to puppet use before the children become loud or aggressive. Merely saying, "These are friendly puppets who have come to help us today," may deter any problems.

Rhyming Games

Read a poem, show objects, or tell the children certain words. Ask them to think of words that rhyme. Some of their responses will be very interesting.

Rhythms

For suggestions, see music and movement activities at the end of Chapter 7.

Role Playing

Encourage a child or children to act out a story or activity. Let others guess what it is. Give a turn to all who want one.

Science

If you are interested in having all the children participate in a science experience, this is an excellent time. Sometimes have the whole group together, and sometimes use small groups for discussion and participation.

For suggested activities, see Chapter 8.

Songs

Most children enjoy singing simple songs. Songs that use the names of the individual children tend to have magical power. (See "Mary Wore Her Red Dress" in Seeger, 1948.)

A review of Chapter 7, including how to teach a song to young children, might be appropriate at this stage.

Stories with Action

Have you ever been on an action walk with children? This activity brings out an element of suspense that delights each child.

The children and teachers sit on the floor, using their hands to make the sound effects: clapping for walking; rubbing the hands together for going through tall grass; gently pounding on the chest for going over a bridge; fists pounding on the legs for running. Use your own imagination and comments from the children to carry you through an enjoyable experience.

Several versions of an animal "hunt" are available. Ramsey and Bayless (1980) take a bear hunt; others take a tiger hunt; still others take a cougar hunt. Here is an original example of how such an activity could be used.

Let's Go Camping   Everyone sits down. The teacher begins; the children repeat what the teacher says and does and participate through entire activity.

"Let's go camping. [Children repeat.] We'll need our sleeping bags, food, _____, _____. [Children repeat. Pretend to gather and pack items.] We have walked a long way. [Children repeat.] I'm getting hungry. [Children repeat. Pretend to fix and eat meal.] I'm getting so sleepy! [Children repeat. Yawn, stretch, and pretend to prepare sleeping bag and self for bed.] Let's crawl into our sleeping bags. [Children repeat. Wiggle as if getting in and going to sleep.] Somebody is snoring! [Children repeat. Snore and blow out air.] Somebody is snoring louder than anyone else! [Children repeat. Snore and blow out air.] _____ [use child's name] isn't sleepy; so he goes for a walk in the woods. As he is walking [slap hands rhythmically on the legs], he goes over some cobble rocks [make click with tongue in mouth]; then he goes over a bridge [pound fists on legs]; then he goes over some dry dirt [rub hands together]. And do you know what he sees when he gets there? He sees a fire in the forest, and the wind is blowing the fire [put arms up in the air and wave back and forth, saying "Whoo-oo-oo, whoo-oo-oo!"].

"When he sees the fire, he runs back over the dry dirt [action], over the bridge [action], and over the cobble rocks [action] to the camp. He wakes everyone up and tells of the fire. All get up and run to the fire, first over the cobble rocks [action], then the bridge [action], and last over the dry dirt [action]. We see the fire with the wind blowing it [action] and decide to go back and get some water [go back through actions]. We get some buckets and pour water into them [say "shh-hhh-hh-pt"] and go back to the fire [with actions]. We pour the water on the fire that the wind is blowing ["whoo-oo-oo," slow down], and the fire goes out.

"Now we're very tired; so we go back to the camp across the dry dirt, bridge, and rocks [very slow actions], crawl into our sleeping bags, and all start to snore [action]. And guess who snores the loudest of all?"

If this activity seems too long for the children, delete parts of it. Usually they respond, "Oh, let's do it again!"

Storybooks

Select an appropriate book, other than one to be used at actual storytime. Show the pictures to the children and stimulate their conversation.

A child may select a book she would like you to read for storytime. Use it while the children are gathering, but use the book you had already prepared for the entire group.

Surprise Box

Occasionally a teacher or a child can bring a surprise or gather up familiar things from the room. Teacher or child feels the object in a box and describes it. Others try to guess its identity.

Talking Time for Children

Many opportunities should be provided for the young child to express himself and his ideas as well as to listen to others. Following are some ideas that have been tried and found to be effective:

➤ Ask which children in the group are absent that day. This helps the children to become more aware of each child.

➤ Talk about the weather. Has there been a recent change? What kinds of wearing apparel are appropriate for today?

➤ If you know a child has done or is about to do something exciting, let him share it with the group.

➤ Casually, get feedback from the children on certain concepts so that you will know if more time and information are needed.

➤ Talk about things the children have been doing during the morning. How did the finger paint feel? Was it fun to climb on the jungle gym? See other ideas presented in Chapter 5.

"Think" Box

Designate a good-sized box as the "think box." Use it as often as the value dictates. The teacher brings the box to group time and encourages verbal expression from the children. "What do you think is in the box today?" As the children guess, the teacher may add clues. For example, one day the box may include gloves—baseball glove, ski glove, boxing glove, lady's dress glove, and child's winter glove. The teacher says to the children, "What does a glove look like?" "How many kinds of gloves do you know about?" As the children name some that are in the box, she takes them out. The teacher may give added clues: "It's a kind of glove you play a game with," or "You wear it in the winter."

Another use of the think box is to have parents and children, the day before you use the box, bring things (something soft, something your favorite color, something about an animal, or a picture of something in your house). The enthusiasm of parents and children is usually high. On the teaching day have the child place his object in the box, unseen by others. At the appropriate time the child shows and tells about his object. The setting is very informal so that even the shy child participates. To prevent boredom, select a few different children to bring objects each time the box is used.

Television

Make a television screen by cutting a hole in a large box. Let the children take turns being the actors. You may want to encourage the children to use props.

Another idea is to use a box that is large enough to cut a screen that is visible to the group. Make a continuous story on butcher paper. Roll the story on a dowel and attach the other end of the story to another dowel. As you tell the story, unroll the pictures from one dowel to the other, showing the pictures through the screen.

Application of Principles

1. For one week, note the different activities which are used for transitions. Which ones do the children respond to best?

2. Be particularly aware of the children's actions, voices, and involvement during transitions. How does the tempo in the room change? Are teachers more concerned with things (cleanup, getting next activity ready) or people? Use examples.

3. Plan and use a new transition activity. Begin it as the first child or children assemble. How do things change as more children join the activity?

4. Learn and use four new finger plays in the next month.

5. Memorize and use four poems. Stimulate children to use rhyming words and to write their own poems.

6. Make and use a plan that will use transition periods as learning experiences for children and teachers.

References

Baker, B. R. (1986, Summer). Transition time: Make it a time of learning for children. *Day Care and Early Education,* 36–38.

Berk, L. (1976, November). How well do classroom practices reflect teacher goals? *Young Children, 32,* 64–81.

Branley, F. M. & Vaughan, E. K. (1956). *Mickey's magnet.* New York: Scholastic Book Services.

Hirsch, E. S. (n.d.). *Transition periods: Stumbling blocks of education.* New York: Early Childhood Education Council of New York City.

Langstaff, J. (1957). *Over in the meadow.* New York: Brace & World.

McAfee, O. D. (1985). Circle Time: Getting Past "Two Little Pumpkins." *Young Children, 40*(6), 24–28.

Ramsey, M. E., & Bayless, K. M. (1980). *Kindergarten: Programs and practices.* St. Louis: MO: Mosby.

Seeger, R. (1948). *American folk songs for children* (pp. 130–131). Garden City, NY: Doubleday.

Suggested Curriculum Topics

These topics are provided for teachers to use to give stimulation to the classroom while focusing on the interests and needs of their students. They can also be used successfully in webbing concepts of depth and breadth. (See Chapter 4, Curriculum Development.)

Animals

➤ Care of animals
➤ Names of young and adult animals
➤ Names of male and female animals
➤ Where and how animals live
➤ How animals help people
➤ Coverings (shell, fur, feathers)
➤ Products obtained from animals
➤ Good pets
➤ Wild animals
➤ Circus animals
➤ Protection (claws, camouflage, hibernation)
➤ Characteristics of animals

Birds

➤ Names of birds
➤ Sounds made by birds
➤ Where birds live
➤ How birds feed their young
➤ How birds help people (beauty, sound, eating insects)
➤ Kinds of nests
➤ Kinds of eggs birds lay (color, size)
➤ Characteristics of birds
➤ Habits of birds (nesting, migrations)

Categories

➤ Grouping (vehicles, food, animals, birds, clothing, furniture, persons, buildings, toys, plants, containers, appliances, things to write with, and building, garden, or household tools)
➤ Multiple classification (things that can be classed in more than one category)

➤ Ways to help discriminate between categories (senses, experiences)
➤ Why categories are useful and helpful

The Children

➤ Learning one's own name and worth
➤ Learning names of other children, teachers, nurse, others
➤ Where to hang clothing
➤ Self-confidence
➤ Good self-image
➤ Parts of the body
➤ Complying with requests
➤ Self-mastery and control

Clothing

➤ Names of garments
➤ Seasons for wearing different types of clothing
➤ Sequence for putting on clothing
➤ Types of fabrics (cotton, wool, leather, plastic)
➤ Clothing for different occasions (play, party, sleeping)
➤ Different types of fasteners on clothing (zippers, buttons, snaps)
➤ Uses of certain pieces of clothing (shoes, hats)
➤ Color or patterns in clothing (printed, woven)
➤ Learning to dress and undress dolls

Color

➤ Names of the primary and secondary colors
➤ How various colors are made
➤ Shades of the same color
➤ How various colors make you feel
➤ Uses of colors (for example, red for danger)
➤ Colors of specific objects (fruits, vehicles, animals)
➤ How colors are made and actually making some (berries, leaves)
➤ Tie-dyeing experience

Communication

➤ Physical and verbal communication
➤ Learning about different languages
➤ Different forms of communication (radio, television, newspaper, books, telephone)
➤ Proper names of people, places, and things so that we understand meanings
➤ How some animals help carry messages (dogs, pigeons)
➤ Learning to recognize objects from verbal descriptions only
➤ Telling something interesting about oneself or an activity
➤ Learning to follow simple directions

The Community

➤ Locations within the community
➤ Kinds of buildings, industries, parks, highways
➤ Recognizing community landmarks
➤ Different communities

Community Helpers

➤ Firefighter, police officer, letter carrier, doctor, nurse, dentist, baker, milk carrier, grocer, merchant, miner, farmer, fisher (places of work, activities, services)
➤ How community helpers work together
➤ Recognizing community helpers by uniforms or clothing

Comparatives

➤ Learning names and relationships by comparing two things (biggest/smallest, hottest/coldest, heaviest/lightest; bigger/smaller, fatter/skinnier, taller/shorter; too loud/too soft, too long/too short)
➤ Learning names and relationships by comparing more than two things (big, bigger, biggest; short, shorter, shortest; long, longer, longest)
➤ Learning that one object can be big when compared to some things and small when compared to others
➤ The concept of *middle*
➤ Ordinal (first, second, third) and cardinal (1, 2, 3) numbers
➤ Learning opposites through comparisons (soft, rough)

Days of the Week

➤ Names of the days of the week
➤ Why days have special names
➤ Sequence of the days
➤ Activities for certain days (for example, Saturday or Sunday)
➤ Learning about the calendar (days, weeks, months)

Environment

➤ Characteristics of the community (lakes, mountains)
➤ What pollution is and how to help prevent it
➤ Natural resources (coal, gas, oil)
➤ Conservation of natural resources (forests, water)
➤ Recycling (water, paper, metal)
➤ How to respect public property

Families

➤ Learning what a family is
➤ Learning the immediate family (mother, father, sister, brother, baby)
➤ Learning the extended family (aunts, uncles, cousins, grandparents)
➤ What families do together
➤ Different jobs and responsibilities of family members
➤ Friends and their names
➤ Learning about people (physical characteristics, abilities, likes, and so on)
➤ How to entertain guests
➤ How to get along with family members
➤ Good social techniques

Food (See the sections on food in Chapter 8 and Chapter 11.)

➤ Names of various foods
➤ Tasting various foods

- ➤ Learning about taste (sweet, sour, salty, bitter)
- ➤ Preparing food in a variety of ways
- ➤ Plant parts used as food (roots, stalk, flower)
- ➤ Things that look alike but taste different (salt, sugar, baking soda)
- ➤ Food consumed by animals
- ➤ Preparing for and participating in lunch or snack
- ➤ Good diet (pyramid group)
- ➤ Where food products come from (animals, farms and gardens, factories)
- ➤ Ways of preparing food (raw, boiled, baked)
- ➤ Learning when food is unripe, ripe, and overripe
- ➤ Things *not* to be eaten (poisons, medicines)

Growing Things (See the sections on plants and nature in Chapter 8.)

- ➤ Names of common flowers and plants
- ➤ How to care for plants
- ➤ Different things that plants grow from (bulb, seed, starts)
- ➤ Parts of the plant (root, stalk, vine, leaf, flower)
- ➤ Parts of plants that are edible (root—carrot, turnip; head—lettuce, cabbage; stalk—celery)
- ➤ Sizes and kinds of seeds
- ➤ Length of growing time (for example, rapid for grass and beans; more slowly for corn and squash)
- ➤ Fruits grown on trees
- ➤ Things needed for growth (sunlight, water, warmth)
- ➤ Food that grows above and below the ground
- ➤ Growing things that are not edible
- ➤ Storing fruits and vegetables
- ➤ Why food is washed or cleaned before eating
- ➤ Growing things for beauty (shrubs, trees, flowers) and consumption (fruit, vegetables)

Health and Cleanliness

- ➤ How to clean various body parts (hair, nails, skin, teeth)
- ➤ Reasons for keeping clean and healthy
- ➤ How to keep healthy (exercise, rest, clothing)
- ➤ Proper diet
- ➤ Poisonous plants
- ➤ Professional people who help us

Holidays

- ➤ Names of holidays
- ➤ Activities unique to holidays
- ➤ Importance of holidays to children (birthdays, religious holidays, national, cultural, local, and other important days. (See also Chapter 10)
- ➤ Which holidays come during which seasons
- ➤ Family customs for various holidays
- ➤ National, religious, cultural, and personal holidays of self and others
- ➤ Preparing for and participating in child-centered holiday activities

Homes

- ➤ Where each child lives
- ➤ What a house looks like (inside and out)

➤ Different types of homes in the community
➤ Care of homes (inside and out)
➤ Household equipment and appliances (brushes, mixers, and so on)
➤ Repair and building tools
➤ Homes in other countries or areas
➤ Furnishing rooms
➤ Building materials
➤ Visiting a home or apartment
➤ Performing tasks

Identification

➤ Matching animals (mother and young)
➤ Categorizing what is sold in a specific type of store
➤ Selecting a type of store for a certain item
➤ Things that belong together (fork and spoon, hat and coat, shoe and sock)
➤ How to recognize something by one or more of the senses
➤ How to group objects with similar characteristics (color, material, shape)
➤ How to distinguish between objects

Machines

➤ Machines for the home or for industry: how they work and what their function is
➤ Learning to operate machines (mixer, eggbeater, gears)
➤ How machines make work easier

Materials

➤ Names of different building materials (brick, wood, fiberglass, cement, steel, cinder blocks)
➤ Names and uses of materials (metal, glass, plaster, paper, cardboard, cloth fabrics, leather, rubber, foil)
➤ Fabrics (waterproof, resilient, inexpensive)

Mathematics (See Chapter 9.)

➤ How to count using familiar things (children, blocks, crackers, clapping)
➤ Counting similar and dissimilar objects
➤ Recognizing written symbols
➤ Learning about parts (fractions) of the whole (for example, a wheel is part of a wagon)
➤ Exploring with unit blocks (using different shapes and numbers to make other shapes)
➤ Making things equal
➤ Learning to tell different things by their number (phone, sport participant, house, time)
➤ Buying by weight, size, amount
➤ Mathematical terms (more, less, how many)

Music (See Chapter 7.)

➤ Singing songs
➤ Playing and listening to records and tapes
➤ Names and uses of musical instruments
➤ Ways of making sounds
➤ Classes of instruments (wind, percussion, string)
➤ Different ways music makes us feel

➤ Learning to participate with music
➤ Discovering rhythm in everyday life (clocks, water dripping, walking)
➤ Observing different instruments being played
➤ Imitating music or movement in nature (trees, animals, water)

Objects

➤ Names of parts of an object (for example, a pencil has a point, lead, a shaft, and an eraser)
➤ Different materials used to make same or different objects
➤ Specific uses of different objects (spoon, screwdriver, belt)
➤ Identifying objects through one or more of the senses
➤ Naming several objects used for the same purpose (for example those that hold water or improve surroundings)

Opposites

➤ Learning opposites (big/little, fat/skinny, loud/soft, hot/cold, long/short, fast/slow, wet/dry, smooth/rough, tall/short, dark/light)
➤ Combining opposites (big, rough, and dark)
➤ Discrimination (an object may be big compared to some things and small compared to others)

Pattern

➤ Learning about different patterns (stripped, flowered, polka-dot, plaid, plain, checked)
➤ Learning whether the pattern is woven into fabric or printed
➤ Creating one's own patterns using art materials
➤ How patterns (shapes) are combined in environment

Plagetian Concepts

➤ Conservation of volume or substance
➤ Reversibility (water to ice to water)
➤ Weight of objects (in hand or on scale)
➤ How objects can be grouped in a variety of ways (color, shape, size, material)
➤ Discovering that learning is enhanced through the senses and movement (sensorimotor skills)

Plurals

➤ Regular plurals (formed by adding *s* or *es*)
➤ Irregular plurals (foot/feet, child/children, man/men, tooth/teeth, mouse/mice, sheep/sheep)
➤ Terms used for more than one of an object (*many, few, group, some*)
➤ When one object is called a pair (scissors, glasses, pants)

Prepositions

➤ Names and relationship of various prepositions (*in, on, over, under, next to, in front of, in back of, inside, outside, between*)
➤ How to carry out simple commands
➤ Using one's body in space to learn prepositions (obstacle course)

The Preschool

➤ Labels for materials and objects in the room
➤ Storage place for toys
➤ Places for certain activities
➤ Learning about adults and children
➤ Limits, responsibilities, and privileges
➤ Learning routine

Safety

➤ Times and places to be careful (roads, around water)
➤ How to prevent accidents
➤ Care of injuries
➤ Professional people who help us
➤ Safety at school and home
➤ Reasons for limits under different circumstances
➤ Using tools and materials

Science (See Chapter 8.)

➤ Magnets
➤ Magnifying glasses
➤ How to measure
➤ Heat and how it changes various things
➤ Light and prisms
➤ Heavy and light objects
➤ Liquids, solids, and gases
➤ Physical science
➤ Social science
➤ Producing and preparing food
➤ Working with levers
➤ Biological science
➤ Discovering things about community, nation, and universe
➤ How to get along with others

Seasons

➤ Naming the seasons and characteristics of each season
➤ What people do during different seasons
➤ What people wear during different seasons
➤ How seasons affect families, animals, and plants
➤ Identifying different seasons from pictures

Shapes

➤ Names of shapes (square, circle, triangle, rectangle, oval, diamond, trapezoid)
➤ Uses of different shapes
➤ Looking for various shapes in the room
➤ Discussing shapes in our daily lives
➤ Why certain things are the shapes they are (for example, a wheel)
➤ How various shapes are formed (two semicircles make a circle; two triangles, a trapezoid)
➤ How similar objects (leaves, flowers) are different shapes

➤ Making an original design using a variety of shapes (an art project or manipulative experience, for example)
➤ Characteristics of various shapes (a triangle has three corners; the lines in a square are the same length)

Sound (See Chapters 6 and 8.)

➤ Listening for sounds in everyday life
➤ Distinguishing things by sound only
➤ Differences in sound (high or low, loud or soft)
➤ Different ways of making sounds
➤ Making sounds of animals
➤ Making sounds of transportation vehicles
➤ Making sounds that express different emotions
➤ Saying rhyming words

Temperature

➤ Terms used with heat (hot/warm, cold/cool, hot/cold)
➤ Temperature and the seasons
➤ Temperature and heat in cooking
➤ How a thermometer registers heat or cold

Time

➤ Learning about the present, past, and future (may be difficult to grasp)
➤ Sequence (before and after)
➤ Ways to tell time (clock, sun, sundial)
➤ Things to do in daylight and in the dark

Transportation

➤ Names of kinds of transportation (boat, airplane, bus, train, automobile)
➤ Ways transportation works
➤ What different vehicles carry and how it feels to ride in each
➤ Learning about vehicles
➤ Wheels and how they work
➤ Transportation in air (airplanes, balloons, helicopters); in water (boats, submarines, ferries); on land (cars, trucks, buses); and underground (subways)
➤ Animals used for transportation (horse, camel, elephant)
➤ Animals used for carrying (burro, llama)

B

Suggested Miniplans for Curriculum Chapters

Build upon the interests and suggestions of children. Avoid rigidity and teacher-directed learning. As a foundation for this information, refer to Chapter 4 for discussion and to review the planning steps as follows:

Step 1: Preassess present knowledge or abilities
Step 2: Identify concepts
Step 3: Overview the schedule and complete the plan
Step 4: Implement the plan in the classroom
Step 5: Evaluate the plan and the day
Step 6: Modify the plan for follow-up or expansion of the theme

From the following suggestions, enhance, select, or abandon any ideas for a personal plan that would better suit you and the children in your classroom. (Suggestions are given here to indicate the variety of ways to preassess, to expedite the use of examples, and to encourage the teacher to be innovative within the interests and skills of the children.) The individual teacher is expected to make a completed plan.

Suggestions Related to Language Arts (Chapter 5)

Language arts include reading, listening, writing, and speaking. Young children are not readers, although they enjoy looking at books and hearing stories. Their writing skills are undeveloped, both in using writing implements and in composing their thoughts. For these reasons, a miniplan is proposed here that encourages children to do what they do best—speak! Young children need to speak fluently and confidently; therefore, this plan is centered on the child's self-image.

These miniplans will follow the previous format; however, they will be in less detail to reduce redundancy—the reader should refer to the previous plan for ideas, sequence, and support.

Step 1: Preassess Present Knowledge or Abilities

➤ Observe the children to determine the ranges of self-image. (Some verbal children are confident and others are insecure. Some nonverbal children are confident and others are insecure.) After making written or mental notes about the confidence and security of each child in your classroom, share your thoughts with other teachers for accuracy, then observe the children again in different activities to solidify or modify the individual assessment.

Step 2: Identify Concepts

➤ Note that sometimes concepts are actual statements or ideas that could be made to children, sometimes they are ideas on which to build, sometimes they remind teachers of goals, sometimes they are forthright statements of fact, and sometimes they indicate a direction that can be used or modified at the time of teaching.

➤ One of your goals in using *this* plan is to help each child feel good about himself. Avoid comparison between children, among cultures, and within personal preference. Each child is special and has individual worth. Aim for personal and group concepts by highlighting individual assets, by helping each child feel more confident than before the topic, and by helping the children acknowledge and appreciate the uniqueness of each child. All comments, actions, and encouragement must be honest and sincere, and teachers must realize that to develop a good self-image is an ongoing—never a one-time—procedure!

➤ After carefully identifying how each child feels about herself, write some proposed individual and group concepts. For example, from observation and consultation, you may note that the children speak in varying degrees of loudness, interact within a select group, avoid certain types of activities, and are either passive or active depending on who is participating or the tone of the activity. For this exercise, assume that the following concepts are appropriate:

Because children use different pitches and kinds of responses, teachers should listen intently when a child is speaking. (Sarah yells for attention, Juan withdraws, Peter speaks too rapidly, Ana is bilingual and gets the languages mixed, and so on.)

Focus: By listening carefully and giving the child full attention, the child will be able to express himself more freely and feel that what is said is of worth.

Different activities encourage or discourage child participation. More active settings (blocks, riding toys, climbing, and so on) discourage younger, less developed, and insecure children from participating.

Focus: Invite reticent children to participate by limiting the size of the group and by staying close by for verbal and physical support, when needed. This will give the children an opportunity to participate without being overwhelmed by the noise and skills of more active children.

Initiate activities by using more quiet children as the nucleus (introducing a new toy, helping with visuals, leading an activity, and so on).

Focus: Avoid putting a child on the spot or insisting he be the center of attention when this is uncomfortable for the child.

Encourage children to talk about themselves and others in a positive and supportive way.

Focus: Help each child think and speak positively, comfortably, and happily about herself and others.

Step 3: Make an Overview, Select and Schedule Activities, and Complete the Plan

➤ Encourage a shy or reticent child to participate in a small group.
➤ Give honest verbal, facial, and physical support to each child.

➤ Provide activities that call the child's attention to constructive things about his body and abilities:

Draw or trace an outline of the child's body and encourage the child to color or cut it out (include ponytails, boots, and so on).

Provide materials and activities that are open-ended (child's choice rather than patterned).

Provide puzzles of body parts, occupations, cultures, and so on.

Help the children to learn about and use tools properly (woodworking, scissors, cooking utensils).

Display the child's work at school and home.

Encourage children to work in pairs, as buddies, or in teams.

Give the child a respectable responsibility, such as preparing snack and tables, holding doors open, watering plants, caring for pets, putting away toys, getting needed items, and so on.

Do a simple game such as "Do as I'm Doing," where the child sets the activity (but be ready with some suggestions).

➤ Talk about similar and different physical characteristics of the children—who has blue eyes, how many have blond hair, and so on. Do this in a way that attracts children to each other—never as a judgment of better or best.

➤ Consider the group carefully to determine which (if any) children are ready for show-and-tell activity or if it will become too teacher-centered. A similar idea could be used with a friend or small group of children so the child does not feel intimidated.

➤ Well-placed pictures in the classroom will give children information about different activities, cultures, locations, and so on. Such pictures often encourage individual or group conversations.

➤ If possible, see the child in settings outside the classroom (home visits, shopping, at the park, and so on).

➤ Occasionally have a parent or family member visit the classroom and tell something special about the child. Or the teacher could have a conversation with a family member and casually mention something special about a child.

➤ Do activities where the names of the children are emphasized or play noncompetitive games where children are described and others try to guess who it is, and so on. Call the children by their names and encourage others to do so also.

Procedures

➤ Focus on some general group concepts or goals and highlight one or two children.

➤ Make children feel that they belong: on the entry door, place a small photograph of each child who belongs in that room, give each one a place for personal items, and identify it with a label, picture, or sticker.

➤ Never compare the children to each other. Rather, help each child to see personal progress—running faster, doing harder activities, verbalizing rather than using physical attacks, getting taller, and so on.

➤ Have quiet areas where children can sit, look at books, play in quiet activities, or visit with one another.

➤ Place appropriate books, flannel boards and characters, and other visual aids where children will use them. Consider such things as developmental abilities of the children, present interests or ideas to be introduced, good cultural and role models, children interacting with other children, and so on.

➤ When possible, assist the children in making rules that are important for specific situations and help them to understand the reasons of rule making. Where rules are necessary, help the children discuss the problems and how to resolve them.

Many of these suggestions could be used on any day with any topic; however, try to fit some, all, or substitutions into a session that would enhance the self-image of each and every child. Incidentally, you could be increasing the self-image of teachers and supporting staff as well!

Step 4: Implement the Plan

➤ With a completed plan, the needed materials, support of teachers, and enthusiasm, you are ready to have a fun and important period with the children. Note their reactions, their comments, and their interactions. What new combinations of children did you see as a result of the activities or ideas? Which children were more or less verbal today? How will you plan to help the children further develop friendships and increase their understanding of themselves and others?

Step 5: Evaluate the Plan

➤ Armed with your plan and your notes, pause for a thoughtful evaluation of what occurred during play and activity periods. Which of your ideas were most successful—and why? Where was the activity or interaction terminated abruptly because of lack of time or too many choices? When did you hear children referring to other children by name—were there increases over previous times?

Step 6: Modify the Plan for Follow-Up or Expansion of the Theme

➤ Promotion of good self-image in children has just begun. Note which children are more popular and which are less popular within the group. Make mental or written notes as to how to help all children learn to interact more favorably with all children. Make a reminder (perhaps a chart) to help you relate with all children. Every single day all teachers should have private or small-group conversations with each child. It may help to focus on one or two children each week, but never overlook any child—whether it is focus week or not. Often feedback from parents will help build a stronger relationship with each child. If a child feels ignored or disliked, she may resort to negative behavior just to be noticed! Don't let this happen in your classroom!
➤ In every session, deliberately plan something that will build good personal and group relationships. (For example, in books, stories, and visual aids, select those that are complimentary, are nonstereotypical, show variety [ethnicity, age, handicaps, abilities, and so on], encourage cooperation, and can be put into immediate use by the children.)

Suggestions Related to a Sensory Experience (Chapter 6)

Step 1: Preassess Present Knowledge About Sound

➤ Show objects that make specific sounds (bell ringing, water dripping, clock ticking, and so on). Have a child imitate a sound of one of the objects and ask the other children to select the proper object. With very young children, make sure the object is familiar and has a definite sound. Some children will describe sounds differently for the same object. Accept their ideas unless they are totally inappropriate.
➤ Have objects behind a screen. Make the sound of each object separately and ask the children to identify the object. Use familiar objects and then introduce a new or slightly more difficult one.
➤ Show pictures of objects and have the children imitate the sound identified with each object. In order to make this an effective experience, include some objects that are

noiseless (a cotton ball dropped on the table, a Band-Aid being applied, a spider walking, and so on).

➤ Prerecord familiar indoor and outdoor sounds on a tape recorder. As the tape is played, have the children imitate the sound (brushing teeth, answering phone, raking leaves, and so on). Then play a series of sounds and help the children make a sequential story using the sounds.

➤ Ask the children to listen to sounds during a play period and then share their findings during a group time. Teachers may need to add visuals or clues to help the children remember over a period of time.

➤ Using one item (perhaps a musical instrument), demonstrate and help the children identify characteristics of that item (fast, slow; high, low; sharp, sustained; loud, soft; and so on).

➤ Talk about how sounds help people: warning (emergency vehicles), schedules (bells, timers, telephones), pleasure (sports whistles, music), and others.

➤ Sing a song that has different sounds, such as "The Wheels on the Bus," "Old McDonald Had a Farm," or others. Accept the sounds the children offer. Even sing the song different ways. For example, the horn on the bus may go "beep, beep, beep" or "honk, honk, honk." It really doesn't have to have *one* specific sound.

Step 2: Identify Concepts

➤ The teacher identifies some basic concepts and begins a tentative plan as to which concepts would interest or bore the children, where the concepts would be most appropriately placed, what would be a reasonable length of time, and other considerations.

Step 3: Make an Overview, Select and Schedule Activities, and Complete the Plan

➤ An inexhaustible list is made of activities and materials that would present clear and accurate concepts about hearing—based on the current developmental level of the children for whom the plan is intended. Some ideas are included in the plan, others are excluded entirely or held for future teaching; however, the entire list is retained for future use.

➤ Suppose the teacher narrows down the prospective ideas to talking with the children at group time; playing a sound game; using a story, a tape recorder, and a workable telephone; placing pictures of noisy and quiet items on the walls; and an art activity. Preassessment is completed and one or more of the ideas suggested in Step 1, or personally developed ideas, are selected.

➤ Prior to the teaching day, the teacher preassesses current knowledge of the children using one or more of the ideas suggested in Step 1 or personally developed ideas. (Items usually included on the plan are general findings of the preassessment, suggested concepts, an outline for the day's activities, evaluation suggestions, and follow-through for parents. (See Figure 4.3 Daily Planning Outline, p. 128.)

For this example, consider the following:

General Findings

➤ Some children readily recognize and imitate sounds in the classroom and home.

➤ Some children need the object and sound to make a clear distinction.

➤ Several of the children offer no comments when listening to sounds in general; others boisterously make requested sounds and volunteer others.

➤ Focusing on sound would be of interest and value to the children at this time.

Concepts to Be Taught

These are broad enough for the needs of individual children, yet specific enough to have a focus.

Suppose the teacher selects one or more of the following:

➤ Sounds are all around us.
➤ Sounds have different meanings.
➤ Different sounds make us feel differently.
➤ Caring for our ears is important because they help us identify sounds.

Outline for the Day's Activities

➤ Assume that the session is for a half day and is divided into four periods: arrival, activity playtime, gathering time, and departure (closing). Activity playtime and gathering time may occur more than once during the day. For some suggestions, see Table B.1

Step 4: Implement the Plan

➤ The plan is carried out. Teachers take *quick* notes of things that went well, things that were troublesome, comments and activities of children, and other occurrences that reflect on the plan and individual children.

Step 5: Evaluate the Plan

➤ In planning (and *before* the plan is implemented), the teacher records some areas of focus for evaluation, hoping or assuming there will be some comments, questions, or

Table B.1   Suggestions for a Miniplan Involving Sound

Curriculum Area	Activity Playtime (large block of time)	Gathering Time (smaller block of time)
Creative, Artistic, and Sensory Expression (Chapter 6)	Transportation vehicles near blocks, housekeeping area with household utensils, pictures placed at eye level, books and tapes in a reading area, prerecorded sound tape and player, self-selection of toys. At this or a selected time the teachers and children could go on a listening walk in their school, on the playground, or nearby. Climbing and riding toys, digging and hauling tools, running and playing activities are available. Some children continue the idea of listening for sounds.	Sound experiences (values of being in a group include: verbalizing and listening, broader understanding of topic, interaction with teacher and group, cooperation); pictures associated with sounds; tape for identifying and/or imitating household, community, transportation, and animal sounds; identifying sounds of items not visible (bell, clock, eggbeater or mixer, squeaky toy, musical instrument, and so on); informal discussion about care, importance, and use of ears using a large model ear; importance of sounds: danger or safety, pleasant and soothing activity, reminders (whistles, bells, warnings), and so on; story and tape "The Listening Walk" by Paul Showers (or an original story and tape) are used; snack of foods that make sounds (crunching of apples or celery, munching of crackers, squeaking of raisins, and so on).

suggestions relating to the plan. These are the items for discussion but may include spontaneous ones as well.

➤ After implementing the plan, teachers use the evaluation as a period of sharing notes and feelings in a discussion rather than as a checklist. Why were some things successful and others unsuccessful? Notations of additions, deletions, substitutions, and so on are made right on the plan for future reference.

Step 6: Modify the Plan for Follow-up or Expansion of the Theme

➤ The teachers discuss the comments and actions of the children, then note on the plan some ideas for future teaching on this same topic. What children understood the concepts? Which ones showed special interest in the topic? How could you increase the knowledge of the immature children *and* the mature children without boring some and frustrating others? Young children need many opportunities to learn about their world as an entity in itself and as a part of their global world. Return to Chapter 1 and review the discussion of the Reflection symbol on p. 13.

➤ The plan, notes, teaching aids, and so on are fields for future use. This gives the teacher incentive to try the topic again soon—either with the same children, with a different group, or as a stepping stone for review or for integrated or more complex information.

Suggestions Related to Music and Movement (Chapter 7)

Although some teachers are very hesitant to teach about music (rhythm, musical instruments, sound, and so on), it seems that even more teachers feel that physical activity will come whether or not there are attempts to promote it. True, many children learn to run, jump, and climb without adult interference; however, because of the impact one feels related to one's body performance, the miniplan for this chapter will be on development for both large and small muscles.

Step 1: Preassess Present Abilities

➤ Focusing on the motor skills of each child, the teacher can determine how the child feels about himself. Age must be a factor in assessing the small- and large-muscle development of each child. Younger and inexperienced children practice large-muscle skills (running, climbing, carrying, and so on). As the child feels more confidence in using large muscles through opportunities and experience, the control and use of small muscles takes on new importance; therefore, expect skills to be at different levels for different children, expect children to use their bodies differently, expect attitudes about their abilities to be different, and expect some children to avoid experiences that may indicate their immaturity.

➤ In determining the small motor skills of the children, provide activities in which eye-hand coordination is important (cutting with *good* scissors, pegs and boards, puzzles, threading, pouring, and so on). Get a feeling for the individual child and for the group (some do this, most do that, none do that).

➤ In determining the large motor skills of the children, provide activities in which arms and legs are used individually or together (climbing, pedaling, catching, running, and so on). Get a feeling for the individual child and for the group (some, most, one).

Step 2: Identify Concepts

➤ Note which children seem deficient in small, large, or both motor skills. Note which children seem proficient in one or both motor skills.

➤ Make this a fun experience—one that the children will enjoy and want to repeat by themselves or through assistance. Emphasis on this topic is not to make children perform better for us but to give them opportunities that increase their self-image, provide additional experiences, and stimulate interaction with peers and adults.

➤ For *this* exercise, concepts will be related to teaching techniques and activities rather than direct statements about the learning of the children.

➤ Activities emphasizing the use of small or large muscles may be inappropriate for some children in their present state of development.

➤ Some activities and materials may be growth-promoting for some children and growth-stunting for others.

➤ Many children practice small- and/or large-muscle development through ideas and opportunities that interest them—not necessarily only those that are teacher-oriented.

Step 3: Make an Overview, Select and Schedule Activities, and Complete the Plan

Overview the supporting activities for this plan; suggestions are given for curriculum areas or time periods.

Activity Playtime

Free Play

➤ *Table toys* (usually small-muscle or eye-hand coordination): puzzles; pegs and boards; stringing objects; small building materials; frames or opportunities (housekeeping area) for lacing, tying, buttoning, zipping, dressing; pouring water or sensory materials (wheat, rice, flour); books and visual aids with flannel boards; and so on

➤ *Floor toys* (usually large-muscle coordination): blocks, transportation vehicles, jungle gyms

➤ *Art:* scissors (good quality), tearing, pasting, painting with brushes, block or stamp printing, collage, crayons, felt pens, finger painting, clothespins for hanging artwork

➤ *Outdoors* (usually large-muscle activities): walking boards, boxes, obstacle course, wheel toys, climbing gyms, nets, ladders, woodworking tools, Frisbees, balls, parachute, gardening, games

Gathering Time

➤ *Stories:* Engage children in physical activities, art activities, activities with pets, and planting (See Chapter 6 for related literature).

➤ *Snack:* soft spreads (butter, peanut butter) with small knives and crackers/bread, pouring own beverage (sponges handy and no pressure), finger foods (vegetables, fruit), and so on. Children can help prepare and serve food.

➤ *Music:* rhythm instruments, participation records, finger plays, songs

➤ *Games:* "Head, Shoulders, Knees, and Toes," "If You're Happy and You Know It," "Hokey Pokey," "Do as I'm Doing," the sponge game. *Note:* Use games that encourage children to participate in their own ways and at their own speed—*avoid* games that teach competition between children or that reveal immaturity of the child ("Simon Says," musical chairs, and so on).

➤ Completing the plan

From these options, a completed plan could be as follows:

Activity Playtime

➤ *Housekeeping area:* Dress-up clothes, dishes, food cartons, dolls, stuffed animals, and so on

➤ *Table toys:* Puzzles of children and activities; small plastic bricks, cash register and tokens, stringing large beads
➤ *Floor toys:* Large unit blocks with various types of vehicles; a portable climbing gym; perhaps hula hoops to define a space for a child
➤ *Quiet area:* Cozy reading corner with books, pillows, stuffed toys
➤ *Sponge game:* Each child is given a sponge approximately 4 by 6 inches. Color is no consideration. The leader (teacher or child) gives ideas and children perform them: "Put the sponge on your head." "Put the sponge on your foot," and so on. Sometimes the instructions include "See if you can walk with the sponge on your head without the sponge falling off," or "Get on your hands and knees, put the sponge on your back, and keep it from falling off."
➤ Tell a story about a child who learns to do more things because he is getting older, more experienced, or more confident (for example, Krauss, *The Growing Story,* published in 1947 by Harper's Children's Books; see Chapter 6, or write an original story appropriate for the children in this classroom).

Now complete the plan following your schedule and the needs of the children in the particular group. Provide for activity time, gathering time, outdoor activities, creative art, music, and so on.

Step 4: Implement the Plan

➤ Note carefully the way the children (individually and collectively) respond to activities, peers, adults, and materials. Make short notes throughout the day.

Step 5: Evaluate the Plan

➤ Using the notes from Step 4 and recalling individual children and activities, share ideas and feelings about the day with other staff members. What indications were there that the plan was successful or unsuccessful? Which children were involved and which children seemed to be discouraged? Give examples. Plan additional moderate stretching for each child, and each day include some type of physical- and self-image-promoting ideas.

Step 6: Modify the Plan for Follow-Up or Expansion of the Theme

➤ From experiencing the day with the children and through careful observation, what would you include or exclude the next time this topic is introduced? How important is it that children are encouraged at their present stage and find success for at least trying the activities? Plan additional moderate stretching activities for each child. Include some type of self-image-promoting ideas daily. Discuss how the staff can give *honest, sincere* praise to each child. Which would be more appropriate: (1) other days focused on large/small-muscle development, or (2) planning carefully for each child? A good self-image is important for children and adults. Begin now to promote healthy concepts in yourself, the children, other staff members, and other contacts.

Add music to activities and have a whole new experience.

Suggestions Related to Biological and Physical Science (Chapter 8)

For simplification, two broad categories of science have been identified: biological and physical. For books and other teaching materials, see both biological and physical references in Chapter 8.

Science can be one of the most exciting, interesting, challenging, and fun topics for young children. They are interested in everything—especially when they discover things for themselves.

Almost everything can fit into science in one or many ways, but as an example, we will use water, a very common, inexpensive, mesmerizing, and versatile medium. It is hoped the reader will be willing to provide simple water experiences for our youngest children and then to develop the topic in a variety of ways for older children. Today adults spend much time researching the properties and benefits of water, results of drought and pollution, and water's other characteristics and uses. It is vital to our survival.

Step 1: Preassess Present Knowledge

➤ Tubs and water for bathing dolls, plastic animals, doll clothes, pouring and measuring, cleanup after art or other activities, painting metal or nonharmful surfaces with a brush and bucket of water, or other water activities more suited to your location, facilities, and staff
➤ Adding water to other media: powdered paint, frozen juices, sensory table, recipes, and so on
➤ Washing fruits and/or vegetables for snack or lunch
➤ An experience related to cleanliness of the body (personal habits) and clothes (washing, frequent changes, proper fit, and so on)
➤ Caring for classroom or family pets
➤ Different weather conditions: heat, snow, rain, fog
➤ Water play outdoors (hose, small wading pool, bathing suits, buckets)
➤ Occupations that depend on water
➤ Caring for plants and gardens
➤ Different climates or physical locations (near bodies of water, deserts, cold regions)
➤ And many more suggestions—some of them more appropriate for some locations, ages, or situations and others less appropriate until the children have more experience and background in the topic
➤ The teacher should have some ideas about what to preassess and what will be presented to the children; otherwise, the preassessment could be long, frustrating, and meaningless. Remember that most children (young and old) thoroughly enjoy pouring and measuring water. Help them to move beyond this stage and still enjoy the simple properties of water.

Step 2: Identify Concepts

➤ For a very young child or one who has had little experience with water except to drink it or splash in it during a bath or on a hot day: This child will thoroughly enjoy pouring, spilling on herself and the floor, and taking an occasional drink. She will be totally absorbed and it will be important for her to have a comfortable feeling about her actions—even though a puddle will occur. The child is learning about the properties of water and what she can do with it. Pouring will be inaccurate as eye-hand coordination begins. When the child tires of the activity, give her a sponge or towel and help her wipe up the excess water, all the time talking about the activity and the feelings it brought. Provide this type of experience frequently along with other pouring and water experiences: helping pour her own beverage, cleaning up, and using water in a variety of ways.
➤ For the older preschool child who has had some water and pouring experiences: He will still want to pour and measure. He will recognize the use of water in other activities: mixing paint, playing at the sensory table, watering plants and animals, and so on. He is now ready for some expanding experiences. One day you may provide ob-

jects for the children to predetermine if the objects will sink or float (providing proper jargon). Another day, experiment with evaporation or the three different properties of water (liquid, solids, gases). Still another day, talk about occupations related to water because of community dependency on water. Your teaching and provision of activities and information will all be on the appropriate level of the children because you have preassessed well and have patiently led the children to this point of understanding.

Step 3: Overview the Schedule, Select Activities and Materials, and Complete the Plan

Few teachers have children of the same developmental and interest level in their preschool classrooms, so plan some basic or repeated experiences for the younger or less mature children and also consider the older and more mature children. Plan to challenge both younger and older children—but at their pace and interest level.

➤ In science activities, plan to use many open-ended materials: those that can be continued for a period of time or can be terminated easily, according to the child's interests. Insisting that a child remain at an activity a certain length of time or to a certain point of completion could discourage him from coming to an activity at another time. Likewise, help the child develop enough interest so that the activity offers something to him now and for the future.

➤ Along with focused activities, set out some familiar activities so the child can move to areas of interest. Help the children to see how ideas fit together. Listen to the children. Pick up on their interests for future science experiences.

➤ In spontaneous ways (singing, poetry, conversation, activities) show the children some of the marvels of our world. Reward the children for showing new interest, curiosity, or discovering something. That's what science is all about!

➤ It certainly isn't necessary to set up a theme or period on science. You can teach it in many ways every day, but once in a while it is stimulating to focus on some scientific ideas.

Step 4: Implement the Plan

➤ Throughout each day, teachers (adults) should be constantly aware of the many planned and spontaneous scientific happenings that are meaningful to the children and their understanding of their environment. Build on them by providing verbal support, physical proximity, and additional materials, and by encouraging the children to work together.

Step 5: Evaluate the Plan

➤ Reflect on how the children approached and used the situations that were provided for them. Could these experiences be enhanced and used again, or were they not on target for these children on this day?

➤ Which children participated in group activities? Which comments of the children led you to believe that they had either understood or misunderstood the concepts presented? Which activities need to be repeated on a simplified level and which ones were too familiar or too easy for the children? How can you tell if any learning occurred? Discuss the feelings (excited, frustrated, challenged, satisfied, indifferent, and so on) of the adults who interacted with the children. How can you encourage children and adults to be excited about science experiences? Which activities or children got out of control, what were the causes, and were these situations healthy or detrimental to the topic?

Step 6: Modify the Plan for Follow-Up or Expansion of the Theme

➤ Teachers should be constantly alert for comments or activities of the children that reflect on scientific concepts. Teachers can reinforce or clarify concepts by having a repertoire of poems, songs, activities, suggestions, and physical and verbal support ready for spontaneous interaction.

➤ Children can learn that there are many ways to solve problems—not just one stereotyped way. But to learn this, they must experience the environment on their own developmental level, according to their own personal time schedule, and in an accepting and loving environment. Children should not be afraid to explore and experiment within guidelines that protect them from harm, that do not impose on the rights of others, and that do not become stagnant.

➤ Become a careful observer and listener. Note the many different ways water could be introduced into your classroom and the many benefits children would gain from such exposure. How can you tie water into snack/lunch? Into a gathering time? Into outdoor play? When would it be better for individual play rather than a group setting? What community activities require water for their success? How could you incorporate water into other curriculum areas, such as language arts, sensory experiences, social science, health, or mathematics?

Suggestions Related to Mathematics (Chapter 9)

The theme for this section is numbers and counting.

Step 1: Preassess Present Knowledge

Adults can determine the understanding and limitations of number symbols, number concepts, and number uses of young children as adults talk with or observe the play of these children.

Here are some quick and easy ways to determine number knowledge of young children.

➤ Count aloud from 1 to 10 with the children (use no visual aids). See how many can count correctly.

➤ Count objects aloud from 1 to 10 with the children.

➤ Invite a couple of children to help set the table for snack or lunch. How many napkins, chairs, and so on will you need at each table? Does the teacher need to place the correct number of chairs and tell the children to put a napkin by each chair, or can the teacher tell the children a number of places to set?

➤ As a table activity, a game, or a one-on-one activity, have a set of number cards. Showing the cards individually, ask the child to say the number of the symbol shown. Or hand the child a set of numbers 1 to 10 and ask that they be put in order. For the child who is having difficulty with these requests, end the experience here for now. For the child who can do this easily, see if she can put them in descending order. For the child who can do both of these things easily, mix some number symbols with some letters of the alphabet and ask the child to make a stack of numbers and one of letters.

➤ Do some finger plays involving numbers. Remember that ascending counting is much easier for young children than descending counting.

➤ Ask a child his age. Note whether he tells a number, shows a number of fingers, or uses both a number and finger gestures: Do they correspond? (For example, does the child say, "I'm two" but display four fingers?) (I had a verbal, intelligent 3-year-old boy in a group who insisted that he was "40" no matter how often or when you asked him.)

➤ Use spinner games. If necessary, help the children relate the number spun on the spinner with the written number and how to move that many spaces.

➤ For less experienced children, do spontaneous counting when appropriate. For more experienced children, help them use numbers in their play. ("There are four boys and one apple. How can we cut the apple so each boy can have an equal part of the apple?") ("How many firefighter hats do we need so everyone can have one?" or "How can we share four hats when there are six children?") Some children think that size has to do with quantity—for example, coin concepts are difficult, some children would rather have a penny or nickel than a dime because of size.

➤ Listen carefully to the conversation of the children. They frequently use numbers. Do they use them correctly? Do the other children understand their meaning?

➤ Be careful to help children build positive concepts about numbers. Drill, excessive repetition, boredom, pressure, or performance can be detrimental to young children.

➤ In ways to improve communication, use stories, songs, and other opportunities to introduce verbal and written language and number concepts. (Examples: After reading *Ask Mr. Bear* by M. Flack [1991, Macmillan Children's Book Group], help the children count the number of animals or suggested gifts for the child's mother; set out a flannel board and number cutouts for manipulation and discussion; display pictures related to number—one dog, two cats, three birds; provide a set of hand puppets, then help the children count them and separate them into groups: family, animals, birds, and so on.)

Step 2: Identify Concepts

There will probably be great variation in the knowledge and use of numbers for young children. Many activities can be provided that will allow the child to explore and experiment at an individual pace. In this way older children are likely to assist younger or less experienced children, but may not be able to explain the reasoning behind number use. For very young children, ability to count or identify number symbols is of limited value.

➤ Children of similar (and different) ages have a different knowledge base regarding numbers and counting.

➤ Using numbers can simplify some tasks.

➤ A healthy attitude about numbers and mathematical concepts sets a good basis for later knowledge.

Note: Identify concepts for a particular group of children based on their present knowledge and good later learning habits. The three suggestions given here are general.

Step 3: Make an Overview, Select and Schedule Activities, and Complete the Plan

➤ Think about the concepts to be emphasized. Carefully consider what activities or parts of the day would be most useful to present information or activities. Make the activities fit naturally into the flow of the schedule—a teacher may see a relationship between concepts and activities, but children might not. Watch for spontaneous opportunities to talk about numbers without unduly promoting them.

➤ Most of the activities should be open-ended: things that a child can do at her present stage of development but that are also slightly challenging. Less experienced children may try to use materials in unique or unrelated ways; more advanced children may go beyond your planning. Make quick but careful notations of the behavior and comments of different children so that follow-up planning will be valuable.

➤ More awareness will be generated on the topic while planning is in progress, so make some questions or identify focal points for discussion that will follow the implementation of the plan.

Step 4: Implement the Plan

➤ Throughout the period when the plan is used, make observations and notations for future building of number concepts, but do not let note taking distract you from interacting with the children. Use number concepts when possible, but do not overload the children by overemphasis on the topic.

Step 5: Evaluate the Plan

➤ This is where the questions or concerns identified in Step 3 will become of value. Were the concerns justified? What changes would make the topic and the plan more appropriate for another time or another group of children? How were the time periods handled? Also raise new questions, ask for feelings and suggestions of staff members, and discuss behavior of individual children as well as the group as a whole.

Step 6: Modify the Plan for Follow-Up or Expansion of the Theme

➤ How can numbers, counting, and mathematical concepts be a part of daily routines without boring the children?
➤ How can staff members help children enjoy and use number concepts in their daily lives?
➤ How can number concepts be integrated naturally into other curriculum areas—art, science, language arts, and so on?
➤ Which children are still in the one-to-one correspondence stage? What are some interesting ideas to give them more experience?
➤ Which children could accurately count to 10 before this experience? Which children can now accurately count to 10? Which children can now accurately count beyond 10? How can number experiences be enriched for them?
➤ How can staff members help children develop a positive attitude toward number use? What are good ways to assist children to count accurately? What are some *spontaneous* ways to introduce numbers? What are some *planned* ways to introduce numbers?
➤ What is the attitude of staff members toward number concepts? Do they need assistance in changing from a negative to a positive attitude? If so, how can this be accomplished?

Suggestions Related to Social Studies (Chapter 10)

There are many lesson plan topics that could easily and profitably be addressed in this chapter. Learning about oneself, one's family and surroundings, varied occupations, field trips, and other subtopics are but a few examples; however, a very timely topic is getting along with others who are similar to or different from us. This topic should be planned for and considered each and every day. Here is a suggested, tentative plan encouraging teachers and children to be more aware of their environment, the people in it, and different sets of circumstances.

Step 1: Preassess Present Knowledge

➤ In most groups of children receiving care and education outside the home, there are children and adults of diverse races, backgrounds, goals, and attitudes. Also, most young children are not yet prejudiced or competitive. Table B.2 shows a number of areas to preassess.
➤ As is very evident, there are many aspects of an anti-bias curriculum. It would be overwhelming and foolish to think one can teach all the necessary concepts *in one day* or *only once*.

Table B.2   Encouraging Harmony, Understanding, and Social Relationships in Young Children

Focus	Considerations
Race	Make notations about the ethnic background of each person in the classroom—not in an effort to categorize individuals, but to plan for diversity in teaching. Lack of ethnic diversity is not an excuse to avoid it. Children need to learn about ethnic and other differences in a warm, accepting atmosphere.
Culture	There are more aspects to culture than how a person dresses or what he eats. These can become more apparent through firsthand experiences.
Gender	It no longer is appropriate to classify people or occupations based on gender.
Age	Individuals of all ages should receive and give respect to others. Very young children have different needs than older children, just as young adults differ from elderly people.
Socioeconomic status	Many young children are unaware of or unconcerned with monetary conditions; however, many young children live in economically deprived situations. Differences can be understood and handled through teaching and learning experiences in the classroom.
Abilities or disabilities	There is much focus on and awareness of individuals with differing abilities and needs. When young children are made aware of these differences, they respond much more positively than when they are exposed to these differences at an older age.
Home situations	No two children experience the same situations at home. Some must deal with low self-esteem, disabilities, divorce and/or dual custody, death of a loved one, absence of one or both parents (war, separation), illness/disease (temporary or terminal), multigenerational living, adoptive or foster homes, poverty, security, hygiene, lack of medical and dental attention, immunizations, and other circumstances.
Personal characteristics	Low self-esteem, physical appearance, skills (physical, verbal, intellectual), social attitude, allergies.

Step 2: Identify Concepts

➤ This type of teaching needs to go on every day, in every activity, and with every person. It is more about teaching *attitudes* than a topic. The teacher needs to carefully consider the composition of the group (children and adults) and make some short-range and long-range plans—then teach with patience, love, and understanding.

➤ No specific concepts are given for this example because each group of children is so different. Teachers can observe situations and then discuss them and children in staff meetings in order to determine a positive approach for this group of children at this particular time.

Step 3: Make an Overview, Select and Schedule Activities, and Complete the Plan

➤ Have individual family members share some of their customs (beginning with food and dress, but going beyond as the children can assimilate the information).

➤ Have pictures, songs, visual aids, and so on available, and talk about how occupations can be performed by males and females.

➤ If someone in the group has a disability, talk about it. If not, visit someone who is disabled.

➤ Openly talk about diseases—communicable, terminal.
➤ See the breakdown in Step 1, p. 484. Write new suggestions/ideas.
➤ Write new pertinent suggestions/ideas.

Step 4: Implement the Plan
Step 5: Evaluate the Plan

When evaluating each plan, note especially the daily focus on the progress of positive attitudes and/or suggestions for creating and promoting an anti-bias curriculum.

➤ Note the attitudes and activities of different children as they enlarge their group of friends, as they build tolerance and acceptance, and as they express themselves verbally.

Step 6: Modify the Plan for Follow-Up or Expansion of the Theme

➤ As it is a lifelong task to help promote love and understanding of other people, watch for children and adults who need extra support because of their diversity or because of their attitudes. (Check Chapter 10 for supplementary books on this topic.)

Suggestions Related to Nutrition and Health (Chapter 11)

The theme for this section is that good food helps build strong bodies.

Step 1: Preassess Present Knowledge

➤ Based on the concepts to be introduced or enhanced, devise a number of ways of finding out what the children already know—without resorting strictly to questioning, especially closed-ended questions. Watch and listen to the children during their play, provide props that will suggest the topic, and note what would be important for them to know about nutrition: Do they appear to be well nourished, have infrequent illnesses, have habits of cleanliness, enjoy various foods, and so on?
➤ List several ways to preassess the children.

Step 2: Identify Concepts

Based on your preassessment, how could a topic on nutrition benefit the children and/or their families? What simple, basic concepts are important for them at this time and stage of development? Introduce some familiarity but slightly stretch their thinking and behavior.

➤ Some foods are better for the body than are other foods.
➤ Children can help select, prepare, and serve healthy foods.
➤ Healthy food helps the body have more energy.
➤ It is important to have clean hands when handling food.
➤ Besides good food, other things help promote a strong body, such as good personal habits, checkups, rest and exercise, the environment, and other things. (This will be a casual mention so the children will realize that *not* just good food keeps them healthy. This could be a later topic.)
➤ For teachers and children: If young children learn about nutrition at a young age and discuss the knowledge often, they may be more conscious of eating good food and developing nutrition goals.

➤ As you identify concepts to emphasize, also think about some discussion questions for the evaluation after the plan has been implemented. (Which children commented about the topic? How could you tell if the children gained *correct* concepts? If you were to use this plan again, on which activities would you put more or less emphasis? How would you make a follow-up plan and how soon would you reintroduce the topic?)

Step 3: Make an Overview, Select and Schedule Activities, and Complete the Plan

➤ Begin with a general schedule overview. Fill in the curriculum and time periods with activities and materials appropriate for the theme. Add, delete, and substitute activities that would be most meaningful to these children. Eliminate activities that do not fit naturally or smoothly into the schedule. (Some diversions from the theme would be expected.)

➤ To give versatility to planning, rather than putting this topic into a time and activity frame, brainstorm how to best support the identified concepts. Consider the following: The first exposure to the topic should be an overview. Then make follow-up plans to discuss specific types of food—perhaps a plan on fruit, one on vegetables, one on grains, one on meat and meat products, one on dairy products, or any combination that meets the needs of the children in the group.

➤ Display and discuss the Food Group Pyramid by the U.S. Department of Agriculture. (Show an example.) Make individual puzzles out of the pyramid so that when the children put them together (or paste them on paper), they get the idea that the food in the bigger pieces should be eaten more frequently than those pictures in the smaller pieces.

➤ In your planning, be sure to include nutritional food and nonnutritional food, so the children have many opportunities to decide between food items. They need to make comparisons and evaluations (would it be healthier to eat potato chips or grapes—and why?). Should candy, for instance, never be consumed? Some families have limited food, cultural preferences, or no knowledge about nutrition. How could this plan make a difference in family buying and eating?

➤ Have empty cartons, packages, and so on of actual food products available in the housekeeping area.

➤ Have pictures of the same food as fresh and processed (for example, a fresh apple, juice, and sauce, or grains in various forms).

➤ Talk about the taste of food without getting too far from today's goal. If appropriate, mention the four tastes (salty, sweet, sour, and bitter), but leave a discussion about the taste buds and specific personal preferences for follow-up topics.

➤ Sometime and somewhere during the day, provide a tasting time for the children. Whenever possible, let the children assist in preparing, serving, and cleaning up snack and/or lunch tables. Would it be possible to make and bake bread, cook applesauce or spaghetti in the classroom, or have each child bring a piece of fruit or a vegetable to make a salad or stone soup? (See Brown, M., *Stone Soup*, Macmillan Children's Book Group, 1986; Chapter 11; and other references related to food.)

➤ Encourage the children to help prepare some nutritious snacks. Stress the importance of cleanliness of hands, surfaces, and utensils when preparing or eating food.

➤ Have a variety of pictures of food, both nutritious and junk. Provide a bulletin board divided into two parts. Talk with the children about which foods help bodies grow strong and which foods are not beneficial. Help them understand why the food is healthy or unhealthy. They may indicate that all their preferences (high sugar, fat, and/or salt content) are healthy just because they like them or eat them often. Watch your terminology carefully so you give the right information and ideas to the children. Bear in mind that adults most often select, serve, and influence the food choices of children.

➤ Plant a garden, but realize that it takes a long time to mature.

➤ Provide good books on food in the reading-browsing area. (See Chapter 11 for suggestions.)

➤ Informally or formally, indoors or outdoors, individually or in groups, sing songs, read poetry, and have informal discussions about good food.

➤ Suggested ideas show how the topic could be used during activity or free-selection play, in gathering times, informally around the classroom and playground, or formally with a group of children. The topic fits well with different curriculum areas—science, art, music, language arts, and so on. Consider carefully whether food items should be used in art projects. Some argue that with food shortages, malnutrition, health problems, and costs, food should not be wasted on art projects when others items could easily be substituted. Perhaps an occasional potato or fruit print or grain collage would invite children to an art activity. You decide. Refer to the section titled "Collage" in Chapter 6 for a discussion of this issue.

Using some, all, or none of the suggestions, write a plan that would be beneficial to the children you will teach.

Step 4: Implement the Plan

➤ Make short notes about various children, activities, and behavior to stimulate discussion at evaluation time.

Step 5: Evaluate the Plan

➤ Throughout the session, record quick notes about the high and low points of the session and follow up with a teacher discussion after the children depart. Begin your evaluation by asking for and making general comments about the concepts and actions of the children. Encourage and listen to comments of other adults in the classroom. Did they see and hear what you saw and heard? How beneficial was the day for the children? Were the concepts and activities appropriate or inappropriate for the children—and why?

Step 6: Modify the Plan for Follow-Up or Expansion of the Theme

➤ While the topic and participation are fresh in your mind, suggest some ways to build a follow-up lesson on this topic or ways to integrate it with other information when the children show interest and readiness.

➤ Return to Step 2 and review your evaluation thoughts. Were the ideas on- or off-target according to the results of the day?

➤ Teachers who feel they have taught a topic "once and for all" need to remember that not only do children learn through appropriate repetition, but they also learn by integrating a topic into other topics, activities, and interactions.

➤ Other contributors to a strong body include cleanliness (hand washing, teeth brushing, and so on); exercise; rest; immunizations; a nonpolluted environment (air, water, soil); proper clothing for an activity and the weather; health care and medical/dental checkups; and others.

➤ Topics related to health and safety include household products; unsafe play activities and toys (ropes, sharp objects); avoiding those who are ill; choosing good friends and activities; understanding making, and supporting rules; reporting hazardous things or unfriendly individuals; and others.

Index